The Library at Warwick School
Please return or renew on or before the last date below

5/17

HarperCollins Publishers
Westerhill Road
Bishopbriggs
Glasgow
G64 2QT

Fifth Edition 2014

10 9 8 7 6 5 4

© HarperCollins Publishers 1999,
2002, 2006, 2009, 2014

ISBN 978-0-00-753509-5

Collins® is a registered trademark of
HarperCollins Publishers Limited

www.collins.co.uk

A catalogue record for this book is
available from the British Library

Typeset by Sharon McTeir,
Creative Publishing Services

Printed and bound in China by
RR Donnelley APS

Acknowledgements
We would like to thank those authors
and publishers who kindly gave
permission for copyright material
to be used in the Collins Corpus.
We would also like to thank Times
Newspapers Ltd for providing
valuable data.

MIX
Paper from
responsible sources
FSC™ C007454
www.fsc.org

FSC™ is a non-profit international organisation established to promote the
responsible management of the world's forests. Products carrying the FSC
label are independently certified to assure consumers that they come from
forests that are managed to meet the social, economic and ecological needs
of present and future generations, and other controlled sources.

Find out more about HarperCollins and the environment at
www.harpercollins.co.uk/green

Contents

Editorial Staff

Editors
Mary O'Neill
Elspeth Summers

For the Publisher
Gerry Breslin
Kerry Ferguson
Sharon McTeir

Computing Support
Thomas Callan
David Wark

Teacher Consultants
Amanda Alexander and Rachel Gee of Lex Education
Ben Fitzgerald
Eilidh Whatley-Marshall

Australian Editor
W. A. Krebs

New Zealand Editor
Elizabeth Gordon

South African Editor
Geoffrey Hughes

Introduction

Since its first publication, *Collins School Thesaurus* has proved itself to be a vital language and literacy tool for today's students. It was created to meet their needs and aspirations through research among teachers. Those features identified as the most helpful were incorporated into its text. This new edition has been revised and expanded to give students even more language and study help.

Collins' unique approach ensures that each entry word is followed by a short explanation of its meaning, which is then followed by an example of real English showing the context in which the word may be used. Furthermore, each synonym given for the entry word is also accompanied by an example showing context. This makes it easier for students to see which synonyms can be directly substituted for the entry word, and which involve a slight shift in sense.

Collins School Thesaurus has even more ways to help. It provides:

- Panels containing more advanced synonyms for the entry word, a suitable antonym where appropriate, and related words

- Themed 'types of' lists relevant to the entry word, such as *shades of red* at **red**, to expand students' vocabulary and enhance their creative writing skills

- A *Word Studies* supplement to help students avoid the most over-used words, offering detailed groups of alternatives for every context and shade of meaning

- The *Essential Guide to Good Writing*, a brand-new supplement to help students hone their writing skills, not just for the English curriculum but for all curriculum subjects

Collins School Thesaurus is even more relevant, accessible, and student-friendly than before, and it's an indispensable companion to the *Collins School Dictionary*.

How to Use the Thesaurus

Collins School Thesaurus is easy to use and understand. On the outer edge of each page there is a marker highlighting the letter of the alphabet featured on that page. At the top of each page, the first and last words entered on the page are clearly shown.

Below are some entries showing the thesaurus's main features, along with an explanation of what they are.

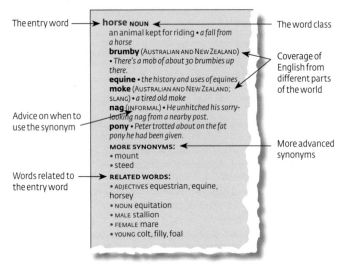

The entry word

horse NOUN
an animal kept for riding • *a fall from a horse*
brumby (AUSTRALIAN AND NEW ZEALAND)
• *There's a mob of about 30 brumbies up there.*
equine • *the history and uses of equines*
moke (AUSTRALIAN AND NEW ZEALAND; SLANG) • *a tired old moke*
nag (INFORMAL) • *He unhitched his sorry-looking nag from a nearby post.*
pony • *Peter trotted about on the fat pony he had been given.*
MORE SYNONYMS:
• mount
• steed
RELATED WORDS:
• ADJECTIVES equestrian, equine, horsey
• NOUN equitation
• MALE stallion
• FEMALE mare
• YOUNG colt, filly, foal

The word class

Coverage of English from different parts of the world

Advice on when to use the synonym

More advanced synonyms

Words related to the entry word

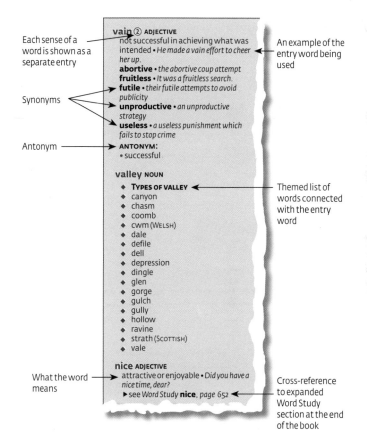

Each sense of a word is shown as a separate entry

vain ② ADJECTIVE
not successful in achieving what was intended • *He made a vain effort to cheer her up.*
abortive • *the abortive coup attempt*
fruitless • *It was a fruitless search.*
futile • *their futile attempts to avoid publicity*
unproductive • *an unproductive strategy*
useless • *a useless punishment which fails to stop crime*

An example of the entry word being used

Synonyms

ANTONYM:
• successful

Antonym

valley NOUN

◆ **TYPES OF VALLEY**
◆ canyon
◆ chasm
◆ coomb
◆ cwm (WELSH)
◆ dale
◆ defile
◆ dell
◆ depression
◆ dingle
◆ glen
◆ gorge
◆ gulch
◆ gully
◆ hollow
◆ ravine
◆ strath (SCOTTISH)
◆ vale

Themed list of words connected with the entry word

nice ADJECTIVE
attractive or enjoyable • *Did you have a nice time, dear?*
▶ see Word Study **nice**, *page 652*

What the word means

Cross-reference to expanded Word Study section at the end of the book

vii

Aa

abandon ① VERB
to leave someone or something
• *His parents had abandoned him.*
desert • *Medical staff have deserted the city's main hospital.*
jilt • *She was jilted by her first fiancé.*
leave • *My husband has left me.*
leave behind • *He walked out and left behind a wife and two young children.*

MORE SYNONYMS:
• forsake
• leave in the lurch

abandon ② NOUN
lack of restraint • *He began to laugh with abandon.*
recklessness • *the headstrong recklessness of youth*
wildness • *Her wildness just needed to be channelled properly.*

ANTONYM:
• control

abate VERB
to become less • *The four-day flood at last abated.*
decrease • *The pain had decreased considerably.*
diminish • *The attacks on the village did not diminish.*
ebb • *Her strength was ebbing fast.*
lessen • *After a while, the cramps lessened.*
subside • *Their enthusiasm was beginning to subside.*
wane • *His popularity shows no sign of waning.*

ability NOUN
the skill needed to do something
• *the ability to get on with others*
capability • *We have the capability of going out and winning.*
competence • *They have a high level of competence.*
expertise • *legal expertise*
skill • *the skill to play at a higher level*
talent • *a talent for music*

MORE SYNONYMS:
• aptitude
• dexterity
• proficiency

ANTONYM:
• inability

able ADJECTIVE
good at doing something • *He proved himself to be an able politician.*
accomplished • *an accomplished pianist*
capable • *a very capable manager*
efficient • *a team of efficient workers*
expert • *My mother was an expert baker.*
first-rate • *This run is only suitable for first-rate skiers.*
skilled • *a skilled craftsman*
talented • *a talented actor*

MORE SYNONYMS:
• competent
• proficient

abolish VERB
to do away with something • *Their*

A
B
C
D
E
F
G
H
I
J
K
L
M
N
O
P
Q
R
S
T
U
V
W
X
Y
Z

objective was to abolish capital gains tax.
annul • *The marriage was annulled last month.*
do away with • *the proposal to do away with nuclear weapons*
overturn • *criminals seeking to overturn their convictions*
put an end to • *efforts to put an end to the traffic in drugs*

MORE SYNONYMS:
• quash
• rescind
• revoke

about ① PREPOSITION
of or concerning • *anxiety about his sick son*
concerning • *documents concerning the estate*
on • *his book on Picasso*
regarding • *strict rules regarding the disposal of food*
relating to • *the rules relating to transfer fees*

about ② ADVERB
not exactly • *The procedure takes about thirty minutes.*
almost • *Their wages have almost doubled.*
approximately • *It was approximately three times the size of a domestic cat.*
around • *The crowd here is around 12,000.*
nearly • *a tradition going back nearly 20 centuries*
roughly • *One unit is roughly equivalent to half a pint of beer.*

above ① PREPOSITION
over or higher than something • *above the clouds*
higher than • *There are no hotels higher than four storeys.*
over • *the picture over the fireplace*

ANTONYM:
• below

RELATED WORDS:
• PREFIXES super-, supra-, sur-

above ② PREPOSITION
greater than a certain level or amount • *The death toll will rise above 50.*
beyond • *I expect to live way beyond 100.*
exceeding • *a floor area exceeding 50,000 square feet*

abrupt ① ADJECTIVE
sudden or unexpected • *the abrupt resignation of the prime minister*
sudden • *this week's sudden thaw*
unexpected • *His career came to an unexpected end.*
unforeseen • *unforeseen difficulties*

MORE SYNONYMS:
• precipitate
• unanticipated

abrupt ② ADJECTIVE
unfriendly and impolite • *He was taken aback by her abrupt manner.*
curt • *"The matter is closed," was the curt reply.*
rude • *He was frequently rude to waiters and servants.*
short • *She seemed tense and was definitely short with me.*
terse • *He received a terse one-line rejection from the Ministry.*

MORE SYNONYMS:
• brusque
• unceremonious

ANTONYM:
• polite

absent ADJECTIVE
not present • *absent from work*
away • *She is away on a business trip.*
elsewhere • *Four witnesses can prove*

he was elsewhere at the time.
gone • I'll only be gone for ten minutes.
missing • Another 44 passengers are still missing.

ANTONYM:
• present

absent-minded ADJECTIVE
forgetful or not paying attention • Her absent-minded stepfather left the camera under the carriage seat.
distracted • He seems distracted, giving the impression of being elsewhere.
forgetful • She's getting rather forgetful, and living mostly in the past.
random (NEW ZEALAND) • I'm sorry, I'm a bit random these days.

absolute ① ADJECTIVE
total and complete • He is talking absolute nonsense.
complete • The operation was a complete success.
downright • That's a downright lie!
pure • a work of pure genius
sheer • It would be sheer madness to carry on after this.
thorough • He has a thorough knowledge of the subject.
total • the total destruction of the city
utter • He stared at me in utter disbelief.

MORE SYNONYMS:
• unmitigated
• unqualified

absolute ② ADJECTIVE
having total power • an absolute ruler
dictatorial • a dictatorial system of government
supreme • humble subjects of her supreme rule
tyrannical • popular uprisings against tyrannical rulers

absorb VERB
to soak up or take in something • Plants absorb carbon dioxide.

digest • Fats are hard to digest.
soak up • Stir until the wheat has soaked up all the water.
take in • A growing tree takes in light and processes it for food.

abstain VERB
to choose not to do something • The patients had to abstain from alcohol.
avoid • Heartburn sufferers should try to avoid fatty foods.
deny oneself • I won't deny myself some celebration tonight.
forgo • My wife and I have to forgo holidays now.
give up • She gave up smoking last year.
refrain • He appealed to all factions to refrain from violence.

MORE SYNONYMS:
• desist
• forbear
• renounce

absurd ADJECTIVE
ridiculous or nonsensical • an absurd waste of money
crazy (INFORMAL) • It would be crazy to tinker with a winning team.
illogical • his completely illogical arguments
ludicrous • It was ludicrous to suggest that the visit could be kept secret.
nonsensical • He says many diets are harmful and nonsensical.
ridiculous • The programme is too ridiculous to take seriously.

MORE SYNONYMS:
• incongruous
• preposterous

abundance NOUN
a great amount of something • an abundance of wildlife
affluence • Pockets of affluence coexist with poverty.

a
b
c
d
e
f
g
h
i
j
k
l
m
n
o
p
q
r
s
t
u
v
w
x
y
z

bounty • *autumn's bounty of fruit, seeds, and berries*

plenty • *Allow plenty of time to get home.*

MORE SYNONYMS:
- cornucopia
- plethora

ANTONYM:
- shortage

abundant ADJECTIVE

present in large quantities • *an abundant supply of cheap labour*

ample • *ample space for a good-sized kitchen*

copious • *copious amounts of red wine*

full • *a full tank of petrol*

plentiful • *a plentiful supply of vegetables*

ANTONYM:
- scarce

abuse ① NOUN

cruel treatment of someone • *child abuse*

exploitation • *Most human life involves the exploitation of animals.*

harm • *the harm smokers willingly do to their own health*

hurt • *The victims suffer mental scars as well as physical hurt.*

ill-treatment • *the ill-treatment of political prisoners*

oppression • *the oppression of black people throughout history*

abuse ② NOUN

unkind remarks directed towards someone • *I was left shouting abuse as the car sped off.*

censure • *a controversial policy which has attracted international censure*

derision • *He was greeted with shouts of derision.*

insults • *They shouted insults at each other.*

invective • *A woman had hurled racist invective at the family.*

abuse ③ VERB

to speak insultingly to someone • *He was verbally abused by other soldiers.*

curse • *We started cursing them under our breath.*

insult • *I did not mean to insult you.*

scold • *Later she scolded her daughter for having talked to her father like that.*

slate (BRITISH; INFORMAL) • *Willis's acting skills have been slated, yet again.*

abusive ADJECTIVE

rude and unkind • *abusive language*

disparaging • *He made some disparaging remarks about the team.*

insulting • *She was charged with insulting behaviour to a police officer.*

offensive • *The book was seen by many Muslims as being deeply offensive to Islam.*

rude • *He is rude to her friends.*

scathing • *He made some particularly scathing comments about the design.*

MORE SYNONYMS:
- censorious
- vituperative

abyss NOUN

a very deep hole • *He crawled to peer over the edge of the abyss.*

chasm • *The climbers strung a rope across the chasm and crawled along it.*

fissure • *The earthquake opened large fissures in the ground.*

gorge • *The valley narrowed to a gorge with cascading crags.*

pit • *Eric lost his footing and began to slide into the pit.*

void • *His feet dangled in the void.*

accelerate VERB

to go faster • *She accelerated away from the kerb.*

hurry • *He shouted at me to hurry.*

quicken • Her pulse quickened in alarm.
speed up • It is designed to speed up credit-card transactions.

ANTONYM:
• decelerate

accept VERB
to receive or agree to something • All those invited to next week's conference have accepted.
acknowledge • He was willing to acknowledge her as his child.
agree to • Hours before the deadline, the Chinese agreed to the conditions.
concur with • I concur with her opinion.
consent to • The Russians consented to the peace treaty.
take • He took the job.

ANTONYM:
• refuse

acceptable ADJECTIVE
good enough to be accepted • an acceptable standard of living
adequate • a lack of adequate facilities
all right • The meal was all right for the price.
fair • He is a fair player, but not outstanding.
good enough • I'm afraid that excuse just isn't good enough.
passable • She can speak fluent Spanish and passable French.
satisfactory • The workmen have done a satisfactory job.
tolerable • a tolerable level of noise

accidental ADJECTIVE
happening by chance • The fire was accidental.
casual • a casual remark
chance • a chance meeting
inadvertent • She giggled at the inadvertent pun.
random • the random nature of death in war

ANTONYM:
• deliberate

accommodate VERB
to provide someone with a place to stay • a hotel built to accommodate guests for the wedding
house • The building will house 12 boys.
put up • I wanted to know if she could put me up for a few days.
shelter • There were no facilities for sheltering the refugees.

accommodating ADJECTIVE
willing to help • his polite, accommodating manner
considerate • I try to be considerate to non-smokers.
helpful • The staff in the Newcastle office are very helpful.
hospitable • He was very hospitable to me when I came to New York.
kind • It was very kind of you to come.
obliging • an extremely pleasant and obliging man

accommodation NOUN
a house or room for living in • Travel and overnight accommodation are included.
digs (BRITISH; INFORMAL) • I was studying and living in digs all round the country.
house • He sold his house in London and moved to the country.
housing • a serious housing shortage
lodgings • At the moment the house provides lodgings for Oxford students.
quarters • the officers' quarters

accompany ① VERB
to go somewhere with someone • Children must be accompanied by an adult.
conduct (FORMAL) • He asked if he might conduct us to the ball.
escort • They were escorted by police to their plane.

go with • *I haven't asked my friend to go with me yet.*
usher • *I ushered him into the office.*

accompany ② VERB
to occur with something • *severe pain accompanied by fever*
come with • *Stress comes with this job.*
go together with • *Poverty and illiteracy go together with high birth rates.*

accomplish VERB
to manage to do something • *If we'd all work together, I think we'd accomplish our goal.*
achieve • *Achieving our aims makes us feel good.*
bring about • *the only way to bring about political change*
complete • *She has just completed her first novel.*
do • *Have you done it yet?*
fulfil • *All the necessary conditions were fulfilled.*
manage • *40% of children managed the required standard in reading.*

MORE SYNONYMS:
• effect
• execute
• realize

accurate ADJECTIVE
correct to a detailed level • *Quartz watches are very accurate.*
correct • *The correct answers can be found at the bottom of the page.*
exact • *an exact copy*
faithful • *a faithful translation*
precise • *precise sales figures*
right • *That clock never tells the right time.*
strict • *He has never been a playboy in the strict sense of the word.*
true • *a true account of what happened*

ANTONYM:
• inaccurate

accuse VERB
to charge someone with doing something wrong • *He accused her of having an affair.*
blame • *The police blamed the explosion on terrorists.*
censure • *The Stock Exchange took the unusual step of censuring him in public.*
charge • *Police have charged Mr Smith with murder.*
cite • *He was banned for 30 days after being cited for foul play.*
denounce • *He publicly denounced government nuclear policy.*

MORE SYNONYMS:
• impeach
• incriminate
• indict

accustomed ADJECTIVE
used to something • *The manager has become accustomed to abuse of late.*
adapted • *The camel's feet, well adapted for dry sand, are useless on mud.*
familiar • *He was very familiar with contemporary music.*
used • *I'm used to having my sleep interrupted.*

ANTONYM:
• unaccustomed

achieve VERB
to gain by hard work or ability • *She has achieved her best tournament result for years.*
accomplish • *halfway towards accomplishing an important career goal*
carry out • *debate about how such reforms should be carried out*
complete • *The commission completed this task in March.*

do • *I have done what I came here to do.*
fulfil • *The army has fulfilled its objective.*
perform • *He has not performed his administrative duties properly.*

achievement NOUN

something which someone has succeeded in doing • *His presence here is an achievement in itself.*
accomplishment • *The list of her accomplishments is staggering.*
deed • *His heroic deeds were celebrated in every corner of India.*
exploit • *His wartime exploits were later made into a TV series.*
feat • *A racing car is an extraordinary feat of engineering.*

acquire VERB

to get something • *I have recently acquired a digital camera.*
attain • *students who attain the required grades*
gain • *He gained valuable experience from the job.*
get • *My video's broken - I'll have to get a new one.*
obtain • *I couldn't obtain a ticket at any price.*
pick up • *You can pick up some real bargains at the January sales.*
procure • *It was still difficult to procure food and fuel.*
secure • *The team have secured a place in the semi-finals.*

act ① VERB

to do something • *The bank acted properly in the best interests of the depositors.*
function • *All the computer systems functioned properly.*
operate • *In the first half he operated effectively in defence.*
perform • *He performed well in a World Cup match last summer.*
work • *All sides will work towards a political solution.*

act ② VERB

to perform in a play or film • *He acted in 91 films altogether.*
act out • *It was made using real people to act out the scene.*
perform • *She performed the role on television twice more.*
play • *He plays agent Lillian Scully in a spoof of The X-Files.*
play the part of • *She agreed to play the part of Evita.*
portray • *His mean, moody looks are perfect for the cynical anti-hero he portrays.*

MORE SYNONYMS:
• characterize
• personify

act ③ NOUN

a single thing someone does • *an act of disloyalty to the King*
accomplishment • *Winning the tournament would be an incredible accomplishment.*
achievement • *She was honoured for her achievements as a film-maker.*
deed • *forgotten deeds of heroism*
feat • *an outstanding feat of athleticism*
undertaking • *Organizing the show has been a massive undertaking.*

action ① NOUN

the process of doing something • *He had to take evasive action to avoid being hit.*
activity • *the electrical activity of the brain*
operation • *It is quite a tricky operation.*
process • *the peace process*

action ② NOUN

something that is done • *He did not like his actions questioned.*

accomplishment • *sporting accomplishments*
achievement • *If we can win the league it will be a great achievement for me.*
deed • *daring and heroic deeds*
exploit • *the stories of his wartime exploits*
feat • *prodigious feats of engineering*

active ① ADJECTIVE
full of energy • *Having an active child around the house can be exhausting.*
energetic • *an energetic, happy young girl*
lively • *a lively and attractive teenager*
restless • *On Christmas Eve the kids are too restless to sleep.*
sprightly • *a small, sprightly 60-year-old*
vivacious • *He was very vivacious and great fun to work with.*

MORE SYNONYMS:
• dynamic
• indefatigable

active ② ADJECTIVE
busy and hardworking • *people who are active in local politics*
busy • *My husband lived a full and busy life.*
engaged • *The contenders are now fully engaged in their campaigns.*
enthusiastic • *As a student he was an enthusiastic member of the Communist party.*
hardworking • *a team of hardworking and dedicated volunteers*
industrious • *It is a happy and industrious community.*
involved • *She is heavily involved in local fundraising projects.*
occupied • *A busy social life will keep you fully occupied in February.*

activity ① NOUN
a situation in which lots of things are happening • *There is an extraordinary level of activity in the office.*
action • *a film full of action and excitement*
bustle • *the hustle and bustle of a busy hospital*
energy • *I love the energy you find in big cities.*
liveliness • *a restaurant with a wonderful atmosphere of liveliness*

activity ② NOUN
something you do for pleasure • *sports and other leisure activities*
hobby • *My hobby is birdwatching.*
interest • *Amongst his many interests are angling and painting.*
pastime • *You need a more active pastime than playing computer games.*
pursuit • *I like art, cooking and outdoor pursuits.*

actual ADJECTIVE
real, rather than imaginary or guessed at • *That is the official figure: the actual figure is much higher.*
authentic • *music played on authentic medieval instruments*
genuine • *a store selling genuine army clothing*
realistic • *a realistic picture of Dublin life*
true • *The film is based on a true story.*
verified • *verified reports of serious human rights violations*

acute ① ADJECTIVE
severe or intense • *an acute shortage of supplies*
critical • *suffering from a critical illness*
extreme • *a crippling disease which causes extreme pain*
grave • *His country faces grave problems.*
great • *He died in great agony.*
intense • *I felt an intense loneliness.*
serious • *It increases the risk of serious injuries.*

severe • *Nuts can trigger off a severe allergic reaction.*

acute ② ADJECTIVE
very intelligent • *an acute mind*
alert • *He is old, but he has a very quick and alert mind.*
astute • *He has a remarkably astute brain.*
bright • *You don't need a bright mind to figure that one out.*
keen • *a competent economist with a keen intellect*
perceptive • *a perceptive analysis of the situation*
quick • *a child with an enquiring mind and a quick intelligence*
sharp • *His gentle manner disguised a sharp mind.*
shrewd • *He demonstrated a shrewd understanding of human nature.*

MORE SYNONYMS:
• discriminating
• discerning
• perspicacious

adapt VERB
to alter for a new use • *Shelves were built to adapt the library for use as an office.*
adjust • *He had to adjust the driver's seat.*
alter • *The government has altered the rules.*
change • *The law needs to be changed.*
convert • *a table that converts into an ironing board*
modify • *Our workshop is busy modifying the tanks for desert conditions.*

add ① VERB
to put something with something else • *Add the grated cheese to the sauce.*
attach • *Don't forget to attach the completed entry form.*

augment • *a way to augment the family income*
supplement • *I suggest supplementing your diet with vitamin A.*

MORE SYNONYMS:
• adjoin
• affix
• append

add ② VERB
to combine numbers or quantities • *Banks add all the interest and other charges together.*
add up • *adding up calories on a calculator*
count up • *They counted up all the hours the villagers worked.*
total • *They will compete for prizes totalling nearly £300.*

ANTONYM:
• subtract

addition NOUN
something that has been added to something else • *recent additions to their range of cars*
increase • *a substantial increase in workload*
supplement • *a supplement to their basic pension*

MORE SYNONYMS:
• addendum
• adjunct
• appendage

adequate ADJECTIVE
enough in amount or quality for a purpose • *an adequate diet*
acceptable • *a company which offers an acceptable benefits package*
ample • *You've had ample time to discuss this matter.*
enough • *enough money to live on*
satisfactory • *a satisfactory bid for the company*

a
b
c
d
e
f
g
h
i
j
k
l
m
n
o
p
q
r
s
t
u
v
w
x
y
z

A

B
C
D
E
F
G
H
I
J
K
L
M
N
O
P
Q
R
S
T
U
V
W
X
Y
Z

sufficient • *One teaspoon of salt should be sufficient.*

ANTONYM:
• insufficient

administer ① VERB
to be responsible for managing something • *people who administer large companies*
be in charge of • *Who is in charge of this division?*
command • *Who would command the troops in the event of war?*
control • *He controls the largest publishing house in the country.*
direct • *Christopher will direct day-to-day operations.*
manage • *Within two years he was managing the shop.*
run • *This is no way to run a business.*
supervise • *the men who supervised the project*

administer ② VERB
to inflict or impose something on someone • *He administered most of the blows.*
carry out • *You are not authorized to carry out disciplinary action.*
deal • *His attacker dealt him a severe blow to the face.*
dispense • *They have set up military courts to dispense swift justice.*
execute • *She leapt up and executed a spinning kick to his head.*
impose • *The judge had no choice but to impose a death sentence.*
inflict • *Inflicting punishment to stop crime is not the answer.*
perform • *He had to perform emergency surgery.*

ANOTHER SYNONYM:
• mete out

admiration NOUN
a feeling of great liking and respect

• *I have always had the greatest admiration for him.*
appreciation • *gifts presented to them in appreciation of their work*
approval • *His son had an obsessive drive to gain his father's approval.*
esteem • *Their public esteem has never been lower.*
regard • *He has always been held in high regard.*
respect • *We all have so much respect for her.*

admire VERB
to like and respect someone or something • *All those who knew him will admire him for his work.*
appreciate • *the need for children to appreciate their mother tongue*
look up to • *A lot of the younger girls look up to you.*
respect • *I want him to respect me as a career woman.*
value • *She genuinely values his opinion.*

MORE SYNONYMS:
• esteem
• venerate

ANTONYM:
• scorn

admit ① VERB
to agree that something is true • *The driver admitted to falling asleep at the wheel.*
accept • *I accepted the truth of all that Nicola had told me.*
acknowledge • *Belatedly the government has acknowledged the problem.*
grant • *The magistrates granted that the RSPCA was justified in bringing the action.*

ANTONYM:
• deny

admit ② VERB

to allow to enter • *He was admitted to university after the war.*

accept • *Stephen was accepted into the family.*

let in • *Turnstile operators were accused of letting in fans without tickets.*

receive • *He was received into the priesthood.*

take in • *The monastery has taken in 26 refugees.*

ANTONYM:
• exclude

adult NOUN

a grown-up person • *Becoming a father signified he was now an adult.*

grown-up • *Las Vegas is the ultimate playground for grown-ups.*

man • *He is now a man of 42.*

woman • *a woman of child-bearing age*

ANTONYM:
• child

advance ① VERB

to move forward or develop • *Rebel forces are advancing on the capital.*

make inroads • *They have made impressive inroads in the movie business.*

press on • *Poland pressed on with economic reform.*

proceed • *He proceeded down the spiral stairway.*

progress • *the ability to progress from one step to the next*

advance ② NOUN

progress in something • *scientific advance*

breakthrough • *a breakthrough in cancer treatment*

development • *the development of the car*

gain • *a gain of nearly 10%*

progress • *signs of progress in his reading*

step • *the first step towards peace*

advantage NOUN

a more favourable position or state • *We have a competitive advantage.*

ascendancy • *The extremists are gaining ascendancy.*

benefit • *For maximum benefit use your treatment every day.*

dominance • *the battle for high-street dominance*

superiority • *military superiority*

ANTONYM:
• disadvantage

advertise VERB

to present something to the public in order to sell it • *Bookmakers cannot advertise on television.*

plug (INFORMAL) • *If I hear another actor plugging his latest book I will scream.*

promote • *What are you doing to promote your new film?*

publicize • *He never publicized his plans.*

push • *a publisher who knows how to push a product*

MORE SYNONYMS:
• blazon
• promulgate

advertisement NOUN

a public announcement to sell or publicize something • *She recently placed an advertisement in the local newspaper.*

ad (INFORMAL) • *an ad for a minicab company*

advert (BRITISH; INFORMAL) • *She appeared in a coffee advert.*

banner ad • *Only one per cent of internet surfers click on banner ads.*

commercial • *She has turned down a small fortune to do TV commercials.*

notice • *The request is published in notices in today's national newspapers.*

plug (INFORMAL) • *a shameless plug for his new film*

a
b
c
d
e
f
g
h
i
j
k
l
m
n
o
p
q
r
s
t
u
v
w
x
y
z

A
B
C
D
E
F
G
H
I
J
K
L
M
N
O
P
Q
R
S
T
U
V
W
X
Y
Z

advice NOUN
a suggestion as to what to do • *Take my advice and stay away from him!*
counsel (FORMAL) • *He had always been able to count on her wise counsel.*
drum (AUSTRALIAN; INFORMAL) • *What's the drum on this?*
guidance • *The nation looks to them for guidance.*
opinion • *You should seek a medical opinion.*
suggestion • *She made suggestions as to how I could improve my diet.*

advise ① VERB
to offer advice to someone • *The minister advised him to leave as soon as possible.*
caution • *The researchers caution against drawing general conclusions from this study.*
counsel • *My advisers counselled me to do nothing.*
recommend • *We strongly recommend reporting the incident to the police.*
suggest • *He suggested a visit to the Cézanne exhibition.*
urge • *We urge that vigorous action be taken immediately.*

MORE SYNONYMS:
• commend
• enjoin
• prescribe

advise ② VERB
to notify someone • *I think it best that I advise you of my decision to retire.*
inform • *My daughter informed me that she was pregnant.*
make known • *The details will be made known by the end of August.*
notify • *The skipper notified the coastguard of the tragedy.*

adviser NOUN
a person whose job is to give advice

• *The President and his advisers spent the day in meetings.*
aide • *a former aide to Ronald Reagan*
consultant • *a management consultant*
guru • *He became Britain's modern design guru after launching Habitat in 1964.*
mentor • *He is my friend and musical mentor.*
tutor • *my college tutor*

advocate VERB
to publicly support a plan or course of action • *Mr Smith advocates corporal punishment for young offenders.*
back • *The newspaper is backing the residents' campaign.*
champion • *He passionately champions our cause.*
endorse • *We are reluctant to endorse such drastic measures.*
favour • *judges who favour the death penalty*
promote • *He promoted the idea of Scottish independence.*
recommend • *I can't recommend such a course of action.*
support • *people who supported his policies*
uphold • *We uphold the capitalist free economy.*

affair ① NOUN
an event or series of events • *The funeral was a sad affair.*
business • *This business has really upset me.*
event • *A wedding should be a joyous event.*
issue • *a major political issue*
matter • *I never interfere in these business matters.*
question • *the difficult question of unemployment*

situation • *The whole situation is now under control.*
subject • *a subject which had worried him for some time*

affair ② NOUN

a secret and romantic relationship • *He had an affair with someone he met on holiday.*
fling • *We had a brief fling, but it was nothing serious.*
liaison • *He denied that he had had a sexual liaison with his secretary.*
relationship • *She went public on her relationship with a Hollywood star.*
romance • *Our company discourages office romances.*

affect VERB

to influence something or someone • *More than 7 million people have been affected by the drought.*
act on • *This drug acts very fast on the central nervous system.*
alter • *The earth's climate appears to have been altered by pollution.*
change • *It was to change the course of my life.*
impinge on • *My private life does not impinge on my professional life.*

affection NOUN

a feeling of fondness for someone or something • *She thought of him with affection.*
attachment • *Mother and child form a close attachment.*
fondness • *his fondness for cats*
liking • *a liking for flashy cars*
love • *My love for all my children is unconditional.*
warmth • *He greeted us both with warmth and affection.*

ANTONYM:
• dislike

affectionate ADJECTIVE

full of fondness for someone • *She gave me a long and affectionate hug.*
caring • *a loving, caring husband*
fond • *She gave him a fond smile.*
loving • *The children were very loving to me.*
tender • *a tender kiss*

ANTONYM:
• cold

afraid ADJECTIVE

scared of something unpleasant happening • *I was afraid of the other boys.*
apprehensive • *People are still terribly apprehensive about the future.*
fearful • *Bankers were fearful of a world banking crisis.*
frightened • *She was frightened of flying.*
nervous • *Emotionally, he left me a wreck, nervous of everyone.*
scared • *I was too scared to move.*

ANTONYM:
• unafraid

after ADVERB

at a later time • *Shortly after, police arrested five suspects.*
afterwards • *He was taken to hospital but died soon afterwards.*
following • *We shared so much, not only during the war, but in the many years following.*
later • *He resigned ten years later.*
subsequently • *She subsequently became honorary secretary.*

ANTONYM:
• before

RELATED WORD:
• PREFIX post-

again ADVERB

happening one more time • *He kissed her again.*
afresh • *The couple moved abroad to start life afresh.*

anew • *She's ready to start anew.*
once more • *Rage overcame him once more.*

against ① PREPOSITION

in opposition to • *I am against animal cruelty.*
averse to • *He's not averse to a drink.*
hostile to • *countries that were once hostile to South Africa*
in opposition to • *radio stations set up in opposition to the BBC*
versus • *Portugal versus England*

RELATED WORDS:
• PREFIXES anti-, contra-, counter-

against ② PREPOSITION

in preparation for or in case of something • *precautions against fire*
in anticipation of • *His school was one of several which closed in anticipation of Arctic conditions.*
in expectation of • *The hotel was being renovated in expectation of a tourist boom.*
in preparation for • *The army massed troops and guns in preparation for a counter-attack.*

aggressive ADJECTIVE

full of hostility and violence • *These fish are very aggressive.*
hostile • *The prisoner eyed him in a hostile silence.*
quarrelsome • *He had been a wild boy and a quarrelsome young man.*

MORE SYNONYMS:
• belligerent
• pugnacious

ANTONYM:
• peaceful

agile ADJECTIVE

able to move quickly and easily • *He is as agile as a cat.*
lithe • *a lithe young gymnast*
nimble • *He built his career around*
quick reflexes and nimble footwork.
sprightly • *She is alert and sprightly despite her 85 years.*
supple • *She is as supple as a dancer.*

MORE SYNONYMS:
• limber
• lissom or
• lissome

ANTONYM:
• clumsy

agitate ① VERB

to campaign energetically for something • *The women had begun to agitate for better conditions.*
campaign • *an organization which campaigns for better consumer rights*
demonstrate • *marchers demonstrating for political reform*
protest • *country dwellers who were protesting for the right to hunt*
push • *Some board members are pushing for the merger.*

agitate ② VERB

to worry or distress someone • *Everything she said was beginning to agitate me.*
bother • *It really bothers me when you talk like that.*
distress • *sudden noises which distressed the animals*
disturb • *These dreams disturb me for days afterwards.*
trouble • *Are you troubled by thoughts of the future?*
upset • *The whole incident upset me dreadfully.*
worry • *I didn't want to worry you with my own problems.*

MORE SYNONYMS:
• discompose
• faze
• perturb

agree ① VERB

to have the same opinion as someone • *So we both agree there's a problem?*
assent • *I assented to the request of the publishers to write this book.*
be of the same opinion • *All the other players are of the same opinion.*
concur • *Four other judges concurred.*
see eye to eye • *He has not always seen eye to eye with his brother.*

ANTONYM:
• disagree

agree ② VERB

to match or be the same as something • *His second statement agrees with facts as stated by the other witnesses.*
accord • *I cannot support policies that no longer accord with my principles.*
conform • *It doesn't conform with current building regulations.*
match • *Attendances do not match the ticket sales.*
square • *Does that explanation square with the facts?*
tally • *The figures don't seem to tally.*

agreeable ① ADJECTIVE

pleasant or enjoyable • *I found it a most agreeable experience.*
delightful • *I've had a delightful time.*
enjoyable • *an enjoyable meal*
lovely • *I hope you have a lovely holiday.*
nice • *It would be very nice to get away from it all for a few days.*
pleasant • *This restaurant offers good food in pleasant surroundings.*
pleasurable • *the pleasurable task of deciding where to go on holiday*

ANTONYM:
• disagreeable

agreeable ② ADJECTIVE

willing to allow or do something • *She said she was agreeable to this plan.*

game • *Are you game to try something a little bit different?*
happy • *I'm happy to go along with what everyone else thinks.*
prepared • *Would you be prepared to queue for hours for a ticket?*
ready • *I'm ready to take over if he resigns.*
willing • *Are you willing to take part in a survey?*

MORE SYNONYMS:
• amenable
• compliant

agreement NOUN

a decision reached by two or more people • *The two countries have signed agreements on fishing and oil.*
arrangement • *Eventually we came to an arrangement that suited us both.*
contract • *She has signed an exclusive solo-album contract.*
deal (INFORMAL) • *The company recently won a five-year deal to build runways.*
pact • *He ruled out any formal pact with the government.*
settlement • *She accepted an out-of-court settlement of £4000.*
treaty • *negotiations over a 1992 treaty on global warming*

MORE SYNONYMS:
• compact
• covenant

aim ① VERB

to plan to do something • *The company aims to sign 1 million customers within five years.*
aspire • *people who aspire to public office*
attempt • *He will attempt to win the title for the second year running.*
intend • *I intend to remarry.*
plan • *Mr Beach was planning to sue over injuries he received.*

a
b
c
d
e
f
g
h
i
j
k
l
m
n
o
p
q
r
s
t
u
v
w
x
y
z

A
B
C
D
E
F
G
H
I
J
K
L
M
N
O
P
Q
R
S
T
U
V
W
X
Y
Z

propose • *And where do you propose building such a huge thing?*
strive • *He strives hard to keep himself very fit.*

aim ② NOUN
what someone intends to achieve
• *Our main aim is to offer a superior product.*
ambition • *His ambition is to sail round the world.*
goal • *I have to keep setting goals for myself.*
intention • *It was always my intention to stay in Italy.*
objective • *His objective was to play golf and win.*
plan • *His plan was to acquire paintings by the best artists in Italy.*
target • *his target of 20 goals this season*

alarm ① NOUN
a feeling of fear • *The cat sprang back in alarm.*
anxiety • *anxiety about crime*
apprehension • *I tensed every muscle in my body in apprehension.*
fright • *The birds smashed into the top of their cages in fright.*
nervousness • *I smiled warmly so he wouldn't see my nervousness.*
panic • *There was panic in the streets of the capital.*
scare • *Despite the scare there are no plans to withdraw the drug.*

MORE SYNONYMS:
• consternation
• trepidation

ANTONYM:
• calm

alarm ② NOUN
a device used to warn people of something • *a burglar alarm*
distress signal • *The pilot was trying*

to send a distress signal when the aircraft crashed.
siren • *a police siren*
warning • *A second air raid warning sounded over the capital.*

alarm ③ VERB
to fill with fear • *We could not see what had alarmed him.*
distress • *He is very distressed by what happened.*
frighten • *The future frightens me.*
panic • *He was panicked by his wife's behaviour.*
scare • *Horses scare me.*
startle • *startled by a gunshot*
unnerve • *Investors had been unnerved by the country's ailing stock market.*

ANTONYM:
• calm

alcohol NOUN
a drink that can make you drunk
• *There wasn't even any alcohol at the party.*
booze (INFORMAL) • *clutching a bottle of booze*
drink • *Too much drink is bad for you.*
grog (AUSTRALIAN AND NEW ZEALAND; INFORMAL) • *They demanded a bottle of grog.*
liquor • *I could smell liquor on his breath.*
spirits • *a voluntary ban on advertising spirits on TV*

RELATED WORD:
• NOUN dipsomania

alert ① ADJECTIVE
paying full attention • *apprehended by alert security staff*
attentive • *an attentive audience*
observant • *an observant policeman*
on guard • *on guard against the threat of invasion*

always ADVERB

all the time or forever • *She's always moaning.*

continually • *Malcolm was continually changing his mind.*

every time • *You can't get it right every time.*

forever • *He was forever attempting to arrange deals.*

invariably • *Their teamwork was invariably good.*

perpetually • *The two groups are perpetually at loggerheads.*

amaze VERB

to surprise greatly • *He amazed us by his knowledge of Welsh history.*

astonish • *I was astonished by his stupidity.*

astound • *I am astounded at the comments made by the Chief Superintendant.*

shock • *She was shocked by the appalling news.*

stagger • *He was staggered by the sheer size of the crowd.*

stun • *Many cinema-goers were stunned by the film's tragic end.*

surprise • *We'll solve the case ourselves and surprise everyone.*

MORE SYNONYMS:
• dumbfound
• flabbergast
• stupefy

amazement NOUN

complete surprise • *Much to my amazement, he arrived on time.*

astonishment • *They looked at each other in astonishment.*

shock • *I am still getting over the shock of winning.*

surprise • *To my surprise, I found I liked it.*

wonder • *Cross shook his head in wonder.*

MORE SYNONYMS:
• perplexity
• stupefaction

amazing ADJECTIVE

very surprising or remarkable • *some of the most amazing stunts you're ever likely to see*

astonishing • *an astonishing display of physical strength*

astounding • *The results are quite astounding.*

staggering • *a staggering 17% leap in sales*

startling • *startling new evidence*

stunning • *a stunning piece of news*

surprising • *A surprising number of customers order the same sandwich every day.*

among ① PREPOSITION

surrounded by • *The bike lay among piles of chains and pedals.*

amid • *a tiny bungalow amid clusters of trees*

amidst • *His parents were found dead amidst the wreckage of the plane.*

in the middle of • *a tiny island in the middle of the Pacific*

in the thick of • *a restaurant built on stilts in the thick of a vast mangrove swamp*

surrounded by • *surrounded by bodyguards*

among ② PREPOSITION

between more than two • *The money will be divided among seven charities.*

between • *Proceeds from the auction will be shared between the artists.*

to each of • *£2,000 to each of the five winners*

amount NOUN

how much there is of something • *I still do a certain amount of work for them.*

a
b
c
d
e
f
g
h
i
j
k
l
m
n
o
p
q
r
s
t
u
v
w
x
y
z

A
B
C
D
E
F
G
H
I
J
K
L
M
N
O
P
Q
R
S
T
U
V
W
X
Y
Z

expanse • *a vast expanse of grassland*
quantity • *vast quantities of food*
volume • *the sheer volume of traffic and accidents*

ample ADJECTIVE

of an amount: more than enough • *There is ample space for a good-sized kitchen.*
abundant • *providing abundant food for local wildlife*
enough • *Do you have enough money for a taxi home?*
plenty of • *You've had plenty of time to make up your mind.*
sufficient • *The police have sufficient evidence to charge him.*

ancestor NOUN

a person from whom someone is descended • *He could trace his ancestors back 700 years.*
forebear • *our Victorian forebears*
forefather • *the land of their forefathers*

MORE SYNONYMS:
• precursor
• progenitor

anger ① NOUN

extreme annoyance • *She vented her anger at the umpire.*
fury • *She screamed, her face distorted in fury.*
outrage • *The decisions provoked outrage from human rights groups.*
rage • *An intense rage was burning inside her.*
wrath • *He incurred the wrath of the referee.*

MORE SYNONYMS:
• choler
• ire
• pique
• spleen
• vexation

anger ② VERB

to make someone angry • *remarks which will anger his critics*
enrage • *He enraged the government by renouncing the agreement.*
infuriate • *Peter's presence had infuriated Gordon.*
outrage • *Customers are outraged by the bank's soaring profits.*

ANTONYM:
• calm

angry ADJECTIVE

very annoyed • *He gets angry with me if I'm late.*
cross • *She was rather cross about having to trail across London.*
enraged • *The enraged crowd stoned the car, then set it on fire.*
furious • *He is furious at the way his wife has been treated.*
mad (INFORMAL) • *I'm pretty mad about it, I can tell you.*

animal NOUN

a living creature • *He was attacked by wild animals.*
beast • *the threat our ancestors faced from wild beasts*
creature • *sea creatures*

RELATED WORD:
• PREFIX ZOO-

animosity NOUN

a feeling of strong dislike towards someone • *There is no animosity between these two players.*
antagonism • *a history of antagonism between the two sides*
antipathy • *our growing antipathy towards our manager*
dislike • *She looked at him with dislike.*
hatred • *He didn't bother to conceal his hatred towards my mother.*
hostility • *unacceptable hostility toward minority groups*

ill will · *He didn't bear anyone any ill will.*

malice · *There was no malice in her voice.*

resentment · *There is growing resentment towards newcomers.*

announce VERB

to make known something publicly · *He will announce tonight that he is resigning from office.*

advertise · *He did not want to advertise his presence in the town.*

make known · *Details will be made known tomorrow.*

proclaim · *He loudly proclaimed his innocence.*

reveal · *They were now free to reveal the truth.*

tell · *She was relieved that she'd finally told the full story.*

MORE SYNONYMS:
• promulgate
• propound

announcement NOUN

a statement giving information about something · *There has been no formal announcement by either government.*

advertisement · *an advertisement placed in the local newspaper*

broadcast · *In a broadcast on state radio the government announced its plans.*

bulletin · *At 3.30pm a bulletin was released announcing the decision.*

declaration · *a public declaration of support*

report · *Local press reports estimate that at least sixteen people have died.*

statement · *a short statement by her solicitors*

annoy VERB

to irritate or displease someone

• *Try making a note of the things which annoy you.*

bother · *I didn't think it would bother me so much to see Brian again.*

displease · *Not wishing to displease her, he avoided answering the question.*

get on someone's nerves (INFORMAL) · *That song gets on my nerves.*

hack off (BRITISH AND NEW ZEALAND; SLANG) · *This will just hack people off more.*

hassle (INFORMAL) · *Then my husband started hassling me.*

irritate · *The flippancy in her voice seemed to irritate him.*

plague · *We were plagued by mosquitoes.*

vex · *Cassandra was vexed at not having noticed it herself.*

annoyance ① NOUN

a feeling of irritation · *He made no secret of his annoyance.*

displeasure · *She voiced her displeasure at her treatment.*

irritation · *He tried not to let his irritation show.*

annoyance ② NOUN

something that causes irritation · *Snoring can be more than an annoyance.*

bore · *It's a bore to be off sick.*

drag (INFORMAL) · *A dry sandwich is a drag to eat.*

nuisance · *He could be a bit of a nuisance when he was drunk.*

pain (INFORMAL) · *The peacocks are a pain - beautiful but noisy.*

pain in the neck (INFORMAL) · *Traffic jams are a pain in the neck.*

pest · *He climbed on the table, pulled my hair, and was generally a pest.*

answer ① VERB

to reply to someone · *I knew Ben was*

lying when he answered me.
reply • *He replied that this was absolutely impossible.*
respond • *"Mind your manners, lady!" I responded.*
retort • *Was he afraid, he was asked. "Afraid of what?" he retorted.*

ANTONYM:
• ask

answer ② NOUN

a reply given to someone • *Without waiting for an answer, he turned and went in through the door.*
reply • *I called out a challenge but there was no reply.*
response • *There has been no response to his remarks from the government.*
retort • *His sharp retort clearly made an impact.*

MORE SYNONYMS:
• rejoinder
• riposte

ANTONYM:
• question

anxiety NOUN

nervousness or worry • *our growing anxiety about their safety*
apprehension • *a feeling of apprehension about the future*
concern • *growing concern about the environment*
fear • *His fears might be groundless.*
misgiving • *She had some misgivings about what she had been asked to do.*
nervousness • *I smiled, trying to hide my nervousness.*
unease • *a deep sense of unease about the coming interview*
worry • *a major source of worry to us all*

MORE SYNONYMS:
• perturbation
• trepidation

anxious NOUN

nervous or worried • *He admitted he was still anxious about the situation.*
apprehensive • *Their families are apprehensive about the trip.*
bothered • *I'm still bothered about what she's going to say.*
concerned • *a phone call from a concerned neighbour*
fearful • *We are all fearful for the security of our jobs.*
nervous • *I still get nervous before a visit to the dentist's.*
troubled • *He was troubled about his son's lifestyle.*
uneasy • *an uneasy feeling that something was wrong*
worried • *His parents are worried about his lack of progress.*

apathetic ADJECTIVE

not interested in anything • *apathetic about politics*
cool • *The idea met with a cool response.*
indifferent • *People have become indifferent to the sufferings of others.*
passive • *His passive attitude made things easier for me.*
uninterested • *unhelpful and uninterested shop staff*

ANTONYM:
• enthusiastic

apologize VERB

to say sorry for something • *I apologize for being late.*
ask forgiveness • *He fell to his knees asking for forgiveness.*
beg someone's pardon • *I was impolite and I do beg your pardon.*
express regret • *Mr Galloway expressed regret that he had caused any offence.*
say sorry • *I wanted to say sorry to her.*

appeal ① VERB

to make an urgent request for

something • *The police appealed for witnesses to come forward.*
beg • *I begged him to leave me alone.*
call upon • *Frequently he was called upon to resolve conflicts.*
plead • *I pleaded to be allowed to go.*
request • *She had requested that the door to her room be left open.*

MORE SYNONYMS:
• entreat
• implore
• pray

appeal ② VERB
to attract or interest • *The idea appealed to him.*
attract • *What attracted you to research work?*
fascinate • *Classical music had fascinated him since the age of three.*
interest • *It was the garden that really interested me.*
please • *It pleased him to talk to her.*

appeal ③ NOUN
a formal request for something • *an appeal for peace*
petition • *The court rejected their petition.*
plea • *his emotional plea for help in solving the killing*
request • *France had agreed to his request for political asylum.*

MORE SYNONYMS:
• entreaty
• supplication

appear ① VERB
to become visible or present • *A woman appeared at the far end of the street.*
come into view • *Nearly fifty gliders came into view to the south of the plateau.*
crop up (INFORMAL) • *Problems will crop up and hit you before you are ready.*

emerge • *The postman emerged from his van soaked to the skin.*
show up (INFORMAL) • *He failed to show up at the ceremony.*
surface • *The same old problems would surface again.*
turn up • *This is like waiting for a bus that never turns up.*

ANTONYM:
• disappear

appear ② VERB
to begin to exist • *small white flowers which appear in early summer*
become available • *In 1950, legal aid became available in Britain.*
be invented • *The lawn mower was invented in 1830.*
come into being • *Fireworks first came into being with the invention of gunpowder.*
come into existence • *before our solar system came into existence*
come out • *This book first came out in 1992.*

appearance ① NOUN
the time when something begins to exist • *the appearance of computer technology*
advent • *the advent of satellite and cable channels*
arrival • *the arrival of modern technologies*
coming • *the coming of the railways*
debut • *the debut of the new channel*
emergence • *the emergence of pay-per-view TV*
introduction • *the introduction of the minimum wage*

appearance ② NOUN
the way that a person looks • *She used to be so fussy about her appearance.*
bearing • *a man of iron will and military bearing*

image • *He urged the rest of the band to update their image.*
look • *She is so much happier with her new look.*
looks • *a young woman with wholesome good looks*

MORE SYNONYMS:
• demeanour
• mien

application NOUN
a computer program designed for a particular purpose • *applications for mobile devices*
app • *The app allows the phone to store songs even without access to the internet.*
killer application • *the development of a killer application*
software • *Download the software onto your phone.*

appointment ① NOUN
an arrangement to meet someone • *She has an appointment with her accountant.*
date • *I have a date with Wendy.*
interview • *a job interview*
meeting • *Can we have a meeting to discuss that?*
rendezvous • *I had almost decided to keep my rendezvous with Tony.*

appointment ② NOUN
the choosing of a person to do a job • *his appointment as manager*
election • *the election of the government in 1997*
naming • *the naming of the new captain*
nomination • *They opposed the nomination of a junior officer to the position.*
selection • *his selection as a parliamentary candidate*

appointment ③ NOUN
a job • *He applied for an appointment in Russia.*

assignment • *my first assignment for The New York Times*
job • *He's trying for a job in the Civil Service.*
place • *All the candidates won places on the ruling council.*
position • *She took up a position at the Arts Council.*
post • *He has held several senior military posts.*

appreciate ① VERB
to value something highly • *He appreciates fine wines.*
admire • *All those who knew him will admire him for his work.*
prize • *Military figures made out of lead are prized by collectors.*
rate highly • *The four-year-old mare is rated highly by her trainer.*
respect • *I respect his talent as a pianist.*
treasure • *She treasures her memories of those joyous days.*
value • *I value the work he gives me.*

ANTONYM:
• scorn

appreciate ② VERB
to understand a situation or problem • *I didn't appreciate the seriousness of it at the time.*
be aware of • *I am well aware of the arguments on the other side.*
perceive • *to get pupils to perceive for themselves the relationship between success and effort*
realize • *People don't realize how serious this is.*
recognize • *They have been slow to recognize it as a problem.*
understand • *They are too young to understand what is going on.*

appropriate ADJECTIVE
suitable or acceptable for a given

situation • *Jeans are not appropriate wear for work.*

apt • *an apt title for his memoirs*
correct • *the importance of correct behaviour and social niceties*
fitting • *a fitting tribute to a great man*
proper • *the proper course for the court to take*
suitable • *a suitable location*

MORE SYNONYMS:
• apposite
• appurtenant
• congruous
• germane

ANTONYM:
• inappropriate

approval ① NOUN
agreement given to something • *The plan will require approval from the local authority.*

agreement • *The clubs are seeking agreement for a provisional deal.*
authorization • *We didn't have authorization to go.*
blessing • *Mr Ryabov appeared to give his blessing to Mr Yeltsin's plan.*
endorsement • *His endorsement has been fervently sought by all the main presidential candidates.*
permission • *They cannot leave the country without permission.*
sanction • *The King cannot enact laws without the sanction of Parliament.*

MORE SYNONYMS:
• assent
• imprimatur
• mandate
• ratification

approval ② NOUN
liking and admiration of a person or thing • *He wanted to gain his father's approval.*

admiration • *a strategy that is winning admiration from around the world*

esteem • *Their public esteem has never been lower.*
favour • *He has won favour with a wide range of groups.*
praise • *She is full of praise for the range of excellent services available.*
respect • *We all have so much respect for her.*

ANTONYM:
• disapproval

approve ① VERB
to think something or someone is good • *Not everyone approves of the festival.*

admire • *I admire him for his work.*
favour • *The opposition parties favour constitutional reform.*
praise • *He praised the fans for their continued support.*
respect • *I want him to respect me as a career woman.*
think highly of • *He thought highly of his brother.*

ANTONYM:
• disapprove

approve ② VERB
to agree formally to something • *The court approved the compensation plan.*

authorize • *to authorize the use of military force*
consent to • *His parents consented to an autopsy.*
endorse • *I can endorse their opinion wholeheartedly.*
permit • *The doorman is not allowed to permit them entry to the film.*
sanction • *He may now be ready to sanction the use of force.*

ANTONYM:
• veto

approximate ADJECTIVE
close but not exact • *We believe that*

an approximate figure of 20% is nearer
the mark.
estimated • Our estimated time of
arrival is 3.30.
inexact • Forecasting is an inexact
science.
loose • a loose translation
rough • a rough estimate

ANTONYM:
• exact

ardent ADJECTIVE
full of enthusiasm and passion • an
ardent supporter of capital punishment
avid • an avid follower of the team
devoted • surrounded by devoted fans
enthusiastic • enthusiastic collectors
of Elvis memorabilia
fervent • a fervent admirer of his
intense • his intense love of football
keen • a keen supporter of the cause
passionate • He developed a
passionate interest in motor racing.

ANOTHER SYNONYM:
• zealous

ANTONYM:
• apathetic

area ① NOUN
a particular part of a place • a
built-up area of the city
district • I drove around the business
district.
locality • All other factories in the
locality went on strike in sympathy.
neighbourhood • She no longer
takes evening strolls around her
neighbourhood.
region • a remote mountainous region
of Afghanistan
zone • a war zone

area ② NOUN
the size of a two-dimensional surface
• The islands cover a total area of 625
square kilometres.

expanse • a huge expanse of blue-green
sea
extent • the extent of the rain forest
range • a driver's range of vision
size • a country nearly three times the
size of ours

argue ① VERB
to disagree with someone in an angry
way • They argued over the cost of the
taxi fare.
bicker • They bickered endlessly about
procedure.
disagree • They can communicate even
when they strongly disagree.
fall out (INFORMAL) • Mum and I used to
fall out a lot.
feud • feuding neighbours
fight • We're always fighting about
money.
quarrel • My brother quarrelled with
my father.
row • We started rowing about whose
turn it was next.
squabble • The children were
squabbling over the remote control.
wrangle • Delegates wrangled over the
future of the organization

argue ② VERB
to try to prove • She argued that her
client had been wrongly accused.
assert • The defendants continue to
assert their innocence.
claim • Statisticians claim that the book
contains inaccuracies.
debate • Parliament will debate the
issue today.
maintain • He had always maintained
his innocence.
reason • I reasoned that if he could do
it, so could I.

MORE SYNONYMS:
• controvert
• expostulate
• remonstrate

argument ① NOUN
an angry disagreement • *She got into an argument with one of the marchers.*
barney (BRITISH, AUSTRALIAN AND NEW ZEALAND; INFORMAL) • *We had such a barney that we nearly split up.*
blue (AUSTRALIAN; SLANG) • *He gets into more blues with authority than I do.*
clash • *clashes between police and demonstrators*
dispute • *a dispute over ticket allocation*
feud • *a two-year feud between neighbours*
fight • *We had another fight about money.*
row • *Maxine and I had a terrible row.*
squabble • *a family squabble over Sunday lunch*

argument ② NOUN
a set of reasons presented for something • *There's a strong argument for lowering the price.*
case • *the case for his defence*
grounds • *facts providing grounds for an unfair dismissal complaint*
logic • *The logic is that, without more growth, the deficit will rise.*
reasoning • *the reasoning behind the decision*

arrange ① VERB
to make plans to do something • *Why don't you arrange to meet him later?*
fix up • *I fixed up an appointment to see her.*
organize • *She organized the trip to the museum.*
plan • *She planned to leave in August.*
schedule • *Our appointment is scheduled for Tuesday.*

arrange ② VERB
to set things out in a particular order • *He started to arrange the books in piles.*

classify • *Weathermen classify clouds into several different groups.*
group • *The fact sheet is grouped into seven sections.*
order • *The French order things differently.*
organize • *He began to organize his materials.*
sort • *The students are sorted into three ability groups.*
MORE SYNONYMS:
• array
• systematize

arrest ① VERB
to take someone into custody • *Police arrested five men in connection with the attack.*
apprehend • *Police have not apprehended her killer.*
capture • *Her accomplice was captured by Dutch police.*
nick (BRITISH; SLANG) • *Keep quiet or we'll all get nicked.*
seize • *Two military observers were seized by rebels yesterday.*
take prisoner • *He was taken prisoner in 1940 at the fall of Dunkirk.*

arrest ② NOUN
the act of arresting someone • *The police made two arrests.*
apprehension • *information leading to the apprehension of the killer*
capture • *He was trying to evade capture by security forces.*
seizure • *the mass seizure of terrorists*

article ① NOUN
a piece of writing in a newspaper or magazine • *There's an article about it in today's paper.*
feature • *a feature about Gulf War syndrome*
item • *I read an item about this only last week.*

A
B
C
D
E
F
G
H
I
J
K
L
M
N
O
P
Q
R
S
T
U
V
W
X
Y
Z

piece • *I disagree with your recent piece about Australia.*

story • *Most newspapers had a story about the film's premiere.*

article ② NOUN

a particular item • *household articles*

item • *Various items have gone missing from my desk.*

object • *everyday objects such as wooden spoons*

thing • *I have a few things to buy for the trip.*

ashamed ADJECTIVE

feeling embarrassed or guilty • *He was not even ashamed of what he had done.*

embarrassed • *I'm not embarrassed to admit I cried.*

guilty • *When she realized I was watching, she looked guilty.*

humiliated • *I felt humiliated at the scene he was causing.*

sheepish • *"I'm afraid it was my idea,"* he admitted, looking sheepish.*

sorry • *She's really sorry for all the trouble she's caused.*

MORE SYNONYMS:
• chagrined
• mortified

ANTONYM:
• proud

ask ① VERB

to put a question to someone • *She asked me if I'd enjoyed my dinner.*

inquire • *I rang up to inquire about train times.*

interrogate • *I interrogated everyone even slightly involved.*

query • *He queried whether it could have been sabotage.*

question • *He was questioned by police.*

quiz • *He was quizzed about his eligibility for benefits.*

ANTONYM:
• answer

ask ② VERB

to make a request to someone • *We had to ask him to leave.*

appeal • *The police appealed for witnesses to come forward.*

beg • *I begged him to leave me alone.*

demand • *I demanded an explanation from him.*

implore • *I implored him not to give it up.*

plead • *She pleaded to be allowed to go.*

seek • *Always seek legal advice before entering into any agreement.*

MORE SYNONYMS:
• beseech
• entreat

ask ③ VERB

to invite someone • *Not everybody had been asked to the wedding.*

bid (LITERARY) • *They all smiled at him and bade him eat.*

invite • *She invited him to her 26th birthday party.*

aspect NOUN

a feature of something • *Exam results are only one aspect of a school's success.*

consideration • *The cost involved will be a chief consideration in our choice.*

element • *Fitness is now an important element in our lives.*

factor • *an important factor in a child's development*

feature • *the most significant feature of his childhood*

part • *Respect is an important part of any relationship.*

point • *There is another point to remember when making your decision.*

side • *He had a darker side to his character.*

assemble ① VERB

to gather together in a group

• *a convenient place for students to assemble between classes*

collect • *We all collected round him to listen.*

come together • *a common room where we can come together and relax*

congregate • *Youngsters love to congregate here in the evenings.*

convene • *A grand jury has convened to gather evidence.*

gather • *We all gathered in the board room.*

mass • *Troops were massing on both sides of the border.*

assemble ② VERB

to fit the parts of something together • *Workers were assembling planes.*

build • *A carpenter built the shelves for us.*

construct • *He had constructed a crude explosive device.*

erect • *Stagehands are employed to erect the scenery.*

make • *I like making model aeroplanes.*

put together • *You can buy the parts and put it together yourself.*

assistant NOUN

a person who helps someone • *His assistant took over while he went out.*

aide • *a presidential aide*

ally • *her political allies*

colleague • *a business colleague*

helper • *volunteer helpers*

right-hand man • *the resignation of the manager's right-hand man*

associate ① VERB

to connect one thing with another • *Poverty is associated with old age.*

connect • *a common problem directly connected with stress*

couple • *The papers coupled the Gulf crisis with the problems facing the former Soviet Union.*

identify • *Candidates want to identify themselves with reform.*

link • *Liver cancer is linked to the hepatitis B virus.*

associate ② VERB

to spend time with a person • *I began associating with different crowds of people.*

hang out (INFORMAL) • *People want to hang out with you for the wrong reasons.*

mingle • *reporters who mingled freely with the crowd*

mix • *local youths who want to mix with the foreign tourists*

run around (INFORMAL) • *What's he doing running around with a teenager?*

socialize • *She made little effort to socialize with other staff.*

MORE SYNONYMS:

• consort
• fraternize

associate ③ NOUN

a person known through work • *the restaurant owner's business associates*

colleague • *learning from more experienced colleagues*

co-worker • *Their Chinese co-workers often worked seven days a week.*

workmate • *employees who expose dishonest workmates*

association ① NOUN

an organization • *a research association*

body • *the chairman of the policemen's representative body*

club • *the local Young Conservatives' club*

company • *a major motor company*

confederation • *the Confederation of British Industry*

group • *an environmental group*

institution • *a member of various financial institutions*

league • *the World Muslim League*

society • *the Royal Society for the Protection of Birds*

A
B
C
D
E
F
G
H
I
J
K
L
M
N
O
P
Q
R
S
T
U
V
W
X
Y
Z

syndicate • *a syndicate of international banks*

ANOTHER SYNONYM:
• fraternity

association ② NOUN

a connection or involvement with a person or group • *his association with a terrorist group*

affiliation • *He has no affiliation with any political party.*

attachment • *Mother and child form a close attachment.*

bond • *There is a special bond between us.*

connection • *He has denied any connection with the organization.*

relationship • *Ours was strictly a professional relationship.*

tie • *I had very close ties with the family.*

MORE SYNONYMS:
• affinity
• liaison

assume ① VERB

to accept that something is true • *I assumed that he would turn up.*

believe • *I believe she'll be back next week.*

guess (INFORMAL) *I guess she thought that was pretty smart.*

imagine • *You tend to imagine that you cannot put a foot wrong.*

suppose • *I see no reason to suppose that it isn't working.*

think • *They thought that they had the match won.*

assume ② VERB

to take responsibility for something • *Mr Cross will assume the role of Chief Executive.*

accept • *He accepted the role of player-captain.*

shoulder • *He has had to shoulder the responsibility of his father's mistakes.*

take on • *Don't take on more responsibilities than you can handle.*

undertake • *He undertook to edit the text himself.*

astute ADJECTIVE

very intelligent or perceptive • *an astute judge of character*

alert • *He is old, but he has a very quick and alert mind.*

clever • *a clever business move*

keen • *a keen understanding of politics*

perceptive • *his perceptive analysis of the situation*

quick • *He has an enquiring mind and a quick intelligence.*

sharp • *His gentle manner disguised a sharp mind.*

shrewd • *He demonstrated a shrewd understanding of human nature.*

smart • *a very smart move*

ANOTHER SYNONYM:
• discerning

attach VERB

to join or fasten things together • *The gadget can be attached to any surface.*

affix • *His name was affixed to the wall of his cubicle.*

connect • *Connect the pipe to the tap.*

couple • *The engine is coupled to a gearbox.*

fasten • *The shelves are fastened to the wall with screws.*

join • *two sticks joined together by a chain*

link • *tree houses linked by ropes*

tie • *He tied the dog to a post with its leash.*

ANTONYM:
• separate

attachment ① NOUN

a feeling of love and affection • *Mother and child form a close attachment.*

affection · *the affection between a pet and its owner*

bond · *There has always been a strong bond between us.*

fondness · *I have a great fondness for all animals.*

liking · *He has never shown any liking for his colleagues.*

love · *A deep love gradually developed between them.*

attachment ② NOUN

a part attached to something else · *The drill comes with a wide range of attachments.*

accessory · *a range of accessories for your mobile phone*

component · *Additional components are available as listed.*

fitting · *bathroom fittings*

fixture · *The box can be adapted to take a light fixture.*

part · *Extra parts can be added later.*

unit · *The unit plugs into any TV set.*

attack ① VERB

to use violence against someone or something · *I thought he was going to attack me.*

assault · *The gang assaulted him with iron bars.*

charge · *He ordered us to charge.*

invade · *The allies invaded the Italian mainland at Anzio.*

raid · *He was found guilty of raiding a bank.*

set upon · *As the lorry drove east it was set upon by bandits.*

storm · *The refugees decided to storm the embassy.*

attack ② VERB

to criticize someone strongly · *She attacked the government's economic policies.*

blast · *He blasted the referee for his inconsistency.*

censure · *The bank has been censured and fined by the authority.*

criticize · *The regime has been harshly criticized.*

have a go at (BRITISH; INFORMAL) · *If they made a mistake the crowd would have a go at them.*

put down (INFORMAL) · *He was always putting me down.*

vilify (FORMAL) · *He was vilified, hounded, and forced into exile.*

MORE SYNONYMS:
• berate
• lambast or
• lambaste
• revile

attack ③ NOUN

violent physical action against someone or something · *a vicious attack on an unarmed man*

assault · *The rebels are poised for a new assault.*

charge · *a bayonet charge*

invasion · *the Roman invasion of Britain*

offensive · *the government's military offensive against the rebels*

onslaught · *civilians trying to flee from the military onslaught*

raid · *a raid on a house by armed police*

attempt ① VERB

to try to do something · *They attempted to escape.*

endeavour · *I will endeavour to arrange it.*

seek · *We have never sought to impose our views.*

strive · *The school strives to treat pupils as individuals.*

try · *I tried hard to persuade him to stay.*

try your hand at · *He'd always wanted to try his hand at writing.*

attempt ② NOUN

an act of trying to do something · *one*

A
B
C
D
E
F
G
H
I
J
K
L
M
N
O
P
Q
R
S
T
U
V
W
X
Y
Z

of his rare attempts at humour
bid • *a bid to save the newspaper*
crack (INFORMAL) • *his third crack at the world heavyweight title*
go (INFORMAL) • *My mum suggested I should have a go at becoming a jockey.*
shot (INFORMAL) • *We'd like a shot at winning the league.*
stab (INFORMAL) • *Several tennis stars have had a stab at acting.*
try • *That makes the scheme worth a try.*

attitude NOUN
someone's way of thinking and behaving • *negative attitudes to work*
outlook • *behaviour that seems contrary to his whole outlook*
perspective • *It gave me a new perspective on life.*
point of view • *Try to look at this from my point of view.*
position • *What's your position on this issue?*
stance • *the Church's stance on contraception*

attract VERB
to appeal to or interest • *The trials have attracted many leading riders.*
appeal to • *The idea appealed to him.*
draw • *The match drew a large crowd.*
entice • *She resisted attempts to entice her into politics.*
lure • *They were being lured into a trap.*
pull (INFORMAL) • *They have to employ performers to pull a crowd.*
tempt • *Can I tempt you with some wine?*

ANTONYM:
• repel

attractive ADJECTIVE
pleasant, especially to look at • *an attractive woman*
appealing • *a sense of humour that I found very appealing*

charming • *a charming little village*
fetching • *a fetching outfit*
handsome • *a handsome man*
lovely • *a lovely island*
pretty • *a shy, pretty girl*

MORE SYNONYMS:
• comely
• prepossessing
• winsome

ANTONYM:
• unattractive

attribute NOUN
a quality or feature • *a normal attribute of human behaviour*
characteristic • *their physical characteristics*
feature • *the most striking feature of his music*
property • *the magnetic properties of iron*
quality • *His humility is one of his most endearing qualities.*
trait • *personality traits*

MORE SYNONYMS:
• idiosyncrasy
• peculiarity

augment VERB
to add something to something else • *a good way to augment your basic wage*
add to • *A fitted kitchen adds to the value of your house.*
boost • *people who boost their earnings by working part-time from home*
complement • *an in-work benefit that complements earnings*
increase • *He is eager to increase his income by any means.*
reinforce • *measures which will reinforce their current strengths*
supplement • *I suggest supplementing your diet with vitamin A.*
top up • *compulsory contributions to top up pension schemes*

authentic ADJECTIVE
real and genuine • *an authentic French recipe*
bona fide • *We are happy to donate to bona fide charities.*
dinkum (AUSTRALIAN AND NEW ZEALAND; INFORMAL) • *a place which serves dinkum Aussie tucker*
genuine • *Experts are convinced the manuscript is genuine.*
real • *It's a real Rembrandt.*
true • *Of course she's not a true blonde.*
ANTONYM:
• fake

automatic ① ADJECTIVE
operating mechanically by itself
• *Modern trains have automatic doors.*
automated • *highly automated production lines*
mechanical • *the oldest working mechanical clock in the world*
robot • *a robot telescope*
self-propelled • *self-propelled artillery*

automatic ② ADJECTIVE
without conscious thought
• *automatic body functions*
instinctive • *an instinctive reaction*
involuntary • *involuntary muscle movements*
natural • *the insect's natural instinct to feed*
reflex • *Blushing is a reflex action linked to the nervous system.*

automobile NOUN (AMERICAN)
a vehicle for carrying a few people
• *the Japanese automobile manufacturer*
car • *My dad's promised me a car if I pass my finals.*
motor • *He's bought himself a flash new motor.*
vehicle • *A child ran straight out in front of the vehicle.*

available ADJECTIVE
ready for use • *There are three small boats available for hire.*
accessible • *This information is accessible on the internet.*
at hand • *Having the right equipment at hand will be enormously useful.*
at someone's disposal • *Do you have all the facts at your disposal?*
free • *There was only one seat free on the train.*
handy • *Keep your keys handy so you can get into your car quickly.*
to hand • *Keep your insurance details to hand when driving.*
ANTONYM:
• unavailable

average ① ADJECTIVE
standard or normal • *the average American teenager*
normal • *I am now back to leading a perfectly normal life.*
regular • *He's just a regular guy.*
standard • *the standard price of a CD*
typical • *A typical day begins at 8.30.*
usual • *This isn't the usual kind of mail-order catalogue.*

average ② : **on average** ADVERB
for the most part • *Men are, on average, taller than women.*
as a rule • *As a rule, the fee is roughly equal to the savings you have made.*
generally • *A glass of fine wine generally costs about £4.*
normally • *Normally, the transport system carries 50,000 passengers a day.*
typically • *In America, estate agents typically charge 5-6% of the sale price.*
usually • *In good condition, these models usually fetch up to 300 dollars at auction.*

avoid ① VERB
to make an effort not to do

something • *We economists always try to avoid giving a straight answer.*
dodge • *dodging military service by feigning illness*
duck out of (INFORMAL) • *ducking out of the post-match press conference*
fight shy of • *She fought shy of confronting her critics.*
refrain from • *Mrs Hardie refrained from making any comment.*
shirk • *We won't shirk our responsibility.*

MORE SYNONYMS:
• circumvent
• give a wide berth to

avoid ② VERB
to keep away from someone or something • *She thought he was trying to avoid her.*
dodge • *He refuses to dodge his critics.*
elude • *an attempt to elude photographers*
eschew (FORMAL) • *He eschewed publicity and avoided nightclubs.*
evade • *He managed to evade the police.*
shun • *Everybody shunned him.*
sidestep • *Rarely does he sidestep a question.*
steer clear of • *It would be best to steer clear of her.*

aware ① : **aware of** ADJECTIVE
conscious of something • *She was acutely aware of the noise of the city.*
acquainted with • *He was well acquainted with American literature.*
conscious of • *She was very*

conscious of Max studying her.
familiar with • *I am not familiar with your work.*
mindful of • *Everyone should be mindful of the dangers.*

ANTONYM:
• unaware

aware ② ADJECTIVE
knowing about something • *Keep me aware of any developments.*
informed • *the importance of keeping the public properly informed*
in the picture • *He's always kept me in the picture.*
knowledgeable • *He's very knowledgeable about new technology.*

MORE SYNONYMS:
• au courant
• in the loop

awful ADJECTIVE
very unpleasant or very bad • *the same awful jokes*
appalling • *living under the most appalling conditions*
dreadful • *They told us the dreadful news.*
frightful • *a frightful ordeal*
ghastly • *a mother accompanied by her ghastly unruly child*
horrendous • *The violence used was horrendous.*
terrible • *Her French is terrible.*

MORE SYNONYMS:
• abysmal
• deplorable

Bb

babble VERB
to talk in an excited way • *He babbled on and on.*
burble • *He burbles on about the goals he has scored.*
chatter • *Jane chattered about the children.*
gabble • *I started to gabble in the interview.*
prattle • *Alan is prattling on again.*

baby NOUN
a very young child • *I've had this birthmark since I was a baby.*
ankle-biter (AUSTRALIAN AND NEW ZEALAND; SLANG) • *I knew him when he was just an ankle-biter.*
bairn (SCOTTISH) • *My wife's expecting a bairn.*
child • *They celebrated the birth of their first child.*
infant • *young mums with infants in prams*

back ① NOUN
the part that is behind the front • *the back of a postcard*
end • *the end of the corridor*
rear • *the rear of the building*
reverse • *the reverse of the sheet*
stern • *the stern of a boat*

ANTONYM:
• front

back ② VERB
to support a person or organization • *His friends are backing him.*

advocate • *Mr Jones advocates longer school days.*
encourage • *The government is encouraging better child care.*
endorse • *Do you endorse his opinion?*
favour • *I favour a different approach.*
promote • *Ann is promoting Alan's ideas.*
support • *We supported his political campaign.*

MORE SYNONYMS:
• champion
• espouse
• second

ANTONYM:
• oppose

background NOUN
where you come from • *a rich background*
culture • *people from different cultures*
environment • *the environment I grew up in*
history • *She has an interesting history.*
upbringing • *a strict upbringing*

bad ① ADJECTIVE
harmful, unpleasant, or upsetting • *I have some bad news.*
▶ see Word Study **bad**, page 635

ANTONYM:
• good

bad ② ADJECTIVE
of poor quality • *bad roads*
▶ see Word Study **bad**, page 635

A
B
C
D
E
F
G
H
I
J
K
L
M
N
O
P
Q
R
S
T
U
V
W
X
Y
Z

ANTONYM:
• satisfactory

bad ③ ADJECTIVE
evil in character • *a bad person*
▶ see Word Study **bad**, page 635
ANTONYM:
• good

badly ① ADVERB
in an inferior way • *This essay is badly written.*
inadequately • *He had been inadequately trained for the job.*
ineptly • *a department which is run ineptly*
poorly • *The event had been poorly organized.*
shoddily • *housing which is ugly and shoddily built*
unsatisfactorily • *an unsatisfactorily regulated system*
ANTONYM:
• well

badly ② ADVERB
seriously • *She was badly hurt in a fall.*
deeply • *I was deeply hurt by these comments.*
desperately • *Felicity looked desperately unhappy.*
gravely • *He was gravely ill following a heart operation.*
seriously • *Four people have been seriously injured.*
ANTONYM:
• slightly

badly ③ ADVERB
in a cruel manner • *He treated his dog badly.*
brutally • *marchers being brutally assaulted by riot police*
callously • *She taunted her husband callously.*
cruelly • *He was cruelly tormented by his older brothers.*

savagely • *an old man savagely beaten by thugs*
viciously • *He struck me viciously across the face.*
ANTONYM:
• well

bait NOUN
something used to tempt someone
• *Charles isn't taking the bait.*
bribe • *a politician who took bribes*
decoy • *He acted as a decoy to trap the murderer.*
inducement • *financial inducements to talk to the newspapers*
lure • *the lure of a huge salary*
temptation • *the temptation of easy money*

balance ① VERB
to make or remain steady • *Balancing on one leg is difficult.*
level • *House prices have levelled.*
stabilize • *attempts to stabilize the economy*
steady • *He steadied himself and shot at goal.*

balance ② NOUN
a stable relationship between things
• *the chemical balance of the brain*
equilibrium • *the political equilibrium of Europe*
equity • *plans for greater equity of incomes*
equivalence • *the lack of equivalence between film and radio*
parity • *She won pay parity with male colleagues.*

ball NOUN
a round object • *a ball of wool*
drop • *a drop of blood*
globe • *the globe of the eyeball*
pellet • *an airgun pellet*
sphere • *a sphere the size of the Earth*

MORE SYNONYMS:
• globule
• orb
• spheroid

ban ① VERB
to disallow something • *I am banned from taking part.*
bar • *The press will be barred from the talks.*
disqualify • *He was disqualified from driving.*
exclude • *They were excluded from the maths class.*
forbid • *The rules forbid the use of force.*
outlaw • *regulations outlawing child labour*
prohibit • *a law that prohibits alcohol*
MORE SYNONYMS:
• banish
• proscribe
• suppress
ANTONYM:
• permit

ban ② NOUN
a rule disallowing something • *a ban on smoking*
disqualification • *a four-year disqualification from athletics*
embargo • *an embargo on trade with the country*
prohibition • *a prohibition on tobacco*
suppression • *the suppression of anti-government protests*
ANTONYM:
• permit

band ① NOUN
a group of musicians who play together • *a singer in a rock and roll band*
group • *They formed the group while they were still at school.*
orchestra • *the National Youth Orchestra*

MORE SYNONYMS:
• combo
• ensemble

band ② NOUN
a group of people who share a common purpose • *a band of rebels*
bunch • *A bunch of protesters were picketing the factory.*
company • *a company of actors*
crowd • *A small crowd of onlookers had gathered.*
gang • *a gang of criminals*
party • *a party of sightseers*
troupe • *She toured with a professional dance troupe.*

bang ① VERB
to hit or put something down hard, with a loud noise • *a toddler banging a saucepan with a wooden spoon*
beat • *They sat in a circle, beating small drums.*
hammer • *The supporters hammered on the windows of the bus.*
hit • *They were hitting the sides of the van with sticks.*
knock • *I knocked on the door for ages, but no-one answered.*
pound • *We pounded on the walls.*
slam • *I slammed down the receiver.*
thump • *The children cheered and thumped on their desks.*

bang ② NOUN
a sudden, short, loud noise • *The TV exploded with a bang.*
blast • *the ear-splitting blast of a cannon*
boom • *There was a boom and a cloud of smoke.*
crack • *the crack of a pistol shot*
detonation • *We heard several loud detonations coming from the building.*
explosion • *the deafening explosion of gunshots*
thump • *She dropped her case to the floor with a loud thump.*

a
b
c
d
e
f
g
h
i
j
k
l
m
n
o
p
q
r
s
t
u
v
w
x
y
z

A
B
C
D
E
F
G
H
I
J
K
L
M
N
O
P
Q
R
S
T
U
V
W
X
Y
Z

bang ③ NOUN
a hard or painful bump against
something • *I got a nasty bang on the
elbow.*
blow • *a blow to the side of the head*
clout (INFORMAL) • *She gave him a
swift clout on the ear.*
knock • *Knocks like this can cause
damage to the spine.*
thump • *Ralph got a thump on the chest.*
whack • *She gave the horse a whack on
the rump.*

banish ① VERB
to exile someone • *She banished him
from the house.*
deport • *Many fans are being
deported from Italy.*
eject • *He was ejected from the club.*
evict • *Police evicted ten families from
the building.*
exile • *He was exiled from Russia.*
expel • *patients expelled from hospitals*
transport • *He was transported to
a prison camp.*

banish ② VERB
to get rid of something or someone
• *to banish illness*
discard • *Read the instructions before
discarding the box.*
dismiss • *I dismissed the idea from
my mind.*
dispel • *The myths are being dispelled.*
eliminate • *They eliminated him from
their enquiries.*
eradicate • *projects to eradicate
certain diseases*
remove • *talks to remove the last
obstacles to the deal*

bank ① NOUN
a store of something • *a blood bank*
fund • *a pension fund*
hoard • *a hoard of treasure*
reserve • *the world's oil reserves*

stock • *stocks of paper and ink*
store • *a secret store of sweets*
MORE SYNONYMS:
• reservoir
• stockpile

bank ② NOUN
the edge of a river or lake • *He sat
fishing on the bank.*
brink • *orchards near the brink of the
sea cliffs*
edge • *She stood too close to the edge
and fell in.*
shore • *He swam towards the shore.*
side • *a picnic by the side of the river*

bar ① NOUN
a piece of metal • *bars across the
windows*
pole • *He was tied to a pole.*
rail • *a curtain rail*
rod • *a fishing rod*
shaft • *the shaft of a spear*

bar ② VERB
to stop someone • *His bodyguards
barred the way.*
obstruct • *Vehicles have obstructed the
entrance.*
prevent • *A fence prevents people from
entering.*

bare ① ADJECTIVE
not covered • *bare legs*
exposed • *His whole back is exposed.*
naked • *a naked body*
nude • *a nude model*
stripped • *I got stripped to have a shower.*
uncovered • *His arms were uncovered.*
undressed • *She got undressed in the
bathroom.*

ANTONYM:
• covered

bare ② ADJECTIVE
with nothing on top or inside • *a small
bare office*

empty • *an empty room*
open • *open country*
spartan • *spartan accommodation*
vacant • *a vacant chair*

barely ADVERB

only just • *She is barely sixteen.*
almost • *I almost didn't make it.*
hardly • *I could hardly believe it.*
just • *They only just won.*
scarcely • *I can scarcely hear her.*

barren ① ADJECTIVE

with nothing growing on it • *a barren desert*
arid • *the arid lands of Botswana*
desert • *desert regions*
desolate • *a desolate place*
dry • *poor, dry countries*
empty • *the empty desert*
waste • *waste land*

MORE SYNONYMS:
• unfruitful
• unproductive

ANTONYM:
• fertile

barren ② ADJECTIVE

unable to produce babies • *women who are barren*
childless • *childless couples*
infertile • *infertile women*
sterile • *sterile females*

ANTONYM:
• fertile

barrier ① NOUN

something preventing entry
• *Demonstrators broke through the barriers.*
barricade • *a barricade of vehicles*
fence • *a garden fence*
obstruction • *Check the exhaust pipe is clear of obstructions.*
wall • *the huge city walls*

MORE SYNONYMS:
• fortification
• obstacle
• rampart

barrier ② NOUN

something that prevents progress
• *plans to reduce the barriers to trade*
handicap • *It is a handicap not knowing a foreign language.*
hindrance • *a potential hindrance to the peace process*
hurdle • *the first hurdle in a job search*
impediment • *a serious impediment to free trade*
obstacle • *the main obstacle to the takeover*

base ① NOUN

the lowest part of something • *the base of the cliffs*
bed • *the river bed*
bottom • *the bottom of the lake*
foot • *the foot of the mountain*
foundation • *They have laid the foundations for the new building.*
pedestal • *The statue is back on its pedestal.*
stand • *a microphone stand*

ANTONYM:
• top

base ② NOUN

the place you work from • *a military base*
camp • *refugee camps*
centre • *a health centre*
headquarters • *army headquarters in Colombo*
post • *a military post in the capital*
station • *the police station*

base ③ VERB

to use as a foundation • *The film is based on a true story.*
build • *a reputation built on lies*
derive • *The name is derived from a Greek word.*

a
b
c
d
e
f
g
h
i
j
k
l
m
n
o
p
q
r
s
t
u
v
w
x
y
z

A
B
C
D
E
F
G
H
I
J
K
L
M
N
O
P
Q
R
S
T
U
V
W
X
Y
Z

found • *My hopes were founded on a mistake.*
ground • *I like a film to be grounded in reality.*
hinge • *The whole play hinges on one character.*

basic ADJECTIVE
most necessary • *the basic requirements for the job*
elementary • *elementary computer training*
essential • *essential reading and writing skills*
fundamental • *fundamental rights*
key • *key skills such as communication and teamwork*
necessary • *They lack the necessary resources.*
vital • *vital supplies*

MORE SYNONYMS:
• central
• indispensable
• primary

basis NOUN
the main principle of something • *The same theme is the basis of several poems.*
core • *the core of Asia's problems*
fundamental • *the fundamentals of road safety*
heart • *the heart of the matter*
premise • *the premise of his argument*
principle • *the principles of Buddhism*

bay ① NOUN
a curve in a coastline • *the Bay of Biscay*
cove • *a sandy cove with white cliffs*
gulf • *the Gulf of Mexico*
inlet • *a deep inlet on the west coast*
sound • *streams that run into the sound*

bay ② VERB
to make a howling noise • *wolves baying in the moonlight*
bark • *a small dog barking at a seagull*
cry • *I heard animals cry in the forest.*

howl • *distant coyotes howling in the night*
yelp • *A dog snapped and yelped at them.*

beach NOUN
an area beside the sea • *making sandcastles on the beach*
coast • *a day at the coast*
sands • *the long white sands of Goa*
seashore • *walks along the seashore*
seaside • *trips to the seaside*
shore • *He swam out from the shore.*
strand • *collecting shells on the strand*

bear ① VERB
to carry something • *The ice wasn't thick enough to bear their weight.*
carry • *He always carried a gun.*
convey • *The taxi conveyed us to the centre.*
shoulder • *He had to shoulder the blame for the mistake.*
support • *Thick wooden posts support the ceiling.*
take • *You'd better take an umbrella.*

bear ② VERB
to have or show something • *The room bore the signs of a violent struggle.*
exhibit • *He began to exhibit symptoms of the disease.*
harbour • *She still harbours feelings of resentment.*
have • *I have a grudge against her.*

bear ③ VERB
to accept something • *He can't bear to talk about it.*
abide • *I can't abide arrogant people.*
endure • *The pain was hard to endure.*
stomach • *He could not stomach violence.*
suffer • *I had to suffer his company all day.*
tolerate • *Women tolerate pain better than men.*

beat ① VERB
to hit someone or something hard
• *He threatened to beat her.*
batter • *The waves kept battering the life raft.*
buffet • *Their plane was buffeted by storms.*
hit • *He hit me on the head.*
pound • *Someone was pounding on the door.*
strike • *She struck him across the mouth.*
thrash • *He was thrashed by his father.*

beat ② VERB
to defeat • *She was easily beaten in the race.*
defeat • *The team hasn't been defeated all year.*
outdo • *One man was trying to outdo the other.*
outstrip • *The company is outstripping its rivals.*
overcome • *Molly had overcome her fear of flying.*
overwhelm • *One attack could overwhelm the enemy.*
vanquish • *the man who helped vanquish Napoleon*
MORE SYNONYMS:
• conquer
• master
• surpass

beat ③ NOUN
a rhythm • *the thumping beat of rock music*
cadence • *the pulsing cadences of his music*
metre • *the strict metre of the poem*
rhythm • *His foot tapped a rhythm on the floor.*
stress • *differences of stress in speech*
time • *a song written in waltz time*

beautiful ADJECTIVE
attractive or pleasing • *beautiful music*
attractive • *an attractive woman*
delightful • *The perfume is delightful.*
fine • *a fine summer's day*
gorgeous • *a gorgeous man*
lovely • *You look lovely.*
pleasing • *a pleasing appearance*
MORE SYNONYMS:
• exquisite
• fair
ANTONYM:
• ugly

beauty ① NOUN
the quality of being beautiful • *an area of outstanding beauty*
attractiveness • *the attractiveness of the region*
charm • *a woman of great charm*
elegance • *the elegance of the overall design*
loveliness • *the loveliness of the scene*
ANTONYM:
• ugliness

beauty ② NOUN
a good-looking person • *a dark-haired beauty*
hunk (INFORMAL) • *The Swedish hunk is back again.*
stunner (INFORMAL) • *the 23-year-old stunner*

beauty ③ NOUN
an attractive feature • *The beauty of the fund is its simplicity.*
advantage • *the advantages of the new system over the old one*
asset • *The one asset the job provided was contacts.*
attraction • *The main attraction of the place is the monument.*
benefit • *Every age has its benefits.*

because CONJUNCTION
for the reason that • *I went home*

because I was tired.
as • *Don't cook for me as I'll be home late.*
since • *Since you didn't listen, I'll repeat that.*

MORE SYNONYMS:
• in that
• on account of
• owing to

before ADVERB
at a previous time • *Have you been to Greece before?*
earlier • *Here is a cake I made earlier.*
formerly • *He had formerly been in the army.*
in advance • *We booked the room well in advance.*
previously • *Previously she had little time to work.*
sooner • *I wish I'd arrived sooner.*

ANTONYM:
• after

RELATED WORDS:
• PREFIXES ante-, fore-, pre-

beg VERB
to ask anxiously for something • *I begged him to leave me alone.*
beseech • *Her eyes beseeched him to show mercy.*
implore • *I implore you not to say anything.*
petition • *He petitioned the Court to let him go free.*
plead • *She was pleading with me to stay.*

MORE SYNONYMS:
• entreat
• importune
• solicit

begin VERB
to start or cause to start • *She began to move around the room.*
commence (FORMAL) • *He commenced his journey.*

inaugurate • *The committee was inaugurated ten days ago.*
initiate • *They wanted to initiate a discussion.*
originate • *Mankind may have originated in Africa.*
set about • *He set about tackling his problems.*
start • *The meeting starts at 10 o'clock.*

MORE SYNONYMS:
• instigate
• institute

ANTONYM:
• end

beginner NOUN
someone learning to do something • *a beginner's course*
apprentice • *an apprentice in a law firm*
learner • *young learners of French*
novice • *Many of us are novices on the computer.*
starter • *new starters at school*
trainee • *a trainee in a newspaper office*

ANTONYM:
• expert

beginning NOUN
where something starts • *the beginning of the city*
birth • *the birth of modern art*
commencement (FORMAL) • *a date for the commencement of talks*
opening • *the opening of the trial*
origin • *the origins of civilization*
outset • *There were lots of problems from the outset.*
start • *the start of all the trouble*

MORE SYNONYMS:
• inauguration
• initiation
• onset

ANTONYM:
• end

behave VERB

to act in a certain way • *They were behaving like animals.*
act • *He is acting like a spoilt child.*
function • *They are functioning as a team.*
operate • *I know how Graham operates.*
work • *My mind is working well today.*

belief ① NOUN

the certainty something is true
• *belief in reincarnation*
confidence • *I have every confidence that you'll do well.*
conviction • *She speaks with conviction.*
judgment • *My judgment is that he should leave.*
opinion • *Robert has strong opinions.*
trust • *She has complete trust that you'll help her.*
view • *In my view, he is wrong.*

belief ② NOUN

a principle of a religion or system • *the culture and beliefs of ancient times*
creed • *people of every race and creed*
doctrine • *Christian doctrine*
dogma • *religious dogma*
faith • *Do you practise any faith?*
ideology • *different political ideologies*
principle • *the principles of Jewish faith*
tenet • *the fundamental tenets of Islam*

believable ADJECTIVE

possible or likely to be the case • *The book is full of believable characters.*
credible • *credible witnesses*
imaginable • *It is scarcely imaginable that it happened here.*
likely • *It's more likely that she forgot.*
plausible • *a plausible explanation*
possible • *It's quite possible that I'm wrong.*
probable • *the most probable outcome*

ANTONYM:
• unbelievable

believe VERB

to accept something is true • *Don't believe everything you read in the papers.*
accept • *He can't accept that he is wrong.*
assume • *I assume these eggs are fresh.*
presume • *The missing person is presumed to be dead.*
swallow (INFORMAL) • *I found their story hard to swallow.*
trust • *I trust that you will manage.*

ANTONYM:
• doubt

belittle VERB

to make someone or something seem less important • *He belittles my opinions.*
deride • *He is derided as weak and incompetent.*
detract from • *Her sour comments detracted from Meg's happiness.*
downgrade • *I fear failure, but I downgrade my successes.*
scorn • *Eleanor scorns the work of others.*
undervalue • *We must never undervalue freedom.*

MORE SYNONYMS:
• denigrate
• disparage
• minimize

ANTONYM:
• praise

beloved ADJECTIVE

dearly loved • *He lost his beloved wife last year.*
adored • *an adored father*
cherished • *his most cherished possession*
darling • *our darling child*
dearest • *my dearest Maria*

a
b
c
d
e
f
g
h
i
j
k
l
m
n
o
p
q
r
s
t
u
v
w
x
y
z

A
B
C
D
E
F
G
H
I
J
K
L
M
N
O
P
Q
R
S
T
U
V
W
X
Y
Z

precious • *I love my precious cat.*
treasured • *treasured memories*

ANTONYM:
• despised

below PREPOSITION OR ADVERB
lower down • *six centimetres below soil level*
beneath • *She hid the letter beneath her mattress.*
down • *I fell down to the bottom.*
lower • *The price will fall lower than this.*
under • *tunnels under the ground*
underneath • *He crawled underneath the table.*

ANTONYM:
• above

bend ① VERB
to make or become curved • *Bend the bar into a horseshoe.*
buckle • *A wave buckled the ship's deck.*
curve • *The wall curves to the left.*
turn • *The road turns right at the end.*
twist • *glass twisted into elaborate patterns*
warp • *The wood had started to warp.*

bend ② VERB
to move forwards and downwards • *I bent over and kissed her cheek.*
arch • *Don't arch your back!*
bow • *He turned and bowed to her.*
crouch • *We were crouching in the bushes.*
incline • *The woman inclined her head to one side.*
lean • *She leant out of the window.*
stoop • *Stooping down, he picked up a stone.*

bend ③ NOUN
a curve in something • *a bend in the road*
arc • *the full arc of a rainbow*
corner • *He drove round the corner.*

curve • *the curve of the stream*
loop • *The river curves in a loop.*
turn • *a turn in the path*

MORE SYNONYMS:
• angle
• arch
• twist

beneficial ADJECTIVE
giving some benefit • *Wine in moderation is beneficial to health.*
advantageous • *an advantageous arrangement*
good for you • *Regular exercise is good for you.*
healthy • *trying to switch to a healthy lifestyle*
helpful • *This treatment is particularly helpful to hay fever sufferers.*
useful • *a useful addition to your first aid kit*
wholesome • *food made with good, wholesome ingredients*

benefit ① NOUN
an advantage • *the benefits of relaxation*
advantage • *The advantages of the new system far outweigh its disadvantages.*
asset • *A second language is an asset in this job.*
boon • *a great boon for busy housewives*
gain • *He used the knowledge for his personal gain.*
good • *Study for your own good!*
help • *It's no help to know I was right.*
profit • *the profits of working hard*
use • *His training was of no use to him.*

ANTONYM:
• disadvantage

benefit ② VERB
to help in something • *The experience will benefit you.*
aid • *measures to aid working mothers*

assist • *The extra money will assist you.*
enhance • *His injury does not enhance our chances.*
further • *His support will further our cause.*
help • *The new laws won't help the environment.*
profit • *It won't profit us to complain.*

ANTONYM:
• harm

benevolent ADJECTIVE
kind and helpful • *a benevolent ruler*
benign • *a benign and loveable man*
charitable • *charitable organizations*
compassionate • *my compassionate friends*
humane • *humane treatment of prisoners*
kind • *You have been kind and helpful to us.*

MORE SYNONYMS:
• altruistic
• beneficent
• philanthropic

beside PREPOSITION
next to • *I stood beside my father and my uncle.*
adjacent to • *a hotel adjacent to the beach*
alongside • *a house alongside the river*
close to • *The restaurant is close to their home.*
near • *He stood very near the front door.*
next to • *She sat down next to him.*

best ① ADJECTIVE
of the highest standard • *the best film I have seen in a long time*
finest • *the finest wines available*
first-rate • *a first-rate musical performance*
foremost • *the foremost painter of his generation*
greatest • *the greatest film ever made*

leading • *He has established himself as one of Britain's leading actors.*
outstanding • *one of England's outstanding tennis players*
pre-eminent • *her status as the pre-eminent pop act of her day*
principal • *London's principal publishing houses*
superlative • *companies that offer superlative products*
supreme • *the supreme achievement of his career*
top • *one of the country's top athletes*

ANTONYM:
• worst

best ② ADJECTIVE
most desirable • *the best thing you could have said*
correct • *the correct thing to do in the circumstances*
most fitting • *the most fitting location for a house*
right • *Are you the right person for the job?*

ANTONYM:
• worst

best ③ NOUN
the preferred thing • *Of all my presents, this is the best.*
cream • *a showcase for the cream of Scottish artists*
elite • *the elite of the sporting world*
finest • *Landlord, wine! And make it the finest!*
pick • *the pick of the crop*

ANTONYM:
• worst

betray ① VERB
to do someone harm • *I was betrayed by someone I had thought a friend.*
be unfaithful • *He's been unfaithful to his wife.*
break your promise • *I broke my promise to help her.*

a
b
c
d
e
f
g
h
i
j
k
l
m
n
o
p
q
r
s
t
u
v
w
x
y
z

A
B
C
D
E
F
G
H
I
J
K
L
M
N
O
P
Q
R
S
T
U
V
W
X
Y
Z

double-cross (INFORMAL) • *I was angry that he double-crossed me.*
inform on • *people who inform on their colleagues*

betray ② VERB
to show feelings • *Jeremy's voice betrayed little emotion.*
expose • *She never exposed her hostile feelings.*
manifest • *Fear can manifest itself in many ways.*
reveal • *Her expression revealed nothing.*
show • *His eyes showed his unhappiness.*

better ① ADJECTIVE
of more worth than another • *Today was much better than yesterday.*
finer • *There is no finer place to live.*
grander • *moving to a much grander house*
greater • *Their eyes are now set on a greater prize.*
higher-quality • *We are trying to provide a higher-quality service.*
nicer • *This is a much nicer room than mine.*
preferable • *Owning property is preferable to renting.*
superior • *His work is far superior to yours.*
surpassing • *a film of surpassing quality*
worthier • *You should save your energies for a worthier cause.*

ANTONYM:
• inferior

better ② ADJECTIVE
well after being ill • *I hope you feel better soon.*
cured • *I used to have insomnia but now I'm cured.*
fitter • *I'm a lot fitter now I've started jogging.*

fully recovered • *He had a back injury but now he's fully recovered.*
healthier • *I'm much healthier since I gave up smoking.*
improving • *His symptoms are not improving despite the treatment.*
on the mend (INFORMAL) • *She's on the mend now.*
recovering • *She's recovering after an attack of appendicitis.*
stonger • *He's slowly getting stronger after his accident.*
well • *I hope you're feeling well again soon*

ANTONYM:
• worse

beware VERB
to be cautious • *Beware of the dog.*
be careful • *Be careful what you say to him.*
be cautious • *Doctors are cautious about using the treatment.*
be wary • *Michelle is wary of marriage.*
guard against • *We have to guard against thieves.*
look out • *Look out, there's a train coming.*
watch out • *Watch out for fog and ice.*

bias NOUN
prejudice for or against a person or group • *bias against women*
bigotry • *religious bigotry*
favouritism • *His promotion was due to favouritism.*
prejudice • *racial prejudice*

biased ADJECTIVE
showing prejudice • *biased attitudes*
one-eyed (AUSTRALIAN AND NEW ZEALAND) • *I may be a bit one-eyed because of the family connection.*
one-sided • *a one-sided argument*
partial • *a very partial view of the situation*

prejudiced · *Don't be prejudiced by what you read.*
slanted · *a slanted newspaper article*
weighted · *a scheme weighted towards those in need*

ANTONYM:
• neutral

big ① ADJECTIVE
of a large size · *a big house*
▶ see Word Study **big**, page 636

ANTONYM:
• small

big ② ADJECTIVE
of great importance · *a big name*
▶ see Word Study **big**, page 636

ANTONYM:
• unimportant

bill NOUN
a statement of how much is owed
· *a huge restaurant bill*
account · *Please charge it to my account.*
charges · *charges for eye tests*
invoice · *They sent an invoice for the damage.*
statement · *a credit card statement*

bit NOUN
a small amount · *a bit of coal*
crumb · *a crumb of comfort*
fragment · *glittering fragments of broken glass*
grain · *His story contains a grain of truth.*
part · *part of the problem*
piece · *The vase was smashed to pieces.*
scrap · *a scrap of evidence*

MORE SYNONYMS:
• iota
• jot
• speck

bite VERB
to cut into something with your teeth · *His cat bit me when I tried to pat it.*

chew · *a video of a man having his leg chewed off by a bear*
gnaw · *The bones had been gnawed by wild animals.*
nibble · *She nibbled a biscuit.*
nip · *There were blotches where the mosquitoes had nipped him.*

bitter ① ADJECTIVE
angry and resentful · *a bitter row*
acrimonious · *an acrimonious discussion*
begrudging · *He gave me begrudging thanks.*
embittered · *an embittered old lady*
rancorous · *the issue that has led to rancorous disputes*
resentful · *She is resentful of others' success.*
sour · *a sour expression*

bitter ② ADJECTIVE
tasting or smelling sharp · *bitter lemons*
acid · *the acid smell of sweat*
acrid · *clouds of acrid smoke*
astringent · *astringent disinfectant*
sharp · *a clean, sharp taste*
sour · *a rich, sour stew*
tart · *the tart qualities of citrus fruit*

ANTONYM:
• sweet

bizarre ADJECTIVE
very strange or eccentric · *He has some bizarre ideas about women.*
curious · *a curious mixture of ancient and modern*
eccentric · *Her eccentric behaviour was beginning to attract attention.*
extraordinary · *What an extraordinary character he is!*
odd · *a series of very odd coincidences*
outlandish · *her outlandish style of dressing*

a b c d e f g h i j k l m n o p q r s t u v w x y z

peculiar • *a peculiar combination of flavours*

queer • *A very queer thing happened to me tonight.*

strange • *She's been behaving in a very strange way lately.*

weird • *his weird theories about UFOs*

ANTONYM:
• ordinary

black NOUN OR ADJECTIVE

◆ **SHADES OF BLACK**
◆ coal-black
◆ ebony
◆ inky
◆ jet
◆ jet-black
◆ pitch-black
◆ raven
◆ sable
◆ sooty

blame ① VERB

to believe someone caused something • *Don't blame me for this trouble.*

accuse • *She accused him of causing the fire.*

charge • *He will be charged with murder.*

hold responsible • *I hold you responsible for this mess.*

blame ② NOUN

the responsibility for something bad • *I'm not going to take the blame for that!*

accountability • *He escaped accountability for his crimes.*

fault • *The fault was all yours.*

guilt • *the sole guilt for the outbreak of war*

liability • *He admitted liability for the crash.*

rap (SLANG) • *A maid took the rap for stealing the letters.*

responsibility • *responsibility for the murder*

MORE SYNONYMS:
• culpability
• incrimination

blank ① ADJECTIVE

with nothing on it • *a blank sheet of paper*

bare • *bare walls*

clean • *a clean sheet of paper*

clear • *a clear patch of floor*

empty • *an empty page*

plain • *a plain envelope*

unmarked • *an unmarked board*

blank ② ADJECTIVE

showing no feeling • *John just looked blank.*

deadpan • *a deadpan expression*

dull • *a dull stare*

empty • *She saw the empty look in his eyes.*

impassive • *her impassive smile*

vacant • *the vacant expression on his face*

blend ① VERB

to mix things so as to form a single item or substance • *Blend the butter with the sugar.*

combine • *Combine the ingredients in a large bowl.*

merge • *how to merge the graphics with the text*

mingle • *the mingled smells of flowers and cigar smoke*

mix • *Mix the two liquids together with a whisk.*

ANTONYM:
• separate

blend ② VERB

to combine in a pleasing way • *The colours blend with the rest of the decor.*

complement • *The flavours complement each other perfectly.*

co-ordinate • *Choose accessories which co-ordinate with your outfit.*

go well • *a wine which goes well with fish*
harmonize • *shades which harmonize with most skin tones*
match • *Those shoes don't match that dress.*
suit • *glasses which suit the shape of your face*

blend ③ NOUN
a mixture or combination of things • *a blend of wine and sparkling water*
alloy • *an alloy of copper and tin*
amalgamation • *Bartók's rich amalgamation of musical styles*
combination • *a fantastic combination of colours*
compound • *a compound of water, sugar and enzymes*
fusion • *a fusion of cooking styles*
mix • *a delicious mix of exotic spices*
mixture • *a sticky mixture of flour and water*

bless VERB
to ask God's protection • *The bishop blessed the congregation.*
anoint • *The priest anointed the child with oil.*
consecrate • *ground that has been consecrated*
dedicate • *The well was dedicated to saints.*
hallow • *A building could be hallowed by prayer.*

ANTONYM:
• curse

blessing ① NOUN
something good • *Good health is a blessing.*
benefit • *the benefits of technology*
boon • *This service is a boon to the elderly.*
gift • *A cheerful nature is a gift.*
godsend • *The extra twenty dollars was a godsend.*

help • *My computer is a real help in my work.*

ANTONYM:
• disadvantage

blessing ② NOUN
approval or permission to do something • *She got married with her parents' blessing.*
approval • *Does this plan have your approval?*
backing • *We can't do anything without his backing.*
consent • *He gave his consent to the article.*
leave • *She gave us leave to start.*
permission • *You have my permission to go.*
support • *My manager has given his full support to my project.*

MORE SYNONYMS:
• approbation
• sanction

ANTONYM:
• disapproval

blob NOUN
a small amount of a thick or sticky substance • *He had a blob of chocolate mousse on his tie.*
bead • *Beads of blood spattered the counter.*
dab • *You've got a dab of glue on your nose.*
drop • *a few thick drops of fluid*
droplet • *droplets of congealed fat*

block ① NOUN
a large piece • *a block of wood*
bar • *a bar of soap*
brick • *concrete bricks*
chunk • *chunks of meat*
ingot • *a gold ingot*
lump • *lumps of metal*
piece • *a big piece of cake*

A
B
C
D
E
F
G
H
I
J
K
L
M
N
O
P
Q
R
S
T
U
V
W
X
Y
Z

block ② VERB
to close by putting something
across • *Mud blocked the river.*
choke • *The town was choked with
cars.*
clog • *Dishes clogged the sink.*
obstruct • *The crash obstructed the
road.*
plug • *Did you plug the leaks?*
ANTONYM:
• unblock

block ③ VERB
to prevent something happening
• *The council blocked his plans.*
bar • *He was barred from entering.*
check • *a policy to check population
growth*
halt • *attempts to halt the spread of
disease*
obstruct • *Lack of funds obstructed
our progress.*
stop • *measures to stop the rising
crime rate*
thwart • *My plans were thwarted by
Taylor.*

blockage NOUN
a thing that clogs something • *a
blockage in the pipe*
block • *a block in the blood vessel*
obstruction • *an obstruction on the
track*
stoppage • *We have to clear the
stoppage.*

blog NOUN
a journal written on the internet • *a
blog about fashion*
chatroom • *writing in an online
chatroom*
microblog • *a huge fan of microblogs*
vlog • *I put up the occasional vlog on my
website.*
weblog • *a weblog that features
whatever is on her mind*

blow ① VERB
to move or cause to move in the
wind • *The wind blew his papers away.*
buffet • *The ship was buffeted by
gales.*
drive • *The strong wind drove us
forward.*
flutter • *The flags are fluttering.*
sweep • *A sudden blast swept away
the cloth.*
waft • *His hair wafted in the breeze.*
whirl • *The fallen leaves whirled
around.*

blow ② NOUN
a hit from something • *a blow to the
head*
bang • *He suffered some bangs and
bumps.*
clout (INFORMAL) • *a clout on the head*
knock • *Knocks can cause damage to
the spine.*
smack • *She gave the child a smack.*
thump • *Ralph got a thump on the
chest.*
whack • *The horse got a whack from
its rider.*

blow ③ NOUN
something disappointing or
upsetting • *Marc's death was a terrible
blow.*
bombshell • *His departure was a
bombshell for the team.*
disappointment • *My exam results
were a real disappointment.*
misfortune • *a series of misfortunes*
setback • *We faced many setbacks
before we got the house.*
shock • *The news came as a shock.*
upset • *The defeat caused an upset.*
MORE SYNONYMS:
• calamity
• catastrophe
• jolt

blue NOUN or ADJECTIVE

◆ **SHADES OF BLUE**
- aqua
- aquamarine
- azure
- cerulean
- cobalt
- cyan
- duck-egg blue
- electric blue
- gentian
- indigo
- lapis lazuli
- midnight blue
- navy
- Nile blue
- peacock blue
- periwinkle
- petrol blue
- royal blue
- sapphire
- saxe blue
- sky-blue
- teal
- turquoise
- ultramarine

blunt ① ADJECTIVE
having rounded edges • *blunt scissors*
dull • *a dull knife*
rounded • *rounded edges*
unsharpened • *an unsharpened pencil*

ANTONYM:
• sharp

blunt ② ADJECTIVE
saying what you think • *a blunt speaker*
bluff • *a bluff old man*
brusque • *His response was brusque.*
forthright • *a forthright reply*
frank • *I'll be frank with you.*
outspoken • *an outspoken critic*
straightforward • *She has a straightforward manner.*

MORE SYNONYMS:
• explicit
• tactless
• trenchant

ANTONYM:
• tactful

blush ① VERB
to go red in the face • *I felt myself blushing.*
colour • *I found myself colouring as I spoke.*
crimson • *He looked at her and she crimsoned.*
flush • *I saw her face flush.*
go red • *His face went red as a beetroot.*
turn red • *He turned red with embarrassment.*
turn scarlet • *She turned scarlet with humiliation.*

blush ② NOUN
a red colour • *Ann took the gift with a blush.*
colour • *The walk will bring colour to your cheeks.*
flush • *A slow flush spread over the man's face.*
glow • *a healthy glow*

boast VERB
to talk proudly • *Carol boasted about her costume.*
brag • *I don't mind bragging about my talents.*
crow • *Stop crowing about your success.*
skite (AUSTRALIAN AND NEW ZEALAND; INFORMAL) • *That's nothing to skite about.*

boastful ADJECTIVE
tending to brag about things • *a boastful liar*
bragging • *bragging stories about his time in the navy*
cocky • *The boxer is cocky and brash.*
conceited • *Young men tend to be conceited.*

a
b
c
d
e
f
g
h
i
j
k
l
m
n
o
p
q
r
s
t
u
v
w
x
y
z

A
B
C
D
E
F
G
H
I
J
K
L
M
N
O
P
Q
R
S
T
U
V
W
X
Y
Z

crowing • *crowing remarks*
egotistical • *egotistical fibs*
swaggering • *He has a swaggering arrogance.*

ANTONYM:
• modest

body ① NOUN

all your physical parts • *My whole body hurt.*
build • *He is of medium build.*
figure • *Janet has a nice figure.*
form • *clothes that flatter your form*
frame • *their bony frames*
physique • *a powerful physique*
shape • *his trim shape*

RELATED WORDS:
• ADJECTIVES corporal, physical

body ② NOUN

a dead body • *Police found a body hidden in the forest.*
carcass • *a sheep's carcass*
corpse • *the corpse of a young man*
dead body • *He'd never seen a dead body.*
remains • *human remains*

body ③ NOUN

an organized group of people • *local voluntary bodies*
association • *the Football Association*
band • *a band of rebels*
company • *the Royal Shakespeare Company*
confederation • *a confederation of workers*
organization • *student organizations*
society • *I joined the local opera society.*

MORE SYNONYMS:
• bloc
• collection
• corporation

boil ① VERB

to bubble • *The water is boiling.*
bubble • *Potatoes bubbled in the pot.*

fizz • *The liquid fizzed and bubbled.*
foam • *When the butter foams, add the onions.*
froth • *The milk frothed over in the pan.*

MORE SYNONYMS:
• effervesce
• seethe

boil ② NOUN

a swelling on the skin • *five boils on his face*
blister • *a blister on my index finger*
swelling • *a swelling under the eye*
tumour • *The tumours had all disappeared.*

MORE SYNONYMS:
• blain
• carbuncle
• pustule

bold ① ADJECTIVE

confident and not shy • *a bold question*
brash • *a brash young sergeant*
brazen • *a brazen young woman*
cheeky • *a cheeky grin*
confident • *I felt confident confronting him.*
forward • *It was forward of you to ask him.*
impudent • *an impudent child*

MORE SYNONYMS:
• barefaced
• pert
• saucy

ANTONYM:
• shy

bold ② ADJECTIVE

unafraid of risk or danger • *a bold attempt*
adventurous • *an adventurous spirit*
brave • *a brave woman*
courageous • *courageous firefighters*
daring • *daring feats*
fearless • *a fearless warrior*
intrepid • *an intrepid explorer*

MORE SYNONYMS:
• audacious
• heroic
• valiant

ANTONYM:
• cowardly

bold ③ ADJECTIVE
clear and noticeable • *bold colours*
bright • *bright light*
flashy • *flashy clothes*
loud • *a loud tie*
striking • *a striking tartan pattern*
strong • *dressed in strong reds and yellows*
vivid • *vivid green and purple*

MORE SYNONYMS:
• conspicuous
• prominent
• pronounced

ANTONYM:
• dull

bolt VERB
to escape or run away • *I bolted towards the exit.*
dash • *He dashed out of the room in a panic.*
escape • *They escaped across the frontier.*
flee • *We fled before the police arrived.*
fly • *She flew down the stairs with her attacker in hot pursuit.*
run away • *I called to him but he just ran away.*
run off • *The children ran off when they spotted me.*
rush • *They all rushed away as we approached.*

bomb ① NOUN
an explosive device • *The bomb exploded in the centre of the city.*
device • *Experts defused the device.*
explosive • *a block of plastic explosive*
missile • *long-range missiles*

rocket • *a rocket launcher*
shell • *Shells began to fall.*
torpedo • *The torpedo struck the ship.*

MORE SYNONYMS:
• grenade
• mine
• projectile

bomb ② VERB
to attack with bombs • *His house was bombed.*
attack • *We are being attacked!*
blow up • *He attempted to blow up the building.*
bombard • *Warships began to bombard the coast.*
destroy • *Helicopters destroyed his village.*
shell • *They shelled the troops.*
torpedo • *His ship was torpedoed.*

bond ① NOUN
a close relationship • *a special bond between us*
attachment • *Mother and child form a close attachment.*
connection • *a family connection*
link • *the links of friendship*
relation • *the relation between husband and wife*
tie • *the ties of blood*
union • *the union of father and son*

MORE SYNONYMS:
• affiliation
• affinity

bond ② NOUN
an obligation to do something • *the social bonds of community*
agreement • *He has broken our agreement.*
contract • *He signed a two-year contract.*
obligation • *your obligation to your father*
pledge • *a pledge of support*

A
B
C
D
E
F
G
H
I
J
K
L
M
N
O
P
Q
R
S
T
U
V
W
X
Y
Z

promise • *You must keep your promises.*
word • *I give you my word.*

MORE SYNONYMS:
• compact
• covenant
• guarantee

bond ③ VERB
to attach separate things • *Strips of wood are bonded together.*
bind • *Tape was used to bind the files.*
fasten • *I fastened the picture to the wall.*
fuse • *The pieces to be joined are melted and fused together.*
glue • *Glue the pieces together.*
paste • *He pasted posters to the wall.*

book ① NOUN
a number of pages in a cover • *I'm reading a great book just now.*
blook • *the blook of her award-winning travel blog*
eBook • *published in hardback and eBook*
iBook® • *It delivered the report as an iBook®*
publication • *publications about job hunting*
textbook • *He wrote a textbook on law.*
volume • *small volumes of poetry*
work • *my favourite work by this author*

◆ TYPES OF BOOK
◆ anthology
◆ atlas
◆ autobiography
◆ biography
◆ dictionary
◆ directory
◆ encyclopedia
◆ gazetteer
◆ glossary
◆ guidebook
◆ manual
◆ novel
◆ phrasebook
◆ thesaurus

◆ PARTS OF A BOOK
◆ appendix
◆ bibliography
◆ blurb
◆ caption
◆ chapter
◆ contents
◆ cover
◆ epilogue
◆ footnote
◆ foreword
◆ glossary
◆ heading
◆ illustration
◆ index
◆ introduction
◆ jacket
◆ layout
◆ line
◆ page
◆ preface
◆ prologue
◆ title

◆ RELIGIOUS BOOKS
◆ Bible (CHRISTIANITY)
◆ Book of Mormon (MORMONISM)
◆ Diamond Scriptures (ZEN BUDDHISM)
◆ Guru Granth or Adi Granth (SIKHISM)
◆ I Ching (CONFUCIANISM and TAOISM)
◆ Mahabharata (HINDUISM)
◆ Qu'ran or Koran (ISLAM)
◆ Ramayana (HINDUISM)
◆ Sutras (BUDDHISM and HINDUISM)
◆ Talmud (JUDAISM)
◆ Tao-te-Ching (TAOISM)
◆ Torah (JUDAISM)
◆ Tripitaka (BUDDHISM)
◆ Veda (HINDUISM)

book ② VERB
to arrange to have or use • *The tickets are booked.*
charter • *A plane was chartered for them.*

engage • *We engaged the services of a plumber.*
organize • *I have organized our flights.*
reserve • *Hotel rooms have been reserved.*
schedule • *A meeting is scheduled for Monday.*

border ① NOUN
a dividing line between things or places • *the border between two countries*
borderline • *the borderline between health and sickness*
boundary • *national boundaries*
frontier • *the American frontier*
line • *the line between fact and fiction*

border ② NOUN
an edge of something • *plain tiles with a bright border*
bounds • *the bounds of good taste*
edge • *the edge of town*
limits • *the city limits*
margin • *the western margins of the island*
rim • *the rim of the lake*

border ③ VERB
to form an edge • *Tall trees bordered the fields.*
edge • *the woods that edge the lake*
fringe • *Street lights fringe the bay.*
hem • *dresses hemmed with feathers*
rim • *the restaurants rimming the harbour*
trim • *coats trimmed with fur collars*

bored ADJECTIVE
impatient and not interested in something • *I am bored with this business.*
fed up • *He is fed up with this country.*
tired • *I am tired of this music.*
uninterested • *He seems uninterested in politics.*
wearied • *He spoke in a wearied voice.*

ANTONYM:
• interested

boredom NOUN
a lack of interest • *the boredom of long trips*
apathy • *political apathy*
dullness • *a period of dullness*
flatness • *a feeling of flatness*
monotony • *the monotony of winter*
tedium • *the tedium of unemployment*
weariness • *a sense of weariness*

ANTONYM:
• interest

boring ADJECTIVE
dull and uninteresting • *a boring job*
dull • *dull tasks*
flat • *a flat performance*
humdrum • *humdrum lives*
monotonous • *the monotonous prison routine*
tedious • *The work is tedious.*
tiresome • *a tiresome old man*

MORE SYNONYMS:
• insipid
• repetitious
• stale

ANTONYM:
• interesting

boss NOUN
a person in charge of something • *He can't stand his boss.*
chief • *the police chief*
director • *the directors of the bank*
employer • *He was sent to Rome by his employer.*
head • *Heads of government met in New York.*
leader • *The party's leader has resigned.*
manager • *the company's marketing manager*

bossy ADJECTIVE
telling people what to do • *a rather bossy little girl*

arrogant • *arrogant behaviour*
authoritarian • *He has an authoritarian approach to parenthood.*
dictatorial • *a dictatorial management style*
domineering • *She is domineering and ruthless.*
imperious • *He has an imperious manner.*
overbearing • *an overbearing mother*

botch VERB
to do something badly • *a botched operation*
bungle • *inefficient people who bungled the job*
mar • *She marred her exit by twisting her ankle.*
mess up • *He manages to mess up his life.*

bother ① VERB
to cause worry or concern • *His lack of money bothers him.*
annoy • *the things that annoy me*
concern • *The future concerns me.*
disturb • *It disturbs me to see you unhappy.*
get on someone's nerves (INFORMAL) • *This place gets on my nerves.*
trouble • *Are you troubled by nightmares?*
worry • *I'm worried by the amount he is drinking.*

MORE SYNONYMS:
• harass
• inconvenience

bother ② NOUN
trouble and difficulty • *I hate the bother of shopping.*
annoyance • *Snoring can be an annoyance.*
difficulty • *The strikes are causing difficulties for commuters.*

inconvenience • *a minor inconvenience*
irritation • *Noise is an irritation.*
trouble • *You've caused me a lot of trouble.*
worry • *It was a time of worry for us.*

MORE SYNONYMS:
• nuisance
• strain

bottom ① NOUN
the lowest part of something • *the bottom of the stairs*
base • *the base of the spine*
bed • *the river bed*
depths • *the depths of the earth*
floor • *the ocean floor*
foot • *the foot of the bed*

ANTONYM:
• top

bottom ② NOUN
the part of the body you sit on • *Sit on your bottom!*
backside (INFORMAL) • *the muscles in your backside*
behind (INFORMAL) • *He kicked me on the behind.*
buttocks • *exercises for your buttocks*
posterior (HUMOROUS) • *He fell on his posterior.*
rear • *I was thrown out on my rear.*

bottom ③ ADJECTIVE
in the lowest place or position • *the bottom drawer*
base • *the base edge of the curtain*
basement • *a basement flat*
ground • *ground level*
lowest • *the lowest part of the brain*

ANTONYM:
• highest

bounce ① VERB
to spring back • *I bounced a ball against the wall.*
bump • *My bicycle bumped along the rough ground.*

ricochet • *The bullets ricocheted off the jeep.*
MORE SYNONYMS:
• rebound
• recoil

bounce ② VERB
to move up and down • *He bounced across the floor.*
bob • *The raft bobbed along.*
bound • *He bounded up the stairway.*
jump • *They jumped up and down to keep warm.*

box NOUN
a container with a firm base and sides • *All her possessions were packed in boxes.*
carton • *cartons full of books*
case • *It is still in its original case.*
chest • *She kept her heirlooms in a carved wooden chest.*
container • *substances kept in heavy metal containers*
trunk • *a trunk full of toys*

boy NOUN
a male child • *I knew him when he was a boy.*
fellow • *a fine little fellow*
lad • *I remember being a lad his age.*
schoolboy • *a group of schoolboys*
youngster • *I was only a youngster in 1970.*
youth • *gangs of youths who cause trouble*

boycott VERB
to refuse to have anything to do with • *Some parties are boycotting the elections.*
blacklist • *He has been blacklisted by various societies.*
embargo • *Imports of fruit were embargoed.*
exclude • *I exclude animal products from my diet.*

reject • *She rejected her parents' religion.*
spurn • *You spurned his last offer.*
MORE SYNONYMS:
• proscribe
• refrain from

brag VERB
to boast about something • *I hate people who brag about their achievements.*
boast • *She kept boasting about how many guys she'd been out with.*
crow • *Stop crowing about your victory.*
skite (AUSTRALIAN AND NEW ZEALAND; INFORMAL) • *That's nothing to skite about.*

braggart NOUN
a person who boasts • *He was a braggart and a liar.*
bigmouth (SLANG) • *He's nothing but a bigmouth.*
boaster • *an idle boaster looking for the main chance*
bragger • *He was quite a bragger.*
show-off • *I've always been a show-off.*
skite or **skiter** (AUSTRALIAN AND NEW ZEALAND; INFORMAL) • *a bit of a skite*

brave ① ADJECTIVE
willing to do dangerous things • *a brave attempt to stop the attack*
bold • *Amrita became a bold rebel.*
courageous • *a courageous decision*
fearless • *his fearless campaigning for justice*
heroic • *The heroic sergeant risked his life.*
plucky • *The plucky schoolgirl amazed the doctors.*
valiant • *a valiant attempt to keep going*
MORE SYNONYMS:
• daring

A
B
C
D
E
F
G
H
I
J
K
L
M
N
O
P
Q
R
S
T
U
V
W
X
Y
Z

• intrepid
• valorous

ANTONYM:
• cowardly

brave ② VERB
to face something without fear
• *Fans braved the rain to hear him sing.*
face • *I can't face another three years of this.*
stand up to • *I have tried to stand up to the bullies.*

bravery NOUN
the quality of being courageous
• *He deserves praise for his bravery.*
boldness • *an outward display of boldness*
courage • *They do not have the courage to apologize.*
fortitude • *He suffered with tremendous fortitude.*
heroism • *acts of heroism*
pluck • *He has pluck and presence of mind.*
valour • *He won a medal for valour.*

MORE SYNONYMS:
• fearlessness
• gallantry
• mettle

ANTONYM:
• cowardice

breach ① NOUN
a breaking of an agreement or law
• *a breach of contract*
infringement • *an infringement of the rules*
offence • *criminal offences*
trespass • *a campaign of trespasses and demonstrations*
violation • *a violation of the peace agreement*

MORE SYNONYMS:
• contravention
• transgression

breach ② NOUN
a gap in something • *the breach in the Berlin Wall*
crack • *a large crack in the ice*
gap • *a narrow gap in the curtains*
hole • *We cut holes in the fabric.*
opening • *an opening in the fence*
rift • *The earthquake caused a deep rift.*
split • *There's a split in my mattress.*

MORE SYNONYMS:
• chasm
• fissure
• rupture

break ① VERB
to separate into pieces • *I broke a plate.*
▶ see Word Study **break**, page 637

break ② VERB
to fail to keep a rule or promise • *He broke his promise to attend.*
breach • *breaches of discipline*
contravene • *His behaviour contravenes our code of conduct.*
infringe • *The judge ruled that he had infringed no rules.*
violate • *They violated the peace agreement.*

break ③ NOUN
a short period of rest or change • *I took a five-minute break from work.*
interlude • *a happy interlude in my life*
interval • *a long interval when no-one spoke*
pause • *After a pause Alex spoke.*
recess • *The court adjourned for a recess.*
respite • *They have had no respite from bombing.*
rest • *I'll start again after a rest.*

breed ① NOUN
a type of animal • *rare breeds of cattle*
kind • *What kind of horse is that?*
species • *Pandas are an endangered species.*

stock • *cattle of Highland stock*
strain • *a special strain of rat*
type • *What type of dog should we get?*
variety • *many varieties of birds*

breed ② VERB
to produce and look after • *He breeds dogs for the police.*
cultivate • *She cultivates fruit and vegetables.*
develop • *A new variety of potato is being developed.*
keep • *He keeps guinea pigs.*
nurture • *trimming and nurturing plants and saplings*
raise • *He raises birds of prey as a hobby.*
rear • *the difficulties of rearing children*

breed ③ VERB
to produce offspring • *Frogs can breed in most ponds.*
multiply • *Rats multiply quickly.*
produce • *She produced a son.*
propagate • *This plant is difficult to propagate.*
reproduce • *the natural desire to reproduce*

MORE SYNONYMS:
• engender
• procreate

brief ① ADJECTIVE
lasting for a short time • *a brief appearance on television*
fleeting • *a fleeting glimpse*
momentary • *There was a momentary silence.*
quick • *a quick look at the newspaper*
short • *a short holiday*
swift • *a swift glance at John's face*

MORE SYNONYMS:
• ephemeral
• temporary
• transitory

ANTONYM:
• long

brief ② VERB
to give necessary information • *A spokesman briefed reporters.*
advise • *I must advise you of my decision to retire.*
fill in (INFORMAL) • *Can you fill me in on Wilbur's visit?*
inform • *They would inform him of their progress.*
instruct • *He instructed us in first aid.*
prepare • *I will prepare you for this exam.*
prime • *Arnold primed him for his duties.*

bright ① ADJECTIVE
strong and startling • *a bright light*
brilliant • *brilliant green eyes*
dazzling • *a dazzling white shirt*
glowing • *the glowing windows of the Cathedral*
luminous • *a luminous star*
radiant • *eyes as radiant as sapphires*
vivid • *strong, vivid colours*

MORE SYNONYMS:
• blazing
• illuminated
• resplendent

ANTONYM:
• dull

bright ② ADJECTIVE
clever and alert • *my brightest student*
brainy (INFORMAL) • *I don't consider myself brainy.*
brilliant • *She has a brilliant mind.*
clever • *a clever child*
ingenious • *an ingenious idea*
intelligent • *Dolphins are an intelligent species.*
smart • *He thinks he's as smart as Sarah.*

MORE SYNONYMS:
• acute
• astute
• sharp

a
b
c
d
e
f
g
h
i
j
k
l
m
n
o
p
q
r
s
t
u
v
w
x
y
z

B

ANTONYM:
• dim

bright ③ ADJECTIVE
cheerful and lively • *a bright smile*
cheerful • *Jack sounded quite cheerful about the idea.*
happy • *a confident, happy child*
jolly • *a jolly nature*
light-hearted • *They are light-hearted and enjoy life.*
lively • *He has a lively personality.*
merry • *bursts of merry laughter*

brilliant ① ADJECTIVE
very bright • *a brilliant light*
bright • *a bright star*
dazzling • *a dazzling white shirt*
gleaming • *gleaming headlights*
glowing • *glowing colours*
luminous • *luminous orange paint*
radiant • *a figure surrounded by a radiant glow*
sparkling • *a choker of sparkling jewels*
vivid • *the vivid hues of tropical flowers*

ANTONYM:
• dull

brilliant ② ADJECTIVE
very clever • *a brilliant pupil*
acute • *His relaxed exterior hides an acute mind.*
brainy (INFORMAL) • *You don't have to be too brainy to work that one out.*
bright • *an exceptionally bright child*
clever • *What a clever idea!*
intelligent • *a lively and extremely intelligent woman*
perceptive • *a perceptive analysis of the situation*
sharp • *a sharp intellect*
smart • *He's the smartest student we've ever had.*

ANTONYM:
• stupid

brilliant ③ ADJECTIVE
wonderful or superb • *It's a brilliant film.*
first-class • *a first-class violinist*
great • *one of the greatest novels of the century*
magnificent • *a magnificent display*
marvellous • *I've had a marvellous time.*
outstanding • *He's an outstanding actor.*
superb • *a superb artist*
tremendous • *a tremendous performance*
wonderful • *the most wonderful music I've ever heard*

ANTONYM:
• terrible

bring ① VERB
to take somewhere • *Bring a friend to the party.*
bear • *They bore the box into the kitchen.*
carry • *She carried her son to the car.*
convey • *Emergency supplies were conveyed by truck.*
lead • *She led him into the house.*
take • *He took cakes to the party.*
transport • *The troops were transported to Moscow.*

bring ② VERB
to cause to happen • *Bring the vegetables to the boil.*
cause • *My mistake caused me some worry.*
create • *The new factory will create more jobs.*
inflict • *The attack inflicted heavy casualties.*
produce • *The drug produces side effects.*
result in • *Many accidents result in serious injuries.*
wreak • *Violent storms wreaked havoc.*

MORE SYNONYMS:
• effect
• occasion

bring about VERB
to cause something to happen
• *It was his arrogance which brought about his downfall.*

cause • *This may cause delays.*
create • *The new scheme will create even more confusion.*
generate • *the excitement generated by this film*
make happen • *If you want change, you have to make it happen yourself.*
produce • *His comments produced a furious response.*
provoke • *a move that has provoked a storm of protest*

broad ① ADJECTIVE
large, especially from side to side
• *His shoulders were broad and his waist narrow.*

expansive • *There are also several swing sets and an expansive grassy play area.*
extensive • *The palace grounds were more extensive than the town itself.*
large • *He was a large man with a thick square head.*
thick • *a finger as thick as a sausage*
vast • *rich families who own vast stretches of land*
wide • *a sunhat with a wide brim*

MORE SYNONYMS:
• ample
• spacious

ANTONYM:
• narrow

broad ② ADJECTIVE
including or affecting many different things or people • *A broad range of issues was discussed.*

comprehensive • *This book is a comprehensive guide to the region.*
extensive • *extensive research into public attitudes to science*
general • *The project should raise general awareness about bullying.*
sweeping • *sweeping economic reforms*
universal • *the universal problem of pollution*
wide • *a major event which brought together a wide range of interest groups*
wide-ranging • *The aims of our campaign are wide-ranging but simple.*

broad ③ ADJECTIVE
general rather than detailed • *These documents provided a broad outline of the Society's development.*

approximate • *They did not have even an approximate idea of what the word meant.*
general • *The figures represent a general decline in employment.*
non-specific • *I intend to use these terms in a deliberately non-specific way.*
rough • *I've got a rough idea of what he looks like.*
sweeping • *a sweeping statement about women drivers*
vague • *They have only a vague idea of the amount of water available.*

broadcast ① NOUN
a programme on radio or television • *this morning's broadcast on Radio 4*

podcast • *the only podcast devoted to snowmobiling*
programme • *Did you see that programme about child geniuses?*
show • *my favourite television show*
transmission • *The radio transmission continued all night long.*
webcast • *a live webcast from the Wimbledon final*

a
b
c
d
e
f
g
h
i
j
k
l
m
n
o
p
q
r
s
t
u
v
w
x
y
z

broadcast ② VERB
to send out so that it can be seen or heard • *Dean and his band are broadcasting live from Brighton.*
air • *The show airs at 9 o'clock every Thursday.*
show • *The television station refused to show the documentary.*
transmit • *The concert will be transmitted on radio and television.*

broadcast ③ VERB
to make known publicly • *You don't need to broadcast your feelings to the entire world.*
advertise • *If you're going on holiday, don't advertise the fact with an uncut lawn.*
announce • *Are you going to announce your engagement tonight?*
make public • *The terms of the agreement were not made public for many years.*
proclaim • *I happily proclaim my ignorance on this one.*

broken ① ADJECTIVE
in pieces • *a broken window*
burst • *a burst pipe*
demolished • *a demolished house*
fractured • *He suffered a fractured skull.*
fragmented • *fragmented images*
shattered • *shattered glass*
smashed • *smashed windows*

broken ② ADJECTIVE
not kept • *a broken promise*
infringed • *a case of infringed human rights*
violated • *a series of violated agreements*

MORE SYNONYMS:
• disobeyed
• traduced
• transgressed

brown NOUN or ADJECTIVE

◆ **SHADES OF BROWN**
◆ auburn
◆ bay
◆ beige
◆ bronze
◆ brunette
◆ buff
◆ burnt sienna
◆ burnt umber
◆ café au lait
◆ camel
◆ chestnut
◆ chocolate
◆ cinnamon
◆ coffee
◆ dun
◆ fawn
◆ ginger
◆ hazel
◆ khaki
◆ mahogany
◆ mocha
◆ oatmeal
◆ ochre
◆ putty
◆ russet
◆ rust
◆ sandy
◆ sepia
◆ tan
◆ taupe
◆ tawny
◆ terracotta
◆ umber

build ① VERB
to make something • *The house was built last year.*
assemble • *Workers were assembling planes.*
construct • *plans to construct a temple on the site*
erect • *The building was erected in 1900.*

fabricate • *All the tools are fabricated from steel.*
form • *hotels formed from cheap cement*
make • *a wall made of bricks*

ANTONYM:
• dismantle

build ② VERB
to develop gradually • *I want to build a relationship with them.*
develop • *These battles could develop into war.*
extend • *Three new products extend the range.*
increase • *The population continues to increase.*
intensify • *The conflict is bound to intensify.*
strengthen • *Cycling strengthens the muscles.*

MORE SYNONYMS:
• augment
• enlarge
• escalate

build ③ NOUN
the size of a body • *He is of medium build.*
body • *a body of average size*
figure • *Janet has a nice figure.*
form • *clothes that flatter your form*
frame • *their bony frames*
physique • *a powerful physique*
shape • *his trim shape*

building NOUN
a structure with walls • *a glass building*
edifice • *historic edifices in the area*
structure • *The museum is an impressive structure.*

bulge ① VERB
to swell out • *He bulges out of his black T-shirt.*
expand • *The pipes expanded in the heat.*
protrude • *His blue eyes protruded from his head.*

stick out • *His stomach stuck out under his jacket.*
swell • *My ankles swelled.*

bulge ② NOUN
a lump in something • *My purse made a bulge in my pocket.*
bump • *a bump in the road*
hump • *a camel's hump*
lump • *itchy red lumps on the skin*
protrusion • *a strange protrusion on his forehead*
swelling • *a swelling on my foot*

bully ① NOUN
someone who deliberately frightens or hurts others • *I fell victim to the class bully.*
oppressor • *They were powerless against their oppressors.*
persecutor • *Eventually he stood up to his persecutors.*

bully ② VERB
to frighten or hurt someone deliberately and repeatedly • *I wasn't going to let him bully me.*
intimidate • *Jones had set out to intimidate and dominate Paul.*
oppress • *men who try to dominate and oppress women*
persecute • *Tom was persecuted by his sisters.*
pick on • *I don't like to see you pick on younger children.*
tease • *The boys in the village had set on him, teasing him.*
torment • *My older brother and sister used to torment me.*

bully ③ VERB
to make someone do something by using force • *She used to bully me into doing my schoolwork.*
force • *I cannot force you in this. You must decide.*
intimidate • *attempts to intimidate*

A
B
C
D
E
F
G
H
I
J
K
L
M
N
O
P
Q
R
S
T
U
V
W
X
Y
Z

people into voting for the governing party
pressurize • *Do not be pressurized into
making your decision immediately.*

MORE SYNONYMS:
• coerce
• dragoon

bump ① VERB
to hit something • *He bumped his
head on the wall.*
bang • *I banged my shin on the edge
of the table.*
collide • *The car collided with a tree.*
hit • *She hit the last barrier and fell.*
jolt • *He jolted my elbow.*
knock • *He knocked on the door.*
strike • *His head struck the windscreen.*

bump ② NOUN
a dull noise • *He heard a bump outside.*
bang • *I heard four or five loud bangs.*
knock • *They heard a knock at the door.*
thud • *She tripped and fell with a thud.*
thump • *There was a loud thump
against the house.*

bump ③ NOUN
a raised part of something • *a bump
in the road*
bulge • *My purse made a bulge in my
pocket.*
hump • *a camel's hump*
knob • *a door with a brass knob*
lump • *itchy red lumps on the skin*
swelling • *a swelling on my foot*

MORE SYNONYMS:
• contusion
• node
• protuberance

bunch ① NOUN
a group of people • *The players were
a great bunch.*
band • *Bands of criminals have been
roaming some neighbourhoods.*
crowd • *All the old crowd have come
out for this occasion.*

gaggle • *A gaggle of journalists sit in a
hotel foyer waiting impatiently.*
gang • *Come on over - we've got lots of
the old gang here.*
group • *The trouble involved a small
group of football supporters.*
lot • *Future generations are going to
think that we were a pretty boring lot.*
multitude • *surrounded by a noisy
multitude*

bunch ② NOUN
several cut flowers held together • *He
had left a huge bunch of flowers in her
hotel room.*
bouquet • *She laid a bouquet on his
grave.*
posy • *a posy of wild flowers*
spray • *a small spray of freesias*

bunch ③ NOUN
a group of things • *George took out a
bunch of keys and went to work on the
lock.*
batch • *She brought a large batch of
newspaper cuttings.*
bundle • *a bundle of sticks tied together
with string*
cluster • *a cluster of shops, cabins and
motels*
heap • *a heap of old boxes for the bonfire*
load • *His people came up with a load of
embarrassing stories.*
pile • *I've got a pile of questions
afterwards for you.*
set • *Only she and Mr Cohen had
complete sets of keys to the shop.*

burden ① NOUN
a load that is carried • *My wet clothes
were an added burden.*
load • *a big load of hay*
weight • *straining to lift heavy weights*

burden ② NOUN
something that worries you • *the
burden of looking after a sick parent*

anxiety • *He expressed his anxieties to me.*

care • *Forget all the cares of the day.*

strain • *I find the travelling a strain.*

stress • *the stress of exams*

trouble • *The Sullivans have money troubles.*

worry • *My son is a worry to me.*

MORE SYNONYMS:
• affliction
• millstone
• trial

RELATED WORD:
• ADJECTIVE onerous

bureaucracy NOUN
complex rules and procedures • *Is there too much bureaucracy in government?*

administration • *high administration costs*

officialdom • *Officialdom is against us.*

red tape • *Our application was delayed by red tape.*

regulations • *absurd regulations about opening hours*

burn ① VERB
to be on fire • *a fire burning in the fireplace*

be ablaze • *The houses were ablaze.*

be on fire • *The ship was on fire.*

blaze • *The wreckage blazed.*

flame • *We watched as the house flamed.*

flare • *The match flared in the dark.*

flicker • *The fire flickered and crackled.*

burn ② VERB
to destroy with fire • *They burned the house down.*

char • *charred bodies*

incinerate • *Hospitals incinerate waste.*

scorch • *The bonfire scorched the grass.*

shrivel • *The papers shrivelled in the flames.*

singe • *Her hair was singed and her coat burnt.*

burst ① VERB
to split apart • *The balloon burst.*

break • *He broke the box open.*

crack • *A water pipe had cracked.*

explode • *The glass exploded.*

puncture • *The nail punctured the tyre.*

rupture • *His appendix ruptured.*

split • *The seam of my dress split.*

burst ② VERB
to happen or appear suddenly • *to burst into flames*

barge • *He barged into the room.*

break • *Her face broke into a smile.*

erupt • *Violence could erupt soon.*

rush • *Water rushed out of the hole.*

burst ③ NOUN
a short period of something • *a burst of energy*

fit • *a fit of rage*

outbreak • *an outbreak of violence*

rush • *a sudden rush of excitement*

spate • *a spate of attacks on horses*

surge • *a surge of emotion*

torrent • *a torrent of words*

business ① NOUN
the buying and selling of goods • *a career in business*

commerce • *commerce between Europe and South America*

dealings • *All dealings with the company were suspended.*

industry • *the American car industry*

trade • *French trade with the West Indies*

trading • *trading between the two countries*

transaction • *We settled the transaction over lunch.*

business ② NOUN
an organization selling goods or services • *a family business*

company • *the Ford Motor Company*

a
b
c
d
e
f
g
h
i
j
k
l
m
n
o
p
q
r
s
t
u
v
w
x
y
z

A
B
C
D
E
F
G
H
I
J
K
L
M
N
O
P
Q
R
S
T
U
V
W
X
Y
Z

corporation • *international corporations*
enterprise • *small industrial enterprises*
establishment • *shops and other commercial establishments*
firm • *a firm of engineers*
organization • *a well-run organization*

MORE SYNONYMS:
• concern
• conglomerate
• venture

business ③ NOUN
any event or situation • *This business has upset me.*
affair • *He handled the affair badly.*
issue • *What is your view on this issue?*
matter • *This is a matter for the police.*
problem • *solutions to the drug problem*
question • *the whole question of TV censorship*
subject • *He raised the subject of money.*

bustle ① VERB
to move hurriedly • *My mother bustled about the room.*
dash • *We dashed about purposefully.*
fuss • *Waiters were fussing round the table.*
hurry • *Claire hurried along the road.*
rush • *I'm rushing to finish the cooking.*
scurry • *rats scurrying around*
scuttle • *Crabs scuttle along the bank.*

bustle ② NOUN
busy and noisy activity • *the bustle of modern life*
activity • *a burst of activity in the building*
commotion • *He heard a commotion outside.*
excitement • *The news created great excitement.*
flurry • *a flurry of activity*
fuss • *He works without any fuss.*

hurry • *the hurry and excitement of the city*

ANTONYM:
• peace

busy ① ADJECTIVE
doing something • *What is it? I'm busy.*
active • *He is active in local politics.*
employed • *He was employed helping me.*
engaged • *He was engaged in conversation.*
engrossed • *She is engrossed in her work.*
occupied • *He is occupied with the packing.*
working • *I am working on a novel.*

ANTONYM:
• idle

busy ② ADJECTIVE
full of activity • *a busy tourist resort*
active • *an active, independent country*
full • *a full life*
hectic • *my hectic work schedule*
lively • *a lively restaurant*
restless • *a restless mind*

busy ③ VERB
to occupy or keep busy • *Kathryn busied herself in the kitchen.*
absorb • *Her career absorbed her completely.*
employ • *You'd be better employed helping me.*
engage • *He was engaged in a meeting when I called.*
immerse • *She immersed herself in her book.*
occupy • *Try to occupy yourself with something.*

but ① CONJUNCTION
although • *Heat the cider until it is very hot but not boiling.*
although • *He was in love with her, although he had not yet admitted it to himself.*

though • *He's very attractive, though not exactly handsome.*
while • *The first two services are free, while the third costs £35.*
yet • *It is completely waterproof, yet light and comfortable.*

but ② PREPOSITION
with the exception of • *The crew gave them nothing but bread to eat.*
except • *I don't take any drugs except aspirin.*
except for • *No-one has complained except for you.*
other than • *This route is not recommended to anyone other than the most experienced cyclist.*

save • *The people had no water at all save that brought up from bore holes.*

buy VERB
to obtain with money • *I'd like to buy him lunch.*
acquire • *I have acquired a new car.*
invest in • *I invested in a house.*
obtain • *She went to obtain a ticket.*
pay for • *He let me pay for his drink.*
procure • *attempts to procure more food*
purchase • *He purchased a sandwich for lunch.*

ANTONYM:
• sell

a
b
c
d
e
f
g
h
i
j
k
l
m
n
o
p
q
r
s
t
u
v
w
x
y
z

Cc

calculate VERB

to work out a number or amount
• *how to calculate the cost of setting up a business*

count • *Shareholders are counting the cost of the slump.*

determine • *calculations to determine the rate of tax*

reckon • *an amount reckoned at 140 billion marks*

work out • *Work out the distance of the journey.*

calculated ADJECTIVE

deliberately planned • *Everything they said was calculated to wound.*

aimed • *The restructuring is aimed at reducing costs.*

designed • *a scheme designed to help poorer families*

intended • *the intended effect of the revised guidelines*

planned • *a carefully planned campaign*

ANTONYM:
• unplanned

call ① VERB

to give a name • *a man called Jeffrey*

christen • *He decided to christen his first-born son Arthur.*

designated • *The wood was designated an "area of natural beauty".*

dubbed • *the man dubbed "the world's greatest living explorer"*

named • *They named their child Anthony.*

call ② VERB

to telephone • *He called me at my office.*

contact • *Contact us immediately if you have any new information.*

phone • *Phone me as soon as you get home.*

ring • *I'll ring you tomorrow.*

telephone • *Please telephone to make an appointment.*

call ③ VERB

to say loudly • *I heard someone calling my name.*

announced • *"Dinner is served," he announced.*

cried • *"Run, Forrest!" she cried.*

cried out • *She cried out to us as she disappeared from view.*

shouted • *He shouted to me from across the room.*

yelled • *"Ahoy there!" the captain yelled over to us.*

call ④ NOUN

an instance of someone shouting out
• *a call for help*

cry • *the cry of a seagull*

shout • *I heard a distant shout.*

yell • *He let out a yell.*

callous ADJECTIVE

not concerned about other people
• *his callous disregard for human life*

cold • *What a cold, unfeeling woman she was.*

heartless • *It was a heartless thing to do.*

indifferent • *indifferent to the suffering of others*
insensitive • *insensitive remarks*

MORE SYNONYMS:
• hard-bitten
• hardhearted
• unsympathetic

ANTONYM:
• caring

calm ① ADJECTIVE
not worried or excited • *Try to keep calm.*
collected • *She was cool and collected during her interrogation.*
composed • *a very composed, business-like woman*
cool • *We have to keep a cool head in this situation.*
impassive • *He remained impassive as his sentence was passed.*
relaxed • *a relaxed manner*

MORE SYNONYMS:
• imperturbable
• unemotional
• unruffled

ANTONYM:
• worried

calm ② ADJECTIVE
still because there is no wind • *Tuesday was a fine, clear and calm day.*
balmy • *balmy summer evenings*
mild • *a mild winter climate*
still • *The air was still.*
tranquil • *a tranquil lake*

ANTONYM:
• rough

calm ③ NOUN
the state of being peaceful • *He liked the calm of the evening.*
calmness • *an aura of calmness*
peace • *a wonderful feeling of peace*
peacefulness • *the peacefulness of the gardens*

quiet • *I need quiet to work.*
serenity • *the peace and serenity of a tropical sunset*
stillness • *the stillness of the summer night*

calm ④ VERB
to make less upset or excited • *We were trying to calm him.*
quieten • *trying to quieten the restless horses*
relax • *This music is supposed to relax you.*
soothe • *I think a bath may soothe me.*

MORE SYNONYMS:
• mollify
• placate

campaign NOUN
actions planned to get a certain result • *a campaign to educate people*
crusade • *the crusade for feminism*
movement • *the human rights movement*
operation • *a full-scale military operation*
push • *an all-out push to promote the show*

cancel ① VERB
to stop something from happening • *We're going to have to cancel our picnic.*
abandon • *He had to abandon his holiday plans.*
call off • *The union has called off the strike.*

cancel ② VERB
to stop something from being valid • *They were forced to cancel their contract.*
annul • *The marriage was annulled.*
quash • *His jail sentence was quashed when new evidence came to light.*
repeal • *The new law was repealed within the year.*
revoke • *His licence was immediately revoked.*

a b c d e f g h i j k l m n o p q r s t u v w x y z

A
B
C
D
E
F
G
H
I
J
K
L
M
N
O
P
Q
R
S
T
U
V
W
X
Y
Z

MORE SYNONYMS:
• abrogate
• countermand
• rescind

candid ADJECTIVE
honest and frank • *a candid interview*
blunt • *She is blunt about his faults.*
frank • *They had a frank discussion about the issue.*
honest • *What is your honest opinion?*
open • *He had always been open with her and she would know if he lied.*
straightforward • *I was impressed by his straightforward manner.*
truthful • *We've all learnt to be fairly truthful about our personal lives.*

candidate NOUN
a person being considered for a position • *a candidate for the presidency*
applicant • *one of thirty applicants for the manager's post*
competitor • *several competitors for the contract*
contender • *a strong contender for the chairmanship*

MORE SYNONYMS:
• nominee
• possibility
• runner

capable ADJECTIVE
able to do something well • *a capable leader*
able • *a very able businessman*
accomplished • *an accomplished painter*
adept • *an adept diplomat*
competent • *a competent and careful driver*
efficient • *efficient administration*
proficient • *proficient with computers*
skilful • *the country's most skilful politician*

ANTONYM:
• incompetent

capacity ① NOUN
the maximum amount that something holds or produces • *the vehicle's fuel capacity*
dimensions • *a car of compact dimensions*
room • *There wasn't enough room in the baggage compartment for all the gear.*
size • *My bedroom is half the size of yours.*
space • *There is space in the back for two people.*
volume • *a container with a volume of two litres*

capacity ② NOUN
a person's power or ability to do something • *Our capacity for giving care, love and attention is limited.*
ability • *The public never had faith in his ability to handle the job.*
capability • *a country with the capability of launching a nuclear attack*
facility • *Humans have lost the facility to use their sense of smell properly.*
gift • *As a youth he discovered a gift for making people laugh.*
potential • *the economic potentials of Eastern and Western Europe*
power • *Human societies have the power to solve the problems confronting them.*

capture ① VERB
to take prisoner • *He was captured by rebels.*
apprehend • *Police have not yet apprehended the killer.*
arrest • *Seven people were arrested.*
catch • *The thief was caught and the money was returned.*
seize • *seized by armed police*
take • *An army unit took the town.*

ANTONYM:
• release

capture ② NOUN
the act of capturing • *He evaded capture for eight years.*
arrest • *Police made two arrests.*
seizure • *the seizure of territory*
taking • *the taking of hostages*
trapping • *The trapping of these animals is illegal.*

car NOUN
a vehicle for carrying a few people • *I finally left the car at the garage.*
automobile (AMERICAN; FORMAL) • *the Japanese automobile manufacturer, Nissan*
motor • *Patricia's new motor*
vehicle • *She managed to scramble out of the vehicle.*

care ① VERB
to be concerned about something • *a company that cares about the environment*
be bothered • *I am not bothered what others think about me.*
be concerned • *We are concerned about the problem.*
be interested • *He's not interested in what anyone else says.*
mind • *I do not mind who wins.*

care ② NOUN
something that causes you to worry • *without a care in the world*
anxiety • *anxieties about money*
concern • *Their main concern is unemployment.*
stress • *the stresses of modern life*
trouble • *She has had her share of troubles.*
woe • *They blame the government for all their woes.*
worry • *My biggest worry is how I will cope on my own.*

MORE SYNONYMS:
• tribulation
• vexation

care ③ NOUN
close attention when doing something • *We took great care in choosing a location.*
attention • *medical attention*
caution • *Proceed with caution.*
pains • *She takes great pains with her appearance.*

MORE SYNONYMS:
• circumspection
• forethought

careful ① ADJECTIVE
acting with care • *Be careful what you say to him.*
cautious • *a cautious approach*
prudent • *prudent management*

MORE SYNONYMS:
• chary
• circumspect
• punctilious

ANTONYM:
• careless

careful ② ADJECTIVE
complete and well done • *It needs careful planning.*
meticulous • *meticulous attention to detail*
painstaking • *a painstaking search*
precise • *precise instructions*
thorough • *a thorough examination*

ANTONYM:
• careless

careless ① ADJECTIVE
not taking enough care • *careless driving*
irresponsible • *an irresponsible attitude*
neglectful • *neglectful parents*
sloppy (INFORMAL) • *sloppy work*

a b c d e f g h i j k l m n o p q r s t u v w x y z

A
B
C
D
E
F
G
H
I
J
K
L
M
N
O
P
Q
R
S
T
U
V
W
X
Y
Z

MORE SYNONYMS:
• cavalier
• lackadaisical
• slapdash
• slipshod
ANTONYM:
• careful

careless ② ADJECTIVE
relaxed and unconcerned • *careless laughter*
casual • *a casual remark*
nonchalant • *a nonchalant attitude*
offhand • *his usual offhand way*

carry VERB
to hold and take something somewhere • *He was carrying a briefcase.*
bear • *He arrived bearing gifts.*
convey (FORMAL) • *The minibus conveyed us to the station.*
lug • *lugging boxes of books around*
take • *Don't forget to take your camera.*
transport • *goods being transported abroad*

carry out VERB
to do and complete something • *the surgeon who carried out the operation*
accomplish • *the desire to accomplish a task*
achieve • *We have achieved our objective.*
fulfil • *to fulfil a promise*
perform • *people who have performed acts of bravery*
MORE SYNONYMS:
• execute
• implement

carve VERB
to make something by cutting • *He carves his figures from pine.*
chisel • *the mason chiselling his stone*
cut • *a figure cut from marble*
engrave • *an engraved crystal goblet*

inscribe • *the words inscribed on his monument*
sculpt • *a sculpted clay figure*
MORE SYNONYMS:
• hew
• whittle

case ① NOUN
a particular situation or example • *a case of mistaken identity*
example • *an example of what can go wrong*
illustration • *a clear illustration of this point*
instance • *a serious instance of corruption*
occasion • *the last occasion on which he appeared*
occurrence • *a frequent occurrence*

case ② NOUN
a container for holding something • *a spectacle case*
box • *a chocolate box*
container • *a huge plastic container*
MORE SYNONYMS:
• holder
• receptacle

case ③ NOUN
a trial or inquiry • *a libel case*
action • *a civil action for damages*
lawsuit • *the rising cost of defending a lawsuit*
proceedings • *criminal proceedings against the former leader*
trial • *Police lied at the trial.*

casual ① ADJECTIVE
happening by chance • *a casual remark*
accidental • *a verdict of accidental death*
chance • *a chance meeting*
incidental • *an incidental effect*
MORE SYNONYMS:
• fortuitous
• serendipitous

- unintentional
- unpremeditated

ANTONYM:
- deliberate

casual ② ADJECTIVE
showing no concern or interest
• *a casual look over his shoulder*
careless • *careless remarks*
cursory • *a cursory glance*
nonchalant • *his nonchalant attitude to life*
offhand • *a deceptively offhand style*
relaxed • *a relaxed manner*

MORE SYNONYMS:
- blasé
- insouciant
- lackadaisical
- perfunctory

ANTONYM:
- concerned

cat NOUN
a small animal kept as a pet • *sharing his flat with four cats*
feline • *Even the most cuddly feline has claws.*
kitty • *a kitty stuck up a tree*
moggy or **moggie** (BRITISH AND NEW ZEALAND; SLANG) • *a grey, long-haired moggy*
pussy or **puss** or **pussycat** (INFORMAL) • *a fluffy little pussycat*

RELATED WORDS:
- ADJECTIVE feline
- MALE tom
- FEMALE queen, tabby
- YOUNG kitten

catch ① VERB
to capture an animal or fish • *We still haven't caught any tuna.*
capture • *Poachers had captured a gorilla.*
snare • *He'd snared a rabbit.*
trap • *Their aim was to trap a tiger.*

catch ② VERB
to capture a person • *another technique for catching criminals*
apprehend • *the force necessary to apprehend a suspect*
arrest • *Police arrested the gunman.*

catch ③ NOUN
a device that fastens something
• *windows fitted with safety catches*
bolt • *the sound of a bolt being slid open*
clasp • *the clasp of her handbag*
clip • *She took the clip out of her hair.*
latch • *You left the latch off the gate.*

catch ④ NOUN
a hidden difficulty • *The catch is that you have to fly via Paris.*
disadvantage • *The disadvantage is that this plant needs frequent watering.*
drawback • *The flat's only drawback was its size.*
snag • *The snag is that you have to pay in advance.*

MORE SYNONYMS:
- fly in the ointment
- stumbling block

category NOUN
a set of things with something in common • *The items were organized into six different categories.*
class • *dividing the stars into six classes of brightness*
classification • *There are various classifications of genres or types of book.*
group • *She is one of the most promising players in her age group.*
set • *Pupils are divided into sets according to ability.*
sort • *What sort of school did you go to?*
type • *The majority of complaints received are of this type.*

a b c d e f g h i j k l m n o p q r s t u v w x y z

cause ① NOUN
what makes something happen • *the most common cause of back pain*
origin • *the origin of the present war*
root • *We need to get to the root of the problem.*
source • *the source of the leak*

cause ② NOUN
an aim supported by a group
• *dedication to the cause of peace*
aim • *political aims*
ideal • *socialist ideals*
movement • *the women's movement*

cause ③ NOUN
the reason for something • *They gave us no cause to believe that.*
basis • *There is no basis for this assumption.*
grounds • *discrimination on the grounds of race or religion*
justification • *There was no justification for what he was doing.*
motivation • *the motivation for his actions*
motive • *Police have ruled out robbery as a motive.*
reason • *You have every reason to be upset.*

cause ④ VERB
to make something happen • *This may cause delays.*
bring about • *We must try to bring about a better world.*
create • *The scheme may create even more confusion.*
generate • *the excitement generated by this film*
produce • *His comments produced a furious response.*
provoke • *a move that has provoked a storm of protest*

MORE SYNONYMS:
• effect
• engender
• give rise to
• lead to
• result in

caution ① NOUN
great care taken in order to avoid danger • *Drivers are urged to exercise extreme caution in icy weather.*
care • *Scissors can be safe for young children if used with care.*
prudence • *A lack of prudence may lead to problems.*

MORE SYNONYMS:
• forethought
• circumspection

caution ② VERB
to scold or warn someone against doing something • *The two men were cautioned but police say they will not be charged.*
reprimand • *He was reprimanded by a teacher for talking in the corridor.*
tick off (INFORMAL) • *Traffic police ticked off a pensioner for jumping a red light.*
warn • *My mother warned me not to talk to strangers.*

cautious ADJECTIVE
acting very carefully to avoid danger
• *a cautious approach*
careful • *Be extremely careful when on holiday abroad.*
guarded • *a guarded response*
tentative • *a tentative approach*
wary • *small firms remain wary of committing themselves to debt*

ANOTHER SYNONYM:
• prudent

ANTONYM:
• daring

cease ① VERB
to stop happening • *Almost miraculously, the noise ceased.*

be over • *The captured planes will be kept until the war is over.*

come to an end • *The strike came to an end.*

die away • *The sound died away and silence reigned.*

end • *The college year ends in March.*

finish • *The teaching day finished at around four o'clock.*

stop • *The rain had stopped.*

ANTONYM:
• begin

cease ② VERB
to stop doing something • *A small number of firms have ceased trading.*

desist from • *His wife never desisted from trying to change his mind.*

discontinue • *Do not discontinue the treatment without consulting your doctor.*

finish • *As soon as he'd finished eating, he excused himself.*

give up • *smokers who give up before the age of 30*

stop • *Stop throwing those stones!*

suspend • *The union suspended strike action this week.*

ANTONYM:
• start

celebrate VERB
to do something special to mark an event • *I was in a mood to celebrate.*

commemorate • *The anniversary of the composer's death was commemorated with a concert.*

party • *It's your birthday - let's party!*

rejoice • *My family rejoiced at the happy outcome to events.*

ANTONYM:
• mourn

celebration NOUN
an event in honour of a special occasion • *his eightieth birthday celebrations*

festival • *a religious festival*

festivity • *the wedding festivities*

gala • *the Olympics' opening gala*

party • *a housewarming party*

MORE SYNONYMS:
• merrymaking
• revelry

celebrity NOUN
a famous person • *At the age of twelve, he was already a celebrity.*

big name • *all the big names in rock and pop*

name • *some of the most famous names in modelling and show business*

personality • *a well-known radio and television personality*

star • *Not all football stars are ill-behaved louts.*

superstar • *a Hollywood superstar*

VIP • *such VIPs as Prince Charles and the former US President*

censure ① NOUN
strong disapproval • *a controversial policy which has attracted international censure*

blame • *I'm the one who'll get the blame if things go wrong.*

condemnation • *There was widespread condemnation of Saturday's killings.*

criticism • *This policy had repeatedly come under strong criticism.*

disapproval • *His action had been greeted with almost universal disapproval.*

reproach • *Those in public life should be beyond reproach.*

censure ② VERB
to criticize severely • *I would not presume to censure him for his views.*

condemn • *He condemned the players for lack of ability and application.*

criticize • *The regime has been harshly*

a
b
c
d
e
f
g
h
i
j
k
l
m
n
o
p
q
r
s
t
u
v
w
x
y
z

A
B
C
D
E
F
G
H
I
J
K
L
M
N
O
P
Q
R
S
T
U
V
W
X
Y
Z

criticized for its human rights violations.
denounce • *The letter called for civil rights, but did not openly denounce the regime.*
reproach • *She had not even reproached him for breaking his promise.*
MORE SYNONYMS:
• berate
• castigate

centre ① **NOUN**
the middle of something • *the centre of the room*
core • *the earth's core*
focus • *Her children are the main focus of her life.*
heart • *the heart of the problem*
hub • *The kitchen is the hub of most households.*
middle • *in the middle of the back row*
ANTONYM:
• edge

centre ② **VERB**
to have as the main subject • *All his thoughts were centred around himself.*
concentrate • *Scientists are concentrating their efforts on finding a cure.*
focus • *Attention is likely to focus on sales growth.*
revolve • *Since childhood, her life has revolved around tennis.*

ceremony ① **NOUN**
formal actions done for a special occasion • *his recent coronation ceremony*
observance • *a Memorial Day observance*
pomp • *His departure was celebrated with suitable pomp.*
rite • *a fertility rite*
ritual • *a Summer Solstice ritual*
service • *The President attended the morning service.*

ceremony ② **NOUN**
formal and polite behaviour • *He hung up without ceremony.*
decorum • *a responsibility to behave with decorum*
etiquette • *the rules of diplomatic etiquette*
formality • *his lack of stuffy formality*
niceties • *social niceties*
protocol • *minor breaches of protocol*

certain ① **ADJECTIVE**
definite or reliable • *One thing is certain - they respect each other.*
definite • *It's too soon to give a definite answer.*
established • *an established medical fact*
guaranteed • *Success is not guaranteed.*
inevitable • *If she wins her case, it is inevitable that other people will sue the company.*
known • *It is not known when the bomb was planted.*
sure • *Sharpe's leg began to ache, a sure sign of rain.*
undeniable • *undeniable proof of guilt*
ANTONYM:
• uncertain

certain ② **ADJECTIVE**
having no doubt in your mind • *She's absolutely certain she's going to succeed.*
clear • *It is important to be clear about what you are doing.*
confident • *I am confident that everything will come out right.*
convinced • *He was convinced that I was part of the problem.*
definite • *Mary is very definite about this fact.*
positive • *I'm as positive as I can be about it.*
satisfied • *People must be satisfied that the treatment is safe.*

sure • *She was no longer sure how she felt about him.*

ANTONYM:
• uncertain

certainly ADVERB
without any doubt • *I'll certainly do all I can to help.*
definitely • *Something should definitely be done.*
undeniably • *Bringing up a baby is undeniably hard work.*
undoubtedly • *He is undoubtedly a great player.*
unquestionably • *He is unquestionably a star.*
without doubt • *The refugees are, without doubt, extremely vulnerable.*

challenge ① NOUN
a suggestion to try something • *They issued a challenge to their rivals.*
dare • *He'd do almost anything for a dare.*

challenge ② VERB
to give someone a challenge • *He challenged his rival to a duel.*
dare • *I dare you to ask him.*
defy • *He looked at me as if he was defying me to argue.*

challenge ③ VERB
to question the truth or value of something • *challenging the authority of the state*
dispute • *He disputed the charge.*
question • *questioning the jury's verdict*

champion ① NOUN
a person who wins a competition • *Kasparov became a world chess champion.*
hero • *the goalscoring hero of the British hockey team*
title holder • *He became the youngest world title holder at the age of 22.*

victor • *the British Grand Prix victors*
winner • *The winner was a horse called Baby Face.*

champion ② NOUN
someone who supports a group, cause, or principle • *He received acclaim as a champion of the oppressed.*
advocate • *He was a staunch advocate of free trade.*
defender • *a strong defender of human rights*
guardian • *The party wants to be seen as a guardian of traditional values.*
protector • *She sees him as a protector and provider.*

champion ③ VERB
to support a group, cause, or principle • *He passionately championed the poor.*
defend • *his courage in defending religious and civil rights*
fight for • *Our Government should be fighting for an end to child poverty.*
promote • *You don't have to sacrifice the environment to promote economic growth.*
stick up for (INFORMAL) • *He has shown courage in sticking up for civil liberties.*
support • *The vice president has always supported the people of New York.*
uphold • *upholding the artist's right to creative freedom*

MORE SYNONYMS:
• advocate
• espouse

chance ① NOUN
a possibility of something happening • *a good chance of success*
likelihood • *the likelihood of infection*
odds • *What are the odds of that happening?*
possibility • *the possibility of pay cuts*
probability • *a probability of victory*

a b c d e f g h i j k l m n o p q r s t u v w x y z

A
B
C
D
E
F
G
H
I
J
K
L
M
N
O
P
Q
R
S
T
U
V
W
X
Y
Z

prospect • *There is little prospect of peace.*

chance ② NOUN
an opportunity to do something
• *He didn't give me a chance to explain.*
occasion • *I had no occasion to speak to her that day.*
opening • *an opening for finding a peaceful outcome to the conflict*
opportunity • *an opportunity to go abroad to study*
time • *There was no time to think.*

chance ③ NOUN
the way things happen without being planned • *events which were merely the result of chance*
accident • *a strange accident of fate*
coincidence • *It was no coincidence that she arrived just then.*
fortune • *a change of fortune*
luck • *His injury was just bad luck.*

RELATED WORD:
• ADJECTIVE fortuitous

change ① NOUN
an alteration in something • *a change in her attitude*
alteration • *some alterations in your diet*
difference • *a noticeable difference in his behaviour*
modification • *Some minor modifications were required.*
transformation • *the transformation of a wilderness into a garden*

MORE SYNONYMS:
• metamorphosis
• mutation
• transition
• transmutation

change ② VERB
to make or become different • *Her views have changed since her husband's death.*

alter • *There is no prospect of the decision being altered.*
convert • *a plan to convert his spare room into an office*
moderate • *They persuaded him to moderate his views.*
modify • *He refused to modify his behaviour.*
reform • *his plans to reform the economy*
transform • *The landscape has been transformed.*

MORE SYNONYMS:
• metamorphose
• mutate
• transmute

change ③ VERB
to exchange one thing for another
• *Can I change this sweater for one a size bigger?*
barter • *bartering wheat for cotton and timber*
exchange • *the chance to sell back or exchange goods*
interchange • *Meat can be interchanged with pulses as a source of protein.*
replace • *His smile was replaced by a frown.*
substitute • *You can substitute honey for the sugar.*
swap • *Let's swap places.*
trade • *They traded land for goods and money.*

changeable ADJECTIVE
likely to change all the time
• *changeable weather*
erratic • *erratic driving*
fickle • *Fashion is a fickle business.*
irregular • *an irregular heartbeat*
unpredictable • *unpredictable behaviour*
unstable • *The political situation is unstable.*

variable • *a variable rate of interest*
volatile • *a volatile atmosphere*

MORE SYNONYMS:
• mercurial
• mutable
• protean

ANTONYM:
• constant

character ① NOUN
the qualities of a person • *He has a dark side to his character.*
make-up • *Determination has always been a part of his make-up.*
nature • *a sunny nature*
personality • *an outgoing personality*
temperament • *his impulsive temperament*

MORE SYNONYMS:
• disposition
• quality
• temper

character ② NOUN
an honourable nature • *She showed real character in her attempt to win over the crowd.*
honour • *He has acted with honour.*
integrity • *a man of integrity*
strength • *He had the strength to turn down the offer.*

characteristic ① NOUN
a typical quality • *His chief characteristic is honesty.*
attribute • *a normal attribute of human behaviour*
feature • *a feature of the local culture*
property • *This liquid has many unique properties.*
quality • *leadership qualities*
trait • *personality traits*

MORE SYNONYMS:
• idiosyncrasy
• peculiarity
• quirk

characteristic ② ADJECTIVE
typical of a person or thing • *He responded with characteristic generosity.*
distinctive • *a distinctive voice*
distinguishing • *no distinguishing marks*
typical • *his typical British modesty*

MORE SYNONYMS:
• idiosyncratic
• peculiar
• singular
• symptomatic

ANTONYM:
• uncharacteristic

charge ① VERB
to ask someone for money as a payment • *The majority of producers charged a fair price.*
ask (for) • *The artist was asking £6,000 for each painting.*
bill • *Are you going to bill me for this?*
levy • *Taxes should not be levied without the authority of Parliament.*

charge ② VERB
to rush forward, often to attack someone • *He charged into the room.*
dash • *She dashed in from the garden.*
rush • *A schoolgirl rushed into the burning flat to help an old man.*
stampede • *The crowd stampeded.*
storm • *He stormed into the shop, demanding to see the manager.*

charge ③ NOUN
the price you have to pay for something • *We can arrange this for a small charge.*
cost • *Badges are available at a cost of £2.50.*
fee • *Pay your solicitor's fees.*
payment • *I'll do it in return for a small payment.*
price • *We negotiated a price for the service.*

a
b
c
d
e
f
g
h
i
j
k
l
m
n
o
p
q
r
s
t
u
v
w
x
y
z

A
B
C
D
E
F
G
H
I
J
K
L
M
N
O
P
Q
R
S
T
U
V
W
X
Y
Z

charm ① NOUN
an attractive quality • *a man of great personal charm*
allure • *the allure of Egypt*
appeal • *confident of his appeal to women*
attraction • *the attractions of living by the sea*
fascination • *It is hard to explain the fascination of this place.*
magnetism • *a man of enormous magnetism*

charm ② VERB
to use charm to please someone • *He charmed his 2,000-strong audience.*
bewitch • *bewitched by her beauty*
captivate • *The crowd was captivated by her honesty.*
delight • *a style of music that has delighted audiences*
entrance • *entranced by her smile*

MORE SYNONYMS:
• beguile
• enchant
• enrapture

chase ① VERB
to try to catch someone or something • *She chased the thief for a hundred yards.*
hunt • *He fled to Portugal after being hunted by police.*
pursue • *She pursued the man who had snatched her bag.*

chase ② VERB
to force to go somewhere • *Angry demonstrators chased him away.*
drive • *The troops drove the rebels into the jungle.*
hound • *He was hounded out of his job.*

MORE SYNONYMS:
• expel
• put to flight

chat ① NOUN
a friendly talk • *We sat around and had a chat.*
conversation • *a telephone conversation*
gossip • *Don't you enjoy a good gossip?*
natter (INFORMAL) • *Let's get together for a natter some time.*
talk • *We will have a talk about it later.*

chat ② VERB
to talk in a friendly way • *He was chatting to his father.*
gossip • *We gossiped into the night.*
natter (INFORMAL) • *His mother would natter to anyone.*
talk • *She's very easy to talk to.*

cheap ① ADJECTIVE
costing very little • *Cheap flights are available.*
bargain • *selling at bargain prices*
economical • *These cars are very economical to run.*
inexpensive • *an inexpensive wine*
reasonable • *His fees were quite reasonable.*

MORE SYNONYMS:
• cut-price
• low-cost
• low-priced

ANTONYM:
• expensive

cheap ② ADJECTIVE
inexpensive but of poor quality • *a suit made of some cheap material*
inferior • *an inferior imitation*
second-rate • *second-rate equipment*
tawdry • *tawdry souvenirs*

cheat VERB
to get something from someone dishonestly • *the people he cheated out of their life savings*
con (INFORMAL) • *He conned his way into a job.*

deceive • *Investors were deceived by a scam.*

defraud • *charges of conspiracy to defraud the government*

dupe • *Stamp collectors were duped into buying fakes.*

fleece • *He fleeced her out of thousands of pounds.*

rip off (SLANG) • *ticket touts ripping off soccer fans*

swindle • *two executives who swindled their employer*

MORE SYNONYMS:
• bilk
• hoodwink

check ① VERB
to examine something • *Check all the details first.*

check out (INFORMAL) • *Check out the financial figures.*

examine • *He examined her passport and stamped it.*

inspect • *the right to inspect company files*

test • *The drug must be tested in clinical trials.*

MORE SYNONYMS:
• inquire into
• look over
• scrutinize

check ② VERB
to reduce or stop something • *a policy to check fast population growth*

control • *a measure to control illegal mining*

curb • *reforms which aim to curb spending*

halt • *an attempt to halt the spread of the disease*

inhibit • *factors which inhibit growth*

restrain • *the need to restrain wage rises*

stop • *measures to stop the trade in ivory*

check ③ NOUN
an examination • *a thorough check of the equipment*

examination • *a medical examination*

inspection • *a routine inspection of the premises*

test • *a test for cancer*

cheek NOUN
speech or behaviour that is rude or disrespectful • *I'm amazed they had the cheek to ask in the first place.*

audacity • *I was shocked at the audacity of the gangsters.*

gall • *She had the gall to claim she had been victimized.*

impudence • *My sister had the impudence to go out wearing my clothes.*

insolence • *The pupil was excluded for insolence.*

nerve • *He had the nerve to ask me to prove who I was.*

rudeness • *Mother was cross at Tom's rudeness.*

MORE SYNONYMS:
• effrontery
• temerity

cheeky ADJECTIVE
rude and disrespectful • *cheeky teenagers*

impertinent • *an impertinent question*

impudent • *his rude and impudent behaviour*

insolent • *a defiant, almost insolent look*

rude • *She was often rude to her mother.*

ANTONYM:
• polite

cheerful ADJECTIVE
in a happy mood • *She was very cheerful despite her illness.*

bright • *"May I help you?" said a bright voice.*

buoyant • *in a buoyant mood*

a
b
c
d
e
f
g
h
i
j
k
l
m
n
o
p
q
r
s
t
u
v
w
x
y
z

A
B
C
D
E
F
G
H
I
J
K
L
M
N
O
P
Q
R
S
T
U
V
W
X
Y
Z

cheery • *a cheery nature*
happy • *a confident, happy child*
jaunty • *a jaunty tune*
jolly • *a jolly, easy-going man*
light-hearted • *They were light-hearted and enjoyed life.*
merry • *a burst of merry laughter*

ANTONYM:
• miserable

cheery ADJECTIVE
happy and cheerful • *He is loved by everyone for his cheery disposition.*
cheerful • *They are both very cheerful in spite of their circumstances.*
chirpy • *She sounded quite chirpy on the phone.*
good-humoured • *Charles was brave and remarkably good-humoured.*
happy • *Marina was a confident, happy child.*
jolly • *She was a jolly, kind-hearted woman.*
sunny • *a nice lad with a sunny disposition*
upbeat • *Neil's colleagues said he was in a joking, upbeat mood.*

MORE SYNONYMS:
• genial
• jovial

ANTONYM:
• gloomy

chew VERB
to break food up with the teeth • *Eat slowly and chew your food properly.*
crunch • *She crunched the ice cube loudly.*
gnaw • *He sat and gnawed at an apple.*
munch • *Sheep were munching the leaves.*

MORE SYNONYMS:
• champ
• chomp
• masticate

chief ① NOUN
the leader of a group or organization
• *the deputy chief of the territory's defence force*
boss • *He cannot stand his boss.*
chieftain • *the legendary British chieftain, King Arthur*
director • *the financial director of the company*
governor • *The incident was reported to the prison governor.*
head • *heads of government from 100 countries*
leader • *the leader of the Conservative Party*
manager • *a retired bank manager*

chief ② ADJECTIVE
most important • *The job went to one of his chief rivals.*
foremost • *one of the world's foremost scholars of ancient Indian culture*
key • *He is expected to be the key witness at the trial.*
main • *one of the main tourist areas of Amsterdam*
prevailing • *the prevailing attitude towards women in this society*
primary • *His language difficulties were the primary cause of his other problems.*
prime • *The police will see me as the prime suspect!*
principal • *The principal reason for my change of mind is this.*

MORE SYNONYMS:
• pre-eminent
• premier

child NOUN
a young person • *I lived in France as a child.*
ankle-biter (AUSTRALIAN AND NEW ZEALAND; SLANG) • *I knew him when he was just an ankle-biter.*
baby • *She took care of me when I was a baby.*

bairn (SCOTTISH) • *a two-year-old bairn*
infant • *young mums with infants in prams*
juvenile • *a prison for juveniles*
kid (INFORMAL) • *They've got three kids.*
minor • *charged with selling cigarettes to minors*
offspring • *parents choosing shoes for their offspring*
toddler • *a toddler in a pushchair*
tot • *The tot was too young to know what was happening.*
youngster • *I was only a youngster in 1965.*

ANTONYM:
• adult

RELATED WORDS:
• ADJECTIVE filial
• PREFIX paedo-

childish ADJECTIVE
immature and foolish • *I don't have time for this childish behaviour.*
immature • *She is emotionally immature.*
infantile • *infantile jokes*
juvenile • *juvenile behaviour*
puerile • *a puerile sense of humour*

ANTONYM:
• mature

china NOUN (SOUTH AFRICAN; INFORMAL)
a friend • *How are you, my old china?*
buddy (INFORMAL) • *We've been buddies since we were kids.*
chum (INFORMAL) • *He went on holiday with his two best chums.*
crony (OLD-FASHIONED) • *She is always surrounded by her cronies.*
friend • *lifelong friends*
mate (BRITISH; INFORMAL) • *Come on mate, things aren't that bad.*
pal (INFORMAL) • *He'd never let a pal down.*

choice ① NOUN
a range of things to choose from
• *available in a choice of colours*
range • *a range of sun-care products*
selection • *an interesting selection of recipes*
variety • *a variety of candidates from which to choose*

choice ② NOUN
the power to choose • *They had little choice in the matter.*
alternative • *He said he could not see any alternative.*
option • *He was given the option of going to jail or paying a fine.*
say • *We don't have a say in the company's decisions.*

choose VERB
to decide to have or do something • *a number of foods to choose from*
opt for • *He opted for early retirement.*
pick • *She was picked for the debating team.*
select • *She paused to select another cookie from the box.*
take • *She took the option he offered her.*

MORE SYNONYMS:
• elect
• fix on
• settle on

chop VERB
to cut down or into pieces • *I heard him chopping wood in the yard.*
cut • *Cut the vegetables up.*
fell • *43,000 square miles of tropical forest are felled each year.*
hack • *They hacked away at the undergrowth.*
lop • *Somebody had lopped the heads off our tulips.*

MORE SYNONYMS:
• cleave
• hew

circulate VERB
to pass around • He circulated rumours about everyone.
distribute • distributing leaflets
propagate • They propagated their political ideas.
spread • spreading malicious gossip
MORE SYNONYMS:
• disseminate
• promulgate

city NOUN
a large town • the city of London
metropolis • a busy metropolis
town • the oldest town in Europe
MORE SYNONYMS:
• conurbation
• municipality
RELATED WORD:
• ADJECTIVE civic

civilized ADJECTIVE
having an advanced society • a highly civilized country
cultured • a mature and cultured nation
enlightened • this enlightened century

claim ① VERB
to say something is the case • He claims to have lived here all his life.
allege • He is alleged to have killed a man.
assert • The defendants continued to assert their innocence.
hold • She holds that these measures are unnecessary.
insist • They insisted that they had no money.
maintain • I still maintain that I am not guilty.
profess • She professed to hate her nickname.

claim ② NOUN
a statement that something is the case • He rejected claims that he had taken bribes.

allegation • allegations of theft
assertion • his assertion that he did not plan to remarry
MORE SYNONYMS:
• pretension
• protestation

clash ① VERB
to fight or argue with another person • A group of 400 demonstrators clashed with police.
battle • In one town thousands of people battled with police officers.
fight • two rival gangs fighting in the streets
quarrel • My brother quarrelled with my father.
wrangle • Delegates wrangled over the future of the organization.

clash ② VERB
of two things: to be so different that they do not go together • Don't make policy decisions which clash with company thinking.
conflict • He held opinions which sometimes conflicted with my own.
contradict • Cut-backs like these surely contradict the Government's commitment to education.
differ • The two leaders differed on several issues.
disagree • Our managers disagreed on several policy issues.
go against • Changes are being made which go against my principles.
jar • They had always been good together and their temperaments seldom jarred.

clash ③ NOUN
a fight or argument • a number of clashes between rival parties
battle • a gun battle between police and drug traffickers
conflict • attempts to prevent a conflict between workers and management

confrontation • *This issue could lead to a military confrontation.*
fight • *He had a fight with Smith and bloodied his nose.*
skirmish (INFORMAL) • *Border skirmishes between the two countries were common.*
squabble • *There have been minor squabbles about phone bills.*
struggle • *a struggle between competing political factions*

clasp ① VERB
to hold something tightly • *Mary clasped the children to her desperately.*
clutch • *She was clutching a photograph.*
embrace • *People were crying for joy and embracing each other.*
grip • *She gripped the rope.*
hold • *He held the pistol in his right hand.*
hug • *She hugged her legs tight to her chest.*
press • *I pressed the child closer to my heart and prayed.*
squeeze • *He longed to just scoop her up and squeeze her.*

clasp ② NOUN
a fastening such as a hook or catch • *She undid the clasp of her hooded cloak.*
buckle • *He wore a belt with a large brass buckle.*
catch • *She fiddled with the catch of her bag.*
clip • *She took the clip out of her hair.*
fastener • *a product range which includes nails, woodscrews, and fasteners*
fastening • *The sundress has a neat back zip fastening.*

class ① NOUN
a group of a particular type • *a new class of vehicle*
category • *different categories of taxpayer*

genre • *films of the horror genre*
grade • *the lowest grade of staff*
group • *a plan to help people in this group*
kind • *the biggest prize of its kind in the world*
set • *The fashionable set all go to this club.*
sort • *several articles of this sort*
type • *various types of vegetable*

class ② VERB
to regard as being in a particular group • *They are officially classed as visitors.*
categorize • *His films are hard to categorize.*
classify • *Carrots are also classified as a fruit.*
designate • *The house is designated as a national monument.*
grade • *This ski-run is graded as easy.*
rank • *She is ranked in the world's top 50 players.*
rate • *He rates the film highly.*

classify VERB
to arrange similar things in groups • *We can classify the differences into three groups.*
arrange • *Arrange the books in neat piles.*
categorize • *This film is hard to categorize.*
grade • *musical pieces graded according to difficulty*
rank • *He was ranked among Britain's best-known millionaires.*
sort • *sorting the material into folders*
MORE SYNONYMS:
• pigeonhole
• systematize
• tabulate

clean ① ADJECTIVE
free from dirt or marks • *clean shoes*

a
b
c
d
e
f
g
h
i
j
k
l
m
n
o
p
q
r
s
t
u
v
w
x
y
z

immaculate • *immaculate white flannels*
impeccable • *dressed in an impeccable trouser suit*
laundered • *freshly laundered shirts*
spotless • *The kitchen was spotless.*
washed • *newly washed hair*

ANTONYM:
• dirty

clean ② ADJECTIVE
free from germs or infection • *a lack of clean water and sanitation*
antiseptic • *an antiseptic hospital room*
hygienic • *a hygienic kitchen*
purified • *Only purified water is used.*
sterilized • *sterilized milk*
uncontaminated • *uncontaminated air*
unpolluted • *unpolluted beaches*

ANTONYM:
• contaminated

clean ③ VERB
to remove dirt from • *She cleaned the house from top to bottom.*
cleanse • *a lotion to cleanse the skin*
dust • *I vacuumed, dusted and polished the living room.*
scour • *He scoured the sink.*
scrub • *I started to scrub off the dirt.*
sponge • *Sponge your face and body.*
swab • *an old man swabbing the floor*
wash • *He got a job washing dishes in a restaurant.*
wipe • *He wiped the sweat from his face.*

ANTONYM:
• soil

clear ① ADJECTIVE
easy to see or understand • *He made it clear he did not want to talk.*
apparent • *There is no apparent reason for the crime.*
blatant • *a blatant piece of cheating*

conspicuous • *one conspicuous difference*
definite • *a definite advantage*
evident • *He ate with evident enjoyment.*
explicit • *He was very explicit about his intentions.*
obvious • *There are obvious dangers.*
plain • *The results are plain to see.*

MORE SYNONYMS:
• incontrovertible
• manifest
• palpable
• patent
• unequivocal

clear ② ADJECTIVE
easy to see through • *a clear liquid*
crystalline • *crystalline green waters*
glassy • *The water was a deep glassy blue.*
translucent • *translucent stones*
transparent • *transparent glass walls*

MORE SYNONYMS:
• limpid
• pellucid
• see-through

ANTONYM:
• cloudy

clear ③ VERB
to prove someone is not guilty • *She was cleared of murder.*
absolve • *He was absolved of all charges.*
acquit • *acquitted of disorderly conduct*

ANTONYM:
• convict

clever ADJECTIVE
very intelligent • *My sister was always a lot cleverer than I was.*
brainy (INFORMAL) • *I don't consider myself to be especially brainy.*
bright • *an exceptionally bright child*
intelligent • *a lively and intelligent woman*

shrewd • *a shrewd businessman*
smart • *a very smart move*

MORE SYNONYMS:
• astute
• quick-witted
• sagacious

ANTONYM:
• stupid

climb VERB
to move upwards over something
• *Climbing the first hill took half an hour.*
ascend • *He ascended the ladder into the loft.*
clamber • *They clambered up the stone walls.*
mount • *He mounted the steps.*
scale • *the first British woman to scale Everest*

close ① VERB
to shut something • *Close the gate behind you.*
secure • *The shed was secured by a padlock.*
shut • *Someone had forgotten to shut the door.*

ANTONYM:
• open

close ② VERB
to block so that nothing can pass
• *All the roads out are closed.*
bar • *Protesters barred the way to his car.*
block • *The road was blocked by debris.*
obstruct • *buskers obstructing the pavement*
seal • *Soldiers had sealed the border.*

close ③ ADJECTIVE
near to something • *a restaurant close to their home*
at hand • *Don't worry, help is at hand.*
adjacent • *The fire spread to adjacent buildings.*
adjoining • *the smell of hamburgers from the adjoining stall*

handy • *Keep a pencil and paper handy.*
near • *The station is quite near.*
nearby • *I dashed into a nearby shop.*
neighbouring • *a man sitting at a neighbouring table*

ANTONYM:
• distant

close ④ ADJECTIVE
friendly and loving • *We became close friends.*
attached • *We've got very attached to one another over the years.*
dear • *a dear and valued companion*
devoted • *My parents were a deeply devoted couple.*
familiar • *I don't like men who try to get too familiar.*
friendly • *We gradually became very friendly.*
intimate • *one of my most intimate friends*
loving • *They forged a loving relationship.*

ANTONYM:
• distant

cloth NOUN
woven or knitted fabric • *a piece of red cloth*
fabric • *waterproof fabric*
material • *This material shrinks badly.*
textiles • *a trader in clothes and textiles*

clothes PLURAL NOUN
the things people wear • *She spends all her money on clothes.*
attire (FORMAL) • *suitable attire*
clothing • *men's clothing*
costume • *national costume*
dress • *traditional dress*
garments • *winter garments*
gear (INFORMAL) • *trendy gear*
outfit • *a stunning scarlet outfit*
wardrobe • *next summer's wardrobe*
wear • *evening wear*

a
b
c
d
e
f
g
h
i
j
k
l
m
n
o
p
q
r
s
t
u
v
w
x
y
z

MORE SYNONYMS:
• apparel
• garb
• raiment

cloud ① NOUN
a mass of vapour or smoke • *The sky was dark with clouds.*
billow • *billows of smoke*
fog • *a fog of cigar smoke*
haze • *a haze of exhaust fumes*
mist • *The valley was wrapped in thick mist.*
vapour • *warm vapour rising from the ground*

cloud ② VERB
to make something confusing • *Anger has clouded his judgement.*
confuse • *You're just confusing the matter by bringing politics into it.*
distort • *a distorted memory*
muddle • *The question muddles two separate issues.*

cloudy ① ADJECTIVE
full of clouds • *a cloudy sky*
dull • *It's always dull and wet here.*
gloomy • *gloomy weather*
leaden • *leaden skies*
overcast • *a damp, overcast morning*
ANTONYM:
• clear

cloudy ② ADJECTIVE
difficult to see through • *a glass of cloudy liquid*
muddy • *a muddy duck pond*
murky • *murky waters*
opaque • *an opaque glass jar*
ANTONYM:
• clear

club ① NOUN
an organization for people with a special interest • *a swimming club*

association • *the Women's Tennis Association*
circle • *a local painting circle*
group • *an environmental group*
guild • *the Screen Writers' Guild*
society • *a historical society*
union • *the International Astronomical Union*

club ② NOUN
a heavy stick • *armed with knives and clubs*
bat • *a baseball bat*
stick • *a crowd carrying sticks and stones*
truncheon • *a policeman's truncheon*

club ③ VERB
to hit with a heavy object • *Two thugs clubbed him with baseball bats.*
bash • *They bashed his head with a spade.*
batter • *battered to death*
beat • *beaten with rifle butts*
bludgeon • *bludgeoning his wife with a hammer*

clumsiness NOUN
awkwardness of movement • *The accident was entirely the result of his own clumsiness.*
awkwardness • *They moved with the awkwardness of mechanical dolls.*
ungainliness • *his physical ungainliness*

clumsy ADJECTIVE
moving awkwardly • *He is big and clumsy in his movements.*
awkward • *an awkward gesture*
gauche • *He makes me feel stupid and gauche.*
lumbering • *a big, lumbering man*
uncoordinated • *an uncoordinated dancer*
ungainly • *As a youth he was lanky and ungainly.*

MORE SYNONYMS:
- accident-prone
- bumbling
- gawky
- maladroit

ANTONYM:
- graceful

coast NOUN
the land next to the sea • *a holiday by the coast*
beach • *a beautiful sandy beach*
border • *the border of the Black Sea*
coastline • *the stunning Caribbean coastline*
seaside • *a day at the seaside*
shore • *a bleak and rocky shore*
strand • *boats fishing from the strand*

coat NOUN
an animal's fur or hair • *She gave the dog's coat a brush.*
fleece • *a blanket of lamb's fleece*
fur • *a kitten with black fur*
hair • *He's allergic to cat hair.*
hide • *rhino hide*
pelt • *a wolf pelt*
skin • *convicted of attempting to sell the skin of a Siberian tiger*
wool • *Lanolin comes from sheep's wool.*

coating NOUN
a layer of something • *a thin coating of ice*
coat • *a coat of paint*
covering • *a covering of dust*
layer • *a layer of dead leaves*

coax VERB
to persuade gently • *We coaxed her into coming with us.*
cajole • *Her sister cajoled her into playing.*
persuade • *My husband persuaded me to come.*
talk into • *They've talked him into getting a new car.*

MORE SYNONYMS:
- inveigle
- prevail upon
- wheedle

cocky ① ADJECTIVE
cheeky or too self-confident • *He was a bit cocky because he was winning all the time.*
arrogant • *an air of arrogant indifference*
brash • *On stage she seems hard and brash.*
conceited • *I thought him conceited.*
overconfident • *She couldn't cope with this new generation of noisy, overconfident teenage girls.*

MORE SYNONYMS:
- egotistical
- swaggering

cocky ② NOUN (AUSTRALIAN AND NEW ZEALAND)
a farmer, especially one whose farm is small • *He got some work with the cane cockies on Maroochy River.*
crofter (SCOTTISH) • *the financial plight of crofters in the islands*
farmer • *He was a simple farmer scratching a living from the soil.*

coil VERB
to wind in loops • *a coiled spring*
curl • *dark, curling hair*
loop • *A rope was looped between his hands.*
spiral • *vines spiralling up towards the roof*
twine • *This lily produces twining stems.*
twist • *She twisted her hair into a bun.*
wind • *a rope wound round her waist*

cold ① ADJECTIVE
having a low temperature • *the coldest winter for ten years*
arctic • *arctic conditions*

A
B
C
D
E
F
G
H
I
J
K
L
M
N
O
P
Q
R
S
T
U
V
W
X
Y
Z

biting • *a biting wind*
bitter • *driven inside by the bitter cold*
bleak • *The weather can be bleak on the coast.*
chilly • *It's chilly for June.*
freezing • *This house is freezing.*
icy • *the icy north wind*
raw • *a raw December morning*
wintry • *wintry showers*

ANTONYM:
• hot

cold ② **ADJECTIVE**
not showing affection • *a cold, unfeeling woman*
aloof • *He seemed aloof and detached.*
distant • *She was polite but distant.*
frigid • *a frigid smile*
lukewarm • *a lukewarm response*
reserved • *emotionally reserved*
stony • *He gave me a stony look.*

MORE SYNONYMS:
• standoffish
• undemonstrative

ANTONYM:
• warm

collapse ① **VERB**
to fall down • *The whole building is about to collapse.*
fall down • *The ceiling fell down.*
give way • *The bridge gave way beneath him.*

collapse ② **VERB**
to fail • *50,000 small businesses collapsed last year.*
fail • *His hotel business has failed.*
fold • *We were laid off when the company folded.*
founder • *a foundering radio station*

collapse ③ **NOUN**
the failure of something • *the collapse of his marriage*
downfall • *the downfall of the government*

failure • *the failure of his business empire*

colleague **NOUN**
a person someone works with • *I'll have to consult my colleagues.*
associate • *business associates*
fellow worker • *She started going out with a fellow worker.*
partner • *her business partner*
workmate • *the nickname his workmates gave him*

collect **VERB**
to gather together • *collecting signatures for a petition*
accumulate • *Most children enjoy accumulating knowledge.*
assemble • *trying to assemble a team*
gather • *gathering information*
raise • *They've raised over £100 for charity.*

MORE SYNONYMS:
• aggregate
• amass

ANTONYM:
• scatter

collection **NOUN**
a group of things collected together • *a collection of paintings*
assortment • *an assortment of pets*
group • *a group of songs*
store • *a vast store of knowledge*

colloquial **ADJECTIVE**
used in conversation • *a colloquial expression*
conversational • *a conversational style*
everyday • *He used plain, everyday English.*
informal • *an informal expression*

MORE SYNONYMS:
• demotic
• idiomatic
• vernacular

colony ① NOUN
a country controlled by another
country • an American colony
dependency • the tiny British
dependency of Montserrat
dominion • The Republic is a dominion
of Brazil.
territory • territories under Israeli
control

colony ② NOUN
a group of settlers in a place • a
colony of Scots
community • the Sikh community in
Britain
outpost • a remote outpost
settlement • a Muslim settlement

colossal ADJECTIVE
very large indeed • a colossal statue
enormous • The main bedroom is
enormous.
gigantic • a gigantic task
huge • They are making huge profits.
immense • an immense cloud of smoke
mammoth • This mammoth
undertaking was completed in 18
months.
massive • a massive steam boat
vast • farmers who own vast stretches
of land

ANTONYM:
• tiny

colour ① NOUN
a shade or hue • Her favourite colour
is blue.
hue • delicate pastel hues
pigmentation • skin pigmentation
shade • walls painted in two shades
of green
tint • a distinct orange tint

colour ② NOUN
a substance used to give colour
• food colour
dye • hair dye

paint • a pot of red paint
pigment • a layer of blue pigment

colour ③ VERB
to give something a colour • Many
women colour their hair.
dye • Only dye clean garments.
paint • She paints her toenails red.
stain • Some foods can stain the teeth.
tint • tinted glass

colour ④ VERB
to affect the way you think • Her
upbringing has coloured her opinion of
marriage.
bias • a biased opinion
distort • The shock of the accident
distorted my judgement.
prejudice • Criticism will prejudice the
Government's decision.
slant • deliberately slanted news
coverage

colourful ① ADJECTIVE
full of colour • colourful clothes
bright • a bright green dress
brilliant • The garden has burst into
brilliant flower.
intense • an intense shade of blue
jazzy (INFORMAL) • a jazzy tie
rich • a rich blue glass bowl
vibrant • vibrant orange shades
vivid • vivid hues

MORE SYNONYMS:
• kaleidoscopic
• multicoloured
• psychedelic

ANTONYM:
• dull

colourful ② ADJECTIVE
interesting or exciting • a colourful
character
graphic • a graphic account of his career
interesting • He has had an interesting
life.
lively • a lively imagination

a
b
c
d
e
f
g
h
i
j
k
l
m
n
o
p
q
r
s
t
u
v
w
x
y
z

A
B
C
D
E
F
G
H
I
J
K
L
M
N
O
P
Q
R
S
T
U
V
W
X
Y
Z

rich • *the rich history of the island*
vivid • *a vivid description*

ANTONYM:
• dull

combination NOUN
a mixture of things • *a combination of charm and skill*
amalgamation • *an amalgamation of two organizations*
blend • *a blend of wine and spring water*
mix • *a mix of fantasy and reality*
mixture • *a mixture of horror, envy and awe*

MORE SYNONYMS:
• amalgam
• coalescence
• composite
• meld

combine VERB
to join or mix together • *trying to combine motherhood with work*
amalgamate • *a plan to amalgamate the two parties*
blend • *The band blends jazz and folk music.*
fuse • *a performer who fuses magic and dance*
integrate • *integrating various styles of art*
merge • *The two countries have merged into one.*
mix • *mixing business with pleasure*
unite • *people uniting to fight racism*

MORE SYNONYMS:
• meld
• synthesize

ANTONYM:
• separate

come ① VERB
to move or arrive somewhere • *Two men came into the room.*
appear • *He appeared at about 9 o'clock.*
arrive • *My brother has just arrived.*

enter • *The class fell silent as the teacher entered.*
materialize • *The car just materialized from nowhere.*
show up (INFORMAL) • *He showed up over an hour late.*
turn up (INFORMAL) • *I'll call you when she turns up.*

come ② VERB
to happen or take place • *Christmas only comes once a year.*
happen • *Nothing ever happens on a Sunday.*
occur • *How did the accident occur?*
take place • *The meeting never took place.*

comfort ① NOUN
a state of ease • *He settled back in comfort.*
ease • *a life of ease*
luxury • *brought up in an atmosphere of luxury*
wellbeing • *a wonderful sense of wellbeing*

comfort ② NOUN
relief from worry or unhappiness • *Her words gave him some comfort.*
consolation • *He knew he was right, but it was no consolation.*
help • *Just talking to you has been a great help.*
relief • *temporary relief from the pain*
satisfaction • *At least I have the satisfaction of knowing I tried.*
support • *His family were a great support to him.*

comfort ③ VERB
to give someone comfort • *trying to comfort the screaming child*
cheer • *The thought did nothing to cheer him.*
console • *"Never mind," he consoled me.*
reassure • *He did his best to reassure her.*

soothe • *She took him in his arms and soothed him.*

comfortable ① ADJECTIVE
physically relaxing • *a comfortable chair*
cosy • *a cosy living room*
easy • *You've had an easy time of it.*
homely • *a homely atmosphere*
relaxing • *a relaxing holiday*
restful • *a restful scene*

ANTONYM:
• uncomfortable

comfortable ② ADJECTIVE
feeling at ease • *I don't feel comfortable around him.*
at ease • *He is not at ease in female company.*
at home • *We soon felt quite at home.*
contented • *a contented life*
happy • *I'm not very happy with that idea.*
relaxed • *a relaxed attitude*

ANTONYM:
• uneasy

command ① VERB
to order someone to do something
• *She commanded me to lie down.*
bid • *The soldiers bade us turn and go back.*
demand • *They demanded that he leave.*
direct • *His doctor has directed him to rest.*
order • *He ordered his men to cease fire.*

MORE SYNONYMS:
• charge
• enjoin

command ② VERB
to be in charge of • *the general who commanded the UN troops*
control • *He now controls the whole company.*
head • *Who heads the firm?*
lead • *He led the country between 1949 and 1984.*

manage • *I manage a small team of workers.*
supervise • *He supervised more than 400 volunteers.*

command ③ NOUN
an order to do something • *The execution was carried out at his command.*
bidding • *They refused to leave at his bidding.*
decree • *a presidential decree*
directive • *a government directive*
injunction • *He left her with the injunction to go to sleep.*
instruction • *They were just following instructions.*
order • *I don't take orders from you.*

MORE SYNONYMS:
• behest
• edict
• fiat

command ④ NOUN
knowledge and ability • *a good command of English*
grasp • *a good grasp of foreign languages*
knowledge • *He has no knowledge of law.*
mastery • *a mastery of grammar*

commemorate VERB
to do something in memory of
• *concerts to commemorate the anniversary of his death*
celebrate • *celebrating their golden wedding*
honour • *celebrations to honour his memory*

MORE SYNONYMS:
• memorialize
• pay tribute to

comment ① VERB
to make a remark • *He refused to comment on the rumours.*

a b c d e f g h i j k l m n o p q r s t u v w x y z

A
B
C
D
E
F
G
H
I
J
K
L
M
N
O
P
Q
R
S
T
U
V
W
X
Y
Z

mention • *I mentioned that I didn't like jazz.*
note • *He noted that some issues remained to be settled.*
observe • *"You're very pale," he observed.*
point out • *I should point out that these figures are approximate.*
remark • *Everyone had remarked on her new hairstyle.*
say • *"Well done," he said.*

MORE SYNONYMS:
• interpose
• opine

comment ② NOUN

something you say • *sarcastic comments*
observation • *a few general observations*
remark • *snide remarks*
statement • *That statement puzzled me.*

commit VERB

to do something • *A crime has been committed.*
carry out • *attacks carried out by terrorists*
do • *They have done a lot of damage.*
perform • *people who have performed acts of bravery*
perpetrate • *A fraud has been perpetrated.*

common ① ADJECTIVE

of many people • *a common complaint*
general • *the general opinion*
popular • *a popular belief*
prevailing • *the prevailing atmosphere*
prevalent • *Smoking is becoming more prevalent among girls.*
universal • *The desire to look attractive is universal.*
widespread • *widespread support*

ANTONYM:
• rare

common ② ADJECTIVE

not special • *the common man*
average • *the average teenager*
commonplace • *a commonplace observation*
everyday • *your everyday routine*
ordinary • *an ordinary day*
plain • *My parents were just plain ordinary folks.*
standard • *standard practice*
usual • *In a usual week I watch about 15 hours of television.*

MORE SYNONYMS:
• run-of-the-mill
• workaday

ANTONYM:
• special

common ③ ADJECTIVE

having bad taste or manners • *a common, rude woman*
coarse • *coarse humour*
rude • *It's rude to stare.*
vulgar • *vulgar remarks*

ANTONYM:
• refined

common sense NOUN

the ability to make good judgments • *Use your common sense.*
good sense • *He had the good sense to call me at once.*
judgment • *I respect your judgment.*
level-headedness • *He prides himself on his level-headedness.*
prudence • *His lack of prudence led to financial problems.*
wit • *They don't have the wit to realize what's happening.*

communicate ① VERB

to be in touch with someone • *We communicate mainly by email.*
be in contact • *I'll be in contact with him next week.*
be in touch • *He hasn't been in touch with me yet.*

correspond • *We correspond regularly.*

communicate ② VERB

to pass on information • *The results will be communicated by post.*

convey • *They have conveyed their views to the government.*

impart • *the ability to impart knowledge*

inform • *Will you inform me of any changes?*

pass on • *I'll pass on your good wishes.*

retweet • *Could you retweet the link to my website?*

spread • *She has spread the news to everyone.*

transmit • *He transmitted his enjoyment to the audience.*

tweet • *He has been tweeting his comments all through the match.*

MORE SYNONYMS:
• disseminate
• make known

companion NOUN

someone you travel with or spend time with • *He has been her constant companion for the last six years.*

comrade • *Unlike so many of his comrades he survived the war.*

crony (OLD-FASHIONED) • *a round of golf with his business cronies*

friend • *Sara's old friend, Charles*

mate • *A mate of mine used to play soccer for Liverpool.*

pal (INFORMAL) • *We've been pals for years.*

partner • *a partner in crime*

company ① NOUN

a business • *a publishing company*

business • *a family business*

corporation • *multi-national corporations*

establishment • *a commercial establishment*

firm • *a firm of engineers*

house • *the world's top fashion houses*

company ② NOUN

a group of people • *the Royal Shakespeare Company*

assembly • *an assembly of citizens*

band • *bands of rebels*

circle • *a large circle of friends*

community • *a community of believers*

crowd • *I don't go around with that crowd.*

ensemble • *an ensemble of young musicians*

group • *an environmental group*

party • *a party of sightseers*

troupe • *a troupe of actors*

MORE SYNONYMS:
• concourse
• coterie

company ③ NOUN

the act of spending time with someone • *I could do with some company.*

companionship • *He keeps a dog for companionship.*

presence • *Your presence is not welcome here.*

compare VERB

to look at things for similarities or differences • *Compare these two illustrations.*

contrast • *In this section we contrast four possible approaches.*

juxtapose • *art juxtaposed with reality*

weigh • *She weighed her options.*

compartment ① NOUN

a section of a railway carriage • *We shared our compartment with a group of businessmen.*

carriage • *Our carriage was full of drunken football fans.*

compartment ② NOUN

one of the separate parts of an object

A
B
C
D
E
F
G
H
I
J
K
L
M
N
O
P
Q
R
S
T
U
V
W
X
Y
Z

• *the freezer compartment of the fridge*
bay • *the cargo bays of the aircraft*
chamber • *the chambers of the heart*
division • *Each was further split into several divisions.*
section • *a toolbox with sections for various items*

compassionate ADJECTIVE
feeling or showing sympathy and pity for others • *My father was a deeply compassionate man.*
caring • *He is a lovely boy, very gentle and caring.*
humane • *She began to campaign for humane treatment of prisoners and their families.*
kind • *I must thank you for being so kind to me.*
kind-hearted • *He was a warm, generous and kind-hearted man.*
merciful • *a merciful God*
sympathetic • *She was very sympathetic to their problems.*
tender • *Her voice was tender, full of pity.*

MORE SYNONYMS:
• benevolent
• humanitarian

compatible ADJECTIVE
going together • *Lifelong partners should be compatible.*
congenial • *congenial company*
consistent • *injuries consistent with a car crash*
harmonious • *a harmonious partnership*
in keeping • *This behaviour was in keeping with his character.*

MORE SYNONYMS:
• accordant
• congruent
• congruous
• consonant

ANTONYM:
• incompatible

compensate ① VERB
to repay someone for loss or damage
• *You will be properly compensated for your loss.*
atone • *He felt he had atoned for what he had done.*
refund • *The company will refund the full cost.*
repay • *collateral with which to repay swindled investors*
reward • *Their patience was finally rewarded.*

MORE SYNONYMS:
• make amends
• make restitution
• recompense
• reimburse
• remunerate

compensate ② VERB
to cancel out • *His lack of skill was compensated for by his enthusiasm.*
balance • *The pros balance the cons.*
cancel out • *The two influences cancel each other out.*
counteract • *pills to counteract high blood pressure*
make up for • *I'll make up for what I've done.*
offset • *The loss is being offset by a new tax.*

MORE SYNONYMS:
• counterbalance
• countervail
• redress

compensation NOUN
something that makes up for loss or damage • *compensation for his injuries*
amends • *an attempt to make amends for his crime*
atonement • *an act of atonement for our sins*

damages • *damages for libel*
payment • *a redundancy payment*

MORE SYNONYMS:
• recompense
• reimbursement
• remuneration
• reparation
• restitution

compete VERB
to try to win • *companies competing for business*
contend • *two groups contending for power*
contest • *the candidates contesting in the election*
fight • *rivals fighting for supremacy*
vie • *The contestants vied to finish first.*

competition ① NOUN
an attempt to win • *There's a lot of competition for places.*
contention • *contention for the gold medal*
contest • *the contest between capitalism and socialism*
opposition • *They are in direct opposition for the job.*
rivalry • *the rivalry between the two leaders*
struggle • *a power struggle*

competition ② NOUN
a contest to find the winner in something • *a surfing competition*
championship • *a swimming championship*
contest • *a beauty contest*
event • *major sporting events*
tournament • *a judo tournament*

competitor NOUN
a person who competes for something • *one of the youngest competitors in the event*
adversary • *his political adversaries*

challenger • *20 seconds faster than the nearest challenger*
competition • *staying ahead of the competition*
contestant • *contestants in the Miss World pageant*
opponent • *the best opponent I've played all season*
opposition • *They can outplay the opposition.*
rival • *a business rival*

complain VERB
to express dissatisfaction • *He came round to complain about the noise.*
carp • *She is constantly carping at him.*
find fault • *He's always finding fault with my work.*
grouse • *You're always grousing about something.*
grumble • *It's not in her nature to grumble.*
kick up a fuss (INFORMAL) • *He kicks up a fuss whenever she goes out.*
moan • *moaning about the weather*
whine • *whining children*
whinge (INFORMAL) • *Stop whingeing and get on with it.*

MORE SYNONYMS:
• bemoan
• bewail

complaint NOUN
an instance of complaining about something • *There have been a number of complaints about the standard of service.*
criticism • *The criticism that we do not try hard enough to learn other languages was voiced.*
grievance • *They had a legitimate grievance against the company.*
grumble • *Her main grumble is over the long hours she has to work.*
objection • *I have no objections about the way I have been treated.*

A
B
C
D
E
F
G
H
I
J
K
L
M
N
O
P
Q
R
S
T
U
V
W
X
Y
Z

protest • *Despite our protests, they went ahead anyway.*

complete ① ADJECTIVE
to the greatest degree possible • *a complete transformation*
absolute • *absolute nonsense*
consummate • *a consummate professional*
outright • *an outright victory*
perfect • *a perfect stranger*
thorough • *a thorough snob*
total • *a total failure*
utter • *an utter shambles*

complete ② ADJECTIVE
with nothing missing • *a complete set of tools*
entire • *the entire plot*
full • *a full report*
intact • *the few buildings which have survived intact*
undivided • *I want your undivided attention.*
whole • *I told him the whole story.*

ANTONYM:
• incomplete

complete ③ VERB
to finish • *He has just completed his first novel.*
conclude • *The judge concluded his summing-up.*
end • *The crowd was in tears as he ended his speech.*
finish • *I'll finish my report this week.*

complex ① ADJECTIVE
having many different parts
• *complex issues*
complicated • *a very complicated voting system*
difficult • *the laborious and difficult process of adopting a child*
intricate • *intricate patterns*
involved • *a long, involved explanation*

tangled • *His personal life has become more tangled than ever.*

MORE SYNONYMS:
• convoluted
• tortuous

ANTONYM:
• simple

complex ② NOUN
an emotional problem • *I have never had a complex about my weight.*
fixation • *She has a fixation about men with beards.*
obsession • *95% of patients know their obsessions are irrational.*
phobia • *The man had a phobia about flying.*
preoccupation • *his total preoccupation with neatness*
problem • *an eating problem*
thing • *He's got this thing about women's shoes.*

complicated ADJECTIVE
complex and difficult • *a complicated situation*
complex • *a complex issue*
convoluted • *a convoluted plot*
elaborate • *an elaborate theory*
intricate • *an intricate process*
involved • *a long, involved explanation*

MORE SYNONYMS:
• Byzantine
• labyrinthine
• perplexing

ANTONYM:
• simple

compose VERB
to create or write • *He has composed a symphony.*
create • *He has created a new ballet.*
devise • *a play devised by the drama company*
invent • *the man who invented gangsta rap*

produce · *He has produced a book about the city.*
write · *I've never been able to write poetry.*

comprehend VERB
to understand or appreciate something · *I just cannot comprehend your attitude.*
appreciate · *She has never really appreciated the scale of the problem.*
fathom · *I really couldn't fathom what Steiner was talking about.*
grasp · *The Government has not yet grasped the seriousness of the crisis.*
see · *I don't see why you're complaining.*
take in · *I try to explain, but you can tell she's not taking it in.*
understand · *They are too young to understand what's going on.*
work out · *It took me some time to work out what was causing the problem.*

compulsory ADJECTIVE
required by law · *School attendance is compulsory.*
mandatory · *the mandatory retirement age*
obligatory · *an obligatory medical examination*
required · *the required reading for this course*
requisite · *the requisite documents*
ANTONYM:
• voluntary

con ① VERB
to trick someone into doing or believing something · *He claimed that the salesman had conned him out of his life savings.*
cheat · *a deliberate attempt to cheat employees out of their pensions*
deceive · *She deceived us into giving her a job.*
mislead · *Ministers must not knowingly mislead the public.*

swindle · *A City businessman swindled investors out of millions of pounds.*
trick · *They tricked him into parting with his life savings.*
MORE SYNONYMS:
• defraud
• dupe

con ② NOUN
a trick intended to mislead or disadvantage someone · *Slimming snacks that offer miraculous weight loss are a con.*
bluff · *The letter was a bluff.*
deception · *You've been the victim of a rather cruel deception.*
fraud · *an investigation into frauds in the world of horseracing*
swindle · *a tax swindle*
trick · *a cheap trick to encourage people to switch energy suppliers*

conceit NOUN
excessive pride · *his insufferable conceit*
egotism · *typical showbiz egotism*
pride · *a blow to his pride*
self-importance · *his bad manners and self-importance*
vanity · *her vanity about her long hair*
MORE SYNONYMS:
• amour-propre
• narcissism
• vainglory

conceited ADJECTIVE
too proud · *a conceited young idiot*
bigheaded (INFORMAL) · *an arrogant, bigheaded man*
cocky · *I was very cocky as a youngster.*
egotistical · *an egotistical show-off*
self-important · *self-important pop stars*
vain · *a shallow, vain woman*
MORE SYNONYMS:
• narcissistic

a b c d e f g h i j k l m n o p q r s t u v w x y z

A
B
C
D
E
F
G
H
I
J
K
L
M
N
O
P
Q
R
S
T
U
V
W
X
Y
Z

• swollen-headed
• vainglorious

ANTONYM:
• modest

concentrate ① VERB
to give something all your attention
• *Concentrate on your studies.*
be engrossed in • *He was engrossed in his work.*
focus your attention on • *focusing his attention on the race*
give your attention to • *I gave my attention to the question.*
put your mind to • *You could do it if you put your mind to it.*

concentrate ② VERB
to be found in one place • *They are mostly concentrated in the urban areas.*
accumulate • *Cholesterol accumulates in the arteries.*
collect • *dust collecting in the corners*
gather • *residents gathered in huddles*

concern ① NOUN
a feeling of worry • *public concern about violence*
anxiety • *anxiety about the economy*
apprehension • *apprehension about the future*
disquiet • *a growing sense of disquiet*
worry • *She has no worries about his health.*

concern ② NOUN
someone's duty or responsibility
• *His private life is not my concern.*
affair • *If you want to go, that's your affair.*
business • *This is none of my business.*
responsibility • *He's not my responsibility.*

concern ③ VERB
to make someone worried • *It concerns me that he doesn't want to go.*

bother • *Nothing bothers me.*
distress • *They are distressed by the accusations.*
disturb • *disturbed by the news*
trouble • *Is anything troubling you?*
worry • *an issue that had worried him for some time*

MORE SYNONYMS:
• disquiet
• perturb

concern ④ VERB
to affect or involve • *This concerns both of us.*
affect • *the ways in which computers affect our lives*
apply to • *This rule does not apply to us.*
be relevant to • *These documents are relevant to the case.*
involve • *meetings which involve most of the staff*

MORE SYNONYMS:
• bear on
• pertain to
• touch

concise ADJECTIVE
using no unnecessary words • *a concise guide*
brief • *a brief description*
short • *a short speech*
succinct • *a succinct explanation*
terse • *a terse statement*

MORE SYNONYMS:
• epigrammatic
• laconic
• pithy

ANTONYM:
• long

conclude ① VERB
to decide something • *He concluded that she had been right.*
decide • *I decided he must be ill.*
deduce • *She deduced that I had written the letter.*

infer • *His feelings were easily inferred from his reply.*
judge • *The doctor judged that he was not fit enough to play.*
reckon (INFORMAL) • *I reckon we should wait a while.*
suppose • *There's no reason to suppose he'll be there.*
surmise • *It is surmised that he must have known.*

conclude ② VERB
to finish something • *He concluded the letter with a postscript.*
close • *They closed the show with a song.*
end • *His speech ended with a prayer for peace.*
finish • *We finished the evening with a walk on the beach.*
round off • *This rounded the afternoon off perfectly.*
wind up • *She quickly wound up her conversation.*

ANTONYM:
• begin

conclusion ① NOUN
a decision made after thinking carefully about something • *I've come to the conclusion that she was lying.*
deduction • *a shrewd deduction about what was going on*
inference • *There were two inferences to be drawn from her letter.*
judgment • *My judgment is that things are going to get worse.*
verdict • *The doctor's verdict was that he was fine.*

conclusion ② NOUN
the finish or ending of something
• *the conclusion of the programme*
close • *bringing the talks to a close*
end • *The war is coming to an end.*
ending • *a dramatic ending*
finish • *the finish of the race*

termination • *the termination of their marriage*

ANTONYM:
• beginning

condemn ① VERB
to say that something is bad or unacceptable • *He was condemned for his arrogance.*
blame • *I blame television for the rise in violence.*
censure • *a motion censuring the government*
criticize • *He was criticized for his failure to act.*
damn • *The report damns the government's handling of the affair.*
denounce • *He was denounced as a traitor.*

condemn ② VERB
to give a punishment • *condemned to death*
damn • *sinners damned to eternal torment*
doom • *doomed to die for his crime*
sentence • *sentenced to ten years in prison*

condition ① NOUN
the state of something • *The house is in good condition.*
form • *The team are not in good form this season.*
shape • *He's in great shape for his age.*
state • *Look at the state of my car!*

condition ② NOUN
something required for something else to be possible • *terms and conditions of the contract*
prerequisite • *A science background is a prerequisite for the job.*
provision • *a provision in his will forbidding the sale of the house*
proviso • *The answer is yes, with one proviso.*

a
b
c
d
e
f
g
h
i
j
k
l
m
n
o
p
q
r
s
t
u
v
w
x
y
z

qualification • *He agreed, but with some qualifications.*
requirement • *The product meets all legal requirements.*
requisite • *the main requisite for membership*
stipulation • *The only dress stipulation was "no jeans".*
terms • *the terms of the agreement*

conduct ① VERB
to carry out an activity or task • *to conduct an experiment*
carry out • *to carry out a survey*
direct • *Christopher will direct day-to-day operations.*
do • *I'm doing a piece of important research right now.*
manage • *his ability to manage the business*
organize • *The initial mobilization was well organized.*
perform • *Several grafts were performed during the operation.*
run • *Each teacher will run a different workshop.*

MORE SYNONYMS:
• execute
• implement
• orchestrate

conduct ② NOUN
the way someone behaves • *Other people judge you by your conduct.*
attitude • *His attitude made me angry.*
behaviour • *Make sure that good behaviour is rewarded.*
manners • *He dressed well and had impeccable manners.*
ways • *I urged him to alter his ways.*

MORE SYNONYMS:
• comportment
• demeanour

conduct yourself VERB
to behave in a particular way • *The*

way he conducts himself reflects on the school.
act • *a gang of youths who were acting suspiciously*
behave • *He'd behaved badly.*

ANOTHER SYNONYM:
• acquit yourself

conference NOUN
a meeting for discussion • *a conference on education*
congress • *a congress of coal miners*
convention • *the Geneva convention*
discussion • *a round of formal discussions*
forum • *a forum for trade negotiations*
meeting • *a meeting of shareholders*

MORE SYNONYMS:
• colloquium
• convocation
• symposium

confess VERB
to admit to something • *Your son has confessed to his crimes.*
acknowledge • *He acknowledged that he was a drug addict.*
admit • *I admit to feeling jealous.*
own up • *The headmaster is waiting for someone to own up.*

ANTONYM:
• deny

confession NOUN
the act of confessing • *a confession of adultery*
acknowledgment • *an acknowledgment of his mistakes*
admission • *an admission of guilt*

confidence ① NOUN
a feeling of trust • *I have complete confidence in you.*
belief • *his belief in his partner*
faith • *He has great faith in her judgment.*
reliance • *I don't put much reliance on that idea.*

trust • *He destroyed my trust in people.*

ANTONYM:
• distrust

confidence ② NOUN
sureness of yourself • *I've never had much confidence.*
aplomb • *She handled the interview with aplomb.*
assurance • *He led the orchestra with great assurance.*
self-assurance • *his supreme self-assurance*
self-possession • *an air of self-possession*

ANTONYM:
• shyness

confident ① ADJECTIVE
sure about something • *confident of success*
certain • *certain of getting a place on the team*
convinced • *He is convinced it's your fault.*
positive • *I'm positive it will happen.*
satisfied • *We must be satisfied that the treatment is safe.*
secure • *secure about his job prospects*
sure • *I'm not sure I understand.*

ANTONYM:
• uncertain

confident ② ADJECTIVE
sure of yourself • *a confident attitude*
assured • *His playing became more assured.*
self-assured • *a self-assured young man*
self-possessed • *a self-possessed career woman*

ANTONYM:
• shy

confine ① VERB
to limit to something specified • *They*

confined themselves to talking about the weather.
limit • *Limit yourself to six units of alcohol a week.*
restrict • *The patient was restricted to a meagre diet.*

confine ② VERB
to prevent from leaving • *confined to bed for two days*
hem in • *hemmed in by spectators*
imprison • *imprisoned in a tiny cell*
restrict • *We were restricted to the building.*
shut up • *He can't stand being shut up in the house.*

MORE SYNONYMS:
• immure
• incarcerate
• intern

confirm ① VERB
to say or show that something is true • *Police confirmed that they had received a call.*
bear out • *The figures bear out his words.*
endorse • *This theory has been endorsed by research.*
prove • *The results prove his point.*
substantiate • *no evidence to substantiate the claims*
validate • *It is difficult to validate this belief.*
verify • *I was asked to verify this statement.*

MORE SYNONYMS:
• authenticate
• corroborate

confirm ② VERB
to make something definite • *Can we confirm the arrangements for tomorrow?*
fix • *The date for the election was fixed.*
settle • *I've settled a time to see him.*

A
B
C
D
E
F
G
H
I
J
K
L
M
N
O
P
Q
R
S
T
U
V
W
X
Y
Z

conflict ① NOUN
disagreement and argument • *conflict between workers and management*
antagonism • *antagonism within the team*
disagreement • *The meeting ended in disagreement.*
discord • *public discord*
friction • *friction between him and his father*
hostility • *hostility between parents and teachers*
opposition • *a wave of opposition*
strife • *a cause of strife in many marriages*

conflict ② NOUN
a war or battle • *the conflict in the Gulf*
battle • *a battle between two gangs*
combat • *men who died in combat*
fighting • *Villagers have left their homes to avoid the fighting.*
strife • *civil strife*
war • *the war between Israel and Egypt*

conflict ③ VERB
to differ or disagree • *conflicting ideas*
be at variance • *His statements are at variance with the facts.*
be incompatible • *These two principles are incompatible.*
clash • *a decision which clashes with official policy*
differ • *The two leaders differ on several issues.*
disagree • *Governments disagree over the need for action.*

confuse ① VERB
to mix two things up • *confusing fact with fiction*
mistake • *I mistook you for someone else.*
mix up • *He sometimes mixes up his words.*
muddle up • *I keep muddling him up with his brother.*

confuse ② VERB
to puzzle or bewilder • *Politics confuse me.*
baffle • *Police are baffled by the murder.*
bewilder • *His silence bewildered her.*
mystify • *I was mystified by his attitude.*
puzzle • *One thing still puzzles me.*
MORE SYNONYMS:
• bemuse
• faze
• nonplus
• perplex

confused ① ADJECTIVE
puzzled or bewildered • *confused about health risks*
baffled • *He stared in baffled amazement.*
bewildered • *bewildered holidaymakers*
muddled • *She was muddled about the date.*
perplexed • *perplexed by recent events*
puzzled • *a puzzled expression*
MORE SYNONYMS:
• at a loss
• at sea
• flummoxed
• nonplussed

confused ② ADJECTIVE
in an untidy mess • *They lay in a confused heap.*
chaotic • *the chaotic mess on his desk*
disordered • *a disordered pile of papers*
disorganized • *a disorganized lifestyle*
untidy • *an untidy room*
ANTONYM:
• tidy

confusing ADJECTIVE
puzzling or bewildering • *a confusing situation*
baffling • *a baffling statement*
bewildering • *a bewildering choice of products*

complicated • *a complicated voting system*
puzzling • *a puzzling problem*

confusion NOUN
an untidy mess • *My life is in confusion.*
chaos • *economic chaos*
disarray • *The nation is in disarray.*
disorder • *The emergency room was in disorder.*
disorganization • *scenes of chaos and disorganization*
mess • *He always leaves the bathroom in a mess.*
ANTONYM:
• order

connect ① VERB
to join together • *Connect the pipe to the tap.*
affix • *His name was affixed to his cubicle.*
attach • *Attach the curtains to the rods with hooks.*
couple • *The engine is coupled to a gearbox.*
fasten • *A hatchet was fastened to his belt.*
join • *two springs joined together*
link • *the Channel Tunnel linking Britain with France*
ANTONYM:
• separate

connect ② VERB
to associate one thing with another • *evidence connecting him with the robberies*
ally • *The new government is allied with the military.*
associate • *symptoms associated with migraine headaches*
link • *research which links smoking with cancer*
relate • *the denial that unemployment is related to crime*

connection ① NOUN
a link or relationship • *a connection between drinking and liver disease*
affiliation • *He has no affiliation with any political party.*
association • *the association between the two companies*
bond • *the bond between a mother and child*
correlation • *the correlation between unemployment and crime*
correspondence • *the correspondence between Eastern and Western religions*
link • *a link between smoking and lung cancer*
relation • *This theory bears no relation to reality.*
relationship • *the relationship between humans and their environment*

connection ② NOUN
a point where things are joined • *The fault was just a loose connection.*
coupling • *The coupling between the railway carriages snapped.*
fastening • *a zip fastening*
junction • *the junction between nerve and muscle*
link • *a link between the city and the motorway*

conscience NOUN
a sense of right and wrong • *He had a guilty conscience.*
principles • *It's against my principles to eat meat.*
scruples • *a man with no moral scruples*
sense of right and wrong • *children with no sense of right and wrong*

conservative ADJECTIVE
unwilling to change • *People get more conservative as they grow older.*
conventional • *conventional tastes*
traditional • *a traditional school*

a
b
c
d
e
f
g
h
i
j
k
l
m
n
o
p
q
r
s
t
u
v
w
x
y
z

A
B
C
D
E
F
G
H
I
J
K
L
M
N
O
P
Q
R
S
T
U
V
W
X
Y
Z

MORE SYNONYMS:
• hidebound
• reactionary

ANTONYM:
• radical

consider ① VERB
to think of someone or something
as • *They do not consider him a
suitable candidate.*
believe • *I believe him to be innocent.*
judge • *His work was judged
unsatisfactory.*
rate • *The film was rated excellent.*
regard as • *They regard the tax as unfair.*
think • *Many people think him arrogant.*
MORE SYNONYMS:
• deem
• hold to be

consider ② VERB
to think carefully • *I will consider
your offer.*
contemplate • *He contemplated
his fate.*
deliberate • *The jury deliberated for
three days.*
meditate • *He meditated on the
problem.*
muse • *She sat musing on how unfair
life was.*
ponder • *pondering how to improve
the team*
reflect • *I reflected on the child's future.*
think about • *I've been thinking about
what you said.*
MORE SYNONYMS:
• cogitate
• mull over
• ruminate

consider ③ VERB
to take into account • *We should
consider her feelings.*
bear in mind • *There are a few points
to bear in mind.*

make allowances for • *Remember to
make allowances for delays.*
respect • *We will respect your wishes.*
take into account • *another factor to
be taken into account*
think about • *more important things
to think about*

consideration ① NOUN
careful thought about something • *a
decision requiring careful consideration*
attention • *I gave the question all my
attention.*
contemplation • *The problem deserves
serious contemplation.*
deliberation • *After much deliberation,
he called the police.*
study • *The proposals need careful
study.*
thought • *I've given the matter a great
deal of thought.*

consideration ② NOUN
concern for someone • *Show some
consideration for other passengers.*
concern • *concern for the homeless*
kindness • *We have been treated with
great kindness.*
respect • *no respect for wildlife*
tact • *a master of tact and diplomacy*

consideration ③ NOUN
something to be taken into account
• *Safety is a major consideration.*
factor • *an important factor in buying
a house*
issue • *Price is not the only issue.*
point • *There is another point to
remember.*

consist: consist of VERB
to be made up of • *The brain consists of
millions of nerve cells.*
be composed of • *The committee is
composed of ten people.*
be made up of • *The bouquet was
made up of roses and carnations.*

comprise • *The show comprises 50 paintings and sketches.*

conspicuous ADJECTIVE
easy to see or notice • *Her conspicuous lack of warmth confirmed her disapproval.*
apparent • *It has been apparent that someone has been stealing.*
blatant • *a blatant disregard for rules*
evident • *He spoke with evident emotion about his ordeal.*
noticeable • *the most noticeable effect of these changes*
obvious • *an obvious injustice*
perceptible • *a perceptible air of neglect*

MORE SYNONYMS:
• patent
• manifest

constant ① ADJECTIVE
going on all the time • *a city under constant attack*
continual • *continual pain*
continuous • *continuous gunfire*
eternal • *an eternal hum in the background*
nonstop • *nonstop music*
perpetual • *her perpetual complaints*
relentless • *relentless pressure*

MORE SYNONYMS:
• incessant
• interminable
• sustained
• unremitting

ANTONYM:
• periodic

constant ② ADJECTIVE
staying the same • *a constant temperature*
even • *an even level of sound*
fixed • *a fixed salary*
regular • *a regular beat*
stable • *a stable condition*

steady • *travelling at a steady 50 miles per hour*
uniform • *a uniform thickness*

MORE SYNONYMS:
• immutable
• invariable

ANTONYM:
• changeable

construct VERB
to build or make something • *The boxes are constructed from rough-sawn timber.*
assemble • *She had been trying to assemble the bomb when it went off.*
build • *Workers at the plant build the F-16 jet fighter.*
create • *We created a makeshift platform for him to stand on.*
erect • *The building was erected in 1900.*
make • *The company now makes cars at two plants in Europe.*
put together • *the mechanic whose job was to put together looms within the plant*
put up • *He was putting up a new fence.*

consult VERB
to go to for advice • *Consult your doctor before undertaking exercise.*
ask for advice • *Ask your bank manager for advice on mortgages.*
confer with • *He is conferring with his lawyers.*
refer to • *I had to refer to the manual.*

contact ① NOUN
the state of being in touch with someone • *We must keep in contact.*
communication • *The leaders were in constant communication.*
touch • *I've lost touch with her over the years.*

contact ② NOUN
someone you know • *a contact in the music business*

acquaintance • We met through a mutual acquaintance.
connection • She had a connection in England.

contact ③ VERB

to get in touch with • We contacted the company to complain.
approach • A journalist has approached me for a story.
communicate with • We communicate mostly by email.
get hold of • I've been trying to get hold of you all week.
get in touch with • I will get in touch with my solicitors.
reach • Where can I reach you in an emergency?

contain ① VERB

to include as a part of • Alcohol contains sugar.
comprise • The band comprises two singers and two guitarists.
include • The price includes VAT.

contain ② VERB

to keep under control • efforts to contain the disease
control • He could hardly control his rage.
curb • measures to curb inflation
repress • people who repress their emotions
restrain • unable to restrain her anger
stifle • stifling the urge to scream

container NOUN

something which holds things • a plastic container for food
holder • a cigarette holder
vessel • storage vessels

MORE SYNONYMS:
• receptacle
• repository

contemplate ① VERB

to think carefully about something

• He cried as he contemplated his future.
consider • She paused to consider her options.
examine • I have examined all the possible alternatives.
muse on • Many of the papers muse on the fate of the President.
ponder • He didn't waste time pondering the question.
reflect on • I reflected on the child's future.
think about • Think about how you can improve the situation.

contemplate ② VERB

to consider doing something • He contemplated a career as a doctor.
consider • Watersports enthusiasts should consider hiring a wetsuit.
envisage • He had never envisaged spending the whole of his life in that job.
plan • I had been planning a trip to the West Coast.
think of • Martin was thinking of taking legal action against his employers.

contempt NOUN

complete lack of respect • I shall treat that remark with the contempt it deserves.
derision • He was greeted with shouts of derision.
disdain • Janet looked at him with disdain.
disregard • total disregard for the safety of the public
disrespect • complete disrespect for authority
scorn • They greeted the proposal with scorn.

ANTONYM:
• respect

contest ① NOUN

a competition or game • Few contests in the history of boxing have been as thrilling.

competition • *a surfing competition*
game • *the first game of the season*
match • *He was watching a football match.*
tournament • *Here is a player capable of winning a world tournament.*

contest ② NOUN
a struggle for power • *a bitter contest over who should control the state's future*
battle • *the eternal battle between good and evil*
fight • *the fight for the US Presidency*
struggle • *locked in a power struggle with his Prime Minister*

contest ③ VERB
to object formally to a statement or decision • *Your former employer has 14 days to contest the case.*
challenge • *The move was immediately challenged.*
dispute • *He disputed the allegations.*
oppose • *Many parents oppose bilingual education in schools.*
question • *It never occurs to them to question the doctor's decisions.*

ANTONYM:
• accept

continual ① ADJECTIVE
happening all the time without stopping • *Despite continual pain, he refused all drugs.*
constant • *She suggests that women are under constant pressure to be abnormally thin.*
continuous • *a continuous stream of phone calls*
endless • *her endless demands for attention*
eternal • *In the background was that eternal hum.*
nagging • *a nagging pain between his shoulder blades*
perpetual • *the perpetual thump of*

music from the flat downstairs
uninterrupted • *five years of uninterrupted growth*

MORE SYNONYMS:
• incessant
• interminable
• unremitting

continual ② ADJECTIVE
happening again and again • *She suffered continual police harassment.*
frequent • *He is prone to frequent bouts of depression.*
recurrent • *buildings in which staff suffer recurrent illness*
regular • *He is a regular visitor to our house.*
repeated • *Mr Smith did not return the money, despite repeated reminders.*

ANTONYM:
• occasional

continue ① VERB
to keep doing something • *Will you continue working after you're married?*
carry on • *The assistant carried on talking.*
go on • *Unemployment is likely to go on rising.*
keep on • *He kept on trying.*
persist • *She persists in using his nickname.*

continue ② VERB
to go on existing • *The fighting continued after they'd left.*
carry on • *My work will carry on after I'm gone.*
endure • *Their friendship has endured for 30 years.*
last • *Nothing lasts forever.*
persist • *The problem persists.*
remain • *The building remains to this day.*
survive • *companies which survived after the recession*

a
b
c
d
e
f
g
h
i
j
k
l
m
n
o
p
q
r
s
t
u
v
w
x
y
z

continue ③ VERB
to start doing again • *After a moment, she continued speaking.*
carry on • *He took a deep breath, then carried on.*
recommence • *He recommenced work on his novel.*
resume • *Police will resume the search today.*

continuous ADJECTIVE
going on without stopping
• *continuous growth*
constant • *under constant pressure*
continued • *a continued improvement*
extended • *conflict over an extended period*
prolonged • *a prolonged drought*
uninterrupted • *uninterrupted rule*

ANTONYM:
• periodic

control ① NOUN
power over something • *He was forced to give up control of the company.*
authority • *You have no authority here.*
command • *He was in command of the ceremony.*
direction • *The team worked well under his direction.*
government • *The entire country is under the government of one man.*
management • *the day-to-day management of the business*
power • *a position of great power*
rule • *15 years of Communist rule*
supremacy • *The party has re-established its supremacy.*

MORE SYNONYMS:
• jurisdiction
• mastery
• superintendence

control ② VERB
to be in charge of • *companies fighting to control the internet*

administer • *the authorities who administer the island*
be in charge of • *She is in charge of the project.*
command • *the general who commanded the troops*
direct • *He will direct day-to-day operations.*
govern • *his ability to govern France*
have power over • *Her husband has total power over her.*
manage • *the government's ability to manage the economy*
rule • *the dynasty which ruled China*

convenient ADJECTIVE
helpful or easy to use • *a convenient mode of transport*
handy • *Credit cards can be handy.*
helpful • *a helpful fact sheet*
useful • *a useful invention*

MORE SYNONYMS:
• labour-saving
• serviceable

ANTONYM:
• inconvenient

convention ① NOUN
an accepted way of behaving or doing something • *It's just a social convention that men don't wear skirts.*
code • *the code of the Shaolin monks*
custom • *The custom of lighting the Olympic flame goes back centuries.*
etiquette • *the rules of diplomatic etiquette*
practice • *It is normal practice not to reveal the sex of the baby.*
tradition • *different cultural traditions from ours*

MORE SYNONYMS:
• propriety
• protocol

convention ② NOUN
a large meeting of an organization

or group • *the annual convention of the Parapsychological Association*
assembly • *an assembly of women Olympic gold-medal winners*
conference • *a conference attended by 450 delegates*
congress • *A lot changed after the party congress.*
meeting • *the annual meeting of company shareholders*

conventional ① ADJECTIVE
having or relating to a very ordinary lifestyle • *a respectable married woman with conventional opinions*
conformist • *He may have to become more conformist if he is to prosper.*
conservative • *The girl was well dressed in a rather conservative style.*
unadventurous • *He was a strong player, but rather unadventurous.*

MORE SYNONYMS:
• bourgeois
• staid

conventional ② ADJECTIVE
familiar, or usually used • *These discs hold 400 times as much information as a conventional floppy disk.*
customary • *the customary one minute's silence*
ordinary • *It has 25 per cent less fat than ordinary ice cream.*
orthodox • *Many of these ideas are being incorporated into orthodox medical treatment.*
regular • *This product looks and tastes like regular margarine.*
standard • *It was standard practice for untrained clerks to deal with serious cases.*
traditional • *traditional teaching methods*

convey VERB
to cause information or ideas to be

known • *I tried to convey the wonder of the experience to my husband.*
communicate • *They successfully communicate their knowledge to others.*
express • *She did her best to express wordless disapproval by scowling.*
get across • *I wanted to get my message across.*
impart • *the ability to impart knowledge*

convince VERB
to persuade that something is true • *I convinced him of my innocence.*
assure • *She assured me that there was nothing wrong.*
persuade • *I had to persuade him of the advantages.*
satisfy • *He had to satisfy the doctors that he was fit to play.*

convincing ADJECTIVE
persuasive • *a convincing argument*
conclusive • *conclusive proof*
effective • *an effective speaker*
persuasive • *persuasive reasons*
plausible • *a plausible explanation*
powerful • *a powerful speech*
telling • *a telling criticism*

MORE SYNONYMS:
• cogent
• incontrovertible

ANTONYM:
• unconvincing

cook VERB
to prepare food for eating by heating it in some way • *I enjoy cooking for friends.*
bake • *a machine for baking bread*
barbecue • *a Korean method of barbecuing meat*
boil • *Boil the fruit and syrup together for half an hour.*
fry • *Garnish the rice with thinly sliced fried onion.*

a
b
c
d
e
f
g
h
i
j
k
l
m
n
o
p
q
r
s
t
u
v
w
x
y
z

grill • *Grill the fish for five minutes.*
microwave • *Microwaved vegetables have a fresher flavour.*
poach • *I had ordered poached eggs on toast for breakfast.*
roast • *Roast the aubergine in the oven for about one hour until soft.*
steam • *mussels on a bed of steamed cabbage*
stew • *You can stew the vegetables in oil.*
toast • *This currant loaf is delicious either fresh or toasted.*

cool ① ADJECTIVE
having a low temperature • *a gust of cool air*
chilled • *a chilled bottle of wine*
chilly • *a chilly afternoon*
cold • *Your dinner's getting cold.*
refreshing • *a refreshing breeze*
ANTONYM:
• warm

cool ② ADJECTIVE
staying calm • *He kept cool through the whole thing.*
calm • *Try to stay calm.*
collected • *She was cool and collected throughout the interview.*
composed • *a composed player*
level-headed • *Simon is level-headed and practical.*
relaxed • *a relaxed manner*
serene • *a serene smile*
MORE SYNONYMS:
• dispassionate
• imperturbable
• unemotional
• unexcited
• unruffled
ANTONYM:
• nervous

cool ③ VERB
to make or become cool • *Put the*

cookies on a wire rack to cool.
chill • *a glass of chilled champagne*
cool off • *Dip the carrots in water to cool them off.*
freeze • *Make double the quantity and freeze half for later.*
refrigerate • *Refrigerate the dough overnight.*
ANTONYM:
• heat

cooperate VERB
to work together • *The family cooperated with the author of the book.*
collaborate • *They collaborated on an album.*
join forces • *The two political parties are joining forces.*
pull together • *The staff and management pull together.*
work together • *industry and government working together*

copy ① NOUN
something made to look like something else • *He had kept a copy of the letter.*
counterfeit • *This credit card is a counterfeit.*
duplicate • *I lost my key and had to get a duplicate made.*
fake • *How do I know this painting isn't a fake?*
forgery • *The letter was a forgery.*
imitation • *Beware of cheap imitations.*
replica • *a replica of the Statue of Liberty*
reproduction • *a reproduction of a famous painting*
MORE SYNONYMS:
• facsimile
• likeness
• replication

copy ② VERB
to do the same thing as someone else

• My little brother copies everything I do.
ape • Generations of women have aped her style and looks.
emulate • Sons are expected to emulate their fathers.
follow • Where America goes, Britain will surely follow.
imitate • Children imitate what they see on TV.
mimic • He mimicked her accent.

MORE SYNONYMS:
• follow suit
• parrot
• simulate

copy ③ VERB
to make a copy of • documents copied by hand
counterfeit • These banknotes are very easy to counterfeit.
duplicate • Videos are being illicitly duplicated all over the country.
reproduce • a new method of reproducing oil paintings

corny ADJECTIVE
unoriginal or sentimental • corny old love songs
banal • banal dialogue
hackneyed • a hackneyed plot
maudlin • a maudlin film
sentimental • a sentimental ballad
stale • stale ideas
stereotyped • a stereotyped image of Britain
trite • a trite ending

MORE SYNONYMS:
• mawkish
• old hat
• unoriginal

correct ① ADJECTIVE
without mistakes • a correct diagnosis
accurate • an accurate description
exact • an exact copy
faultless • Hans's English was faultless.

flawless • a flawless performance
precise • precise calculations
right • That clock never shows the right time.
true • a true account

correct ② ADJECTIVE
socially acceptable • correct behaviour
acceptable • It is becoming more acceptable for women to drink.
appropriate • appropriate dress
fitting • behaving in a manner not fitting for a lady
okay or **OK** (INFORMAL) • Is it okay if I bring a friend with me?
proper • In those days it was not proper for women to go on the stage.
seemly • It is not seemly to joke about such things.

ANTONYM:
• wrong

correct ③ VERB
to make right • trying to correct his faults
amend • They want to amend the current system.
cure • an operation to cure his limp
improve • We must improve the situation.
rectify • attempts to rectify the problem
reform • He promised to reform his wicked ways.
remedy • What is needed to remedy these deficiencies?
right • I intend to right these wrongs.

MORE SYNONYMS:
• emend
• redress

correction NOUN
the act of making something right
• the correction of obvious mistakes
adjustment • My car needs a brake adjustment.

a b **c** d e f g h i j k l m n o p q r s t u v w x y z

amendment • *He has made lots of amendments to the script.*

righting • *the righting of the country's domestic troubles*

MORE SYNONYMS:
• emendation
• rectification

correspond VERB

to be similar or connected to something else • *The two maps correspond closely.*

agree • *His statement agrees with those of other witnesses.*

be related • *These philosophical problems are closely related.*

coincide • *He was delighted to find that her feelings coincided with his own.*

correlate • *Obesity correlates with increased risk for diabetes.*

fit • *The punishment must always fit the crime.*

match • *Our value system does not match with theirs.*

tally • *This description did not tally with what we saw.*

corrupt ① ADJECTIVE

acting dishonestly or illegally
• *corrupt politicians*

crooked • *a crooked cop*

dishonest • *a dishonest scheme*

fraudulent • *fraudulent trading*

shady (INFORMAL) • *shady deals*

unscrupulous • *unscrupulous landlords*

MORE SYNONYMS:
• unethical
• unprincipled
• venal

ANTONYM:
• honest

corrupt ② VERB

to make dishonest • *Organized crime has corrupted local government.*

bribe • *accused of bribing officials*

buy off • *Police were bought off by drugs dealers.*

fix (INFORMAL) • *He fixed the match by bribing the players.*

corrupt ③ VERB

to make immoral • *TV is corrupting our children.*

deprave • *material likely to deprave those who watch it*

pervert • *perverted by their contact with criminals*

corruption NOUN

dishonest and illegal behaviour
• *charges of corruption*

bribery • *on trial for bribery*

dishonesty • *She accused the government of dishonesty and incompetence.*

fraud • *jailed for fraud*

MORE SYNONYMS:
• extortion
• profiteering
• venality

cost ① NOUN

the amount of money needed • *The cost of petrol has increased.*

charge • *We can arrange this for a small charge.*

expense • *household expenses*

outlay • *Buying wine in bulk is well worth the outlay.*

payment • *an initial payment of just $100*

price • *House prices are expected to rise.*

rate • *specially reduced rates*

cost ② NOUN

loss or damage • *the total cost in human misery*

detriment • *These changes are to the detriment of staff morale.*

expense • *I supported my husband's career at the expense of my own.*

penalty • *paying the penalty for someone else's mistakes*

cost ③ VERB
to involve a cost of • *The air fares were going to cost a lot.*
come to • *Lunch came to nearly 15.*
sell at • *The books are selling at £1 per copy.*
set someone back (INFORMAL) • *This wedding will set us back thousands of pounds.*

cosy ① ADJECTIVE
warm and comfortable • *Guests can relax in the cosy bar.*
comfortable • *a comfortable fireside chair*
snug • *a snug log cabin*
warm • *warm blankets*

cosy ② ADJECTIVE
pleasant and friendly • *a cosy chat between friends*
friendly • *a friendly little get-together*
informal • *The house has an informal atmosphere.*
intimate • *an intimate candlelit dinner for two*
relaxed • *a relaxed evening in*

council NOUN
a governing group of people • *the city council*
assembly • *the National Assembly*
board • *the Pakistan Cricket Board*
committee • *the management committee*
panel • *a panel of judges*
MORE SYNONYMS:
• conclave
• convocation
• quango
• synod

count ① VERB
to add up • *I counted the money.*

add up • *Add up the sales figures.*
calculate • *First, calculate your monthly living expenses.*
tally • *Computers now tally the votes.*
MORE SYNONYMS:
• compute
• enumerate
• tot up

count ② VERB
to be important • *Our opinions don't count.*
carry weight • *a politician whose words carry weight*
matter • *It doesn't matter what she thinks.*
rate • *This does not rate as one of my main concerns.*
signify • *His absence does not signify much.*
weigh • *This evidence did not weigh with the jury.*

count ③ NOUN
a counting or number counted • *The count revealed that our party had the majority.*
calculation • *I did a quick calculation in my head.*
reckoning • *By my reckoning we were about two miles from camp.*
sum • *I've never been good at sums.*
tally • *They keep a tally of visitors to the castle.*
MORE SYNONYMS:
• computation
• enumeration

counteract VERB
to reduce the effect of something • *pills to counteract high blood pressure*
act against • *The immune system acts against infection.*
offset • *The slump was offset by a surge in exports.*

a
b
c
d
e
f
g
h
i
j
k
l
m
n
o
p
q
r
s
t
u
v
w
x
y
z

A
B
C
D
E
F
G
H
I
J
K
L
M
N
O
P
Q
R
S
T
U
V
W
X
Y
Z

MORE SYNONYMS:
• counterbalance
• countervail
• negate
• neutralize

countless ADJECTIVE
too many to count • *the star of countless films*
infinite • *an infinite number of atoms*
innumerable • *innumerable problems*
myriad • *pop music in all its myriad forms*
untold • *untold wealth*

MORE SYNONYMS:
• incalculable
• limitless
• measureless
• multitudinous

country ① NOUN
a political area • *the boundary between the two countries*
kingdom • *The kingdom's power declined.*
land • *America, land of opportunity*
state • *a communist state*

country ② NOUN
land away from towns and cities • *He lives right out in the country.*
bush (NEW ZEALAND AND SOUTH AFRICAN) • *a trip out to the bush*
countryside • *surrounded by beautiful countryside*
outback (AUSTRALIAN AND NEW ZEALAND) • *nostalgic paintings of the outback*
outdoors • *He loves the great outdoors.*

RELATED WORDS:
• ADJECTIVES pastoral, rural

courage NOUN
lack of fear • *His courage impressed everyone.*
bravery • *an act of bravery*
daring • *tales of daring and adventure*

guts (INFORMAL) • *He didn't have the guts to admit he was wrong.*
heroism • *the young soldier's heroism*
nerve • *I didn't have the nerve to complain.*
pluck • *You have to admire her pluck.*
valour • *He was decorated for valour in the war.*

MORE SYNONYMS:
• dauntlessness
• fearlessness
• grit
• intrepidity

ANTONYM:
• fear

course ① NOUN
a series of lessons • *a course in computing*
classes • *I go to dance classes.*
curriculum • *the history curriculum*

course ② NOUN
a policy of action • *He took the only course left open to him.*
plan • *Your best plan is to see your doctor.*
policy • *She decided the best policy was to wait.*
procedure • *He did not follow the correct procedure.*

course ③ NOUN
a way taken to get somewhere • *She sensed the plane had changed course.*
direction • *He went off in the opposite direction.*
line • *the birds' line of flight*
path • *the path of an oncoming car*
route • *the most direct route*
trajectory • *the trajectory of the missile*
way • *What way do you go home?*

court ① NOUN
a place where legal matters are decided • *He ended up in court for theft.*
bench • *He was brought before the bench.*

law court • *prisoners tried by a law court*
tribunal • *The claim was thrown out by a European tribunal.*

court ② VERB (OLD-FASHIONED)
to intend to marry • *I was courting Billy at 19 and married him at 21.*
go steady • *They've been going steady for six months now.*
woo • *He wooed and married his first love.*

courtesy NOUN
polite and considerate behaviour • *a lack of courtesy to other drivers*
civility • *Handle customers with tact and civility.*
courteousness • *his courteousness and kindness*
gallantry • *He treated me with old-fashioned gallantry.*
good manners • *the rules of good manners*
grace • *He didn't even have the grace to apologize.*
graciousness • *The team displayed graciousness in defeat.*
politeness • *basic standards of politeness*

cover ① VERB
to protect or hide • *He covered his face.*
cloak • *a land cloaked in mist*
conceal • *The hat concealed her hair.*
cover up • *I covered him up with a blanket.*
hide • *His sunglasses hid his eyes.*
mask • *A cloud masked the sun.*
obscure • *One wall was obscured by a huge banner.*
screen • *The road was screened by a block of flats.*
shade • *shading his eyes from the glare*

ANTONYM:
• reveal

cover ② VERB
to form a layer over • *Tears covered his face.*
coat • *Coat the fish with batter.*
overlay • *The floor was overlaid with rugs.*

cover ③ NOUN
something which protects or hides • *a duvet cover*
case • *a spectacle case*
coating • *steel covered with a coating of zinc*
covering • *a plastic covering*
jacket • *the jacket of a book*
mask • *a surgical mask*
screen • *They put a screen round me.*
wrapper • *Take the product from its sealed wrapper.*

cow NOUN
a farm animal kept for milk or meat • *a herd of dairy cows*
bovine • *a herd of deranged bovines*
cattle • *fields where cattle graze*

coward NOUN
someone who is easily scared • *He's too much of a coward to fight.*
chicken (SLANG) • *We called him a chicken.*
wimp (INFORMAL) • *He seems like a wimp to me.*

cowardly ADJECTIVE
easily scared • *too cowardly to tell the truth*
chicken (SLANG) • *I was too chicken to complain.*
faint-hearted • *This is no time to be faint-hearted.*
gutless (INFORMAL) • *a gutless coward*
sookie (NEW ZEALAND) • *a sookie thing to do*

MORE SYNONYMS:
• craven
• lily-livered

a
b
c
d
e
f
g
h
i
j
k
l
m
n
o
p
q
r
s
t
u
v
w
x
y
z

A
B
C
D
E
F
G
H
I
J
K
L
M
N
O
P
Q
R
S
T
U
V
W
X
Y
Z

- pusillanimous
- spineless
- timorous

ANTONYM:
- brave

cower VERB
to bend down with fear • *The hostages cowered in their seats.*
cringe • *I cringed in horror.*
quail • *She quailed at the sight.*
shrink • *He shrank back in terror.*

crack ① VERB
to become damaged, with lines on the surface • *A gas main has cracked.*
break • *She broke her leg playing rounders.*
fracture • *You've fractured a rib.*
snap • *The mast snapped like a dry twig.*

crack ② VERB
to find the answer to something • *We've managed to crack the problem.*
decipher • *trying to decipher the code*
solve • *attempts to solve the mystery*
work out • *I've worked out where I'm going wrong.*

crack ③ NOUN
a line or gap caused by damage • *a large crack in the wall*
break • *a train crash caused by a break in the rails*
cleft • *a cleft in the rocks*
crevice • *a crevice in the cliff-face*
fracture • *a hip fracture*
MORE SYNONYMS:
- fissure
- interstice

crafty ADJECTIVE
clever and rather dishonest • *That crafty old devil has taken us for a ride.*
artful • *the smiles and schemes of an artful woman*
cunning • *I have a cunning plan to get us out of this mess.*

devious • *By devious means she obtained the address.*
scheming • *You're a scheming little devil, aren't you?*
slippery • *a slippery customer*
sly • *He is a sly old beggar if ever there was one.*
wily • *the wily manoeuvring of the President*

cram VERB
to stuff something into a container or place • *She crammed her mouth with nuts.*
jam • *The place was jammed with people.*
pack • *The drawers were packed with clothes.*
squeeze • *The two of us were squeezed into one seat.*
stuff • *wallets stuffed with dollars*

crash ① NOUN
an accident involving a moving vehicle • *a plane crash*
accident • *a serious car accident*
bump • *I had a bump in the car park.*
collision • *a head-on collision*
pile-up (INFORMAL) • *a 54-car pile-up*
smash • *He nearly died in a car smash.*

crash ② NOUN
a loud noise • *There was a sudden crash outside.*
bang • *The door slammed with a bang.*
clash • *the clash of cymbals*
din • *the din of battle*
smash • *the smash of falling crockery*

crash ③ NOUN
the failure of a business • *a stock market crash*
bankruptcy • *Many firms are now facing bankruptcy.*
collapse • *The economy is on the edge of collapse.*
depression • *the Great Depression of the 1930s*

failure · *a major cause of business failure*
ruin · *Inflation has driven them to the brink of ruin.*

crash ④ VERB
to have an accident · *His car crashed into the rear of a van.*
bump · *I've just bumped my car.*
collide · *Two trains collided in London today.*
drive into · *He drove his car into a tree.*
have an accident · *My brother's had an accident on his moped.*
hurtle into · *The racing car hurtled into the spectator enclosure.*
plough into · *The plane had ploughed into the mountainside.*
wreck · *He's wrecked his van.*

crawl VERB
to be full of · *The place is crawling with drunks.*
be alive with · *The river was alive with frogs.*
be full of · *The place was full of insects.*
be overrun (SLANG) · *The area is overrun with tourists.*
swarm · *The wood was swarming with police officers.*
teem · *ponds teeming with fish*

craze NOUN
a brief enthusiasm for something
· *the latest fitness craze*
fad · *a new-age fad*
fashion · *the fashion for Seventies toys*
trend · *the latest trend among film stars*
vogue · *a vogue for so-called health drinks*

crazy ① ADJECTIVE (INFORMAL)
very strange or foolish · *People thought we were crazy when we told them our plans.*
foolish · *It is foolish to risk skin cancer for the sake of a tan.*

insane · *If you want my opinion, I think your idea is completely insane.*
mad · *You'd be mad to work with him again.*
ridiculous · *It was an absolutely ridiculous decision.*
wild · *all sorts of wild ideas*
zany · *zany humour*

ANTONYM:
· sensible

crazy ② ADJECTIVE (INFORMAL)
very keen on something · *He's crazy about football.*
fanatical · *fanatical about computer games*
mad · *She's not as mad about sport as I am.*
obsessed · *He was obsessed with American gangster movies.*
passionate · *He is passionate about the project.*
smitten · *They were totally smitten with each other.*
wild · *I'm just wild about Peter.*

MORE SYNONYMS:
· enamoured
· zealous

create ① VERB
to make something happen · *His reaction created a bad atmosphere.*
bring about · *helping to bring about peace*
cause · *Sugar causes dental decay.*
lead to · *The takeover led to widespread redundancies.*
occasion · *the distress occasioned by her dismissal*

create ② VERB
to invent something · *creating a new style of painting*
coin · *the man who coined the term "virtual reality"*

a b c d e f g h i j k l m n o p q r s t u v w x y z

A
B
C
D
E
F
G
H
I
J
K
L
M
N
O
P
Q
R
S
T
U
V
W
X
Y
Z

compose • *Vivaldi composed many concertos.*
devise • *We devised a scheme to help him.*
formulate • *He formulated his plan for escape.*
invent • *He invented the first electric clock.*
originate • *the designer who originated platform shoes*

creative ADJECTIVE
able to invent • *her creative talents*
fertile • *a fertile imagination*
imaginative • *an imaginative writer*
inspired • *his inspired use of colour*
inventive • *an inventive storyline*

credit NOUN
praise for something • *He took all the credit for my idea.*
commendation • *Both teams deserve commendation.*
glory • *basking in reflected glory*
praise • *Praise is due to all concerned.*
recognition • *She got no recognition for her work.*
thanks • *He received no thanks for his efforts.*

MORE SYNONYMS:
• acclaim
• Brownie points
• kudos

ANTONYM:
• disgrace

creepy ADJECTIVE (INFORMAL)
strange and frightening • *This place is really creepy at night.*
disturbing • *There was something about him she found disturbing.*
eerie • *I walked down the eerie dark path.*
macabre • *macabre stories*
scary (INFORMAL) • *We watched scary movies.*

sinister • *There was something sinister about him.*
spooky • *The whole place has a slightly spooky atmosphere.*
unnatural • *The altered landscape looks unnatural and weird.*

crime NOUN
an act that breaks the law • *the problem of organized crime*
misdemeanour • *a financial misdemeanour*
offence • *a serious offence*
violation • *tax law violations*
wrong • *I intend to right that wrong.*

MORE SYNONYMS:
• felony
• malfeasance
• misdeed
• transgression

criminal ① NOUN
someone who has committed a crime • *the country's most dangerous criminals*
crook (INFORMAL) • *The man is a crook and a liar.*
culprit • *the true culprit's identity*
delinquent • *juvenile delinquents*
offender • *a first-time offender*
skelm (SOUTH AFRICAN) • *a skelm from the city*
villain • *He tackled an armed villain single-handed.*

MORE SYNONYMS:
• evildoer
• felon
• lawbreaker
• malefactor

criminal ② ADJECTIVE
involving crime • *criminal activities*
corrupt • *corrupt practices*
crooked • *crooked business deals*
illegal • *an illegal action*
illicit • *illicit dealings*
unlawful • *unlawful entry*

MORE SYNONYMS:
• culpable
• felonious
• indictable
• iniquitous
• nefarious

ANTONYM:
• legal

cripple ① VERB
to injure severely • *crippled in a car accident*
disable • *disabled by polio*
lame • *He was lamed for life.*
maim • *mines maiming and killing civilians*
paralyse • *paralysed in a riding accident*

cripple ② VERB
to prevent from working • *The crisis may cripple the Irish economy.*
bring to a standstill • *The strike brought France to a standstill.*
impair • *Their actions will impair France's national interests.*
put out of action • *The port has been put out of action.*

critical ① ADJECTIVE
very important • *a critical point in history*
crucial • *a crucial election campaign*
deciding • *Price was a deciding factor.*
decisive • *a decisive moment in my life*
momentous • *a momentous decision*
pivotal • *He played a pivotal role in the match.*
vital • *vital information*

ANTONYM:
• unimportant

critical ② ADJECTIVE
very serious • *a critical illness*
grave • *grave danger*
precarious • *a precarious financial situation*
serious • *His condition is said to be serious.*

critical ③ ADJECTIVE
finding fault with something or someone • *critical remarks*
carping • *carping comments*
derogatory • *derogatory references to women*
disapproving • *a disapproving look*
disparaging • *He spoke in disparaging tones.*
scathing • *a scathing attack*
MORE SYNONYMS:
• captious
• cavilling
• censorious
• fault-finding
ANTONYM:
• complimentary

criticism NOUN
expression of disapproval • *public criticism of his actions*
censure • *They deserve praise rather than censure.*
disapproval • *a chorus of disapproval*
disparagement • *their disparagement of this book*
fault-finding • *her husband's constant fault-finding*
flak (INFORMAL) • *I got a lot of flak for that idea.*
panning (INFORMAL) • *a panning from the critics*
MORE SYNONYMS:
• animadversion
• denigration
• stricture
ANTONYM:
• praise

criticize VERB
to find fault • *The regime has been harshly criticized.*
censure • *a decision for which she was censured*

A
B
C
D
E
F
G
H
I
J
K
L
M
N
O
P
Q
R
S
T
U
V
W
X
Y
Z

condemn • *He refused to condemn their behaviour.*
find fault with • *She keeps finding fault with my work.*
knock (INFORMAL) • *Don't knock it till you've tried it.*
pan (INFORMAL) • *Critics panned the show.*
put down • *She's always putting him down in front of the kids.*

MORE SYNONYMS:
• disparage
• excoriate
• lambast *or*
• lambaste

ANTONYM:
• praise

crook ① NOUN (INFORMAL)
a criminal • *The man is a crook and a liar.*
cheat • *a rotten cheat*
rogue • *Mr Scott wasn't a rogue at all.*
scoundrel (OLD-FASHIONED) • *He is a lying scoundrel!*
shark • *Beware the sharks when you are deciding how to invest.*
swindler • *Swindlers have cheated investors out of £12 million.*
thief • *The thieves snatched the camera.*
villain • *As a copper, I've spent my life putting villains behind bars.*

crook ② ADJECTIVE (AUSTRALIAN AND NEW ZEALAND; INFORMAL)
ill • *He admitted to feeling a bit crook.*
ill • *I was feeling ill.*
nauseous • *The drugs may make the patient feel nauseous.*
poorly • *Julie's still poorly.*
queasy • *He was very prone to seasickness and already felt queasy.*
sick • *The very thought of food made him feel sick.*
under the weather • *I was still feeling a bit under the weather.*
unwell • *He felt unwell as he was travelling home this afternoon.*

crooked ① ADJECTIVE
bent or twisted • *a crooked tree*
bent • *a bent back*
deformed • *born with a deformed right leg*
distorted • *a distorted image*
irregular • *irregular and discoloured teeth*
out of shape • *The wires were bent out of shape.*
twisted • *bits of twisted metal*
warped • *warped wooden shutters*

ANTONYM:
• straight

crooked ② ADJECTIVE
dishonest or illegal • *crooked business practices*
corrupt • *corrupt police officers*
criminal • *criminal activities*
dishonest • *dishonest salespeople*
fraudulent • *a fraudulent claim*
illegal • *illegal trading*
shady (INFORMAL) • *shady deals*

MORE SYNONYMS:
• dishonourable
• nefarious
• unprincipled

ANTONYM:
• honest

cross ① VERB
to go across • *the bridge which crosses the river*
ford • *trying to find a safe place to ford the stream*
go across • *going across the road*
span • *the iron bridge spanning the railway*
traverse • *a valley traversed by streams*

cross ② VERB
to meet and go across • *the intersection where the roads cross*
crisscross • *Phone wires crisscross the street.*

intersect • *The circles intersect in two places.*

cross ③ NOUN

a mixture of two things • *a cross between a collie and a retriever*
blend • *a blend of the old and the new*
combination • *a combination of fear and anger*
mixture • *a mixture of two factors*

cross ④ ADJECTIVE

rather angry • *I'm very cross with him.*
angry • *Are you angry with me?*
annoyed • *I'm annoyed with myself for being so stupid.*
fractious • *The children were getting fractious.*
fretful • *the fretful expression on her face*
grumpy • *a grumpy old man*
in a bad mood • *He's in a bad mood about something.*
irritable • *She had been restless and irritable all day.*

MORE SYNONYMS:
• irascible
• peevish
• splenetic
• testy
• tetchy

crouch VERB

to squat down • *A man was crouching behind the car.*
bend down • *I bent down and touched the grass.*
squat • *He squatted on his heels to talk to the children.*

crowd ① NOUN

a large group of people • *A huge crowd gathered in the square.*
horde • *hordes of tourists*
host • *a host of fans*
mass • *a heaving mass of people*
mob • *a mob of demonstrators*
multitude • *surrounded by a noisy multitude*

swarm • *swarms of visitors*
throng • *An official pushed through the throng.*

crowd ② VERB

to gather close together • *Hundreds of fans crowded into the hall.*
congregate • *A large crowd congregated outside the stadium.*
gather • *Dozens of people gathered to watch.*
swarm • *Police swarmed into the area.*
throng • *The crowds thronged into the mall.*

crowded ADJECTIVE

full of people • *a crowded room*
congested • *congested cities*
full • *The train was full.*
overflowing • *buildings overflowing with students*
packed • *By 10.30 the shop was packed.*

crucial ADJECTIVE

very important • *a crucial moment in his career*
central • *central to the whole process*
critical • *a critical point in the campaign*
decisive • *ready to strike at the decisive moment*
momentous • *a momentous event*
pivotal • *He played a pivotal role in the match.*
vital • *vital information*

crude ① ADJECTIVE

rough and simple • *a crude weapon*
primitive • *They managed to make a primitive harness.*
rough • *a rough sketch*
rudimentary • *some form of rudimentary heating*
simple • *a simple stringed instrument*

crude ② ADJECTIVE

rude and offensive • *a crude sense of humour*
coarse • *coarse speech*

a
b
c
d
e
f
g
h
i
j
k
l
m
n
o
p
q
r
s
t
u
v
w
x
y
z

dirty • *a dirty joke*
indecent • *indecent lyrics*
obscene • *obscene language*
tasteless • *a tasteless remark*
vulgar • *a vulgar phrase*

MORE SYNONYMS:
• boorish
• crass
• smutty

ANTONYM:
• refined

cruel ADJECTIVE
deliberately causing hurt • *I hate
people who are cruel to animals.*
barbarous • *a barbarous attack*
brutal • *a brutal murder*
callous • *callous treatment*
cold-blooded • *a cold-blooded killer*
heartless • *It was a heartless thing
to do.*
inhumane • *He was kept under
inhumane conditions.*
sadistic • *mistreated by sadistic guards*
vicious • *a vicious blow*

ANTONYM:
• kind

cruelty NOUN
cruel behaviour • *an act of
unbelievable cruelty*
barbarity • *the barbarity of war*
brutality • *police brutality*
callousness • *the callousness of his
murder*
inhumanity • *man's inhumanity to
man*
savagery • *scenes of unimaginable
savagery*
viciousness • *the viciousness of the
attacks*

ANTONYM:
• kindness

crumple VERB
to squash and wrinkle • *She
crumpled the paper in her hand.*

crease • *Don't crease the material.*
crush • *Andrew crushed his empty can.*
screw up • *He screwed the letter up in
anger.*
wrinkle • *trying not to wrinkle her silk
skirt*

crush ① VERB
to destroy the shape of by squeezing
• *Their car was crushed by an army tank.*
crumble • *Crumble the stock cubes
into a jar.*
crumple • *She crumpled the note up and
threw it away.*
mash • *Mash the bananas with a fork.*
squash • *She squashed the wasp under
her heel.*

crush ② VERB
to defeat completely • *his bid to crush
the uprising*
overcome • *working to overcome the
enemy forces*
put down • *Soldiers moved in to put
down the rebellion.*
quell • *Troops eventually quelled the
unrest.*
stamp out • *steps to stamp out
bullying in schools*
vanquish • *his vanquished foe*

cry ① VERB
to have tears coming from your eyes
• *Stop crying and tell me what's wrong.*
▶ see Word Study **cry**, page 638

cry ② VERB
to call out loudly • *"See you soon!" they
cried.*
call • *She called to me across the square.*
exclaim • *"You must be mad!" she
exclaimed.*
shout • *"Over here!" they shouted.*
yell • *He yelled out of the window.*

cry ③ NOUN
a loud or high shout • *a cry of pain*
call • *the call of a seagull*

exclamation • *an exclamation of surprise*
shout • *I heard a distant shout.*
yell • *Bob let out a yell.*

cunning ① ADJECTIVE
clever and deceitful • *a cunning and ruthless businessman*
artful • *an artful old woman*
crafty • *a crafty plan*
devious • *a devious mind*
sly • *a sly trick*
wily • *a wily politician*

MORE SYNONYMS:
• foxy
• Machiavellian

ANTONYM:
• open

cunning ② NOUN
cleverness and deceit • *the cunning of today's criminals*
deviousness • *the deviousness of drug traffickers*
guile • *She was without guile or pretence.*

curb ① VERB
to keep something within limits • *He must learn to curb that temper of his.*
check • *an attempt to check the spread of the disease*
contain • *A hundred firefighters are still trying to contain the fire.*
control • *the need to control environmental pollution*
limit • *He limited payments on the country's foreign debt.*
restrain • *efforts to restrain corruption*
suppress • *The Government is suppressing inflation by devastating the economy.*

curb ② NOUN
an attempt to keep something within limits • *He called for stricter curbs on immigration.*

brake • *Illness had put a brake on his progress.*
control • *price controls*
limit • *limits on government spending*
limitation • *We need a limitation on the powers of the government.*
restraint • *new restraints on trade unions*

cure ① VERB
to make well • *a treatment which cures eczema*
heal • *plants used to heal wounds*
remedy • *an operation to remedy a blood clot on his brain*

cure ② NOUN
something that makes an illness better • *a cure for cancer*
medicine • *herbal medicines*
remedy • *a remedy for colds and flu*
treatment • *the most effective treatment for malaria*

curiosity ① NOUN
the desire to know • *a curiosity about the past*
inquisitiveness • *the inquisitiveness of children*
interest • *a lively interest in current affairs*

curiosity ② NOUN
something unusual • *a museum displaying relics and curiosities*
freak • *a freak of nature*
marvel • *a marvel of science*
novelty • *in the days when a motor car was a novelty*
oddity • *Tourists are still something of an oddity here.*
rarity • *Mexican restaurants are a rarity here.*

curious ① ADJECTIVE
wanting to know • *He was curious about my family.*
inquiring • *He gave me an inquiring look.*

a
b
c
d
e
f
g
h
i
j
k
l
m
n
o
p
q
r
s
t
u
v
w
x
y
z

A
B
C
D
E
F
G
H
I
J
K
L
M
N
O
P
Q
R
S
T
U
V
W
X
Y
Z

inquisitive • *Cats are very inquisitive.*
interested • *A crowd of interested villagers gathered.*
nosy (INFORMAL) • *nosy neighbours*
ANTONYM:
• incurious

curious ② ADJECTIVE
strange and unusual • *a curious mixture of the old and the new*
bizarre • *his bizarre behaviour*
extraordinary • *an extraordinary story*
odd • *an odd coincidence*
peculiar • *a peculiar smell*
singular • *a singular talent*
strange • *a strange taste*
unusual • *an unusual name*
ANTONYM:
• ordinary

current ① NOUN
a strong continuous movement of water • *swept away by the strong current*
flow • *the quiet flow of the olive-green water*
tide • *We will sail with the tide.*
undertow • *Dangerous undertows make swimming unsafe along the coastline.*

current ② ADJECTIVE
happening, being done, or being used now • *current trends*
contemporary • *He has adopted a more contemporary style.*
fashionable • *the fashionable theory about this issue*
ongoing • *an ongoing debate on inner city problems*
present • *skilfully renovated by the present owners*
present-day • *Even by present-day standards these are large aircraft.*
today's • *In today's America, health care is big business.*

up-to-the-minute • *up-to-the-minute information on sales and stocks*
ANTONYM:
• past

curve ① NOUN
a bending line • *a curve in the road*
arc • *The ball rose in an arc.*
bend • *a bend in the river*
trajectory • *the trajectory of an artillery shell*
turn • *every turn in the road*
RELATED WORD:
• ADJECTIVE sinuous

curve ② VERB
to move in a curve • *The road curved sharply to the left.*
arc • *A rainbow arced over the town.*
arch • *a domed ceiling arching overhead*
bend • *The path bent to the right.*
swerve • *His car swerved off the road.*

custom ① NOUN
a traditional activity • *an ancient Chinese custom*
convention • *the conventions of Western art*
practice • *an old Jewish practice*
ritual • *an ancient Shintoist ritual*
tradition • *different cultural traditions*

custom ② NOUN
something a person always does • *It was his custom to start work at 8.30.*
habit • *his habit of making tactless remarks*
practice • *her usual practice of attending church*
routine • *his daily routine*
wont • *Paul woke early, as was his wont.*

customer NOUN
someone who buys something • *The shop was filled with customers.*
buyer • *show homes to tempt potential buyers*

client • *a solicitor and his client*
consumer • *the increasing demands of consumers*
patron • *the restaurant's patrons*
purchaser • *a prospective purchaser*
shopper • *late-night shoppers on their way home*

cut ① VERB
to mark, injure, or remove part of (something or someone) with something sharp • *The thieves cut a hole in the fence.*
▶ see Word Study **cut**, *page 639*

cut ② VERB
to reduce something • *The department's first priority is to cut costs.*
cut back • *The Government has decided to cut back on defence spending.*
decrease • *calls to decrease income tax*
lower • *The Central Bank has lowered interest rates.*
reduce • *Gradually reduce the dosage.*
slash • *Holiday prices have been slashed.*

MORE SYNONYMS:
• abridge
• downsize
• rationalize

ANTONYM:
• increase

cut ③ NOUN
a mark or injury made by cutting
• *a cut on his left eyebrow*
gash • *There was a deep gash across his forehead.*
incision • *a tiny incision in the skin*

slash • *jeans with slashes in the knees*
slit • *Make a slit along the stem.*

cut ④ NOUN
a reduction in something • *another cut in interest rates*
cutback • *cutbacks in funding*
decrease • *a decrease in foreign investment*
lowering • *the lowering of taxes*
reduction • *reductions in staff*
saving • *household savings on energy use*

ANTONYM:
• increase

cute ADJECTIVE
pretty or attractive • *You were such a cute baby!*
appealing • *an appealing kitten*
attractive • *I thought he was very attractive.*
charming • *a charming little cottage*
dear • *Look at their dear little faces!*
good-looking • *Cassandra noticed him because he was so good-looking.*
gorgeous • *All the girls think Ryan's gorgeous.*
pretty • *She's a very pretty girl.*

ANTONYM:
• ugly

cynical ADJECTIVE
always thinking the worst of people
• *a cynical attitude*
distrustful • *distrustful of all politicians*
sceptical • *a sceptical response*

a
b
c
d
e
f
g
h
i
j
k
l
m
n
o
p
q
r
s
t
u
v
w
x
y
z

Dd

daft ADJECTIVE
extremely silly • *Now there's a daft suggestion!*
crazy • *He has this crazy idea about his neighbours.*
foolish • *It would be foolish to raise his hopes unnecessarily.*
ludicrous • *It was ludicrous to suggest that the visit could be kept a secret.*
preposterous • *their preposterous claim that they had discovered a plot*
ridiculous • *It was an absolutely ridiculous decision.*
silly • *That's a silly question.*
stupid • *I made a stupid mistake.*

ANTONYM:
• sensible

damage ① VERB
to cause harm to something • *A fire had severely damaged the school.*
harm • *a warning that the product may harm the environment*
hurt • *He had hurt his back in an accident.*
injure • *Several policemen were injured in the clashes.*

damage ② NOUN
harm that is done to something • *The bomb caused extensive damage to the restaurant.*
harm • *All dogs are capable of doing harm to human beings.*
injury • *He escaped without injury.*

damp ① ADJECTIVE
slightly wet • *a damp towel*

clammy • *clammy hands*
dank • *The kitchen was dank and cheerless.*
humid • *Visitors can expect hot and humid conditions.*
moist • *The soil is reasonably moist after the September rain.*
sodden • *We stripped off our sodden clothes.*
soggy • *soggy cheese sandwiches*
wet • *My hair was still wet.*

damp ② NOUN
slight wetness • *There was damp all over the walls.*
dampness • *I could see big circles of dampness under each arm.*
humidity • *The heat and humidity were intolerable.*
moisture • *Compost helps the soil retain moisture.*

MORE SYNONYMS:
• clamminess
• dankness

danger NOUN
the possibility of harm • *Your life is in danger.*
hazard • *a health hazard*
jeopardy • *A series of setbacks have put the whole project in jeopardy.*
menace • *In my view you are a menace to the public.*
peril • *the perils of the sea*
risk • *There is a small risk of brain damage.*
threat • *Some couples see single women as a threat to their relationship.*

ANTONYM:
• safety

dangerous ADJECTIVE
likely to cause harm • *It's dangerous to drive when you're tired.*
hazardous • *They have no way to dispose of the hazardous waste they produce.*
perilous • *a perilous journey across the war-zone*
risky • *Investing is risky.*
treacherous • *Blizzards had made the roads treacherous.*

ANTONYM:
• safe

dare ① VERB
to challenge someone to do something • *I dare you to ask him his name.*
challenge • *He left a note at the scene of the crime, challenging detectives to catch him.*
defy • *I defy you to watch it on your own.*
throw down the gauntlet • *Jaguar has thrown down the gauntlet to competitors by giving the best guarantee on the market.*

dare ② VERB
to have the courage to do something • *Nobody dared to complain.*
risk • *The skipper was not willing to risk taking his ship through the straits.*
venture • *the few Europeans who had ventured beyond the Himalayas*

daring ① ADJECTIVE
willing to take risks • *a daring escape by helicopter*
adventurous • *an adventurous skier*
audacious • *an audacious plan to win the presidency*
bold • *bold economic reforms*
brave • *He was not brave enough to report the loss of the documents.*

fearless • *They were young and strong and fearless.*

MORE SYNONYMS:
• intrepid
• valiant

ANTONYM:
• cautious

daring ② NOUN
the courage to take risks • *His daring may have cost him his life.*
audacity • *He had the audacity to make a 200-1 bet on himself to win.*
boldness • *the boldness of his economic programme*
bravery • *He deserves the highest praise for his bravery.*
courage • *He impressed everyone with his personal courage.*
guts (INFORMAL) • *I haven't got the guts to tell him.*
nerve (INFORMAL) • *He didn't have the nerve to meet me.*

MORE SYNONYMS:
• fearlessness
• intrepidity
• temerity

ANTONYM:
• caution

dark ① ADJECTIVE
lacking light • *It was too dark to see what was happening.*
cloudy • *a cloudy sky*
dim • *the dim outline of a small boat*
dingy • *a dingy bedsit*
murky • *the murky waters of the loch*
overcast • *a cold, windy, overcast afternoon*
shadowy • *a shadowy corner*

ANTONYM:
• light

dark ② ADJECTIVE
dull in colour • *a dark suit*

black • *a black leather coat*
swarthy • *a broad swarthy face*

dark ③ NOUN
lack of light • *I've always been afraid of the dark.*
darkness • *The room was plunged into darkness.*
dimness • *I squinted to adjust my eyes to the dimness.*
dusk • *She disappeared into the dusk.*
gloom • *the gloom of a foggy November morning*

MORE SYNONYMS:
• murk
• murkiness

ANTONYM:
• light

dash ① VERB
to rush somewhere • *Suddenly she dashed out into the garden.*
bolt • *I bolted for the exit.*
fly • *She flew downstairs.*
race • *The hares raced away out of sight.*
run • *The gunmen ran off into the woods.*
rush • *Someone rushed out of the building.*
sprint • *Sergeant Greene sprinted to the car.*
tear • *He tore off down the road.*

MORE SYNONYMS:
• make haste
• hasten

dash ② VERB
to throw or be thrown violently against something • *The waves dashed against the rocks.*
break • *Danny listened to the waves breaking against the shore.*
crash • *The door swung inwards and crashed against a cupboard behind it.*
hurl • *He hurled the vase to the ground in rage.*
slam • *They slammed me on to the ground.*

smash • *smashing the bottle against a wall*

dash ③ VERB
to ruin or frustrate someone's hopes or ambitions • *They had their hopes raised and then dashed.*
crush • *My dreams of becoming an actor have been crushed.*
destroy • *Even the most gifted can have their confidence destroyed by the wrong teacher.*
disappoint • *His hopes have been disappointed many times before.*
foil • *Our idea of building a water garden was foiled by the planning authorities.*
frustrate • *The government has deliberately frustrated his efforts.*
shatter • *A failure would shatter all our hopes.*
thwart • *Her ambition to be an artist was thwarted by failing eyesight.*

MORE SYNONYMS:
• confound
• quash

dash ④ NOUN
a sudden movement or rush • *a 160-mile dash to the hospital*
bolt • *He made a bolt for the door.*
race • *a race for the finishing line*
run • *One of the gang made a run for it.*
rush • *the mad rush not to be late for school*
sprint • *a last-minute sprint to catch the bus*
stampede • *There was a stampede for the exit.*

dash ⑤ NOUN
a small quantity of something • *a dash of wine vinegar*
drop • *I'll have a drop of that milk in my tea.*
pinch • *a pinch of salt*

splash • *add a splash of lemon juice*
sprinkling • *a light sprinkling of sugar*

daydream ① NOUN

a series of pleasant thoughts • *He learnt to escape into daydreams.*
dream • *My dream is to have a house in the country.*
fantasy • *fantasies of romance and true love*

MORE SYNONYMS:
• castle in Spain
• castle in the air
• pipe dream
• reverie

daydream ② VERB

to think about pleasant things • *He daydreams of being a famous journalist.*
dream • *She used to dream of becoming an actress.*
fantasize • *I fantasized about writing music.*

dazed ADJECTIVE

unable to think clearly • *At the end of the interview I was dazed and exhausted.*
bewildered • *Some shoppers looked bewildered by the sheer variety.*
confused • *Things were happening too quickly and Brian was confused.*
dizzy • *Her head hurt and she felt dizzy.*
light-headed • *If you miss breakfast, you may feel light-headed.*
numbed • *I'm so numbed with shock that I can hardly think.*
stunned • *a stunned silence*

MORE SYNONYMS:
• disorientated
• punch-drunk
• stupefied

dead ① ADJECTIVE

no longer alive • *My husband's been dead a year now.*
deceased • *his recently deceased mother*
departed • *my dear departed father*
extinct • *the bones of extinct animals*
late • *my late husband*

ANTONYM:
• alive

dead ② ADJECTIVE

no longer functioning • *a dead language*
defunct • *the now defunct Social Democratic Party*
not working • *The radio is not working.*

deadly ADJECTIVE

causing death • *a deadly disease*
destructive • *the destructive power of nuclear weapons*
fatal • *a fatal heart attack*
lethal • *a lethal dose of sleeping pills*
mortal • *Our lives were in mortal danger.*

deal VERB

to cope successfully with something • *He must learn to deal with stress.*
attend to • *We have business to attend to first.*
cope with • *She has had to cope with losing all her money.*
handle • *I have learned how to handle pressure.*
manage • *As time passed I learned to manage my grief.*
see to • *Sarah saw to the packing while Jim fetched the car.*
take care of • *Malcolm took care of all the arrangements.*

dear ① NOUN

a person for whom you have affection • *What's the matter, dear?*
angel • *Be an angel and fetch my bag.*
beloved (OLD-FASHIONED) • *He took his beloved into his arms.*
darling • *Thank you, darling.*
treasure (INFORMAL) • *Charlie? Oh, he's a treasure.*

a
b
c
d
e
f
g
h
i
j
k
l
m
n
o
p
q
r
s
t
u
v
w
x
y
z

A
B
C
D
E
F
G
H
I
J
K
L
M
N
O
P
Q
R
S
T
U
V
W
X
Y
Z

dear ② ADJECTIVE
much loved • *a dear friend of mine*
beloved • *He lost his beloved wife last year.*
cherished • *his most cherished possession*
darling • *his darling daughter*
esteemed • *my esteemed colleagues*
precious • *Her family's support is very precious to her.*
prized • *one of the gallery's most prized possessions*
treasured • *one of my most treasured memories*

dear ③ ADJECTIVE
costing a lot • *They're too dear.*
costly • *Having curtains professionally made can be costly.*
expensive • *Wine's so expensive in this country.*
pricey (INFORMAL) • *Medical insurance is very pricey.*

deceive VERB
to make someone believe something untrue • *I was really hurt that he had deceived me.*
con (INFORMAL) • *The British motorist has been conned by the government.*
double-cross • *They were frightened of being double-crossed.*
dupe • *a plot to dupe stamp collectors into buying fake rarities*
fool • *They tried to fool you into coming after us.*
mislead • *He was furious with his doctors for having misled him.*
take in • *I wasn't taken in for one moment.*
trick • *His family tricked him into going to Pakistan.*

MORE SYNONYMS:
• bamboozle
• beguile
• hoodwink

decent ① ADJECTIVE
of an acceptable standard • *He gets a decent pension.*
adequate • *an adequate diet*
passable • *She speaks passable French.*
reasonable • *He couldn't make a reasonable living from his writing.*
respectable • *investments that offer respectable rates of return*
satisfactory • *I never got a satisfactory answer.*
tolerable • *to make life more tolerable*

decent ② ADJECTIVE
correct and respectable • *the decent thing to do*
proper • *It is right and proper to do this.*
respectable • *He came from a perfectly respectable middle-class family.*

ANTONYM:
• improper

deceptive ADJECTIVE
likely to make people believe something untrue • *First impressions can be deceptive.*
false • *"Thank you," she said with false enthusiasm.*
fraudulent • *fraudulent claims about being a nurse*
illusory • *They argue that freedom is illusory.*
misleading • *It would be misleading to say that we were friends.*
unreliable • *His account is quite unreliable.*

MORE SYNONYMS:
• delusive
• specious

decide VERB
to choose to do something • *She decided to do a secretarial course.*
choose • *The council chose to inform the public about the risks.*
come to a decision • *Have you come*

to a decision about where you're going
tonight?

determine (FORMAL) • *He determined
to rescue his two countrymen.*
elect (FORMAL) • *I have elected to stay.*
make up your mind • *He simply can't
make his mind up whether he should stay.*
reach a decision • *He demanded to
know all the facts before reaching any
decision.*
resolve (FORMAL) • *She resolved to
report the matter to the authorities.*

decision NOUN

a judgment about something • *The
editor's decision is final.*
conclusion • *I've come to the conclusion
that she's a great musician.*
finding • *It is the finding of this court
that you are guilty.*
judgment • *a landmark judgment by
the Court of Appeal*
resolution • *a resolution
condemning violence*
ruling • *He tried to have the court
ruling overturned.*
verdict • *The judges will deliver their
verdict in October.*

declaration NOUN

a forceful or official announcement
• *a declaration of war*
affirmation • *her first public
affirmation of her decision*
protestation (FORMAL) • *his
protestations of innocence*
statement • *He made a formal
statement to the police.*
testimony • *His testimony was an
important element in the case.*

MORE SYNONYMS:
• assertion
• avowal

declare VERB

to state something forcefully or

officially • *He declared that he was going
to be famous.*
affirm • *a speech in which he affirmed a
commitment to lower taxes*
announce • *She was planning to
announce her engagement.*
assert • *He asserted his innocence.*
certify • *The president certified that the
project would receive $650m.*
proclaim • *He still proclaims himself a
believer in the Revolution.*
profess (FORMAL) • *Why do
organisations profess that they care?*
pronounce • *The authorities took time
to pronounce their verdict.*
state • *Please state your name.*

MORE SYNONYMS:
• attest
• aver
• avow

decline ① VERB

to become smaller or weaker • *a
declining birth rate*
decrease • *The number of independent
firms decreased from 198 to 96.*
diminish • *The threat of nuclear war has
diminished.*
drop • *His blood pressure had dropped.*
fall • *Output will fall by six per cent.*
go down • *Crime has gone down 70
per cent.*
plummet • *The Prime Minister's
popularity has plummeted to an all-time
low.*
reduce • *The number of students fluent
in Latin has been steadily reducing.*

MORE SYNONYMS:
• dwindle
• wane

ANTONYM:
• increase

decline ② VERB

to refuse politely to accept or do
something • *He declined their invitation.*

abstain • *I will abstain from voting in the ballot.*

excuse yourself • *I was invited, but I excused myself.*

refuse • *He refused to comment after the trial.*

turn down • *I thanked him for the offer but turned it down.*

ANTONYM:
• accept

decline ③ NOUN

a gradual weakening or decrease • *economic decline*

decrease • *a decrease in the number of young people out of work*

downturn • *a sharp downturn in the industry*

drop • *a drop in support for the Conservatives*

fall • *a sharp fall in the value of the pound*

recession • *pull the economy out of recession*

shrinkage • *a shrinkage in industrial output*

slump • *a slump in property prices*

ANTONYM:
• increase

decorate ① VERB

to make more attractive • *He decorated his room with pictures.*

adorn • *Several oil paintings adorn the walls.*

deck • *The house was decked with flowers.*

ornament • *a high ceiling, ornamented with plaster fruits and flowers*

MORE SYNONYMS:
• beautify
• bedeck
• embellish
• festoon

decorate ② VERB

to put paint or wallpaper on • *when they came to decorate the bedroom*

do up (INFORMAL) • *He spent the summer doing up the barn.*

renovate • *The couple spent thousands renovating the house.*

decrease ① VERB

to become or make less • *Population growth is decreasing by 1.4% each year.*

cut down • *He cut down his coffee intake.*

decline • *The number of staff has declined.*

diminish • *The threat of nuclear war has diminished.*

drop • *Temperatures can drop to freezing at night.*

dwindle • *his dwindling authority*

lessen • *changes to their diet that would lessen the risk of disease*

lower • *The Central Bank has lowered interest rates.*

reduce • *It reduces the risk of heart disease.*

shrink • *The forests have shrunk to half their size.*

MORE SYNONYMS:
• abate
• curtail
• subside
• wane

ANTONYM:
• increase

decrease ② NOUN

a lessening in the amount of something • *a decrease in the number of unemployed*

cutback • *cutbacks in defence spending*

decline • *the rate of decline in tobacco consumption*

drop • *a drop in temperature*

lessening • *a lessening of tension*

reduction • *dramatic reductions in staff*

MORE SYNONYMS:
• abatement
• curtailment
• diminution

ANTONYM:
• increase

deep ① ADJECTIVE
having a long way to the bottom
• *a deep hole*
bottomless • *a bottomless pit*
yawning • *a yawning chasm*

ANTONYM:
• shallow

deep ② ADJECTIVE
great or intense • *his deep love of Israel*
extreme • *extreme poverty*
grave • *a grave crisis*
great • *the great gulf between the two teams*
intense • *The pain was intense.*
profound • *discoveries which had a profound effect on medicine*
serious • *a serious problem*

deep ③ ADJECTIVE
low in sound • *a deep voice*
bass • *a beautiful bass voice*
low • *Her voice was so low she was sometimes mistaken for a man.*

MORE SYNONYMS:
• resonant
• sonorous

ANTONYM:
• high

defeat ① VERB
to win a victory over someone • *His guerrillas defeated the colonial army in 1954.*
beat • *the team that beat us in the final*
conquer • *During 1936, Mussolini conquered Abyssinia.*
crush • *in his bid to crush the rebels*

rout • *the battle at which the Norman army routed the English*
trounce • *Australia trounced France by 60 points to 4.*
vanquish (FORMAL) • *after the hero had vanquished the dragon*

defeat ② NOUN
a failure to win • *a 2-1 defeat by Sweden*
conquest • *He had led the conquest of southern Poland.*
debacle (FORMAL) • *It will be hard for them to recover from this debacle.*
rout • *The retreat turned into a rout.*
trouncing • *after a 6-2 trouncing on Sunday*

ANTONYM:
• victory

defect NOUN
a fault or flaw • *A defect in the aircraft caused the crash.*
deficiency • *the most serious deficiency in NATO's air defence*
failing • *She blamed the country's failings on its culture of greed.*
fault • *a minor technical fault*
flaw • *The only flaw in his character is a short temper.*
imperfection • *my physical imperfections*
shortcoming • *The book has its shortcomings.*
weakness • *His only weakness is his laziness.*

defence ① NOUN
action to protect something • *The flat land offered no scope for defence.*
cover • *They could not provide adequate air cover for ground operations.*
protection • *Such a diet is believed to offer protection against cancer.*
resistance • *Most people have a natural resistance to the disease.*

a b c d e f g h i j k l m n o p q r s t u v w x y z

safeguard • *legislation that offers safeguards against discrimination*
security • *Airport security was tightened.*

defence ② NOUN

an argument in support of something • *Chomsky's defence of his approach*
argument • *There's a strong argument for lowering the price.*
excuse • *There's no excuse for behaviour like that.*
explanation • *The authorities have given no explanation for his arrest.*
justification • *The only justification for a zoo is educational.*
plea • *a plea of insanity*

defend ① VERB

to protect from harm • *They would have killed him if he hadn't defended himself.*
cover • *travel insurance covering you against theft*
guard • *A few men were left outside to guard her.*
protect • *What can women do to protect themselves from heart disease?*
safeguard • *action to safeguard the ozone layer*
shelter • *a wooden house, sheltered by a low roof*
shield • *He shielded his head from the sun with an old sack.*

defend ② VERB

to argue in support of • *I can't defend what he did.*
endorse • *I can endorse their opinion wholeheartedly.*
justify • *No argument can justify a war.*
stick up for (INFORMAL) • *Why do you always stick up for her?*
support • *Would you support such a move?*
uphold • *upholding the artist's right to creative freedom*

defender NOUN

a person who argues in support of something • *a committed defender of human rights*
advocate • *a strong advocate of free market policies*
champion • *a champion of women's causes*
supporter • *a major supporter of the tax reform*

deficiency NOUN

a lack of something • *signs of vitamin deficiency*
deficit • *a staffing deficit*
deprivation • *sleep deprivation*
inadequacy • *the inadequacies of the current system*
lack • *a lack of people wanting to start new businesses*
want (FORMAL) • *a want of manners and charm*

ANTONYM:
• abundance

deficient ADJECTIVE

lacking in something • *a diet deficient in vitamins*
inadequate • *inadequate staffing*
lacking • *Why was military intelligence so lacking?*
poor • *soil that is poor in zinc*
short • *The proposals were short on detail.*
wanting • *He analysed his game and found it wanting.*

definite ① ADJECTIVE

unlikely to be changed • *It's too soon to give a definite answer.*
assured • *Victory was still not assured.*
certain • *Very little in life is certain.*
decided • *Is anything decided yet?*
fixed • *a world without fixed laws*
guaranteed • *Success is not guaranteed.*
settled • *Nothing is settled yet.*

definite ② ADJECTIVE
certainly true • *The police had nothing definite against her.*
clear • *It was a clear case of homicide.*
positive • *We have positive proof that he was a blackmailer.*

MORE SYNONYMS:
• black-and-white
• clear-cut
• cut-and-dried

deformed ADJECTIVE
abnormally shaped • *a deformed right leg*
disfigured • *the scarred, disfigured face*
distorted • *the distorted image caused by the projector*

degrade VERB
to humiliate someone • *the notion that pornography degrades women*
demean • *I wasn't going to demean myself by acting like a suspicious wife.*
humiliate • *He enjoyed humiliating me.*

delay ① VERB
to put something off until later • *the decision to delay the launch until tomorrow*
defer • *Customers often defer payment for as long as possible.*
postpone • *The visit has been postponed indefinitely.*
put off • *women who put off having a baby*
shelve • *The project has now been shelved.*
suspend • *Relief convoys will be suspended until the fighting stops.*

delay ② VERB
to slow or hinder something • *Various setbacks delayed production.*
check • *a policy to check fast population growth*
hinder • *Further investigation was hindered by the loss of all documentation.*

impede • *Fallen rocks are impeding the progress of rescue workers.*
obstruct • *The authorities are obstructing a UN investigation.*
set back • *public protests that could set back reforms*

MORE SYNONYMS:
• hold up
• retard

ANTONYM:
• hurry

delay ③ NOUN
a time when something is delayed • *a 7-hour stoppage that caused delays on most flights*
interruption • *interruptions in the supply of food*
obstruction • *Obstruction of justice is a criminal offence.*
setback • *a setback for the peace process*

delete VERB
to remove something written • *The word 'exploded' had been deleted.*
cross out • *He crossed out the first sentence and wrote it again.*
erase • *It was unfortunate that she had erased the message.*
rub out • *She rubbed out the marks in the margin.*

MORE SYNONYMS:
• blue-pencil
• cancel
• edit out
• strike out

deliberate ① ADJECTIVE
done on purpose • *a deliberate act of sabotage*
calculated • *a calculated attempt to cover up her crime*
conscious • *I made a conscious decision not to hide.*
intentional • *The kick was intentional.*

A
B
C
D
E
F
G
H
I
J
K
L
M
N
O
P
Q
R
S
T
U
V
W
X
Y
Z

premeditated • *a premeditated attack*
studied • *"It's an interesting match," he said with studied understatement.*

ANTONYM:
• accidental

deliberate ② ADJECTIVE

careful and not hurried • *His movements were gentle and deliberate.*
careful • *The trip needs careful planning.*
cautious • *a cautious approach*
measured • *walking at the same measured pace*
methodical • *Da Vinci was methodical in his research.*

ANTONYM:
• casual

deliberate ③ VERB

to think carefully about something • *The jury deliberated for five days before reaching a verdict.*
debate • *He was debating whether or not he should tell her.*
meditate • *She meditated on the uncertainties of his future.*
mull over • *McLaren had been mulling over an idea to make a movie.*
ponder • *He was pondering the problem when Phillipson drove up.*
reflect • *I reflected on the child's future.*

delicious ADJECTIVE

tasting very nice • *a wide selection of delicious meals*
appetizing • *the appetizing smell of freshly baked bread*
delectable • *delectable wine*
luscious • *luscious fruit*
tasty • *The food was very tasty.*

MORE SYNONYMS:
• ambrosial
• mouthwatering
• scrumptious

delight ① NOUN

great pleasure or joy • *To my great delight, it worked.*
glee • *His victory was greeted with glee by his supporters.*
happiness • *Our happiness at being reunited knew no bounds.*
joy • *the joys of being a parent*
pleasure • *the pleasure of seeing her face*
rapture • *gasps of rapture*
satisfaction • *I felt a glow of satisfaction at my achievement.*

delight ② VERB

to give someone great pleasure • *The report has delighted environmentalists.*
amuse • *a selection of toys to amuse your baby*
captivate • *captivated the world with her radiant looks*
charm • *He charmed his landlady, chatting and flirting with her.*
enchant • *Dena was enchanted by the house.*
please • *It pleased him to talk to her.*
thrill • *The electric atmosphere thrilled him.*

demand VERB

to need or require something • *This situation demands hard work.*
involve • *Running a kitchen involves a great deal of discipline.*
need • *a problem that needs careful handling*
require • *Then he'll know what's required of him.*
take • *Walking across the room took all her strength.*
want • *The windows wanted cleaning.*

MORE SYNONYMS:
• call for
• entail
• necessitate

deny ① VERB

to say that something is untrue • *She denied both accusations.*

contradict • *Her version contradicted the Government's claim.*

refute • *He angrily refutes the charge.*

MORE SYNONYMS:

• abjure
• disavow
• disclaim
• gainsay
• rebut
• repudiate

ANTONYM:

• admit

deny ② VERB

to refuse to believe something • *He denied the existence of God.*

reject • *children who rejected their parents' religious beliefs*

renounce • *after she renounced terrorism*

deny ③ VERB

to refuse to give something • *His ex-partner denies him access to the children.*

refuse • *The council had refused permission for the march.*

withhold • *Financial aid for Russia has been withheld.*

department NOUN

a section of an organization • *the marketing department*

division • *the bank's Latin American division*

office • *Contact your local tax office.*

section • *a top-secret section of the Foreign Office*

unit • *the health services research unit*

depend ① VERB

to rely on • *You can depend on me.*

bank on • *The government is banking on the Olympics to save the city money.*

count on • *I can always count on you to cheer me up.*

rely on • *They can always be relied on to turn up.*

trust • *I knew I could trust him to meet a tight deadline.*

depend ② VERB

to be affected by • *Success depends on the quality of the workforce.*

be determined by • *Social status is largely determined by occupation.*

hinge on • *Victory or defeat hinged on her final putt.*

MORE SYNONYMS:

• be subject to
• hang on
• rest on

deposit VERB

to put down or leave somewhere • *The barman deposited a bottle in front of him.*

drop • *He dropped me outside the hotel.*

lay • *The table was spread with a cloth, and the box was laid on top.*

leave • *Leave your key with a neighbour.*

place • *I placed the book on the counter.*

put down • *Mishka put down her heavy shopping bag.*

derelict ADJECTIVE

abandoned and in poor condition • *a derelict warehouse*

abandoned • *a network of abandoned mines*

dilapidated • *a dilapidated castle*

neglected • *a neglected garden*

ruined • *a ruined church*

descend VERB

to move downwards • *as we descend to the cellar*

dip • *The sun dipped below the horizon.*

dive • *The shark dived down and under the boat.*

fall • *Bombs fell in the town.*

go down • *after the sun has gone down*

plummet • *as the plane plummeted through the air*

a b c d e f g h i j k l m n o p q r s t u v w x y z

A
B
C
D
E
F
G
H
I
J
K
L
M
N
O
P
Q
R
S
T
U
V
W
X
Y
Z

sink • *A fresh egg will sink and an old egg will float.*

ANTONYM:
• ascend

describe VERB
to give an account of something
• *We asked her to describe what she did in her spare time.*
define • *Culture can be defined in many ways.*
depict • *a novel depicting a gloomy, futuristic America*
portray • *a writer who accurately portrays provincial life*

MORE SYNONYMS:
• characterize
• detail

deserve VERB
to have a right to something • *He deserves a rest.*
be entitled to • *She is entitled to feel proud.*
be worthy of • *The bank might think you're worthy of a loan.*
earn • *You've earned this holiday.*
justify • *The decision was fully justified by economic conditions.*
merit • *Such ideas merit careful consideration.*
warrant • *no evidence to warrant a murder investigation*

design ① VERB
to make a plan of something • *They wanted to design a machine that was both attractive and practical.*
draft • *The legislation was drafted by Democrats.*
draw up • *a working party to draw up a formal agreement*
plan • *when we plan road construction*

design ② NOUN
a plan or drawing • *his design for a new office*

model • *an architect's model of a wooden house*
plan • *when you have drawn a plan of the garden*

MORE SYNONYMS:
• blueprint
• schema

design ③ NOUN
the shape or style of something • *a new design of clock*
form • *the form of the human body*
pattern • *a pattern of coloured dots*
shape • *a kidney shape*
style • *Several styles of hat were available.*

desire ① VERB
to want something • *We can stay longer if you desire.*
crave • *I crave her approval.*
fancy • *She fancied living in Canada.*
long for • *He longed for the winter to be over.*
want • *I want a drink.*
wish • *We wished to return.*
yearn • *He yearned to sleep.*

MORE SYNONYMS:
• ache for
• covet

desire ② NOUN
a feeling of wanting something • *I had a strong desire to help people.*
appetite • *She had lost her appetite for air travel.*
craving • *a craving for sugar*
hankering • *a hankering to be an actress*
longing • *her longing to return home*
wish • *Her wish is to be in films.*
yearning • *a yearning for a child of my own*
yen (INFORMAL) • *Mike had a yen to try cycling.*

despair ① NOUN
a loss of hope • *feelings of despair*

dejection · *There was an air of dejection about her.*
despondency · *There's a mood of despondency in the country.*
gloom · *the deepening gloom over the economy*
hopelessness · *She had a feeling of hopelessness about the future.*

despair ② VERB
to lose hope · *I despair at the attitude with which their work is received.*
feel dejected · *Everyone has days when they feel dejected.*
feel despondent · *John often felt despondent after visiting the job centre.*
lose heart · *He appealed to his countrymen not to lose heart.*
lose hope · *You mustn't lose hope.*

despite PREPOSITION
in spite of · *He fell asleep despite all the coffee he'd drunk.*
in spite of · *In spite of all the gossip, Virginia stayed behind.*
notwithstanding (FORMAL) · *Notwithstanding his age, Sikorski had an important job.*
regardless of · *He led from the front, regardless of the danger.*

destroy VERB
to ruin something completely · *The building was completely destroyed.*
annihilate · *The lava annihilates everything in its path.*
demolish · *A storm moved over the island, demolishing buildings.*
devastate · *A fire had devastated large parts of Windsor castle.*
obliterate · *Whole villages were obliterated by fire.*
raze · *The town was razed to the ground during the occupation.*
ruin · *My wife was ruining her health through worry.*

wreck · *the injuries which nearly wrecked his career*

destruction NOUN
the act of destroying something · *the destruction of the ozone layer*
annihilation · *Leaders fear the annihilation of their people.*
demolition · *the demolition of an old bridge*
devastation · *A huge bomb blast brought chaos and devastation.*
obliteration · *the obliteration of three rainforests*

detail NOUN
an individual feature of something · *We discussed every detail of the performance.*
aspect · *Climate affects every aspect of our lives.*
element · *one of the key elements of the peace plan*
particular · *You will find all the particulars in Chapter 9.*
point · *Many of the points in the report are correct.*
respect · *At least in this respect we are equals.*

MORE SYNONYMS:
• fine point
• nicety

determination NOUN
a firm decision to do something · *the government's determination to beat inflation*
perseverance · *Adam's perseverance proved worthwhile.*
persistence · *She was determined to be a doctor and her persistence paid off.*
resolution · *She acted with resolution and courage.*
resolve (FORMAL) · *the American public's resolve to go to war if necessary*

a b c d e f g h i j k l m n o p q r s t u v w x y z

tenacity • *Hard work and sheer tenacity are crucial to career success.*

MORE SYNONYMS:
• doggedness
• single-mindedness
• steadfastness
• willpower

determine ① VERB
to cause or control a situation or result • *The size of the chicken pieces will determine the cooking time.*

control • *Scientists may soon be able to control the ageing process.*

decide • *The results will decide if he will win a place on the course.*

dictate • *A number of factors will dictate how long the tree will survive.*

govern • *the rules governing eligibility for unemployment benefit*

shape • *the role of key leaders in shaping the future of Europe*

determine ② VERB
to decide or settle something firmly • *The final wording had not yet been determined.*

arrange • *It was arranged that the party would gather in the Royal Garden Hotel.*

choose • *Houston was chosen as the site for the convention.*

decide • *Her age would be taken into account when deciding her sentence.*

fix • *The date of the election was fixed.*

resolve • *She resolved to report the matter to the authorities.*

settle • *That's settled then. We'll do it tomorrow.*

determine ③ VERB
to find out the facts about something • *The investigation will determine what really happened.*

ascertain (FORMAL) • *We need to ascertain the true facts.*

confirm • *X-rays have confirmed that he has not broken any bones.*

discover • *It was difficult for us to discover the reason for the decision.*

establish • *an autopsy to establish the cause of death*

find out • *one family's campaign to find out the truth*

verify • *A clerk verifies that the payment and invoice amount match.*

determined ADJECTIVE
firmly decided • *She was determined not to repeat her error.*

bent on • *They seem bent on destroying the city.*

dogged • *dogged persistence*

intent on • *He is intent on repeating his victory.*

persistent • *He phoned again this morning. He's very persistent.*

purposeful • *She had a purposeful air.*

resolute (FORMAL) • *a decisive and resolute leader*

single-minded • *a single-minded determination to win*

tenacious • *a tenacious and persistent interviewer*

MORE SYNONYMS:
• steadfast
• unflinching
• unwavering

develop ① VERB
to grow or become more advanced • *Children develop at different rates.*

advance • *tracing how medical technology has advanced to its present state*

evolve • *As scientific knowledge evolves, beliefs change.*

grow • *The boys grew into men.*

mature • *Other changes occur as the child matures physically.*

progress • *His disease progressed quickly.*
result • *Ignore the warnings and illness could result.*
spring • *His anger sprang from his childhood suffering.*

develop ② VERB
to become affected by an illness or fault • *He developed pneumonia.*
catch • *to catch a cold*
contract (FORMAL) • *He contracted AIDS from a blood transfusion.*
fall ill • *She fell ill with measles.*
get • *When I was five I got mumps.*
go down with • *Three members of the band went down with flu.*
pick up • *They've picked up an infection from something they've eaten.*
succumb • *I was determined not to succumb to the virus.*

devious ADJECTIVE
getting what you want by sly methods • *a devious politician*
calculating • *a calculating businessman*
scheming • *He was branded a "scheming liar".*
underhand • *He used underhand tactics to win the election.*
wily • *a wily old statesman*

devoted ADJECTIVE
very loving and loyal • *a devoted father*
constant • *her constant companion*
dedicated • *dedicated followers of classical music*
doting • *His doting parents bought him a racing bike.*
faithful • *I'm very faithful when I love someone.*
loving • *Jim was a loving husband.*
loyal • *a loyal friend*
true • *David was true to his wife.*

dictionary NOUN
- ◆ **PARTS OF A DICTIONARY OR**
- ◆ **THESAURUS**
- ◆ antonym
- ◆ definition
- ◆ entry
- ◆ example
- ◆ headword
- ◆ homonym
- ◆ homophone
- ◆ inflection
- ◆ label
- ◆ part of speech
- ◆ pronunciation
- ◆ root word
- ◆ synonym
- ◆ word derivation

die ① VERB
to stop living • *My mother died of cancer.*
cark it (AUSTRALIAN AND NEW ZEALAND; INFORMAL) • *You think you're about to cark it.*
expire (FORMAL) • *before he finally expired*
pass away • *He passed away last year.*
pass on • *My mother passed on four years ago.*
perish (FORMAL) • *the ferry disaster in which 193 passengers perished*

die ② VERB
to fade away • *My love for you will never die.*
fade away • *With time, they said, the pain will fade away.*
fade out • *Thanks to supermarkets, the corner shop is gradually fading out.*
peter out • *The six-month strike seemed to be petering out.*

die out VERB
to cease to exist • *That custom has died out now.*
disappear • *Huge areas of the countryside are disappearing.*

A
B
C
D
E
F
G
H
I
J
K
L
M
N
O
P
Q
R
S
T
U
V
W
X
Y
Z

fade • *Prospects for peace had already started to fade.*
vanish • *those species which have vanished*

difference ① NOUN

a lack of similarity between things • *the vast difference in size*
contrast • *the real contrast between the two poems*
discrepancy • *discrepancies between their statements*
disparity • *disparities between poor and wealthy districts*
distinction • *a distinction between the body and the soul*
divergence • *There's a substantial divergence of opinion within the party.*
variation • *a wide variation in the prices charged*

ANTONYM:
• similarity

difference ② NOUN

the amount by which two quantities differ • *The difference is 8532.*
balance • *They were due to pay the balance on delivery.*
remainder • *They own a 75% stake. The remainder is owned by the bank.*

different ① ADJECTIVE

unlike something else • *We have totally different views.*
contrasting • *painted in contrasting colours*
disparate (FORMAL) • *The republics are very disparate in size and wealth.*
dissimilar • *His methods were not dissimilar to those used by Freud.*
divergent (FORMAL) • *divergent opinions*
opposed • *two opposed ideologies*
unlike • *This was a foreign country, so unlike San Jose.*

MORE SYNONYMS:
• at odds
• at variance

ANTONYM:
• similar

different ② ADJECTIVE

unusual and out of the ordinary • *The result is interesting and different.*
special • *a special variety of strawberry*
unique • *Each person's signature is unique.*

different ③ ADJECTIVE

distinct and separate • *The lunch supports a different charity each year.*
another • *Her doctor referred her to another therapist.*
discrete (FORMAL) • *two discrete sets of nerves*
distinct • *A word may have two quite distinct meanings.*
individual • *Each family needs individual attention.*
separate • *The word 'quarter' has two completely separate meanings.*

difficult ① ADJECTIVE

not easy to do or solve • *a difficult decision to make*
arduous • *a long, arduous journey*
demanding • *a demanding job*
hard • *He found it hard to get work.*
intractable (FORMAL) • *an intractable problem*
laborious • *a laborious task*
uphill • *an uphill battle*

MORE SYNONYMS:
• knotty
• problematic
• thorny

ANTONYM:
• easy

difficult ② ADJECTIVE

not easy to deal with • *I hope she isn't going to be difficult.*
demanding • *a demanding child*
troublesome • *a troublesome teenager*

trying • *The whole business has been very trying.*

MORE SYNONYMS:
• obstreperous
• refractory
• unmanageable

difficulty ① NOUN
a problem • *The central difficulty is his drinking.*
complication • *An added complication is the growing concern for the environment.*
hassle (INFORMAL) • *all the usual hassles at the airport*
hurdle • *preparing a CV, the first hurdle in a job search*
obstacle • *To succeed, you must learn to overcome obstacles.*
pitfall • *the pitfalls of working abroad*
problem • *He left home because of family problems.*
snag • *The only snag was that he had no transport.*
trouble • *What seems to be the trouble?*

MORE SYNONYMS:
• impediment
• stumbling block

difficulty ② NOUN
the quality of being difficult • *the difficulty of the problem*
hardship • *economic hardship*
strain • *the stresses and strains of a busy career*
tribulation (FORMAL) • *the trials and tribulations of everyday life*

MORE SYNONYMS:
• arduousness
• laboriousness

dig ① VERB
to break up soil or sand • *He dug a hole in the ground.*
burrow • *The larvae burrow into cracks in the floor.*

excavate • *A contractor was hired to excavate soil from the area.*
gouge • *quarries which have gouged great holes in the hills*
hollow out • *They hollowed out crude dwellings from the soft rock.*
quarry • *The caves are quarried for cement.*
till • *freshly tilled fields*
tunnel • *The rebels tunnelled out of jail.*

dig ② VERB
to push something in • *He could feel the beads digging into his palm.*
jab • *A needle was jabbed into the baby's arm.*
poke • *She poked a fork into the turkey skin.*
thrust • *She thrust her hand into the sticky mess.*

dig ③ NOUN
a push or poke • *She silenced him with a dig in the ribs.*
jab • *a swift jab in the stomach*
poke • *a playful poke in the arm*
prod • *He gave the donkey a prod in the backside.*
thrust • *knife thrusts*

dim ① ADJECTIVE
not bright or well-lit • *a dim outline of a small boat*
dark • *a dark corridor*
dull • *The stamp was a dark, dull blue.*
grey • *a grey, wet, April Sunday*
murky • *one murky November afternoon*
poorly lit • *a poorly lit road*
shadowy • *a shadowy corner*

dim ② ADJECTIVE
vague or unclear • *a dim memory*
faint • *a faint recollection*
hazy • *Many details remain hazy.*
indistinct • *the indistinct murmur of voices*

a
b
c
d
e
f
g
h
i
j
k
l
m
n
o
p
q
r
s
t
u
v
w
x
y
z

A
B
C
D
E
F
G
H
I
J
K
L
M
N
O
P
Q
R
S
T
U
V
W
X
Y
Z

obscure • *The origin of the custom is obscure.*
shadowy • *the shadowy world of spies*
vague • *I have a vague memory of shots being fired.*

MORE SYNONYMS:
• fuzzy
• ill-defined
• indistinguishable

ANTONYM:
• clear

dim ③ ADJECTIVE (INFORMAL)
slow to understand • *He is rather dim.*
dumb (INFORMAL) • *I've met a lot of dumb people.*
obtuse • *I've really been very obtuse.*
slow • *He got hit on the head and he's been a bit slow since.*
stupid • *How could I have been so stupid?*
thick (INFORMAL) • *I must have seemed incredibly thick.*

ANTONYM:
• bright

diminish VERB
to reduce or become reduced • *The threat of war has diminished.*
contract • *Output fell last year and is expected to contract further.*
decrease • *Gradually decrease the amount of vitamin C you are taking.*
lessen • *The attention he gets will lessen when the new baby is born.*
lower • *This drug lowers cholesterol levels.*
reduce • *It reduces the risk of heart disease.*
shrink • *the entertainment giant's intention to shrink its interest in the venture*
weaken • *The Prime Minister's authority has been fatally weakened.*

dinkum ADJECTIVE (AUSTRALIAN AND NEW ZEALAND; INFORMAL)
genuine or right • *a fair dinkum bloke with no pretensions*

genuine • *If this offer is genuine I will gladly accept.*
guileless • *She was so guileless that he had to believe her.*
honest • *My dad was the most honest man I ever met.*
sincere • *a sincere desire to reform*

direct ① ADJECTIVE
in a straight line or with nothing in between • *the direct route*
first-hand • *She has little first-hand knowledge of Quebec.*
immediate • *his immediate superior*
personal • *I have no personal experience of this.*
straight • *Keep the boat in a straight line.*
uninterrupted • *an uninterrupted view*

ANTONYM:
• indirect

direct ② ADJECTIVE
open and honest • *He can be very direct sometimes.*
blunt • *She is blunt about her personal life.*
candid • *I haven't been completely candid with you.*
forthright • *forthright language*
frank • *She is always very frank.*
straight • *He never gives you a straight answer.*
straightforward • *his straightforward manner*

ANTONYM:
• devious

direct ③ VERB
to control and guide something • *Christopher will direct day-to-day operations.*
control • *He now controls the entire company.*
guide • *He should have let his instinct guide him.*

lead • *He led the country between 1949 and 1984.*
manage • *Within two years he was managing the store.*
oversee • *an architect to oversee the work*
run • *Is this any way to run a country?*
supervise • *I supervise the packing of all mail orders.*

direction ① NOUN
the line in which something is moving • *ten miles in the opposite direction*
course • *The captain altered course.*
path • *He stepped into the path of a reversing car.*
route • *We took the wrong route.*
way • *Does anybody know the way to the bathroom?*

direction ② NOUN
control and guidance of something • *He was chopping vegetables under the chef's direction.*
charge • *A few years ago he took charge of the company.*
command • *In 1942 he took command of 108 Squadron.*
control • *The restructuring involves Ronson giving up control of the company.*
guidance • *the reports which were produced under his guidance*
leadership • *The agency doubled in size under her leadership.*
management • *The zoo needed better management.*

dirt ① NOUN
dust or mud • *I started to scrub off the dirt.*
dust • *The furniture was covered in dust.*
filth • *tons of filth and sewage*
grime • *Kelly got the grime off his hands.*
muck • *This congealed muck was interfering with the filter.*
mud • *Their lorry got stuck in the mud.*

dirt ② NOUN
earth or soil • *He drew a circle in the dirt with the stick.*
earth • *a huge pile of earth*
soil • *an area with very good soil*

dirty ① ADJECTIVE
marked with dirt • *The kids have got their clothes dirty.*
filthy • *a pair of filthy jeans*
grimy • *a grimy industrial city*
grubby • *kids with grubby faces*
mucky • *a mucky floor*
muddy • *his muddy boots*
soiled • *a soiled white apron*
unclean • *unclean water*
ANTONYM:
• clean

dirty ② ADJECTIVE
unfair or dishonest • *a dirty fight*
corrupt • *corrupt practices*
crooked • *crooked business deals*
ANTONYM:
• honest

dirty ③ ADJECTIVE
sexually explicit • *a dirty joke*
blue • *a blue movie*
filthy • *a filthy book*
pornographic • *pornographic videos*
rude • *a rude joke*
MORE SYNONYMS:
• risqué
• salacious
• smutty

disadvantage NOUN
an unfavourable circumstance • *the advantages and disadvantages of allowing their soldiers to marry*
drawback • *The apartment's only drawback was that it was too small.*
handicap • *The tax issue was undoubtedly a handicap to Labour.*
minus • *The pluses and minuses were about equal.*

weakness • *the strengths and weaknesses of the argument*

MORE SYNONYMS:
• downside
• hindrance

ANTONYM:
• advantage

disagree ① VERB

to have a different opinion • *They can communicate even when they disagree.*

differ • *They differ on lots of issues.*
dispute • *Nobody disputed that Davey was clever.*
dissent • *dissenting views*

ANTONYM:
• agree

disagree ② VERB

to think that something is wrong • *I disagree with drug laws in general.*

object • *We objected strongly but were outvoted.*
oppose • *protesters opposing nuclear tests*
take issue with • *I take issue with much of what he said.*

disagreeable ADJECTIVE

unpleasant in some way • *a disagreeable odour*

horrible • *a horrible small boy*
horrid • *What a horrid smell!*
nasty • *What a nasty little snob you are!*
objectionable • *an objectionable, stuck-up young woman*
obnoxious • *One of the parents was a most obnoxious character.*
unfriendly • *She spoke in a loud, rather unfriendly voice.*
unpleasant • *The side-effects can be unpleasant.*

ANTONYM:
• agreeable

disagreement ① NOUN

a dispute about something • *My driving instructor and I had a brief disagreement.*

altercation (FORMAL) • *an altercation with the referee*
argument • *an argument about money*
difference • *We have our differences but we get along.*
dispute • *a pay dispute*
quarrel • *I had a terrible quarrel with my brother.*
row • *a major diplomatic row*
squabble • *minor squabbles about phone bills*
tiff • *a lovers' tiff*

ANTONYM:
• agreement

disagreement ② NOUN

an objection to something • *Britain and France have expressed some disagreement with the proposal.*

dissent • *voices of dissent*
objection • *I have no objection to banks making money.*
opposition • *their opposition to the scheme*

disappear ① VERB

to go out of sight • *The aircraft disappeared off the radar.*

be lost to view • *They observed the comet for 70 days before it was lost to view.*
drop out of sight • *After his first film he dropped out of sight.*
fade • *We watched the harbour fade into the mist.*
recede • *Luke receded into the distance.*
vanish • *Anne vanished from outside her home the Wednesday before last.*

ANTONYM:
• appear

disappear ② VERB

to stop existing • *The pain has finally disappeared.*

cease (FORMAL) • *At 1 o'clock the rain ceased.*
die out • *How did the dinosaurs die out?*
go away • *All she wanted was for the pain to go away.*
melt away • *His anger melted away.*
pass • *He told her the fear would pass.*
vanish • *species which have vanished*

disappointed ADJECTIVE
sad because something has not happened • *I was disappointed that Kluge was not there.*
dejected • *Her refusal left him feeling dejected.*
despondent • *After the interview John was despondent.*
disenchanted • *She has become very disenchanted with the marriage.*
disillusioned • *I've become very disillusioned with politics.*
downcast • *After his defeat Mr Rabin looked downcast.*
saddened • *He is saddened that they did not win anything.*

MORE SYNONYMS:
• disheartened
• let down

ANTONYM:
• satisfied

disappointment ① NOUN
a feeling of being disappointed • *Book early to avoid disappointment.*
dejection • *There was an air of dejection about her.*
despondency • *a mood of gloom and despondency*
regret • *my one great regret in life*

MORE SYNONYMS:
• disenchantment
• disillusionment

disappointment ② NOUN
something that disappoints you • *The reunion was a bitter disappointment.*

blow • *It was a terrible blow when he was made redundant.*
setback • *a setback for the peace process*

disapproval NOUN
the belief that something is wrong • *his mother's disapproval of his marriage*
censure • *He deserves support, not censure.*
condemnation • *the universal condemnation of French nuclear tests*
criticism • *actions which have attracted fierce criticism*

ANTONYM:
• approval

disapprove VERB
to think that something is wrong • *Everyone disapproved of their marrying so young.*
condemn • *Political leaders condemned the speech.*
deplore (FORMAL) • *He deplores violence.*
dislike • *Her father seemed to dislike all her boyfriends.*
find unacceptable • *I find such behaviour totally unacceptable.*
take a dim view of • *They took a dim view of local trade unionists.*

MORE SYNONYMS:
• frown on
• take exception to

ANTONYM:
• approve

disaster NOUN
a very bad accident • *another air disaster*
calamity (FORMAL) • *It could only end in calamity.*
catastrophe • *War would be a catastrophe.*
misfortune • *She seemed to enjoy the misfortunes of others.*

a b c d e f g h i j k l m n o p q r s t u v w x y z

A
B
C
D
E
F
G
H
I
J
K
L
M
N
O
P
Q
R
S
T
U
V
W
X
Y
Z

tragedy • *They have suffered an enormous personal tragedy.*

discard VERB
to get rid of something • *Read the instructions before discarding the box.*
cast aside • *In America we seem to cast aside our elderly people.*
dispose of • *how he disposed of the murder weapon*
dump (INFORMAL) • *The getaway car was dumped near the motorway.*
jettison • *The crew jettisoned excess fuel.*
shed • *a snake that has shed its skin*
throw away • *I never throw anything away.*
throw out • *Why don't you throw out all those old magazines?*

discern VERB (FORMAL)
to notice or understand something clearly • *trying to discern a pattern in his behaviour*
detect • *Arnold could detect a certain sadness in the old man's face.*
make out • *I could just make out a shadowy figure through the mist.*
notice • *Mrs Shedden noticed a bird sitting on the garage roof.*
observe • *In 1664 Hooke observed a reddish spot on the planet's surface.*
perceive • *Get pupils to perceive the relationship between success and effort.*
see • *Supporters saw in him a champion of the oppressed.*
spot • *I've spotted an error in your calculations.*

discharge ① VERB
to send something out • *The resulting salty water will be discharged at sea.*
emit • *the amount of greenhouse gases emitted*
empty • *companies which empty toxic by-products into rivers*

expel • *Poisonous gas is expelled into the atmosphere.*
flush • *Flush out all the sewage.*
give off • *natural gas, which gives off less carbon dioxide than coal*
release • *a weapon which releases toxic nerve gas*

discharge ② VERB
to allow someone to leave hospital or prison • *He has a broken nose but may be discharged today.*
free • *The country is set to free more prisoners.*
let go • *They held him for three hours and then let him go.*
liberate • *They promised to liberate prisoners held in detention camps.*
release • *He was released on bail.*
set free • *More than ninety prisoners have been set free.*

discharge ③ VERB
to dismiss someone from a job • *He was discharged from the military.*
dismiss • *The military commander has been dismissed.*
eject • *He was ejected from his first job for persistent latecoming.*
fire (INFORMAL) • *If he wasn't so good at his job, I'd fire him.*
sack (INFORMAL) • *The teacher was sacked for slapping a schoolboy.*

discharge ④ NOUN
a sending away from a job or institution • *They face a dishonourable discharge from the Army.*
dismissal • *shock at the director's dismissal from his post*
ejection • *These actions led to his ejection from office.*
expulsion • *his expulsion from the party in 1955*
the sack (INFORMAL) • *People who make mistakes can be given the sack.*

discourage VERB

to make someone lose enthusiasm
• *Don't let these problems discourage you.*
daunt • *He was not the type of man to be daunted by adversity.*
deter • *Tougher sentences would do nothing to deter crime.*
dissuade • *He considered emigrating, but his family managed to dissuade him.*
put off • *I wouldn't let it put you off applying.*

MORE SYNONYMS:
• demoralize
• dishearten

ANTONYM:
• encourage

discover VERB

to find something or find out about something • *He discovered that she had a brilliant mind.*
come across • *He came across the jawbone of a carnivorous dinosaur.*
find • *The police also found a pistol.*
find out • *Watch the next episode to find out what happens.*
learn • *The Admiral, on learning who I was, wanted to meet me.*
realize • *As soon as we realized something was wrong, we took action.*
stumble on or **stumble across** • *They stumbled on a magnificent waterfall.*
unearth • *Researchers have unearthed documents implicating her in the crime.*

discuss VERB

to talk about something • *I will be discussing the situation with colleagues tomorrow.*
debate • *The UN Security Council will debate the issue today.*
exchange views on • *They exchanged views on a wide range of subjects.*
go into • *We didn't go into that.*
talk about • *What did you talk about?*

discussion NOUN

a talk about something • *informal discussions*
consultation • *consultations between lawyers*
conversation • *I struck up a conversation with him.*
debate • *There has been a lot of debate among scholars about this.*
dialogue • *a direct dialogue between the two nations*
discourse • *a long tradition of political discourse*
talk • *We had a long talk about it.*

disgrace ① NOUN

lack of respect • *She has brought disgrace upon the whole team.*
scandal • *They often abandoned their children because of fear of scandal.*
shame • *I don't want to bring shame on the family name.*

MORE SYNONYMS:
• discredit
• dishonour

ANTONYM:
• credit

disgrace ② VERB

to bring shame upon • *I have disgraced my family's name.*
discredit • *He said such methods discredited the communist fight worldwide.*
shame • *I wouldn't shame my father by doing that.*

disgraceful ADJECTIVE

deserving of shame • *disgraceful behaviour*
scandalous • *a scandalous waste of money*
shameful • *the most shameful episode in US naval history*
shocking • *a shocking invasion of privacy*

A
B
C
D
E
F
G
H
I
J
K
L
M
N
O
P
Q
R
S
T
U
V
W
X
Y
Z

MORE SYNONYMS:
• discreditable
• dishonourable

disgust ① NOUN
a strong feeling of dislike • *his disgust at the incident*
nausea • *I was overcome with a feeling of nausea.*
repulsion • *a shudder of repulsion*
revulsion • *They expressed their shock and revulsion at his death.*

disgust ② VERB
to cause someone to feel disgust • *He disgusted many with his behaviour.*
repel • *a violent excitement that frightened and repelled her*
revolt • *The smell revolted him.*
sicken • *What he saw there sickened him.*

MORE SYNONYMS:
• nauseate
• turn your stomach

disgusting ADJECTIVE
very unpleasant or unacceptable • *one of the most disgusting sights I had ever seen*
foul • *a foul stench*
gross • *Don't be so gross!*
obnoxious • *a most obnoxious character*
repellent • *a very large, repellent toad*
revolting • *The smell was revolting.*
sickening • *a sickening attack on a pregnant woman*
vile • *a vile odour*

MORE SYNONYMS:
• nauseating
• repugnant

dishonest ADJECTIVE
not truthful • *It would be dishonest to mislead people.*
corrupt • *corrupt police officers*
crooked • *crooked business deals*
deceitful • *The ambassador called the report deceitful and misleading.*

fraudulent • *fraudulent claims about being a nurse*
lying • *He called her 'a lying little twit'.*

MORE SYNONYMS:
• mendacious
• untruthful

ANTONYM:
• honest

dishonesty NOUN
dishonest behaviour • *She accused the government of dishonesty.*
cheating • *He was accused of cheating.*
corruption • *The President faces 54 charges of corruption.*
deceit • *the deceit and lies of the past*
trickery • *They resorted to trickery in order to impress their clients.*

MORE SYNONYMS:
• duplicity
• fraudulence
• mendacity

ANTONYM:
• honesty

disintegrate VERB
to break into many pieces • *At 420 mph the windscreen disintegrated.*
break up • *There was a danger of the ship breaking up completely.*
crumble • *The flint crumbled into fragments.*
fall apart • *Bit by bit the building fell apart.*
fall to pieces • *The radio handset fell to pieces.*
fragment • *The clouds fragmented and out came the sun.*

dislike ① VERB
to consider something unpleasant • *We don't serve it often because many people dislike it.*
abhor (FORMAL) • *a man who abhorred violence*

be averse to • *He's not averse to a little publicity.*
detest • *Jean detested being photographed.*
hate • *Most people hate him.*
loathe • *a play loathed by the critics*
not be able to abide • *I can't abide liars.*
not be able to bear • *I can't bear people who speak like that.*
not be able to stand • *He can't stand the sound of her voice.*

ANTONYM:
• like

dislike ② NOUN
a feeling of not liking something • *She looked at him with dislike.*
animosity • *The animosity between the two men grew.*
antipathy • *their antipathy to my smoking*
aversion • *I've always had an aversion to being part of a group.*
distaste • *Roger looked at her with distaste.*
hatred • *her hatred of authority*
hostility • *hostility to ethnic groups*
loathing • *He made no secret of his loathing of her.*

ANTONYM:
• liking

disobey VERB
to deliberately refuse to follow instructions • *He was forever disobeying the rules.*
break • *drivers breaking speed limits*
defy • *the first time that I dared to defy my mother*
flout • *illegal campers who persist in flouting the law*
infringe • *He was adamant that he had infringed no rules.*
violate • *They violated the ceasefire agreement.*

MORE SYNONYMS:
• contravene (FORMAL)
• transgress

ANTONYM:
• obey

disorder ① NOUN
a state of untidiness • *Inside, all was disorder.*
clutter • *She prefers the worktop to be free of clutter.*
disarray • *Her clothes were in disarray.*
muddle • *a general muddle of pencils and boxes*

ANTONYM:
• order

disorder ② NOUN
a lack of organization • *The men fled in disorder.*
chaos • *Their concerts often ended in chaos.*
confusion • *There was confusion when a man fired shots.*
disarray • *The nation is in disarray following rioting.*
turmoil • *the political turmoil of 1989*

disorder ③ NOUN
a disease or illness • *a rare nerve disorder*
affliction • *an affliction which can ruin a young man's life*
complaint • *a common skin complaint*
condition • *a heart condition*
disease • *heart disease*
illness • *mental illness*

dispose of VERB
to get rid of something • *Fold up the nappy and dispose of it.*
discard • *Read the instructions before discarding the box.*
dispense with • *We got a CD-player and dispensed with our old-fashioned record-player.*
dump • *The government declared that it*

a
b
c
d
e
f
g
h
i
j
k
l
m
n
o
p
q
r
s
t
u
v
w
x
y
z

did not dump radioactive waste at sea.
get rid of · The owner needs to get rid of the car for financial reasons.
jettison · The crew jettisoned excess fuel and made an emergency landing.
throw away · I never throw anything away.

disprove VERB
to show that something is not true · the statistics that will prove or disprove the hypothesis
discredit · There would be difficulties in discrediting the evidence.
give the lie to · This survey gives the lie to the idea that the economy is recovering.
invalidate · Some of the other criticisms were invalidated years ago.
prove false · It is hard to prove such claims false.
refute · the kind of rumour that is impossible to refute

ANTONYM:
• prove

dispute ① NOUN
an argument · The dispute between them is settled.
argument · a heated argument
clash · the clash between trade union leaders and the government
conflict · Avoid any conflict between yourself and your ex-partner.
disagreement · disagreements among the member states
feud · a bitter feud between the state government and the villagers
row · a major diplomatic row with France
wrangle · a legal wrangle

dispute ② VERB
to question something's truth or wisdom · He disputed the allegations.
challenge · I challenge the wisdom of this decision.

contest · Your former employer wants to contest the case.
contradict · Her version contradicted the Government's claim.
deny · She denied both accusations.
query · No one queried my decision.
question · It never occurred to me to question the doctor's diagnosis.

ANTONYM:
• accept

distant ① ADJECTIVE
far away in space or time · a distant land
far · Is it very far?
outlying · outlying districts
out-of-the-way · an out-of-the-way spot
remote · a remote village

MORE SYNONYMS:
• faraway
• far-flung
• far-off

ANTONYM:
• close

distant ② ADJECTIVE
cold and unfriendly · He is polite but distant.
aloof · He seemed aloof and detached.
detached · He observed me with a detached curiosity.
reserved · She's quite a reserved person.
withdrawn · Her husband had become withdrawn and moody.

MORE SYNONYMS:
• standoffish
• unapproachable

ANTONYM:
• friendly

distinguish ① VERB
to see the difference between things · Could he distinguish right from wrong?
differentiate · At this age your baby cannot differentiate one person from another.

discriminate • *He is unable to discriminate a good idea from a terrible one.*

tell • *How do you tell one from another?*

tell apart • *I can only tell them apart by the colour of their shoes.*

tell the difference • *I can't tell the difference between their policies and ours.*

distinguish ② VERB

to recognize something • *I heard shouting but was unable to distinguish the words.*

discern • *We could just discern a narrow ditch.*

make out • *He couldn't make out what she was saying.*

pick out • *Through my binoculars I picked out a group of figures.*

recognize • *He did not think she could recognize his car in the snow.*

distract VERB

to stop someone from concentrating • *Playing video games distracts him from his homework.*

divert • *They want to divert our attention from the real issues.*

draw away • *to draw attention away from the crime*

MORE SYNONYMS:
• sidetrack
• turn aside

distress ① NOUN

great suffering • *Jealousy causes distress and painful emotions.*

heartache • *the heartache of her divorce*

pain • *eyes that seemed filled with pain*

sorrow • *a time of great sorrow*

suffering • *to put an end to his suffering*

distress ② NOUN

the state of needing help • *The ship might be in distress.*

difficulty • *rumours about banks being in difficulty*

need • *When you were in need, I loaned you money.*

straits • *The company's closure left them in desperate financial straits.*

trouble • *a charity that helps women in trouble*

distress ③ VERB

to cause someone unhappiness • *Her death had profoundly distressed me.*

bother • *It bothered me that boys weren't interested in me.*

disturb • *dreams so vivid that they disturb me for days*

grieve • *It grieved her to be separated from her son.*

pain • *It pains me to think of you struggling all alone.*

sadden • *The cruelty in the world saddens me deeply.*

trouble • *He was troubled by the lifestyle of his son.*

upset • *I'm sorry if I've upset you.*

worry • *I didn't want to worry you.*

distribute ① VERB

to hand something out • *They publish and distribute brochures.*

circulate • *He has circulated a discussion document.*

hand out • *One of my jobs was to hand out the prizes.*

pass around • *Sweets were being passed around.*

pass round • *She passed her holiday photos round.*

distribute ② VERB

to spread something through an area • *Distribute the topping evenly over the fruit.*

diffuse • *Interest in books is more widely diffused than ever.*

disperse • *The leaflets were dispersed throughout the country.*

A
B
C
D
E
F
G
H
I
J
K
L
M
N
O
P
Q
R
S
T
U
V
W
X
Y
Z

scatter • *She scattered the petals over the grave.*

spread • *A thick layer of wax was spread over the surface.*

distribute ③ VERB

to divide and share something • *Distribute chores evenly among all family members.*

allocate • *funds allocated for nursery education*

allot • *The seats are allotted to the candidates who have won the most votes.*

dispense (FORMAL) • *The Union had already dispensed £400 in grants.*

divide • *Paul divides his spare time between the bedroom and the study.*

dole out • *I got out my wallet and began to dole out the money.*

share out • *You could share out the food a bit more equally.*

MORE SYNONYMS:
• apportion
• mete out

disturb ① VERB

to intrude on someone's peace • *She slept in a separate room so as not to disturb him.*

bother • *I'm sorry to bother you.*

disrupt • *Protesters disrupted the debate.*

intrude on • *I don't want to intrude on your parents.*

disturb ② VERB

to upset or worry someone • *Some scenes may disturb you.*

agitate • *The thought agitated her.*

distress • *Her death had profoundly distressed me.*

shake • *Well, it shook me quite a bit.*

trouble • *He was troubled by the lifestyle of his son.*

unsettle • *The presence of the two policemen unsettled her.*

upset • *I'm sorry if I've upset you.*

worry • *I didn't want to worry you.*

dive VERB

to jump or fall into water • *She was standing by the pool, about to dive in.*

jump • *He ran along the board and jumped in.*

leap • *as she leapt into the water*

submerge • *Hippos are unable to submerge in the few remaining water holes.*

divide ① VERB

to split something up • *The idea is to divide the country into four sectors.*

cut up • *Halve the tomatoes, then cut them up.*

partition • *a plan to partition the country*

segregate • *Police were used to segregate the two rival camps.*

separate • *Fluff the rice with a fork to separate the grains.*

split • *Split the chicken in half.*

split up • *He split up the company.*

ANTONYM:
• join

divide ② VERB

to form a barrier between things • *the frontier dividing Mexico from the USA*

bisect • *The main street bisects the town.*

separate • *the fence that separated the yard from the paddock*

divide ③ VERB

to cause people to disagree • *the enormous differences that still divide them*

come between • *It's difficult to imagine anything coming between them.*

set against one another • *The case has set neighbours against one another in the village.*

split • *Women priests are accused of splitting the church.*

division ① NOUN

separation into parts • *the unification of Germany after its division into two states*
partition • *fighting which followed the partition of India*
separation • *the separation of church and state*

division ② NOUN

a disagreement • *There were divisions in the Party on economic policy.*
breach • *a serious breach in relations between the two countries*
difference of opinion • *Was there a difference of opinion over what to do with the money?*
rupture • *a rupture of the family unit*
split • *They accused both sides of trying to provoke a split in the party.*

division ③ NOUN

a section of something • *the Research Division*
department • *the company's chemicals department*
section • *a top-secret section of the Foreign Office*
sector • *the nation's manufacturing sector*

dizzy ADJECTIVE

about to lose your balance • *He kept getting dizzy spells.*
giddy • *She felt slightly giddy.*
light-headed • *If you skip breakfast, you may feel light-headed.*

do ① VERB

to carry out a task • *He just didn't want to do any work.*
carry out • *Police believe the attacks were carried out by nationalists.*
execute (FORMAL) • *The landing was skilfully executed.*
perform • *people who have performed outstanding acts of bravery*

undertake • *She undertook the arduous task of monitoring the elections.*

do ② VERB

to be sufficient • *Home-made stock is best, but cubes will do.*
be adequate • *The western diet should be perfectly adequate for most people.*
be sufficient • *One teaspoon of sugar should be sufficient.*
suffice (FORMAL) • *Often a far shorter letter will suffice.*

do ③ VERB

to perform well or badly • *Connie did well at school.*
fare • *Some later expeditions fared better.*
get on • *I asked him how he had got on.*
manage • *How did your mother manage after your father died?*

dodge ① VERB

to move out of the way • *We dodged behind a pillar out of sight of the tourists.*
duck • *I wanted to duck down and slip past but they saw me.*
swerve • *He swerved to avoid a truck.*

dodge ② VERB

to avoid doing something • *dodging military service by feigning illness*
avoid • *They managed to avoid paying their fares.*
elude • *He eluded the police for 13 years.*
evade • *by evading taxes*
get out of • *He'll do almost anything to get out of paying his share.*
shirk • *We can't shirk our responsibility.*
sidestep • *Rarely, if ever, does he sidestep a question.*

dog NOUN

an animal often kept as a pet • *a children's book about dogs*
brak (SOUTH AFRICAN) • *a rabid brak*
canine • *a new canine was needed*
mongrel • *a rescued mongrel called Chips*

a
b
c
d
e
f
g
h
i
j
k
l
m
n
o
p
q
r
s
t
u
v
w
x
y
z

A
B
C
D
E
F
G
H
I
J
K
L
M
N
O
P
Q
R
S
T
U
V
W
X
Y
Z

mutt (SLANG) • *the most famous mutts in the western world*
pooch (SLANG) • *Julian's pet pooch*
RELATED WORDS:
• ADJECTIVE canine
• FEMALE bitch
• YOUNG pup, puppy

doomed ADJECTIVE
certain to fail • *a doomed attempt to rescue the children*
condemned • *Many women are condemned to poverty.*
hopeless • *I don't believe your situation is as hopeless as you think.*
ill-fated • *his ill-fated attempt on the world record*

double ① ADJECTIVE
twice the usual size • *a double whisky*
twice • *Unemployment in Northern Ireland is twice the national average.*
twofold • *a twofold risk*

double ② ADJECTIVE
consisting of two parts • *a double album*
dual • *dual nationality*
twin • *twin beds*
twofold • *Their concern was twofold: personal and political.*

doubt ① NOUN
a feeling of uncertainty • *This raises doubts about the point of advertising.*
misgiving • *I had misgivings about his methods.*
qualm • *I have no qualms about recommending this approach.*
scepticism • *The report has been greeted with scepticism.*
uncertainty • *the uncertainties regarding the future funding of the company*
ANTONYM:
• certainty

doubt ② VERB
to feel uncertain about something • *No one doubted his ability.*
be dubious • *I was dubious about the entire proposition.*
be sceptical • *Other archaeologists are sceptical about his findings.*
query • *No one queried my decision.*
question • *It never occurs to them to question the doctor's decisions.*
ANTONYM:
• believe

doubtful ADJECTIVE
unlikely or uncertain • *It is doubtful whether he will appear again.*
debatable • *Whether the Bank of England would do any better is highly debatable.*
dubious • *This claim seems to us rather dubious.*
questionable • *It is questionable whether the expenditure is justified.*
uncertain • *It's uncertain whether they will accept the plan.*
ANTONYM:
• certain

down ① ADVERB
towards the ground, or in a lower place • *We went down in the lift.*
downwards • *She gazed downwards.*
downstairs • *Denise went downstairs and made some tea.*
ANTONYM:
• up

down ② ADJECTIVE
depressed • *He sounded really down.*
dejected • *Everyone has days when they feel dejected.*
depressed • *She's been very depressed about this situation.*
dispirited • *I left feeling utterly dispirited.*
fed up (INFORMAL) • *I'm just fed up and I don't know what to do.*

glum • *She was very glum and was missing her children.*

melancholy • *It was in the afternoon that Tom felt most melancholy.*

miserable • *My work was making me really miserable.*

MORE SYNONYMS:
• despondent
• morose
• pessimistic

downfall NOUN
the failure of a person or thing • *His lack of experience had led to his downfall.*

collapse • *The medical system is facing collapse.*

fall • *the fall of the military dictator*

ruin • *Inflation has driven them to the brink of ruin.*

drab ADJECTIVE
dull and unattractive • *the same drab grey dress*

dingy • *his rather dingy office*

dismal • *a dark dismal day*

dreary • *a dreary little town*

gloomy • *the gloomy days of winter*

grey • *a New Year that will be grey and cheerless*

sombre • *a worried official in sombre black*

MORE SYNONYMS:
• cheerless
• lacklustre

ANTONYM:
• bright

drag VERB
to pull something along the ground • *He dragged his chair towards the table.*

draw • *He drew his chair nearer the fire.*

haul • *A crane was used to haul the car out of the stream.*

lug • *Nobody wants to lug around huge suitcases.*

tow • *They threatened to tow away my car.*

trail • *She came down the stairs slowly, trailing the coat behind her.*

drain ① VERB
to cause a liquid to flow somewhere • *Miners built the tunnel to drain water out of the lakes.*

draw off • *The fluid can be drawn off with a syringe.*

pump • *to get rid of raw sewage by pumping it out to sea*

drain ② VERB
to flow somewhere • *rivers that drain into lakes*

discharge • *Blood was discharging from his nostrils.*

empty • *The Washougal empties into the Columbia River.*

flow • *The waters of Lake Erie now flow into the Niagara River.*

seep • *Radioactive water has seeped into underground reservoirs.*

drain ③ VERB
to use something up • *The prolonged boardroom battle drained him of energy and money.*

consume • *plans which will consume hours of time*

exhaust • *People are now living longer and exhausting natural resources.*

sap • *The illness sapped his strength.*

tax • *Overcrowding has taxed the city's ability to deal with waste.*

use up • *They aren't the ones who use up the world's resources.*

drastic ADJECTIVE
severe and urgent • *It's time for drastic action.*

extreme • *I would rather die than do anything so extreme.*

harsh • *harsh new measures to combat drink-driving*

radical • *radical economic reforms*

a
b
c
d
e
f
g
h
i
j
k
l
m
n
o
p
q
r
s
t
u
v
w
x
y
z

A
B
C
D
E
F
G
H
I
J
K
L
M
N
O
P
Q
R
S
T
U
V
W
X
Y
Z

severe • *a severe shortage of drinking water*

draw ① VERB
to make a picture • *He starts a drawing by painting simplified shapes.*
paint • *He is painting a huge volcano.*
sketch • *He sketched a map on the back of a menu.*
trace • *She learned to draw by tracing pictures out of old storybooks.*

draw ② VERB
to move somewhere • *as the car drew away*
move • *She moved away from the window.*
pull • *He pulled into the driveway.*

draw ③ VERB
to pull something • *He drew his chair nearer the fire.*
drag • *He dragged his chair towards the table.*
haul • *A crane was used to haul the car out of the stream.*
pull • *a freight train pulling waggons*

drawback NOUN
a problem that makes something less than perfect • *The only drawback was that the apartment was too small.*
difficulty • *There is only one difficulty - I don't have the key.*
hitch • *It's a great idea but I can see a serious hitch.*
problem • *The main problem with the house is its inaccessibility.*
snag • *It's a great school - the snag is the fees are £9,000 a year.*
trouble • *The trouble is that he might not agree with our plans.*

dreadful ADJECTIVE
very bad or unpleasant • *He told us the dreadful news*
appalling • *living under the most appalling conditions*

atrocious • *The food here is atrocious.*
awful • *Jeans look awful on me.*
frightful • *The war had been so frightful he couldn't talk about it.*
ghastly • *a ghastly pair of shoes*
horrendous • *the most horrendous experience of his life*
terrible • *Thousands more people suffered terrible injuries.*

ANTONYM:
• wonderful

dream ① NOUN
mental pictures while sleeping • *He had a dream about Claire.*
hallucination • *The drug induces hallucinations at high doses.*
trance • *She seemed to be in a trance.*
vision • *seeing the Virgin Mary in a vision*

MORE SYNONYMS:
• delusion
• reverie

dream ② NOUN
something that you want very much • *his dream of winning the lottery*
ambition • *His ambition is to sail round the world.*
aspiration • *one of his greatest aspirations*
daydream • *He learned to escape into daydreams of becoming a writer.*
fantasy • *fantasies of romance and true love*

MORE SYNONYMS:
• Holy Grail
• pipe dream

dreary ADJECTIVE
dull or boring • *the dreary winter months*
boring • *a boring job*
drab • *The rest of the day's activities often seem drab.*
dull • *There was scarcely a dull moment.*

humdrum • *The new government seemed rather humdrum.*
monotonous • *It's monotonous work, like most factory jobs.*
tedious • *Such lists are tedious to read.*
uneventful • *her dull, uneventful life*

ANTONYM:
• exciting

dress ① NOUN
a piece of clothing • *a black dress*
frock • *a party frock*
gown • *wedding gowns*
robe • *a fur-lined robe*

dress ② NOUN
clothing in general • *evening dress*
attire (FORMAL) • *women dressed in their finest attire*
clothes • *casual clothes*
clothing • *protective clothing*
costume • *women in traditional costume*
garb (FORMAL) • *his usual garb of a dark suit*

MORE SYNONYMS:
• apparel
• raiment

dress ③ VERB
to put on clothes • *a tall woman dressed in black*
attire (FORMAL) • *He was attired in a smart blue suit.*
clothe • *He lay down on the bed fully clothed.*
garb (FORMAL) • *He was garbed in sweater, jacket and boots.*

ANTONYM:
• undress

drink ① VERB
to swallow liquid • *He drank some tea.*
gulp • *She quickly gulped her coffee.*
guzzle • *She guzzled gin and tonics like they were lemonade.*
sip • *She sipped from her coffee mug.*

swig (INFORMAL) • *I swigged down two white wines.*

MORE SYNONYMS:
• imbibe
• quaff
• sup

drink ② VERB
to drink alcohol • *He drinks little and eats carefully.*
booze (INFORMAL) • *drunken businessmen who had been boozing all afternoon*
tipple • *We saw a woman tippling from the sherry bottle.*

drip ① VERB
to fall in small drops • *Rain dripped from the brim of his cap.*
dribble • *Sweat dribbled down his face.*
splash • *Tears splashed into her hands.*
trickle • *A tear trickled down the old man's cheek.*

drip ② NOUN
a small amount of a liquid • *drips of water*
bead • *beads of sweat*
drop • *a drop of blue ink*
droplet • *water droplets*

MORE SYNONYMS:
• dribble
• globule

drive ① VERB
to operate or power a machine or vehicle • *Don't drive a car or operate heavy machinery after taking this medication.*
operate • *A rock fall trapped the men as they operated a tunnelling machine.*
pilot • *He piloted his own plane to Washington.*
power • *The flywheel's battery could be used to power an electric car.*
propel • *Attached is a tiny rocket designed to propel the spacecraft towards Mars.*

a b c d e f g h i j k l m n o p q r s t u v w x y z

A
B
C
D
E
F
G
H
I
J
K
L
M
N
O
P
Q
R
S
T
U
V
W
X
Y
Z

run • *I ran a Rover 100 from 1977 until 1983.*
steer • *What is it like to steer a ship this size?*
work • *I learned how to work the forklift.*

drive ② VERB
to force someone to do something • *Depression drove him to self-harm.*
compel • *He felt compelled to speak out against their actions.*
force • *A back injury forced her to withdraw from the tournament.*
lead • *His abhorrence of racism led him to write his first book.*
motivate • *What motivates people to behave like this?*
prompt • *The recession has prompted consumers to cut back on spending.*
push • *James did not push her into stealing the money.*
spur • *It's the money that spurs these fishermen to take such risks.*

drive ③ VERB
to force something pointed into a surface • *I used the sledgehammer to drive the pegs in.*
hammer • *Hammer a wooden peg into the hole.*
knock • *He knocked a couple of nails into the wall.*
ram • *He rammed the stake with all his strength into the creature's heart.*
sink • *He sinks the needle into my arm.*
thrust • *thrusting a knife into his ribs*

drive ④ NOUN
a journey in a vehicle • *We might go for a drive on Sunday.*
excursion • *an excursion to a local vineyard*
jaunt • *Let's take a jaunt down to the beach.*
journey • *The journey from Manchester to Plymouth took a few hours.*
ride • *We took some friends for a ride in the family car.*

run • *We went for a run in the new car to try it out.*
spin • *I was thinking about going for a spin.*
trip • *We went on a coach trip to the seaside.*

drive ⑤ NOUN
energy and determination • *He is best remembered for his drive and enthusiasm.*
ambition • *When I was young I never had any ambition.*
determination • *her natural determination to succeed*
energy • *At 54 years old, her energy is magnificent.*
enterprise • *the group's lack of enterprise*
initiative • *We were disappointed by his lack of initiative.*
motivation • *His poor performance may be attributed to lack of motivation.*
vigour • *He played with great vigour.*

drop ① VERB
to fall downwards • *She let her head drop.*
descend • *as the aircraft descended*
fall • *Bombs fell in the town.*
plummet • *His parachute failed to open and he plummeted to the ground.*
sink • *She sank to her knees.*
tumble • *The gun tumbled out of his hand.*

drop ② VERB
to become less • *Temperatures can drop to freezing at night.*
decline • *The number of staff has declined.*
decrease • *Population growth is decreasing by 1.4% each year.*
diminish • *diminishing resources*
fall • *Her weight fell to under seven stone.*
plummet • *Share prices have plummeted.*

sink • *Pay increases have sunk to around 7%.*
slump • *Net profits slumped by 41%.*
tumble • *House prices have tumbled by almost 30%.*

ANTONYM:
• rise

drop ③ NOUN
a small amount of a liquid • *a drop of blue ink*
bead • *beads of sweat*
drip • *drips of water*
droplet • *water droplets*

MORE SYNONYMS:
• dribble
• globule

drug ① NOUN
a treatment for disease • *a new drug in the fight against AIDS*
medication • *She is not on any medication.*
medicine • *herbal medicines*

RELATED WORD:
• COMBINING FORM pharmaco-

drug ② NOUN
an illegal substance • *She was sure Leo was taking drugs.*
narcotic • *He was indicted for dealing in narcotics.*
stimulant • *the use of stimulants in sport*

drunk ① ADJECTIVE
having consumed too much alcohol • *I got drunk.*
babalas (SOUTH AFRICAN) • *He was babalas again last night.*
intoxicated (FORMAL) • *He appeared intoxicated.*
tipsy • *I'm feeling a bit tipsy.*

MORE SYNONYMS:
• bacchic
• inebriated

ANTONYM:
• sober

drunk ② NOUN
someone who consumes too much alcohol • *A drunk lay in the alley.*
alcoholic • *after admitting that he was an alcoholic*
boozer (INFORMAL) • *He's a bit of a boozer.*

dry ① ADJECTIVE
without any liquid • *The path was dry after the sunshine.*
arid • *arid conditions*
dried-up • *a dried-up river bed*
parched • *parched brown grass*

ANTONYM:
• wet

dry ② VERB
to remove liquid from something • *Wash and dry the lettuce.*
dehydrate • *Avoid alcohol, which dehydrates the body.*
drain • *The authorities have mobilized vast numbers of people to drain flooded land.*

MORE SYNONYMS:
• dehumidify
• desiccate

ANTONYM:
• moisten

dubious ① ADJECTIVE
not entirely honest or reliable • *a rather dubious claim*
crooked • *expose his crooked business deals*
dishonest • *He had become rich by dishonest means.*
questionable • *allegations of questionable business practices*
suspect • *The whole affair is highly suspect.*
suspicious • *two characters who looked suspicious*

a
b
c
d
e
f
g
h
i
j
k
l
m
n
o
p
q
r
s
t
u
v
w
x
y
z

unreliable • *a notoriously unreliable source of information*

dubious ② ADJECTIVE
doubtful about something • *My parents were a bit dubious about it all.*
doubtful • *I was still very doubtful about our chances for success.*
nervous • *The party has become nervous about its prospects of winning.*
sceptical • *Other archaeologists are sceptical about his findings.*
suspicious • *I'm a little suspicious about his motives.*
unconvinced • *Most consumers seem unconvinced that the recession is over.*
undecided • *After university she was still undecided as to what career she wanted.*
unsure • *Fifty-two per cent were unsure about the idea.*

dull ① ADJECTIVE
not interesting • *I found him rather dull.*
boring • *a boring job*
drab • *The rest of the day's activities often seem drab.*
humdrum • *The new government seemed rather humdrum.*
monotonous • *It's monotonous work, like most factory jobs.*
tedious • *Such lists are tedious to read.*
uninteresting • *Their media has a reputation for being dull and uninteresting.*

ANTONYM:
• interesting

dull ② ADJECTIVE
not bright or clear • *a dark, dull blue colour*
drab • *the same drab grey dress*
gloomy • *Inside it's gloomy after all that sunshine.*
muted • *He likes sombre, muted colours.*

sombre • *an official in sombre black*
subdued • *subdued lighting*

ANTONYM:
• bright

dull ③ ADJECTIVE
covered with clouds • *It's always dull and raining.*
cloudy • *In the morning it was cloudy.*
leaden • *a leaden sky*
murky • *one murky November afternoon*
overcast • *For three days it was overcast.*

ANTONYM:
• bright

dumb ① ADJECTIVE
unable to speak • *We were all struck dumb for a minute.*
mute • *a mute look of appeal*
silent • *Suddenly they both fell silent.*
speechless • *Alex was almost speechless with rage.*

dumb ② ADJECTIVE (INFORMAL)
slow to understand • *I've met a lot of pretty dumb people.*
dim • *He is rather dim.*
obtuse (FORMAL) • *I've really been very obtuse.*
stupid • *How could I have been so stupid?*
thick (INFORMAL) • *I must have seemed incredibly thick.*

ANTONYM:
• smart

dump ① VERB
to get rid of something • *The getaway car was dumped near the motorway.*
discharge • *The resulting salty water will eventually be discharged at sea.*
dispose of • *how he disposed of the murder weapon*
get rid of • *The cat had kittens, which they got rid of.*
jettison • *The crew jettisoned their excess fuel.*

throw away • *You should have thrown the letter away.*

throw out • *You ought to throw out those empty bottles.*

dump ② VERB

to put something down • *We dumped our bags at the hotel and went for a walk.*

deposit • *Imagine if you were suddenly deposited on a desert island.*

drop • *Many children had been dropped outside the stadium by their parents.*

dupe VERB

to trick someone • *Some of the offenders duped the psychologists.*

cheat • *Many brokers were charged with cheating customers.*

con (INFORMAL) • *The British people have been conned by the government.*

deceive • *He has deceived us all.*

delude • *Television deludes you into thinking you are experiencing reality.*

fool • *Art dealers fool a lot of people.*

play a trick on • *She realized he had played a trick on her.*

trick • *He'll be upset when he finds out you tricked him.*

duty ① NOUN

something that you ought to do • *We have a duty as adults to listen to children.*

obligation • *He had not felt an obligation to help save his old friend.*

responsibility • *work and family responsibilities*

duty ② NOUN

a task associated with a job • *My main duty as librarian was the acquisition of books.*

assignment • *dangerous assignments*

job • *One of my jobs was to make the tea.*

responsibility • *He handled his responsibilities as a counsellor very well.*

role • *Both sides had important roles to play.*

duty ③ NOUN

tax paid to the government • *customs duties*

excise • *These products are excused VAT and excise.*

levy (FORMAL) • *An annual motorway levy is imposed on all drivers.*

tariff • *America wants to eliminate tariffs on such items as electronics.*

tax • *the tax on new cars and motorcycles*

dying: be dying for VERB

to want something very much • *I'm dying for a breath of fresh air.*

ache for • *She still ached for the lost intimacy of marriage.*

hunger for • *Jules hungered for adventure.*

long for • *He longed for the winter to be over.*

pine for • *I pine for the countryside.*

yearn for • *He yearned for freedom.*

a
b
c
d
e
f
g
h
i
j
k
l
m
n
o
p
q
r
s
t
u
v
w
x
y
z

Ee

eager ADJECTIVE
wanting very much to do or have
something • *Robert is eager to earn
some extra money.*
anxious • *She was anxious to leave
early.*
ardent • *one of the government's most
ardent supporters*
avid • *He's always been an avid reader.*
enthusiastic • *Tom usually seems very
enthusiastic.*
keen • *Kirsty has always been a keen
swimmer.*
raring to go (INFORMAL) • *They're all
ready and raring to go.*

MORE SYNONYMS:
• fervent
• hungry
• zealous

early ① ADJECTIVE
before the arranged or expected time
• *You're not late - I'm early!*
advance • *We got an advance copy of
her new book.*
premature • *The injury put a premature
end to his sporting career.*
untimely • *her untimely death in a car
crash at the age of 21*

ANTONYM:
• late

early ② ADJECTIVE
near the beginning of a period of
time • *the early 1970's*
primeval • *These insects first appeared
in the primeval forests of Europe.*

primitive • *We found a fossil of a
primitive bird-like creature.*

early ③ ADVERB
before the arranged or expected time
• *We left early so we wouldn't have to
queue.*
ahead of time • *The bus always arrives
ahead of time.*
beforehand • *If you'd let me know
beforehand, you could have come with us.*
in advance • *You need to book in
advance to get a good seat.*
in good time • *We arrived at the airport
in good time.*
prematurely • *men who go
prematurely bald*

earn ① VERB
to get money in return for doing work
• *He earns a lot more than I do.*
bring in • *My job brings in just enough
to pay the bills.*
draw • *I draw a salary, so I can afford to
run a car.*
get • *How much do you get if you're a
lorry driver?*
make • *She makes a lot of money.*
obtain • *the profits obtained from
buying and selling shares*

MORE SYNONYMS:
• net
• procure
• reap

earn ② VERB
to receive something that you

deserve • *He earned the respect of his troops.*

acquire • *She has acquired a reputation as a liar and a cheat.*

attain (FORMAL) • *He finally attained his pilot's licence.*

win • *She won the admiration of all her colleagues.*

earth ① NOUN

the planet on which we live • *the tallest mountain on earth*

globe • *from every corner of the globe*

planet • *the effects of pollution on the atmosphere of our planet*

world • *the first person to cycle round the world*

RELATED WORD:
• ADJECTIVE terrestrial

earth ② NOUN

soil from the ground • *He filled a pot with earth and popped the seeds in it.*

clay • *lumps of clay that stuck to his boots*

dirt • *kneeling in the dirt*

ground • *digging potatoes out of the ground*

soil • *We planted some bulbs in the soil around the pond.*

MORE SYNONYMS:
• loam
• topsoil
• turf

ease ① NOUN

lack of difficulty or worry • *He passed his driving test with ease.*

leisure • *living a life of leisure*

relaxation • *The town has a feeling of relaxation and tranquillity about it.*

simplicity • *The simplicity of the new scheme has made it popular with motorists.*

ease ② VERB

to make or become less severe or intense • *The doctor gave him another injection to ease the pain.*

abate • *By morning the storms had abated.*

calm • *The government is taking steps to calm the situation.*

relax • *He relaxed his grip on the axe and smiled.*

relieve • *The pills will help relieve the pain for a while.*

slacken • *Her grip on the rope slackened and she fell back.*

MORE SYNONYMS:
• allay
• alleviate
• assuage

ease ③ VERB

to move slowly or carefully • *He eased the door open and peered outside.*

creep • *The car crept down the ramp.*

edge • *I edged the van slowly back into the garage.*

guide • *Bob guided the plane out onto the tarmac.*

inch • *The ambulance inched its way through the crowds of shoppers.*

lower • *He lowered himself into the armchair.*

manoeuvre • *We attempted to manoeuvre his canoe towards the shore.*

squeeze • *They squeezed him into his seat and strapped him in.*

easy ① ADJECTIVE

able to be done without difficulty • *The software is very easy to install.*

light • *a few light exercises to warm up*

painless • *Finding somewhere to stay was pretty painless in the end.*

simple • *All you have to do is answer a few simple questions.*

smooth • *a smooth changeover to the new system*

straightforward • *The route is fairly straightforward so you shouldn't need a map.*

a
b
c
d
e
f
g
h
i
j
k
l
m
n
o
p
q
r
s
t
u
v
w
x
y
z

ANTONYM:
• hard

easy ② ADJECTIVE
comfortable and without worries
• *He has not had an easy life.*
carefree • *a carefree summer spent on the beach*
comfortable • *a comfortable teaching job at a small private school*
leisurely • *a leisurely weekend spent with a few close friends*
quiet • *a quiet weekend in the sun*
relaxed • *It's very relaxed here, you can do what you like.*

eat ① VERB
to chew and swallow food • *For lunch he ate a cheese sandwich.*
▶ see Word Study **eat**, page 640

eat ② VERB
to have a meal • *We like to eat early.*
breakfast (FORMAL) • *The ladies like to breakfast in their rooms.*
dine • *We usually dine at about six.*
feed • *Leopards only feed when they are hungry.*
have a meal • *We could have a meal at Pizza Palace after the film.*
lunch (FORMAL) • *We lunched at El Greco's.*
picnic • *After our walk, we picnicked by the river.*

eat away VERB
to destroy something slowly • *The front of the car had been eaten away by rust.*
corrode • *buildings corroded by acid rain*
destroy • *Areas of the coast are being destroyed by the sea.*
dissolve • *Chemicals in the water are dissolving the bridge.*
erode • *the floods that erode the dry, loose soil*

rot • *Too many sweets will rot your teeth.*
wear away • *The weather soon wears away the paintwork.*

eccentric ① ADJECTIVE
regarded as odd or peculiar • *His maths teacher was considered a bit eccentric.*
bizarre • *He's quite a bizarre character.*
outlandish • *His outlandish behaviour sometimes puts people off.*
quirky • *a quirky, delightful film that is full of surprises*
strange • *his strange views about UFOs*
weird • *His taste in music is a bit weird.*
whimsical • *a whimsical old gentleman*

eccentric ② NOUN
someone who is regarded as odd or peculiar • *He's always been regarded as a bit of an eccentric.*
character (INFORMAL) • *a well-known character who lived in Johnson Street*
crank • *People regarded vegetarians as cranks in those days.*

economic ① ADJECTIVE
concerning the way money is managed • *the need for economic reforms*
budgetary • *a summit meeting to discuss various budgetary matters*
commercial • *a purely commercial decision*
financial • *The financial pressures on the government are mounting.*

MORE SYNONYMS:
• fiscal
• monetary

economic ② ADJECTIVE
making a profit • *goods that happen to be economic to produce*
productive • *the need to make these industries more productive*
profitable • *a new venture that has proved highly profitable*

viable • *businesses that are no longer viable*

MORE SYNONYMS:
• money-making
• profit-making
• remunerative

economical ① ADJECTIVE

cheap to use and saving you money • *Our car may not be fast, but it's very economical.*

cheap • *This isn't a very cheap way of buying stationery.*

cost-effective • *the most cost-effective way of shopping*

economic • *the most economic way to see the museum*

inexpensive • *There are several good inexpensive restaurants in town.*

economical ② ADJECTIVE

careful and sensible with money or materials • *He's never been very economical about housekeeping.*

careful • *She's very careful with her pocket money.*

frugal • *his frugal lifestyle*

prudent • *the prudent use of precious natural resources*

thrifty • *My mother was very thrifty because she had so little spare cash.*

economy NOUN

the careful use of things to save money • *improvements in the fuel economy of new cars*

frugality (FORMAL) • *We must live with strict frugality if we are to survive.*

prudence • *A lack of prudence could seriously affect his finances.*

restraint • *We need to exercise some restraint in our spending.*

thrift • *He was widely praised for his thrift and imagination.*

ecstasy NOUN

extreme happiness • *his feeling of ecstasy after winning the medal*

bliss • *husband and wife living together in bliss and harmony*

delight • *He squealed with delight when we told him.*

elation • *His supporters reacted to the news with elation.*

euphoria • *There was a sense of euphoria after our election victory.*

exaltation • *the mood of exaltation that affected everyone*

joy • *her joy at finding him after so long*

rapture • *His speech was received with rapture by a huge crowd.*

edge ① NOUN

the place where something ends or meets something else • *on the edge of the forest*

border • *a pillowcase with a lace border*

boundary • *The area beyond the western boundary belongs to Denmark.*

brim • *He kept climbing until he reached the brim of the crater.*

fringe • *the rundown areas on the fringes of the city*

lip • *The lip of the jug was badly cracked.*

margin • *standing on the margin of the land where it met the water*

rim • *a large round mirror with a gold rim*

MORE SYNONYMS:
• perimeter
• periphery

ANTONYM:
• centre

edge ② VERB

to move somewhere slowly • *He edged towards the phone, ready to grab it if it rang.*

creep • *The car crept forward a few feet, then stopped.*

inch • *The ambulance inched its way through the crowds.*

sidle • *A man sidled up to him and tried to sell him a ticket.*

a
b
c
d
e
f
g
h
i
j
k
l
m
n
o
p
q
r
s
t
u
v
w
x
y
z

educated ADJECTIVE
having a high standard of learning
• *He is an educated, tolerant and reasonable man.*
cultivated • *His mother was an elegant, cultivated woman.*
cultured • *a cultured man with a wide circle of friends*
intellectual • *He is the intellectual type.*
learned • *He was a scholar, a very learned man.*

MORE SYNONYMS:
• erudite
• well-educated

education NOUN
the process of learning or teaching
• *the importance of a good education*
coaching • *extra coaching to help him pass his exams*
e-learning • *The company wants to encourage staff to take e-learning courses.*
instruction • *All instruction is provided by qualified experts.*
schooling • *He began to wish he'd paid more attention to his schooling.*
training • *His military training was no use to him here.*
tuition • *personal tuition in the basics of photography*

effect NOUN
a direct result of something • *the effect that divorce has on children*
consequence • *aware of the consequences of their actions*
end result • *The end result of this process is still unclear.*
fruit • *The new software is the fruit of three years' hard work.*
result • *The result of all this uncertainty is that no-one is happy.*
upshot • *The upshot is that we have a very unhappy workforce.*

efficient ADJECTIVE
able to work well without wasting time or energy • *The new hatchback has a much more efficient engine.*
businesslike • *a highly businesslike approach that impressed everyone*
competent • *an extremely competent piece of work*
economic • *The new system is much more economic, and will save millions.*
effective • *effective use of the time we have left*
organized • *Tony seemed very organized, and completely in control of the situation.*
productive • *the need to make farmers much more productive*

ANTONYM:
• inefficient

effort ① NOUN
physical or mental energy • *It took a lot of effort, but we managed in the end.*
application • *His talent, application and energy are a credit to the school.*
energy • *He decided to devote his energy to writing another book.*
exertion • *Is it really worth all the exertion?*
trouble • *It's not worth the trouble.*
work • *All the work I put in has now been wasted!*

effort ② NOUN
an attempt or struggle • *an unsuccessful effort to ban Sunday shopping*
attempt • *an attempt to obtain an interview with the President*
bid • *a last-minute bid to stop the trial going ahead*
stab (INFORMAL) • *his latest stab at acting*
struggle • *his struggle to clear his name*

elaborate ① ADJECTIVE

having many different parts • *an elaborate research project*

complex • *a complex explanation*

complicated • *a complicated plan of the building's security system*

detailed • *the detailed plans that have been drawn up*

intricate • *an intricate system of levers and pulleys*

involved • *a very involved operation, lasting many hours*

ANTONYM:
• simple

elaborate ② ADJECTIVE

highly decorated • *elaborate wooden carvings*

fancy • *the fancy plasterwork on the ceiling*

fussy • *a rather fussy design*

ornate • *an ornate wrought-iron staircase*

elaborate ③ VERB

to add more information about something • *He promised to elaborate on what had been said last night.*

develop • *Maybe we should develop this idea.*

enlarge • *He was enlarging on proposals made earlier.*

expand • *a view that I will expand on later*

eliminate ① VERB

to get rid of someone or something • *We've eliminated two of the four options so far.*

cut out • *His guilty plea cut out the need for a long, costly trial.*

do away with • *the attempt to do away with nuclear weapons altogether*

eradicate • *Efforts to eradicate malaria seem to be failing.*

get rid of • *Why don't we just get rid of the middlemen altogether?*

remove • *You should try and remove these fatty foods from your diet.*

stamp out • *We need to stamp out this disgusting practice.*

eliminate ② VERB

to beat someone in a competition • *His team was eliminated in the first round.*

knock out • *We were knocked out by the Dutch champions.*

put out • *Decker finally put her fellow American out in the quarter final.*

embarrass VERB

to make someone feel ashamed or awkward • *You always embarrass me in front of my friends!*

disconcert • *The way Anderson was smirking disconcerted her.*

fluster • *Nothing could fluster him.*

humiliate • *How dare you humiliate me like that!*

shame • *Her son's behaviour had upset and shamed her.*

MORE SYNONYMS:
• discomfit
• faze
• mortify

embarrassed ADJECTIVE

ashamed and awkward • *I'm not embarrassed about taking my clothes off.*

ashamed • *I felt so ashamed I wanted to die.*

awkward • *It was a very awkward occasion.*

humiliated • *A humiliated Mr Stevens admitted that the concert had been cancelled.*

red-faced • *Red-faced executives had to explain this fact.*

self-conscious • *I always feel self-conscious when I'm having my picture taken.*

a
b
c
d
e
f
g
h
i
j
k
l
m
n
o
p
q
r
s
t
u
v
w
x
y
z

A
B
C
D
E
F
G
H
I
J
K
L
M
N
O
P
Q
R
S
T
U
V
W
X
Y
Z

sheepish • *He looked very sheepish when he finally appeared.*

MORE SYNONYMS:
• abashed
• bashful
• discomfited
• mortified

embarrassment NOUN
shame and awkwardness • *I laughed loudly to cover my embarrassment.*
awkwardness • *the awkwardness of our first meeting*
bashfulness • *Overcome with bashfulness, he lowered his voice.*
humiliation • *the humiliation of having to ask for money*
self-consciousness • *her painful self-consciousness*
shame • *the shame he felt at having let her down*

MORE SYNONYMS:
• chagrin
• discomfiture
• mortification

emergency NOUN
an unexpected and difficult situation
• *This is an emergency!*
crisis • *the economic crisis affecting parts of Africa*
pinch • *I don't mind working late in a pinch.*

emit VERB
to give out or release something
• *Polly blinked and emitted a long sigh.*
exude • *a plant that exudes an extremely unpleasant smell*
give off • *The fumes it gives off are poisonous, so watch out.*
give out • *The alarm gave out a series of bleeps, then stopped.*
release • *The factory is still releasing toxic fumes.*

send out • *The volcano has been sending out smoke for weeks.*
utter • *He uttered a loud snort and continued eating.*

MORE SYNONYMS:
• produce
• radiate
• send forth

emphasis NOUN
special or extra importance • *too much emphasis on commercialism*
accent • *In the new government the accent will be on co-operation.*
importance • *There's not enough importance being given to environmental issues.*
prominence • *Crime prevention has to be given more prominence.*
weight • *This adds more weight to the government's case.*

emphasize VERB
to make something seem specially important or obvious • *He emphasized the need for everyone to remain calm.*
accent • *a white dress accented by a coloured scarf*
accentuate • *His shaven head accentuates his round face.*
highlight • *This disaster has highlighted the difficulty faced by the government.*
play up • *He played up his bad-boy image.*
stress • *I would like to stress that we are in complete agreement.*
underline • *This underlines how important the new trade deal really is.*

MORE SYNONYMS:
• foreground
• prioritize
• underscore

employ ① VERB
to pay someone to work for you

• *Mollison was employed by Mr Darnley as a bodyguard.*
appoint • *We need to appoint a successor to Mr Stevens.*
commission • *He has been commissioned to design a new bridge.*
engage (FORMAL) • *They have finally engaged a suitable nanny.*
hire • *I was hired as a gardener on the estate.*
take on • *the need to take on more workers for the summer*

employ ② VERB
to use something • *the tactics employed by the police*
bring to bear • *We can bring two very different techniques to bear on this.*
make use of • *He makes use of several highly offensive terms to describe them.*
use • *the methods used in the investigation*
utilize • *Engineers will utilize a range of techniques to improve the signal.*

employee NOUN
someone who is paid to work for someone else • *the way they look after their employees*
hand • *He's been working as a farm hand down south.*
worker • *Workers at the plant have been laid off.*
workman • *A council workman finally arrived to fix the door.*

employer NOUN
someone that other people work for • *a meeting with her employer to discuss the issue*
boss • *My boss has always been very fair.*
gaffer (INFORMAL) • *You'll need to speak to the gaffer about that.*

employment NOUN
the fact of employing people • *the employment of children to work in shops*

engagement • *the engagement of suitable staff*
enlistment • *Enlistment in the armed forces is falling.*
hiring • *The hiring of new staff is our top priority.*
recruitment • *new policies on recruitment and training*
taking on • *Taking on extra staff would make life a lot easier.*

empty ① ADJECTIVE
having no people or things in it • *The roads were empty.*
bare • *When she got there, the cupboard was bare.*
blank • *all the blank pages in his diary*
clear • *The runway must be kept clear at all times.*
deserted • *By nightfall, the square was deserted.*
unfurnished • *The flat was unfurnished when we moved in.*
uninhabited • *The house has remained uninhabited since she moved out.*
vacant • *two vacant lots on the industrial estate*
ANTONYM:
• full

empty ② ADJECTIVE
boring or without value or meaning • *My life is empty without him.*
inane • *a series of inane remarks*
meaningless • *the feeling that his existence was meaningless*
worthless • *a worthless film with nothing to say about anything*

empty ③ VERB
to remove people or things • *He emptied all the cupboards before Tony arrived.*
clear • *The police cleared the building just in time.*
drain • *She drained the bottles and washed them out.*

evacuate • *Fortunately the building had been evacuated.*

unload • *It only took twenty minutes to unload the van.*

ANTONYM:
• fill

enclose VERB

to surround a thing or place completely • *The book arrived enclosed in a red plastic bag.*

encircle • *The area had been encircled by barbed wire.*

fence off • *We decided to fence off the land.*

hem in • *We were hemmed in by walls and hedges.*

surround • *the low wall that surrounded the rose garden*

wrap • *Wrap the chicken in foil and bake it in a medium oven.*

encourage ① VERB

to give someone confidence • *We were very encouraged by the response.*

cheer • *This news cheered us all and helped us keep going.*

hearten • *I am heartened to hear that.*

reassure • *He always reassures me when I'm feeling down.*

ANTONYM:
• discourage

encourage ② VERB

to support a person or activity • *the need to encourage people to be sensible*

aid • *I tried to aid his creative efforts.*

boost • *Efforts to boost investment seem to be succeeding.*

favour • *conditions which favour growth in the economy*

help • *policies aimed at helping small businesses*

incite • *He incited his followers to attack the police station.*

support • *Rowe will support me in this campaign.*

MORE SYNONYMS:
• foster
• further
• promote
• strengthen

end ① NOUN

the last part of a period or event • *the end of the 20th century*

close • *The company made £100 million by the close of last year.*

ending • *the ending of a great era*

expiry • *the expiry of his period of training*

finish • *The college basketball season is nearing its finish.*

climax • *the dramatic climax of the trial*

close • *the close of the festival*

conclusion • *the conclusion of this fascinating tale*

culmination • *the remarkable culmination of a glittering career*

ending • *a film with a tragic ending*

finale • *a grand finale to the week-long celebrations*

finish • *a disappointing finish to our adventures*

ANTONYM:
• beginning

RELATED WORDS:
• ADJECTIVES final, terminal, ultimate

end ② NOUN

the furthest point of something • *the room at the end of the corridor*

boundaries • *We worked along the boundaries of the paths.*

bounds • *the landscape beyond the bounds of London*

edge • *He fell off the edge of the cliff.*

extremity • *the western extremity of the continent*

limits • *an area outside the official city limits*

margin • *agricultural regions well beyond the forest margin*

end ③ NOUN
the purpose for which something is done • *The army is being used for political ends.*
aim • *groups united by a common aim*
goal • *We're all working towards the same goal.*
intention • *He concealed his real intentions.*
object • *the stated object of the mission*
objective • *the objective of all this effort*
purpose • *the true purpose of their visit*
reasons • *Are you here on holiday, or for business reasons*

end ④ VERB
to come or bring to a finish • *talks being held to end the fighting*
bring to an end • *The treaty brought to an end fifty years of conflict.*
cease • *By one o'clock the storm had ceased.*
conclude • *The evening concluded with the usual speeches.*
finish • *waiting for the film to finish*
stop • *When is it all going to stop?*
terminate • *the decision to terminate their contract*

ANTONYM:
• begin

endanger VERB
to put someone or something in danger • *a dispute that could endanger the peace talks*
compromise • *We will not allow safety to be compromised.*
jeopardize • *a scandal that could jeopardize his government*
put at risk • *those who were put at risk by her stupidity*
risk • *He is risking the lives of others.*
threaten • *A breakdown in this system could threaten the whole project.*

endure ① VERB
to experience something difficult • *He had to endure hours of discomfort.*
cope with • *We've had a lot to cope with in the last few weeks.*
experience • *The company has experienced heavy financial losses.*
go through • *having to go through the public humiliation of a court case*
stand • *I don't know how he stood it for so long.*
suffer • *Steven has suffered years of pain from arthritis.*

endure ② VERB
to continue to exist • *Our friendship has endured through everything.*
last • *a car that is built to last*
live on • *His name will live on as an inspiration to others.*
remain • *When all the rest is forgotten, this fact will remain.*
survive • *the few traces of their civilization that have survived*

enemy NOUN
someone who is against you • *She has many enemies in the government.*
adversary • *face to face with his old adversary*
antagonist • *He killed his antagonist in a duel.*
foe • *He plays Dracula's foe, Dr. Van Helsing.*
opponent • *Her political opponents will be delighted at this news.*

ANTONYM:
• friend

energetic ADJECTIVE
full of energy • *an able, energetic and very determined politician*
animated • *an animated conversation about politics and sport*
dynamic • *a dynamic and ambitious businessman*

a b c d e f g h i j k l m n o p q r s t u v w x y z

indefatigable • *trying to keep up with their indefatigable boss*
spirited • *a spirited defence of his new tax proposals*
tireless • *a tireless campaigner for the homeless*
vigorous • *a vigorous campaign*

energy NOUN
the ability and strength to do things • *I'm saving my energy for tomorrow.*
drive • *a man with immense drive and enthusiasm*
life • *At 96, she's still as full of life as ever.*
spirit • *Despite trailing 6-2, they played with a lot of spirit.*
strength • *She put all her strength into finding a new job.*
vigour • *They returned to their work with renewed vigour.*
vitality • *a woman with considerable charm and endless vitality*

MORE SYNONYMS:
• élan
• verve
• zeal
• zest

enjoy VERB
to find pleasure in something • *I haven't enjoyed a film as much as that in ages!*
appreciate • *people who don't appreciate Satie's music*
delight in • *He delights in playing practical jokes.*
like • *Kirsty likes shopping.*
love • *He loves skiing.*
relish • *She relished the opportunity to get back at him.*
revel in • *Stevens was revelling in the attention.*
take pleasure from • *He took no pleasure from the knowledge that he had won.*
take pleasure in • *She seemed to take pleasure in my discomfort.*

enlarge VERB
to make something larger • *plans to enlarge the 30,000 seat stadium*
add to • *We've decided to add to this house rather than move again.*
expand • *If we want to stay in business, we need to expand.*
extend • *They extended the house by adding a conservatory.*
increase • *They have increased the peace-keeping force to 2000.*
magnify • *A more powerful lens will magnify the image.*

MORE SYNONYMS:
• augment
• broaden
• distend
• elongate
• lengthen
• widen

enlarge on VERB
to give more information about something • *I'd like you to enlarge on that last point.*
develop • *Maybe I should develop this idea a little bit further.*
elaborate on • *He refused to elaborate on what he had said earlier.*
expand on • *an idea that I will expand on later*

enormous ADJECTIVE
very large in size or amount • *an enormous dust cloud*
colossal • *a colossal waste of public money*
gigantic • *The road is bordered by gigantic rocks.*
huge • *Several painters were working on a huge piece of canvas.*
immense • *an immense cloud of smoke*
massive • *The scale of the problem is massive.*
tremendous • *I felt a tremendous pressure on my chest.*

vast • *vast stretches of land*

ANTONYM:
• tiny

ensure VERB
to make sure about something • *We must ensure that this never happens again.*
guarantee • *Further investment should guarantee that profits will rise.*
make certain • *to make certain that he'll get there*
make sure • *I will personally make sure that the job gets done.*

enterprise ① NOUN
a business or company • *a small enterprise with a high turnover*
business • *a medium-sized business*
company • *a company that was doing very well*
concern • *It's not a large concern, but it makes a profit.*
establishment • *a modest establishment dedicated to sailing*
firm • *a clothing firm*
operation • *a one-man operation*

enterprise ② NOUN
a project or task • *a risky enterprise such as horse breeding*
effort • *her latest fund-raising effort for cancer research*
endeavour • *an endeavour that was bound to end in failure*
operation • *He'd set up a small mining operation.*
project • *a project that will attract a lot of media attention*
undertaking • *This undertaking will rely on the hard work of our volunteers.*
venture • *a venture that few were willing to invest in*

entertain VERB
to keep people amused or interested • *things that might entertain children in the school holidays*

amuse • *He amused us all evening, singing and telling jokes.*
charm • *He charmed Mrs Nisbet with his tales of life on the road.*
delight • *a routine that will delight everyone*
enthral • *He enthralled audiences all over Europe.*
please • *He certainly knows how to please a crowd.*

entertainment NOUN
enjoyable activities • *Their main form of entertainment is the TV.*
amusement • *looking for some amusement on a Saturday night*
enjoyment • *We need a bit of enjoyment to cheer us up.*
fun • *It's not really my idea of family fun.*
pleasure • *Hours of pleasure can be had with a pack of cards.*
recreation • *a healthy and enjoyable form of recreation*

enthusiasm NOUN
eagerness and enjoyment in something • *We were disappointed by their lack of enthusiasm.*
eagerness • *He could barely contain his eagerness.*
excitement • *Her excitement got the better of her.*
interest • *He doesn't show much interest in football.*
keenness • *I don't doubt his keenness, it's his ability that worries me.*
warmth • *He greeted us with his usual warmth and affection.*

MORE SYNONYMS:
• ardour
• fervour
• relish
• zeal

enthusiastic ADJECTIVE
showing great excitement and

eagerness for something • *He was very enthusiastic about the new scheme.*

ardent • *one of the government's most ardent supporters*

avid • *an avid reader*

devoted • *a devoted Star Trek fan*

eager • *He is eager to learn more about computers.*

excited • *We are very excited about getting a new dog.*

keen • *Dave is a keen angler.*

passionate • *a passionate opponent of the government*

MORE SYNONYMS:
- fervent
- wholehearted
- zealous

ANTONYM:
- apathetic

entrance ① NOUN

the way into a particular place • *I met Barry at the entrance to the station.*

door • *She was waiting by the front door.*

doorway • *the mass of people blocking the doorway*

entry • *Kevin had been hanging round the back entry for hours.*

gate • *the security guard at the main gate*

way in • *Is this the way in?*

entrance ② NOUN

a person's arrival somewhere • *She had failed to notice her father's entrance.*

appearance • *She had timed her appearance at the dinner to perfection.*

arrival • *journalists awaiting the arrival of the team*

entry • *He was arrested on his entry into Mexico.*

entrance ③ NOUN

the right to enter somewhere • *He gained entrance to the hotel where the band were staying.*

access • *We were denied access to the stadium.*

admission • *no admission without a ticket*

entry • *I was unable to gain entry to the meeting.*

entrance ④ VERB

to amaze and delight someone • *The audience was entranced by her voice.*

bewitch • *Young Gordon's smile bewitched everyone.*

captivate • *I was captivated by her piercing blue eyes.*

charm • *He charmed Mr Darnley and made him feel young again.*

delight • *a CD that will delight her many fans*

enthral • *Audiences were enthralled by his spectacular stage act.*

fascinate • *She never failed to fascinate him.*

MORE SYNONYMS:
- enchant
- enrapture
- spellbind

entry ① NOUN

a person's arrival somewhere • *her dramatic entry*

appearance • *She made her appearance to tumultuous applause.*

arrival • *He apologized for his late arrival.*

entrance • *My entrance was spoiled when I tripped over the carpet.*

entry ② NOUN

the way into a particular place • *He was hanging around at the entry to the station.*

door • *I'll meet you at the front door.*

doorway • *A bicycle was blocking the doorway.*

entrance • *The bomb had been left outside the entrance to the building.*

gate · *Guards were posted at the main gate.*
way in · *I can't find the way in.*

entry ③ NOUN
something that has been written down · *the final entry in his journal*
item · *A number of interesting items appear in his diary.*
note · *He grunted and made a note in his pocket book.*
record · *There is no record for 13 October in the log book.*

envy ① NOUN
a feeling of resentment about what someone else has · *his feelings of envy towards Kevin*
jealousy · *the jealousy people felt towards him because of his money*
resentment · *All the anger, bitterness and resentment suddenly melted away.*

envy ② VERB
to want something that someone else has · *I don't envy you one bit.*
be envious · *people who were envious of her good fortune*
begrudge · *Surely you don't begrudge me one night out.*
be jealous · *I couldn't help being jealous when I knew he had won.*
covet · *She coveted his job.*
resent · *Anyone with money was resented and ignored.*

equal ① ADJECTIVE
the same in size, amount, or value · *equal numbers of men and women*
equivalent · *A kilogram is equivalent to 2.2 pounds.*
identical · *glasses containing identical amounts of water*
the same · *different areas of research that have the same importance*

equal ② : **equal to** ADJECTIVE
having the necessary ability for

something · *She was equal to any task they gave her.*
capable of · *I'm no longer capable of this kind of work.*
up to · *He said he wasn't up to a long walk.*

equal ③ VERB
to be as good as something else · *a time that equalled the European record*
be equal to · *The final score is equal to his personal best.*
match · *able to match her previous time for the 100m*

equip VERB
to supply someone with something · *The boat was equipped with an outboard motor.*
arm · *The children arrived armed with a range of gardening tools.*
endow · *The male bird is endowed with a vicious-looking eagle.*
fit out · *the amount spent on fitting out their offices*
provide · *We provided them with waterproofs and sandwiches.*
supply · *They supplied us with camping gear and a stove.*

equipment NOUN
the things you need for a particular job · *a shed full of gardening equipment*
apparatus · *All the firemen were wearing breathing apparatus.*
gear · *Police in riot gear have sealed off the area.*
paraphernalia · *ashtrays, lighters and other paraphernalia associated with smoking*
stuff · *The builders had left all their stuff in the garden.*
tackle · *Martin kept all his fishing tackle in the spare room.*

MORE SYNONYMS:
• accoutrements
• appurtenances

a
b
c
e
f
g
h
i
j
k
l
m
n
o
p
q
r
s
t
u
v
w
x
y
z

A
B
C
D
E
F
G
H
I
J
K
L
M
N
O
P
Q
R
S
T
U
V
W
X
Y
Z

e-reader or **eReader** NOUN
a portable device for reading books
• *an e-reader with a full colour display*
Kindle® • *reading a paper on Kindle®*
Reader® • *The book is available for your Reader®*

erode VERB
to wear something away and destroy it • *The cliffs were being eroded by the constant pounding of the sea.*
corrode • *buildings corroded by acid rain*
destroy • *ancient monuments destroyed by pollution*
deteriorate • *The tapestry had deteriorated badly where the roof was leaking.*
disintegrate • *Once they were exposed to light the documents rapidly disintegrated.*

err VERB
to make a mistake • *The builders had erred considerably in their original estimate.*
blunder • *Fletcher had obviously blundered.*
go wrong • *We must have gone wrong somewhere in our calculations.*
make a mistake • *Okay, I made a mistake, I'm only human.*
miscalculate • *They miscalculated, and now they're in deep trouble.*

error NOUN
a mistake • *a mathematical error*
blunder • *He made a tactical blunder by announcing his intentions.*
fault • *It is a fault to think you can learn how to manage people in business school.*
lapse • *a serious security lapse*
mistake • *spelling mistakes*
slip • *We must be careful - we can't afford any slips.*

escape ① VERB
to manage to get away • *Three prisoners who escaped have given themselves up.*
break free • *He was handcuffed to his bed, but somehow managed to break free.*
break out • *two prisoners who broke out of the maximum security wing*
get away • *She got away from her guards.*
make your escape • *We made our escape down a drainpipe using knotted sheets.*
run away • *I called him but he just ran away.*
run off • *The children ran off when they spotted me.*
MORE SYNONYMS:
• abscond
• bolt

escape ② VERB
to manage to avoid something • *He was lucky to escape injury.*
avoid • *She has managed to avoid arrest so far.*
dodge • *He dodged his military service by pretending to be ill.*
duck • *a pathetic attempt to duck her responsibilities*
elude • *He managed to elude the police for 13 years.*
evade • *He has now been charged with evading tax.*

escape ③ NOUN
something that distracts you from something unpleasant • *Cycling gives me an escape from the routine of work.*
distraction • *a distraction from his troubles*
diversion • *a pleasant diversion from my studies*
relief • *The piano provides relief from all the stress.*

essence ① NOUN
the most basic and important part
of something • *The essence of good
management is the ability to listen.*
core • *the need to get to the core of the
problem*
heart • *a problem that reaches to the
very heart of the party*
nature • *the nature of what it is to be
European*
soul • *a song that captures the soul of
this proud nation*
spirit • *the spirit of modern manhood*

MORE SYNONYMS:
• crux
• kernel
• quintessence
• substance

essence ② NOUN
a concentrated liquid • *vanilla essence*
concentrate • *orange concentrate*
extract • *lemon extract*

essential ① ADJECTIVE
extremely important • *Good
ventilation is essential in a greenhouse.*
crucial • *Her speech was a crucial part
of the campaign.*
indispensable • *She has become
indispensable to the department.*
vital • *a vital aspect of the plans that
everyone has overlooked*

essential ② ADJECTIVE
basic and important • *an essential
part of any child's development*
basic • *the basic laws of physics*
cardinal • *He had broken one of the
cardinal rules of business.*
fundamental • *the fundamental
principles of democracy*
key • *Mollison had a key role to play in
the negotiations.*
main • *an attempt to analyse the main
points of his theory*

principal • *the principal idea that
underpins their argument*

essentials PLURAL NOUN
the things that are most important
• *We only had enough money for the
essentials.*
basics • *We need to get back to basics.*
fundamentals • *the fundamentals of
road safety*
necessities • *Water, food, and shelter
are the necessities of life.*
prerequisites • *Self-confidence is one
of the prerequisites for a happy life.*
rudiments • *teaching him the
rudiments of car maintenance*

esteem NOUN
admiration and respect for another
person • *He is held in high esteem by his
colleagues.*
admiration • *I have always had the
greatest admiration for him.*
estimation • *He has gone down in my
estimation.*
regard • *I had a very high regard for him
and his work.*
respect • *I have tremendous respect
for Dean.*
reverence • *He is still spoken of with
reverence by those who knew him.*

MORE SYNONYMS:
• honour
• veneration (FORMAL)

estimate NOUN
a guess at an amount, quantity, or
outcome • *This figure is five times the
original estimate.*
appraisal • *an appraisal of your
financial standing*
assessment • *assessments of
mortgaged property*
estimation • *The first group were
correct in their estimation of the man's
height.*

a
b
c
d
e
f
g
h
i
j
k
l
m
n
o
p
q
r
s
t
u
v
w
x
y
z

guess • *He examined her and made a guess at her temperature.*
quote • *Never agree to a job without getting a quote first.*
reckoning • *By my reckoning we were seven kilometres from the town.*
valuation • *The valuations reflect prices at the end of the fiscal year.*

eternal ADJECTIVE
lasting forever • *the secret of eternal life*
everlasting • *everlasting love*
immortal • *your immortal soul*
unchanging • *the unchanging laws of the cosmos*

even ① ADJECTIVE
flat and level • *I need an even surface to write on.*
flat • *a small hut with a flat roof*
horizontal • *He drew a series of horizontal lines on the paper.*
level • *checking the floor to make sure it was level*
smooth • *the smooth marble floor tiles*
ANTONYM:
• uneven

even ② ADJECTIVE
without changing or varying • *an even flow of liquid*
constant • *The temperature remained more or less constant.*
regular • *her quiet, regular breathing*
smooth • *He caught the ball and passed it in one smooth motion.*
steady • *a steady stream of people*
uniform • *The prices rises are not uniform across the country.*

even ③ ADJECTIVE
the same • *At halftime the scores were still even.*
equal • *The two teams shared equal points into the second round.*
identical • *At the end of the contest, our scores were identical.*

level • *The scores were level at halftime.*
neck and neck • *They're still neck and neck with two minutes to go.*

event ① NOUN
something that happens • *still amazed at the events of last week*
affair • *He preferred to forget the whole affair.*
business • *Do you remember that business with Jim?*
circumstance • *due to circumstances beyond our control*
episode • *a rather embarrassing episode at Yvonne's wedding*
experience • *an experience that changed his mind about going to university*
incident • *the incident in the restaurant*
matter • *She doesn't seem to be taking this matter seriously.*

event ② NOUN
a competition • *The next event is the long jump.*
bout • *This is his fifth heavyweight bout in three months.*
competition • *the first competition of the afternoon*
contest • *She's out of the contest for good.*

everyday ADJECTIVE
usual or ordinary • *the drudgery of everyday life*
common • *a common occurrence*
daily • *In our daily life we follow predictable patterns of behaviour.*
day-to-day • *I use a lot of spices in my day-to-day cooking.*
mundane • *the mundane realities of life*
ordinary • *ordinary tableware*
routine • *routine maintenance of the machine*
MORE SYNONYMS:
• banal
• unexceptional

evident ADJECTIVE

easily noticed or understood • *He spoke with evident emotion about his ordeal.*

apparent • *He spoke with apparent nonchalance about his experience.*

clear • *It became clear that I hadn't convinced Mike.*

noticeable • *a noticeable effect*

obvious • *It's obvious that he doesn't like me.*

palpable • *The tension between Jim and Amy is palpable.*

plain • *It was plain to him that she was having a nervous breakdown.*

visible • *the most visible sign of her distress*

MORE SYNONYMS:
• conspicuous
• manifest
• patent

evil ① NOUN

the force that causes bad things to happen • *the conflict between good and evil*

badness • *behaving that way out of sheer badness*

immorality • *the immorality that is typical of the arms trade*

sin • *The whole town is a den of sin and corruption.*

vice • *a place long associated with vice and immorality*

wickedness • *the wickedness of his behaviour*

MORE SYNONYMS:
• baseness
• depravity
• sinfulness

ANTONYM:
• good

evil ② NOUN

something unpleasant or harmful • *a lecture on the evils of alcohol*

affliction • *Hay fever is an affliction that affects thousands.*

ill • *Many of the nation's ills are his responsibility.*

misery • *the misery of drug addiction*

sorrow • *the joys and sorrows of family life*

evil ③ ADJECTIVE

morally wrong or bad • *an utterly evil man*

bad • *He's not a bad man, he's just very unhappy.*

depraved • *a throughly depraved film*

malevolent • *a malevolent influence on the whole school*

sinful • *He is a good person in a sinful world.*

vile • *vile acts of brutality*

wicked • *a wicked attack on a helpless child*

ANTONYM:
• good

exact ① ADJECTIVE

correct in every detail • *It's an exact reproduction of the first steam engine.*

accurate • *an accurate description of the man*

authentic • *authentic Elizabethan costumes*

faithful • *faithful copies of ancient stone tools*

faultless • *She spoke with a faultless French accent.*

precise • *It's difficult to give a precise date for the painting.*

true • *Is this a true picture of life in the Middle Ages?*

ANTONYM:
• approximate

exact ② VERB (FORMAL)

to demand and obtain something • *They are certain to exact a high price for their cooperation.*

a
b
c
d
e
f
g
h
i
j
k
l
m
n
o
p
q
r
s
t
u
v
w
x
y
z

A
B
C
D
E
F
G
H
I
J
K
L
M
N
O
P
Q
R
S
T
U
V
W
X
Y
Z

command • *an excellent surgeon who commanded the respect of all his colleagues*
extract • *to extract the maximum political advantage from this situation*
impose • *the first council to impose a fine for dropping litter*
insist on • *She insisted on conducting all the interviews herself.*
insist upon • *He insists upon good service.*
wring • *attempts to wring concessions from the government*

exactly ① ADVERB

with complete accuracy and precision • *He arrived at exactly five o'clock.*
accurately • *We cannot accurately predict where the missile will land.*
faithfully • *I translated the play as faithfully as I could.*
just • *There are no statistics about just how many people won't vote.*
on the dot • *At nine o'clock on the dot, they have breakfast.*
precisely • *No-one knows precisely how many people are in the camp.*
quite • *That wasn't quite what I meant.*

ANTONYM:
• approximately

exactly ② INTERJECTION

an expression implying total agreement • *"We'll never know the answer." – "Exactly. So let's stop speculating."*
absolutely • *"It's worrying, isn't it?" – "Absolutely."*
indeed • *"That's a topic that's getting a lot of media coverage." – "Indeed."*
precisely • *"So, you're suggesting we do away with these laws?" – "Precisely."*
quite • *"It's your choice, isn't it?" – "Quite."*

exaggerate VERB

to make things seem worse than they are • *He thinks I'm exaggerating, but I'm not!*
overdo • *I think he's overdoing it a bit when he complains like that.*
overestimate • *I think we're overestimating their desire to cooperate.*
overstate • *It's impossible to overstate the seriousness of this situation.*

exam NOUN

a test to find out how much you know • *a maths exam*
examination • *a three-hour written examination*
oral • *I got good marks for my French oral.*
test • *I failed my history test again.*

examination ① NOUN

a careful inspection of something • *The Navy is carrying out an examination of the wreck.*
analysis • *An analysis of the ash revealed traces of lead oxide.*
inspection • *The police inspection of the vehicle found no fingerprints.*
study • *A study of the wreckage has thrown new light on the crash.*

examination ② NOUN

a check carried out on someone by a doctor • *The doctor suggested an immediate examination of his ear.*
check • *a quick check just to make sure everything's working properly*
checkup • *my annual checkup at the clinic*
medical • *He had a medical before leaving England.*

examine ① VERB

to look at something very carefully • *Police scientists are examining the scene of the crash.*
analyse • *We haven't had time to analyse all the samples yet.*

go over • *I'll go over your report tomorrow.*
go through • *We went through his belongings and found a notebook.*
inspect • *Customs officials inspected the vehicle.*
look over • *Once we've looked the house over we should know what caused the fire.*
study • *Experts are studying the frozen remains of a mammoth.*

MORE SYNONYMS:
• peruse
• scrutinize

examine ② NOUN
to give someone a medical examination • *I was examined by several specialists.*
check • *Dr Mollison checked my nose and throat.*
inspect • *I was inspected twice by Dr Stevens.*
look at • *He said he wanted to look at my chest again just to make sure.*
test • *They tested my eyes but my vision was fine.*

example ① NOUN
something that represents a group of things • *some examples of medieval wood carving*
illustration • *Lo's success is an illustration of how well China is doing.*
sample • *This drawing is a sample of his early work.*
specimen • *I had to submit a specimen of my handwriting for analysis.*

example ② NOUN
something that people can imitate • *His dedication is an example to us all.*
ideal • *a woman who was the American ideal of beauty*
model • *His conduct at the talks was a model of dignity.*

paragon • *She is a paragon of neatness and efficiency.*
prototype • *He was the prototype of the English gentleman.*

MORE SYNONYMS:
• archetype
• exemplar
• paradigm

excellent ADJECTIVE
extremely good • *It's an excellent book, one of my favourites.*
beaut (AUSTRALIAN AND NEW ZEALAND; INFORMAL) • *a beaut spot to live*
brilliant • *What a brilliant film!*
cracking (BRITISH, AUSTRALIAN AND NEW ZEALAND; INFORMAL) • *You've done a cracking job in the garden!*
fine • *There's a fine view from the bedroom window.*
first-class • *a first-class effort*
great • *He's a great player and we'll be sorry to lose him.*
outstanding • *an outstanding performance*
superb • *a superb craftsman*

ANTONYM:
• terrible

except PREPOSITION
apart from • *I don't drink, except for the occasional glass of wine.*
apart from • *The room was empty apart from one man seated by the fire.*
but • *He didn't speak anything but Greek.*
other than • *She makes no reference to any research other than her own.*
save (FORMAL) • *We had almost nothing to eat, save the few berries and nuts we could find.*
with the exception of • *Yesterday was a day off for everybody, with the exception of Tom.*

A
B
C
D
E
F
G
H
I
J
K
L
M
N
O
P
Q
R
S
T
U
V
W
X
Y
Z

exceptional ① ADJECTIVE
unusually excellent, talented, or clever • *His piano playing is exceptional.*
excellent • *The recording quality is excellent.*
extraordinary • *He is an extraordinary musician.*
outstanding • *an outstanding athlete*
phenomenal • *The performances have been absolutely phenomenal.*
remarkable • *a remarkable achievement*
talented • *He is a talented violinist.*

ANOTHER SYNONYM:
• extraordinary

ANTONYM:
• mediocre

exceptional ② ADJECTIVE
unusual and likely to happen very rarely • *The courts hold that this case is exceptional.*
isolated • *They said the allegations related to an isolated case.*
out of the ordinary • *I've noticed nothing out of the ordinary.*
rare • *those rare occasions when he did eat alone*
special • *In special cases, an exception to this rule may be made.*
unheard-of • *buying rum at the unheard-of rate of $2 per bottle*
unusual • *To be appreciated as a parent is unusual.*

ANOTHER SYNONYM:
• unprecedented (FORMAL)

ANTONYM:
• common

excess ① NOUN
behaviour that goes beyond what is acceptable • *a life of excess*
extravagance • *Examples of her extravagance were everywhere.*
indulgence • *a moment of sheer indulgence*

MORE SYNONYMS:
• debauchery
• dissipation
• intemperance
• overindulgence

excess ② NOUN
a larger amount than necessary • *An excess of houseplants made the room look like a jungle.*
glut • *the current glut of dairy products in Europe*
overdose • *An overdose of sun can lead to skin problems later.*
surfeit • *A surfeit of rich food did not help his digestive problems.*
surplus • *Germany suffers from a surplus of teachers at the moment.*

MORE SYNONYMS:
• overabundance
• plethora
• superabundance
• superfluity

ANTONYM:
• shortage

excess ③ ADJECTIVE
more than is needed • *problems associated with excess weight*
extra • *Pour any extra liquid into a bowl and set aside.*
superfluous • *all our superfluous belongings, things we don't need*
surplus • *Farmers have to sell off their surplus stock cheap.*

excessive ADJECTIVE
too great • *an excessive reliance on government funding*
enormous • *She spent an enormous amount on clothes.*
exaggerated • *the exaggerated claims made by their supporters*
needless • *a film that is full of needless violence*
undue • *the need to avoid undue expense*

unreasonable • *unreasonable increases in the price of petrol*

MORE SYNONYMS:
• disproportionate
• exorbitant
• immoderate
• inordinate
• profligate

exchange ① VERB
to give something in return for something else • *We exchanged phone numbers.*
barter • *Traders came from everywhere to barter in the markets.*
change • *Can you change pesetas for pounds?*
swap • *I wouldn't swap places with her for anything!*
switch • *They switched cars and were away before the alarm was raised.*
trade • *a secret deal to trade arms for hostages*

exchange ② NOUN
the act of giving something for something else • *a ceasefire to allow the exchange of prisoners*
interchange • *a meeting at which the interchange of ideas was encouraged*
swap • *They agreed to a swap and made the necessary arrangements.*
switch • *The switch went ahead as planned.*
trade • *I am willing to make a trade with you.*

excite ① VERB
to make someone feel enthusiastic or nervous • *The idea of visiting America really excited the kids.*
agitate • *I've no idea what has agitated him.*
animate • *There was plenty about this match to animate the capacity crowd.*

thrill • *The reception he got at the meeting thrilled him.*
titillate • *a meal that will titillate the taste buds of every gourmet*

excite ② VERB
to cause a particular feeling or reaction • *The meeting failed to excite strong feelings in anyone.*
arouse • *a move that has aroused deep public anger*
elicit • *His proposal elicited a storm of protest.*
evoke • *The film has evoked a sense of nostalgia in many older people.*
incite • *a crude attempt to incite racial hatred*
inspire • *The handling of the new car quickly inspires confidence.*
provoke • *The suggestion has provoked anger.*
stir up • *He's just trying to stir up trouble.*

MORE SYNONYMS:
• fire
• foment
• inflame
• kindle
• rouse

excited ADJECTIVE
happy and unable to relax • *We are very excited about getting a new dog.*
agitated • *in an excited and agitated state*
enthusiastic • *Tom usually seems very enthusiastic.*
feverish • *a state of feverish anticipation*
high (INFORMAL) • *I was feeling really high after Lorraine's party.*
thrilled • *The children were thrilled when the snow came.*

ANTONYM:
• bored

A
B
C
D
E
F
G
H
I
J
K
L
M
N
O
P
Q
R
S
T
U
V
W
X
Y
Z

excitement NOUN

interest and enthusiasm • *The release of his latest film has caused great excitement.*

activity • *a scene of frenzied activity*

adventure • *setting off in search of adventure*

agitation • *He reacted to the news with considerable agitation.*

commotion • *We decided to find out what all the commotion was about.*

enthusiasm • *They greeted our arrival with enthusiasm.*

thrill • *the thrill of scuba diving*

MORE SYNONYMS:
• animation
• elation
• furore
• tumult

exciting ADJECTIVE

making you feel happy and enthusiastic • *the most exciting race I've ever seen*

dramatic • *Their arrival was dramatic and exciting.*

electrifying • *It was an electrifying performance.*

exhilarating • *an exhilarating walk along the cliff tops*

rousing • *a rousing speech*

stimulating • *It's a stimulating book, full of ideas.*

thrilling • *a thrilling opportunity to watch the lions as they feed*

MORE SYNONYMS:
• intoxicating
• sensational
• stirring

ANTONYM:
• boring

exclude ① VERB

to decide not to include something

• *We cannot exclude this possibility altogether.*

eliminate • *We can eliminate Mr Darnley from our list of suspects.*

ignore • *We cannot afford to ignore this option.*

leave out • *We can narrow it down by leaving out everywhere that's too expensive.*

omit • *His name seems to have been omitted from the list.*

rule out • *The police have already ruled out a retrial.*

ANTONYM:
• include

exclude ② VERB

to stop someone going somewhere or doing something • *The university used to exclude women from all lectures.*

ban • *Tony was banned from driving for three years.*

bar • *She was barred from the tennis club.*

forbid • *Carver was forbidden to attend any of the society's meetings.*

keep out • *We need to keep out troublemakers.*

MORE SYNONYMS:
• blackball
• debar

exclusive ADJECTIVE

available only to a few rich people • *one of Britain's most exclusive golf clubs*

chic • *a chic nightclub in Monaco*

classy • *a very classy restaurant*

posh (INFORMAL) • *She took me to a posh hotel to celebrate.*

select • *a very lavish and very select party*

up-market • *The area is much more up-market than it used to be.*

excuse ① NOUN

a reason or explanation • *Stop making excuses and get on with it!*

explanation • *You'd better have a good explanation for your conduct.*
justification • *What possible justification can there be for this?*
pretext • *His pretext for leaving early was an upset stomach.*
reason • *This gave me the perfect reason for visiting London.*

excuse ② VERB
to forgive someone or someone's behaviour • *Please excuse my late arrival.*
forgive • *Forgive me, I'm so sorry.*
overlook • *the need to overlook each other's failings*
pardon • *Pardon my ignorance, but who is Cliff Hanley?*
turn a blind eye to • *We can't be expected to turn a blind eye to this behaviour.*

exempt ADJECTIVE
excused from a duty or rule • *Teachers were exempt from military service.*
excused • *Some MPs will have been officially excused attendance.*
immune • *Members of the parliament are immune from prosecution.*
not liable • *They are not liable to pay income tax.*

exercise NOUN
activity that keeps you fit • *I need to get more exercise.*
activity • *a bit of physical activity to get the heart going*
exertion • *I'm tired out by all this exertion.*
training • *He needs to do a bit more training before the match.*
work • *I'm doing a lot more work at the gym now I'm feeling better.*

exhaust ① VERB
to make very tired • *I mustn't exhaust myself as I did last time.*

drain • *My emotional turmoil had drained me.*
fatigue • *He is easily fatigued.*
tire out • *a great new job that tires me out*
wear out • *Living out of a suitcase wears you out.*

exhaust ② VERB
to use something up completely • *She has exhausted all my patience.*
consume • *plans which will consume hours of time*
deplete • *chemicals that deplete the earth's protective ozone shield*
run through • *The project ran through its funds in months.*
use up • *The gas has all been used up.*

expand VERB
to make or become larger • *The rails expanded and buckled in the fierce heat.*
develop • *We need to develop the company's engineering division.*
enlarge • *Plans to enlarge the stadium have been approved.*
extend • *We're trying to extend our range of sports wear.*
fill out • *The balloon had filled out and was already almost airborne.*
grow • *The Japanese share of the market has grown dramatically.*
increase • *We will need to increase our overseas operations.*
swell • *The river had swollen rapidly.*
ANTONYM:
• decrease

expand on VERB
to give more information about something • *an idea that I will expand on later*
develop • *You should develop this theme a little bit further.*
elaborate on • *He refused to elaborate on what he had said earlier.*

A
B
C
D
E
F
G
H
I
J
K
L
M
N
O
P
Q
R
S
T
U
V
W
X
Y
Z

enlarge on • *I'd like you to enlarge on that last point.*

expect ① VERB
to believe that something is going to happen • *The trial is expected to last several weeks.*
anticipate • *We do not anticipate any problems.*
assume • *He assumed that they would wait for him.*
believe • *Experts believe the comet will pass close to the earth.*
imagine • *The meal cost more than we had imagined.*
presume • *I presume they'll be along shortly.*
reckon • *We reckon it'll be a fairly quick journey.*
think • *I thought the concert would be cancelled.*
MORE SYNONYMS:
• envisage
• forecast
• foresee
• predict

expect ② VERB
to believe that something is your right • *I was expecting to have a bit of time to myself.*
demand • *a job that demands a lot of time and money*
rely on • *I'm relying on you to help me.*
require • *They require a lot of her, may be too much.*

expensive ADJECTIVE
costing a lot of money • *a very expensive Italian suit*
costly • *a costly court case*
dear • *Those trainers are far too dear.*
pricey • *Medical insurance can be very pricey.*
MORE SYNONYMS:
• exorbitant
• overpriced

ANTONYM:
• cheap

experience ① NOUN
knowledge or skill in a particular activity • *We're looking for someone with engineering experience.*
expertise • *They lack the expertise to deal with such a complex case.*
know-how • *Her technical know-how was invaluable.*
knowledge • *We need someone with knowledge of computing.*
training • *His military training made the difference between life and death.*
understanding • *someone with considerable understanding of the law*

experience ② NOUN
something that happens to you • *a terrifying experience that she still talks about*
adventure • *a series of hair-raising adventures during the war*
affair • *He seemed keen to forget the affair and never discussed it.*
encounter • *his first encounter with alcohol*
episode • *The episode has proved deeply embarrassing for her.*
incident • *an incident he would rather forget*
ordeal • *a painful ordeal that is now over*

experience ③ VERB
to have something happen to you • *We are experiencing a few technical problems.*
encounter • *The storms were the worst they had ever encountered.*
have • *We're having a few difficulties with the computer.*
meet • *The next time you meet a situation like this, be careful.*
undergo • *The market is now undergoing a severe recession.*

experienced ADJECTIVE
very skilful as a result of practice • *an experienced diver*
expert • *an expert pilot*
knowledgeable • *He's very knowledgeable in this field.*
practised • *a practised and accomplished surgeon*
seasoned • *a seasoned climber*
well-versed • *He is well-versed in many styles of jazz.*

ANTONYM:
• inexperienced

expert ① NOUN
a skilled or knowledgeable person • *A team of experts will be on hand to offer advice.*
ace (INFORMAL) • *former motor-racing ace Stirling Moss*
authority • *an authority on ancient Egypt*
buff (INFORMAL) • *Cliff is a bit of a film buff.*
geek • *a new site designed by dog-loving computer geeks*
guru • *fashion gurus who predicted a 70's revival*
master • *He is a master in the art of office politics.*
professional • *He's widely respected in the theatre as a true professional.*
specialist • *a specialist in tropical diseases*
wizard • *a financial wizard who made millions in the early 80's*

ANTONYM:
• beginner

expert ② ADJECTIVE
skilled and knowledgeable • *Mollison's expert approach impressed everyone.*
able • *an able and dedicated surgeon*
adept • *He's an adept guitar player.*
experienced • *He was an experienced traveller and knew the area well.*

knowledgeable • *He's very knowledgeable about Chinese pottery.*
proficient • *Jackson is proficient in several European languages.*
skilful • *the skilful use of light in his early paintings*
skilled • *Ian is a highly skilled photographer.*

MORE SYNONYMS:
• adroit
• dexterous
• masterly
• practised

explain VERB
to give extra information about something • *He explained to us how the system worked.*
define • *Can you define what you mean by 'excessive'?*
describe • *an attempt to describe the whole process*
illustrate • *Let me illustrate this point with an example.*

MORE SYNONYMS:
• elucidate
• expound

explanation NOUN
a helpful or clear description • *his lucid explanation of Einstein's theories*
clarification • *Her clarification has done little to help matters.*
definition • *a definition of what we actually mean by 'symbolism'*
description • *a fascinating description of how the pyramids were built*
exposition • *the fullest available exposition of Coleridge's ideas*

explode ① VERB
to burst or cause to burst loudly • *the sound of a bomb exploding nearby*
blow up • *Their boat blew up as they slept.*
burst • *Joey blew up the balloon until it burst.*

a
b
c
d
e
f
g
h
i
j
k
l
m
n
o
p
q
r
s
t
u
v
w
x
y
z

detonate • *Troops managed to detonate the mine safely.*

go off • *The bomb went off without any warning.*

set off • *No-one knows who planted the bomb, or how it was set off.*

explode ② VERB

to become angry suddenly • *I asked him if he'd finished and he just exploded.*

blow up • *When she finally told him, he blew up and walked out.*

go berserk • *He'll go berserk if he ever finds out.*

go mad • *He went mad when I mentioned the kids.*

explode ③ VERB

to increase suddenly and rapidly • *Sales of computer games have exploded in recent years.*

rocket • *Inflation has rocketed in the last few months.*

shoot up • *Prices shot up and the shelves were soon empty.*

soar • *Demand for shares in his new company has soared.*

explosion NOUN

a violent burst of energy • *The explosion shattered windows all along the street.*

bang • *A loud bang made me run for cover.*

blast • *Three people were killed in the blast.*

expose ① VERB

to make something visible • *The wreck was exposed by the action of the tide.*

reveal • *His shirt was open, revealing his tattooed chest.*

show • *a short skirt which showed too much of her legs*

uncover • *She removed her scarf and uncovered her head.*

expose ② VERB

to tell the truth about someone or

something • *He has been exposed as a liar and a cheat.*

bring to light • *The truth will be brought to light eventually.*

reveal • *an investigation that revealed widespread corruption*

show up • *She was finally shown up as a hypocrite.*

uncover • *We uncovered evidence of fraud.*

unearth • *Investigators have unearthed new evidence.*

express ① VERB

to say what you think • *She expressed interest in the plans for the new dam.*

communicate • *People must learn to communicate their feelings.*

couch • *Their demands, though extreme, are couched in moderate language.*

phrase • *It sounds fine, but I would have phrased it differently.*

put • *Absolutely - I couldn't have put it better.*

put across • *the need to put across your message without offending anyone*

voice • *Local people have voiced their concern over plans for a bypass.*

MORE SYNONYMS:
• articulate
• enunciate
• utter
• verbalize

express ② ADJECTIVE

very fast • *a special express delivery service*

direct • *There's also a direct train.*

fast • *delays due to an accident in the fast lane*

high-speed • *the high-speed rail link between London and Paris*

nonstop • *the new nonstop service to New York*

expression ① NOUN
the look on your face that shows
your feelings • *an aggrieved expression*
countenance • *the beaming
countenance of the prime minister*
face • *Why are you all wearing such long
faces?*

MORE SYNONYMS:
• aspect
• mien

expression ② NOUN
a word or phrase used to
communicate • *a good old American
expression*
idiom • *talking in the idiom of the Home
Counties*
phrase • *What is the origin of the phrase?*
remark • *her passing remark to the
camera*
term • *a derogatory term for an Arab*

extend ① VERB
to have a particular size or position
• *The region will extend way beyond the
capital.*
continue • *The caves continue for miles
beneath the hills.*
hang • *The branches hang down to the
ground.*
reach • *a long shirt that reached to her
knees*
stretch • *an area of forest stretching
as far as the eye could see*

extend ② VERB
to stick out • *a brass peg that extended
from the end of the mast*
jut out • *The tip of the island juts out like
a finger into the sea.*
project • *the ruins of a fort which
projected from the mud*
protrude (FORMAL) • *a huge rock
protruding from the surface of the lake*
stick out • *pieces of rough metal that
stuck out like spikes*

extend ③ VERB
to make something larger • *We'd
like to extend the house and build a
conservatory.*
add to • *They will be adding to their
range of children's wear.*
develop • *He developed the US arm of
the company.*
enlarge • *plans to enlarge the conference
centre*
expand • *an unsuccessful attempt to
expand the store's range of footwear*
widen • *the need to widen the appeal of
the scheme*

MORE SYNONYMS:
• augment
• broaden
• supplement

extensive ① ADJECTIVE
covering a large area • *a manor house
set in extensive grounds*
broad • *a broad expanse of green lawn*
expansive • *an expansive grassy play
area*
large • *a large country estate*
spacious • *a spacious dining area*
sweeping • *the sweeping curve of the bay*
vast • *vast stretches of land*
wide • *Worktops should be wide enough
to allow food preparation.*

extensive ② ADJECTIVE
very great in effect • *The blast caused
extensive damage.*
comprehensive • *comprehensive
television coverage of last week's events*
considerable • *He has considerable
powers within the party.*
far-reaching • *a decision with far-
reaching consequences*
great • *great changes in British society*
pervasive • *the pervasive influence of
the army in national life*
untold • *This might do untold damage
to her health.*

A
B
C
D
E
F
G
H
I
J
K
L
M
N
O
P
Q
R
S
T
U
V
W
X
Y
Z

widespread • *There is widespread support for the proposals.*

extent NOUN
the length, area, or size of something • *The full extent of the losses was revealed yesterday.*
degree • *To what degree were you in control of these events?*
level • *the level of public concern over this issue*
measure • *The full measure of the government's dilemma has become apparent.*
scale • *He underestimates the scale of the problem.*
size • *the size of the task*

MORE SYNONYMS:
• expanse
• magnitude

extra ① ADJECTIVE
more than is usual or expected • *The company is taking on extra staff for the summer.*
added • *The Tandoori Cottage has the added advantage of being cheap.*
additional • *the need for additional funding*
excess • *If there's any excess sauce, you can freeze it.*
further • *the introduction of further restrictions*
more • *We need three more places at the table.*
new • *the burden of new legislation on top of all the recent changes*
spare • *There are spare blankets in the cupboard.*

MORE SYNONYMS:
• ancillary
• auxiliary
• supplementary

extra ② NOUN
something that is not included with

other things • *Air conditioning is an optional extra.*
accessory • *the accessories you have to buy to make the place look good*
addition • *the latest addition to the team*
bonus • *The view from the hotel was an added bonus.*

extract ① VERB
to take or get something out of somewhere • *Citric acid can be extracted from orange juice.*
draw • *Villagers still have to draw their water from wells.*
mine • *the finest gems, mined from all corners of the world*
obtain • *Opium is obtained from poppies.*
pull out • *I can pull that information out of the database for you.*
remove • *Three bullets were removed from his wounds.*
take out • *I got an abscess so he took the tooth out.*

extract ② VERB
to get information from someone • *He tried to extract further information from the witness.*
draw • *They finally drew a confession from him.*
elicit (FORMAL) • *the question of how far police should go to elicit a confession*
get • *How did you get an admission like that out of her?*
glean • *We're gleaning information from all sources.*
obtain • *Police have obtained statements from several witnesses.*

extract ③ NOUN
a small section of music or writing • *an extract from his latest novel*
excerpt • *an excerpt from Tchaikovsky's Nutcracker*
passage • *He read out a passage from Milton.*

reading · *The author treated us to a reading from his latest novel.*

section · *Let's study a section of the text in more detail.*

snatch · *We played them a snatch of a violin concerto.*

snippet · *snippets of popular classical music*

extraordinary ADJECTIVE

unusual or surprising · *He really is an extraordinary man.*

amazing · *What an amazing coincidence!*

bizarre · *It's such a bizarre thing to happen.*

odd · *It's an odd combination of colours.*

singular · *Cathy gave me a smile of singular sweetness.*

strange · *It's a strange piece of music.*

surprising · *A surprising number of women prefer to wear trousers to work.*

unusual · *It's a most unusual way to spend your holiday.*

ANTONYM:
• ordinary

extreme ① ADJECTIVE

very great in degree or intensity
· *those people living in extreme poverty*

acute · *a mistake that caused acute embarrassment for everyone concerned*

deep · *a decision that caused deep resentment*

dire · *He is in dire need of hospital treatment.*

great · *a change in the law that could cause many people great hardship*

intense · *A number of people collapsed in the intense heat that day.*

profound · *feelings of profound shock and anger*

severe · *a business with severe financial problems*

extreme ② ADJECTIVE

unusual or unreasonable · *I think that's rather an extreme reaction.*

drastic · *Let's not do anything too drastic.*

exceptional · *I think this is an exceptional case.*

excessive · *a newspaper feature about the use of excessive force by the police*

extravagant · *All that money being spent on hospitality seemed a bit extravagant.*

radical · *The government is introducing a series of radical economic reforms.*

unreasonable · *I don't think she's being the least bit unreasonable.*

extreme ③ NOUN

the highest or furthest degree or point · *We're just going from one extreme to the other.*

boundary · *the boundaries of artistic freedom*

depth · *the beauty of the countryside in the depths of winter*

end · *There are extremist groups at both ends of the political spectrum.*

height · *His behaviour was the height of bad manners.*

limit · *The ordeal tested the limits of their endurance.*

ultimate · *A Rolls-Royce is the ultimate in luxury.*

MORE SYNONYMS:
• acme
• apex
• nadir
• pinnacle
• zenith

a
b
c
d
e
f
g
h
i
j
k
l
m
n
o
p
q
r
s
t
u
v
w
x
y
z

Ff

face ① NOUN
the front part of the head • *A strong wind was blowing in my face.*
countenance • *He met each enquiry with an impassive countenance.*
features • *Her features were strongly defined.*
mug (SLANG) • *He managed to get his ugly mug on the telly.*

MORE SYNONYMS:
• lineaments
• physiognomy

face ② NOUN
a surface or side of something • *the north face of Everest*
aspect • *The house had a south-west aspect.*
exterior • *The exterior of the building was made of brick.*
front • *There was a large veranda at the front of the house.*
side • *narrow valleys with steep sides*
surface • *tiny waves on the surface of the water*

face ③ VERB
to look towards something or someone • *a room that faces on to the street*
be opposite • *I was opposite her at the breakfast table.*
look at • *She turned to look at the person who was speaking.*
overlook • *The pretty room overlooks a beautiful garden.*

fact NOUN
a piece of information that is true • *a statement of verifiable fact*
certainty • *A general election became a certainty three weeks ago.*
reality • *Fiction and reality became increasingly blurred.*
truth • *In the town, very few know the whole truth.*

ANTONYM:
• lie

factor NOUN
something that helps to cause a result • *Physical activity is an important factor in maintaining fitness.*
aspect • *Exam results illustrate only one aspect of a school's success.*
cause • *Smoking is the biggest preventable cause of death and disease.*
consideration • *Money was also a consideration.*
element • *Fitness has now become an important element in our lives.*
influence • *Van Gogh was a major influence on the development of modern painting.*
part • *Respect is a very important part of any relationship.*

MORE SYNONYMS:
• circumstance
• determinant

factory NOUN
a building where goods are made • *He owned furniture factories in several areas.*

mill • *a textile mill*
plant • *The plant produces most of the company's output.*
works • *the steel works*

fade
to make or become less intense
• *The fabric had faded in the bright sunlight.*
die away • *The sound died away gradually.*
dim • *The house lights dimmed.*
discolour • *Exposure to bright light can cause wallpaper to discolour.*
dull • *Repeated washing had dulled the bright finish.*
wash out • *This dye won't wash out.*

fail ① VERB
to be unsuccessful • *He failed in his attempt to take over the company.*
be defeated • *The vote to change the law was defeated.*
be in vain • *It became clear that his efforts had been in vain.*
be unsuccessful • *My job application was unsuccessful.*
come to grief • *Many marriages have come to grief over lack of money.*
fall through • *Negotiations with business leaders fell through last night.*
flunk (INFORMAL) • *He flunked all his exams.*

ANTONYM:
• succeed

fail ② VERB
to omit to do something • *They failed to phone her.*
neglect • *They never neglect their duties.*
omit • *He had omitted to tell her of the change in his plans.*

fail ③ VERB
to become less effective • *His eyesight began to fail.*

cease • *The secrecy about his condition had ceased to matter.*
crash • *My computer's screen keeps crashing.*
decline • *His power declined as he grew older.*
give out • *All machines give out eventually.*
sink • *Her spirits sank lower and lower.*
stop working • *The boat came to a halt when the engine stopped working.*

failure ① NOUN
a lack of success • *to end in failure*
breakdown • *a breakdown of the talks between the parties*
defeat • *It is important not to admit defeat.*
downfall • *people wishing to see the downfall of the government*
fiasco • *The evening was a total fiasco.*
miscarriage • *a miscarriage of justice*

ANTONYM:
• success

failure ② NOUN
an unsuccessful person or thing • *The venture was a complete failure.*
disappointment • *a disappointment to his family*
flop (INFORMAL) • *The play turned out to be a flop.*
loser • *He had always been a loser.*
no-hoper (AUSTRALIAN AND NEW ZEALAND) • *hanging around a group of no-hopers*

MORE SYNONYMS:
• incompetent
• ne'er-do-well

failure ③ NOUN
a weakness in something • *a failure in the insurance system*
deficiency • *a serious deficiency in their defence system*

shortcoming • *The book has many shortcomings.*

faint ① ADJECTIVE
lacking in intensity • *a faint smell of tobacco*
dim • *dim lighting*
faded • *a faded sign on the side of the building*
indistinct • *The lettering was worn and indistinct.*
low • *She spoke in a low voice.*
muted • *some muted cheers from the gallery*
vague • *a vague memory*

ANTONYM:
• strong

faint ② ADJECTIVE
feeling dizzy and unsteady • *Feeling faint is one of the symptoms.*
dizzy • *suffering from dizzy spells*
giddy • *He felt giddy after the ride.*
light-headed • *She felt light-headed because she hadn't eaten.*

MORE SYNONYMS:
• enervated
• vertiginous

faint ③ VERB
to lose consciousness temporarily • *to faint from shock*
black out • *The blood drained from his head and he blacked out.*
collapse • *I collapsed when I heard the news.*
pass out • *to pass out with pain*
swoon (LITERARY) • *Women in the '20s swooned over Valentino.*

fair ① ADJECTIVE
reasonable and just • *a fair trial*
equal • *the commitment to equal opportunities*
equitable • *an equitable allocation of resources*
impartial • *an impartial observer*

legitimate • *a legitimate claim to the money*
proper • *It's right and proper that he should be here.*
upright • *an upright and trustworthy man*

MORE SYNONYMS:
• disinterested
• dispassionate
• unbiased

ANTONYM:
• unfair

fair ② ADJECTIVE
having light-coloured hair or pale skin • *long fair hair*
blonde *or* **blond** • *she had blonde tresses*
light • *He had a light complexion and blue eyes.*

ANTONYM:
• dark

fair ③ NOUN
an outdoor entertainment • *a country fair*
bazaar • *a fundraising bazaar*
carnival • *the annual Antigua Carnival*
exhibition • *an international trade exhibition*
festival • *a rock festival*
fete • *The church fete was a popular attraction.*
show • *an agricultural show*

faith ① NOUN
trust in a thing or a person • *to have great faith in something*
confidence • *They had no confidence in the police.*
trust • *His trust in them was misplaced.*

faith ② NOUN
a person's or community's religion • *They believed in the old faith.*
belief • *united by belief*
creed • *open to all, regardless of creed*

persuasion • *people of all religious persuasions*
religion • *the Christian religion*

faithful ① ADJECTIVE
loyal to someone or something • *a faithful dog*
devoted • *They are devoted to each other.*
loyal • *a sign of true and loyal friendship*
staunch • *a staunch member of the party*
true • *a true believer*

MORE SYNONYMS:
• steadfast
• unwavering

ANTONYM:
• unfaithful

faithful ② ADJECTIVE
accurate and truthful • *The film was faithful to the novel.*
accurate • *an accurate description of the event*
exact • *an exact copy of the original*
strict • *We demand strict adherence to the rules.*
true • *The film was quite true to life.*

fake ① NOUN
a deceitful imitation of a thing or person • *These paintings are fakes.*
copy • *It wasn't real, just a copy.*
forgery • *The signature was a forgery.*
fraud • *Many psychics are frauds.*
imitation • *The "antique" chair is in fact a clever imitation.*
reproduction • *a reproduction of a famous painting*
sham • *The election was denounced as a sham.*

fake ② ADJECTIVE
imitation and not genuine • *fake fur*
artificial • *It's made with artificial sweeteners.*
counterfeit • *a large number of counterfeit documents*

false • *a false passport*
imitation • *bound in imitation leather*
phoney or **phony** (INFORMAL) • *He used a phoney accent.*

ANOTHER SYNONYM:
• assumed

ANTONYM:
• real

RELATED WORD:
• PREFIX pseudo-

fake ③ VERB
to pretend to experience something • *He faked his own death.*
feign • *to feign illness*
pretend • *Todd shrugged with pretended indifference.*
simulate • *writhing around in simulated agony*

fall ① VERB
to descend towards the ground • *The tile fell from the roof.*
collapse • *The bridge collapsed on to the road.*
drop • *bombs dropping from the sky*
plunge • *A bus plunged into the river.*
topple • *He toppled slowly backwards.*
trip • *She tripped and broke her leg.*

ANTONYM:
• rise

fall ② VERB
to become lower or less • *Output fell by more than half.*
decline • *a declining birth rate*
decrease • *The number of bankruptcies decreased last year.*
diminish • *Resources are diminishing steadily.*
dwindle • *his dwindling authority*
plummet • *plummeting share prices*
subside • *The flood waters have subsided.*

MORE SYNONYMS:
• abate

A
B
C
D
E
F
G
H
I
J
K
L
M
N
O
P
Q
R
S
T
U
V
W
X
Y
Z

• depreciate
• ebb

ANTONYM:
• increase

fall ③ NOUN
a reduction in amount • *a fall in the exchange rate*
decline • *signs of economic decline*
decrease • *an overall decrease of 10%*
drop • *the sharp drop in export sales*
reduction • *The bank announced a reduction in interest rates.*
slump • *a slump in property prices*

ANTONYM:
• rise

false ① ADJECTIVE
not true or correct • *He gave a false name and address.*
erroneous • *to arrive at an erroneous conclusion*
fictitious • *the source of the fictitious rumours*
incorrect • *a decision based on incorrect information*
mistaken • *I had a mistaken view of what had happened.*
untrue • *The remarks were completely untrue.*

ANTONYM:
• true

false ② ADJECTIVE
not genuine but intended to seem so • *false hair*
artificial • *an artificial limb*
bogus • *their bogus insurance claim*
fake • *a fake tan*
forged • *They crossed the frontier using forged documents.*
simulated • *a simulated display of affection*

MORE SYNONYMS:
• ersatz
• spurious

ANTONYM:
• genuine

RELATED WORD:
• PREFIX pseudo-

false ③ ADJECTIVE
unfaithful and deceitful • *They turned out to be false friends.*
deceitful • *deceitful and misleading remarks*
disloyal • *He was accused of being disloyal to the company.*
insincere • *A lot of actors are insincere.*
unfaithful • *left alone by her unfaithful husband*

MORE SYNONYMS:
• duplicitous
• perfidious

fame NOUN
the state of being very well-known • *The film brought him international fame.*
eminence • *to achieve eminence as a politician*
glory • *my moment of glory*
prominence • *He came to prominence with his bestselling novel.*
renown • *a singer of great renown*
reputation • *the city's reputation as a place of romance*

familiar ADJECTIVE
knowing something well • *Most children are familiar with the stories.*
acquainted with • *Peter was well acquainted with Wordsworth.*
aware of • *aware of the dangers of smoking*
knowledgeable about • *They were very knowledgeable about gardening.*
versed in • *She was well versed in company law.*

ANTONYM:
• unfamiliar

family ① NOUN
a group of relatives • *My family are always supportive of me.*
descendants • *Their descendants lived there for centuries.*
relations • *friends and relations*
relatives • *She had relatives in many countries.*

RELATED WORD:
• ADJECTIVE familial

family ② NOUN
a group of related species • *Tigers are members of the cat family.*
class • *several classes of butterflies*
classification • *The classification includes conifers.*
kind • *different kinds of roses*

famous ADJECTIVE
very well-known • *the most famous woman of her time*
celebrated • *his most celebrated film*
distinguished • *a distinguished academic family*
illustrious • *the most illustrious scientists of the century*
legendary • *His skills are legendary.*
noted • *He is noted for his generosity.*
renowned • *The area is renowned for its cuisine.*

MORE SYNONYMS:
• lionized
• signal

ANTONYM:
• unknown

fan NOUN
an enthusiast about something or someone • *a fan of the new band*
adherent • *The movement was gaining adherents everywhere.*
admirer • *one of her many admirers*
devotee • *a devotee of chamber music*
lover • *an art lover*

supporter • *rival football supporters*
zealot • *a religious zealot*

MORE SYNONYMS:
• aficionado
• buff
• enthusiast

fanatic NOUN
someone who is extremely enthusiastic about something • *a football fanatic*
activist • *political activists*
devotee • *a devotee of the movement*
extremist • *groups of religious extremists*
militant • *The militants took over the organization.*
zealot • *He was a supporter but not a zealot.*

fanatical ADJECTIVE
showing extreme support for something • *a fanatical patriot*
fervent • *a fervent supporter*
obsessive • *obsessive about motor racing*
passionate • *a passionate interest*
rabid • *a rabid racist group*
wild • *I am wild about this band.*

MORE SYNONYMS:
• immoderate
• zealous

fancy ① VERB
to want to have or do something • *He fancied a drink.*
be attracted to • *I am attracted to the idea of emigrating.*
hanker after • *to hanker after a bigger car*
have a yen for • *She had a yen for some new clothes.*
would like • *I would really like some ice cream.*

fancy ② ADJECTIVE
special and elaborate • *dressed up in fancy clothes*

A
B
C
D
E
F
G
H
I
J
K
L
M
N
O
P
Q
R
S
T
U
V
W
X
Y
Z

decorated • *She preferred decorated surfaces to plain ones.*
elaborate • *his elaborate costume ideas*
extravagant • *the extravagant frescoes in the upper church*
intricate • *covered with intricate patterns*
ornate • *an ornate picture frame*

MORE SYNONYMS:
• baroque
• embellished
• ornamented

ANTONYM:
• plain

far ① ADVERB
at a great distance from something
• *The sea was far below us.*
afar • *seen from afar*
a great distance • *They travelled a great distance.*
a long way • *The guy's lonely and a long way from home.*
deep • *deep into the jungle*
miles • *He lived miles away.*

far ② ADVERB
to a great extent or degree • *far better than the others*
considerably • *The dinners were considerably less formal than before.*
incomparably • *South Africa seems incomparably richer than the rest of Africa.*
much • *I feel much better now.*
very much • *Things got very much worse.*

far ③ ADJECTIVE
very distant • *in the far south of the country*
distant • *the distant horizon*
long • *a long distance from here*
outlying • *The outlying areas are accessible only by air.*
remote • *a cottage in a remote village*

ANTONYM:
• near

fascinate VERB
to be of intense interest to someone
• *He was fascinated by the new discovery.*
absorb • *totally absorbed by her career*
bewitch • *Bill was bewitched by her charm.*
captivate • *Her looks captivated the whole world.*
enthral • *She sat enthralled by the actors.*
intrigue • *Her story intrigued them.*

MORE SYNONYMS:
• beguile
• enchant
• spellbind
• transfix

fashion ① NOUN
a popular style of dress or behaviour
• *changing fashions in clothing*
craze • *the latest health craze*
fad • *just a passing fad*
style • *a revival of an old style*
trend • *the current trend in footwear*
vogue • *a vogue for fitness training*

fashion ② NOUN
a manner or way of doing something
• *It works in a similar fashion.*
manner • *in a friendly manner*
method • *He did it by his usual method.*
mode • *a different mode of life*
way • *in her usual resourceful way*

fashion ③ VERB
to make and shape something
• *fashioned from rough wood*
construct • *an inner frame constructed from timber*
create • *It was created from odds and ends.*
make • *a doll made from fabric*
mould • *They moulded the cups from clay.*

shape · *Shape the dough into a loaf.*
work · *a machine for working the stone*

fashionable ADJECTIVE
very popular · *a fashionable restaurant*
current · *the current thinking on the subject*
in (INFORMAL) · *Jogging was the in thing.*
latest · *all the latest hairstyles*
popular · *the most popular movie*
prevailing · *contrary to prevailing attitudes*

MORE SYNONYMS:
• chic
• in vogue
• trendsetting

ANTONYM:
• old-fashioned

fast ① ADJECTIVE
moving at great speed · *a fast train*
accelerated · *at an accelerated pace*
hurried · *He ate a hurried breakfast.*
quick · *a quick learner*
rapid · *a rapid rise through the company*
speedy · *best wishes for a speedy recovery*
swift · *as swift as an arrow*

MORE SYNONYMS:
• fleet
• mercurial
• winged

ANTONYM:
• slow

fast ② ADVERB
quickly and without delay · *You'll have to move fast.*
hastily · *sheltering in hastily erected tents*
hurriedly · *students hurriedly taking notes*
quickly · *She worked quickly and methodically.*
rapidly · *moving rapidly across the field*

swiftly · *They had to act swiftly to save him.*

ANTONYM:
• slowly

fast ③ ADVERB
firmly and strongly · *She held fast to the rail.*
firmly · *with windows firmly shut*
securely · *The door was securely locked and bolted.*
tightly · *held tightly in his arms*

fasten VERB
to close or attach something · *Fasten your seat belts.*
attach · *He attached a label to the plant.*
fix · *It was fixed on the wall.*
join · *joined together by string*
lock · *a locked door*
secure · *The chest was secured with a lock and chain.*
tie · *Tie your shoelaces.*

fat ADJECTIVE
weighing too much · *a fat man*
▶ see Word Study **fat**, page 641

ANTONYM:
• thin

fatal ① ADJECTIVE
causing death · *fatal injuries*
deadly · *a deadly disease*
incurable · *It was regarded as an incurable illness.*
lethal · *a lethal dose of sleeping pills*
mortal · *They were in mortal danger.*
terminal · *terminal cancer*

fatal ② ADJECTIVE
having an undesirable effect · *The mistake was fatal to my plans.*
calamitous · *a calamitous air crash*
catastrophic · *The water shortage is potentially catastrophic.*
disastrous · *This could have disastrous consequences for industry.*
lethal · *a lethal left hook*

a
b
c
d
e
f
g
h
i
j
k
l
m
n
o
p
q
r
s
t
u
v
w
x
y
z

A
B
C
D
E
F
G
H
I
J
K
L
M
N
O
P
Q
R
S
T
U
V
W
X
Y
Z

fate NOUN
a power believed to control events
• *the fickleness of fate*
chance • *a victim of chance*
destiny • *We are masters of our own destiny.*
fortune • *Remember, fortune favours the brave.*
providence • *His death was an act of providence.*

MORE SYNONYMS:
• kismet
• nemesis
• predestination

fault ① NOUN
something for which someone is responsible • *It was all my fault.*
blame • *They put the blame on her.*
liability • *The company was forced to admit liability.*
responsibility • *He accepted full responsibility for the error.*

fault ② NOUN
a defective quality in something • *a minor technical fault*
blemish • *a blemish on an otherwise outstanding career*
defect • *a manufacturing defect*
deficiency • *serious deficiencies in the system*
drawback • *The plan had one major drawback.*
failing • *the country's many failings*
flaw • *serious character flaws*
imperfection • *small imperfections on the surface*
weakness • *his one weakness*

ANTONYM:
• strength

fault ③ VERB
to find reasons to be critical of someone • *Her conduct cannot be faulted.*

blame • *I don't blame him.*
censure • *He was censured by the committee.*
criticize • *The minister criticized the police.*

faulty ADJECTIVE
containing flaws or errors • *Faulty goods should be sent back.*
defective • *a lorry with defective brakes*
flawed • *The test results were seriously flawed.*
imperfect • *an imperfect specimen*
invalid • *That's an invalid argument.*
unsound • *a building that is structurally unsound*

MORE SYNONYMS:
• fallacious
• imprecise
• malfunctioning

favour ① NOUN
a liking or approval of something
• *The proposals met with favour.*
approval • *to gain his father's approval*
esteem • *in high esteem*
grace • *to fall from grace*
support • *They gave us their full support.*

ANTONYM:
• disapproval

favour ② NOUN
a kind and helpful action • *Can you do me a favour?*
courtesy • *the courtesy of a personal response*
good turn • *to do someone a good turn*
kindness • *She did me the kindness of calling.*
service • *a service to your country*

ANTONYM:
• wrong

favour ③ VERB
to prefer something or someone
• *They favoured the eldest child.*
prefer • *the preferred candidate*

single out · *He is always being singled out for special treatment.*

favourable ① ADJECTIVE
of advantage and benefit to someone · *favourable conditions*
advantageous · *the most advantageous course of action*
beneficial · *a beneficial effect on our health*
good · *He got a very good deal.*
opportune · *an opportune moment to attack*
suitable · *Conditions were not suitable for life to flourish.*

MORE SYNONYMS:
• auspicious
• propitious
• timely

ANTONYM:
• unfavourable

favourable ② ADJECTIVE
positive and expressing approval · *a favourable response*
affirmative · *to give an affirmative answer*
amicable · *amicable discussions*
approving · *a warm, approving glance*
friendly · *The proposal was given a friendly reception.*
positive · *a positive effect on the situation*
sympathetic · *He got a sympathetic hearing.*
welcoming · *a welcoming atmosphere*

ANTONYM:
• unfavourable

favourite ① ADJECTIVE
being someone's best-liked person or thing · *my favourite hotel*
best-loved · *our best-loved music*
dearest · *Her dearest wish was fulfilled.*
favoured · *the favoured child of elderly parents*

preferred · *his preferred method of exercise*

favourite ② NOUN
the thing or person someone likes best · *The youngest was always her favourite.*
darling · *the spoilt darling of the family*
idol · *the idol of his fans*
pet · *the teacher's pet*
pick · *the pick of the bunch*

favouritism NOUN
unfair favour shown to a person or group · *There was never a hint of favouritism.*
bias · *political bias in broadcasting*
one-sidedness · *The committee must show no one-sidedness.*

MORE SYNONYMS:
• nepotism
• partiality
• partisanship

ANTONYM:
• impartiality

fear ① NOUN
an unpleasant feeling of danger · *shivering with fear*
alarm · *I looked at him with growing alarm.*
awe · *in awe of his great powers*
dread · *She thought with dread of the coming storm.*
fright · *He jumped with fright at the noise.*
panic · *a moment of panic*
terror · *to shake with terror*

MORE SYNONYMS:
• apprehensiveness
• cravenness
• trepidation

fear ② VERB
to feel frightened of something · *There is nothing to fear.*
be afraid · *The dog was afraid of him.*

be frightened • *I am frightened of thunder.*
be scared • *Are you scared of snakes?*
dread • *He dreaded angry scenes.*
take fright • *The horse took fright at the sudden noise.*

feature ① NOUN
a particular characteristic of something • *an unusual feature of the room*
aspect • *every aspect of our lives*
attribute • *a normal attribute of human behaviour*
characteristic • *their physical characteristics*
mark • *distinguishing marks*
property • *the magnetic properties of iron*
quality • *skills and personal qualities*

feature ② NOUN
a special article or programme • *a news feature*
article • *a travel article*
column • *the advice column*
item • *an item about chemical waste*
piece • *a specially-written piece*
report • *a film report on the scandal*
story • *front-page news stories*

feature ③ VERB
to include and draw attention to something • *featuring an interview with the president*
emphasize • *to emphasize their differences*
give prominence to • *The Times is alone in giving prominence to the visit.*
spotlight • *a book spotlighting female singers*
star • *starring a major Australian actor*

feel ① VERB
to experience emotionally • *I felt enormous happiness.*
experience • *They seem to experience*

more distress than the others.
suffer • *suffering from pangs of conscience*
undergo • *to undergo a change of heart*

feel ② VERB
to believe that something is the case • *She feels she is in control of her life.*
believe • *I believe they are right.*
consider • *We consider them to be our friends.*
deem • *I deemed it best to cancel the party.*
judge • *She was judged to be capable of anything.*
think • *I think I am very lucky.*

feel ③ VERB
to touch something physically • *Feel this lovely material!*
finger • *He was fingering the coins in his pocket.*
fondle • *She fondled the dog's ears.*
stroke • *I stroked the smooth wooden surface.*
touch • *He touched my face.*

feeling ① NOUN
the experiencing of an emotion • *feelings of envy*
emotion • *trembling with emotion*
fervour • *religious fervour*
heat • *He spoke with some heat about his experiences.*
passion • *She argued with great passion.*
sentiment • *I'm afraid I don't share your sentiments.*

feeling ② NOUN
a physical sensation • *a feeling of pain*
sensation • *a very pleasant sensation*
sense • *a slight sense of heat at the back of my throat*

feeling ③ NOUN
an opinion on something • *strong feelings on politics*

inclination • *neither the time nor the inclination*
opinion • *a consensus of opinion*
point of view • *an unusual point of view on the subject*
view • *Make your views known.*

fellowship ① NOUN
a feeling of friendliness within a group • *a sense of community and fellowship*
brotherhood • *a symbolic act of brotherhood*
camaraderie • *the camaraderie among soldiers*
companionship • *the companionship between old friends*

fellowship ② NOUN
a group of people with a common interest • *a fellowship of writers*
association • *a trade association*
brotherhood • *a secret international brotherhood*
club • *a youth club*
league • *the League of Nations*
society • *the historical society*

female ① NOUN
a person or animal which can have babies • *Hay fever affects males more than females.*
girl • *a girls' school*
lady • *a nice young lady*
sheila (AUSTRALIAN AND NEW ZEALAND; INFORMAL) • *his role as a sheila in his own play*
woman • *the number of women in the police force*
ANTONYM:
• male

female ② ADJECTIVE
relating to females • *the world's greatest female distance runner*
feminine • *the traditional feminine role*

girlish • *She gave a girlish giggle.*
womanly • *a womanly shape*
ANTONYM:
• male

fertile ADJECTIVE
capable of producing plants or offspring • *fertile soil*
fruitful • *The fruitful earth gave forth its treasures.*
productive • *the most productive vineyards*
prolific • *Chinchillas are prolific breeders.*
rich • *This plant grows in moist rich ground.*
MORE SYNONYMS:
• fecund
• generative
ANTONYM:
• barren

fervent ADJECTIVE
showing sincere and enthusiastic feeling • *a fervent admirer of her work*
ardent • *one of the most ardent supporters of the policy*
committed • *a committed socialist*
devout • *She was a devout Christian.*
enthusiastic • *a huge and enthusiastic crowd*
impassioned • *an impassioned appeal for peace*
passionate • *I'm a passionate believer in public art.*
zealous • *He was a recent convert, and very zealous.*

festival ① NOUN
an organized series of events • *an arts festival*
carnival • *The carnival lasted for three days.*
entertainment • *theatrical entertainments*
fair • *The book fair attracted many visitors.*

fete • *a church fete*
gala • *the May Day gala*

festival ② NOUN
a day or period of religious
celebration • *open except on days of
religious festivals*
anniversary • *The anniversary is
celebrated each spring.*
holiday • *the Easter holiday*

◆ **CHRISTIAN FESTIVALS**
◆ Advent
◆ Ascension Day
◆ Ash Wednesday
◆ Candlemas
◆ Christmas
◆ Corpus Christi
◆ Easter
◆ Epiphany
◆ Good Friday
◆ Lent
◆ Maundy Thursday
◆ Michaelmas
◆ Palm Sunday
◆ Pentecost
◆ Quadragesima
◆ Shrove Tuesday
◆ Trinity
◆ Whitsun

◆ **JEWISH FESTIVALS**
◆ Feast of Tabernacles
◆ Hanukkah, Hanukah *or*
Chanukah
◆ Passover *or* Pesach
◆ Purim
◆ Rosh Hashanah
◆ Shavuot, Shabuoth *or* Pentecost
◆ Sukkoth *or* Succoth
◆ Yom Kippur *or* Day of Atonement

◆ **HINDU FESTIVALS**
◆ Diwali
◆ Durga-puja
◆ Dussehra
◆ Ganesh Chaturthi

◆ Holi
◆ Janmashtami
◆ Navaratri
◆ Raksha Bandhan
◆ Ramanavami
◆ Sarasvati-puja

◆ **MUSLIM FESTIVALS**
◆ Al Hijrah
◆ Ashura
◆ Eid-ul-Adha *or* Id-ul-Adha
◆ Eid-ul-Fitr *or* Id-ul-Fitr
◆ Lailat-ul-Isra' wa'l Mi'raj
◆ Lailat-ul-Qadr
◆ Mawlid al-Nabi
◆ Ramadan

◆ **SIKH FESTIVALS**
◆ Baisakhi Mela
◆ Diwali Mela
◆ Hola Mohalla Mela
◆ the Gurpurabs

◆ **BUDDHIST FESTIVALS**
◆ Wesak

few ADJECTIVE
small in number • *a few moments
ago*
infrequent • *at infrequent intervals*
meagre • *a society with meagre
resources*
not many • *Not many people attended
the meeting.*
scanty • *scanty memories of his
childhood*
scarce • *Resources are scarce.*
sparse • *a bare landscape with sparse
trees*
ANTONYM:
• many

fidget VERB
to move and change position
restlessly • *fidgeting in his seat*
fiddle (INFORMAL) • *She fiddled with her
pencil.*
jiggle • *He's jiggling his keys.*

squirm • *He squirmed and wriggled with impatience.*
twitch • *Everybody twitched in their seats.*

field ① NOUN
an area of farm land • *a field full of sheep*
green • *on the village green*
meadow • *a grassy meadow*
pasture • *cows grazing in the pasture*

field ② NOUN
a particular subject or interest • *a breakthrough in the field of physics*
area • *a politically sensitive area*
department • *Health care isn't my department.*
domain • *in the domain of art*
province • *This is the province of a different section.*
speciality • *His speciality was mythology.*
territory • *an expert in his own territory of history*

MORE SYNONYMS:
• bailiwick
• discipline
• metier

fierce ① ADJECTIVE
wild and aggressive • *a fierce lion*
aggressive • *encouraging aggressive behaviour in later life*
dangerous • *These birds are dangerous.*
ferocious • *two and a half days of ferocious violence*
murderous • *a murderous attack*

MORE SYNONYMS:
• barbarous
• fell
• feral

ANTONYM:
• gentle

fierce ② ADJECTIVE
very intense • *a fierce contest*

intense • *We found ourselves standing in intense heat.*
keen • *a keen interest in cars*
relentless • *The pressure was relentless.*
strong • *a strong dislike*

fight ① VERB
to take part in a battle or contest • *He fought the world champion.*
battle • *The gang battled with the police.*
brawl • *men brawling drunkenly in the street*
grapple • *grappling with an alligator*
struggle • *He was struggling with police outside the club.*

fight ② NOUN
an aggressive struggle • *a fight to the death*
action • *wounded in action*
battle • *a gun battle*
bout • *a wrestling bout*
combat • *the end of a long combat*
duel • *He was killed in a duel.*
skirmish • *a minor border skirmish*

fight ③ NOUN
an angry disagreement • *a fight with my mother*
argument • *an argument over a boyfriend*
blue (AUSTRALIAN; SLANG) • *a bloke I'd had a blue with years ago*
dispute • *a dispute over ticket allocation*
row • *Maxine and I had a terrible row.*
squabble • *a family squabble over Sunday lunch*

fighter NOUN
someone who physically fights another person • *a tough street fighter*
soldier • *well-equipped soldiers*
warrior • *a brave warrior*

figure ① NOUN
a number, or amount represented

figure | 210

by a number • *No one really knows the true figures.*
amount • *Postal money orders are available in amounts up to $700.*
digit • *a code made up of letters and digits*
number • *A lot of marriages end in divorce, but we don't know the exact number.*
numeral • *the numeral six*
statistic • *Official statistics show wages declining by 24%.*
total • *Then he added everything together to arrive at the final total.*

figure ② NOUN

a shape, or the shape of someone's body • *A figure appeared in the doorway.*
body • *She's got nice hair and a great body.*
build • *a tall woman with a naturally slim build*
form • *The shadowy form receded into the darkness.*
physique • *He has the physique and energy of a man half his age.*
shape • *tall, dark shapes moving in the mist*
silhouette • *Tuck the shirt in to give yourself a streamlined silhouette.*

figure ③ NOUN

a person • *international political figures*
character • *What a sad character that Nigel is.*
dignitary • *a visiting dignitary of great importance*
person • *My grandfather was a person of some influence.*
personality • *The event was attended by many showbiz personalities.*
player • *a key player in the negotiations*

figure ④ VERB (INFORMAL)

to guess or conclude something • *I figure I'll learn from experience.*
expect • *I expect you're just tired.*
guess • *I guess he's right.*

reckon (INFORMAL) • *Toni reckoned that it must be about three o'clock.*
suppose • *What do you suppose he's up to?*

fill VERB

to make something full • *Fill it up with water.*
cram • *Mourners crammed the small church.*
gorge • *gorged with food*
pack • *a lorry packed with explosives*
stock • *a lake stocked with carp*
stuff • *Stuff the pillow with feathers.*

ANTONYM:
• empty

final ① ADJECTIVE

being the last one in a series • *the fifth and final day*
closing • *in the closing stages of the race*
concluding • *the concluding part of the serial*
eventual • *the eventual aim of their policies*
last • *his last chance*
ultimate • *The ultimate outcome will be different.*

ANTONYM:
• first

final ② ADJECTIVE

unable to be changed or questioned • *The judges' decision is final.*
absolute • *absolute authority*
conclusive • *conclusive proof*
definite • *too soon to give a definite answer*
definitive • *the definitive account of the war*

finally ① ADVERB

happening after a long time • *It finally arrived.*
at last • *He came at last.*
at the last moment • *They changed their minds at the last moment.*

eventually • *The flight eventually left.*
in the end • *It all turned out right in the end.*
in the long run • *a success in the long run*

finally ② ADVERB
in conclusion of something • *Finally, I'd like to talk about safety measures.*
in conclusion • *In conclusion, we have to agree.*
in summary • *It was, in summary, a satisfactory outcome.*
lastly • *Lastly, I would like to thank my agent.*

finance ① VERB
to provide the money for something • *financed by the government*
back • *a fund backed by local businesses*
fund • *The scheme is funded by the banks.*
pay for • *He paid for his trip out of his savings.*
support • *She supported herself through university.*

finance ② NOUN
the managing of money and investments • *the world of high finance*
banking • *the international banking system*
budgeting • *We must exercise caution in our budgeting this year.*
commerce • *industry and commerce*
economics • *the economics of the third world*
investment • *tax incentives to encourage investment*

financial ADJECTIVE
relating to money • *financial difficulties*
economic • *an economic crisis*
fiscal • *the long-term fiscal policy of this country*
money • *on the money markets*

MORE SYNONYMS:
• budgetary
• monetary
• pecuniary

find ① VERB
to discover something • *I can't find my notes.*
come across • *He came across the book by chance.*
discover • *They discovered the body in the bushes.*
locate • *locating the position of the gene*
track down • *to track down her parents*
turn up • *They failed to turn up any evidence.*
unearth • *to unearth the missing copy*
MORE SYNONYMS:
• descry
• espy
• ferret out
ANTONYM:
• lose

find ② VERB
to realize or learn something • *We found that we got on well.*
become aware • *I became aware of his work last year.*
detect • *I detected a note of envy in her voice.*
discover • *It was discovered that the goods were missing.*
learn • *I flew from New York on learning of his death.*
realize • *They realized too late that it was wrong.*

fine ① ADJECTIVE
very good and admirable • *fine clothes*
admirable • *with many admirable qualities*
beautiful • *a beautiful view of the river*
excellent • *inns with excellent cuisine*
magnificent • *his magnificent country house*

outstanding • *an area of outstanding natural beauty*
splendid • *a splendid collection of cartoons*

fine ② ADJECTIVE
small in size or thickness • *powder with very fine particles*
delicate • *delicate curtains to let in the light*
lightweight • *certain lightweight fabrics*
powdery • *soft powdery dust*
sheer • *a sheer chiffon shirt*
small • *netting with a small mesh*

MORE SYNONYMS:
• diaphanous
• gauzy
• gossamer

fine ③ ADJECTIVE
subtle and precise • *the fine details*
fastidious • *fastidious attention to detail*
keen • *a keen eye for a bargain*
precise • *a gauge with precise adjustment*
refined • *a woman of refined tastes*
sensitive • *The radio had very sensitive tuning.*
subtle • *a very subtle distinction*

finish ① VERB
to complete something • *to finish a report*
close • *They have closed the deal.*
complete • *She completed her first novel.*
conclude • *He concluded his speech.*
end • *That ended our discussion.*
finalize • *to finalize an agreement*

ANTONYM:
• start

finish ② NOUN
the last part of something • *to see it through to the finish*

close • *to bring to a close*
completion • *The project is nearing completion.*
conclusion • *at the conclusion of the programme*
end • *the end of the race*
ending • *The film had an unexpected ending.*
finale • *the grand finale of the evening*

MORE SYNONYMS:
• culmination
• denouement
• termination

ANTONYM:
• start

finish ③ NOUN
the surface appearance of something • *a glossy finish*
grain • *the smooth grain of the wood*
lustre • *a similar lustre to silk*
polish • *The bodywork had a high polish.*
shine • *It gives a beautiful shine to the hair.*
surface • *a polished surface*
texture • *paper with a linen-like texture*

fire ① NOUN
the flames produced when something burns • *a ball of fire*
blaze • *The firemen were hurt in the blaze.*
combustion • *Energy is released by combustion.*
flames • *rescued from the flames*
inferno • *The building was an inferno.*

fire ② VERB
to shoot or detonate something • *to fire a cannon*
detonate • *to detonate an explosive device*
explode • *They exploded a bomb.*
launch • *The protesters launched the missile from a boat.*

set off • *the largest nuclear explosion ever set off on Earth*

shoot • *people shooting guns in all directions*

fire ③ VERB (INFORMAL)
to dismiss someone from a job • *She was fired yesterday.*
discharge • *A trooper has been discharged from the army.*
dismiss • *He was dismissed by the bank.*
make redundant • *Many people were made redundant.*
sack (INFORMAL) • *Jones was sacked for disciplinary reasons.*

firm ① ADJECTIVE
solid and not soft • *Leave the ice cream until it is firm.*
compressed • *compressed wood pulp made into cardboard*
congealed • *a bowl of congealed grease*
hard • *The snow was hard and slippery.*
rigid • *Pour the mixture into a rigid plastic container.*
set • *The glue wasn't completely set.*
solid • *a block of solid wax*
stiff • *egg whites beaten until stiff*

ANTONYM:
• soft

firm ② ADJECTIVE
resolute and determined • *The department needs a firm manager.*
adamant • *He was adamant that he would not resign.*
determined • *She was determined to finish the game.*
inflexible • *his inflexible routine*
resolute • *a willingness to take resolute action*
staunch • *many staunch supporters*
unshakable • *an unshakable belief in democracy*

MORE SYNONYMS:
• obdurate

• steadfast
• unwavering

firm ③ NOUN
a commercial organization • *a firm of builders*
business • *a stockbroking business*
company • *his software development company*
corporation • *one of the leading banking corporations*
enterprise • *small business enterprises*
organization • *a multinational organization*

first ① ADJECTIVE
done or in existence before anything else • *the first moon landing*
earliest • *The earliest settlers lived there.*
initial • *our initial meeting*
opening • *There was a standing ovation on opening night.*
original • *She was one of the original cast.*
primeval • *the primeval forests of Europe*

ANTONYM:
• last

first ② ADVERB
done or occurring before anything else • *You must do that first.*
beforehand • *Bill had prepared beforehand.*
earlier • *I did that one earlier.*
firstly • *Firstly, I'd like to thank you all for coming.*
initially • *not as bad as they initially predicted*
to begin with • *To begin with, we must prepare the soil.*

first ③ ADJECTIVE
more important than anything else • *our first responsibility*
chief • *the chief pilot*

Sidebar: A B C D E F G H I J K L M N O P Q R S T U V W X Y Z

foremost • *one of our foremost thinkers*
leading • *the team's leading scorer*
prime • *He was the prime suspect.*
principal • *the principal reason*

first-rate ADJECTIVE
excellent • *They were dealing with a first-rate professional.*
excellent • *She does an excellent job as Fred's personal assistant.*
exceptional • *His piano playing is exceptional.*
first-class • *The food was first-class.*
marvellous • *He certainly is a marvellous actor.*
outstanding • *an outstanding athlete*
splendid • *We had a splendid meal.*
superb • *a superb 18-hole golf course*

MORE SYNONYMS:
• superlative (FORMAL)
• unparalleled

fissure NOUN
a deep crack in rock or the ground • *There was a rumbling, and a fissure opened up.*
cleft • *a narrow cleft in the rocks*
crack • *The building developed large cracks in walls and ceilings.*
crevice • *a huge boulder with ferns growing in every crevice*
fault • *the San Andreas Fault*
rift • *In the open bog are many rifts and potholes.*
split • *The slate has a few small splits around the edges.*

fit ① VERB
to be the right shape or size • *made to fit a child*
belong • *I just didn't belong there.*
correspond • *The two angles didn't correspond exactly.*
dovetail • *The movement's interests dovetailed with her own.*
go • *small enough to go in your pocket*
match • *Match the pegs with the holes.*

fit ② VERB
to place something in position • *a fitted carpet*
adapt • *shelves adapted to suit the smaller books*
arrange • *Arrange the pieces to form a picture.*
place • *Place the card in the slots.*
position • *plants which are carefully positioned in the alcove*

fit ③ ADJECTIVE
in good physical condition • *a reasonably fit person*
healthy • *a healthy mind in a healthy body*
in good condition • *in good condition for his age*
robust • *a strong, robust man*
trim • *a trim figure*
well • *Alison was looking well.*

ANTONYM:
• unfit

fitting ① ADJECTIVE
appropriate and suitable for something • *a fitting end*
appropriate • *an appropriate outfit for the occasion*
correct • *the correct thing to say*
proper • *It isn't proper that she should be here.*
right • *He always said just the right thing.*
suitable • *some hymns suitable for a wedding*

MORE SYNONYMS:
• apposite
• decorous
• seemly

fitting ② NOUN
a part attached to something else
• *fixtures and fittings*

accessory • *bathroom accessories*
attachment • *a wide range of attachments*
component • *special components*
part • *Extra parts can be added later.*
unit • *The unit plugs into any TV set.*

fix ① VERB
to attach or secure something
• *fixed to the wall*
attach • *The label was attached with glue.*
bind • *sticks bound together with string*
fasten • *Fasten the two parts securely.*
secure • *firmly secured by strong nails*
stick • *She stuck the pictures into the book.*

fix ② VERB
to repair something broken • *The bike is fixed now.*
correct • *to correct our mistakes*
mend • *They finally got round to mending the roof.*
patch up • *Patch up those holes.*
repair • *I had my shoes repaired.*

fix ③ NOUN (INFORMAL)
a difficult situation • *in a bit of a fix*
difficulty • *He was in real difficulties with money.*
mess • *Their economy was in a mess.*
predicament • *a tricky predicament*
quandary • *in a quandary about what to do*

flabby ADJECTIVE
fat and with loose flesh • *a flabby stomach*
floppy • *the floppy bodies in tracksuits*
sagging • *a sagging double chin*
slack • *The skin around her eyelids is now slack and baggy.*

MORE SYNONYMS:
• flaccid
• pendulous

ANTONYM:
• taut

flash ① NOUN
a sudden short burst of light • *a flash of lightning*
burst • *a burst of fire*
flare • *the sudden flare of a match*
sparkle • *sparkles from her sequinned dress*

flash ② VERB
to shine briefly and often repeatedly
• *They signalled by flashing a light.*
flare • *matches flaring in the darkness*
glint • *the low sun glinting off the windscreens*
glitter • *the glittering crown on his head*
sparkle • *Diamonds sparkled on her wrists.*
twinkle • *stars twinkling in the night sky*

flashy ADJECTIVE
showy in a vulgar way • *flashy clothes*
flamboyant • *an unsuitably flamboyant outfit*
garish • *curtains in garish colours*
showy • *an expensive and showy watch*
tacky (INFORMAL) • *tacky red sunglasses*
tasteless • *a house with tasteless decor*

MORE SYNONYMS:
• meretricious
• ostentatious

ANTONYM:
• modest

flat ① NOUN
a set of rooms for living in • *a two-bedroomed flat*
apartment • *a huge apartment overlooking the park*
rooms • *We shared rooms while we were students.*

flat ② ADJECTIVE
level and smooth • *a flat surface*

a
b
c
d
e
f
g
h
i
j
k
l
m
n
o
p
q
r
s
t
u
v
w
x
y
z

A
B
C
D
E
F
G
H
I
J
K
L
M
N
O
P
Q
R
S
T
U
V
W
X
Y
Z

horizontal • *horizontal with the ground*
level • *a completely level base*
levelled • *The floor must be levelled before you start.*
smooth • *a smooth marble top*
unbroken • *the unbroken surface of the sea*

ANTONYM:
• uneven

flat ③ ADJECTIVE
without emotion or interest • *a dreadfully flat speech*
boring • *a boring menu*
dull • *He told some really dull stories.*
insipid • *an insipid performance*
monotonous • *an interesting story expressed in a monotonous voice*
weak • *A weak ending spoiled the story.*

flatter ① VERB
to praise someone insincerely • *flattering remarks*
compliment • *She was often complimented for her looks.*
fawn • *surrounded by fawning attendants*

flatter ② VERB
to make more attractive • *clothes that flatter your figure*
enhance • *an enhancing neckline*
set off • *Blue sets off the colour of your eyes.*
suit • *That shade really suits your skin tone.*

flattery NOUN
flattering words and behaviour • *susceptible to flattery*
adulation • *received with adulation by the critics*
fawning • *the constant fawning of her courtiers*

MORE SYNONYMS:
• blandishment

• obsequiousness
• sycophancy

flaw NOUN
an imperfection in something • *The program contained serious flaws.*
blemish • *A small blemish spoiled the surface.*
defect • *a manufacturing defect*
fault • *a fault in the engine*
imperfection • *slight imperfections in the weave*

flee VERB
to run away from something • *to flee the country*
bolt • *He bolted for the exit.*
escape • *They escaped across the frontier.*
fly • *to fly from war*
leave • *to leave the scene of the crime*
run away • *to run away from the police*
take flight • *250,000 took flight from the floods.*

flexible ① ADJECTIVE
able to bend or be bent easily • *long flexible bristles*
elastic • *an elastic rope*
lithe • *lithe and graceful movements*
pliable • *baskets made from pliable cane*
supple • *exercises to keep you supple*

MORE SYNONYMS:
• ductile
• lissom or
• lissome
• pliant

flexible ② ADJECTIVE
able to adapt or change • *flexible working hours*
adaptable • *an adaptable attitude to work*
discretionary • *the discretionary powers of the courts*
open • *an open mind*

flinch VERB

to move suddenly with fear or pain • *The sharp pain made her flinch.*
cringe • *to cringe in terror*
shrink • *She shrank from the flames.*
start • *They started at the sudden noise.*
wince • *I could see him wincing with pain.*

float ① VERB

to be supported by water • *leaves floating on the river*
be on the surface • *The oil is on the surface of the sea.*
bob • *toys bobbing in the bath*
drift • *to drift in on the tide*
lie on the surface • *The boat lay on the surface of the lake.*
stay afloat • *They could stay afloat without swimming.*

ANTONYM:
• sink

float ② VERB

to be carried on the air • *floating on the breeze*
drift • *The music drifted in through the window.*
glide • *eagles gliding above us*
hang • *A haze of perfume hung in the room.*
hover • *Butterflies hovered above the flowers.*

flood ① NOUN

a large amount of water coming suddenly • *Many people were drowned in the floods.*
deluge • *houses overwhelmed by the deluge*
downpour • *a downpour of torrential rain*
spate • *The river was in spate.*
torrent • *Torrents of water gushed into the reservoir.*

flood ② NOUN

a sudden large amount of something • *a flood of angry letters*
rush • *a sudden rush of panic*
stream • *a stream of bad language*
torrent • *He replied with a torrent of abuse.*

flood ③ VERB

to overflow with water • *The river flooded its banks.*
deluge • *Heavy rain deluged the capital.*
drown • *a drowned village*
overflow • *an overflowing bath*
submerge • *to prevent water submerging the cobbled streets*
swamp • *His small boat was swamped by the waves.*

flourish ① VERB

to develop or function successfully or healthily • *Business was flourishing.*
bloom • *Not many economies bloomed during that period.*
boom • *Sales are booming.*
come on • *He is coming on very well at his new school.*
do well • *Out-of-town superstores are doing well.*
prosper • *The high street banks continue to prosper.*
succeed • *the qualities needed in small businesses to succeed*
thrive • *Today the company continues to thrive.*

ANTONYM:
• fail

flourish ② VERB

to wave or display something • *He flourished his glass.*
brandish (LITERARY) • *He appeared brandishing a sword.*
display • *She proudly displayed the letter and began to read.*
hold aloft • *He held the cup aloft.*

a
b
c
d
e
f
g
h
i
j
k
l
m
n
o
p
q
r
s
t
u
v
w
x
y
z

wave • *Crowds were waving flags and applauding.*

flourish ③ NOUN

a bold sweeping or waving movement • *with a flourish of his hand*

flick • *a flick of the whip*

sweep • *With one sweep of her hand she threw back the sheets.*

wave • *Steve stopped him with a wave of the hand.*

flow ① VERB

to move or happen in a continuous stream • *a river flowing gently down into the valley*

circulate • *to circulate round the entire house*

glide • *models gliding down the catwalk*

roll • *rolling gently to the sea*

run • *A stream ran beside the road.*

slide • *Tears slid down her cheeks.*

flow ② NOUN

a continuous movement of something • *traffic flow*

current • *currents of air*

drift • *the drift towards the cities*

flood • *a flood of complaints*

stream • *a constant stream of visitors*

tide • *to slow the tide of change*

fluent ADJECTIVE

expressing yourself easily and without hesitation • *a fluent speaker of French*

articulate • *an articulate young woman*

easy • *the easy flow of his argument*

effortless • *He spoke with effortless ease.*

flowing • *a smooth, flowing presentation*

ready • *a ready answer*

ANTONYM:
• hesitant

fly ① VERB

to move through the air • *to fly to Paris*

flit • *butterflies flitting among the flowers*

flutter • *The birds fluttered on to the feeder.*

sail • *a kite sailing above the trees*

soar • *eagles soaring in the sky*

fly ② VERB

to move very quickly • *She flew down the stairs.*

dart • *She darted to the window.*

dash • *We had to dash.*

hurry • *They hurried to catch the train.*

race • *I had to race round the shops.*

rush • *rushing off to work*

speed • *The car sped off.*

tear • *He tore off down the road.*

foam ① NOUN

a mass of tiny bubbles • *waves tipped with foam*

bubbles • *She liked to have bubbles in the bath.*

froth • *Yeast swells up to form a froth.*

head • *the foamy head on beer*

lather • *It took a lot of shampoo to get a good lather.*

foam ② VERB

to swell and form bubbles • *a foaming river*

bubble • *The boiling liquid bubbled up.*

fizz • *a drink fizzing in the glass*

froth • *It frothed up over the top.*

focus ① VERB

to concentrate your vision on something • *His eyes began to focus.*

aim • *Astronomers aimed optical telescopes in their direction.*

concentrate • *concentrating his gaze on a line of ants*

direct • *He directed the light on to the roof.*

fix • *Their radar was fixed on the enemy ship.*

focus ② NOUN
the centre of attention • *the focus of the conversation*
centre • *She was the centre of an admiring crowd.*
focal point • *the focal point of the whole room*
hub • *the hub of the financial world*
target • *the target of the attack*

foil ① VERB
to prevent something from happening • *The police foiled an armed robbery.*
check • *to check the rise in crime*
counter • *countering the threat of strike action*
defeat • *an important role in defeating the rebellion*
frustrate • *a frustrated attempt*
thwart • *to thwart someone's plans*
MORE SYNONYMS:
• circumvent
• nullify

foil ② NOUN
a contrast to something • *a perfect foil for his temperament*
antithesis • *the antithesis of his crooked brother*
background • *a fitting background for her beauty*
complement • *the perfect complement to the antique furniture*
contrast • *The green woodwork is a stunning contrast to the black walls.*

fold ① VERB
to bend something • *He folded the paper carefully.*
bend • *Bend the top towards you.*
crease • *Crease along the dotted line.*
crumple • *He crumpled the note and put it in his pocket.*
tuck • *Tuck in the top and bottom.*
turn under • *The end was turned under.*

fold ② NOUN
a crease in something • *hanging in folds*
bend • *There was a bend in the photograph.*
crease • *sharp creases in his shirt*
pleat • *a skirt with pleats*
wrinkle • *all the little wrinkles on Paul's face*

follow ① VERB
to pursue someone • *We were being followed.*
hound • *constantly hounded by photographers*
pursue • *He was pursued across several countries.*
stalk • *Her former husband was stalking her.*
track • *They tracked him to his home.*

follow ② VERB
to come after someone or something • *Night follows day.*
come after • *Summer comes after spring.*
succeed • *He was succeeded by his son.*
supersede • *Horses were superseded by cars.*
ANTONYM:
• precede

follow ③ VERB
to act in accordance with something • *Follow the instructions carefully.*
comply • *in order to comply with EC regulations*
conform • *conforming to the new safety requirements*
obey • *You must obey the law.*
observe • *The army was observing a ceasefire.*

follower NOUN
a supporter of a person or belief • *a loyal follower of the movement*
believer • *many devout believers in the faith*

a b c d e f g h i j k l m n o p q r s t u v w x y z

A
B
C
D
E
F
G
H
I
J
K
L
M
N
O
P
Q
R
S
T
U
V
W
X
Y
Z

disciple • *one of his disciples*
fan • *football fans*
henchman • *always surrounded by his henchmen*
supporter • *He was a major supporter of the plan.*

MORE SYNONYMS:
• adherent
• protagonist

ANTONYM:
• leader

fond ① ADJECTIVE
feeling affection or liking • *a fond father*
adoring • *an adoring husband*
affectionate • *an affectionate smile*
devoted • *a devoted couple*
doting • *doting grandparents*
having a liking for • *She had a great liking for chocolate.*
loving • *a loving son*

fond ② ADJECTIVE
unlikely to happen or be fulfilled • *fond wishes for a better life*
deluded • *a deluded belief in future improvement*
empty • *empty promises of full employment*
foolish • *What foolish dreams we have!*
naive • *her naive belief in others' goodness*
vain • *the vain hope that he might lose weight*

MORE SYNONYMS:
• delusory
• overoptimistic

food NOUN
things eaten to provide nourishment • *our favourite food*
diet • *a healthy balanced diet*
fare • *traditional regional fare*
foodstuffs • *basic foodstuffs*
kai (AUSTRALIAN AND NEW ZEALAND;

INFORMAL) • *There's no kai in the house.*
nourishment • *unable to take nourishment*
provisions • *provisions for two weeks*
refreshment • *Refreshments will be provided.*
tucker (AUSTRALIAN AND NEW ZEALAND; INFORMAL) • *some of the cheapest pub tucker in town*

MORE SYNONYMS:
• provender
• subsistence
• victuals

RELATED WORDS:
• ADJECTIVE alimentary
• NOUN gastronomy

fool ① NOUN
an unintelligent person • *What a stupid fool he is!*
dope (INFORMAL) • *He felt such a dope.*
dunce • *I was a complete dunce at chemistry.*
idiot • *acting like an idiot*
ignoramus • *the ignoramus of the group*
moron • *They treated him like a moron.*

fool ② VERB
to trick someone • *Don't let him fool you.*
con (INFORMAL) • *conned out of all his money*
deceive • *deceiving the audience*
dupe • *in order to dupe the medical staff*
mislead • *a deliberately misleading statement*
trick • *They tricked him into believing it.*

MORE SYNONYMS:
• bamboozle
• hoodwink

foolish ADJECTIVE
silly and unwise • *feeling foolish*
inane • *an inane remark*
nonsensical • *a nonsensical thing to say*

senseless • *It would be senseless to stop her.*
silly • *a silly thing to say*
unintelligent • *a weak and unintelligent man*
unwise • *He had made some unwise investments.*

ANTONYM:
• wise

forbid VERB
to order someone not to do something • *forbidden to go out*
ban • *banned from driving*
exclude • *Women were excluded from the classes.*
outlaw • *the outlawed political parties*
prohibit • *Fishing is prohibited.*
veto • *Their application was vetoed.*

ANTONYM:
• allow

force ① VERB
to compel someone to do something • *We were forced to turn right.*
compel • *I felt compelled to act.*
drive • *They are driving the company into bankruptcy.*
make • *They made me do it.*
oblige • *We were obliged to abandon the car.*
pressurize • *trying to pressurize them*

MORE SYNONYMS:
• coerce
• impel
• obligate

force ② NOUN
a pressure to do something • *They made him agree by force.*
compulsion • *a compulsion to write*
duress • *carried out under duress*
pressure • *under pressure to resign*

force ③ NOUN
the strength of something • *the force of the explosion*

impact • *the impact of the blast*
might • *the full might of the army*
power • *massive computing power*
pressure • *the pressure of work*
strength • *The storm was gaining strength.*

foreign ADJECTIVE
relating to other countries • *foreign travel*
distant • *in that distant land*
exotic • *filmed in an exotic location*
overseas • *a long overseas trip*

foremost ADJECTIVE
most important or best • *one of the world's foremost scholars*
best • *He was the best player in the world throughout the 1950s.*
chief • *my chief reason for objecting to the plan*
first • *The first priority is to defeat inflation.*
greatest • *one of the West Indies' greatest cricketers*
leading • *the leading researchers in this area*
most important • *the country's most important politicians and philosophers*
prime • *I regard this as my prime duty.*
principal • *one of the country's principal publishing houses*
top • *The President met with his top military advisers.*

forest NOUN

◆ **TYPES OF FOREST**
◆ bush
◆ coppice
◆ copse
◆ grove
◆ jungle
◆ spinney
◆ thicket
◆ wood
◆ woodland

a
b
c
d
e
f
g
h
i
j
k
l
m
n
o
p
q
r
s
t
u
v
w
x
y
z

forget VERB
  to fail to remember something • *I forgot to lock the door.*
  fail to remember • *He failed to remember my name.*
  omit • *omitting to mention the details*
  overlook • *to overlook an important fact*

  ANTONYM:
  • remember

forgive VERB
  to stop blaming someone for something • *Can you ever forgive me?*
  absolve • *The verdict absolved him from blame.*
  condone • *We cannot condone violence.*
  excuse • *Please excuse our bad behaviour.*
  pardon • *Relatives had begged the authorities to pardon him.*

  ANTONYM:
  • blame

forgiveness NOUN
  the act of forgiving • *I ask for your forgiveness.*
  acquittal • *The jury voted for acquittal.*
  mercy • *to beg for mercy*
  pardon • *a presidential pardon*
  remission • *with remission for good behaviour*

  MORE SYNONYMS:
  • absolution
  • exoneration

form ① NOUN
  a type or kind • *He contracted a rare form of cancer.*
  class • *a new class of nuclear-powered submarine*
  kind • *a new kind of leadership*
  sort • *Try to do some sort of exercise every day.*
  type • *There are various types of this disease.*

variant • *The quagga was a beautiful variant of the zebra.*
  variety • *an unusual variety of this common garden flower*

form ② NOUN
  the shape or pattern of something • *Valleys often take the form of deep canyons.*
  contours • *the contours of the body*
  layout • *He tried to recall the layout of the farmhouse.*
  outline • *I could just see the outline of a building in the mist.*
  shape • *little pens in the shape of baseball bats*
  structure • *the chemical structure of this molecule*

form ③ VERB
  to be the elements that something consists of • *the articles that formed the basis of his book*
  compose • *The force would be composed of troops from NATO countries.*
  constitute • *The country's ethnic minorities constitute about 7% of its total population.*
  make up • *Women officers make up 13 per cent of the police force.*
  serve as • *an arrangement of bricks and planks that served as a bookshelf*

form ④ VERB
  to organize, create, or come into existence • *The bowl was formed out of clay.*
  assemble • *a model assembled entirely from matchsticks*
  create • *These patterns were created by the action of water.*
  develop • *We must develop closer ties with Germany.*
  draw up • *We've drawn up a plan of action.*
  establish • *The school was established in 1989 by an Italian professor.*

A B C D E F G H I J K L M N O P Q R S T U V W X Y Z

fashion · *Stone Age settlers fashioned necklaces from animals' teeth.*
make · *The organic waste decomposes to make compost.*

formal ① ADJECTIVE
in accordance with convention · *a formal dinner*
conventional · *a conventional style of dress*
correct · *polite and correct behaviour*
precise · *They spoke very precise English.*
stiff · *his stiff manner and lack of humour*

ANTONYM:
· informal

formal ② ADJECTIVE
official and publicly recognized · *No formal announcement has been made.*
approved · *a legally approved method of dealing with these*
legal · *They have a legal responsibility.*
official · *according to the official figures*
prescribed · *There is a prescribed procedure for situations like this.*
regular · *through the regular channels*

former ADJECTIVE
existing in the past · *a former tennis champion*
ancient · *the ancient civilizations*
bygone · *memories of a bygone age*
old · *our old school*
past · *a long list of past winners*

formidable ADJECTIVE
difficult to overcome · *They faced formidable obstacles.*
challenging · *a more challenging job*
daunting · *a daunting prospect*
difficult · *A difficult task lay ahead.*
intimidating · *She was an intimidating opponent.*
mammoth · *a mammoth undertaking*
onerous · *onerous responsibilities*

fort NOUN
a building for defence and shelter
· *They had to abandon the fort.*
castle · *a heavily-guarded castle*
citadel · *The citadel towered above the river.*
fortification · *fortifications along the border*
fortress · *an ancient fortress*

fossick VERB (AUSTRALIAN AND NEW ZEALAND)
to search for something · *If you fossick around in some specialist music stores, you may find a copy.*
forage · *They were forced to forage for clothing and fuel.*
hunt · *A forensic team was hunting for clues.*
look · *I've looked through all my drawers and I can't find it anywhere.*
rummage · *He rummaged around the post room and found the document.*
search · *We've searched through the whole house for the keys.*

fragile ADJECTIVE
easily broken or damaged · *fragile china*
breakable · *Anything breakable or sharp had to be removed.*
dainty · *a dainty Japanese tea service*
delicate · *a delicate instrument*
flimsy · *packed in a flimsy box*
frail · *a frail shell*

MORE SYNONYMS:
· frangible
· infirm

ANTONYM:
· tough

fragrance NOUN
a pleasant smell · *the fragrance of the roses*
aroma · *the aroma of fresh bread*
bouquet · *a wine with a lively fruit bouquet*

perfume • *enjoying the perfume of the lemon trees*
scent • *flowers chosen for their scent*
smell • *a sweet smell of pine*

fragrant ADJECTIVE
having a pleasant smell • *fragrant oils*
aromatic • *a plant with aromatic leaves*
perfumed • *perfumed body cream*
sweet-smelling • *posies of sweet-smelling flowers*

ANTONYM:
• smelly

frank ADJECTIVE
open and straightforward • *a frank discussion*
blunt • *his blunt approach*
candid • *She was completely candid with me.*
honest • *my honest opinion*
open • *an open, trusting nature*
plain • *plain talking*
straightforward • *spoken in a straightforward manner*

fraud ① NOUN
the act of deceiving someone • *electoral fraud*
deceit • *deliberate deceit*
deception • *obtaining money by deception*
guile • *children's lack of guile*
hoax • *a bomb hoax*
trickery • *They had to resort to trickery.*

MORE SYNONYMS:
• chicanery
• duplicity
• spuriousness

fraud ② NOUN
someone or something that deceives you • *Many psychics are frauds.*
charlatan • *exposed as a charlatan*
cheat • *Cheats will be disqualified.*
fake • *The painting was a fake.*
forgery • *just a clever forgery*

imposter • *an imposter with false documents*
quack • *He tried all sorts of quacks.*

free ① ADJECTIVE
not being held prisoner • *a free man*
at large • *Three prisoners are at large.*
at liberty • *the last top Nazi still at liberty*
liberated • *newly liberated slaves*
loose • *He broke loose from his bonds.*

ANTONYM:
• captive

free ② ADJECTIVE
available without payment • *a free brochure*
complimentary • *complimentary tickets*
gratis • *The meal was gratis.*
unpaid • *unpaid voluntary work*
without charge • *They mended it without charge.*

free ③ VERB
to release from captivity • *to free the slaves*
discharge • *discharged from prison*
liberate • *liberated under the terms of the amnesty*
release • *The hostages were soon released.*
set at liberty • *He was set at liberty after ten years.*
set loose • *The animals were set loose after treatment.*

MORE SYNONYMS:
• emancipate
• unfetter

ANTONYM:
• imprison

freedom ① NOUN
the ability to choose • *freedom of action*
discretion • *Use your own discretion.*
latitude • *There is more latitude for personal opinions.*

leeway • *granted more leeway to pass reforms*
licence • *a licence to kill*
scope • *plenty of scope for improvement*

freedom ② NOUN
the state of being free or being set free • *gaining their freedom after months of captivity*
emancipation • *the emancipation of the slaves*
liberty • *three months' loss of liberty*
release • *the immediate release of the captives*

MORE SYNONYMS:
• deliverance
• manumission

ANTONYM:
• captivity

freedom ③ NOUN
the absence of something unpleasant • *freedom from pain*
exemption • *granted exemption from all taxes*
immunity • *information in exchange for immunity from prosecution*

frenzy NOUN
wild and uncontrolled behaviour • *gripped by a frenzy of nationalism*
agitation • *in a state of intense agitation*
fury • *She stalked out in a fury.*
hysteria • *mass hysteria*
madness • *a moment of madness*
rage • *She flew into a rage.*

MORE SYNONYMS:
• delirium
• paroxysm

frequent ① ADJECTIVE
happening often • *his frequent visits*
common • *a common occurrence*
continual • *continual demands for money*
everyday • *an everyday event*

habitual • *a habitual daydreamer*
recurrent • *a recurrent theme in her work*
repeated • *His parents made repeated attempts to visit.*

ANTONYM:
• rare

frequent ② VERB
to go somewhere often • *a restaurant which he frequents*
attend • *He often attends their meetings.*
haunt • *She haunted their house.*
patronize • *to patronize a hotel*
visit • *a place we often visit*

ANTONYM:
• avoid

friend NOUN
a person you know and like • *lifelong friends*
china (SOUTH AFRICAN; INFORMAL) • *a drinking session with his chinas*
companion • *my constant companion*
confidant or **confidante** • *her only confidant*
crony • *surrounded by her cronies*
mate (INFORMAL) • *going out with his mates*
pal • *We are great pals.*

MORE SYNONYMS:
• alter ego
• soul mate

ANTONYM:
• enemy

friendly ADJECTIVE
kind and pleasant • *a very friendly crowd*
affectionate • *on affectionate terms*
amiable • *He was very amiable company.*
close • *The two were very close.*
cordial • *a most cordial welcome*
genial • *a genial host*
welcoming • *a welcoming house*

a b c d e f g h i j k l m n o p q r s t u v w x y z

A
B
C
D
E
F
G
H
I
J
K
L
M
N
O
P
Q
R
S
T
U
V
W
X
Y
Z

MORE SYNONYMS:
• companionable
• comradely
• convivial

ANTONYM:
• unfriendly

friendship NOUN
a state of being friendly with someone • *I value our friendship.*
affection • *to win their affection*
attachment • *the deep attachment between them*
closeness • *her closeness to her sister*
goodwill • *as a gesture of goodwill*

ANTONYM:
• hostility

frighten VERB
to make someone afraid • *trying to frighten us*
alarm • *alarmed by the noise*
intimidate • *She is intimidated by her boss.*
scare • *You aren't scared of mice, are you?*
startle • *I didn't mean to startle you.*
terrify • *Heights terrified her.*
terrorize • *The gunmen terrorized the villagers.*
unnerve • *an unnerving silence*

frightened ADJECTIVE
having feelings of fear about something • *frightened of thunder*
afraid • *Jane was afraid of the other children.*
alarmed • *Don't be alarmed.*
petrified • *petrified of wasps*
scared • *scared of being alone in the house*
startled • *a startled animal*
terrified • *a terrified look*

MORE SYNONYMS:
• cowed

• panicky
• terror-stricken

frightening ADJECTIVE
causing someone to feel fear • *a frightening experience*
alarming • *an alarming increase*
hair-raising • *at hair-raising speed*
intimidating • *threatening and intimidating behaviour*
menacing • *a menacing glance*
terrifying • *one of the most terrifying diseases*

frivolous ADJECTIVE
not serious or sensible • *a frivolous young person*
flippant • *a flippant comment*
foolish • *saying foolish and inappropriate things*
juvenile • *juvenile behaviour*
puerile • *your puerile schoolboy humour*
silly • *making silly jokes*

ANTONYM:
• serious

front ① NOUN
the part that faces forward • *the front wall of the house*
face • *the face of the building*
frontage • *a restaurant with a river frontage*

ANTONYM:
• back

front ② NOUN
the outward appearance of something • *a respectable front*
appearance • *the appearance of fair treatment*
exterior • *his tough exterior*
face • *a brave face*
show • *a convincing show of affection*

front ③: **in front** PREPOSITION
further forward • *too close to the car in front*

ahead • *ahead of the rest of the field*
before • *I'm before you.*
leading • *the leading rider*

frown VERB
to draw the eyebrows together
• *She frowned in concentration.*
glare • *The woman glared angrily at him.*
glower • *She glowered but said nothing.*
knit your brows • *He knitted his brows in concentration.*
scowl • *He scowled at the waiter.*

frozen ADJECTIVE
extremely cold • *frozen to the bone*
arctic • *arctic weather conditions*
chilled • *chilled to the marrow*
frigid • *frigid temperatures*
icy • *an icy wind*
numb • *numb with cold*

frustrate VERB
to prevent something from happening • *His efforts were frustrated.*
block • *They are blocking the peace process.*
check • *to check the spread of the virus*
foil • *They foiled all my plans.*
thwart • *his way to thwart your club's ambitions*

MORE SYNONYMS:
• forestall
• nullify

fulfil VERB
to carry out or achieve something
• *He decided to fulfil his dream and go to college.*
accomplish • *If they all work together they can accomplish their goal.*
achieve • *We will strive to achieve these goals.*
carry out • *They seem to have very little intention of carrying out their commitments.*
perform • *Each component performs a different function.*

realize • *The question is, will our hopes ever be realized?*
satisfy • *The procedures should satisfy certain basic requirements.*

full ① ADJECTIVE
filled with something • *full of books*
filled • *filled up to the top*
loaded • *The van was loaded with furniture.*
packed • *The train was packed.*
saturated • *completely saturated with liquid*

ANTONYM:
• empty

full ② ADJECTIVE
missing nothing out • *I want a full account of what happened.*
comprehensive • *a comprehensive guide to the area*
detailed • *a detailed description*
exhaustive • *an exhaustive treatment of the subject*
extensive • *extensive coverage of the earthquake*
maximum • *the way to take maximum advantage of pay TV*
thorough • *a thorough search*

full ③ ADJECTIVE
loose-fitting • *a full skirt*
baggy • *a baggy sweater*
loose • *hidden under his loose shirt*
voluminous • *voluminous sleeves*

fun ① NOUN
an enjoyable activity • *It was great fun.*
amusement • *There is no amusement for teenagers in this village.*
enjoyment • *It gave us much enjoyment.*
entertainment • *little opportunity for entertainment*
pleasure • *to mix business and pleasure*
recreation • *time for recreation*

fun ② : **make fun of** VERB
to tease someone • Don't make fun
of him.
deride • This theory is widely derided.
laugh at • They laughed at his hat.
mock • He was often mocked by his
classmates.
ridicule • She allowed them to ridicule her.
taunt • a fellow pupil who had
taunted him about his height

MORE SYNONYMS:
• lampoon
• rib
• satirize

function ① NOUN
the useful thing that something or
someone does • The main function of
merchant banks is to raise capital.
duty • My duty is to look after the
animals.
job • Their main job is to keep us healthy.
purpose • The purpose of the occasion
was to raise money for charity.
remit • The centre's remit is to advise
businesses.
responsibility • He handled his
responsibilities as a counsellor in an
intelligent fashion.
role • information about the drug's
role in preventing infection

function ② NOUN
a large formal dinner, reception, or
party • We were going down to a
function in London.
dinner • a series of official dinners
gathering • I'm always shy at formal
gatherings like that.
party • They met at a party.
reception • At the reception they
served smoked salmon.

function ③ VERB
to operate or work • The heater was
not functioning properly.

go • My car won't go in fog.
operate • Ceiling and wall lights can
operate independently.
perform • When there's snow, how is
this car going to perform?
run • The system is now running
smoothly.
work • Is the telephone working today?

fund ① NOUN
an amount of money • the pension
fund
capital • difficulty in raising capital
foundation • money from a research
foundation
pool • a reserve pool of cash
reserve • a drain on the cash reserves
supply • to curb money supply and
inflation

fund ② NOUN
a large amount of something • an
extraordinary fund of energy
hoard • his hoard of supplies
mine • a mine of information
reserve • oil reserves
reservoir • the body's short-term
reservoir of energy
store • a store of fuel

fund ③ VERB
to provide the money for something
• to raise money to fund research into
breast cancer
finance • big projects financed by
foreign aid
pay for • His parents paid for his
holiday.
subsidize • heavily subsidized by the
government
support • He is supporting himself
through college.

fundi NOUN (SOUTH AFRICAN)
an expert • The local fundis are
wonderfully adept and have created a car
for hunting.

expert • *our team of experts*
geek • *a new site designed by dog-loving computer geeks*
guru • *Fashion gurus dictate some crazy ideas.*
master • *a master of the English language*
specialist • *a specialist in diseases of the nervous system*
virtuoso • *He was gaining a reputation as a piano virtuoso.*

funny ① ADJECTIVE
being strange or odd • *They heard a funny noise.*
mysterious • *in mysterious circumstances*
odd • *There was something odd about her.*
peculiar • *It tasted very peculiar.*
puzzling • *a puzzling development*
strange • *A strange thing happened.*
unusual • *a most unusual man*

funny ② ADJECTIVE
causing amusement • *a funny story*
amusing • *a most amusing lecturer*
comic • *comic moments*
comical • *the comical expression on his face*
hilarious • *We thought it was hilarious.*
humorous • *a humorous magazine*
witty • *a very witty speech*

MORE SYNONYMS:
• droll
• jocular
• risible

ANTONYM:
• serious

furious ① ADJECTIVE
extremely angry • *He is furious at the way his wife has been treated.*
enraged • *I got more and more enraged at my father.*

fuming • *He was still fuming over the remark.*
infuriated • *He knew how infuriated the conversation had made me.*
livid • *She was absolutely livid about it.*
mad • *I'm pretty mad about this, I can tell you.*
raging • *Inside, Sally was raging.*

MORE SYNONYMS:
• frenzied
• incensed
• tumultuous

furious ② ADJECTIVE
involving great energy, effort, or speed • *a furious gunbattle*
breakneck • *Jack drove to Mayfair at breakneck speed.*
fierce • *Competition has been fierce between the rival groups.*
frantic • *There was frantic activity behind the scenes.*
frenzied • *the frenzied run-up to the general election*
intense • *The military on both sides are involved in intense activity.*
manic • *Preparations continued at a manic pace.*

ANOTHER SYNONYM:
• frenetic

fuss ① NOUN
anxious or excited behaviour • *What's all the fuss about?*
agitation • *in a state of intense agitation*
bother • *I don't want any bother.*
commotion • *a commotion in the market*
confusion • *in the confusion after an ammunition dump blew up*
stir • *The play caused a stir here.*
to-do • *a big to-do*

MORE SYNONYMS:
• ado

a
b
c
d
e
f
g
h
i
j
k
l
m
n
o
p
q
r
s
t
u
v
w
x
y
z

• fluster
• palaver

fuss ② VERB
to behave in a nervous or restless way
• *Waiters fussed around the table.*
bustle • *shoppers bustling around the store*
fidget • *He was fidgeting with his tie.*
fret • *Stop fretting about the details.*

fussy ADJECTIVE
difficult to please • *fussy about his food*
choosy (INFORMAL) • *Cats can be choosy about what they eat.*
discriminating • *a discriminating visitor*
exacting • *She failed to meet his exacting standards.*
fastidious • *Disney was also fastidious about cleanliness.*
particular • *very particular about the colours he used*

MORE SYNONYMS:
• faddish
• finicky
• pernickety

futile ADJECTIVE
having no chance of success • *a futile effort to run away*
abortive • *the abortive coup attempt*
forlorn • *forlorn hopes of future improvement*
unsuccessful • *an unsuccessful bid for independence*
useless • *It was useless to even try.*
vain • *in the vain hope of success*

ANTONYM:
• successful

future ADJECTIVE
relating to a time after the present
• *to predict future growth*
approaching • *concerned about the approaching winter*
coming • *in the coming months*
forthcoming • *candidates for the forthcoming elections*
impending • *her impending marriage*
later • *We'll discuss it at a later date.*
prospective • *my prospective employers*

ANTONYM:
• past

Gg

a b c d e f **g** h i j k l m n o p q r s t u v w x y z

gadget NOUN
a small machine or tool • *kitchen gadgets such as toasters and kettles*
appliance • *Switch off all electrical appliances when they're not in use.*
device • *a device that warns you when the batteries need changing*
machine • *a machine for slicing vegetables*
tool • *a tool for cutting wood, metal or plastic*

MORE SYNONYMS:
• implement
• instrument
• utensil

gain ① VERB
to get something gradually • *Students can gain valuable experience by working.*
achieve • *Achieving our goals makes us feel good.*
acquire • *Companies should reward workers for acquiring more skills.*
earn • *She has earned the respect of the world's top women cyclists.*
obtain • *You would need to obtain permission to copy the design.*
secure • *He failed to secure enough votes for outright victory.*
win • *The long-term aim is to win promotion.*

MORE SYNONYMS:
• attain
• capture
• reap

gain ② VERB
to get an advantage • *Areas of the world would actually gain from global warming.*
benefit • *Both sides have benefited from the talks.*
profit • *Frankie is now profiting from his crimes.*

gain ③ NOUN
an increase or improvement in something • *The Party has made substantial gains in local elections.*
advance • *advances in computer technology*
growth • *The area has seen a rapid population growth.*
improvement • *a major improvement in standards*
increase • *an increase of 7% in visitors to the UK*
rise • *a 3% rise in electricity prices*

gamble ① VERB
to bet money on something • *John gambled heavily on the horses.*
back • *I backed Germany to win 1-0.*
bet • *He bet them £500 they would lose.*

gamble ② VERB
to take a risk • *Few firms will be willing to gamble on new products.*
chance • *Armstrong chanced a gallop to the water.*
risk • *One of his daughters risked everything to join him in exile.*
stake • *He has staked his reputation on the outcome.*

MORE SYNONYMS:
• hazard
• take a chance
• venture

gamble ③ NOUN
a risk that someone takes • *We are taking a gamble on a young player.*
chance • *You take a chance on the weather when you holiday in the UK.*
lottery • *Robinson described the final as a bit of a lottery.*
risk • *How much risk are you prepared to take?*

game NOUN
an occasion on which people compete • *South Africa's first game of the season*
clash • *the clash between Australia and the West Indies*
contest • *The rain spoiled a good contest.*
match • *a football match*

gap ① NOUN
a space or a hole in something • *They squeezed through a gap in the fence.*
break • *stars twinkling between the breaks in the clouds*
chink • *All the walls have wide chinks in them.*
crack • *a crack in the curtains*
hole • *a hole in the wall*
opening • *an opening in the trees*
space • *the space between their car and the one in front*
MORE SYNONYMS:
• cleft
• cranny
• crevice

gap ② NOUN
a period of time • *After a gap of nearly a decade, Manley was back.*
hiatus (FORMAL) • *The shop is open again after a two-year hiatus.*

interlude • *a happy interlude in the Kents' life*
interval • *There was a long interval of silence.*
lull • *a lull in the conversation*
pause • *Then, after a pause, he goes on.*

gap ③ NOUN
a difference between people or things • *the gap between rich and poor*
difference • *He denied there were any major differences between them.*
disparity (FORMAL) • *disparities between poor and wealthy school districts*
inconsistency • *There were major inconsistencies in his evidence.*

garbage ① NOUN
things that people do not want • *piles of garbage*
debris • *screws, bolts and other debris from a scrapyard*
junk (INFORMAL) • *What are you going to do with all that junk?*
litter • *If you see litter in the corridor, pick it up.*
refuse (FORMAL) • *refuse collection and street cleaning*
rubbish • *household rubbish*
trash • *I forgot to take out the trash.*
waste • *industrial waste*

garbage ② NOUN (INFORMAL)
ideas and opinions that are untrue or unimportant • *I personally think this is complete garbage.*
drivel • *What absolute drivel!*
gibberish • *a politician talking gibberish*
nonsense • *all that poetic nonsense about love*
rubbish • *He's talking rubbish.*

garbled ADJECTIVE
confused or incorrect • *A garbled message awaited us at the desk.*

confused • *the latest twist in a murky and confused story*
distorted • *a distorted version of what was said*
incomprehensible • *Her speech was incomprehensible.*
jumbled • *his jumbled account of how Jack had been hired*
unintelligible • *He muttered something unintelligible.*

gasp ① VERB
to breathe in quickly through your mouth • *She gasped for air.*
choke • *People began to choke as smoke filled the air.*
gulp • *She gulped air into her lungs.*
pant • *Amy climbed rapidly until she was panting with the effort.*
puff • *I could see he was unfit because he was puffing.*

MORE SYNONYMS:
• catch your breath
• fight for breath

gasp ② NOUN
a short quick breath of air • *An audible gasp went round the court.*
gulp • *I took in a large gulp of air.*
pant • *Her breath came in pants.*
puff • *He blew out a little puff of air.*

gather ① VERB
to come together in a group • *We gathered around the fireplace.*
assemble • *a place for students to assemble between classes*
congregate • *Youngsters love to congregate here in the evenings.*
flock • *The criticisms will not stop people flocking to see the film.*
mass • *The General was massing his troops for a counterattack.*
round up • *The police rounded up a number of suspects.*

MORE SYNONYMS:
• convene
• marshal
• muster

ANTONYM:
• scatter

gather ② VERB
to bring things together • *I suggest we gather enough firewood to last the night.*
accumulate • *In five years it has accumulated a huge debt.*
amass • *She has amassed a personal fortune of $38 million.*
collect • *1.5 million signatures have been collected.*
hoard • *They've begun to hoard food and gasoline.*
stockpile • *People are stockpiling food for the coming winter.*

gather ③ VERB
to learn or believe something • *"He speaks English." "I gathered that."*
assume • *I assume the eggs are fresh.*
conclude • *He concluded that Oswald was somewhat abnormal.*
hear • *I heard that he was forced to resign.*
learn • *She wasn't surprised to learn that he was involved.*
understand • *I understand that he's just taken early retirement.*

gathering NOUN
a meeting with a purpose • *polite social gatherings*
assembly • *an assembly of party members*
congregation • *The congregation sang hymns and said prayers.*
get-together (INFORMAL) • *family get-togethers*
meeting • *Can we have a meeting to discuss that?*
rally • *a pre-election rally*

a
b
c
d
e
f
g
h
i
j
k
l
m
n
o
p
q
r
s
t
u
v
w
x
y
z

A
B
C
D
E
F
G
H
I
J
K
L
M
N
O
P
Q
R
S
T
U
V
W
X
Y
Z

MORE SYNONYMS:
• conference
• congress
• convention

gaudy ADJECTIVE
colourful in a vulgar way • *gaudy fake jewellery*
bright • *fake fur, dyed in bright colours*
flashy • *women in flashy satin suits*
garish • *They climbed the garish purple-carpeted stairs.*
loud • *a loud checked shirt*
showy • *He favoured large showy flowers.*
tacky (INFORMAL) • *tacky red sunglasses*
vulgar • *I think it's a very vulgar house.*

MORE SYNONYMS:
• jazzy
• ostentatious
• tasteless
• tawdry

general ① ADJECTIVE
relating to the whole of something • *a general decline in employment*
broad • *a broad outline of the Society's development*
comprehensive • *a comprehensive guide to the region*
overall • *The overall quality of pupils' work had shown a marked improvement.*

MORE SYNONYMS:
• generic
• indiscriminate
• panoramic
• sweeping

ANTONYM:
• specific

general ② ADJECTIVE
widely true, suitable or relevant • *The project should raise general awareness about bullying.*
accepted • *the accepted version of events*

broad • *a film with broad appeal*
common • *Such behaviour is common to all young people.*
universal • *Music and sports programmes have a universal appeal.*
widespread • *The proposals have attracted widespread support.*

ANTONYM:
• special

generosity NOUN
willingness to give money, time or help • *She is well known for her generosity.*
benevolence • *Banks are not known for their benevolence.*
charity • *private acts of charity*
kindness • *We have been treated with such kindness by everybody.*

MORE SYNONYMS:
• bounty
• liberality
• munificence
• open-handedness

ANTONYM:
• meanness

generous ① ADJECTIVE
willing to give money, time or help • *The gift is generous by any standards.*
charitable • *Individuals can be charitable and help their neighbours.*
hospitable • *He was very hospitable to me when I came to New York.*
kind • *She is warm-hearted and kind to everyone.*
lavish • *The Princess received a number of lavish gifts from her hosts.*
liberal • *Don't be too liberal with your spending.*

MORE SYNONYMS:
• munificent
• open-handed
• prodigal
• unstinting

ANTONYM:
• mean

generous ② ADJECTIVE
very large • *a generous portion of spaghetti*
abundant • *an abundant supply of hot food*
ample • *There is ample space for a good-sized kitchen.*
plentiful • *a plentiful supply of beer*

ANTONYM:
• meagre

genius ① NOUN
a very clever or talented person • *a mathematical genius*
brain • *the financial brain behind the company*
master • *Spiro Rosakis is a master of his craft.*
mastermind • *the mastermind of the plot to kill the ex-prime minister*
virtuoso • *The man is a virtuoso of pop music.*

genius ② NOUN
extraordinary ability or talent • *a poet of genius*
brains • *She has brains as well as beauty.*
brilliance • *his brilliance as a director*
intellect • *people of great intellect*

gentle ADJECTIVE
not violent or rough • *a quiet and gentle man*
benign • *a good-looking chap with a benign expression*
kind • *I fell in love with him because of his kind nature.*
kindly • *a kindly old gentleman*
meek • *He was a meek, mild-mannered fellow.*
mild • *Alexis was quiet, mild and happy-go-lucky.*
placid • *a look of impatience on her normally placid face*

soft • *She had a very soft heart.*
tender • *Her voice was tender.*

MORE SYNONYMS:
• compassionate
• humane
• lenient
• sweet-tempered

ANTONYM:
• cruel

genuine ADJECTIVE
not false or pretend • *They're convinced the picture is genuine.*
authentic • *an authentic French recipe*
bona fide • *We are happy to donate to bona fide charities.*
dinkum (AUSTRALIAN AND NEW ZEALAND; INFORMAL) • *They are all dinkum stolen bank notes.*
real • *a real Rembrandt*

ANTONYM:
• fake

get ① VERB
to fetch or receive something • *I'll get us all a cup of coffee.*
acquire • *I have recently acquired a new camera.*
fetch • *Sylvia fetched a towel from the bathroom.*
obtain • *Evans was trying to obtain a false passport.*
procure (FORMAL) • *It remained very difficult to procure food.*
receive • *I received your letter of November 7.*
secure (FORMAL) • *He failed to secure enough votes for outright victory.*

get ② VERB
to change from one state to another • *People draw the curtains once it gets dark.*
become • *The wind became stronger.*
grow • *He grew to love his work.*

a
b
c
d
e
f
g
h
i
j
k
l
m
n
o
p
q
r
s
t
u
v
w
x
y
z

turn • *The leaves have turned golden-brown.*

get on VERB

to enjoy someone's company • *I get on very well with his wife.*
be compatible • *Mary and I are very compatible.*
hit it off (INFORMAL) • *They hit it off straight away.*

ghost NOUN

the spirit of a dead person • *the ghost of the drowned girl*
apparition • *She felt as if she were seeing a ghostly apparition.*
phantom • *She was relentlessly pursued by a grossly disfigured phantom.*
spectre • *The Tower is said to be haunted by the spectre of Anne Boleyn.*
spirit • *the spirits of our dead ancestors*
RELATED WORD:
• ADJECTIVE spectral

gidday or g'day INTERJECTION

(AUSTRALIAN AND NEW ZEALAND)
hello • *Gidday, mate!*
hello • *Hello, Trish. Glad you could make it.*
hi (INFORMAL) • *Hi, how are you doing?*
good morning (FORMAL) • *Good morning, class.*
good afternoon (FORMAL) • *Good afternoon, Miss Bates.*
good evening (FORMAL) • *Good evening, ladies and gentlemen!*

gift ① NOUN

something you give someone • *He showered her with gifts.*
bequest (FORMAL) • *They received a bequest of $310,000.*
bonsela (SOUTH AFRICAN) • *a generous bonsela*
contribution • *companies that make charitable contributions*
donation • *donations of food and clothing for victims of the hurricane*

legacy • *What about the legacy from your uncle?*
present • *This book would make a great Christmas present.*

gift ② NOUN

a natural skill or ability • *a gift for comedy*
ability • *It's obvious he has an exceptional ability.*
aptitude • *She realised she had an aptitude for writing.*
flair • *Tony found he had a real flair for design.*
talent • *Both her children have a talent for music.*

give ① VERB

to provide someone with something • *I gave her a CD.*
award • *The Mayor awarded him a medal.*
deliver • *The Canadians plan to deliver more food to southern Somalia.*
donate • *Others donated second-hand clothes.*
grant • *Permission was granted a few weeks ago.*
hand • *Isabel handed me a glass of orange juice.*
present • *The Queen presented the prizes.*
provide • *The government was not in a position to provide them with food.*
supply • *a contract to supply radar equipment to the Philippines*
MORE SYNONYMS:
• accord
• administer
• bestow
• confer
ANTONYM:
• take

give ② VERB

to collapse or break under pressure

• *My knees gave under me.*
buckle • *His left wrist buckled under the strain.*
cave in • *Half the ceiling caved in.*
collapse • *The roof supports had collapsed.*
give way • *He fell when a ledge gave way beneath him.*
yield • *The handle yielded to her grasp.*

give in VERB
to admit that you are defeated • *Juppe should not give in to the strikers.*
capitulate • *Cohen capitulated to virtually every demand.*
concede • *Mr Pyke is not prepared to concede defeat.*
submit • *Mrs Jones submitted to an operation on her right knee.*
succumb • *The Minister said his country would never succumb to pressure.*
surrender • *He surrendered to American troops.*
yield • *an enemy who had shown no desire to yield*

glad ADJECTIVE
happy about something • *They'll be glad to get away from it all.*
delighted • *Frank will be delighted to see you.*
happy • *Jacques is very happy that you are here.*
joyful • *a joyful reunion with his mother*
overjoyed • *Shelley was overjoyed to see me.*
pleased • *They're pleased to be going home.*

ANTONYM:
• sorry

glance ① NOUN
a brief look at something • *The boys exchanged glances.*
glimpse • *They caught a glimpse of their hero.*

look • *Lucille took a last look in the mirror.*
peek • *Could I just have another quick peek at the bedroom?*
peep • *Would you take a peep out of the window?*

glance ② VERB
to look at something quickly • *He glanced at his watch.*
glimpse • *I soon glimpsed the doctor in his garden.*
look • *Bethan looked quickly at the elegant people around her.*
peek • *She had peeked at him through a crack in the wall.*
peep • *Now and then she peeped to see if he was noticing her.*
scan • *She scanned the advertisement pages of the newspaper.*

glance ③ VERB
to hit something quickly and bounce away • *My fist glanced off his jaw.*
bounce • *The ball bounced off the opposite post.*
brush • *She brushed her lips across Michael's cheek.*
skim • *pebbles skimming across the water*

MORE SYNONYMS:
• rebound
• ricochet

glare ① VERB
to look angrily at someone • *Joe glared at his brother.*
frown • *She looked up to see Vic frowning at her.*
glower • *He glowered at me but said nothing.*
scowl • *Robert scowled, and slammed the door behind him.*

glare ② NOUN
an angry look • *The waiter lowered his eyes to avoid Harold's furious glare.*

frown • *There was a deep frown on the boy's face.*
scowl • *Chris met the remark with a scowl.*

glare ③ NOUN
very bright light • *the glare of the headlights*
blaze • *There was a sudden blaze of light.*
glow • *the glow of the fire*

gloomy ① ADJECTIVE
feeling very sad • *They are gloomy about their chances of success.*
dejected • *Everyone has days when they feel dejected.*
down • *The old man sounded really down.*
glum • *What on earth are you looking so glum about?*
miserable • *She went to bed, miserable and depressed.*
sad • *You must feel sad about what's happened.*

MORE SYNONYMS:
• blue
• despondent
• downhearted

ANTONYM:
• cheerful

gloomy ② ADJECTIVE
dark and depressing • *a gloomy house on the edge of Phoenix Park*
dark • *The house looked dark and unwelcoming.*
dismal • *damp and dismal weather*
dreary • *the dreary, industrial city of Ludwigshafen*
dull • *It's always dull and raining.*

ANTONYM:
• sunny

glory ① NOUN
fame and admiration that someone gets • *It was her moment of glory.*

fame • *The film earned him international fame.*
honour • *the honour of captaining one's country*
immortality • *Some people want to achieve immortality through their work.*
praise • *Holbrooke deserves full praise for his efforts.*
prestige • *I'm not in this job for the prestige.*

MORE SYNONYMS:
• acclaim
• eminence
• renown

ANTONYM:
• disgrace

glory ② NOUN
something impressive or beautiful • *Spring arrived in all its glory.*
grandeur • *the grandeur of the country mansion*
magnificence • *the magnificence of the sunset*
majesty • *the majesty of Niagara Falls*
splendour • *the splendour of the palace of Versailles*

glory ③ VERB
to enjoy something very much • *The workers were glorying in their new-found freedom.*
gloat • *Their rivals were gloating over their triumph.*
relish • *He relished the idea of getting some cash.*
revel • *a ruthless killer who revels in his job*

gloss NOUN
a bright shine on a surface • *aluminium foil with a high gloss surface*
brilliance • *ceramic tiles of great brilliance*
gleam • *the gleam of brass*
polish • *His boots had a high polish.*

sheen • *The carpet had a silvery sheen to it.*
shine • *This gel gives a beautiful shine to the hair.*

glossy ADJECTIVE
smooth and shiny • *The leaves were dark and glossy.*
bright • *Her eyes were bright with excitement.*
brilliant • *The woman had brilliant green eyes.*
polished • *a highly polished floor*
shiny • *a shiny new sports car*
sleek • *sleek black hair*

glow ① NOUN
a dull steady light • *the glow of the fire*
gleam • *the first gleam of dawn*
glimmer • *In the east there was the slightest glimmer of light.*
light • *the light of the evening sun*

glow ② VERB
to shine with a dull steady light • *A light glowed behind the curtains.*
gleam • *Lights gleamed in the deepening mist.*
glimmer • *A few stars still glimmered.*
shine • *Scattered lights shone on the horizon.*
smoulder • *A very small fire was smouldering in the grate.*

glue VERB
to stick things together • *Glue the two halves together.*
fix • *Fix the fabric to the roller.*
paste • *The children were busy pasting gold stars on a chart.*
seal • *He sealed the envelope and put on a stamp.*
stick • *I stuck the notice on the board.*

go ① VERB
to move or travel somewhere • *I went home at the weekend.*

advance • *Rebel forces are advancing on the capital.*
drive • *My husband and I drove to Liverpool to see my mum.*
fly • *He flew to Los Angeles.*
journey (FORMAL) • *They intended to journey up the Amazon.*
leave • *What time are you leaving?*
proceed (FORMAL) • *The taxi proceeded along a lonely road.*
set off • *He set off for the station.*
travel • *Students often travel hundreds of miles to get here.*

go ② VERB
to work properly • *stuck on the motorway with a car that won't go*
function • *All the instruments functioned properly.*
work • *The pump doesn't work and we have no running water.*

go ③ NOUN
an attempt to do something • *I always wanted to have a go at waterskiing.*
attempt • *one of his rare attempts at humour*
shot (INFORMAL) • *a shot at winning a brand new car*
stab (INFORMAL) • *Several sports stars have had a stab at acting and singing.*
try • *After a few tries, Patrick had given up.*

goal NOUN
something that a person hopes to achieve • *The goal is to make as much money as possible.*
aim • *The aim of the festival is to raise awareness of this issue.*
end • *This is another policy designed to achieve the same end.*
intention • *He announced his intention of standing for parliament.*
object • *The object of the exercise is to raise money for charity.*
objective • *His objective was to play golf and win.*

purpose • *His purpose was to make a profit.*

target • *She failed to achieve her target of losing 20 pounds.*

gobble VERB

to eat food very quickly • *Pete gobbled all the beef stew.*

bolt • *Being under stress can cause you to bolt your food.*

devour • *She devoured two bars of chocolate.*

wolf • *Pitt wolfed down a peanut butter sandwich.*

good ① ADJECTIVE

pleasant, acceptable, or satisfactory • *We had a really good time.*

▶ see *Word Study* **good**, page 642

ANTONYM:
• bad

good ② ADJECTIVE

skilful or successful • *I'm not very good at art.*

▶ see *Word Study* **good**, page 642

ANTONYM:
• incompetent

good ③ ADJECTIVE

kind, thoughtful, and loving • *You are so good to me.*

▶ see *Word Study* **good**, page 642

ANTONYM:
• unkind

goodwill NOUN

kindness and helpfulness towards other people • *I invited them to dinner as a gesture of goodwill.*

benevolence • *He chuckles often and radiates benevolence.*

favour • *in order to gain the favour of whoever is in power*

friendliness • *Visitors remarked on the friendliness of the people.*

friendship • *The two countries signed treaties of friendship.*

gossip NOUN

informal conversation about other people • *Don't you like a good gossip?*

dirt • *the latest dirt on the other candidates*

hearsay • *They have had only hearsay and rumour to go on.*

MORE SYNONYMS:
• chitchat
• prattle
• scandal
• tittle-tattle

go through VERB

to experience an unpleasant event • *I was going through a very difficult time.*

endure • *He'd endured years of pain and sleepless nights.*

experience • *British business was experiencing a severe recession.*

undergo • *Magee underwent emergency surgery.*

grab VERB

to take hold of something roughly • *I grabbed him by the neck.*

clutch • *Michelle clutched my arm.*

grasp • *He grasped both my hands.*

seize • *She seized a carving fork and advanced in my direction.*

snatch • *Mick snatched the cards from Archie's hand.*

grace NOUN

an elegant way of moving • *He moved with the grace of a trained boxer.*

elegance • *She is elegance personified.*

poise • *Ballet classes are important for poise and grace.*

ANTONYM:
• clumsiness

grade VERB

to arrange things according to quality • *The oil is tasted and graded according to quality.*

A
B
C
D
E
F
G
H
I
J
K
L
M
N
O
P
Q
R
S
T
U
V
W
X
Y
Z

class • *They are officially classed as visitors.*
classify • *Rocks can be classified according to their origin.*
group • *The fact sheets are grouped into seven sections.*
rate • *He was rated as one of the country's top young players.*
sort • *The students are sorted into three ability groups.*

MORE SYNONYMS:
• evaluate
• sequence

gradual ADJECTIVE
happening or changing slowly • *the gradual improvement in communications*
continuous • *Our policy is one of continuous improvement.*
progressive • *One symptom of the disease is progressive loss of memory.*
slow • *The distribution of passports has been a slow process.*
steady • *a steady rise in sales*

ANTONYM:
• sudden

grammar NOUN

◆ **GRAMMAR WORDS**
◆ active
◆ aspect
◆ comparative
◆ passive
◆ person
◆ plural
◆ possessive
◆ singular
◆ superlative
◆ tense
◆ voice

grand ① ADJECTIVE
very impressive in size or appearance • *a grand building in the centre of town*
imposing • *the imposing gates at the entrance to the estate*

impressive • *The old boat presented an impressive sight.*
magnificent • *magnificent views over the San Fernando valley*
majestic • *a stupendous vista of majestic peaks*
monumental • *a monumental sculpture of a human face*
splendid • *a splendid Victorian mansion*

MORE SYNONYMS:
• glorious
• grandiose
• palatial

grand ② ADJECTIVE (INFORMAL)
pleasant or enjoyable • *It was a grand day.*
brilliant (INFORMAL) • *I've had a brilliant time.*
great (INFORMAL) • *I had a great time at university.*
marvellous (INFORMAL) • *It was a marvellous day and we were all so happy.*
terrific (INFORMAL) • *Everybody there was having a terrific time.*
wonderful • *It was a wonderful experience.*

grant ① NOUN
a money award given for a particular purpose • *My application for a grant has been accepted.*
allocation • *The aid allocation for that country is under review.*
allowance • *She gets an allowance for looking after Lillian.*
award • *a study award worth £2,000*
handout • *a cash handout of six thousand rupees*
subsidy • *state subsidies to public transport companies*

grant ② VERB
to allow someone to have something • *France has agreed to grant him political asylum.*

a
b
c
d
e
f
g
h
i
j
k
l
m
n
o
p
q
r
s
t
u
v
w
x
y
z

allocate • *The budget allocated $7 billion for development programmes.*

allow • *Children should be allowed the occasional treat.*

award • *A High Court judge awarded him £6 million damages.*

give • *We have been given permission to attend the meeting.*

permit • *The doorman said he could not permit them entry to the film.*

MORE SYNONYMS:
• accord
• bestow

ANTONYM:
• deny

grant ③ VERB
to admit that something is true • *I grant that you had some justification for your actions.*

accept • *I do not accept that there is a crisis in British science.*

acknowledge • *He acknowledged that he had been partly to blame.*

admit • *I admit that I do make mistakes.*

allow • *He allows that capitalist development may result in social inequality.*

concede • *Bess finally conceded that Nancy was right.*

ANTONYM:
• deny

grasp ① VERB
to hold something firmly • *He grasped both my hands.*

clutch • *I staggered and had to clutch at a chair for support.*

grab • *I grabbed him by the neck.*

grip • *She gripped the rope.*

hold • *He held the pistol tightly in his right hand.*

seize • *He seized my arm to hold me back.*

snatch • *I snatched at a hanging branch and pulled myself up.*

grasp ② VERB
to understand an idea • *The Government has not yet grasped the seriousness of the crisis.*

absorb • *He only absorbed about half the information we gave him.*

appreciate • *She never really appreciated the bitterness of the conflict.*

assimilate • *My mind could only assimilate one concept at a time.*

realize • *People don't realize how serious this recession has been.*

take in • *She listens to the explanation, but you can see she's not taking it in.*

understand • *They are too young to understand what is going on.*

grasp ③ NOUN
a firm hold • *She slipped her hand from his grasp.*

clasp • *He gripped my hand in a strong clasp.*

embrace • *He held her in a passionate embrace.*

grip • *His strong hand eased the bag from her grip.*

hold • *He released his hold on the camera.*

grasp ④ NOUN
a person's understanding of something • *They have a good grasp of foreign languages.*

awareness • *The children demonstrated their awareness of green issues.*

comprehension (FORMAL) • *This was utterly beyond her comprehension.*

grip • *He has lost his grip on reality.*

knowledge • *She has a good knowledge of these processes.*

understanding • *a basic understanding of computers*

grateful ADJECTIVE
pleased and wanting to thank

someone • *I am grateful to you for your help.*
appreciative • *We have been very appreciative of their support.*
indebted • *I am deeply indebted to him for his help.*
thankful • *I'm just thankful that I've got a job.*

ANTONYM:
• ungrateful

gratitude NOUN
the feeling of being grateful • *I wish to express my gratitude to Kathy Davis for her help.*
appreciation • *their appreciation of his efforts*
recognition • *an honour given in recognition of his help to the college*
thanks • *They accepted their certificates with words of thanks.*

ANTONYM:
• ingratitude

grave ① NOUN
a place where a corpse is buried • *They visited her grave twice a year.*
mausoleum • *the great mausoleum at the top of the hill*
pit • *The bodies were buried in a shallow pit.*
sepulchre • *Death holds him in his sepulchre.*
tomb • *the tomb of the Unknown Soldier*

RELATED WORD:
• ADJECTIVE sepulchral

grave ② ADJECTIVE (FORMAL)
very serious • *The situation in his country is very grave.*
acute • *The report has caused acute embarrassment to the government.*
critical • *Its finances are in a critical state.*
heavy (INFORMAL) • *Things were just starting to get heavy when the police arrived.*

serious • *The government faces very serious difficulties.*
sober • *a room filled with sad, sober faces*
solemn • *His solemn little face broke into smiles.*
sombre • *His expression became increasingly sombre.*

graze ① VERB
to slightly injure your skin • *He fell heavily and grazed his left arm.*
scrape • *She stumbled and fell, scraping her palms and knees.*
scratch • *The branches scratched my hands and face.*
skin • *He fell and skinned both his knees.*

graze ② NOUN
a slight injury to your skin • *He just has a slight graze.*
abrasion (FORMAL) • *He had severe abrasions to his right cheek.*
scratch • *She had scratches to her face.*

great ① ADJECTIVE
very large in size • *great columns of ice*
big • *He lives in a big house.*
colossal • *a colossal tomb*
huge • *a huge marquee in the grounds*
large • *a large pile of logs*
enormous • *They entered an enormous hall.*
extensive • *an extensive range of stock*
gigantic • *a gigantic theme park*
immense • *an immense building*
stupendous • *a stupendous sum of money*
tremendous • *It's a tremendous challenge*
vast • *The fire destroyed a vast area of forest.*

ANTONYM:
• small

great ② ADJECTIVE
important or famous • *the great novels of the nineteenth century*

celebrated • *the celebrated author of "Lord of the Rings"*
chief • *one of our chief problems*
celebrated • *the celebrated author of "Lord of the Rings"*
distinguished • *a distinguished baritone*
eminent • *two eminent French scientists*
famed • *the famed Australian actor*
famous • *a famous artist*
illustrious • *some of the world's most illustrious ballerinas*
important • *an important question*
main • *our main competitor*
major • *a major issue in the next election*
momentous • *a momentous occasion*
notable • *a notable chess player*
principal • *Our principal aim*
prominent • *Scotland's most prominent historian*
renowned • *the renowned heart surgeon*
serious • *a serious deficiency in the system*
significant • *This is a significant step towards peace.*

great ③ ADJECTIVE (INFORMAL)
very good • *I thought it was a great idea.*
beaut (AUSTRALIAN AND NEW ZEALAND) • *a beaut place to live*
fine • *He enjoys good food and fine wines.*
excellent • *an excellent pasta sauce*
superb • *The room was full of superb works of art.*
fantastic (INFORMAL) • *a fantastic firework display*
first-rate • *They pride themselves on their first-rate service.*
marvellous (INFORMAL) • *a marvellous rooftop restaurant*
outstanding • *outstanding works of art*
superb • *a superb staircase made from oak*

terrific (INFORMAL) • *It was a terrific party.*
tremendous (INFORMAL) • *You've done a tremendous job.*
wonderful • *I've had a wonderful time.*

ANTONYM:
• terrible

greedy ADJECTIVE
wanting more than you need • *greedy bosses who award themselves huge pay rises*
materialistic • *During the 1980s Britain became a very materialistic society.*
snoep (SOUTH AFRICAN; INFORMAL) • *a bunch of snoep businessmen*

MORE SYNONYMS:
• acquisitive
• avaricious
• grasping
• voracious

green ADJECTIVE
concerned with environmental issues • *Children and adolescents are now aware of green issues.*
conservationist • *a chorus of protest from conservationist groups*
ecological • *shared interest in ecological issues*

MORE SYNONYMS:
• eco-friendly
• environmentally friendly
• non-polluting
• ozone-friendly

♦ **SHADES OF GREEN**
♦ apple green
♦ avocado
♦ bottle-green
♦ chartreuse
♦ eau de nil
♦ emerald
♦ grass-green
♦ jade
♦ khaki

- lime
- Lincoln green
- olive
- pea green
- pistachio
- sage
- sea green
- turquoise

RELATED WORD:
- ADJECTIVE verdant

greet VERB

to say hello to someone when they arrive • *The president was greeted by local political leaders.*

meet • *A nurse met me at the entrance.*
receive (FORMAL) • *250 guests were received by the bride and bridegroom.*
welcome • *She was there to welcome him home.*

MORE SYNONYMS:
- hail
- salute

grey NOUN or ADJECTIVE

- **SHADES OF GREY**
- ash
- charcoal
- gunmetal
- hoary
- leaden
- pewter
- platinum
- silver
- silvery
- slate
- steel grey
- stone
- taupe
- whitish

grief NOUN

a feeling of extreme sadness • *a huge outpouring of national grief*
distress • *the intense distress they were causing my family*

heartache • *She has suffered more heartache than anyone deserves.*
misery • *All that money brought nothing but misery.*
sadness • *It is with a mixture of sadness and joy that I say farewell.*
sorrow • *a time of great sorrow*
unhappiness • *There was a lot of unhappiness in my adolescence.*

MORE SYNONYMS:
- anguish
- dejection
- heartbreak
- woe

ANTONYM:
- happiness

grieve ① VERB

to feel extremely sad • *He still grieves for his wife.*
lament • *All who knew Spender will lament his death.*
mourn • *The whole nation mourns the death of their great leader.*

grieve ② VERB

to make someone feel extremely sad • *It grieved Elaine to be separated from her son.*
distress • *It distresses me that the President has not tackled crime.*
pain • *It pains me to think of you struggling all alone.*
sadden • *The cruelty in the world saddens me.*
upset • *The news upset me.*

ANTONYM:
- cheer

grim ADJECTIVE

looking very serious • *Her face was grim.*
grave • *Mrs Williams was looking very grave.*
severe • *He leaned towards me, a severe expression on his face.*

A
B
C
D
E
G
H
I
J
K
L
M
N
O
P
Q
R
S
T
U
V
W
X
Y
Z

solemn • *What a solemn-faced kid he had been.*

stern • *Michael gave the dog a stern look.*

grip ① NOUN

a firm hold on something • *His strong hand eased the bag from her grip.*

clasp • *With one last clasp of his hand, she left him.*

grasp • *The spade slipped from her grasp and fell to the ground.*

hold • *He released his hold on the camera.*

grip ② NOUN

someone's control over something • *The president maintains an iron grip on his country.*

clutches • *She fell into the clutches of the wrong sort of person.*

control • *The port area is under the control of rebel forces.*

influence • *Alexandra fell under the influence of Grigori Rasputin.*

power • *I was really in the power of my mother.*

grip ③ VERB

to hold something firmly • *Alison gripped the steering wheel and stared straight ahead.*

clutch • *Michelle clutched my arm.*

grasp • *He grasped both my hands.*

hold • *He was struggling to hold on to the rope.*

ground NOUN

the surface of the earth • *We slid down the roof and dropped to the ground.*

dirt • *They sat on the dirt in the shade of a tree.*

earth • *The road winds for miles through parched earth.*

land • *800 acres of agricultural land*

soil • *In Southern India the soil is fertile.*

terrain • *Farms give way to hilly terrain.*

grounds ① PLURAL NOUN

the land surrounding a building • *the grounds of the university*

estate • *Lord Wyville's estate in Yorkshire*

gardens • *an elegant Regency house set in beautiful gardens*

land • *Their home is on his father's land.*

grounds ② PLURAL NOUN

the reason for doing or thinking something • *Owen was against it on the grounds of expense.*

basis • *Could you tell me on what basis the fee is calculated?*

cause • *No one had cause to get angry or unpleasant.*

excuse • *There's no excuse for behaviour like that.*

justification • *There was no justification for what I was doing.*

reason • *Who would have a reason to want to kill her?*

MORE SYNONYMS:
• foundation
• pretext
• rationale

group ① NOUN

a number of people or things • *a group of football supporters*

band • *a band of rebels*

bunch • *They're a nice bunch of lads.*

collection • *a collection of essays from foreign affairs experts*

crowd • *A small crowd of onlookers has gathered.*

gang • *Gangs of teenagers hang out in shop doorways.*

pack • *a pack of cards*

party • *a party of sightseers*

set • *Different sets of people often use the same buildings.*

MORE SYNONYMS:
• aggregation

- assemblage
- coterie

group ② VERB

to link people or things together
• *Their responses are grouped into 11 categories.*
arrange • *He started to arrange the books in piles.*
class • *They are officially classed as visitors.*
classify • *Rocks can be classified according to their origin.*
organize • *I was organizing the vast array of junk we had collected.*
sort • *The students are sorted into three ability groups.*

MORE SYNONYMS:
- assort
- marshal

grow ① VERB

to increase in size or amount
• *Bacteria grow more quickly once food is contaminated.*
develop • *These clashes could develop into open warfare.*
expand • *Will the universe continue to expand forever?*
increase • *Industrial output increased by 2%.*
multiply • *Her husband multiplied his demands on her time.*

ANTONYM:
- shrink

grow ② VERB

to be alive or exist • *Trees and bushes grew down to the water's edge.*
flourish • *The plant flourishes in slightly harsher climates.*
germinate • *Heat will encourage seeds to germinate.*
sprout • *It only takes a few days for beans to sprout.*

MORE SYNONYMS:
- shoot
- spring up

grow ③ VERB

to pass gradually into a particular state • *I grew a little afraid of the guy next door.*
become • *The wind became stronger.*
get • *The boys were getting bored.*
turn • *In October it turned cold.*

growth NOUN

the act of getting bigger • *the growth of the fishing industry*
development • *What are your plans for the development of your company?*
enlargement • *the enlargement of the European Union*
expansion • *a new period of economic expansion*
increase • *a sharp increase in the number of homeless people*

grumble ① VERB

to complain in a bad-tempered way
• *"This is very inconvenient," he grumbled.*
carp • *the man whom other actors love to carp about*
complain • *They complained about the high cost of visiting Europe.*
groan • *parents groaning about the price of college tuition*
moan • *moaning about the weather*
mutter • *She could hear the old woman muttering about young people.*
whine • *children who whine that they are bored*
whinge • *All she ever does is whinge.*

grumble ② NOUN

a bad-tempered complaint • *I didn't hear any grumbles from anyone at the time.*
complaint • *I get nothing but complaints about my cooking.*

moan • *Sometimes it helps to have a good old moan.*
murmur • *She paid without a murmur.*
objection • *If you have any objections, please raise them now.*
protest • *Despite our protests, they went ahead with the plan.*
whinge • *It's depressing listening to everybody's whinges.*

grumpy ADJECTIVE

bad-tempered and annoyed • *a grumpy old man*
irritable • *He had missed his dinner and grew irritable.*
sulky • *She still looked like a sulky teenager.*
sullen • *Several leading players have maintained a sullen silence.*
surly • *They were surly, sometimes downright rude to me.*

MORE SYNONYMS:
• bad-tempered
• cantankerous
• ill-tempered

guarantee ① NOUN

something that makes another thing certain • *The package offered a guarantee of job security.*
assurance • *a written assurance that he would start work at once*
pledge • *a pledge of support from the Ministry of Culture*
promise • *I'd made him a promise that I'd write a book for him.*
undertaking • *She gave an undertaking not to repeat the allegations.*
word • *He simply cannot be trusted to keep his word.*

guarantee ② VERB

to make it certain that something will happen • *Reports of this kind are guaranteed to cause anxiety.*

ensure • *We need to ensure that every student has basic literacy skills.*
pledge • *Both sides pledged that a nuclear war would never be fought.*
promise • *He promised that the rich would not get preferential treatment.*

guard ① VERB

to protect someone • *Police were guarding his home yesterday.*
defend • *He and his friends defended themselves against racist thugs.*
protect • *What can women do to protect themselves from heart disease?*
safeguard • *measures to safeguard their forces from chemical weapons*
shelter • *A neighbour sheltered the boy for seven days.*
shield • *She had shielded him from the terrible truth.*
watch over • *two policewomen to watch over him*

guard ② VERB

to stop someone making trouble or escaping • *The soldiers had been guarding paramilitary prisoners.*
patrol • *Prison officers continued to patrol the grounds.*
police • *It is extremely difficult to police the border.*
supervise • *Only two staff were supervising over 100 prisoners.*

guard ③ NOUN

someone who guards people or places • *The prisoners overpowered their guards and locked them in a cell.*
sentry • *We can sneak past the sentries.*
warden • *The siege began when the prisoners seized three wardens.*

MORE SYNONYMS:
• sentinel
• warder
• watchman

guess ① VERB
to form an idea or opinion about
something • *Wood guessed that he was
a very successful banker.*
estimate • *It's difficult to estimate
how much money is involved.*
imagine • *"Was he meeting
someone?" "I imagine so."*
reckon • *Toni reckoned that it must be
about three o'clock.*
speculate • *The reader can speculate
what will happen next.*
suppose • *I supposed you would have a
meal somewhere.*
suspect • *I suspect they were right.*
think • *Nora thought he was
seventeen years old.*

MORE SYNONYMS:
• conjecture
• hazard
• surmise

guess ② NOUN
an attempt to give the right answer
• *My guess is that the answer will be
negative.*
feeling • *My feeling is that everything
will come right for us.*
reckoning • *By my reckoning, 50% of
the team will be available.*
speculation • *speculations about
the future of the universe*

MORE SYNONYMS:
• conjecture
• hypothesis

guide ① VERB
to lead someone somewhere • *He
took Elliott by the arm and guided him
out.*
accompany • *We accompanied Joe to
the magazine's midtown offices.*
direct • *Officials directed him to the
wrong airport.*
escort • *I escorted him to the door.*
lead • *The nurse led me to a large room.*

MORE SYNONYMS:
• conduct
• convoy
• shepherd
• usher

guide ② VERB
to influence someone • *He should have
let his instinct guide him.*
counsel (FORMAL) • *Green was
counselled not to talk to reporters.*
govern • *Our thinking is as much
governed by habit as by behaviour.*
influence • *My dad influenced me to do
electronics.*

guilty ① ADJECTIVE
having done something wrong • *They
were found guilty of murder.*
convicted • *a convicted drug
dealer*
criminal • *He had a criminal record for
petty theft.*

MORE SYNONYMS:
• blameworthy
• culpable
• felonious

ANTONYM:
• innocent

guilty ② ADJECTIVE
unhappy because you have done
something bad • *When she saw me she
looked guilty.*
ashamed • *Zumel said he was not
ashamed of what he had done.*
regretful • *Surprisingly, she didn't feel
regretful about her actions.*
remorseful (FORMAL) • *He felt
remorseful for what he had done.*
sorry • *She was very sorry about all the
trouble she'd caused.*

MORE SYNONYMS:
• conscience-stricken

a
b
c
d
e
f
g
h
i
j
k
l
m
n
o
p
q
r
s
t
u
v
w
x
y
z

• contrite
• shamefaced

gullible ADJECTIVE
easily tricked • *I'm so gullible I would have believed him.*
naive • *It would be naive to believe Mr Gonzalez's statement.*
trusting • *She has an open, trusting nature.*

MORE SYNONYMS:
• credulous
• unsuspecting

ANTONYM:
• suspicious

gush VERB
to flow in large quantities • *Piping-hot water gushed out.*
flow • *Tears flowed down his cheeks.*
pour • *Blood was pouring from his broken nose.*
spurt • *a fountain that spurts water nine stories high*
stream • *water streaming from the pipes*

MORE SYNONYMS:
• cascade
• issue
• jet

A
B
C
D
E
F
G
H
I
J
K
L
M
N
O
P
Q
R
S
T
U
V
W
X
Y
Z

Hh

habit ① NOUN
something that is done regularly
• *his habit of smiling at everyone he saw*
convention • *It's just a social
convention that men don't wear skirts.*
custom • *an ancient Japanese custom*
practice • *the practice of clocking in
at work*
routine • *my daily routine*
tradition • *a family tradition at
Christmas*

habit ② NOUN
an addiction to something • *her
cocaine habit*
addiction • *his addiction to gambling*
dependence • *the effects of drug
dependence*

habitat NOUN
the natural home of a plant or
animal • *the habitat of the spotted owl*
environment • *a safe environment for
marine mammals*
territory • *a bird's territory*

hackneyed ADJECTIVE
used too often to be meaningful
• *hackneyed postcard snaps of lochs
and glens*
banal • *banal lyrics*
clichéd • *clichéd slogans*
stale • *Her relationship with Mark has
become stale.*
tired • *a tired excuse*
trite • *The film is teeming with trite
ideas.*

MORE SYNONYMS:
• run-of-the-mill
• threadbare
• timeworn

ANTONYM:
• original

hail ① NOUN
a lot of things falling together • *a hail
of bullets*
barrage • *a barrage of angry questions*
bombardment • *the sound of heavy
aerial bombardment*
shower • *a shower of rose petals*
storm • *The announcement provoked a
storm of protest.*
volley • *A volley of shots rang out.*

hail ② VERB
to attract someone's attention • *He
hailed me from across the street.*
call • *He called me over the Tannoy.*
signal to • *The lollipop lady signalled to
me to stop.*
wave down • *I ran on to the road and
waved down a taxi.*

halt ① VERB
to come or bring to a stop • *She held
her hand out to halt him.*
draw up • *The car drew up outside the
house.*
pull up • *The cab pulled up, and the
driver jumped out.*
stop • *The event literally stopped the
traffic.*

A
B
C
D
E
F
G
H
I
J
K
L
M
N
O
P
Q
R
S
T
U
V
W
X
Y
Z

halt ② VERB

to bring something to an end
• *Production was halted.*

cease • *A small number of firms have ceased trading.*

check • *We have managed to check the spread of terrorism.*

curb • *efforts to curb the spread of nuclear weapons*

cut short • *They had to cut short a holiday abroad.*

end • *They decided to end the ceasefire.*

terminate • *His contract has been terminated.*

ANTONYM:
• begin

halt ③ NOUN

an interruption or end to something
• *He brought the car to a halt.*

close • *Their 18-month marriage was brought to a close.*

end • *The war came to an end.*

pause • *There was a pause before he replied.*

standstill • *The country was brought to a standstill by strikes.*

stop • *He slowed the car almost to a stop.*

stoppage • *Air and ground crew are staging a 24-hour stoppage today.*

MORE SYNONYMS:
• impasse
• termination

hamper VERB

to make movement or progress difficult for someone • *I was hampered by a lack of information.*

frustrate • *His attempt was frustrated by the weather.*

hinder • *A thigh injury hindered her mobility.*

impede • *Their work was being impeded by shortages of supplies.*

obstruct • *charged with obstructing the course of justice*

restrict • *Her life is restricted by asthma.*

MORE SYNONYMS:
• encumber
• fetter

hand down VERB

to pass from one generation to another • *Recipes are handed down from mother to daughter.*

bequeath • *He bequeathed all his silver to his children.*

give • *a typewriter given to me by my father*

pass down • *an heirloom passed down from generation to generation*

pass on • *My parents passed on their love of classical music to me.*

MORE SYNONYMS:
• bestow
• will

handicap ① NOUN

a physical or mental disability • *He learnt to overcome his handicap.*

defect • *a rare birth defect*

disability • *children with learning disabilities*

handicap ② NOUN

something that makes progress difficult • *Being a foreigner was not a handicap.*

barrier • *Taxes are the most obvious barrier to free trade.*

disadvantage • *the disadvantage of unemployment*

drawback • *The flat's only drawback was that it was too small.*

hindrance • *She was a help rather than a hindrance to my work.*

impediment • *an impediment to economic development*

obstacle • *the main obstacle to the deal*

handicap ③ VERB

to make something difficult for

someone • *Greater levels of stress may seriously handicap some students.*
burden • *We decided not to burden him with the news.*
hamper • *I was hampered by a lack of information.*
hinder • *A thigh injury hindered her mobility.*
impede • *Fallen rocks impeded the progress of the rescue workers.*
restrict • *laws to restrict foreign imports*

handle ① NOUN
the part of an object by which it is held • *a broom handle*
grip • *He fitted new grips to his golf clubs.*
hilt • *the hilt of the small, sharp knife*

handle ② VERB
to hold or move with the hands • *Wear rubber gloves when handling cat litter.*
feel • *The doctor felt his arm.*
finger • *He fingered the few coins in his pocket.*
grasp • *Grasp the end firmly.*
hold • *Hold it by the edge.*
touch • *She touched his hand reassuringly.*

handle ③ VERB
to deal with or control something • *She handled the travel arrangements.*
administer • *The project is administered by the World Bank.*
conduct • *This is no way to conduct a business.*
deal with • *The matter has been dealt with by the school.*
manage • *Within two years he was managing the store.*
supervise • *I supervise the packing of all mail orders.*
take care of • *He took care of the catering arrangements.*

handsome ① ADJECTIVE
very attractive in appearance • *a handsome man*
attractive • *an attractive young woman*
good-looking • *good-looking actors*
ANTONYM:
• ugly

handsome ② ADJECTIVE
large and generous • *a handsome profit*
ample • *ample space for a good-sized kitchen*
considerable • *his considerable wealth*
generous • *a generous gift*
liberal • *a liberal donation*
plentiful • *a plentiful supply of vegetables*
sizable or **sizeable** • *He inherited the house and a sizeable chunk of land.*
ANTONYM:
• small

handy ① ADJECTIVE
conveniently near • *Keep a pencil and paper handy.*
at hand • *Having the right equipment at hand will be enormously useful.*
at your fingertips • *Firms need information at their fingertips.*
close • *a secluded area close to her home*
convenient • *Martin drove along until he found a convenient parking space.*
nearby • *He tossed the match into a nearby wastepaper bin.*
on hand • *Experts are on hand to offer advice.*

handy ② ADJECTIVE
easy to handle or use • *handy hints on looking after indoor plants*
convenient • *a convenient way of paying*
easy to use • *This ice cream maker is cheap and easy to use.*
helpful • *helpful instructions*

a b c d e f g h i j k l m n o p q r s t u v w x y z

A
B
C
D
E
F
G
H
I
J
K
L
M
N
O
P
Q
R
S
T
U
V
W
X
Y
Z

neat • *It had been such a neat, clever plan.*

practical • *the most practical way of preventing crime*

useful • *useful information*

hang ① VERB

to be attached at the top with the lower part free • *His jacket hung from a hook behind the door.*

dangle • *A gold bracelet dangled from his left wrist.*

droop • *Pale wilting roses drooped from a vase.*

hang ② VERB

to fasten something to another thing by its top • *She came out of the house to hang clothes on the line.*

attach • *He attached the picture to the wall with a nail.*

drape • *He draped the coat round his shoulders.*

fasten • *stirrups fastened to the saddle*

fix • *He fixed a pirate flag to the mast.*

suspend • *The TV is suspended from the ceiling on brackets.*

happen VERB

to take place • *The accident happened on Wednesday.*

come about • *It came about almost by accident.*

follow • *He was arrested in the confusion which followed.*

occur • *The crash occurred on a sharp bend.*

result • *Ignore the early warnings and illness could result.*

take place • *The festival took place last September.*

MORE SYNONYMS:
• ensue
• materialize

happiness NOUN

a feeling of great pleasure • *Money can't buy happiness.*

delight • *To my delight, it worked perfectly.*

ecstasy • *a state of almost religious ecstasy*

elation • *His supporters reacted to the news with elation.*

joy • *tears of joy*

pleasure • *Everybody takes pleasure in eating.*

satisfaction • *job satisfaction*

MORE SYNONYMS:
• exuberance
• felicity
• merriment

ANTONYM:
• sadness

happy ① ADJECTIVE

feeling or causing joy • *a happy atmosphere*

▶ see Word Study **happy**, page 644

ANTONYM:
• sad

happy ② ADJECTIVE

fortunate or lucky • *a happy coincidence*

auspicious • *It was not an auspicious start to his new job.*

convenient • *a convenient outcome for all concerned*

favourable • *a favourable result*

fortunate • *We're in a very fortunate situation.*

lucky • *It was a lucky chance that you were here.*

opportune • *It was hardly an opportune moment to bring the subject up.*

timely • *his timely arrival*

ANTONYM:
• unlucky

hard ① ADJECTIVE
firm, solid, or rigid • *a hard piece of cheese*
firm • *a firm mattress*
rigid • *rigid plastic containers*
solid • *solid rock*
stiff • *stiff metal wires*
strong • *It has a strong casing which won't crack or chip.*
tough • *dark brown beans with a rather tough outer skin*

ANTONYM:
• soft

hard ② ADJECTIVE
requiring a lot of effort • *hard work*
arduous • *a long, arduous journey*
exhausting • *It's a pretty exhausting job.*
laborious • *Keeping the garden tidy can be a laborious task.*
rigorous • *rigorous military training*
strenuous • *Avoid strenuous exercise in the evening.*
tough • *Change is often tough to deal with.*

ANTONYM:
• easy

hard ③ ADJECTIVE
difficult to understand • *That's a very hard question.*
baffling • *a baffling remark*
complex • *a complex problem*
complicated • *a complicated system of voting*
difficult • *It was a very difficult decision to make.*
puzzling • *Some of this book is rather puzzling.*

ANTONYM:
• simple

harden VERB
to make or become stiff or firm • *Give the cardboard two coats of varnish to harden it.*
bake • *The soil had been baked solid by the heatwave.*
cake • *The blood had begun to cake and turn brown.*
freeze • *The lake freezes in winter.*
set • *Lower the heat and allow the omelette to set.*
stiffen • *paper that had been stiffened with paste*

MORE SYNONYMS:
• anneal
• solidify

ANTONYM:
• soften

hardly ADVERB
almost not or not quite • *I could hardly believe what I was seeing.*
barely • *His voice was barely audible.*
just • *Her hand was just visible under her coat.*
only just • *For centuries farmers there have only just managed to survive.*
scarcely • *He could scarcely breathe.*

hardship NOUN
difficult circumstances • *Many people are suffering economic hardship.*
adversity • *They manage to enjoy life despite adversity.*
destitution • *a life of poverty and destitution*
difficulty • *Many new golf clubs are in serious financial difficulty.*
misfortune • *She seemed to enjoy the misfortunes of others.*
want • *They were fighting for freedom of speech and freedom from want.*

MORE SYNONYMS:
• oppression

a b c d e f g h i j k l m n o p q r s t u v w x y z

- privation
- tribulation

harm ① VERB
to injure someone or damage
something • *The hijackers seemed
anxious not to harm anyone.*
abuse • *Animals are still being
exploited and abused.*
damage • *He damaged his knee
during training.*
hurt • *He fell and hurt his back.*
ill-treat • *They thought he had been
ill-treating is wife.*
ruin • *My wife was ruining her health
through worry.*
wound • *The bomb killed six people and
wounded another five.*

harm ② NOUN
injury or damage • *All dogs are capable
of doing harm to human beings.*
abuse • *The abuse of animals is
inexcusable.*
damage • *The bomb caused extensive
damage.*
hurt • *an evil desire to cause hurt and
damage*
injury • *The two other passengers
escaped serious injury.*

harmful ADJECTIVE
having a bad effect on something
• *Whilst most stress is harmful, some is
beneficial.*
damaging • *damaging allegations
about his personal life*
destructive • *the awesome destructive
power of nuclear weapons*
detrimental • *levels of radioactivity
which are detrimental to public health*
hurtful • *Her comments can only be
hurtful to the family.*
pernicious • *the pernicious influence
of secret societies*

MORE SYNONYMS:
- baleful
- baneful
- deleterious
- injurious

ANTONYM:
- harmless

harmless ADJECTIVE
safe to use or be near • *This experiment
was harmless to the animals.*
innocuous • *Both mushrooms look
innocuous but are in fact deadly.*
nontoxic • *a cheap and nontoxic
method of cleaning up our water*
not dangerous • *The tests are not
dangerous to the environment.*
safe • *The doll is safe for children.*

ANTONYM:
- harmful

harsh ADJECTIVE
severe, difficult, and unpleasant
• *harsh weather conditions*
austere • *The life of the troops was still
comparatively austere.*
cruel • *an unusually cruel winter*
hard • *He had a hard life.*
ruthless • *the ruthless treatment of
staff*
severe • *My boss gave me a severe
reprimand.*
stern • *a stern warning*

MORE SYNONYMS:
- Draconian
- Spartan

ANTONYM:
- mild

hassle ① NOUN (INFORMAL)
something that is difficult or causes
trouble • *It's not worth the hassle.*
bother • *I buy sliced bread - it's less
bother.*

effort • *This chore is well worth the effort.*

inconvenience • *the expense and inconvenience of having central heating installed*

trouble • *You've caused us a lot of trouble.*

upheaval • *Moving house is always a big upheaval.*

hassle ② VERB (INFORMAL)
to annoy someone by nagging or making demands • *My husband started hassling me.*

badger • *They kept badgering me to go back.*

bother • *Go away and don't bother me about all that just now.*

go on at • *She's always going on at me to have a baby.*

harass • *We are routinely harassed by the police.*

nag • *She had stopped nagging him about his drinking.*

pester • *the creep who's been pestering you to go out with him*

hasty ADJECTIVE
done or happening suddenly and quickly • *The signs of their hasty departure could be seen everywhere.*

brisk • *a brisk walk*

hurried • *a hurried breakfast*

prompt • *It is not too late, but prompt action is needed.*

rapid • *a rapid retreat*

swift • *my swift departure*

hate ① VERB
to have a strong dislike for something or someone • *Most people hate him, but they don't care to say so.*

abhor • *He abhorred violence.*

be sick of • *We're sick of being ripped off.*

despise • *A lot of people despise and loathe what I do.*

detest • *Jean detested being photographed.*

dislike • *those who dislike change*

loathe • *a play universally loathed by the critics*

ANTONYM:
• love

hate ② NOUN
a strong dislike • *a violent bully, destructive and full of hate*

animosity • *The animosity between the two men grew.*

aversion • *I've always had an aversion to being part of a group.*

dislike • *Consider what your likes and dislikes are about your job.*

hatred • *her hatred of authority*

hostility • *He looked at her with open hostility.*

loathing • *Critics are united in their unmitigated loathing of the band.*

MORE SYNONYMS:
• animus
• detestation
• enmity
• odium

ANTONYM:
• love

hateful ADJECTIVE
extremely unpleasant • *It was a hateful thing to say.*

abhorrent • *Discrimination is abhorrent to my council and our staff.*

despicable • *a despicable crime*

horrible • *a horrible little boy*

loathsome • *the loathsome spectacle we were obliged to witness*

obnoxious • *He was a most obnoxious character. No-one liked him.*

offensive • *an offensive remark*

hatred NOUN
an extremely strong feeling of dislike

a
b
c
d
e
f
g
h
i
j
k
l
m
n
o
p
q
r
s
t
u
v
w
x
y
z

• He has been accused of inciting racial hatred.

animosity • The animosity between the two men grew.

antipathy • public antipathy towards scientists

aversion • my aversion to housework

dislike • his dislike of modern buildings

hate • These people are so full of hate.

revulsion • They expressed their revulsion at his violent death.

ANTONYM:
• love

haughty ADJECTIVE

showing excessive pride • He spoke in a haughty tone.

arrogant • an air of arrogant indifference

conceited • They had grown too conceited and pleased with themselves.

disdainful • She cast a disdainful glance at me.

proud • She was said to be proud and arrogant.

snobbish • They had a snobbish dislike for their intellectual inferiors.

stuck-up (INFORMAL) • She was a famous actress, but she wasn't a bit stuck-up.

ANTONYM:
• humble

have ① VERB

to own something • We have two tickets for the concert.

hold • He does not hold a firearm certificate.

keep • We keep chickens.

own • His father owns a local pub.

possess • He is said to possess a fortune.

have ② VERB

to experience something • He had a marvellous time.

endure • The company endured heavy losses.

enjoy • The average German will enjoy 40 days' paid holiday this year.

experience • Widows seem to experience more distress than do widowers.

feel • I felt a sharp pain in my shoulder.

sustain • He had sustained a cut on his left eyebrow.

undergo • He recently underwent brain surgery.

head ① NOUN

a person's mind and mental abilities • I don't have a head for business.

aptitude • an aptitude for accountancy

brain • If you stop using your brain you'll go stale.

common sense • Use your common sense.

intelligence • Try to use your intelligence to solve the puzzle - don't just guess.

mind • I'm trying to clear my mind of all this.

wits • She has used her wits to get where she is today.

MORE SYNONYMS:
• intellect
• rationality

head ② NOUN

the top, front, or start of something • the head of the queue

beginning • the beginning of this chapter

front • Stand at the front of the line.

source • the source of this great river

start • Go back to the start of this section.

top • the top of the stairs

ANTONYM:
• tail

head ③ NOUN

the person in charge of something
• heads of government

boss • the boss of the new company
chief • the President's chief of security
director • the director of the intensive
care unit
leader • the leader of the Conservative
Party
manager • the manager of our division
president • the president of the
medical commission
principal • the principal of the school

head ④ VERB

to be in charge of something • He
heads the department.

be in charge of • She's in charge of
the overseas division.
control • He controls the largest fast
food empire in the world.
direct • Christopher will direct day-to-
day operations.
lead • leading a campaign to save the
rainforest
manage • Within two years he was
managing the store.
run • Each teacher will run a different
workshop.

health ① NOUN

the condition of your body • Smoking
is bad for your health.

condition • He remains in a critical
condition in hospital.
constitution • He must have an
extremely strong constitution.
shape • He was still in better shape
than many younger men.

health ② NOUN

a state in which a person is feeling
well • In hospital they nursed me back
to health.

fitness • He has fitness problems.

good condition • He is in great
condition for a man of 56.
wellbeing • Singing can create a sense
of wellbeing.

ANTONYM:
• illness

healthy ① ADJECTIVE

having good health • She was a very
healthy child.

active • an active lifestyle
fit • A short, physically fit man of 61.
in good shape (INFORMAL) • I kept
myself in good shape by swimming.
robust • a robust and vibrant young
man
strong • a strong constitution
well • I'm not very well today.

ANTONYM:
• ill

healthy ② ADJECTIVE

producing good health • a healthy diet
beneficial • Wine in moderation is
beneficial to health.
bracing • a bracing walk
good for you • Regular, moderate
exercise is good for you.
nourishing • sensible, nourishing food
nutritious • a hot, nutritious meal
wholesome • fresh, wholesome
ingredients

MORE SYNONYMS:
• invigorating
• salubrious
• salutary

ANTONYM:
• unhealthy

heap ① NOUN

a pile of things • a heap of rubble
hoard • a hoard of silver and jewels
mass • a mass of flowers
mound • The bulldozers piled up huge
mounds of dirt.

a
b
c
d
e
f
g
h
i
j
k
l
m
n
o
p
q
r
s
t
u
v
w
x
y
z

pile • *a pile of betting slips*

stack • *stacks of books on the bedside table*

heap ② VERB

to pile things up • *She heaped vegetables onto his plate.*

pile • *He was piling clothes into the suitcase.*

stack • *They stacked up pillows behind his back.*

heaps PLURAL NOUN (INFORMAL)

plenty of something • *heaps of cash*

loads (INFORMAL) • *I've got loads of money.*

lots (INFORMAL) • *lots of fun*

plenty • *We've got plenty of time for a drink.*

stacks • *stacks of magazines*

tons (INFORMAL) • *I've got tons of work to do.*

hear ① VERB

to listen to something • *I heard the sound of gunfire.*

catch • *I don't believe I caught your name.*

eavesdrop • *The government illegally eavesdropped on his phone conversations.*

heed • *Few at the conference heeded his warning.*

listen in • *Secret agents listened in on his phone calls.*

listen to • *He spent his time listening to the radio.*

overhear • *I overheard two doctors discussing my case.*

hear ② VERB

to learn about something • *I heard that he was forced to resign.*

ascertain • *They had ascertained that he was not a spy.*

discover • *She discovered that they'd escaped.*

find out • *As soon as we found this out, we closed the ward.*

gather • *I gather the report is critical of the judge.*

learn • *She wasn't surprised to learn that he was involved.*

understand • *I understand that she's just taken early retirement.*

heat ① NOUN

the quality of being warm or hot • *the heat of the sun*

high temperature • *The suffering caused by the high temperature has been great.*

warmth • *the warmth of the sand between her toes*

ANTONYM:
• cold

RELATED WORD:
• ADJECTIVE thermal

heat ② NOUN

a state of strong emotion • *in the heat of the election campaign*

excitement • *in a state of great excitement*

fervour • *religious fervour*

intensity • *the intensity of feeling about this issue*

passion • *He spoke with great passion.*

vehemence • *I was surprised by the vehemence of his criticism.*

heat ③ VERB

to raise the temperature of something • *Heat the oil in a frying pan.*

reheat • *Reheat the soup to a gentle simmer.*

warm up • *Just before serving, warm up the tomato sauce.*

ANTONYM:
• cool

heathen NOUN (OLD-FASHIONED)
someone who does not believe in an established religion • *She called us all heathens and hypocrites.*
pagan • *the sky-god of the ancient pagans*
unbeliever • *punishing unbelievers and traitors*

MORE SYNONYMS:
• idolater
• infidel

ANTONYM:
• believer

heaven ① NOUN
the place where good people are believed to go when they die • *She told them their mother was now in heaven.*
next world • *He said, "We will see each other again in the next world."*
paradise • *They believed they would go to paradise if they died in battle.*

MORE SYNONYMS:
• Elysium (GREEK MYTH)
• happy hunting ground (NATIVE AMERICAN LEGEND)
• nirvana (BUDDHISM and HINDUISM)
• Valhalla (NORSE)
• Zion (CHRISTIANITY)

ANTONYM:
• hell

heaven ② NOUN
a place or situation liked very much • *I was in cinematic heaven.*
bliss • *a scene of domestic bliss*
ecstasy • *the ecstasy of being in love*
paradise • *The Algarve is a golfer's paradise.*
rapture • *the sheer rapture of listening to Bach's music*

heavy ① ADJECTIVE
great in weight or force • *a heavy frying pan*

bulky • *a bulky grey sweater*
massive • *a massive blue whale*

ANTONYM:
• light

heavy ② ADJECTIVE
serious or important • *a heavy speech*
deep • *a period of deep personal crisis*
grave • *the grave crisis facing the country*
profound • *Anna's patriotism was profound.*
serious • *It was a question which deserved serious consideration.*
solemn • *a simple, solemn ceremony*
weighty • *Surely such weighty matters merit a higher level of debate.*

ANTONYM:
• trivial

heed ① VERB
to pay attention to someone's advice • *Few at the conference heeded his warning.*
follow • *If you are not going to follow my advice, we are both wasting our time.*
listen to • *They won't listen to my advice.*
pay attention to • *The food industry is now paying attention to young consumers.*
take notice of • *We want the government to take notice of what we think.*

heed ② NOUN
careful attention • *He pays too much heed to her.*
attention • *He never paid much attention to his audience.*
notice • *So do they take any notice of public opinion?*

hell ① NOUN
the place where souls of evil people are believed to go after death

a
b
c
d
e
f
g
h
i
j
k
l
m
n
o
p
q
r
s
t
u
v
w
x
y
z

• Milton's Satan would rather "reign in Hell, than serve in Heaven".

abyss • Satan rules over the dark abyss.

inferno • an inferno described in loving detail by Dante

MORE SYNONYMS:
• fire and brimstone
• Gehenna (NEW TESTAMENT and JUDAISM)
• Hades (GREEK MYTH)
• hellfire
• Tartarus (GREEK MYTH)
• underworld

ANTONYM:
• heaven

hell ② NOUN (INFORMAL)
an unpleasant situation or place
• Bullies can make your life hell.

agony • the agony of divorce

anguish • the anguish of families unable to trace relatives who've disappeared

misery • All that money brought nothing but sadness and misery.

nightmare • The years in prison were a nightmare.

ordeal • the painful ordeal of the last year

hello INTERJECTION
a greeting • I popped my head in to say hello.

gidday (AUSTRALIAN AND NEW ZEALAND)
• Gidday, mate! How you doing?

hi (INFORMAL) • She smiled and said, "Hi".

how do you do? (FORMAL) • "How do you do, Mrs Brown?" Sam said, holding out his hand.

good morning (FORMAL) • Good morning, everyone.

good afternoon (FORMAL) • Good afternoon. Won't you sit down?

good evening (FORMAL) • Good evening, and welcome!

ANTONYM:
• goodbye

help ① VERB
to make something easier or better for someone • He began to help with the chores.

aid • a software system to aid managers

assist • information to assist you

lend a hand • I'd be glad to lend a hand.

support • He thanked everyone who had supported the strike.

help ② NOUN
assistance or support • The books were not much help.

advice • He has given me lots of good advice in my time here.

aid • millions of dollars of aid

assistance • I would be grateful for any assistance.

guidance • the reports which were produced under his guidance

helping hand • Most mums would be grateful for a helping hand.

support • Only 60 clubs pledged their support for the scheme.

helper NOUN
a person who gives assistance
• There is an adult helper for every two children.

aide • a presidential aide

assistant • a research assistant

deputy • I can't make it so I'll send my deputy.

henchman • Adolf Eichmann, Hitler's notorious henchman

right-hand man • He was the perfect right-hand man for the president.

supporter • He is a strong supporter of the plan.

helpful ① ADJECTIVE
giving assistance or advice • The staff in the office are very helpful.

accommodating • *Lindi seemed a nice, accommodating girl.*
cooperative • *I made every effort to be cooperative.*
kind • *I must thank you for being so kind to me.*
supportive • *Her boss was very supportive.*

ANTONYM:
• unhelpful

helpful ② ADJECTIVE
making a situation better • *Having the right equipment will be enormously helpful.*
advantageous • *an advantageous arrangement*
beneficial • *beneficial changes in the tax system*
constructive • *constructive criticism*
profitable • *a profitable exchange of ideas*
useful • *useful information*

helpless ADJECTIVE
weak or unable to cope • *a helpless baby*
defenceless • *a savage attack on a defenceless girl*
powerless • *He was powerless to help.*
unprotected • *She felt unprotected and defenseless.*
vulnerable • *the most vulnerable members of society*
weak • *taking ruthless advantage of a weak old man*

hesitant ADJECTIVE
uncertain about something • *At first he was hesitant to accept the role.*
diffident • *John was as outgoing as Helen was diffident.*
doubtful • *I was very doubtful about the chances for success.*
reluctant • *She was reluctant to get involved.*

unsure • *He made her feel awkward and unsure of herself.*
wavering • *wavering voters*

MORE SYNONYMS:
• irresolute
• vacillating

hesitate VERB
to pause or show uncertainty • *She hesitated before replying.*
dither • *We're still dithering over whether to marry.*
pause • *The crowd paused for a minute, wondering what to do next.*
waver • *Louise never wavered in her determination to take up the post.*

hide ① VERB
to put something where it cannot be seen • *She hid her face in her hands.*
cache • *He has £289 million cached away.*
conceal • *The hat concealed her hair.*
secrete • *She secreted the gun in the kitchen cabinet.*
stash (INFORMAL) • *He had stashed money away in a secret offshore account.*

hide ② NOUN
the skin of a large animal • *the process of tanning hides*
pelt • *a bed covered with beaver pelts*
skin • *a leopard-skin coat*

high ① ADJECTIVE
tall or a long way above the ground • *a high tower*
elevated • *an apartment in an elevated position overlooking the docks*
lofty • *lofty towers and spires*
soaring • *a 14th-century church with a soaring spire*
steep • *the steep hill leading up to her house*
tall • *a garden screened by tall walls*
towering • *towering red sandstone cliffs*

ANTONYM:
• low

high ② ADJECTIVE
great in degree, quantity, or intensity
• There is a high risk of heart disease.
acute • a state of acute anxiety
excessive • He was driving at excessive
speed.
extraordinary • drinking extraordinary
quantities of alcohol
extreme • acting under extreme
emotional pressure
great • These products created a great
level of interest.
severe • There are severe penalties for
drug smuggling.

ANTONYM:
• low

hill NOUN
◆ **TYPES OF HILL**
◆ brae (SCOTTISH)
◆ down
◆ dune
◆ elevation
◆ fell
◆ foothill
◆ height
◆ hillock
◆ hummock
◆ knoll
◆ kopje (SOUTH AFRICAN)
◆ mound
◆ prominence
◆ tor

hinder VERB
to get in the way of someone or
something • A thigh injury hindered her
mobility.
block • The President is blocking the
release of the two men.
check • We have managed to check the
spread of terrorism.

delay • Various problems have delayed
production.
frustrate • They have frustrated his
efforts to gain a work permit.
hamper • I was hampered by a lack of
information.
impede • Fallen rocks are impeding the
progress of rescue workers.

MORE SYNONYMS:
• encumber
• stymie

hint ① NOUN
an indirect suggestion • He gave
a strong hint that there would be a
referendum sooner rather than later.
clue • How a man shaves may be a
telling clue to his age.
indication • He gave no indication that
he was ready to compromise.
intimation • I did not have any
intimation that he was going to resign.
suggestion • We reject any suggestion
that the law needs amending.

hint ② NOUN
a helpful piece of advice • I hope to get
some fashion hints.
advice • Don't be afraid to ask for advice.
pointer • Here are a few pointers to help
you make your choice.
suggestion • Can I give you a few
suggestions?
tip • tips for busy managers

hint ③ VERB
to suggest something indirectly
• Criticism is hinted at but never made
explicit.
imply • The report implied that his death
was inevitable.
indicate • She has indicated that she
may resign.
insinuate • an article which insinuated
that he was lying

intimate • *He intimated that he was contemplating a shake-up of the company.*
suggest • *Are you suggesting that I need to lose some weight?*

hire ① VERB
to pay money to use something • *She hired the car for three days.*
charter • *They chartered a jet to fly her home.*
lease • *He went to Toronto, where he leased an apartment.*
rent • *She rents a house with three other girls.*

hire ② VERB
to employ the services of someone • *The staff have been hired on short-term contracts.*
appoint • *The Prime Minister has appointed a civilian as defence minister.*
commission • *You can commission her to paint something especially for you.*
employ • *They employed me as a nanny.*
engage • *We engaged the services of a recognized engineer.*
sign up • *He persuaded the company to sign her up.*

hit ① VERB
to strike someone or something forcefully • *Both men had been hit with baseball bats.*
▶ see Word Study **hit**, page 645

hit ② VERB
to collide with something • *The car had apparently hit a traffic sign.*
bang into • *She fell after another skier banged into her.*
bump • *The boat bumped against something.*
collide with • *He almost collided with Daisy.*
meet head-on • *Their cars met head-on down a narrow alleyway.*

run into • *The mail train ran into a derailed goods train at 75mph.*
smash into • *The car plunged down a cliff and smashed into a tree.*

hit ③ NOUN
the action of hitting something • *Give it a good hard hit with the hammer.*
blow • *He went to hospital after a blow to the face.*
knock • *a painful knock on the knee*
rap • *There was a rap on the door.*
slap • *She reached forward and gave him a slap.*
smack • *a smack with a ruler*
stroke • *six strokes of the cane*

hoard ① VERB
to store for future use • *People have begun to hoard food and petrol.*
save • *Save some fuel in case of emergencies.*
stockpile • *People are stockpiling food for the coming winter.*
store • *It's perfect for storing eggs or vegetables.*

hoard ② NOUN
a store of things • *a hoard of silver and jewels*
cache • *a cache of weapons and explosives*
fund • *a scholarship fund for engineering students*
reserve • *the world's oil reserves*
stockpile • *stockpiles of nuclear warheads*
store • *I have a store of food and water here.*
supply • *food supplies*

hoarse ADJECTIVE
rough and unclear • *Nick's voice was hoarse with screaming.*
croaky • *He sounds a bit croaky today.*

a b c d e f g h i j k l m n o p q r s t u v w x y z

gruff • *his gruff Scottish growl*
husky • *Her deep husky voice was her trademark.*
rasping • *Both men sang in a deep rasping tone.*

ANTONYM:
• clear

hobby NOUN

an enjoyable activity pursued in your spare time • *My hobbies are music and photography.*
diversion • *Finger painting is very messy but an excellent diversion.*
leisure activity • *America's top leisure activity is watching television.*
leisure pursuit • *His main leisure pursuit is hill walking.*
pastime • *His favourite pastime is golf.*

hold ① VERB

to carry or support something • *Hold the baby while I load the car.*
carry • *He was carrying a briefcase.*
clasp • *She clasped the children to her.*
clutch • *He was clutching a photograph.*
embrace • *The couple in the corridor were embracing each other.*
grasp • *He grasped both my hands.*
grip • *They gripped the rope tightly.*

hold ② NOUN

power or control over someone or something • *The party has a considerable hold over its own leader.*
control • *He will have to give up his control of the company.*
dominance • *the gang's dominance of the London underworld*
sway • *ideas that held sway for centuries*

hold ③ NOUN

the act or a way of holding something • *He grabbed the rope and got a hold on it.*
grasp • *His hand was taken in a warm, firm grasp.*
grip • *His strong hand eased the bag from her grip.*

hole ① NOUN

an opening or hollow in something • *The builders had cut holes into the stone.*
gap • *The wind was tearing through gaps in the window frames.*
hollow • *Water gathers in a hollow and forms a pond.*
opening • *He squeezed through a narrow opening in the fence.*
pit • *He lost his footing and began to slide into the pit.*
split • *The seat has a few small splits around the corners.*
tear • *I peered through a tear in the van's curtains.*

hole ② NOUN

a weakness in a theory or argument • *There are some holes in that theory.*
defect • *A defect in the aircraft caused the crash.*
error • *NASA discovered an error in its calculations.*
fault • *There is a fault in the computer program.*
flaw • *Almost all of these studies have serious flaws.*
loophole • *They exploited a loophole in the law.*

hole ③ NOUN (INFORMAL)

a difficult situation • *He admitted that the government was in a hole.*
fix (INFORMAL) • *This will put homeowners in a fix.*
hot water (INFORMAL) • *They have already been in hot water over high prices this year.*
mess • *the many reasons why the economy is in such a mess*

predicament • *the once great club's current predicament*

tight spot • *This was one tight spot he couldn't get out of.*

holiday NOUN

time spent away from home for enjoyment • *I'm exhausted - I really need a holiday.*

break • *They are currently taking a short break in Spain.*

leave • *Why don't you take a few days' leave?*

recess • *Parliament returns today after its summer recess.*

staycation • *The recession has made the staycation very popular.*

time off • *He took time off to go sailing with wife.*

vacation • *We went on vacation to Puerto Rico.*

holy ① ADJECTIVE

relating to God or a particular religion • *All Christian holy places were closed for a day in protest.*

blessed • *Blessed are the peacemakers, for they shall be called the children of God.*

consecrated • *the consecrated bread from the Eucharist*

hallowed • *hallowed ground*

sacred • *sacred music*

sacrosanct • *For him the Sabbath was sacrosanct.*

venerated • *Jerusalem is Christianity's most venerated place.*

holy ② ADJECTIVE

religious and leading a good life • *In the East, holy men have always had long hair.*

devout • *She is a devout Catholic.*

pious • *He was brought up by pious female relatives.*

religious • *They are both very religious.*

saintly • *his saintly mother*

virtuous • *a virtuous family man*

MORE SYNONYMS:
• god-fearing
• godly

ANTONYM:
• wicked

home ① NOUN

the building in which someone lives • *They stayed at home and watched TV.*

abode • *a luxurious abode*

dwelling • *One thousand new dwellings are planned for the area.*

house • *our new house*

residence • *the Royal Family's private residence*

home ② ADJECTIVE

involving your own country • *the home news pages of this newspaper*

domestic • *over 100 domestic flights a day to 15 UK destinations*

internal • *The government stepped up internal security.*

national • *major national and international issues*

native • *He was glad to be back on his native soil.*

ANTONYM:
• foreign

homely ADJECTIVE

simple, ordinary and comfortable • *The room was small and homely.*

comfortable • *A home should be warm and comfortable.*

cosy • *Guests can relax in the cosy bar.*

modest • *the modest home of a family who lived off the land*

simple • *They celebrated mass in a simple chapel.*

welcoming • *The restaurant is small and very welcoming.*

a
b
c
d
e
f
g
h
i
j
k
l
m
n
o
p
q
r
s
t
u
v
w
x
y
z

A
B
C
D
E
F
G
H
I
J
K
L
M
N
O
P
Q
R
S
T
U
V
W
X
Y
Z

ANTONYM:
• grand

honest ADJECTIVE
truthful and trustworthy • *He is a very honest, decent man.*
law-abiding • *law-abiding citizens*
reputable • *a reputable car dealer*
trustworthy • *He is a trustworthy and level-headed leader.*
truthful • *She could not give him a truthful answer.*
virtuous • *a virtuous family man*
ANTONYM:
• dishonest

honour ① NOUN
personal integrity • *I can no longer serve with honour in your government.*
decency • *No-one had the decency to tell me to my face.*
goodness • *He retains a faith in human goodness.*
honesty • *His reputation for honesty and integrity is second to none.*
integrity • *He was praised for his fairness and high integrity.*
ANTONYM:
• dishonour

honour ② NOUN
an award or mark of respect • *He was showered with honours - among them an Oscar.*
accolade • *the ultimate international accolade, the Nobel Peace prize*
commendation • *The officer received a commendation for brave conduct.*
homage • *films that pay homage to our literary heritage*
praise • *He had won consistently high praise for his theatre work.*
recognition • *At last, her father's work has received popular recognition.*

tribute • *He paid tribute to the organizing committee.*
MORE SYNONYMS:
• acclaim
• kudos

honour ③ VERB
to give someone special praise • *He was honoured by the French government with the Legion d'Honneur.*
commemorate • *a plaque commemorating the servicemen who died*
commend • *I commended her for that action.*
decorate • *He was decorated for his gallantry by the General.*
glorify • *My philosophy of life is to glorify God in all I do.*
praise • *He praised their excellent work.*

hooligan NOUN
a destructive and violent young person • *English football hooligans*
delinquent • *a nine-year-old delinquent*
hoon (AUSTRALIAN AND NEW ZEALAND; INFORMAL) • *the rocks hurled by hoons*
lout • *He was attacked by stone-throwing louts.*
tough • *Residents may be too terrified of local toughs to protest.*
vandal • *The Scout hut was burnt down by vandals.*
yob (BRITISH AND AUSTRALIAN; SLANG)
• *drunken yobs chanting football songs*

hope NOUN
a wish or feeling of desire and expectation • *There was little hope of recovery.*
ambition • *His ambition is to sail around the world.*
dream • *his dream of becoming a pilot*
expectation • *The hotel was being renovated in expectation of a tourist boom.*

hopeless ① ADJECTIVE
certain to fail or be unsuccessful
• Our situation is hopeless.
forlorn • the forlorn hope of finding a
better life
futile • their futile attempts to avoid
publicity
impossible • The tax is impossible to
administer.
pointless • a pointless exercise that
would only waste more time
useless • She knew it was useless to
protest.
vain • a vain attempt to sign a
goalkeeper

hopeless ② ADJECTIVE
bad or inadequate • I don't drive and
the buses are hopeless.
inadequate • The problem lies with
inadequate staffing.
pathetic • the pathetic state of the rail
network
poor • The flat was in a poor state of repair.
useless (INFORMAL) • My husband is
useless around the house.

horrible ① ADJECTIVE
disagreeable or unpleasant • a horrible
little boy
awful • I had an awful time.
disagreeable • a disagreeable odour
horrid • My parents are horrid to each
other.
mean • Why are you always so mean
to me?
nasty • This divorce could turn nasty.
unpleasant • He's a very unpleasant
little man.

horrible ② ADJECTIVE
causing shock, fear, or disgust
• horrible crimes
appalling • They have been living under
the most appalling conditions.

dreadful • She told me the dreadful news.
grim • a grim discovery
gruesome • gruesome murders
terrifying • a terrifying experience

horrify VERB
to cause to feel horror or shock • a
crime trend that will horrify parents
appal • I was appalled by her behaviour.
disgust • He disgusted everyone with
his boorish behaviour.
dismay • He was deeply dismayed by
the decision.
outrage • Human rights campaigners
were outraged by the execution.
shock • Pictures of emaciated prisoners
shocked the world.
sicken • What he saw at the accident
sickened him.

horror ① NOUN
a strong feeling of alarm or disgust
• He gazed in horror at the knife.
alarm • She sat up in alarm.
dread • She thought with dread of the
cold winter to come.
fear • I stood there crying and shaking
with fear.
fright • He uttered a shriek and jumped
with fright.
panic • He felt a sudden rush of panic at
the thought.
terror • She shook with terror.

horror ② NOUN
a strong fear of something • his horror
of death
abhorrence • their abhorrence of
racism
aversion • Many people have a natural
aversion to insects.
disgust • I threw the book aside in
disgust.
hatred • My hatred for him is intense.
loathing • She looked at him with
loathing.

a
b
c
d
e
f
g
h
i
j
k
l
m
n
o
p
q
r
s
t
u
v
w
x
y
z

revulsion • *They expressed their revulsion at his violent death.*

MORE SYNONYMS:
• abomination
• odium
• repugnance

horse NOUN
an animal kept for riding • *a fall from a horse*
brumby (AUSTRALIAN AND NEW ZEALAND) • *There's a mob of about 30 brumbies up there.*
equine • *the history and uses of equines*
moke (AUSTRALIAN AND NEW ZEALAND; SLANG) • *a tired old moke*
nag (INFORMAL) • *He unhitched his sorry-looking nag from a nearby post.*
pony • *Peter trotted about on the fat pony he had been given.*

MORE SYNONYMS:
• mount
• steed

RELATED WORDS:
• ADJECTIVES equestrian, equine, horsey
• NOUN equitation
• MALE stallion
• FEMALE mare
• YOUNG colt, filly, foal

hostile ADJECTIVE
unfriendly, aggressive, and unpleasant • *The Governor faced hostile crowds.*
antagonistic • *They were nearly all antagonistic to the idea.*
belligerent • *a belligerent war of words between India and Pakistan*
malevolent • *He fixed our photographer with a malevolent stare.*
unkind • *All last summer he'd been unkind to her.*

ANTONYM:
• friendly

hostility NOUN
aggressive or unfriendly behaviour towards someone or something • *hostility to Black and ethnic groups*
animosity • *The animosity between the two men grew.*
antagonism • *a history of antagonism between the two sides*
hatred • *her lifelong hatred of authority*
ill will • *He didn't bear anyone any ill will.*
malice • *There was no malice in her voice.*
resentment • *There is growing resentment against newcomers.*

MORE SYNONYMS:
• animus
• detestation
• enmity

ANTONYM:
• friendship

hot ① ADJECTIVE
having a high temperature • *a hot climate*
boiling • *It's boiling in here.*
heated • *a heated swimming pool*
scalding • *Her son was burned by scalding tea.*
scorching • *It was a scorching hot day.*
warm • *a warm, dry summer*

ANTONYM:
• cold

hot ② ADJECTIVE
very spicy • *a hot, aromatic Thai red curry*
peppery • *a rich, peppery extra virgin olive oil*
spicy • *a spicy Cajun sauce*

ANTONYM:
• bland

house NOUN
a building where a person or family

lives • *They live in a large house with eight rooms.*

abode • *I went round the streets and found his new abode.*

building • *Their flat was on the first floor of the building.*

dwelling • *One thousand new dwellings are planned for the area.*

home • *One in four people are without adequate homes.*

residence • *the Royal Family's private residence*

hug ① VERB

to hold someone close to you • *Lynn and I hugged each other.*

clasp • *She clasped the children to her.*

cuddle • *They used to kiss and cuddle in front of everyone.*

embrace • *The couple in the corridor were embracing each other.*

squeeze • *He kissed her on the cheek and squeezed her tight.*

hug ② NOUN

the act of holding someone close to you • *She gave him a hug.*

clinch (SLANG) • *They were caught in a clinch when her parents returned home.*

embrace • *a young couple locked in an embrace*

huge ADJECTIVE

extremely large in amount, size, or degree • *a huge crowd*

colossal • *a colossal waste of money*

enormous • *The main bedroom is enormous.*

giant • *a giant statue*

immense • *He wielded immense power.*

massive • *a massive surge in popularity*

vast • *this vast area of northern Canada*

MORE SYNONYMS:
• gargantuan
• prodigious

ANTONYM:
• tiny

hui NOUN (NEW ZEALAND)

a meeting • *He arranged a hui which called together a broad span of Maori tribes.*

assembly • *an assembly of prizewinning journalists*

conference • *a conference attended by 280 delegates*

congress • *a congress of coal miners*

convention • *the annual convention of the Society of Professional Journalists*

gathering • *the annual gathering of the South Pacific Forum*

meeting • *Can we have a meeting to discuss that?*

rally • *They held a rally to mark International Human Rights Day.*

humane ADJECTIVE

showing kindness and sympathy towards others • *a more just and humane society*

benevolent • *a most benevolent employer*

caring • *a very caring boy*

charitable • *charitable work*

compassionate • *a deeply compassionate man*

kind • *She is warmhearted and kind.*

merciful • *a merciful God*

thoughtful • *a very thoughtful gesture*

MORE SYNONYMS:
• altruistic
• humanitarian

humble ① ADJECTIVE

not vain or boastful • *He gave a great performance, but he was very humble.*

meek • *He was a meek, mild-mannered fellow.*

A
B
C
D
E
F
G
H
I
J
K
L
M
N
O
P
Q
R
S
T
U
V
W
X
Y
Z

modest • *He's modest, as well as being a great player.*
unassuming • *She has a gentle, unassuming manner.*
ANTONYM:
• haughty

humble ② ADJECTIVE
ordinary or unimportant • *A splash of wine will transform a humble casserole.*
lowly • *He was irked by his lowly status.*
modest • *his modest beginnings*
ordinary • *It was just an ordinary weekend.*
simple • *a simple dinner of rice and beans*

humble ③ VERB
to make someone feel humiliated • *the little car company that humbled the industry giants*
disgrace • *I have disgraced the family's name.*
humiliate • *His teacher continually humiliates him in maths lessons.*

humid ADJECTIVE
damp and hot • *a hot, humid Italian summer*
clammy • *My shirt was clammy with sweat.*
muggy • *The weather was muggy and overcast.*
steamy • *The air was hot and steamy from the heat of a hundred bodies.*
sticky • *four hot, sticky days in the middle of August*

humiliate VERB
to hurt someone's pride • *He enjoyed humiliating me.*
disgrace • *I have disgraced my family.*
embarrass • *It embarrassed him that he had no idea of what was going on.*
humble • *The champion was humbled by the unseeded qualifier.*

put down • *I know that I do put people down occasionally.*
shame • *Her son's affair had shamed her.*

humour ① NOUN
something which is thought to be funny • *The film's humour contains a serious message.*
comedy • *his career in comedy*
wit • *She was known for her biting wit.*
MORE SYNONYMS:
• drollery
• jocularity

humour ② NOUN
the mood someone is in • *He hasn't been in a good humour lately.*
frame of mind • *Clearly, she was not in the right frame of mind to continue.*
mood • *Lily was in one of her aggressive moods.*
spirits • *He was in very low spirits.*
temper • *Lee stormed off the field in a furious temper.*

humour ③ VERB
to please someone so that they will not become upset • *I nodded, partly to humour him.*
flatter • *I knew she was just flattering me.*
indulge • *He did not agree with indulging children.*
mollify • *The investigation was undertaken primarily to mollify pressure groups.*
pander to • *politicians who pander to big business*

hungry ADJECTIVE
wanting to eat • *I didn't have any lunch, so I'm really hungry.*
famished • *Isn't dinner ready? I'm famished.*
ravenous • *a pack of ravenous animals*
starving • *starving refugees*

hurry ① VERB

to move or do something as quickly as possible • *She hurried through the empty streets.*

dash • *He dashed upstairs.*

fly • *I must fly or I'll miss my train.*

get a move on (INFORMAL) • *Get a move on because my car's on a double yellow line.*

rush • *I've got to rush. I've got a meeting in a few minutes.*

scurry • *Reporters scurried to find telephones.*

hurry ② VERB

to make something happen more quickly • *his attempt to hurry the process of independence*

accelerate • *They must now accelerate the development of their new car.*

hasten • *This will hasten the closure of small pubs.*

quicken • *He quickened his pace a little.*

speed up • *an effort to speed up the negotiations*

ANTONYM:
• slow down

hurt ① VERB

to cause someone to feel pain • *I didn't mean to hurt her.*

harm • *The hijackers seemed anxious not to harm anyone.*

injure • *motorists who kill, maim, and injure*

wound • *The bomb killed six people and wounded another five.*

hurt ② VERB

to upset someone or something • *What you said really hurt me.*

distress • *I did not want to frighten or distress the horse.*

sadden • *He is saddened that they did not win anything.*

upset • *I'm sorry if I've upset you.*

wound • *My relatives have wounded me in the past.*

hurt ③ ADJECTIVE

upset or offended • *He felt hurt by all the lies.*

aggrieved • *He felt aggrieved at what happened.*

offended • *He was offended at being left out.*

upset • *I'm upset by your attitude.*

wounded • *I think she feels desperately wounded and unloved.*

MORE SYNONYMS:
• piqued
• rueful

hygiene NOUN

the principles and practice of health and cleanliness • *Be extra careful about personal hygiene.*

cleanliness • *Many of the beaches fail to meet minimum standards of cleanliness.*

sanitation • *the hazards of contaminated water and poor sanitation*

hypnotize VERB

to put someone into a state in which they seem to be asleep but can respond to suggestions • *She will hypnotize you and will stop you from smoking.*

put in a trance • *A stage hypnotist put her in a trance.*

put to sleep • *First the hypnotist will put you to sleep.*

MORE SYNONYMS:
• entrance
• mesmerize

hysterical ① ADJECTIVE

in a state of uncontrolled excitement or panic • *Calm down. Don't get hysterical.*

frantic • A bird had been locked in and was by now quite frantic.

frenzied • her frenzied attempts to get free

overwrought • One overwrought man had to be restrained by friends.

raving • He looked at her as if she were a raving lunatic.

hysterical ② ADJECTIVE (INFORMAL)
extremely funny • His stand-up routine was hysterical.

comical • Her expression is almost comical.

hilarious • He had a fund of hilarious jokes on the subject.

Ii

icon NOUN

a picture that represents a person
or thing • *Click on the icon to start the
program.*
avatar • *This game lets you create
your own avatar.*
representation • *an ancient
representation of a spear*
thumbnail • *You can make thumbnails
of your photographs with this
application.*

idea ① NOUN

a plan or suggestion for something
• *She said she'd had a brilliant idea.*
plan • *I have a cunning plan.*
recommendation • *a range of
recommendations for change*
scheme • *a proposed scheme*
solution • *He came up with a solution
to the problem.*
suggestion • *Do you have a better
suggestion?*

MORE SYNONYMS:
• hypothesis
• theory

idea ② NOUN

an opinion or belief about something
• *old-fashioned ideas about women*
belief • *my religious beliefs*
conviction • *a firm conviction that
things have improved*
impression • *your first impressions of
college*
notion • *I have a notion of what he is
like.*

opinion • *a favourable opinion of our
neighbours*
view • *Make your views known to local
politicians.*

idea ③ NOUN

what you know about something
• *They had no idea where they were.*
clue • *I don't have a clue what you mean.*
guess • *My guess is he went east.*
hint • *He gave no hint about where he was.*
inkling • *We had an inkling that
something was happening.*
notion • *I have a notion how it is done.*
suspicion • *I have a strong suspicion
they are lying.*

ideal ① NOUN

a principle or idea you try to achieve
• *I don't live up to my ideal of myself.*
principle • *acts that go against your
principles*
standard • *My father has high moral
standards.*
value • *the values of liberty and equality*

ideal ② NOUN

the best example of something • *She
remains his feminine ideal.*
epitome • *The hotel was the epitome
of luxury.*
example • *He was held up as an
example of courage.*
model • *a model of good manners*
paragon • *You are not a paragon of
virtue.*
prototype • *He was the prototype of a
strong leader.*

standard • *the standard by which we are compared*

MORE SYNONYMS:
• archetype
• criterion
• paradigm

ideal ③ ADJECTIVE

being the best example of something • *the ideal person for the job*

classic • *a classic example of hypocrisy*

complete • *She is the complete athlete.*

consummate • *a consummate politician*

model • *She is a model pupil.*

perfect • *He is the perfect husband for her.*

supreme • *a supreme method of cooking vegetables*

identify ① VERB

to recognize or name someone or something • *I tried to identify her perfume.*

diagnose • *This illness is easily diagnosed.*

label • *Poisonous substances should be labelled as such.*

name • *The victims of the fire have been named.*

pinpoint • *They could not pinpoint the cause of death.*

place • *The man was familiar, but I couldn't place him.*

recognize • *a man I recognized as Luke's father*

identify ②: **identify with** VERB

to understand someone's feelings • *I can't identify with the characters.*

associate with • *I associate myself with the green movement.*

empathize with • *I empathize with the people who live here.*

feel for • *I pitied and felt for him.*

relate to • *We have difficulty relating to each other.*

respond to • *She responded to his pain.*

idiot NOUN

a stupid person • *You're an idiot!*

fool • *He'd been a fool to get involved.*

galah (AUSTRALIAN; INFORMAL) • *sounding like an illiterate galah*

imbecile • *I don't want to deal with these imbeciles.*

moron • *I think that Gordon is a moron.*

oaf • *You clumsy oaf!*

twit (INFORMAL) • *I feel such a twit.*

idiotic ADJECTIVE

extremely foolish or silly • *an idiotic thing to do*

crazy • *You were crazy to leave then.*

daft (INFORMAL) • *He's not so daft as to listen to them.*

dumb (INFORMAL) • *I've met a lot of dumb people.*

foolish • *It is foolish to risk injury.*

senseless • *acts of senseless violence*

stupid • *stupid ideas*

MORE SYNONYMS:
• foolhardy
• insane
• moronic

idle ADJECTIVE

doing nothing • *a popular occupation for idle, wealthy young women*

jobless • *One in four people are now jobless.*

redundant • *redundant workers*

unemployed • *jobs for unemployed people*

MORE SYNONYMS:
• inactive
• stationary

ANTONYM:
• busy

ignorant ① ADJECTIVE

not knowing about something • *He*

was completely ignorant of the rules.
inexperienced • I am inexperienced at decorating.
innocent • Like a young child, she's innocent about the world.
oblivious • John appeared oblivious to his surroundings.
unaware • She was unaware that she was being filmed.
unconscious • He was unconscious of his failure.

ignorant ② ADJECTIVE
not knowledgeable about things
• People are afraid to appear ignorant.
green • The new boy is very green and immature.
naive • a shy, naive man
unaware • Young children are fairly unaware.

MORE SYNONYMS:
• uneducated
• unlearned
• untutored

ignore VERB
to take no notice of someone or something • Her husband ignored her.
blank (SLANG) • The crowd blanked her for the first four numbers.
discount • They simply discounted his feelings.
disregard • He disregarded his father's advice.
neglect • They never neglect their duties.
overlook • a fact that we all tend to overlook

ill ADJECTIVE
unhealthy or sick • Payne was seriously ill with pneumonia.
ailing • The President is said to be ailing.
poorly (BRITISH; INFORMAL) • Julie is still poorly.
queasy • I feel queasy on boats.

sick • He's very sick and he needs treatment.
unhealthy • an unhealthy-looking fellow
unwell • She felt unwell back at the office.

MORE SYNONYMS:
• indisposed
• infirm
• under the weather

ANTONYM:
• healthy

illegal ADJECTIVE
forbidden by the law • an illegal organization
banned • banned substances
criminal • a criminal offence
illicit • illicit drugs
outlawed • a place where hunting is outlawed
prohibited • a country where alcohol is prohibited
unlawful • unlawful acts

MORE SYNONYMS:
• proscribed
• unauthorized
• wrongful

ANTONYM:
• legal

illness NOUN
a particular disease • a mystery illness
affliction • a severe mental affliction
ailment • common ailments
complaint • a skin complaint
disease • He has been cured of the disease.
disorder • a rare nervous disorder
lurgy (BRITISH, AUSTRALIAN AND NEW ZEALAND; INFORMAL) • It's only a matter of days before Joan gets the lurgy as well.
sickness • radiation sickness

illusion ① NOUN
a thing that you think you can see

a b c d e f g h i j k l m n o p q r s t u v w x y z

A
B
C
D
E
F
G
H
I
J
K
L
M
N
O
P
Q
R
S
T
U
V
W
X
Y
Z

• *Painters create the illusion of space.*
hallucination • *Perhaps the footprint was a hallucination.*
mirage • *I began to see mirages.*
semblance • *A semblance of normality has been restored.*

MORE SYNONYMS:
• chimera
• phantasm

illusion ② NOUN
a false belief • *Their hopes proved to be an illusion.*
delusion • *I was under the delusion that I could win.*
fallacy • *It's a fallacy that the rich are generous.*
fancy • *childhood fancies*
misconception • *There are many misconceptions about school.*

imaginary ADJECTIVE
existing in your mind but not in real life • *an imaginary friend*
fictional • *a fictional character*
fictitious • *a fictitious illness*
hypothetical • *a hypothetical situation*
ideal • *in an ideal world*
illusory • *Freedom is illusory.*
invented • *distorted or invented stories*
mythological • *mythological creatures*

ANTONYM:
• real

imagination NOUN
the ability to form new ideas • *a girl who lacks imagination*
creativity • *She paints with great creativity.*
ingenuity • *the ingenuity of engineers*
inventiveness • *the artistic inventiveness of Mozart*
originality • *a composer of great originality*
vision • *a leader with vision*

imagine ① VERB
to have an idea of something • *He could not imagine a more peaceful scene.*
conceive • *I can't even conceive of that much money.*
envisage • *I envisage them staying together.*
fantasize • *I fantasized about writing music.*
picture • *I tried to picture the place.*
visualize • *He could not visualize her as old.*

imagine ② VERB
to believe that something is the case • *I imagine you're talking about my brother.*
assume • *Don't assume we are similar.*
believe • *I believe you have my pen.*
gather • *I gather that his mother was Scottish.*
guess (INFORMAL) • *I guess he's right.*
suppose • *He supposed I would be back at school.*
suspect • *Susan suspected things would get worse.*

MORE SYNONYMS:
• fancy
• surmise

imitate VERB
to copy someone or something • *She imitated her parents.*
ape • *She is aping her sister's style.*
copy • *I used to copy everything my big brother did.*
emulate • *Sons are expected to emulate their fathers.*
impersonate • *He could impersonate all the other students.*
mimic • *He mimicked her accent.*
simulate • *a machine which simulates natural sounds*

MORE SYNONYMS:
• mirror

- mock
- parody

immediate ① ADJECTIVE

happening or done without delay
• *My immediate reaction was fear.*

instant • *He took an instant dislike to Mark.*

instantaneous • *The applause was instantaneous.*

immediate ② ADJECTIVE

most closely connected to you
• *my immediate family*

close • *I have a few close friends.*

direct • *your direct descendants*

near • *near relatives*

immediately ① ADVERB

right away • *Ingrid answered Peter's letter immediately.*

at once • *You must come at once.*

directly • *He will be there directly.*

instantly • *She'd been knocked down in the street and died almost instantly.*

now • *Get out, now!*

promptly • *The telephone was answered promptly.*

right away • *You'd better tell them right away.*

straightaway • *I'd like to see you straightaway.*

MORE SYNONYMS:
- forthwith
- posthaste

immediately ② ADVERB

very near in time or position
• *immediately behind the house*

closely • *He rushed out, closely followed by Kemp.*

directly • *James stopped directly under the window.*

right • *He stood right behind me.*

immense ADJECTIVE

very large or huge • *an immense cloud of smoke*

colossal • *a colossal waste of money*

enormous • *The main bedroom is enormous.*

giant • *a giant oak table*

gigantic • *a gigantic task*

huge • *Several painters were working on a huge piece of canvas.*

massive • *a massive cruise liner*

vast • *a vast expanse of water*

ANTONYM:
- tiny

imminent ADJECTIVE

going to happen very soon • *my sister's imminent arrival*

close • *My birthday is quite close.*

coming • *the coming dawn*

forthcoming • *their forthcoming marriage*

impending • *impending doom*

looming • *My exams are looming.*

near • *in the near future*

immune ADJECTIVE

not subject to or affected by something • *He seems immune to pressure.*

exempt • *She is exempt from blame.*

free • *He was not completely free of guilt.*

protected • *He is protected from the law.*

resistant • *crops that are resistant to disease*

safe • *I was safe from punishment.*

unaffected • *She is unaffected by the sight of blood.*

MORE SYNONYMS:
- insusceptible
- invulnerable

impatient ① ADJECTIVE

easily annoyed • *You are too impatient with others.*

brusque • *a brusque manner*

curt • *He had spoken in a very curt tone of voice.*

a
b
c
d
e
f
g
h
i
j
k
l
m
n
o
p
q
r
s
t
u
v
w
x
y
z

A
B
C
D
E
F
G
H
I
J
K
L
M
N
O
P
Q
R
S
T
U
V
W
X
Y
Z

irritable • *Brian was nervous and irritable with her.*

MORE SYNONYMS:
• intolerant
• snappy

ANTONYM:
• patient

impatient ② ADJECTIVE
eager to do something • *He was impatient to leave.*

eager • *Children are eager to learn.*
restless • *The kids were bored and restless.*

impede VERB
to make someone's or something's progress difficult • *Fallen rocks are impeding the progress of rescue workers.*

block • *The country has been trying to block these imports.*
delay • *Various set-backs delayed production.*
disrupt • *The drought has severely disrupted agricultural production.*
get in the way • *She had a job which never got in the way of her hobbies.*
hamper • *The bad weather hampered rescue operations.*
hinder • *The investigation was hindered by the loss of vital documents.*
obstruct • *The authorities are obstructing the inquiry.*

imperfect ADJECTIVE
having faults or problems • *We live in an imperfect world.*

broken • *broken toys*
damaged • *damaged goods*
defective • *defective eyesight*
faulty • *a car with faulty brakes*
flawed • *a flawed character*

MORE SYNONYMS:
• deficient
• impaired
• rudimentary

ANTONYM:
• perfect

impersonal ADJECTIVE
not concerned with people and their feelings • *I found him strangely distant and impersonal.*

aloof • *His manner was aloof.*
cold • *Sharon was very cold with me.*
detached • *He felt emotionally detached from the victims.*
formal • *Business relationships are usually formal.*
neutral • *He told me the news in a neutral manner.*
remote • *She was beautiful but remote.*

MORE SYNONYMS:
• bureaucratic
• businesslike
• dispassionate

implore VERB
to beg someone to do something • *"Tell me what to do!" she implored him.*

beg • *I begged him to come with me.*
beseech (LITERARY) • *I beseech you to show him mercy.*
plead with • *The lady pleaded with her daughter to come home.*

important ① ADJECTIVE
necessary or significant • *Her sons are the most important thing to her.*

momentous • *the momentous decision to go to war*
serious • *a serious matter*
significant • *a significant discovery*
weighty • *We discussed weighty matters.*

MORE SYNONYMS:
• salient
• seminal

ANTONYM:
• unimportant

important ② ADJECTIVE
having great influence or power • *the*

most important person in the country
eminent • *an eminent scientist*
foremost • *a foremost expert in American history*
influential • *one of the most influential books ever written*
leading • *a leading nation in world politics*
notable • *notable celebrities*
powerful • *large, powerful countries*

MORE SYNONYMS:
• pre-eminent
• prominent

impose ① VERB
to force something on someone
• *Fines were imposed on the culprits.*
dictate • *The policy is dictated from the top.*
enforce • *It is a difficult law to enforce.*
inflict • *Inflicting punishment to stop crime is not the answer.*
levy • *a tax levied on imported goods*
ordain • *the task of trying to ordain parliamentary behaviour*

impose ② : **impose on** VERB
to take advantage of someone • *I should stop imposing on your hospitality.*
abuse • *They abused my hospitality by eating everything.*
take advantage of • *He took advantage of her generosity.*
use • *She's just using you.*

impossible ADJECTIVE
unable to happen or be believed • *You shouldn't promise impossible things.*
absurd • *absurd claims to have met big stars*
hopeless • *a hopeless task*
inconceivable • *It's inconceivable that people can still be living in those conditions.*
ludicrous • *his ludicrous plan to build a house*

out of the question • *Is a pay increase out of the question?*
unthinkable • *The idea of splitting up is unthinkable.*

MORE SYNONYMS:
• outrageous
• unattainable
• unworkable

ANTONYM:
• possible

impression ① NOUN
the way someone or something seems to you • *your first impressions of college*
feeling • *the feeling that she was wasting her life*
hunch • *Was your hunch right or wrong?*
idea • *I had my own ideas about what had happened.*
notion • *I have a notion of what he is like.*
sense • *She had the sense that she was in trouble.*

impression ② : **make an impression** VERB
to have a strong effect on people • *He certainly made an impression on his teachers.*
cause a stir • *News of her death caused a stir.*
influence • *You can't do anything to influence him.*
make an impact • *Events can make an impact on our lives.*

impressionable ADJECTIVE
easy to influence • *impressionable teenagers*
gullible • *I'm so gullible I'd have believed him.*
open • *an open, trusting nature*
receptive • *moulding their young, receptive minds*
sensitive • *Ouija boards can be*

a
b
c
d
e
f
g
h
i
j
k
l
m
n
o
p
q
r
s
t
u
v
w
x
y
z

dangerous, especially to sensitive people.
susceptible • *Children can be susceptible to advertisements.*
vulnerable • *vulnerable old people*

MORE SYNONYMS:
• ingenuous
• suggestible

impressive ADJECTIVE
tending to impress • *an impressive achievement*
awesome • *awesome mountains, deserts and lakes*
exciting • *He tells the most exciting stories.*
grand • *a grand old building*
powerful • *a powerful image*
stirring • *stirring music*
striking • *her striking personality*

MORE SYNONYMS:
• dramatic
• moving

imprison VERB
to lock someone up • *He was imprisoned for murder.*
confine • *Keep your dog confined to the house.*
detain • *They'll be detained and charged.*
incarcerate • *Prisoners were incarcerated in terrible conditions.*
jail • *An innocent man was jailed.*
lock up • *You people should be locked up!*
send to prison • *The judge sent him to prison for life.*

MORE SYNONYMS:
• constrain
• immure
• intern

ANTONYM:
• free

improbable ADJECTIVE
unlikely or unbelievable • *improbable stories*

doubtful • *It was doubtful if they would arrive on time.*
dubious • *dubious evidence*
far-fetched • *This all sounds a bit far-fetched.*
implausible • *a film with an implausible ending*
unbelievable • *an unbelievable storyline*
unlikely • *It is unlikely that he is alive.*

ANTONYM:
• probable

improve VERB
to get or make better • *He improved their house.*
advance • *Medical technology has advanced.*
better • *They tried to better their working conditions.*
enhance • *Good jewellery enhances your outfits.*
look up (INFORMAL) • *Things are looking up for me now.*
progress • *Jack's condition is progressing well.*
upgrade • *You'll have to upgrade your image.*

MORE SYNONYMS:
• ameliorate
• develop
• reform

ANTONYM:
• worsen

improvement NOUN
the fact or process of getting better • *dramatic improvements in conditions*
advance • *the advances in air safety since the 1970s*
development • *monitoring her language development*
enhancement • *the enhancement of the human condition*
progress • *The doctors are pleased with her progress.*
upturn • *an upturn in the economy*

impudence NOUN

disrespectful talk or behaviour towards someone • *Have you ever heard such impudence?*
audacity • *He had the audacity to speak up.*
boldness • *I was amazed at her boldness towards him.*
cheek (INFORMAL) • *I can't believe he had the cheek to complain.*
chutzpah (AMERICAN; INFORMAL) • *He had the chutzpah to ask us to leave.*
gall • *the most presumptuous question any interviewer has ever had the gall to ask*
impertinence • *His words sounded like impertinence.*
insolence • *I got punished for insolence.*
nerve • *You've got a nerve coming round here after what you've done.*

inability NOUN

a lack of ability to do something • *an inability to concentrate*
impotence • *a sense of impotence in the situation*
inadequacy • *my inadequacy as a gardener*
incompetence • *the incompetence of government officials*
ineptitude • *political ineptitude*

ANTONYM:
• ability

inadequate ① ADJECTIVE

not enough in quantity • *Supplies of medicine are inadequate.*
insufficient • *insufficient evidence to justify criminal proceedings*
lacking • *Why was military intelligence so lacking?*
poor • *poor wages*
scarce • *the region's scarce supplies of water*
short • *Deliveries are unreliable and food is short.*

ANTONYM:
• adequate

inadequate ② ADJECTIVE

not good enough • *She felt painfully inadequate in the crisis.*
deficient • *He made me feel deficient as a mother.*
incapable • *He lost his job for being incapable.*
incompetent • *the power to sack incompetent teachers*
inept • *He was inept and lacked the intelligence to govern.*
pathetic • *She made some pathetic excuse.*
useless • *I'm useless around the house.*

inappropriate NOUN

not suitable for a purpose or occasion • *This behaviour is inappropriate.*
improper • *the improper use of resources*
incongruous • *an incongruous assortment of clothes*
unfit • *houses that are unfit for living in*
unseemly • *He thought crying was unseemly.*
unsuitable • *food that is unsuitable for children*
untimely • *their unjustified and untimely interference*

ANTONYM:
• appropriate

incentive NOUN

something that encourages you to do something • *the incentive to work*
bait • *He added some bait to make the agreement sweeter.*
encouragement • *She didn't get much encouragement to do anything.*
inducement • *Are gangster films an inducement to crime?*
motivation • *Money is my motivation.*

stimulus • *He needed all the stimulus he could get.*

MORE SYNONYMS:
• lure
• motive
• spur

incident NOUN
an event • *Little incidents can shape our lives.*
circumstance • *This is a fortunate circumstance.*
episode • *I'm glad this episode is over.*
event • *recent events in Europe*
happening • *the latest happenings in sport*
occasion • *I remember that occasion fondly.*
occurrence • *Nancy wondered about the strange occurrence.*

incite VERB
to excite someone into doing something • *The campaigners incited a riot.*
agitate for • *Workers agitated for better conditions.*
goad • *He tried to goad me into a response.*
instigate • *The violence was instigated by a few people.*
provoke • *I provoked him into doing something stupid.*
whip up • *an attempt to whip up public hostility to the president*

include VERB
to have as a part • *A British breakfast always includes sausages.*
contain • *This sheet contains a list of names.*
cover • *The books covers many topics.*
embrace • *a small county embracing two cities*
encompass • *classes which encompass a wide range of activities*

incorporate • *The new cars incorporate many improvements.*
involve • *a high-energy workout which involves nearly every muscle*

ANTONYM:
• exclude

income NOUN
the money someone or something earns • *families on low incomes*
earnings • *his earnings as an accountant*
pay • *We complained about our pay.*
profits • *The bank made profits of millions of dollars.*
salary • *The lawyer was paid a good salary.*
takings • *The shop had huge takings that week.*
wages • *His wages have gone up.*

MORE SYNONYMS:
• proceeds
• receipts
• revenue

incomparable ADJECTIVE
too good to be compared with anything else • *an area of incomparable beauty*
inimitable • *his inimitable style*
peerless (LITERARY) • *He gave a peerless performance.*
superlative • *The hotel has superlative views.*
supreme • *the supreme piece of writing about the war*
unparalleled • *unparalleled happiness*
unrivalled • *an unrivalled knowledge of music*

MORE SYNONYMS:
• matchless
• unequalled

incompetent ADJECTIVE
lacking the ability to do something properly • *You are incompetent, and you know it.*

bungling • *a bungling amateur*
cowboy (BRITISH; INFORMAL) • *cowboy builders*
incapable • *an incapable leader*
inept • *an inept performance*
unable • *He felt unable to handle the situation.*
useless • *I felt useless and a failure.*

MORE SYNONYMS:
• ineffectual
• inexpert
• unskilful

ANTONYM:
• competent

incomplete ADJECTIVE
not finished or whole • *an incomplete book*
deficient • *a deficient diet*
half-pie (NEW ZEALAND; INFORMAL) • *His report was half-pie.*
insufficient • *insufficient information*
partial • *The concert was a partial success.*

MORE SYNONYMS:
• imperfect
• undeveloped
• unfinished

ANTONYM:
• complete

increase ① VERB
to make or become larger in amount • *The population continues to increase.*
enlarge • *They are trying to enlarge their customer base.*
expand • *We will expand the size of the picture.*
extend • *She plans to extend her stay.*
grow • *The sound grew in volume.*
multiply • *viruses which can multiply rapidly in the human body*
swell • *His anger swelled within him.*

MORE SYNONYMS:
• augment
• escalate

ANTONYM:
• decrease

increase ② NOUN
a rise in the amount of something • *a pay increase*
gain • *a gain in speed*
growth • *the growth of unemployment*
increment • *tiny increments of movement*
rise • *a rise in prices*
upsurge • *an upsurge of interest in books*

ANTONYM:
• decrease

incredible ① ADJECTIVE
totally amazing • *a champion with incredible skill*
amazing • *an amazing success*
astonishing • *an astonishing piece of good luck*
astounding • *an astounding discovery*
extraordinary • *extraordinary beauty*
marvellous • *a marvellous thing to do*
sensational (INFORMAL) • *a sensational performance*

incredible ② ADJECTIVE
impossible to believe • *the incredible stories of some children*
absurd • *absurd ideas*
far-fetched • *This all sounds very far-fetched to me.*
improbable • *highly improbable claims*
unbelievable • *The film has an unbelievable plot.*
unimaginable • *unimaginable wealth*
unthinkable • *It's unthinkable that Tom forgot your birthday.*

MORE SYNONYMS:
• implausible
• inconceivable
• preposterous

indecent ADJECTIVE
shocking or rude • *indecent lyrics*

a
b
c
d
e
f
g
h
i
j
k
l
m
n
o
p
q
r
s
t
u
v
w
x
y
z

A
B
C
D
E
F
G
H
I
J
K
L
M
N
O
P
Q
R
S
T
U
V
W
X
Y
Z

crude • *crude pictures*
dirty • *dirty jokes*
improper • *improper behaviour*
lewd • *lewd comments*
rude • *a rude gesture*
vulgar • *vulgar language*

independent ① ADJECTIVE
separate from other people or things
• *an independent political party*
autonomous • *an autonomous country*
free • *Do we have a free press?*
separate • *We live separate lives.*
unrelated • *two unrelated incidents*

independent ② ADJECTIVE
not needing other people's help • *a fiercely independent woman*
individualistic • *individualistic behaviour*
liberated • *a genuinely liberated woman*
self-sufficient • *I am quite self-sufficient.*
unaided • *his first unaided walk through the park*

indicate VERB
to show something • *a gesture which indicates his relief*
denote • *Messy writing denotes a messy mind.*
reveal • *His diary revealed his disturbed state of mind.*
show • *I would like to show my appreciation.*
signal • *Ted signalled that everything was all right.*
signify • *A white flag signifies surrender.*
MORE SYNONYMS:
• imply
• manifest
• point to

indication NOUN
a sign of something • *He gave no indication that he had heard me.*
clue • *Did she give any clue as to how she was feeling?*
hint • *The Minister gave a strong hint that he intended to resign.*
sign • *Your blood will be checked for any sign of kidney failure.*
signal • *They saw the visit as an important signal of support.*
suggestion • *There is no suggestion that the two sides are any closer to agreeing.*
warning • *a warning of impending doom*

ANOTHER SYNONYM:
• intimation

indirect ADJECTIVE
not done or going directly but by another way • *the indirect effects of smoking*
meandering • *the meandering course of the river*
oblique • *oblique threats*
rambling • *In a rambling answer, he denied the charge.*
roundabout • *a roundabout way of getting information*
tortuous • *a tortuous path*
wandering • *a wandering route through the woods*

ANTONYM:
• direct

individual ① ADJECTIVE
relating to separate people or things
• *individual dishes of trifle*
discrete (FORMAL) • *breaking down the job into discrete steps*
independent • *two independent studies*
separate • *Use separate chopping boards for different foods.*
single • *every single house in the street*

individual ② ADJECTIVE
different and unusual • *Develop your own individual writing style.*
characteristic • *a characteristic feature*
distinctive • *His voice was very distinctive.*
idiosyncratic • *a highly idiosyncratic personality*
original • *a chef with an original touch*
personal • *his own personal method of playing*
special • *her own special way of doing things*
unique • *Each person's signature is unique.*

individual ③ NOUN
a person, different from any other person • *the rights of the individual*
character • *a remarkable character*
party • *Who is the guilty party?*
person • *One person died and several others were injured.*
soul • *He's a jolly soul.*
ANOTHER SYNONYM:
• personage

industrious ADJECTIVE
tending to work hard • *industrious groups of students*
busy • *an exceptionally busy man*
conscientious • *Sherry was slow but conscientious.*
diligent • *Williams was diligent in the writing of letters.*
hard-working • *an exceptionally disciplined and hard-working young man*
tireless • *a tireless and willing worker*
ANTONYM:
• lazy

inefficient ADJECTIVE
badly organized and slow • *an inefficient government*
disorganized • *My boss is completely disorganized.*

incapable • *If he fails he will be considered incapable.*
incompetent • *an incompetent officer*
inept • *an inept use of power*
sloppy • *sloppy management*
MORE SYNONYMS:
• ineffectual
• inexpert
• slipshod
ANTONYM:
• efficient

inexperienced ADJECTIVE
lacking experience of a situation or activity • *inexperienced drivers*
green (INFORMAL) • *He was a young lad, and very green.*
new • *a new mother*
raw • *raw talent*
unaccustomed • *Kate is unaccustomed to being on TV.*
ANTONYM:
• experienced

infect VERB
to cause disease in something • *One mosquito can infect many people.*
affect • *Neil has been affected by the virus.*
blight • *trees blighted by pollution*
contaminate • *These substances can contaminate fish.*
taint • *blood that had been tainted with HIV*

infectious ADJECTIVE
spreading from one person to another • *infectious diseases*
catching • *There is no suggestion that multiple sclerosis is catching.*
contagious • *a highly contagious disease of the lungs*
spreading • *The spreading virus is threatening the population.*

A
B
C
D
E
F
G
H
I
J
K
L
M
N
O
P
Q
R
S
T
U
V
W
X
Y
Z

MORE SYNONYMS:
• communicable
• virulent

inferior ① ADJECTIVE
having a lower position than
something or someone else • Women
were given inferior status.
  lesser • the work of lesser writers
  lower • lower animals
  minor • a minor celebrity
  secondary • He was relegated to a
  secondary position.
  second-class • second-class citizens
  subordinate • His subordinate officers
  followed his example.

ANTONYM:
• superior

inferior ② ADJECTIVE
of low quality • inferior quality cassette
tapes
  mediocre • mediocre music
  poor • a poor standard of service
  second-class • a second-class
  education
  second-rate • second-rate restaurants
  shoddy • Customers no longer tolerate
  shoddy goods.

ANTONYM:
• superior

inferior ③ NOUN
a person in a lower position than
another • You must still be polite to your
inferiors.
  junior • the office junior
  menial • menials in poorly paid jobs
  subordinate • All her subordinates
  adored her.
  underling • Every underling feared him.

ANTONYM:
• superior

infinite ADJECTIVE
without any limit or end • an infinite
number of possibilities

  boundless • boundless energy
  eternal • the secret of eternal youth
  everlasting • our everlasting friendship
  inexhaustible • an inexhaustible
  supply of ideas
  perpetual • a perpetual source of worry
  untold • untold wealth

MORE SYNONYMS:
• bottomless
• interminable
• limitless

influence ① NOUN
power over other people • He has quite
a lot of influence.
  authority • You have no authority over
  me.
  control • Teachers have a lot of control
  over students.
  importance • a politician of great
  importance
  power • a position of power
  sway • My mother holds sway at home.

MORE SYNONYMS:
• ascendancy
• domination

influence ② NOUN
an effect that someone or something
has • under the influence of alcohol
  effect • Your age has an effect on your
  views.
  hold • He is losing his hold on the public.
  magnetism • a man of great personal
  magnetism
  spell • under the spell of one of his
  teachers
  weight • the weight of the law

influence ③ VERB
to have an effect on someone or
something • I never try to influence my
children.
  affect • He will not let personal
  preference affect his choice.
  control • I can't control him.

direct • I don't need you directing my life.
guide • Let your instinct guide you.
manipulate • I hate the way he manipulates people.
sway • efforts to sway voters

inform VERB
to tell someone about something
• Please inform me of your progress.
advise (FORMAL) • I can advise you of his whereabouts.
enlighten • a history lesson which enlightens you
notify • Ann was notified of her sister's illness.
tell • Tell me what is going on.

MORE SYNONYMS:
• apprise
• communicate

informal ADJECTIVE
relaxed and casual • His manner was informal and relaxed.
casual • a casual attitude towards money
colloquial • colloquial language
easy • easy conversation
familiar • John was too familiar towards his teacher.
natural • Beth was friendly and natural with us.
relaxed • a relaxed atmosphere in class

ANTONYM:
• formal

information NOUN
the details you know about something • Pat would not give any information about Sarah.
data • The survey provided valuable data.
drum (AUSTRALIAN; INFORMAL) • I don't have the drum on this yet.
facts • Pass on all the facts to the police.
material • highly secret material
news • We have news of your brother.

notice • advance notice of the event
word • I received word that the guests had arrived.

inform on VERB
to tell the police about someone who has committed a crime • Somebody must have informed on the thieves.
betray • They betrayed their associates to the police.
denounce • He was denounced as a dangerous rebel.
grass on (BRITISH; SLANG) • He grassed on the members of his own gang.
tell on (INFORMAL) • It's all right, I won't tell on you.

ingredient NOUN
a thing that something is made from
• Place all the ingredients in a pan.
component • the components of hamburgers
constituent • the main constituent of fish oil
element • the various elements in a picture

inhabit VERB
to live in a place • the people who inhabit these islands
dwell • the people who dwell in the forest
live • She has lived here for ten years.
lodge • Some people lodged permanently in the hallway.
occupy • Forty tenants occupy the block.
populate • a swamp populated by huge birds
reside (FORMAL) • He resides in the country.

inhabitant NOUN
someone who lives in a place • an inhabitant of Norway
citizen • American citizens
inmate • prison inmates

a
b
c
d
e
f
g
h
i
j
k
l
m
n
o
p
q
r
s
t
u
v
w
x
y
z

native • *Dr Brown is a native of New Zealand.*
occupant • *the previous occupant of the house*
resident • *the residents of the retirement home*

inheritance NOUN

something that is passed on • *The house would be his son's inheritance.*
bequest • *His aunt left a bequest for him in her will.*
heritage • *This building is part of our heritage.*
legacy • *His politeness was the legacy of his upbringing.*

injure VERB

to damage part of someone's body • *A bomb exploded, injuring five people.*
harm • *The hijackers did not harm anyone.*
hurt • *He hurt his back in an accident.*
maim • *Mines in rice paddies maim and kill civilians.*
wound • *wounded by shrapnel*

injury NOUN

damage to part of the body • *He sustained serious injuries in the accident.*
damage • *brain damage*
harm • *Dogs can do harm to human beings.*
wound • *a head wound*

injustice NOUN

unfairness and lack of justice • *the injustice of the system*
bias • *He shows bias against women.*
discrimination • *racial discrimination*
inequality • *people concerned about social inequality*
prejudice • *prejudice against workers over 45*
unfairness • *the unfairness of the decision*
wrong • *I intend to right past wrongs.*

ANTONYM:
• justice

innocence NOUN

inexperience of evil or unpleasant things • *the innocence of babies*
gullibility • *I'm paying for my gullibility back then.*
inexperience • *their inexperience of the real world*
naivety • *There was a youthful naivety to his honesty.*
simplicity • *She prayed with childlike simplicity.*

MORE SYNONYMS:
• artlessness
• ingenuousness
• unworldliness

innocent ① ADJECTIVE

not guilty of a crime • *the arrest of innocent suspects*
blameless • *I have led a blameless life.*
clear • *He was clear of blame for the accident.*
not guilty • *Both men were found not guilty.*

ANTONYM:
• guilty

innocent ② ADJECTIVE

without experience of evil or unpleasant things • *They seem so young and innocent.*
childlike • *childlike trust*
guileless • *Her eyes were as guileless as a doll's.*
naive • *I was young and naive when I left home.*
pure • *She had led a pure life.*
spotless • *a spotless, pure child*
virginal • *a shy, virginal princess*

MORE SYNONYMS:
• artless
• ingenuous
• unworldly

insane ADJECTIVE

mad • *Some people can't take the pressure and go insane.*

crazy • *If I sat home and worried, I'd go crazy.*

deranged • *a deranged man who shot 14 people in the main square*

mad • *She was afraid of going mad.*

mentally ill • *a patient who is mentally ill*

out of your mind • *I wonder if I'm going out of my mind.*

unhinged • *an experience which left her completely unhinged*

insert VERB

to put something into something else • *He inserted the key into the lock.*

enter • *Enter your name in the box.*

implant • *a device implanted in the arm*

introduce • *Scientists introduced new genes into mice.*

place • *Cover the casserole tightly and place in the oven.*

put • *She put a coin in the slot.*

set • *diamonds set in gold*

inside ADJECTIVE

surrounded by the main part and often hidden • *We booked an inside cabin.*

inner • *the inner ear*

innermost • *the innermost parts of the galaxy*

interior • *a car with plenty of interior space*

internal • *your internal organs*

ANTONYM:
• outside

insides PLURAL NOUN (INFORMAL)

the parts inside your body • *My insides ached from eating too much.*

entrails • *chicken entrails*

guts • *fish guts*

innards • *the innards of a human body*

internal organs • *damage to internal organs*

MORE SYNONYMS:
• viscera
• vitals

insignificant ADJECTIVE

small and unimportant • *a small, insignificant village*

irrelevant • *irrelevant details*

little • *It seems such a little thing to get upset over.*

minor • *Western officials say the problem is minor.*

petty • *Rows can start over petty things.*

trifling • *These difficulties may seem trifling to you.*

trivial • *He tried to wave aside these issues as trivial matters.*

unimportant • *The age difference seemed unimportant.*

ANOTHER SYNONYM:
• inconsequential

ANTONYM:
• significant

insincere ADJECTIVE

saying things you do not mean • *A lot of actors are insincere.*

deceitful • *deceitful and misleading remarks*

dishonest • *dishonest salespeople*

false • *a false confession*

two-faced • *the most two-faced politicians in the world*

ANTONYM:
• sincere

insist VERB

to demand something forcefully • *My family insisted I should not give in.*

demand • *The teacher demanded an explanation.*

press • *She is pressing for improvements to education.*

a
b
c
d
e
f
g
h
i
j
k
l
m
n
o
p
q
r
s
t
u
v
w
x
y
z

urge • *We urge vigorous action be taken immediately.*

inspect VERB

to examine something carefully • *the right to inspect company files*

check • *Check each item for obvious flaws.*

examine • *He examined her passport and stamped it.*

eye • *We eyed each other thoughtfully.*

investigate • *Police are investigating the scene of the crime.*

scan • *The officer scanned the room.*

survey • *He surveyed the ruins of the building.*

MORE SYNONYMS:
• audit
• scrutinize
• vet

instant ① NOUN

a short period of time • *The pain disappeared in an instant.*

flash • *It was all over in a flash.*

minute • *I'll see you in a minute.*

moment • *In a moment he was gone.*

second • *Seconds later, firemen reached his door.*

split second • *Her gaze met Michael's for a split second.*

trice • *She was back in a trice.*

instant ② ADJECTIVE

immediate and without delay • *He had taken an instant dislike to her.*

immediate • *We need an immediate reply.*

instantaneous • *an explosion resulting in the instantaneous deaths of all crew members*

prompt • *Prompt action is needed.*

instinct NOUN

a natural tendency to do something • *My first instinct was to protect myself.*

feeling • *You seem to have a feeling for drawing.*

impulse • *Peter resisted an impulse to smile.*

intuition • *You should trust your intuition.*

sixth sense • *Some sixth sense told him to keep going.*

urge • *He fought the urge to panic.*

instruct ① VERB

to tell someone to do something • *They have instructed solicitors to sue.*

command • *He commanded his troops to attack.*

direct • *They have been directed to give attention to this problem.*

order • *Williams ordered him to leave.*

tell • *A passer-by told him to move his car.*

ANTONYM:
• forbid

instruct ② VERB

to teach someone about a subject or skill • *He instructs therapists in relaxation techniques.*

coach • *He coached me in French.*

educate • *We need to educate people about the destructive effects of alcohol.*

school • *She's been schooling her kids herself.*

teach • *She taught children French.*

train • *We train them in a range of building techniques.*

tutor • *He was tutoring her in the stringed instruments.*

insufficient ADJECTIVE

not enough for a particular purpose • *insufficient information*

deficient • *a deficient diet*

inadequate • *The problem lies with inadequate staffing.*

lacking • *My confidence is lacking.*

scant • *Gareth paid scant attention to what was going on.*

short • *She was short of breath.*

ANTONYM:
• sufficient

insult ① VERB
to offend someone by being rude to them • *I did not mean to insult you.*
abuse • *footballers abusing referees*
affront • *He pretended to be affronted by what I said.*
offend • *I had no intention of offending the community.*
put down • *They seemed to delight in putting me down.*
slag (BRITISH; INFORMAL) • *He's always slagging me in front of his mates.*
slight • *They felt slighted by not being consulted.*
snub • *He snubbed her in public and made her feel foolish.*

ANTONYM:
• compliment

insult ② NOUN
a rude remark that offends someone • *The two men exchanged insults.*
abuse • *Raft hurled verbal abuse at his co-star.*
affront • *She took my words as a personal affront.*
offence • *I meant no offence to Mr Hardy.*
slight • *She is very sensitive to slights.*
snub • *This was a deliberate snub to me.*

ANTONYM:
• compliment

intelligence NOUN
the ability to understand and learn things • *students of high intelligence*
cleverness • *Her cleverness gets in the way of her emotions.*
comprehension • *an idea beyond human comprehension*
intellect • *Lucy's lack of intellect disappointed her father.*
perception • *You have brilliant perception and insight.*

sense • *They have the sense to seek help.*
understanding • *I've got no sense, no understanding.*
wit • *He had the wit to see this was a good idea.*

MORE SYNONYMS:
• acumen
• capacity
• nous

intelligent ADJECTIVE
able to understand and learn things • *Dolphins are an intelligent species.*
acute • *His relaxed exterior hides a very acute mind.*
brainy (INFORMAL) • *I don't consider myself brainy.*
bright • *an exceptionally bright child*
clever • *a clever girl*
quick • *His quick mind soon grasped the situation.*
sharp • *a very sharp intellect*
smart • *He thinks he's as smart as Sarah.*

ANTONYM:
• stupid

intend ① VERB
to decide or plan to do something • *She intended to move back to Cape Town.*
aim • *We aim to raise funds for charity.*
be determined • *Kate was determined to enjoy the day.*
mean • *I didn't mean any harm.*
plan • *He planned to leave Adelaide on Monday.*
propose • *Where do you propose building such a huge thing?*
resolve • *She resolved to report the matter.*

intend ② VERB
to mean for a certain use • *a book intended for serious students*
aim • *children's games aimed at developing quickness*

design • *The house had been designed for a large family.*

earmark • *That money was earmarked for house repairs.*

mean • *I was not meant for domestic life.*

intense ① ADJECTIVE

very great in strength or amount • *intense heat*

acute • *an acute shortage of accommodation*

deep • *He felt a deep sense of relief.*

extreme • *Proceed with extreme caution.*

fierce • *There was fierce competition for the job.*

great • *Dawes felt a great pain and weakness.*

powerful • *I had a powerful urge to scream at him.*

profound • *The book had a profound effect in the USA.*

severe • *I had severe problems.*

intense ② ADJECTIVE

tending to have strong feelings • *He was dark-haired and intense.*

ardent • *one of his most ardent supporters*

earnest • *Ella was a pious, earnest woman.*

fervent • *a fervent admirer of Beethoven's music*

fierce • *fierce loyalty to his friends*

impassioned • *He made an impassioned appeal for peace.*

passionate • *He is very passionate about the project.*

vehement • *a vehement critic of the plan*

intention NOUN

a plan to do something • *He announced his intention of retiring.*

aim • *The aim of this book is to inform you.*

goal • *The goal is to raise a lot of money.*

idea • *I bought books with the idea of reading them.*

object • *It was his object in life to find the island.*

objective • *His objective was to play golf and win.*

purpose • *He did not know the purpose of Vincent's visit.*

interest ① NOUN

a feeling of wanting to know about something • *I have a great interest in that period of history.*

attention • *The book attracted considerable attention.*

concern • *How it happened is of little concern to me.*

curiosity • *His reply satisfied our curiosity.*

fascination • *a lifelong fascination with the sea*

interest ② NOUN

a hobby • *He has a wide range of sporting interests.*

activity • *I enjoy outdoor activities like canoeing and climbing.*

hobby • *My hobbies are football, photography and tennis.*

pastime • *His favourite pastime is golf.*

pursuit • *his favourite childhood pursuits*

interest ③ VERB

to attract someone's attention and curiosity • *This part of the book interests me most.*

appeal • *The bright colours seem to appeal to children.*

captivate • *this author's ability to captivate young minds*

fascinate • *Politics fascinated my father.*

intrigue • *The situation intrigued him.*

stimulate • *Bill was stimulated by the challenge.*

ANTONYM:
• bore

interesting ADJECTIVE
making you want to know, learn or hear more • *an interesting hobby*
absorbing • *an absorbing conversation*
compelling • *compelling drama*
entertaining • *a cheerful and entertaining companion*
gripping • *a gripping story*
intriguing • *the intriguing character of the author*
stimulating • *My trip to India had been stimulating.*

ANTONYM:
• boring

interfere ① VERB
to try to influence a situation • *Stop interfering and leave me alone.*
butt in • *I butted in where I didn't belong.*
intervene • *Soldiers don't like civilians intervening in their affairs.*
intrude • *I don't want to intrude on your meeting.*
meddle • *Scientists should not meddle in such matters.*
tamper • *the price we pay for tampering with the environment*

interfere ② VERB
to have a damaging effect on a situation • *His problems interfered with his work.*
conflict • *an evening that conflicted with my work schedule*
disrupt • *Strikes disrupted air traffic in Italy.*

internet NOUN
a worldwide network of computers • *posting photos on the internet*
blogosphere • *an event that set the blogosphere buzzing*

cloud • *downloading software from the cloud*
cyberspace • *The volume of business which takes place in cyberspace is growing.*
net • *comments on the net*
web • *one of the biggest sites on the web*
world wide web • *articles published on the world wide web*

interrogate VERB
to question someone thoroughly • *I interrogated everyone involved.*
examine • *Lawyers examined the witnesses.*
grill (INFORMAL) • *Jenkins kept telling police who grilled him: "I didn't kill her."*
question • *He was questioned by police.*
quiz • *She quizzed me quite closely for a while.*

MORE SYNONYMS:
• cross-examine
• cross-question

interrupt ① VERB
to start talking when someone else is talking • *He tried to speak, but she interrupted him.*
butt in • *Mirella butted in without a greeting.*
heckle • *It is easy to heckle from the safety of the audience.*

interrupt ② VERB
to stop a process or activity for a time • *The match was interrupted by rain.*
break • *allowing passengers to break their journey in Fiji*
discontinue • *Do not discontinue the treatment without seeing your doctor.*
suspend • *Relief convoys will be suspended until the fighting stops.*

interval NOUN
a period of time between two moments or dates • *There was a long interval of silence.*

break • *a short break from work*
gap • *the gap between school terms*
hiatus • *There was a momentary hiatus in the sounds.*
interlude • *It was a happy interlude in the Kents' life.*
intermission • *There will be a short intermission between acts.*
pause • *a pause between two periods of intense activity*

intervene VERB

to step in to prevent conflict • *I relied on them to intervene if anything happened.*
arbitrate • *A committee was set up to arbitrate in the dispute.*
mediate • *efforts to mediate between the two communities*

introduction ① NOUN

the act of presenting someone or something new • *the introduction of a single European currency*
establishment • *the establishment of a democratic system*
inauguration • *the inauguration of the President*
initiation • *your initiation into adulthood*
institution • *the institution of new laws*
launch • *the launch of this popular author's new book*

introduction ② NOUN

a piece of writing at the beginning of a book • *The book contains a new introduction by the author.*
foreword • *I am happy to write the foreword to this collection.*
preface • *I read through the preface quickly.*
prologue • *the General Prologue to The Canterbury Tales*

intrude VERB

to disturb someone or something • *I*
don't want to intrude on your parents.
butt in • *I butted in where I didn't belong.*
encroach • *Does your work encroach on your private life?*
infringe • *She promised not to infringe on his space.*
interrupt • *Georgina interrupted his thoughts.*
trespass • *I don't like to trespass on your time.*
violate • *These men were violating her family's privacy.*

invade VERB

to enter a country by force • *The allies invaded the Italian mainland at Anzio.*
attack • *Government planes attacked the town.*
enter • *The Taleban entered western Kabul.*
occupy • *Soldiers occupied the town within a few minutes.*
violate • *A helicopter violated Greek territory yesterday.*

invent ① VERB

to be the first person to think of a device or idea • *He invented the first electric clock.*
coin • *Lanier coined the term "virtual reality".*
come up with (INFORMAL) • *He came up with a gadget to relieve hay fever.*
conceive • *He conceived the first portable computer.*
create • *The company decided to create a new perfume.*
formulate • *He formulated his plan for escape.*
originate • *the designer who originated platform shoes*

MORE SYNONYMS:
• design

- devise
- improvise

invent ② VERB

to make up a story or excuse • *I tried to invent a plausible excuse.*
concoct • *A newspaper concocted an imaginary interview.*
fabricate • *The evidence against them was fabricated.*
make up • *Donna was known for making up stories about herself.*
manufacture • *The children manufactured an elaborate tale.*

investigate VERB

to find out all the facts about something • *Police are still investigating the incidents.*
examine • *I have examined all the possible alternatives.*
explore • *a book which explores the history of technology*
probe • *He probed into her private life.*
research • *I'm researching for an article on New England.*
sift • *I sifted the evidence for conclusions.*
study • *Experts are studying the security in the building.*

invincible ADJECTIVE

unable to be defeated • *When Woods is on form he is invincible.*
impregnable • *an impregnable fortress*
indomitable • *the indomitable spirit of the Polish people*
unbeatable • *a performance record that is unbeatable*

MORE SYNONYMS:
- indestructible
- insurmountable
- unassailable

invisible ADJECTIVE

unable to be seen • *His face was invisible beneath his hat.*
concealed • *a concealed weapon*

disguised • *a disguised panel in the wall*
hidden • *a hidden camera*
inconspicuous • *She tried to make herself inconspicuous.*
unseen • *His work was guided by an unseen hand.*

MORE SYNONYMS:
- imperceptible
- indiscernible

ANTONYM:
- visible

involve VERB

to have as a necessary part • *Running a kitchen involves a great deal of discipline.*
incorporate • *The program incorporates a range of activities.*
require • *Caring for a baby requires special skills.*
take in • *This study takes in a number of areas.*

MORE SYNONYMS:
- entail
- necessitate

irrational ADJECTIVE

not based on logical reasons
• *irrational fears*
absurd • *It was an absurd over-reaction.*
crazy • *crazy ideas*
illogical • *his completely illogical arguments*
nonsensical • *Such an idea sounds paradoxical, if not downright nonsensical.*
unsound • *The thinking is good-hearted, but muddled and unsound.*

MORE SYNONYMS:
- silly
- unreasoning

irregular ① ADJECTIVE

not smooth or even • *an irregular surface*
asymmetrical • *She has asymmetrical features.*

a
b
c
d
e
f
g
h
i
j
k
l
m
n
o
p
q
r
s
t
u
v
w
x
y
z

bumpy • *bumpy roads*
jagged • *jagged fragments of stained glass*
lopsided • *his lopsided smile*
ragged • *the ragged edges of a tear*
uneven • *uneven teeth*

ANTONYM:
• regular

irregular ② ADJECTIVE
not forming a regular pattern • *He worked irregular hours.*
erratic • *a planet with an erratic orbit*
haphazard • *a haphazard system*
occasional • *occasional rain showers*
patchy • *Her career has been patchy.*
random • *The stock market is random and unpredictable.*
variable • *a variable rate of interest*

MORE SYNONYMS:
• fitful
• sporadic

ANTONYM:
• regular

irresponsible ADJECTIVE
not concerned with the consequences of your actions • *an irresponsible attitude*
careless • *a careless driver*
reckless • *reckless spending*
thoughtless • *a thoughtless remark*
wild • *a night of wild abandon*

ANTONYM:
• responsible

irritable ADJECTIVE
easily annoyed • *Nicol was unusually tense and irritable.*
bad-tempered • *You're very bad-tempered today.*
cantankerous • *a cantankerous old man*
petulant • *He was like a petulant child.*
ratty (BRITISH AND NEW ZEALAND; INFORMAL) • *There's no need to get ratty.*

MORE SYNONYMS:
• irascible
• tetchy

irritate VERB
to annoy someone • *Their attitude irritates me.*
anger • *This article angered me.*
annoy • *It just annoyed me to hear him going on.*
bother • *Nothing bothers me.*
exasperate • *Bertha was exasperated by the delay.*
needle (INFORMAL) • *If her remark needled him, he didn't show it.*
ruffle • *He doesn't get ruffled by anything.*

MORE SYNONYMS:
• gall
• provoke

issue ① NOUN
a subject that people are talking about • *important issues of the day*
concern • *Political concerns continue to dominate the news.*
matter • *He touched on many matters in his speech.*
problem • *the energy problem*
question • *The whole question of aid is a tricky one.*
subject • *the president's views on the subject*
topic • *the main topic for discussion*

issue ② NOUN
a particular edition of a newspaper or magazine • *the latest issue of the Lancet*
copy • *a copy of "USA Today"*
edition • *There's an article about the film in next month's edition.*
instalment • *a magazine published in monthly instalments*

issue ③ VERB
to make a formal statement • *They have issued a statement denying the allegations.*

deliver • *He delivered a speech to his fellow union members.*

give • *The minister gave a warning that war should be avoided at all costs.*

make • *He says he was depressed when he made the statement.*

pronounce • *The authorities took time to pronounce their verdicts.*

read out • *She read out an announcement outside the court.*

release • *The police are not releasing any more details about the attack.*

ANTONYM:
• withdraw

issue ④ VERB

to give something officially • *Staff will be issued with badges.*

equip • *plans to equip the reserve army with guns*

furnish (FORMAL) • *They will furnish you with the necessary items.*

give out • *The prizes were given out by a local dignitary.*

provide • *The government was unable to provide them with food.*

supply • *an agreement not to supply these countries with chemical weapons*

item ① NOUN

one of a collection or list of things • *an item on the agenda*

article • *articles of clothing*

matter • *He dealt with a variety of matters.*

point • *Many of the points in the report are correct.*

thing • *Big things are paid for by the government.*

item ② NOUN

a newspaper or magazine article • *There was an item in the paper about him.*

article • *a short article in one of the papers*

feature • *The magazine contained a special feature on the project.*

notice • *notices in today's national newspapers*

piece • *I disagree with your recent piece about Australia.*

report • *a film report on the scandal*

a
b
c
d
e
f
g
h
i
j
k
l
m
n
o
p
q
r
s
t
u
v
w
x
y
z

Jj

jagged ADJECTIVE
sharp and spiky • *jagged black cliffs*
barbed • *barbed wire*
craggy • *craggy mountains*
rough • *the rough surface of the rock*
serrated • *a serrated knife*

ANTONYM:
• smooth

jail ① NOUN
a place where prisoners are held
• *sentenced to 18 months in jail*
nick (BRITISH, AUSTRALIAN AND NEW
ZEALAND; SLANG) • *He spent seven years
in the nick.*
prison • *his release from prison*

MORE SYNONYMS:
• lockup
• penal institution
• penitentiary

jail ② VERB
to put in prison • *He was jailed for
twenty years.*
detain • *Police can detain a suspect
for 48 hours.*
imprison • *imprisoned for 18 months
on charges of theft*
incarcerate • *They have been
incarcerated as political prisoners.*

jam ① NOUN
a crowded mass of people or things
• *stuck in a jam on the motorway*
crowd • *elbowing his way through
the crowd*
crush • *We got separated in the crush.*

mass • *a mass of excited fans*
mob • *a growing mob of demonstrators*
multitude • *surrounded by a noisy
multitude*
throng • *An official pushed through the
throng.*

jam ② NOUN
a difficult situation • *We're in a real
jam now.*
dilemma • *faced with a dilemma*
fix (INFORMAL) • *a difficult economic fix*
hole (SLANG) • *He admitted that the
government was in a hole.*
plight • *the plight of the Third World
countries*
predicament • *a way out of our
predicament*
quandary • *We're in a quandary over
our holiday plans.*
trouble • *You are in serious trouble.*

jam ③ VERB
to push something somewhere
roughly • *He jammed his hat on to his
head.*
cram • *He crammed the bank notes into
his pocket.*
force • *I forced the key into the ignition.*
ram • *He rammed the muzzle of the gun
against my forehead.*
stuff • *She stuffed the newspaper into a
litter bin.*

jam ④ VERB
to become stuck • *The second time he
fired, his gun jammed.*
stall • *The engine stalled.*

stick • *She tried to open the window but it was stuck.*

jealous ADJECTIVE
wanting to have something which someone else has • *She was jealous of his success.*
envious • *envious of the attention his brother was getting*
resentful • *resentful of her husband's hobby*
MORE SYNONYMS:
• covetous
• emulous

job ① NOUN
the work someone does to earn money • *I'm still looking for a job.*
employment • *unable to find employment*
occupation • *his occupation as a carpenter*
position • *He's leaving to take up a position abroad.*
post • *She has resigned her post as his assistant.*
profession • *She chose nursing as her profession.*
trade • *her trade as a jeweller*

job ② NOUN
a duty or responsibility • *It's your job to find out what's going on.*
concern • *The technical aspects are the concern of the engineers.*
duty • *I consider it my duty to write and thank you.*
function • *an important function to fill*
responsibility • *It's not my responsibility to look after your mother.*
role • *Our role is to keep the peace.*
task • *She had the task of breaking the bad news.*

join ① VERB
to become a member of something • *He joined the Army five years ago.*

enlist • *He was 18 when he enlisted in the US Navy.*
enrol • *She has enrolled in an acting class.*
sign up • *I've signed up as a member.*
ANTONYM:
• resign

join ② VERB
to fasten two things together • *two sticks joined together by a chain*
attach • *The gadget can be attached to any surface.*
connect • *two rooms connected by a passage*
couple • *an engine coupled to a gearbox*
fasten • *a wooden bench fastened to the floor*
link • *tree houses linked by ropes*
tie • *He tied the dog to a post by its leash.*
MORE SYNONYMS:
• append
• knit
• splice
ANTONYM:
• separate

joke ① NOUN
something that makes people laugh • *I heard a great joke today.*
gag (INFORMAL) • *a gag about unscrupulous lawyers*
jest • *It was only intended as a jest.*
lark • *They just did it for a lark.*
prank • *an end-of-term prank*
quip • *a famous quip by Groucho Marx*
wisecrack (INFORMAL) • *She was tempted to make a wisecrack.*
witticism • *laughing at each other's witticisms*
MORE SYNONYMS:
• jape
• sally

joke ② VERB
to say something funny • *She was*

always joking about her appearance.
banter • *He played trick shots and bantered with the crowd.*
chaff • *They chaffed us about our chances of winning.*
jest • *drinking and jesting with his cronies*
kid (INFORMAL) • *Don't worry, I'm only kidding.*
quip • *"You'll have to go on a diet," he quipped.*
tease • *"You must be in love," she teased.*

journey ① NOUN
the act of travelling from one place to another • *the journey from Paris to Bordeaux*
excursion • *The trip includes an excursion to Zermatt.*
expedition • *an expedition to the South Pole*
passage • *a 10-hour passage from Swansea*
tour • *a two-month tour of Europe*
trek • *a trek through the Gobi desert*
trip • *a business trip*
voyage • *the first space shuttle voyage*

journey ② VERB
to travel from one place to another • *In 1935, she journeyed through Turkey and Africa.*
go • *We went from Glasgow to London in six hours.*
proceed • *proceeding along the road in the wrong direction*
tour • *He toured China in 1993.*
travel • *Gran travelled down by train.*
trek • *trekking through the jungle*
voyage • *They voyaged as far as Spain.*

joy NOUN
great happiness • *Her face shone with joy.*
bliss • *an expression of pure bliss*
delight • *He let out a yell of delight.*
ecstasy • *Her eyes closed in ecstasy.*

elation • *He felt a surge of elation at the news.*
rapture • *His speech was received with rapture.*

MORE SYNONYMS:
• exaltation
• exultation
• felicity

ANTONYM:
• misery

joyful ADJECTIVE
extremely happy • *a joyful smile*
delighted • *I'm delighted to be here.*
elated • *the elated faces of the freed hostages*
jubilant • *the jubilant crowds*
over the moon (INFORMAL) • *I was over the moon to hear about your promotion.*

MORE SYNONYMS:
• cock-a-hoop
• enraptured

judge ① NOUN
the person in charge of a law court • *The judge awarded him £2000 in damages.*
beak (BRITISH; SLANG) • *a third appearance before the beak*
justice • *his appointment as a Justice of the High Court*
magistrate • *defendants appearing before a magistrate*

RELATED WORD:
• ADJECTIVE judicial

judge ② NOUN
someone who picks the winner or keeps control of a competition • *A panel of judges are selecting the finalists.*
referee • *The referee awarded a free kick against Rourke.*
umpire • *The umpire's decision is final.*

judge ③ VERB
to form an opinion about someone

or something • *Don't judge people by
their looks.*
appraise • *The teachers are appraised
by an official.*
assess • *It is too early to assess the
impact of the change.*
consider • *We consider him to be
dangerous.*
estimate • *The cost of the damage is
estimated at over a million dollars.*
evaluate • *a test to evaluate a
candidate's potential*
rate • *The film was rated a hit.*

judge ④ VERB
to pick the winner or keep control
in a competition • *Entrants will be
judged in two age categories.*
referee • *He has refereed in two World
Cups.*
umpire • *He umpired baseball games.*
MORE SYNONYMS:
• adjudge
• adjudicate

judgment NOUN
an opinion or decision based on
evidence • *It's hard to form a judgment
without all the facts.*
appraisal • *a calm appraisal of the
situation*
assessment • *my own personal
assessment of our position*
conclusion • *I've come to the conclusion
that she knows what she's talking about.*
opinion • *Seek a medical opinion before
you travel.*
ruling • *a High Court ruling*
verdict • *The doctor's verdict was that
he was entirely healthy.*
view • *In my view, things aren't going
to get any better.*

jump ① VERB
to leap up or over something • *I
jumped over the fence.*

303 | junk

bound • *He bounded up the steps.*
clear • *The horse cleared the gate by
inches.*
hurdle • *He crossed the lawn and
hurdled the fence.*
leap • *He had leapt from a window and
escaped.*
spring • *The lion roared once and
sprang.*
vault • *Ned vaulted over a fallen tree.*

jump ② VERB
to increase suddenly • *Sales jumped by
25% last year.*
escalate • *Costs escalated dramatically.*
increase • *Trading has increased by 20%
this month.*
rise • *Unemployment is rising rapidly.*
surge • *The party's share of the vote
surged from 10% to 17%.*

jump ③ NOUN
a leap into the air • *the longest ever
jump by a man*
bound • *With one bound Jack was free.*
leap • *Smith took the gold medal with a
leap of 2.37 metres.*
vault • *She regained the record with a
vault of 3.80 metres.*

junior ADJECTIVE
having a relatively low position
compared to others • *a junior minister*
inferior • *inferior status*
lesser • *He resigned to take a lesser
position and a cut in wages.*
lower • *the lower ranks of council
officers*
subordinate • *sixty of his subordinate
officers*
ANTONYM:
• senior

junk NOUN
old articles that people usually throw
away • *What are you going to do with all
that junk?*

clutter • *She likes her worktops to be clear of clutter.*

odds and ends • *My handbag's full of useless odds and ends.*

refuse • *a weekly collection of refuse*

rubbish • *They piled most of their rubbish into skips.*

scrap • *a small yard containing a heap of scrap*

trash • *cluttered with trash*

justice ① NOUN

fairness in the way that people are treated • *He wants freedom, justice and equality.*

equity • *Income should be distributed with some sense of equity.*

fairness • *concern about the fairness of the election campaign*

impartiality • *a system lacking impartiality*

ANTONYM:
• injustice

justice ② NOUN

the person in charge of a law court • *his appointment as a Justice of the High Court*

judge • *The judge awarded him £2000 in damages.*

magistrate • *defendants appearing before a magistrate*

justify VERB

to show that something is reasonable or necessary • *How can you justify what you've done?*

defend • *Her conduct is hard to defend.*

excuse • *That still doesn't excuse his behaviour.*

explain • *She left a note explaining her actions.*

vindicate • *Ministers are confident their decision will be vindicated.*

warrant • *These allegations warrant an investigation.*

Essential Guide to Good Writing

WRITING EFFECTIVELY

Planning your writing

Whatever you are writing, it is important to think about it first. If you plan your writing well, it will be clear, accurate, and effective.

You may think that planning your writing is just one extra job and a waste of time, but in fact good planning will probably save you time as well as make your writing better.

Planning does not necessarily take a lot of time, and a plan will help you:

- organize your thoughts
- make sure you are clear about what you want to write
- make sure you have all the information you need
- make sure you don't leave anything out

> **Key point to remember**
> Planning will save you time and make your writing more effective.

Before you start to write, the most important question to ask yourself is: What am I trying to achieve?

The best way to be clear about this is to ask three questions:

1. **Who** is this writing for?
2. **What** do I want to say?
3. **Why** do I want to say it?

Imagine, for example, that you really like animals, and you need a holiday job, so you decide to write to the local zoo. In this case, the answers to the questions above could be:

1. The manager or personnel officer of the zoo.
2. That you want a summer holiday job. That you love animals and worked on a farm last year.
3. Because you want to get a holiday job in a zoo.

There are important points to remember about each of these questions:

- **Who?** Make sure that you use a suitable style and tone for your audience. Informal language and jokes are fine for your friends, but a job application needs to be more formal.
- **What?** Make sure that what you say is absolutely clear, and that you have included everything you wanted to include.
- **Why?** Make sure your writing achieves its purpose. Be clear about what you want to happen: do you want to persuade someone that your point of view is correct? Do you want to inform people about something or explain it to them?

Before starting to write, it can sometimes be helpful to make a brief **summary** of what you are trying to achieve. This can help you to concentrate on the most important points of your writing.

When you have finished your writing, you can go back to your summary and check that what you have written achieves what you wanted it to. A good summary will always answer the questions *who?*, *what?*, and *why?*

> **Key point to remember**
> Always be clear about the purpose of your writing.

Writing in sentences

Sentences are the building blocks of our texts. The length of your sentences will depend on who you are writing for, but very long sentences can be confusing, while very short sentences can sound quite childish. If your sentence is longer than about 15–20 words, see if you can divide it into shorter sentences.

The basic rule is that each sentence should have a **verb** and a **subject**:

The vase smashed on the floor. (vase = subject, smashed = verb)
My Mum plays the violin. (My Mum = subject, plays = verb)

It is best not to start a sentence with a conjunction such as 'and', 'but', or, 'or', especially in formal writing, as some people thing this is incorrect.

Some people also think it is wrong to end a sentence with a preposition such as 'on', 'up', or 'in'. However, avoiding this can sometimes sound a bit too formal for the context. Compare the following sentences:

We were shocked to see the conditions they live in.
We were shocked to see the conditions in which they live.

Always think about the purpose of your document and your audience, and this will help you choose the appropriate style and tone.

> **Tip for success**
>
> Try reading your work aloud. If your sentences work well, it will be easy to read. See where you make natural pauses, and think about whether you need to add commas.

Writing clearly

If you use a clear writing style, especially when giving information, your writing will be easier for your audience to understand. Try to follow these rules:

* **Don't use technical words if it isn't necessary**. Your audience may not understand technical jargon, even if you do.

   Of course, sometimes technical terms *are* appropriate. If you are writing a science essay, you must use the correct terminology. Always think of your audience.

* **Don't be too formal.** Ask yourself if there is a simpler word or phrase that would be appropriate for your reader.

very formal	simpler
prior to	*before*
in excess of	*more than*
in the vicinity of	*near*

* **Try to use active verbs instead of nouns.** This will make your sentences sound less complicated and formal.

noun form	active verb form
give encouragement to	*encourage*
ensure the completion of	*complete*
make provision for	*provide*

Active or passive verbs?

It is usually better to use active verbs in your writing because it will make the structure of your sentences simple, and it sounds less formal. Compare these two sentences, for example:

> New recycling methods have been introduced by the council. (passive)
> The council has introduced new recycling methods. (active)

However, the passive can be useful sometimes. For instance, you might use the passive if you do not want to appear to be blaming someone or criticizing someone:

> You have not paid the money. (active and accusing)
> The money has not been paid. (passive and more neutral)

The passive is also used when you do not know who carried out an action or it does not matter who carried out the action. You might use the passive in essays and reports in which a slightly more formal style is appropriate:

> The results were analyzed in the laboratory.
> The buildings were knocked down in 1989.

Avoiding repetition

One simple rule applies to all your work:

Avoid repeating words.

Whatever you are writing, it will sound dull and clumsy if you use the same words over and over again. If you read your work aloud, you will notice when you have done this.

Too much repetition	Better ...
Team A discovered ..., Team B discovered ..., Team C discovered	Team A discovered ..., Team B found ..., Team C's results showed ...

Use your Collins School Thesaurus to find interesting alternatives to use.

Sometimes the easiest way to avoid repetition is simply to replace one of the words with a pronoun:

Too much repetition	Better ...
We intend to invite all our friends and ask each friend to bring some food.	We intend to invite all our friends and ask each of them to bring some food.

Avoiding clichés

A **cliché** is a word or phrase that has been used too often. If you use clichés, your writing will be boring. When readers see them, they may lose interest and miss your main message. They may think that if your writing is not original, your ideas cannot be original either.

You may find that clichés slip into the first draft of your writing – after all, it is because they are so well-known and come so easily to mind that they have become clichés. Read through your document and try to identify any phrases that seem to fit into this category.

Then ask yourself: what does this phrase actually mean? It may not really have much meaning at all, in which case you can probably delete it. Examples of this sort of cliché are:

> *at the end of the day*
> *at this moment in time*
> *with all due respect*

Or it may be that the phrase has been used so much that it has lost all its power, and may well annoy your reader. Examples of this sort of cliché are:

> *an emotional rollercoaster*
> *moving the goalposts*
> *the best thing since sliced bread*

Sometimes a simple combination of adjective and noun can be so overused that it becomes a cliché, for example:

> *a roaring fire*
> *a vice-like grip*
> *a long-lost friend*

This does not mean that such combinations should never be used, but try not to use too many obvious combinations, and choose something more original if you can.

One area of language where it is very easy to fall into the trap of using a cliché is the **simile**.

Look at the following similes:

> *as cold as ice*
> *as fresh as a daisy*

They are so overused that they are not powerful descriptions. Now look at the following similes, all found in real writing:

> *as cold as a Siberian winter*
> *as cold as a statue of stone*
> *as fresh as green shoots in the morning*
> *as fresh as a big green shiny cucumber*

Of course, imaginative similes like these are not suitable for all types of writing. In formal writing, it is probably best to avoid similes altogether. In more creative writing, you should aim to be descriptive and original, but your similes should fit into the overall style of the text.

Avoiding unnecessary words

It is very easy to use more words than you need, but too many words will make your writing less effective and may annoy your readers.

Compare the following:

> *Jack and I are of the same opinion on this matter.*
> *Jack and I agree.*
> *Due to the fact that the train was delayed, we were late for the concert.*
> *We were late for the concert because the train was delayed.*

- **Avoid 'empty' words and phrases** that do not add meaning to your sentences, for example *in terms of, the fact of the matter*.
- **Avoid saying the same things twice.** This is known as **tautology**. Here are some examples of this:

9 a.m. in the morning	a.m. means 'in the morning' – choose one or the other
re-examine again	just say 're-examine' – the 'again' is expressed in the prefix 're-'
my personal opinion	if it's your opinion, it's personal – you don't need to say so

- **Avoid adding illogical extra words.** Here are some examples:

in actual fact	if it is a fact, it must be 'actual' – just say 'in fact'
very unique	something unique is the *only* one of its kind – there are no degrees of uniqueness

Avoiding ambiguity

Ambiguity is when something could possibly be understood in more than one way. It is an easy trap to fall into because *you* know what you mean when you write, but try to put yourself in the reader's place and make sure there is no room for doubt.

- Be careful with words that have more than one meaning. Often the context will be enough to make it clear which meaning you intended. If you write that you are going to the bank, nobody is likely to think you are going to a river bank. However, consider the following:

   My teacher is really funny. (Is the teacher humorous or strange?)

- Make it clear whether you are using words and phrases in a **literal** or **figurative** way:

   He was in debt to his friend. (Did he owe his friend money or simply feel grateful?)

- Use pronouns carefully to make sure it is clear who or what they refer to:

   Rosie had an argument with Sarah, and she started crying. (Was it Rosie or Sarah who cried?)

- Check the structure of your sentence to make sure it is clear how the parts relate to each other. Compare these sentences:

   We talked about bullying at school. (This is ambiguous – were we at school or not?)

   We talked about school bullying.

   At school, we talked about bullying.

- Make sure it is clear what your adjectives are describing:

   a large man's briefcase (Is it the man or the briefcase that is large?)

Using the right register

The word **register** refers to aspects of language such as how **formal** or **informal** it is. Compare these sentences:

   They furnished us with the requisite implements. (very formal)

   They gave us the necessary tools. (neutral)

   They let us have the gear we needed. (informal)

You should match the register of your language to the type of writing you are doing. Using the wrong register can make your writing sound odd and your audience might not take it seriously.

Register can often be shown by the choice of words or phrases:

formal	neutral	informal
wax lyrical	speak enthusiastically	go on about
of one's own volition	voluntarily	off your own bat
in the ascendancy	becoming successful	on the up

Dictionaries mark words which are formal or informal, so you can check if you are not sure. Many idioms and phrasal verbs are either informal or slightly informal, so take care to use them appropriately.

Informal language is fine for personal letters, social-network posts, texts, etc, but for most forms of writing in school, a neutral or slightly formal style is more appropriate. Remember, though, that you shouldn't use very formal language to try to impress – it is more important to put your ideas over clearly.

> **Tip for success**
> Do not use different registers within the same piece of writing.

Some types of writing need to use very specific **technical terms**. For example, a document for medical professionals might use a word such as '*suprarenal*' instead of saying '*above the kidneys*' because this word will be understood by its readers. In scientific documents, the use of technical terms can be necessary to avoid any ambiguity.

At the other end of the scale, **literary** or **poetic language** such as '*bewail*' or '*flaxen*' may be appropriate in creative writing.

Emphasizing important points

We use emphasis to draw a reader's attention to the points which are most important. There are a number of ways of doing this:

- **Order within the whole text**. Start with the most important points.
- **Order within a sentence or paragraph**. The first part of the sentence is seen as the most important. Compare these sentences:

> *A thorough safety assessment is needed urgently, following a number of accidents on the site.*
>
> *Following a number of accidents on the site, a thorough safety assessment is needed urgently.*

In the first example, the fact that the safety assessment is needed is emphasized by coming first in the sentence. In the second example, the fact that there have been some accidents comes across as the more important point.

- **A summary of the main points**. You can put this in the conclusion or even as a list at the beginning. For example, you might begin a detailed report with a section on 'key findings' – simply a list of the main points you want to make.

- **Amount of text**. The more important a point, the more space you are likely to use discussing it. If you add too much detail about less important points, your readers may be confused about what is most important.

- **Typeface**. It is very simple to highlight words and phrases by using different forms of typefaces such as **bold**, *italics*, or <u>underlining</u>. Italics are probably the most commonly used:

    Please note that pupils should not bring mobile phones to school *at any time*.

  Fonts can also be made larger or smaller for emphasis, or a different colour may be used to make certain parts of a document stand out.

- **Repetition**. Repetition can be used to emphasize points. You could make a point and then repeat it immediately, using phrases such as:

    In other words ...
    Put more simply ...

  This is a useful way to stress the point you are making and also to explain it in a different way so that you can be certain that your readers will understand it.

  If you are writing a long document, you may want to repeat certain points throughout it, using phrases such as:

    This demonstrates yet again ...
    Again we see ...

  Repetition can also be a useful stylistic device, in writing as well as in speech. You might repeat a word, a phrase or part of a phrase:

    They said local businesses would close – not true. They claimed jobs would be lost – not true. They claimed traffic would increase – not true.

- **Headings**. Headings can be used to reinforce the main point that will be made in the parts they refer to.

- **Sudden change of style**. If readers are surprised by a sudden change of style, they may pay more attention to what is being said. One example would be to use a very short, snappy sentence after one or more longer sentences:

    Architects and engineers had assured officials and residents that the techniques used in constructing the bridge would ensure that it remained solid during an earthquake. It did not.

- **Emphatic words and phrases**. These can highlight the most important points, for example:

    Our priority now is ...
    The crucial advantage that this scheme offers is ...

    In a similar way, words such as 'crucially' or 'above all' at the start of a sentences signal the importance of what follows, as do adjectives such as 'urgent', 'vital', or 'essential'.

- **Punctuation**. The most obvious way to emphasize a sentence is to end it with an exclamation mark:

    We won over a thousand pounds!

    Be careful with exclamation marks, though. It is fine to use them in informal letters, emails, etc, but do not use them too often. It is not usually appropriate to use them in more formal writing.

    Structuring a sentence with a dash or a colon can also emphasize part of it:

    Critics described the film as terrible.
    Critics had one word for the film: terrible.

Increasing your vocabulary

- The best way to increase your vocabulary is to **read a lot**. As you read, notice the words that are being used.
- If you find a word you do not know, you will sometimes be able to get a good idea of its meaning from the other words around it. If not, **look it up in a dictionary**. It is not always a good idea to look up every new word as you find it, because it can be distracting, but you could **underline or highlight** some of the words and look them up at the end.
- It can be useful to **keep a vocabulary notebook**, to record new words you have learned. You can arrange the words in the order that is best for you: alphabetically or by subject.
- Try to develop an interest in words, and ask yourself questions about them. For instance, you can widen your vocabulary by **learning words in groups**. If you know that *canine* means 'relating to dogs', see if you know the word meaning 'relating to cats' (*feline*) or 'relating to cows' (*bovine*). Similarly,

if you know that *carnivorous* means 'meat-eating', do you know the word for 'plant-eating' (*herbivorous*) or for creatures that eat anything (*omnivorous*)?

- **Notice the context** that words are in. You can often make your writing more elegant by choosing which words go together, such as the interesting verbs with the common nouns in these examples:

  abandon an attempt
  draw to a close
  adopt a method

- Word games such as **crossword puzzles** can help to develop an interest in words and can introduce words you did not know before.

- A good **dictionary** will help a lot with your writing. Try to use a dictionary that is suitable for you. *Collins School Dictionary* should have all the words you need for all your subjects, but will not be too big to carry around. If English is not your first language, you could use a learner's dictionary, which will have simple definitions, lots of example sentences, and all the grammar information you need.

- A **thesaurus** such as this one, the *Collins School Thesaurus*, gives you lots of interesting alternative words to use instead of very common and over-used ones. The more you consult your thesaurus for alternatives, the more familiar the words will become, and soon they will be part of your vocabulary.

CHECKING YOUR WRITING

General checks

It is important to leave time to check your work, so that the finished quality is as high as possible. Checking falls into two main areas:

- **Overall structure and content**
- **Points of spelling, grammar, punctuation, etc**

If you have planned your work carefully and written one or more drafts, your work should already be logical and well structured. However, even for a short piece of writing, such as a letter or email, it is worth asking yourself the following questions:

- Has my writing achieved what I wanted to achieve?
- Have I expressed my points clearly?
- Do my ideas or pieces of information come in a logical sequence?
- Do I have enough evidence to support my points?
- Is the tone of my writing what I wanted it to be?
- Have I included everything I wanted to include?

It can often be a good idea to ask someone else to correct your work – your eyes will see what you *intended* to write, whereas someone else may spot errors more easily.

> **Tip for success**
> Most people find it easier to check their work on paper rather than on a computer screen, so if it is important that it is correct, consider printing it out.

Checking spelling

It is important to make sure your spelling is correct.

Use your instinct: if a word looks wrong, check it in a dictionary. You can also use a spellchecker on your computer, but make sure that it is set to the variety of English you want – for example, British or American.

General points to look out for include:

- **Homophones**. These are words which sound the same but are spelt differently, for example their/there, flour/flower, bare/ bear. Remember that the spellchecker on your computer will not be able to correct errors in homophones because they are both correct words.
- **Letters that are the wrong way round**. It is very easy to make this kind of error when you are typing your work, for instance typing *'form'* instead of *'from'*.
- **Missing letters**. Make sure you do not miss out silent letters in words such as 'gover**n**ment', or forget to double the consonant in words such as 'swi**mm**ing'.

> **Tip for success**
> Take particular care with typed writing – it is much easier to make a mistake with fingers on keys than with a pen.

Checking grammar and punctuation

It is important that your writing is grammatically correct and properly punctuated.

General points to look out for include:

- **Apostrophes**. Make sure you have put them in where they are needed and left them out where they are not.
- **Capital letters**. Make sure that all proper nouns have capital letters. It is also a common error to put a lower case 'i' where the upper case pronoun 'I' is needed.
- **Repeated words**. These are often found at the end of one line and the beginning of another.
- **Missing words**. It can be very easy to miss out little words such as 'of' or 'in', and equally difficult to spot that they are missing, since your brain can compensate by adding them in unconsciously when you read.
- **Agreement**. This means making sure that all the parts of a sentence relate correctly to each other, avoiding mistakes such as *'We was asked to contribute.'* (Should be: *We were asked to contribute.*)

If you are using your computer to write, you will probably have a grammar checker available. This will pick up some common problems, but you should still check your work yourself.

> **Tip for success**
> Do not try to correct huge pieces of text in one go – you need to be fresh to be able to spot errors.

Other things to check

- **Facts and information**. If there is any doubt about the source of your information, for instance if it came from a website you are not sure is reliable, make sure you can confirm it in another, more reliable source.
- **Numbers**. Always check numbers, especially long ones such as telephone numbers. It is very easy to make a mistake when you type these.
- **Dates**. If you tell people a meeting is on Thursday 6th, but the 6th is a Wednesday, you will cause confusion.
- **Repetition of words and phrases**. As you were writing, you may not have realized that you used the same word or phrase over and over again, but when you check at the end, you will notice this, and can vary your words if you want to.

Checking work on a computer

In many ways, computers make all sorts of writing much easier, especially because we can correct mistakes and move around sections of text without having to write everything out again. However, this does mean that it is very easy to bring in mistakes.

If you correct one word in a sentence or one part of a sentence, take great care to make sure that the whole sentence is still correct. For instance, it is very easy to leave in words that are not needed. Look at the following example:

She had an important role in his career.
His mother played had an important role in his career.

The writer only deleted 'she' instead of 'she had' when making this correction, leading to an extra verb in the sentence.

Remember, too, to make sure that agreement within a sentence is not affected by a change to part of it:

I gave my passport to the officer, who looked at it closely.
I gave my passport and driving licence to the officer, who looked at it closely.

In this case, the writer has added the words '*and driving licence*' but has forgotten to change the pronoun '*it*' later in the sentence to '*them*'.

Tip for success

If you decide to move a section of text, do make sure that you have deleted it from where it was originally.

DIFFERENT TYPES OF WRITING

You have to vary your style according to the type of text you are writing: the kind of original, descriptive writing you would use for a piece of creative writing would not be appropriate for an essay or report!

Imaginative writing

When you use your imagination to write creatively, your main purpose is to entertain your audience.

If you are writing a story, make an outline of your plot before you begin. This way, you will keep to a structure and sequence of events and not ramble.

- **Decide who the main characters are**, what happens to them and what they do, and how any conflict at the centre of your story is resolved.
- **Decide where and when the action takes place**. Use the setting to create a **mood** or **atmosphere**. For example, a city in a foggy evening has an eerie aspect; a crowded beach could be either lively or claustrophobic, depending on the point of view of the narrator.
- **Decide who is narrating the events**. A **first-person narrator** (*I*) has immediacy and can convey a personal response, so you are likely to use one if you are retelling a personal experience. However, a first-person narrator cannot convey the thoughts of another person or events outside of his or her own perception. A **third-person narrator** (*he/she*) allows you to describe events happening elsewhere and the thoughts of other people, which gives you more options when writing a story.

Here are some things to think about and try applying to your imaginative writing once you start.

- Open the text with an arresting or engaging sentence or image:
    You've got to love summer, haven't you?
- If you are writing a story, it is important to develop and describe the **characters** involved. Think about what they look like, how they dress, how they move.
- Use vivid words and **imagery** to create an atmosphere or mood. You might do this through **simile**, **metaphor**, or **personification**, for example:
    The shy sun finally revealed itself and spread its warm blanket over us.
  You can also do this through colour:
    The steely grey sky seemed to bear down on us.

- Remember to describe using as many **senses** as possible. Create an image for your reader of how something looks, tastes, sounds, smells, or feels.

- If you are describing an event, bring in your own **feelings** and personal **reactions** to the situation you are describing. Were you angry, excited, sad? You might write in the first person:

  I was delighted to see …

- Use **vivid adjectives and adverbs**. If appropriate, use an unexpected or unusual word or phrase that will make the reader take notice. Your thesaurus will help you to find interesting and lively words to use.

> **Tip for success**
>
> Don't use too many adjectives to describe one thing. It is better to pick a strong adjective that captures a feeling or impression rather than using three less punchy ones.

- As well as using adjectives and adverbs to describe, use **nouns and verbs** to reveal something about character and mood. For example, you could say that a character *strides*, rather than *walks*, to suggest an air of purpose or confidence.

- Leave out any details that do not contribute to the overall plot or atmosphere, or the piece will not cohere and the reader will be distracted.

- Any **dialogue** you include should also be relevant or useful to the story, perhaps to reveal more about a character or create a tense situation.

- Vary your sentence and paragraph **lengths** to change the pace of your writing. Longer paragraphs and sentences can help 'slow down' your text, while shorter sentences seem more dynamic and can be used to describe exciting action.

- Vary the **structure** of your sentences so your text is not repetitive. For example, change:

  He opened the door cautiously to *Cautiously, he opened the door.*

- You can also vary the structure of your sentences to change their **emphasis**. For example, moving the subject of your sentence to the end can create tension:

  Down the alley, onto the street and across the road, he ran for his life.

- End the text with a memorable sentence or image:

  It was the best summer of my life.

Formal letters

So much communication is done through phone calls, emails, and websites that many people have forgotten how to write formal letters. However, letters are still used in some situations.

Here is general layout for a formal letter. The layout of formal letters varies but this format is generally accepted. The numbers in the letter refer to points made on the following page.

---

7 Molden Rd
(1)   Bristol
BR2 4UP

(2) 18 November 2013

The Manager (3)
Fabby Fashions
2 North Row
Bristol
BR1 3GY

Dear Sir or Madam (4)

Faulty jumper – refund requested (5)

On Saturday 16 November 2013 I bought a blue Bartleby and Snitch jumper from your shop. It cost £45 and I paid for it in cash.

When I put it on at home I noticed that there was a hole in the left sleeve.

I would appreciate it if you would refund the full cost to me. I enclose the receipt for my purchase.

Yours faithfully (6)

Sylvie Marks

(7)
Ms Sylvie Marks

---

1. Write your address in the top right corner of the letter. Do not write your name here.

2. Write the date on the right, under your address. Write the month in full as a word.

3. Write the name and address of the person that you are writing to on the left, under your address and date.

4. If you know the name of the person you are writing to, use the title and the family name to address them. If you do not know the name of the person you are writing to, write 'Dear Sir or Madam'.

5. The heading goes here in bold, giving the subject matter of the letter. This will not be appropriate for all formal letters but is useful in cases where the letter clearly relates to a particular subject.

6. Write 'Yours sincerely' to end the letter if you know the surname of the person you are writing to. Write 'Yours faithfully' if you do not. Remember to start 'Yours' with a capital letter.

7. Write your signature by hand and then type your name under it. Put your given name first and family name second.

> **Key point to remember**
> If you know that the person you are sending the letter to is a woman but you do not know how she prefers to be addressed, use the title 'Ms'. 'Ms' is used for both married and single women.

- Most formal letters have a similar structure, having an introduction, a main part, and a conclusion.
- The language that you use in a formal letter must be appropriate. It should be polite, whatever subject you are writing about. It does not need to be very formal but it must not be informal. Do not use:
  - ▷ slang or informal language
  - ▷ contractions, such as 'I'm' and 'can't'
- Make sure that you spell the name of the person that you are writing to correctly. People can feel offended when their names are spelt wrongly.
- It is helpful to write a clear heading before the main part of your letter. This tells the reader exactly what the letter is about. There is a greater chance that the reader will pay attention to your letter if they know from the start what they are dealing with.

- Take care over the appearance of your letter. Present the text in short blocks and leave plenty of white space between them. Prepare a letter that looks easy to read.

> **Key point to remember**
> Make sure that you use the reader's correct title. For example, do not write 'Mr...' if the reader is a doctor and likes to be addressed with that title.

You must try to help the reader by making the message of the letter as clear as possible. You can do this by:

- giving the main point (or points) first. Your reader will immediately want to know why you are writing to them and may feel impatient with your letter if they have to read through a lot of text in order to find this out.
- not including too much information. Only write what the reader needs to know. Do not include a lot of details or the reader may struggle to understand the main point of the letter.
- not including irrelevant information. This might confuse the reader or make them impatient.
- keeping your sentences short and simple. Short sentences with a simple structure are easier to understand.

> **Tip for success**
> Write a clear letter that can be easily understood.

Personal letters

Again, so much communication is done through texting and social networking that informal letters between friends are becoming quite rare. Still, some people like to write letters – or at least notes – to their friends.

(1) 18th December, 2013

Dear Sara (2)

(3) It was great to speak to you last week – thanks for phoning. I'm so sorry I haven't been in touch this year. It's been quite hectic with one thing and another!

(4) We're both really excited that you're coming to see us in the new year - it's been far too long. I just thought I'd better remind you to bring your walking boots. There are some fantastic walks we can do round here (if we have the energy!). Also, make sure you bring warm sweaters and coats. The scenery here is gorgeous but it is very cold, especially in January (and I seem to remember from our college days together that you feel the cold!).

(5) Did I mention I bumped into Steve Washington in Manchester earlier this year? He looked so different I almost didn't recognize him. Anyway, I'll tell you more when I see you…

Really looking forward to seeing you both. I'll call you nearer the time with directions.

(6) Much love
Emma xxx
(7) PS Can't wait to see you with short hair!

① You do not need to write your address here, although some people do. If you want to give the reader a new or different address, you can write it here. If you sometimes write from one place and sometimes another, you may show which of these addresses you are writing from by putting, for example:

> *London*
> *18th December, 2013*

② You can use the traditional greeting for an informal letter, which is 'Dear Paolo/Greta, etc' or you may like to write simply, 'Hi Paolo/Greta, etc'.

③ You can start an informal letter by referring to a previous communication with the reader. You can also start by asking after the health of the reader or by saying sorry for not having written to or telephoned the reader recently:

- How are you?
- How are you doing?
- I hope you're both well.
- I'm sorry it's been so long since my last letter.

④ The tone of an informal letter is very often conversational. Just as in conversation, you can use informal words and phrases freely. You can use contractions (for example 'I'm', 'won't', etc) and you do not have to write in full sentences.

⑤ You can end a letter by saying how pleased you are that you are going to see the reader soon. You may also encourage the reader to write or to call you:

- It'll be great to see you.
- It would be great to meet up one of these days.
- Can't wait to see you.
- Hope to hear from you soon.
- Stay in touch.
- Write soon.

⑥ If you are writing to a close friend, before you sign your name, you will want to show affection by using a word or phrase such as:

- Love
- Lots of love
- Much love
- All my love
- Love from

If you are writing to a friend that you do not know so well, you may prefer:

- Best wishes
- All the best
- Kind regards
- Regards

⑦ If, when you have finished writing your letter, you think of something else that you want to add, you can put it after the letters, 'PS'.

Blogs

A blog is a website where someone regularly writes their thoughts and opinions in the form of a *post*. Blogs usually contain text, images, and links to other websites.

The style and tone of a blog will depend very much on its content. A cycling blog written by a keen cyclist might have an informative and factual tone. The blogger wants to provide useful information for other cyclists and to share their experiences with them. They may not be so interested in entertaining their readers.

A political blog, on the other hand, might be very funny, using humour in order to criticize politicians.

The blog that someone writes about their daily life will probably have an informal tone and be written in the style of a conversation, 'chatting' to its readers as if they were friends.

Whatever the content or subject matter of the blog that you are writing, there are a few general rules.

The first – and possibly the most important – is to **consider your audience**. *Who* do you intend to read this? What are their interests and opinions, and **what do they want from your blog**? Do they want:

- information on a particular subject?
- entertainment?
- to hear your opinions?
- all of the above?

By providing what your reader wants, you will keep them coming back for more.

It might help to think of your blog as a *resource* for the reader. For example, if you are writing a blog about a particular sport, you might like to **share tips** with the reader about techniques that you have discovered that have improved your performance. Or you might **provide links** to websites that sell equipment that you have found useful. Give your reader the advantages of your experience and knowledge.

> **Key point to remember**
> If you give links to other blogs or websites, make sure you have visited them first and are certain of their content.

- **Talk to your reader**. Most blogs are written in slightly informal, conversational English. This is what readers expect. It gives them the feeling that they have formed a relationship with the writer. Try to imagine that you are *chatting* to your reader. Use the sort of words and phrases that you would naturally use in conversation with a friend. This may include words and phrases that you would not use in other forms of writing.

- **Be yourself**. People want to read blogs with original writing and original ideas. If they come back to your blog, it is because they like reading about what *you* have to say and they want to see how *you* say it. Be confident in your style and never try to write like someone else.

- **Do not be afraid to start your sentences with 'I'**. Generally, people do not expect blogs to read like newspapers. In other words, they do not visit a blog to read a report of facts. Most people read blogs because they give them a chance to learn about other people. They want to know *what the writer has done* and *how the writer feels* about things. Tell your reader in the first person about your experiences and opinions.

> **Tip for success**
> Once you have developed a style of writing that you are happy with, keep using that style.

- **Keep your blog short.** Most people spend only a few minutes of their day or week reading blogs. They simply do not have time to read a lot, no matter how interesting or amusing the writing is. Do not fill the screen with text. Leave some white space and create a clean, simple screen that the reader knows they can deal with quickly.

- **Write a post that readers can scan.** Remember that many people who visit a blog do not read the whole text word for word. Instead they scan the screen, looking for particular words and phrases. They may want to get the general idea of what you have written or they may want only to find particular information. Present your blog in such a way that people scanning the text can get the most from it. You can do this by:

▷ writing in **short paragraphs**. It is much easier to scan a text that is broken up into many short chunks rather than one long block of text.

▷ providing **lists of information**, introduced by bullet points. Lists are quick and easy to understand.

▷ providing a number of **relevant titles** to break up your text. Titles naturally attract the eye and can help guide the reader to a particular part of the post.

- **Communicate your message quickly.** Whatever message or information you are trying to communicate in your post, make sure you do it within the first few lines. Do not assume that the reader has the time or the interest to read through a long introduction. Start your point immediately you start writing.

- **Make use of pictures.** Select attractive and relevant images to break up blocks of text. Even if your images are only for decoration, they will still make the screen look more professional and more appealing.

- Finally, when you have finished writing your post, **edit your writing.** The tone of your blog might be relaxed and informal but you still need the writing itself to be correct. Some readers will stop visiting a blog because the English is poor even though they are interested in the topic. Take time to:

▷ remove phrases or words that are not needed

▷ change the order of paragraphs if this improves the post

▷ correct errors

▷ correct punctuation

> **Key point to remember**
> Get your reader's attention by saying what is most important within the first few lines.

Essays

Writing essays can be difficult and a lot of students struggle with some aspect of it. However, there are a number of things that you can do to make the task easier.

- **Read and then re-read the essay title.** Before you start even to plan your essay make absolutely sure that you understand the title and what it is asking you to do. Remember that this is one of the main points on which your essay will be judged. This point may sound obvious but failure to answer the question is one of the commonest reasons for essays being marked down.

  As you write more essays, you will notice that certain verbs are used again and again in essay titles. Make sure that you know exactly what each verb means in the context of an essay title:

▷ **analyse**: to examine something in detail for the purposes of explaining it
▷ **assess**: to judge how valuable, important, or successful something is
▷ **compare**: to look for similarities between
▷ **contrast**: to look for differences between
▷ **evaluate**: to judge how valuable, important, or successful something is
▷ **illustrate**: to explain something by using examples
▷ **outline**: to describe the most important points
▷ **relate**: to show how two or more issues are connected
▷ **summarize**: to describe the most important points

> **Key point to remember**
> No matter how well written your essay is, if you fail to answer the question, you will lose marks.

- Take time to **plan your essay**. Proper planning will help you to organize and develop your thoughts so that you are clear about what you want to write. It will also ensure that you do not leave anything out.
- **Keep to the point**. Do not introduce unrelated subjects or aspects of a subject that are not relevant. Even if your points are interesting, you will not gain marks for them! Ask yourself before you make each new point, how does this point answer the essay title?

- **Make every word count.** Write clearly and concisely, avoiding over-long sentences and unnecessary adjectives. You will want to show that you have a varied vocabulary but do not be tempted to use a lot of words where a few well-chosen words will do!
- **Remember paragraphs.** As a general rule, every time you make a separate point, start a new paragraph. Do not make your paragraphs too long. If a paragraph is very long, consider dividing it into separate points.
- Remember that the type of English that is right for essays is **slightly formal English**. It is more formal than the English that we usually use for speaking and writing emails. The English generally used in essays does not:

▷ include informal or slang words (unless you are quoting someone).

▷ include contractions, such as 'isn't' and 'won't'.

▷ generally include phrases that use the words 'I', 'me', or 'my'.

- Finally, when you have finished your essay, make sure you **read it carefully** at least twice. Be prepared at this point to make changes to it. Consider:

▷ the order of the points that you make. Is this logical and does the essay 'flow'?

▷ your choice of language. Is it clear and does it say exactly what you intended it to say?

Tip for success

Use your computer's spellchecker to check your finished work but make sure that you read your essay for spelling errors too. Remember that a spellchecker will not find a typo such as 'from' where the intended word is 'form'.

Essay phrases and words

There are different stages to an essay and each stage of the essay requires you to do different things. Under the relevant heading below, you will see a range of words and phrases that can be used at a particular stage or for a particular purpose. Use these words and phrases to express your ideas in a way that is more precise and more varied.

Introductions

Introducing the topic and purpose of an essay
Here you say briefly what you will discuss, making sure that it fits exactly with the title of your essay:

- *This essay will examine/look at …*
- *This essay focuses on/discusses …*
- *This essay considers/explores …*

Defining key terms used in the essay
If there is any doubt about the meaning of a word or phrase that is important in your essay, explain in your introduction what *you* mean by that word or phrase:

- *Throughout this essay the term 'x' will refer to …*
- *The term 'x' refers here to …*
- *For the purposes of this essay, the term 'x' is used to mean …*

Explaining how the essay is organized
You may like to give a very brief summary of the structure of your essay. This shows the teacher or examiner that you have arranged your thoughts and arguments in an organized way. It will also make it easier for them to understand exactly what you are saying:

- *This essay has been divided into three parts. The first part looks at …*
- *There are three parts to this essay. The first part deals …*
- *This essay begins by… It then looks at …*

Saying why the topic is particularly interesting or important
You may like to put the topic in context, especially if the topic is of particular relevance now:

- *We live in a world in which …*
- *The issue of x is one that affects everyone …*
- *Recent years have seen an increasing interest in …*
- *One of the most important developments in recent years is …*

Raising an area of your topic where there is disagreement or controversy
You might like to offer arguments against a statement in the essay title, especially if you know of recent findings that seem to contradict it.

- *This is not always true, however.*
- *However, recent evidence suggests that this may not be the case.*
- *More recently, research has emerged that seems to contradict …*
- *There is increasing concern about …*
- *Not everyone agrees with this statement, however …*

The main part of the essay
This is the part of the essay where you discuss and develop the ideas that you outlined in your introduction. In this part of the essay, you will need to do several things, for example, give facts and make statements, justify or disagree with statements, give reasons, and suggest causes.

Stating what is generally considered to be true
You will probably want to introduce a statement that everyone – or most people – agree is true. (You might then develop the point or go on to argue against that point.)

- *It is often said that ...*
- *It is certainly true that ...*
- *It is undoubtedly the case that ...*
- *Few people would argue that ...*

Stating that something is partly true
You may only partly agree with a statement:

- *There is an element of truth in this statement.*
- *There is some degree of truth in this.*
- *This is to some extent true.*

> ### Key point to remember
> When giving personal opinions in academic essays, it is generally better to avoid phrases that use the words 'I', 'me', or 'my':
> ✗ *I think that keeping animals in captivity is wrong for the following reasons.*
> ✗ *It's my opinion that keeping animals in captivity is wrong for the following reasons.*
> ✓ *Keeping animals in captivity is wrong for the following reasons.*

Providing facts
You might like to refer to some new information or statistics that relate to your topic:

- *Recent research clearly indicates/shows ...*
- *Recent research suggests ...*
- *A new study confirms that ...*
- *A recent report revealed ...*
- *It has recently emerged that ...*

The verbs 'seem' and 'appear' can be used to make claims less definite, for example:

Government-funded research into this area appears to confirm this theory.

Suggesting reasons for something

You might want to suggest an explanation – or more than one explanation – for a situation or problem that you have described:

- *This may be because of/caused by ...*
- *This may be a result/consequence of ...*
- *It is likely/possible that ...*
- *One possible explanation is that ...*
- *We might deduce from this that ...*

Describing the result of something

If you have stated the cause of something, you might want to say what the result is. These words can be used to start sentences that link the cause of something with the outcome.

- *Consequently ...*
- *As a result/consequence ...*
- *The result is ...*
- *It follows that ...*
- *Therefore ...*

Adding to a point that you made before

You might like to add to a previous point, either by saying something that you think is equally important:

- *Besides, ...*
- *In addition, ...*
- *Similarly, ...*
- *In the same way, ...*

or by giving a point that is even more important:

- *What is more, ...*
- *Furthermore, ...*
- *Moreover, ...*
- *More importantly, ...*

Introducing examples

You will almost certainly want to provide examples of what you are claiming. Examples provide proof for your claim and can be introduced with the following words:

- *For example ...*
- *For instance ...*
- *A good example of this is ...*
- *An illustration/instance of this is ...*

  Alternatives to the phrase *'good example'* are *'notable example'* and *'prime example'*.

Giving different opinions

Whatever your view on a subject, you will probably need to show that you are aware of different views, with phrases such as:

- *It could/might be argued that ...*
- *It is sometimes said that ...*
- *There are those who claim that ...*
- *Another way of looking at/viewing this is ...*

Conclusions

The conclusion brings together all the ideas and information you have discussed. It shows the reader that the essay is complete and that the aims of the essay have been achieved. In a conclusion, you summarize the main points and say what the consequences of your evidence are:

- *In summary, ...*
- *To summarize, ...*
- *In conclusion, ...*
- *To conclude, ...*
- *We can therefore conclude that ...*

Kk

kai NOUN (NEW ZEALAND; INFORMAL)
food • *I'm starving - let's have some kai.*
food • *Enjoy your food.*
grub (INFORMAL) • *Get yourself some grub.*
provisions • *enough provisions for two weeks*
rations • *The soldiers sampled the officers' rations.*
tucker (AUSTRALIAN AND NEW ZEALAND; INFORMAL) • *I haven't had any decent tucker for days.*

MORE SYNONYMS:
• sustenance (FORMAL)
• victuals

keen ① ADJECTIVE
showing eagerness and enthusiasm for something • *a keen amateur photographer*
ardent • *one of his most ardent supporters*
avid • *an avid reader*
eager • *We're eager to have another baby.*
enthusiastic • *Tom was very enthusiastic about the place.*
fond of • *Are you fond of Chinese cuisine?*
into (INFORMAL) • *I'm really into football.*

keen ② ADJECTIVE
quick to notice or understand things • *a keen intellect*
astute • *an astute judge of character*
brilliant • *She had a brilliant mind.*
perceptive • *a perceptive gaze*

quick • *His quick mind soon grasped the situation.*
shrewd • *Her questions showed a shrewd perception.*

keep ① VERB
to have and look after something • *His father keeps a small shop.*
care for • *vintage cars lovingly cared for by their owners*
maintain • *The house costs a fortune to maintain.*
preserve • *the need to preserve the rainforests*

keep ② VERB
to store something • *She kept her money under the mattress.*
deposit • *You are advised to deposit your valuables in the hotel safe.*
hold • *Our stock is held in a warehouse.*
store • *Store the cookies in an airtight tin.*

keep ③ VERB
to do what you said you would do • *I always keep my promises.*
carry out • *He carried out his threat.*
fulfil • *He fulfilled all his responsibilities.*
honour • *The two sides have agreed to honour a new ceasefire.*

kidnap VERB
to take someone away by force • *Four tourists have been kidnapped by rebels.*
abduct • *people claiming to have been abducted by aliens*
capture • *The guerrillas shot down one*

plane and captured the pilot.
seize • *hostages seized by terrorists*

kill VERB
to make someone or something die
• *The earthquake killed 62 people.*
assassinate • *the plot to assassinate Martin Luther King*
butcher • *The guards butchered hundreds of prisoners.*
destroy • *The jockey was unhurt but his horse had to be destroyed.*
execute • *He was executed for treason.*
exterminate • *an effort to exterminate all the rats*
massacre • *300 civilians have been massacred by the rebels.*
murder • *the widow of the murdered leader*
slaughter • *Whales are being slaughtered for commercial gain.*
slay • *a painting of Saint George slaying the dragon*

MORE SYNONYMS:
• annihilate
• dispatch

kin PLURAL NOUN
the people who are related to you
• *She has gone to live with her husband's kin.*
family • *There's a history of heart disease in our family.*
kindred • *his loyalty to his friends and kindred*
people • *She was reunited with her people.*
relations • *I was staying with relations in Atlanta.*
relatives • *On Sundays his relatives come to visit.*

kind ① NOUN
a particular type of person or thing
• *I don't like that kind of film.*
brand • *his favourite brand of whisky*
breed • *a rare breed of cattle*

category • *Cereal bars are the fastest-growing category of breakfast products.*
class • *a better class of restaurant*
classification • *the cost of coverage for different classifications of motorcycle*
genre • *a writer who does not confine himself to one particular genre*
grade • *an improved grade of fertilizer*
sort • *a dozen trees of various sorts*
species • *a rare species of moth*
type • *What type of guns were they?*
variety • *a new variety of rose*

kind ② ADJECTIVE
considerate towards other people
• *Thank you for being so kind to me.*
benevolent • *a very benevolent employer*
benign • *a benign ruler*
charitable • *a charitable nature*
compassionate • *My father was a deeply compassionate man.*
considerate • *a caring and considerate husband*
good • *a good man driven to a desperate act*
humane • *the humane treatment of prisoners*
kind-hearted • *Mark was kind-hearted, generous, and loved life.*
kindly • *a kindly old man*
thoughtful • *a thoughtful gesture*
unselfish • *his generous and unselfish attitude towards others*

MORE SYNONYMS:
• lenient
• philanthropic

ANTONYM:
• cruel

kindness NOUN
the quality of being considerate towards other people • *Everyone has treated me with great kindness.*
benevolence • *an act of selfless benevolence*

charity • *Ms Rubens writes with warmth and charity.*
compassion • *He showed no compassion to his victim.*
gentleness • *the gentleness with which she treated her mother*
humanity • *Her speech showed great maturity and humanity.*

MORE SYNONYMS:
• kindliness
• magnanimity
• philanthropy
• tenderness

ANTONYM:
• cruelty

king NOUN
a man who is the head of a royal family • *the king and queen of Spain*
monarch • *the coronation of the new monarch*
sovereign • *the first British sovereign to visit the country*

RELATED WORDS:
• ADJECTIVES royal, regal, monarchical

know ① VERB
to understand or be aware of something • *I don't know anything about cars.*

apprehend • *It is impossible to apprehend the whole painting at once.*
be aware of • *Smokers are aware of the risks they run.*
comprehend • *They do not comprehend the nature of the problem.*
perceive • *the world as we perceive it*
see • *Don't you see what he's up to?*
understand • *too young to understand what was happening*

know ② VERB
to be familiar with a person or thing • *I believe you two already know each other.*
be acquainted with • *Are you acquainted with my husband?*
be familiar with • *I am familiar with his work.*
recognize • *She recognized him at once.*

knowledge NOUN
all you know about something • *She had no knowledge of French.*
education • *a man with little education*
learning • *people of great learning*
scholarship • *a lifetime of scholarship*
wisdom • *a source of wisdom and knowledge*

Ll

label ① NOUN
a piece of paper or plastic attached to something for information • *He peered at the label on the bottle.*
sticker • *She's got a disabled sticker on her car.*
tag • *a name tag*
ticket • *a price ticket*

label ② VERB
to put a label on something • *The produce was labelled "Made in China".*
flag • *Flag the pages which need corrections.*
sticker • *products stickered at a special price*
tag • *The pigeon was tagged with a numbered band.*

labour ① NOUN
very hard work • *the labour of weeding and digging*
effort • *legs aching with the effort of the climb*
exertion • *She felt dizzy with the exertion of walking.*
industry • *At last his industry was rewarded.*
toil • *their day's toil in the fields*
work • *All our work is starting to pay off.*

labour ② NOUN
the workforce of a country or industry • *unskilled labour*
employees • *Only a third of all employees are union members.*
workers • *Thousands of workers have been laid off.*

workforce • *a country where half the workforce is unemployed*

labour ③ VERB
to work very hard • *peasants labouring in the fields*
slave • *We've been slaving half the night to finish this.*
toil • *workers toiling in wretched conditions*
work • *He works twelve hours a day.*

ANTONYM:
• relax

lack ① NOUN
the shortage or absence of something which is needed • *a lack of funds*
absence • *an absence of evidence*
deficiency • *tests for vitamin deficiency*
scarcity • *a scarcity of water*
shortage • *a food shortage*
want • *becoming weak from want of rest*

MORE SYNONYMS:
• dearth
• insufficiency
• scantiness

ANTONYM:
• abundance

lack ② VERB
to be without something that is needed • *She lacks confidence.*
be deficient in • *Your diet is deficient in vitamins.*
be short of • *I'm short of cash.*
miss • *Your jacket is missing a button.*

lag VERB

to make slower progress than other people or things • *He is now lagging 10 points behind the champion.*
fall behind • *The city is falling behind in attracting tourists.*
trail • *The Communist party is trailing badly in the opinion polls.*

lake NOUN

♦ **TYPES OF LAKE**
♦ lagoon
♦ loch (SCOTTISH)
♦ lough (IRISH)
♦ mere
♦ reservoir
♦ tarn

lame ① ADJECTIVE

unable to walk properly because of an injured leg • *She was lame in one leg.*
crippled • *a woman crippled by arthritis*
hobbling • *a hobbling old man*
limping • *limping from a hamstring injury*

lame ② ADJECTIVE

weak or unconvincing • *a lame excuse*
feeble • *his feeble attempt at humour*
flimsy • *MPs condemned his evidence as flimsy.*
pathetic • *a pathetic attempt at humour*
poor • *a poor effort*
unconvincing • *an unconvincing argument*
weak • *a weak performance*

lament ① VERB

to express sorrow or regret over something • *She lamented the death of her brother.*
grieve • *grieving over his dead wife and son*
mourn • *We mourned the loss of our home.*

wail • *a mother wailing for her lost child*
weep • *She wept for her lost love.*

MORE SYNONYMS:
• bemoan
• bewail

lament ② NOUN

something you say to express sorrow or regret • *a lament for a vanished age*
moan • *a moan of sorrow*
wail • *wails of grief*

MORE SYNONYMS:
• lamentation
• plaint

land ① NOUN

an area of ground which someone owns • *a dispute over land*
estate • *a shooting party on his estate in Yorkshire*
grounds • *the palace grounds*
property • *travellers who camped on his property*

land ② NOUN

a region or country • *America is the land of opportunity.*
country • *the boundary between the two countries*
nation • *the nation's financial crisis*
province • *The Algarve is Portugal's southernmost province.*
region • *the region of Tuscany*
territory • *the disputed territory of Kashmir*

land ③ VERB

to arrive on the ground after flying or sailing • *We landed in New York around noon.*
alight • *A thrush alighted on a nearby branch.*
dock • *The ship docked in Le Havre.*
touch down • *The plane touched down in Barbados.*

a b c d e f g h i j k l m n o p q r s t u v w x y z

language ① NOUN
the system of words people use to communicate • *She speaks four languages.*
dialect • *the Cantonese dialect*
idiom • *the Australian idiom*
jargon • *scientific jargon*
lingo (INFORMAL) • *I don't speak the lingo.*
tongue • *The French feel passionately about their native tongue.*
vernacular • *an Indian vernacular derived from Sanskrit*
vocabulary • *a new word in the German vocabulary*

MORE SYNONYMS:
• argot
• cant
• lingua franca
• patois

language ② NOUN
the style in which you speak or write • *He explained the process in plain language.*
phrasing • *The phrasing of this report is confusing.*
style • *a simple writing style*
wording • *The wording of the contract was ambiguous.*

MORE SYNONYMS:
• phraseology
• terminology

large ADJECTIVE
of a greater size or amount than usual • *a large room*
big • *Her husband was a big man.*
colossal • *a colossal task*
enormous • *an enormous house*
giant • *a giant bird*
gigantic • *a gigantic spider*
great • *a great hall as long as a church*
huge • *huge profits*
immense • *an immense chamber*
massive • *a massive ship*
vast • *a vast desert*

MORE SYNONYMS:
• gargantuan
• sizable *or*
• sizeable

ANTONYM:
• small

last ① ADJECTIVE
the most recent • *last year*
latest • *his latest thriller*
most recent • *her most recent film*
preceding • *The bank's turnover had risen during the preceding year.*
previous • *his previous marriage*

ANTONYM:
• first

last ② ADJECTIVE
happening or remaining after all the others of its kind • *the last three chapters of the book*
closing • *the closing years of this century*
concluding • *the concluding scene of the film*
final • *This is your final chance.*
ultimate • *the ultimate result of the move*

ANTONYM:
• first

last ③ VERB
to continue to exist or happen • *The film lasted for two and a half hours.*
carry on • *Our marriage can't carry on like this.*
continue • *The exhibition continues till 25 November.*
endure • *Somehow their friendship endures.*
persist • *The problem persists.*
remain • *The building remains to this day.*
survive • *companies which survived after the recession*

late ① ADJECTIVE
after the expected time • *The train was late.*

behind • *I've got behind with my payments.*
behind time • *Hurry up. We're behind time already.*
belated • *a belated birthday card*
delayed • *The kick-off was delayed by 10 minutes.*
last-minute • *buying some last-minute Christmas presents*
overdue • *The birth is two weeks overdue.*

MORE SYNONYMS:
• behindhand
• tardy
• unpunctual

ANTONYM:
• early

late ② ADJECTIVE
dead, especially recently • *my late husband*
dead • *He has been dead for a year now.*
deceased • *his recently deceased mother*
departed • *memories of departed friends*

MORE SYNONYMS:
• defunct
• perished

laugh ① VERB
to make a noise which shows you are amused or happy • *You never laugh at my jokes.*
▶ see Word Study **laugh**, page 647

laugh ② NOUN
the noise you make when amused or happy • *She has a very infectious laugh.*
chortle • *"That's what you think," he said with a chortle.*
chuckle • *We had a quiet chuckle at his mistake.*
giggle • *She gave a nervous giggle.*
guffaw • *He let out a huge guffaw of amusement.*

snigger • *barely able to stifle a snigger*
titter • *A titter went round the room.*

law ① NOUN
a country's system of rules • *The use of this drug is against the law.*
charter • *a citizen's charter for France*
code • *a code of conduct*
constitution • *proposed changes to the constitution*

RELATED WORDS:
• ADJECTIVES legal, judicial

law ② NOUN
one of the rules of a country • *The anti-stalking law was introduced in 1990.*
act • *A new act has been passed by Parliament.*
code • *a code designed to protect the rights of children*
decree • *a decree lifting sanctions against China*
regulation • *regulations outlawing child labour*
rule • *a rule that was imposed in 1962*
statute • *a practice regulated by statute*

MORE SYNONYMS:
• edict
• ordinance

lawyer NOUN
someone who advises people about the law • *I'm discussing the matter with my lawyers.*
advocate • *A public advocate will be appointed to represent you.*
attorney • *a prosecuting attorney*
barrister • *The author is a practising barrister.*
counsel • *His counsel advised him to appeal against the verdict.*
solicitor • *She took advice from a solicitor.*

lay ① VERB
to put something somewhere • *Lay a sheet of newspaper on the floor.*

a b c d e f g h i j k l m n o p q r s t u v w x y z

place • *She placed a mug of coffee in front of him.*
put • *He put the photograph on the desk.*
set • *He set his briefcase on the floor.*
set down • *I set the glasses down on the table.*
settle • *He settled his coat over my shoulders.*
spread • *She spread a towel over the sand and lay down.*

lay ② VERB
to arrange or set something out • *A man came to lay the carpet.*
arrange • *He started to arrange the books in piles.*
set out • *The flower garden was set out with large beds of roses.*

layer NOUN
something that covers a surface or comes between two other things • *A fresh layer of snow covered the street.*
blanket • *a blanket of fog*
coat • *a coat of paint*
coating • *a crisp chocolate coating*
covering • *a thin covering of dust*
film • *a film of plastic*
sheet • *a sheet of ice*
stratum • *the correct geological stratum*

layout NOUN
the way in which something is arranged • *the layout of the garden*
arrangement • *the arrangement of a room*
design • *the design of the museum*
format • *the format of the book*
plan • *a detailed plan of the house*

laze VERB
to relax and do no work • *We spent a few days lazing around by the pool.*
idle • *We spent hours idling in one of the cafés.*
loaf • *loafing around the house all day*

lounge • *They lounged in the shade.*
ANTONYM:
• work

lazy ADJECTIVE
not willing to work • *a lazy and incompetent employee*
idle • *an idle young layabout*
slack • *Many workers have simply become too slack.*

MORE SYNONYMS:
• good-for-nothing
• indolent
• shiftless
• slothful
• workshy

ANTONYM:
• industrious

lead ① VERB
to guide or take someone somewhere • *She led him into the house.*
conduct • *He asked if he might conduct us to the ball.*
escort • *They were escorted by police to their plane.*
guide • *He took me by the arm and guided me out.*
steer • *Nick steered them towards the door.*
usher • *I ushered him into the office.*

lead ② VERB
to be in charge of • *He led the country between 1949 and 1984.*
command • *the general who commanded the troops*
direct • *He will direct day-to-day operations.*
govern • *his ability to govern the country*
head • *Who heads the firm?*
manage • *I manage a small team of workers.*
supervise • *He supervised more than 400 volunteers.*

lead ③ NOUN

a clue which may help solve a crime
• The police are following up several leads.
clue • a vital clue to the killer's identity
indication • All the indications suggest that he is the murderer.
trace • No traces of violence were found on the body.

leader NOUN

the person in charge of something
• the leader of the Republican Party
boss (INFORMAL) • Who's the boss around here?
captain • the captain of the team
chief • the chief of police
commander • a commander in the Royal Navy
director • the director of the film
head • Heads of government met in New York.
principal • the principal of the school
ringleader • the ringleader of the gang

ANTONYM:
• follower

leading ADJECTIVE

particularly important, respected, or advanced • a leading industrial nation
chief • one of his chief rivals
eminent • an eminent surgeon
key • the key witness at the trial
main • one of the main tourist areas of Amsterdam
major • Exercise has a major part to play in preventing disease.
principal • one of the principal figures in politics today
prominent • a prominent member of the Law Society
top • a top model

MORE SYNONYMS:
• foremost
• pre-eminent

lead to VERB

to cause something to happen
• Smoking leads to heart disease and cancer.
cause • Knocks can cause damage to the spine.
contribute to • injuries which contributed to his death
produce • The drug produces side effects.

MORE SYNONYMS:
• bring on
• conduce to
• result in

leaflet NOUN

a piece of paper with information about a subject • Protesters were handing out leaflets in the street.
booklet • a booklet about mortgage rates
brochure • a travel brochure
circular • A circular was sent out to shareholders.
pamphlet • an anti-vivisection pamphlet

MORE SYNONYMS:
• handbill
• mailshot

leak ① VERB

to escape from a container or other object • The gas had leaked from a cylinder.
escape • A vent was opened to let some air escape.
ooze • Blood was oozing from the wound.
seep • Radioactive water has seeped into underground reservoirs.
spill • 70,000 tonnes of oil spilled from the tanker.

leak ② NOUN

a hole which lets gas or liquid escape
• Have you plugged the leaks?

A
B
C
D
E
F
G
H
I
J
K
L
M
N
O
P
Q
R
S
T
U
V
W
X
Y
Z

chink • *A mist rose from the chinks in the pavement.*

crack • *The lava oozed through cracks in the rock.*

fissure • *Water trickled out of fissures in the limestone.*

hole • *The sea was flowing in through the hole in the ship's hull.*

puncture • *My tyre has a slow puncture.*

leap ① VERB

to jump a great distance or height • *The deer leapt into the air.*

bounce • *She bounced up and down on the spot, looking for attention.*

bound • *The dog came bounding up the stairs.*

jump • *I jumped over the fence.*

spring • *He sprang to his feet.*

vault • *He could easily vault the wall.*

leap ② NOUN

a jump of great distance or height • *a leap of 2.37 metres*

jump • *the longest jumps by a man and a woman*

bound • *With one bound, Jack was free.*

spring • *The cheetah gave a great spring into the air.*

learn ① VERB

to gain knowledge by studying or training • *I am trying to learn French.*

grasp • *The basics of the language are easy to grasp.*

master • *He's having trouble mastering the piano.*

pick up • *You'll soon pick up enough German to get by.*

learn ② VERB

to find out about something • *On learning who she was, I asked to meet her.*

ascertain • *They had ascertained that he was not a spy.*

determine • *calculations to determine the rate of tax*

discover • *She discovered that they'd escaped.*

find out • *As soon as we found this out, we closed the ward.*

gather • *I gather the report is critical of the judge.*

hear • *I heard he had moved away.*

understand • *I understand that she's just taken early retirement.*

learned ADJECTIVE

having gained a lot of knowledge by studying • *a very learned man*

academic • *I feel intimidated by academic people.*

erudite • *a witty and erudite leader*

intellectual • *an artistic and intellectual couple*

literate • *a literate and educated readership*

scholarly • *a scholarly researcher*

MORE SYNONYMS:
• lettered
• well-read

least ADJECTIVE

as small or few as possible • *Stick to foods with the least fat.*

fewest • *Which product has the fewest calories?*

lowest • *the lowest temperatures on record for this time of year*

minimum • *the minimum height for a policeman*

slightest • *He showed only the slightest hint of emotion.*

smallest • *the smallest measurable unit of light*

ANTONYM:
• most

leave ① VERB

to go away from a person or place • *He is not allowed to leave the country.*

abandon • *He claimed that his parents had abandoned him.*
depart • *A number of staff departed during his time as director.*
desert • *Medical staff have deserted the city's main hospital.*
forsake • *I would never forsake my children.*
go • *Let me know when you're ready to go.*
quit • *He quit his job as an office boy.*
withdraw • *Troops withdrew from the country last month.*

MORE SYNONYMS:
• abscond
• decamp

leave ② NOUN
a period of time off work • *Why don't you take a few days' leave?*
holiday • *I still have several days' holiday to take.*
time off • *He took time off to go sailing with his wife.*
vacation • *We went on vacation to Puerto Rico.*

MORE SYNONYMS:
• furlough
• sabbatical

lecture ① NOUN
a formal talk about a particular subject • *In his lecture he covered several topics.*
address • *an address to the American people*
discourse • *a lengthy discourse on market strategy*
presentation • *a business presentation*
sermon • *his first sermon as a bishop*
speech • *He delivered his speech in French.*
talk • *a brief talk on the history of the site*

MORE SYNONYMS:
• exposition
• oration

lecture ② NOUN
a talk intended to tell someone off
• *The police gave us a stern lecture on safety.*
reprimand • *He has been given a severe reprimand.*
scolding • *given a scolding for offending his opponents*
ticking-off (INFORMAL) • *We were given a ticking-off for running in the corridors.*
warning • *He was given a severe warning from the referee.*

lecture ③ VERB
to teach by giving formal talks to audiences • *She has lectured all over the world.*
give a talk • *He set about campaigning, giving talks and fund-raising.*
speak • *He's been invited to speak at the Democratic Convention.*
talk • *Today, I plan to talk about the issues of education and nursery care.*
teach • *She has taught at the university for 34 years.*

left-wing ADJECTIVE
believing in socialist policies • *a left-wing demonstration*
leftist • *three leftist guerrilla groups*
liberal • *a politician with liberal views*
radical • *a radical feminist*
socialist • *Europe's last socialist state*

legacy NOUN
property someone leaves you when they die • *He left his sons a generous legacy.*
bequest • *He made a bequest to his favourite charity.*
estate • *documents concerning the estate*
heirloom • *a family heirloom*
inheritance • *She was worried she'd lose her inheritance to her stepmother.*

a
b
c
d
e
f
g
h
i
j
k
l
m
n
o
p
q
r
s
t
u
v
w
x
y
z

A
B
C
D
E
F
G
H
I
J
K
L
M
N
O
P
Q
R
S
T
U
V
W
X
Y
Z

legal ① ADJECTIVE
relating to the law • *the Dutch legal system*
forensic • *the forensic skill of a good barrister*
judicial • *a judicial review*
judiciary • *various levels of the judiciary system*

legal ② ADJECTIVE
allowed by the law • *The strike was perfectly legal.*
authorized • *an authorized procedure*
lawful • *What I did was lawful and proper.*
legitimate • *a legitimate business*
permissible • *the current permissible levels of pesticide in food*
rightful • *the rightful owner of the property*
valid • *a valid passport*

MORE SYNONYMS:
• constitutional
• licit
• sanctioned

ANTONYM:
• illegal

leisure NOUN
time when you can relax • *There wasn't a lot of time for leisure.*
free time • *He played piano in his free time.*
recreation • *Saturday afternoons are for recreation.*
relaxation • *Make time for a bit of relaxation.*
time off • *I haven't had any time off all day.*

ANTONYM:
• work

leisurely ADJECTIVE
unhurried or calm • *a leisurely walk along the beach*

comfortable • *going at a comfortable speed*
easy • *an easy pace*
gentle • *His movements were gentle and deliberate.*
relaxed • *a relaxed meal*
unhurried • *an unhurried way of life*

ANTONYM:
• hasty

lekker ADJECTIVE (SOUTH AFRICAN; SLANG)
pleasant or tasty • *We had a really lekker meal.*
delectable • *delectable chocolates*
delicious • *a wide selection of delicious desserts*
luscious • *luscious fruit*
pleasant • *a pleasant dinner*
tasty • *Try this tasty dish for supper.*

length ① NOUN
the distance from one end of something to the other • *The fish was about a metre in length.*
distance • *Work out the distance of the journey.*
extent • *the extent of the rain forest*
span • *a butterfly with a two-inch wing span*

length ② NOUN
the amount of time something lasts for • *The film is over two hours in length.*
duration • *The duration of the course is one year.*
period • *for a limited period only*
space • *A dramatic change takes place in the space of a few minutes.*
span • *The batteries have a life span of six hours.*
term • *a 12-month term of service*

lengthen VERB
to make something longer • *The runway had to be lengthened.*
extend • *They have extended the deadline.*

make longer • *You can make your hair longer by using extensions.*
prolong • *a move which will prolong the strike*
stretch • *Take care not to stretch the fabric.*

MORE SYNONYMS:
• elongate
• protract

ANTONYM:
• shorten

lessen VERB
to decrease in size or amount
• *changes to their diet that would lessen the risk of disease*
abate • *The storm gradually abated.*
decrease • *Population growth is decreasing by 1.4% each year.*
diminish • *The threat of war has diminished.*
dwindle • *his dwindling authority*
lower • *The Central Bank has lowered interest rates.*
minimize • *attempts to minimize the risk of developing cancer*
reduce • *Gradually reduce the dosage.*
shrink • *The forests have shrunk to half their size.*

MORE SYNONYMS:
• de-escalate
• downsize

ANTONYM:
• increase

lesson NOUN
a period of time for being taught
• *Johanna took piano lessons.*
class • *I go to dance classes.*
coaching • *He needs extra coaching in maths.*
lecture • *a series of lectures on art*
period • *We get six periods of French a week.*
tutoring • *a growing demand for private tutoring*

let ① VERB
to allow someone to do something
• *The authorities won't let her leave the country.*
allow • *I pleaded to be allowed to go.*
give permission • *Who gave you permission to come here?*
permit • *Permit me to express my opinion.*
sanction • *He may now be ready to sanction the use of force.*

ANTONYM:
• forbid

let ② VERB
to let someone use your property for money • *She always lets her house for the summer.*
hire out • *The machines are hired out to farmers.*
lease • *She plans to lease the building to students.*
rent • *He rents rooms to backpackers.*

level ① ADJECTIVE
completely flat • *a plateau of level ground*
flat • *Cricket should be played on a totally flat field.*
horizontal • *Every horizontal surface was covered with plants.*

ANTONYM:
• uneven

level ② VERB
to make something flat • *We levelled the ground.*
flatten • *Flatten the dough and cut it into four pieces.*
plane • *planing the surface of the wood*
smooth • *He smoothed his hair.*

level ③ NOUN
a point on a scale which measures something • *Crime levels have started to decline.*
grade • *the lowest grade of staff*

a b c d e f g h i j k l m n o p q r s t u v w x y z

rank • He rose to the rank of captain.
stage • an early stage of development
standard • a decent standard of living
status • We were reduced to the status of animals.

lie ① VERB
to rest somewhere horizontally • The injured man was lying on his back.
loll • He was lolling on the sofa.
lounge • We lounged on the beach all day.
recline • She reclined on the couch.
sprawl • They sprawled in a lawn chair, snoozing.

MORE SYNONYMS:
• be prostrate
• be recumbent
• be supine
• repose

lie ② VERB
to say something that is not true • She always lies about her age.
fib • He fibbed when she asked him where he'd been.
perjure oneself • All of the witnesses perjured themselves.
tell a lie • He could never tell a lie or do anything devious.

MORE SYNONYMS:
• dissimulate
• equivocate
• forswear oneself
• prevaricate

lie ③ NOUN
something you say which is not true • His whole story was a lie.
deceit • the deceits of political leaders
fabrication • She described the magazine interview as "a complete fabrication".
falsehood • He accused them of spreading falsehoods about him.
fib • I caught him out in another fib.

fiction • His account of events is a complete fiction.

life NOUN
the time during which you are alive • a long and active life
existence • a very miserable existence
life span • This species of snake has a life span of up to 25 years.
lifetime • a lifetime devoted to service for others
time • If I had my time again, I would do things differently.

RELATED WORDS:
• ADJECTIVES animate, vital

lift ① VERB
to move something to a higher position • straining to lift heavy weights
elevate • a mechanism to elevate the platform
hoist • I hoisted my rucksack on to my shoulder.
pick up • Anthony picked up his case from the floor.
raise • He raised his hand to wave.

ANTONYM:
• lower

lift ② VERB
to remove something such as a ban or law • the decision to lift sanctions against Iran
cancel • The government has cancelled the state of emergency.
end • pressure to end the embargo
relax • an attempt to persuade the US Congress to relax the law
remove • an amendment to remove the ban on divorce

MORE SYNONYMS:
• rescind
• revoke

light ① NOUN
brightness that enables you to see

things • *Cracks of light filtered through the shutters.*
brightness • *the brightness of the full moon*
brilliance • *the brilliance of the noonday sun*
glare • *shading his eyes from the glare*
glow • *the red glow of the dying fire*
illumination • *The only illumination came from a small window.*
radiance • *The bedside lamp cast a soft radiance over her face.*

MORE SYNONYMS:
• incandescence
• luminescence
• luminosity
• phosphorescence

ANTONYM:
• dark

RELATED WORD:
• PREFIX photo-

light ② ADJECTIVE
pale in colour • *a light blue shirt*
bleached • *bleached pine tables*
blonde or **blond** • *blonde hair*
fair • *to protect my fair skin*
pale • *dressed in pale pink*
pastel • *delicate pastel shades*

ANTONYM:
• dark

light ③ ADJECTIVE
not weighing much • *working out with light weights*
flimsy • *a flimsy cardboard box*
lightweight • *They will carry lightweight skis on their backs.*
portable • *a portable television*
slight • *She is small and slight.*

ANTONYM:
• heavy

light ④ VERB
to make a place bright • *The room was lit by a single candle.*

brighten • *The late afternoon sun brightened the room.*
illuminate • *No streetlights illuminated the road.*
light up • *Fireworks lit up the sky.*

ANTONYM:
• darken

light ⑤ VERB
to make a fire start burning • *It's time to light the barbecue.*
ignite • *A stray spark ignited the fireworks.*
kindle • *I kindled a fire in the stove.*

ANTONYM:
• extinguish

like ① PREPOSITION
similar to • *He looks just like my father.*
akin • *She looked at me with something akin to hatred.*
analogous • *a process analogous to the curing of tobacco*
parallel • *Our situation is parallel to yours.*
similar • *a taste similar to that of celery*

ANTONYM:
• unlike

like ② VERB
to find someone or something pleasant • *I really like this music.*
adore (INFORMAL) • *All her employees adored her.*
appreciate • *I know you appreciate good food.*
be fond of • *Are you fond of Chinese cuisine?*
be keen on • *I'm not very keen on sport.*
be partial to • *I'm partial to men with dark hair.*
enjoy • *Most children enjoy cartoons.*
go for • *What kind of man do you go for?*
have a soft spot for • *I've always had a soft spot for him.*

have a weakness for • *I have a weakness for slushy romantic novels.*
love • *She loves reading.*
relish • *He relished the idea of proving me wrong.*
revel in • *She appears to revel in being unpopular.*

ANTONYM:
• dislike

likely ADJECTIVE
having a good chance of happening
• *It seems likely that he will come back.*
anticipated • *the anticipated result*
expected • *the expected response*
liable • *He is liable to be a nuisance.*
possible • *It's quite possible that I'm wrong.*
probable • *the probable outcome*

ANTONYM:
• unlikely

limit ① NOUN
a point beyond which something cannot go • *the speed limit*
bounds • *the bounds of good taste*
deadline • *We finished the job within the deadline.*
maximum • *He was given two years in prison, the maximum allowed for the charges.*
ultimate • *This hotel is the ultimate in luxury.*
utmost • *His skills were tested to the utmost.*

limit ② VERB
to prevent something from going any further • *Limit yourself to six units of alcohol a week.*
confine • *Damage was confined to a small portion of the building.*
curb • *measures to curb inflation*
fix • *The mortgage rate is fixed at 8.5%.*
ration • *I'm rationing myself to ten cigarettes a day.*

restrict • *The patient was restricted to a meagre diet.*

MORE SYNONYMS:
• circumscribe
• delimit
• demarcate
• straiten

limp ADJECTIVE
not stiff or firm • *a limp lettuce leaf*
drooping • *the drooping branches of a birch*
flabby • *a flabby stomach*
floppy • *She fondled the dog's floppy ears.*
slack • *his slack belly*
soft • *a soft dough*

MORE SYNONYMS:
• flaccid
• pliable

ANTONYM:
• stiff

line ① NOUN
a long thin mark on something • *Draw a line down the centre of the page.*
rule • *He drew a rule under the last name.*
score • *There was a long score on the car's bonnet.*
streak • *dark streaks on the surface of the moon*
stripe • *a green jogging suit with white stripes down the sides*

line ② NOUN
a row of people or things • *a line of spectators*
column • *a column of figures*
file • *A file of mourners walked behind the coffin.*
queue • *a long queue of angry motorists*
rank • *ranks of police in riot gear*
row • *a row of pretty little cottages*

line ③ NOUN
the route along which something

moves • *the line of flight*
course • *the course of the river*
path • *The lava annihilates everything in its path.*
route • *the most direct route*
track • *a railway track*
trajectory • *the trajectory of the missile*

link ① NOUN
a connection between two things • *the link between sunbathing and skin cancer*
affiliation • *He has no affiliation with any political party.*
association • *the association between the two companies*
attachment • *Mother and child form a close attachment.*
bond • *The experience created a bond between us.*
connection • *He has denied any connection to the bombing.*
relationship • *the relationship between humans and their environment*
tie • *She has ties with this town.*

MORE SYNONYMS:
• affinity
• liaison

link ② VERB
to connect two things • *tree houses linked by ropes*
attach • *Attach the curtains to the rods with hooks.*
connect • *two rooms connected by a passage*
couple • *The engine is coupled to a gearbox.*
fasten • *a wooden bench fastened to the floor*
join • *the skin which joins the eye to the eyelid*
tie • *He tied the dog to the tree by its lead.*

ANTONYM:
• separate

liquid ① NOUN
a substance which is not solid and can be poured • *Drink plenty of liquids for the next few days.*
fluid • *The fluid can be removed with a syringe.*
liquor • *Pour the liquor off into the pan.*
solution • *a solution of honey and vinegar*

liquid ② ADJECTIVE
in the form of a liquid • *wash in warm water with liquid detergent*
fluid • *a fluid fertilizer*
molten • *molten metal*
runny • *a dessertspoon of runny honey*

list ① NOUN
a set of things written down one below the other • *There were six names on the list.*
catalogue • *a chronological catalogue of the Beatles' songs*
directory • *a telephone directory*
index • *The book includes a comprehensive subject index.*
inventory • *an inventory of stolen goods*
listing • *a listing of all the schools in the area*
record • *Keep a record of everything you eat and drink.*
register • *a register of births, deaths and marriages*

list ② VERB
to set things down in a list • *All the ingredients are listed on the label.*
catalogue • *I was cataloguing my video collection.*
index • *Most of the archive has been indexed.*
record • *400 species of fungi have been recorded.*
register • *a registered charity*

MORE SYNONYMS:
• enumerate

a b c d e f g h i j k l m n o p q r s t u v w x y z

A
B
C
D
E
F
G
H
I
J
K
L
M
N
O
P
Q
R
S
T
U
V
W
X
Y
Z

• itemize
• tabulate

listen VERB
to hear and pay attention to
something • *I'll repeat that for those of
you who weren't listening.*
attend • *Close your books and attend
to me.*
hark • *Hark! I hear the sound of footsteps.*
hear • *Will you hear me saying my lines?*
pay attention • *Pay attention or you
won't know what to do.*

little ① ADJECTIVE
small in size or amount • *a little old
lady*
dainty • *dainty sandwiches and cakes*
dwarf • *He grows dwarf tulips.*
mini • *a machine which resembles a
mini laptop computer*
miniature • *a collection of miniature
toy boats*
minute • *minute particles of soil*
pygmy • *a children's zoo with pygmy
goats*
skimpy • *dressed only in a skimpy bikini*
small • *They sat at a small table.*
tiny • *He tore the paper into tiny pieces.*
wee • *Would you like a wee bit of cake?*
ANTONYM:
• large

little ② NOUN
a small amount or degree • *We offered
her plenty to eat but she would only take
a little.*
hardly any • *He's done hardly any
work today.*
not much • *There's not much
difference between them.*
meagre • *a meagre pay increase*
measly • *a measly ration of food*
paltry • *a boring job with a paltry salary*
scant • *He paid scant attention to his
colleagues.*

live ① VERB
to have your home somewhere • *She
has lived here for 20 years.*
dwell • *the people who dwell in the forest*
inhabit • *the fish that inhabit the coral
reefs*
reside • *He used to reside in England.*
stay (SCOTTISH AND SOUTH AFRICAN)
• *We've stayed in this house since we got
married.*

live ② VERB
to be alive • *He will not live much longer.*
be alive • *You are lucky to be alive.*
exist • *the chances of finding life existing
on Mars*

live ③ ADJECTIVE
not dead or artificial • *a live spider*
alive • *It is unlikely that he is still alive.*
animate • *an animate object*
living • *living tissue*

lively ADJECTIVE
full of life and enthusiasm • *a lively
personality*
active • *an active youngster*
animated • *an animated discussion*
energetic • *She gave an energetic
performance.*
perky • *He wasn't quite as perky as
usual.*
sparkling • *I was enjoying a sparkling
conversation.*
sprightly • *a sprightly old man*
vivacious • *She is vivacious and
charming.*
ANTONYM:
• dull

load ① NOUN
something being carried • *This truck
can carry a load of up to 10 tons.*
cargo • *The boat was carrying its usual
cargo of bananas.*
consignment • *The first consignment
of food has been sent.*

freight · *Most of the freight was carried by rail.*
shipment · *a shipment of weapons*

load ② VERB
to put a lot of things on or into · *The trucks were loaded with blankets and supplies.*
fill · *The van was filled with crates.*
pack · *helicopters packed with medical supplies*
pile · *Her trolley was piled with groceries.*
stack · *stalls stacked with wares*

loan ① NOUN
a sum of money that you borrow · *a small business loan*
advance · *She was paid a $100,000 advance on her next novel.*
credit · *He can't get credit to buy the equipment.*
mortgage · *I took out a second mortgage on the house.*

loan ② VERB
to lend something to someone · *He loaned us the painting for our exhibition.*
advance · *I advanced him some money till we got home.*
lend · *Will you lend me your jacket?*

local ① ADJECTIVE
belonging to the area where you live · *This is a local shop for local people.*
community · *the revival of family and community life*
district · *the district council*
neighbourhood · *a neighbourhood watch scheme*
parish · *the parish priest*
regional · *the regional elections*

local ② NOUN
a person who lives in a particular area · *That's what the locals call the place.*
inhabitant · *the inhabitants of Glasgow*

native · *She is proud to be a native of Sydney.*
resident · *a protest by residents of the village*

locate VERB
to find out where someone or something is · *We have been unable to locate him.*
find · *They can't find it on the map.*
pinpoint · *Computers pinpointed where the shells came from.*
track down · *She has spent years trying to track down her parents.*

located ADJECTIVE
existing or standing in a particular place · *The restaurant is located near the cathedral.*
placed · *The hotel is wonderfully placed right in the city centre.*
sited · *a castle romantically sited on a river estuary*
situated · *His hotel is situated in a lovely place.*

location NOUN
a place or position · *a house with a beautiful location*
place · *the place where the temple used to stand*
point · *a popular meeting point for tourists*
position · *The ship radioed its position to the coastguard.*
site · *the site of the murder*
situation · *The hotel has a superb isolated situation.*
spot · *Can you show me the spot where it happened?*
whereabouts · *His exact whereabouts are still not known.*

MORE SYNONYMS:
· locale
· locus

a b c d e f g h i j k l m n o p q r s t u v w x y z

A
B
C
D
E
F
G
H
I
J
K
L
M
N
O
P
Q
R
S
T
U
V
W
X
Y
Z

lock ① VERB
to close and fasten something with a
key • *Are you sure you locked the door?*
latch • *He latched the gate.*
padlock • *The box has been padlocked
shut.*

ANTONYM:
• unlock

lock ② NOUN
a device used to fasten something
• *The lock had been burst open.*
latch • *A key clicked in the latch of the
front door.*
padlock • *He put a padlock on the door
of his flat.*

logical ① ADJECTIVE
using logic to work something out • *a
logical argument*
consistent • *a consistent and well-
presented theory*
rational • *a rational analysis*
reasoned • *a reasoned discussion*
sound • *His reasoning is sound, but he
has missed the point.*
valid • *Both sides put forward valid
points.*

MORE SYNONYMS:
• cogent
• coherent

ANTONYM:
• illogical

logical ② ADJECTIVE
sensible in the circumstances • *a
logical deduction*
judicious • *the judicious use of military
force*
obvious • *I jumped to the obvious
conclusion.*
plausible • *a plausible explanation*
reasonable • *a reasonable course of
action*
sensible • *the sensible thing to do*
wise • *a wise decision*

ANTONYM:
• illogical

lonely ① ADJECTIVE
unhappy because of being alone
• *She's lonely and just wants to talk.*
alone • *scared of being alone in the
house*
forlorn • *He looked a forlorn figure as he
left the pitch.*
forsaken • *a forsaken and bitter man*
lonesome • *I'm lonesome without you.*

lonely ② ADJECTIVE
isolated and not visited by many
people • *a lonely hillside*
deserted • *a deserted farmhouse*
desolate • *a desolate place*
isolated • *Many of the villages are in
isolated areas.*
remote • *a remote outpost*
secluded • *a secluded area close to her
home*
uninhabited • *an uninhabited island*
MORE SYNONYMS:
• godforsaken
• out-of-the-way
• unfrequented

long ① ADJECTIVE
continuing for a great amount of
time • *a long interval when no-one spoke*
extended • *an extended period of
unemployment*
interminable • *the interminable
debate about GM foods*
lengthy • *a lengthy delay*
lingering • *a lingering death from
cancer*
long-drawn-out • *the effects of a long-
drawn-out war*
prolonged • *A prolonged labour is
dangerous for both mother and child.*
protracted • *protracted negotiations
over pay rises*
slow • *Writing music is a slow process.*

sustained • *a sustained run of bad luck*

ANTONYM:
• short

long ② ADJECTIVE
great in length or distance • *a long line of people*
elongated • *The catfish has an elongated body.*
extensive • *an extensive list of products*
lengthy • *lengthy queues*

ANTONYM:
• short

long ③ VERB
to want something very much • *He longed for a cigarette.*
ache • *She still ached for her dead husband.*
covet • *She coveted his job.*
crave • *I crave her approval.*
hunger • *Jules hungered for adventure.*
lust • *She lusted after a designer kitchen.*
pine • *I pine for the countryside.*
yearn • *He yearned for freedom.*

longing NOUN
a strong wish for something • *her longing to return home*
craving • *a craving for sugar*
desire • *her desire for a child of her own*
hankering • *a hankering to be an actress*
hunger • *a hunger for success*
thirst • *a thirst for adventure*
yearning • *a yearning to be part of a normal family*

look ① VERB
to turn your eyes towards something and see it • *She looked at me with something like hatred.*
▶ see Word Study **look**, *page 648*

look ② VERB
to appear or seem to be • *the desire to look attractive*

appear • *He appeared intoxicated.*
look like • *You look like you need a good night's sleep.*
seem • *She seemed tense.*
seem to be • *They seem to be lacking in enthusiasm.*

look ③ NOUN
the action of turning your eyes towards something • *Lucy took a last look in the mirror.*
gaze • *her concentrated gaze*
glance • *a cursory glance*
glimpse • *a fleeting glimpse*
peek • *Give me a peek at his letter.*

look ④ NOUN
the way someone or something appears • *He had the look of a desperate man.*
air • *a nonchalant air*
appearance • *He was fastidious about his appearance.*
bearing • *a man of military bearing*
expression • *I saw his puzzled expression.*
face • *Why are you all wearing such long faces?*
semblance • *a semblance of normality*

look after VERB
to take care of someone or something • *Will you look after my cats when I go on holiday?*
care for • *vintage cars lovingly cared for by their owners*
mind • *Jim will mind the shop while I'm away.*
nurse • *My mother nursed him while he was ill.*
take care of • *I'll take care of the house for you.*
tend • *He tended his flower beds.*
watch • *My mother will watch the kids while we're out.*

a b c d e f g h i j k l m n o p q r s t u v w x y z

A
B
C
D
E
F
G
H
I
J
K
L
M
N
O
P
Q
R
S
T
U
V
W
X
Y
Z

lookalike NOUN
a person who looks like someone else • *an Elvis lookalike*
dead ringer (INFORMAL) • *a dead ringer for his brother*
double • *He's the exact double of his father at that age.*
spitting image (INFORMAL) • *She is the spitting image of me.*

look for VERB
to try to find a person or thing • *I'm looking for my son.*
forage • *foraging for food*
hunt • *Police are hunting for clues.*
search • *Rescue teams are searching for the missing crew members.*
seek • *They have had to seek work as labourers.*

loose ① ADJECTIVE
not firmly held or fixed • *a loose tooth*
free • *She broke her fall with her free hand.*
unsecured • *corridors blocked by unsecured objects*
wobbly • *a wobbly bridge*
ANTONYM:
• secure

loose ② ADJECTIVE
not fitting closely • *Wear loose clothes for comfort.*
baggy • *a baggy black jumper*
slack • *Those trousers are very slack on you.*
sloppy • *wearing a sloppy t-shirt, jeans and trainers*
ANTONYM:
• tight

loosen VERB
to make something looser • *He loosened his tie.*
slacken • *We slackened the guy-ropes.*
undo • *She began to undo the tiny buttons.*

untie • *He untied his shoes and slipped them off.*
ANTONYM:
• tighten

loot ① VERB
to steal from a place during a riot or battle • *Gangs began breaking windows and looting shops.*
pillage • *The bandits pillaged the church.*
plunder • *They plundered and burned the town.*
raid • *Rustlers have raided a village in the region.*
ransack • *The three raiders ransacked the house.*

loot ② NOUN
stolen or illegal money or goods • *The loot was never recovered.*
booty • *They divided the booty between them.*
haul • *the biggest haul of cannabis ever seized*
plunder • *pirates in search of easy plunder*
spoils • *the spoils of war*
swag (SLANG) • *The thieves carried the swag off in a stolen car.*

lose ① VERB
to be unable to find • *I've lost my keys.*
drop • *She's dropped a contact lens.*
mislay • *I seem to have mislaid my glasses.*
misplace • *Somehow my suitcase was misplaced.*
ANTONYM:
• find

lose ② VERB
to be beaten • *We lost the match.*
be beaten • *He was soundly beaten in the election.*
be defeated • *They were defeated in the final.*

ANTONYM:
• win

lost ① ADJECTIVE

not knowing where you are • *I think we're lost.*
adrift • *two men adrift on a raft in the middle of the sea*
astray • *I am lost and astray in the world.*
off-course • *After a while I realized I was completely off-course.*

lost ② ADJECTIVE

unable to be found • *a mother wailing for her lost child*
mislaid • *searching for his mislaid keys*
misplaced • *I've found your misplaced glasses.*
missing • *a missing person*
vanished • *unable to contact the vanished convoy*

lot ①: a lot or lots NOUN

a large amount of something • *Remember to drink lots of water.*
abundance • *an abundance of food*
a great deal • *I've spent a great deal of time on this project.*
masses (INFORMAL) • *There were masses of flowers at her funeral.*
piles (INFORMAL) • *He's got piles of money.*
plenty • *We've got plenty of time.*
quantities • *She drank quantities of hot, sweet tea.*
scores • *There were scores of witnesses.*

lot ② NOUN

an amount or number • *We've just sacked one lot of builders.*
batch • *a batch of cookies*
bunch (INFORMAL) • *My neighbours are a noisy bunch.*
crowd • *They're a real crowd of villains.*
group • *a small group of football supporters*

quantity • *a quantity of water*
set • *a set of photographs*

loud ① ADJECTIVE

having a high level of sound • *a loud explosion*
blaring • *a blaring television*
deafening • *a deafening roar*
noisy • *a noisy old car*
resounding • *a resounding slap*
strident • *her strident voice*
thunderous • *thunderous applause from the crowd*

MORE SYNONYMS:
• clamorous
• sonorous
• stentorian

ANTONYM:
• quiet

loud ② ADJECTIVE

too brightly coloured • *a loud tie*
flamboyant • *a flamboyant outfit*
flashy • *flashy clothes*
garish • *a garish three-piece suite*
gaudy • *a gaudy purple-and-orange hat*
lurid • *She painted her toenails a lurid pink.*

ANTONYM:
• dull

lovable ADJECTIVE

easy to love • *His vulnerability makes him very lovable.*
adorable • *an adorable black kitten*
charming • *a charming young Frenchman*
enchanting • *He was an enchanting baby.*
endearing • *one of his most endearing qualities*
sweet • *a sweet little girl*

MORE SYNONYMS:
• captivating
• engaging
• winsome

a
b
c
d
e
f
g
h
i
j
k
l
m
n
o
p
q
r
s
t
u
v
w
x
y
z

A
B
C
D
E
F
G
H
I
J
K
L
M
N
O
P
Q
R
S
T
U
V
W
X
Y
Z

ANTONYM:
• hateful

love ① VERB
to feel strong affection for someone
• I loved my husband very much.
adore • She adored her parents.
cherish • He genuinely loved and cherished her.
worship • She had worshipped him from afar for years.

MORE SYNONYMS:
• be in love with
• dote on
• hold dear
• idolize

ANTONYM:
• hate

love ② VERB
to like something very much • We both love fishing.
appreciate • I know you appreciate good food.
enjoy • Do you enjoy opera?
like • I've always liked horror films.
relish • I relish the challenge of dangerous sports.

MORE SYNONYMS:
• delight in
• have a weakness for
• take pleasure in

ANTONYM:
• hate

love ③ NOUN
a strong feeling of affection • a mother's love for her children
adoration • He had been used to female adoration all his life.
affection • She thought of him with great affection.
ardour • an attempt to rekindle their lost ardour
devotion • At first she was flattered by his devotion.

infatuation • consumed with infatuation for her
passion • the object of her passion

ANTONYM:
• hatred

love ④ NOUN
a strong liking for something • her love of animals
devotion • his devotion to literature
fondness • a fondness for good wine
liking • my liking for classical music
weakness • He had a weakness for cats.

MORE SYNONYMS:
• partiality
• penchant

ANTONYM:
• hatred

lovely ADJECTIVE
very attractive and pleasant • You look lovely.
attractive • Polperro is an attractive harbour village.
beautiful • She's a very beautiful woman.
delightful • a delightful garden
enjoyable • I've had a very enjoyable time.
pleasant • a pleasant little apartment
pretty • a pretty room overlooking a beautiful garden

ANTONYM:
• horrible

loving ADJECTIVE
feeling or showing love • a loving husband and father
affectionate • openly affectionate with each other
devoted • a devoted couple
doting • a doting father
fond • She gave him a fond smile.
tender • Her voice was tender.
warm • a warm and loving mother

MORE SYNONYMS:
• demonstrative

- solicitous
- warm-hearted

ANTONYM:
- cold

low ① ADJECTIVE

short or not far above the ground
• *The sun was low in the sky.*
little • *a little table*
short • *a short flight of steps*
small • *a small stool*
squat • *squat stone houses*
stunted • *stunted trees*
sunken • *a sunken garden*

ANTONYM:
- high

low ② ADJECTIVE

small in degree or quantity • *low prices*
minimal • *minimal expenditure*
modest • *a modest rate of unemployment*
poor • *working for poor wages*
reduced • *reduced customer demand*
scant • *scant stocks of fish*
small • *produced in small numbers*

ANTONYM:
- high

low ③ ADJECTIVE

not considered respectable • *a man of low birth*
common • *She might be a little common, but at least she wasn't boring.*
contemptible • *He mixes with the most contemptible people in society.*
despicable • *a despicable wretch*
disreputable • *the company of disreputable women*
lowly • *his lowly status*
vulgar • *She considers herself to be above the vulgar rabble.*

lower ① VERB

to move something downwards
• *They lowered the coffin into the grave.*

drop • *He dropped his plate into the sink.*
let down • *They let the barrier down.*
take down • *The pilot took the helicopter down.*

ANTONYM:
- raise

lower ② VERB

to make something less in amount • *a commitment to lower taxes*
cut • *The first priority is to cut costs.*
decrease • *The government plans to decrease interest rates.*
diminish • *to diminish the prestige of the monarchy*
lessen • *a diet that would lessen the risk of disease*
minimize • *attempts to minimize the risk of cancer*
reduce • *Gradually reduce the dosage.*
slash • *We're slashing our prices.*

ANTONYM:
- increase

loyal ADJECTIVE

firm in your friendship or support • *a loyal friend*
constant • *I've lost my best friend and constant companion.*
dependable • *a cheerful, dependable mate*
faithful • *She remained faithful to her husband.*
staunch • *a staunch supporter*
true • *a true friend*
trusty • *a trusty ally*

MORE SYNONYMS:
- steadfast
- true-hearted
- unswerving
- unwavering

ANTONYM:
- treacherous

luck NOUN

something that happens by chance

• It was just luck that we happened to meet.

accident • It came about almost by accident.

chance • We only met by chance.

destiny • Is it destiny that brings people together?

fate • a simple twist of fate

fortune • smiled on by fortune

MORE SYNONYMS:
• fortuity
• predestination

lucky ① ADJECTIVE

having a lot of good luck • He had always been lucky at cards.

blessed • being blessed with good looks

charmed • She seems to have a charmed life.

fortunate • He was extremely fortunate to survive.

ANTONYM:
• unlucky

lucky ② ADJECTIVE

happening by chance with good consequences • a lucky break

fortuitous • a fortuitous combination of circumstances

fortunate • a fortunate accident

opportune • I had arrived at an opportune moment.

timely • his timely intervention

MORE SYNONYMS:
• adventitious
• propitious
• providential

ANTONYM:
• unlucky

lump ① NOUN

a solid piece of something • a big lump of dough

ball • a ball of clay

cake • a cake of soap

chunk • a chunk of bread

hunk • a hunk of beef

piece • a piece of cake

wedge • a wedge of cheese

lump ② NOUN

a bump on the surface of something • I've got a big lump on my head.

bulge • My purse made a bulge in my pocket.

bump • a bump in the road

hump • a hump on his back

swelling • a swelling over one eye

MORE SYNONYMS:
• protrusion
• protuberance
• tumescence

lure ① VERB

to attract someone somewhere or into doing something • We are being lured into a trap.

attract • Warm weather attracts the fish close to the shore.

beckon • The mermaids beckoned the sailors towards the rocks.

draw • What drew him to the area was its proximity to London.

entice • Retailers will do anything to entice shoppers through their doors.

tempt • trying to tempt American tourists back to Britain

lure ② NOUN

something that you find very attractive • the lure of rural life

attraction • the attraction of living on the waterfront

bait • using cheap bread and milk as a bait to get people into the shop

magnet • The park is a magnet for health freaks.

pull • feel the pull of the past

temptation • the many temptations to which they will be exposed

lustful ADJECTIVE

feeling or showing strong sexual

desire • *lustful thoughts*
carnal • *carnal desires*
lecherous • *a lecherous old man*
lewd • *his arrest for lewd behaviour*

MORE SYNONYMS:
• lascivious
• libidinous
• wanton

luxurious ADJECTIVE
expensive and full of luxury • *a luxurious lifestyle*
de luxe • *de luxe cars*
lavish • *a lavish party*
opulent • *an opulent office*
plush (INFORMAL) • *a plush hotel*
sumptuous • *a sumptuous feast*

ANTONYM:
• plain

luxury ① NOUN
comfort in expensive surroundings
• *a life of luxury*
affluence • *the trappings of affluence*
opulence • *the sheer opulence of her new life*
sumptuousness • *The hotel lobby was sumptuousness itself.*

luxury ② NOUN
something enjoyable which you do not have often • *Telephones are still a luxury in poor countries.*
extra • *The car is a basic model with no extras.*
extravagance • *Eating out is an extravagance.*

indulgence • *This car is one of my few indulgences.*
treat • *I only eat cakes as a treat.*

lying ① NOUN
the action of telling lies • *I've had enough of your lying.*
deceit • *the deceits of political leaders*
dishonesty • *deliberate dishonesty*
fabrication • *His story is pure fabrication.*
fibbing • *Her fibbing eventually got her into trouble.*
perjury • *This witness has committed perjury.*

MORE SYNONYMS:
• dissimulation
• duplicity
• mendacity

lying ② ADJECTIVE
telling lies • *The man is just a lying cheat.*
deceitful • *deceitful and misleading remarks*
dishonest • *a dishonest account of events*
false • *a false confession*
untruthful • *She unwittingly gave untruthful answers.*

MORE SYNONYMS:
• dissembling
• mendacious

ANTONYM:
• honest

a b c d e f g h i j k l m n o p q r s t u v w x y z

Mm

machine NOUN
a piece of equipment • *a machine to pump water out of mines*
apparatus • *an apparatus for use in fires*
appliance • *electrical appliances*
contraption • *a strange contraption called the General Gordon Gas Bath*
device • *a timer device for a bomb*
instrument • *navigation instruments*
mechanism • *the locking mechanism*

mad ① ADJECTIVE
mentally ill • *She was afraid of going mad.*
barmy (SLANG) • *Bill used to say I was barmy.*
batty (SLANG) • *some batty uncle of theirs*
crazy (INFORMAL) • *If I worried about all this stuff, I'd go crazy.*
deranged • *after a deranged man shot 14 people*
insane • *The King is surely insane.*
loony (SLANG) • *She's as loony as her brother!*

ANTONYM:
• sane

mad ② ADJECTIVE
very foolish or unwise • *He'd be mad to refuse.*
barmy (SLANG) • *a barmy idea*
crazy (INFORMAL) • *People thought they were crazy to try it.*
daft (INFORMAL) • *That's a daft question.*
foolhardy • *Some described the act as foolhardy.*

foolish • *It would be foolish to raise hopes unnecessarily.*
stupid • *It would be stupid to pretend otherwise.*

mad ③ ADJECTIVE (INFORMAL)
angry about something • *They both got mad at me for interfering.*
angry • *She was angry at her husband.*
enraged • *I got more and more enraged at my father.*
fuming • *Mrs Vine was still fuming.*
furious • *He is furious at the way his wife has been treated.*
incensed • *Mum was incensed at his lack of compassion.*
infuriated • *He knew how infuriated this would make me.*
irate • *Bob was very irate, shouting and screaming about the flight delay.*
livid (INFORMAL) • *I am absolutely livid about it.*

magic NOUN
a special power • *They believe in magic.*
sorcery • *the use of sorcery to combat evil influences*
witchcraft • *people who practise witchcraft*

MORE SYNONYMS:
• necromancy
• occultism

magical ADJECTIVE
wonderful and exciting • *Paris is a magical city.*
bewitching • *bewitching brown eyes*
enchanting • *an enchanting child*

MORE SYNONYMS:
- entrancing
- spellbinding

main ADJECTIVE

most important • *the main reason*
cardinal • *one of the cardinal rules of movie reviewing*
chief • *one of his chief rivals*
foremost • *one of the foremost scholars on ancient Indian culture*
leading • *a leading industrial nation*
major • *one of the major causes of cancer*
predominant • *Her predominant emotion was confusion.*
primary • *the primary source of water in the region*
prime • *the prime suspect*
principal • *the principal source of sodium in our diets*

mainly ADVERB

true in most cases • *The staff were mainly Russian.*
chiefly • *He painted chiefly portraits.*
generally • *It is generally true that the darker the fruit the higher its iron content.*
largely • *The early studies were done on men, largely by male researchers.*
mostly • *Cars are mostly metal.*
predominantly • *Business is conducted predominantly by phone.*
primarily • *The body is made up primarily of bone, muscle, and fat.*
principally • *This is principally because the market is weak.*

MORE SYNONYMS:
- for the most part
- in general
- on the whole

major ADJECTIVE

very important or serious • *a major problem*

critical • *a critical factor*
crucial • *He took the crucial decisions himself.*
leading • *a leading industrial nation*
outstanding • *an outstanding contribution*
significant • *Her upbringing had a significant effect on her relationships.*

ANTONYM:
- minor

majority NOUN

more than half • *The majority of our cheeses are made with pasteurized milk.*
best part • *for the best part of 24 hours*
better part • *I spent the better part of £100 on her.*
bulk • *the bulk of the world's great poetry*
mass • *the mass of the population*
most • *Most of the book is completely true.*

MORE SYNONYMS:
- lion's share
- preponderance

make ① VERB

to construct something • *Sheila makes all her own clothes.*
assemble • *Workers were assembling planes.*
build • *Workers at the site build the F-16 jet fighter.*
construct • *the campaign to construct a temple on the site*
create • *It's great for a radio producer to create a show like this.*
fabricate • *All the tools are fabricated from high quality steel.*
fashion • *Stone Age settlers fashioned necklaces from sheep's teeth.*
form • *a figure formed from clay*
manufacture • *They manufacture plastics.*
produce • *We try to produce items that are the basics of a stylish wardrobe.*

a b c d e f g h i j k l m n o p q r s t u v w x y z

A
B
C
D
E
F
G
H
I
J
K
L
M
N
O
P
Q
R
S
T
U
V
W
X
Y
Z

make ② VERB
to force someone to do something
• *Mary made him clean up the plate.*
compel • *legislation to compel cyclists to wear a helmet*
drive • *Jealousy drives people to murder.*
force • *A back injury forced her to withdraw from the competition.*
oblige • *Finally I was obliged to abandon the car.*

MORE SYNONYMS:
• coerce
• impel

make ③ NOUN
a particular type • *a certain make of wristwatch*
brand • *a brand of cigarette*
model • *To keep the cost down, opt for a basic model.*

make up ① VERB
to form the parts of something
• *Women police officers make up 13% of the police force.*
compose • *The force would be composed of troops from NATO countries.*
comprise • *a crowd comprised of the wives and children of scientists*
constitute • *Hindus constitute 83% of India's population.*
form • *Cereals form the staple diet.*

make up ② VERB
to invent a story • *It's very unkind of you to make up stories about him.*
concoct • *The prisoner concocted the story to get a lighter sentence.*
fabricate • *Officers fabricated evidence against them.*
invent • *I must invent something I can tell my mother.*

MORE SYNONYMS:
• formulate
• manufacture

making ① NOUN
the act of creating something • *the making of this movie*
assembly • *the assembly of an explosive device*
building • *The building of the airport continues.*
construction • *boat construction*
creation • *the creation of large parks and forests*
fabrication • *the design and fabrication of the space shuttle*
manufacture • *the manufacture of nuclear weapons*
production • *These proteins stimulate the production of blood cells.*

making ②: **in the making**
ADJECTIVE
about to become something • *a captain in the making*
budding • *a budding author*
emergent • *an emergent state*
potential • *a potential champion*
up-and-coming • *an up-and-coming golfer*

male ADJECTIVE
relating to men • *a deep male voice*
manly • *He was the ideal of manly beauty.*
masculine • *masculine characteristics like facial hair*

ANTONYM:
• female

malicious ADJECTIVE
having the intention of hurting someone • *She described the charges as malicious.*
cruel • *Children can be so cruel.*
malevolent (FORMAL) • *She gave me a malevolent stare.*
mean • *Someone's played a mean trick on you.*
spiteful • *spiteful telephone calls*

vicious • *a vicious attack on an innocent man's character*

MORE SYNONYMS:
• malignant
• rancorous (FORMAL)

man ① NOUN

an adult male human being • *a young man*

bloke (BRITISH, AUSTRALIAN AND NEW ZEALAND; INFORMAL) • *a really nice bloke*

chap (INFORMAL) • *I am a very lucky chap.*

gentleman • *It seems this gentleman was waiting for the doctor.*

guy (INFORMAL) • *a guy from Manchester*

male • *A high proportion of crime is perpetrated by young males.*

ANTONYM:
• woman

man ② NOUN

people in general • *All men are equal.*

humanity • *He has rendered a great service to humanity.*

human race • *Can the human race carry on expanding?*

mankind • *the evolution of mankind*

MORE SYNONYMS:
• Homo sapiens
• humankind

mana NOUN (NEW ZEALAND)

the authority and influence of an important person • *a leader of great mana*

authority • *figures of authority*

influence • *He denies using any political influence.*

power • *positions of great power*

standing • *The Prime Minister's standing was high in the US.*

stature • *his stature as the world's greatest cellist*

status • *the status of a national hero*

ANOTHER SYNONYM:
• sway (LITERARY)

manage ① VERB

to succeed in doing something • *We managed to find somewhere to sit.*

cope with • *how my mother coped with bringing up three children*

succeed in • *We have succeeded in persuading cinemas to show the video.*

manage ② VERB

to be in charge of something • *Within two years he was managing the store.*

be in charge of • *Who's in charge of the canteen?*

command • *Who would command the troops in the event of war?*

control • *He now controls the largest retail development empire in southern California.*

direct • *Christopher will direct day-to-day operations.*

run • *Is this any way to run a country?*

management ① NOUN

the act of running an organization • *The zoo needed better management.*

control • *The restructuring involves Mr Ronson giving up control of the company.*

direction • *Organizations need clear direction.*

running • *the day-to-day running of the clinic*

management ② NOUN

the people who run an organization • *The management is doing its best.*

administration • *They would like the college administration to exert more control.*

board • *a recommendation which he wants to put before the board*

bosses (INFORMAL) • *a dispute between workers and bosses*

directors • *the board of directors of a local bank*

A
B
C
D
E
F
G
H
I
J
K
L
M
N
O
P
Q
R
S
T
U
V
W
X
Y
Z

employers • *Employers are said to be considering the demand.*

manager NOUN
a person in charge of running an organization • *the manager of Daiwa's New York branch*
boss (INFORMAL) • *He cannot stand his boss.*
director • *the financial director of Braun UK*
executive • *an advertising executive*

manifest ADJECTIVE (FORMAL)
obvious or easily seen • *the manifest failure of the policy*
blatant • *a blatant attempt to spread the blame*
clear • *a clear case of homicide*
conspicuous • *Politics has changed in a conspicuous way.*
glaring • *a glaring example of fraud*
obvious • *an obvious injustice*
patent • *This was patent nonsense.*
plain • *He's made it plain that he wants to be involved.*

manner ① NOUN
the way that you do something • *She smiled again in a friendly manner.*
fashion • *another drug that works in a similar fashion*
mode • *He switched automatically into interview mode.*
style • *Kenny's writing style*
way • *He had a strange way of talking.*

manner ② NOUN
the way that someone behaves • *his kind manner*
bearing • *his military bearing*
behaviour • *her anti-social behaviour*
conduct • *principles of civilized conduct*
demeanour • *a cheerful demeanour*
MORE SYNONYMS:
• comportment
• deportment

manoeuvre ① VERB
to move something skilfully • *It took expertise to manoeuvre the boat so close to the shore.*
guide • *He took Elliott by the arm and guided him out.*
navigate • *He attempted to navigate his way through the crowds.*
negotiate • *I negotiated my way out of the airport.*
steer • *I steered him towards the door.*

manoeuvre ② NOUN
a clever action • *manoeuvres to block the electoral process*
dodge • *a tax dodge*
ploy • *a cynical marketing ploy*
ruse • *This was a ruse to divide them.*
tactic • *The tactic paid off.*
MORE SYNONYMS:
• machination
• stratagem
• subterfuge

manufacture ① VERB
to make goods in a factory • *Several models are being manufactured here.*
assemble • *a factory where they assemble tractors*
fabricate • *a plant which fabricates aeroplane components*
make • *making cars at two plants in Europe*
mass-produce • *the invention of machinery to mass-produce footwear*
produce • *The company produced computer parts.*
process • *The material will be processed into plastic pellets.*

manufacture ② NOUN
the making of goods in a factory • *the manufacture of nuclear weapons*
assembly • *the assembly of cars by robots*
fabrication • *the design and fabrication of the shuttle*

making • *the steps that go into the making of a book*
mass production • *the mass production of baby food*
production • *We need to maintain the production of cars at last year's level.*

many ① ADJECTIVE
a large number • *Among his many hobbies was the breeding of fine horses.*
countless • *She brought joy to countless people.*
innumerable • *He has invented innumerable excuses.*
myriad • *the myriad other tasks we are trying to perform*
numerous • *Sex crimes were just as numerous as they are today.*
umpteen (INFORMAL) • *He has produced umpteen books.*

MORE SYNONYMS:
• multifarious
• multitudinous

ANTONYM:
• few

many ② PRONOUN
a large number of people or things • *in many of these neighbourhoods*
a lot • *A lot of people would agree with you.*
a mass • *a mass of books and papers*
a multitude • *for a multitude of reasons*
large numbers • *Large numbers of people stayed away.*
lots (INFORMAL) • *lots of strange new animals*
plenty • *plenty of vegetables*
scores • *Scores of people were injured.*

ANTONYM:
• few

mark ① NOUN
a small stain • *I can't get this mark off the curtain.*
blot • *an ink blot*

line • *A line of dirt ran across his face like a scar.*
smudge • *a lipstick smudge on his collar*
spot • *He noticed a grease spot on his trousers.*
stain • *a stain on the front of his shirt*
streak • *A streak of mud smudged her cheek.*

mark ② VERB
to stain something • *to stop the pen from marking her shirt*
smudge • *Her face was smudged with dirt.*
stain • *His clothing was stained with mud.*
streak • *Rain had begun to streak the window-panes.*

market NOUN
a place to buy or sell things • *the fish market at Billingsgate*
bazaar • *an Eastern bazaar*
fair • *a craft fair*

marriage NOUN
the relationship between a husband and wife • *six years of marriage*
matrimony (FORMAL) • *the bonds of matrimony*
wedlock (FORMAL) • *a child conceived out of wedlock*

RELATED WORDS:
• ADJECTIVES conjugal, connubial, marital, nuptial

marsh NOUN
◆ **TYPES OF MARSH**
◆ bog
◆ fen
◆ mire
◆ morass
◆ mudflats
◆ quagmire
◆ quicksands
◆ saltmarsh
◆ slough
◆ swamp
◆ wetland

a b c d e f g h i j k l **m** n o p q r s t u v w x y z

marvellous ADJECTIVE
wonderful or excellent • *a marvellous actor*
brilliant • *a brilliant performance*
excellent • *She does an excellent job as Bill's secretary.*
first-rate • *The meal was absolutely first-rate.*
magnificent • *She was magnificent as Lady Macbeth.*
remarkable • *a remarkable achievement*
splendid • *splendid photographs*
superb • *a superb novel*
wonderful • *It's wonderful to see you.*
ANTONYM:
• terrible

mass ① NOUN
a large number or amount • *a mass of papers*
crowd • *A huge crowd of people gathered in the square.*
heap • *a heap of bricks*
load • *a load of kids*
lump • *a lump of clay*
mob • *a growing mob of demonstrators*
pile • *a pile of sand*
throng • *A shout went up from the throng of spectators.*

mass ② ADJECTIVE
involving a large number of people • *mass unemployment*
general • *We are trying to raise general awareness about this issue.*
popular • *popular anger at the decision*
universal • *universal health care*
widespread • *widespread support for the proposals*

mass ③ VERB
to gather together in a large group • *Police began to mass at the shipyard.*
assemble • *Thousands of people assembled in the stadium.*

congregate • *Youngsters congregate here in the evenings.*
gather • *In the evenings, we gathered round the fireplace.*
group • *The children grouped together under the trees.*

master ① NOUN
a male schoolteacher • *a retired maths master*
instructor • *a college instructor*
teacher • *her chemistry teacher*
tutor • *an adult education tutor in German*

master ② VERB
to learn how to do something • *She found it easy to master the typewriter.*
become proficient in • *He quickly became proficient in the language.*
get the hang of (INFORMAL) • *It's a bit tricky till you get the hang of it.*
grasp • *It took him a while to grasp the basics of the process.*
learn • *He enjoyed learning new skills.*

match ① NOUN
an organized game • *a football match*
competition • *a surfing competition*
contest • *one of the best contests in recent boxing history*
game • *England's first game of the new season*

match ② VERB
to be similar to • *The shoes matched her dress.*
agree • *Their statements do not agree.*
correspond • *The two maps correspond closely.*
fit • *The punishment must always fit the crime.*
go with • *The curtains didn't go with the carpet.*
suit • *the best package to suit your needs*
tally • *The figures didn't seem to tally.*

MORE SYNONYMS:
• accord
• harmonize

material ① NOUN
any type of cloth • *the thick material of her skirt*
cloth • *a piece of cloth*
fabric • *silk and other delicate fabrics*

material ② NOUN
a solid substance • *the materials to make red dye*
matter • *waste matter from industries*
stuff • *the stuff from which the universe is made*
substance • *a crumbly black substance*

matter ① NOUN
something that you have to deal with • *business matters*
affair • *The funeral was a sad affair.*
business • *This whole business has upset me.*
issue • *a major political issue*
question • *the difficult question of unemployment*
situation • *The situation is now under control.*
subject • *a difficult subject on which to reach a compromise*

matter ② NOUN
any substance • *The atom is the smallest divisible particle of matter.*
material • *a conducting material such as metal*
stuff • *a dress made from some flimsy stuff*
substance • *a poisonous substance*

matter ③ VERB
to be important • *It does not matter how long their hair is.*
be of consequence • *Their choice of partner is of no consequence to anyone but themselves.*
count • *It's as if my opinions just don't count.*

make a difference • *Exercise makes all the difference.*

mature ① VERB
to become fully developed • *Children mature earlier these days.*
come of age • *The money was held in trust until he came of age.*
grow up • *She grew up in Tokyo.*
reach adulthood • *She died before reaching adulthood.*

mature ② ADJECTIVE
fully developed • *He's very mature for his age.*
adult • *a pair of adult birds*
full-grown • *a full-grown male orangutan*
fully-fledged • *He has developed into a fully-fledged adult.*
grown • *a grown man*
grown-up • *They have two grown-up children.*

maximum ① ADJECTIVE
being the most that is possible • *the maximum recommended intake*
top • *a top speed of 200 mph*
utmost • *a question of the utmost importance*

ANTONYM:
• minimum

maximum ② NOUN
the most that is possible • *a maximum of fifty men*
ceiling • *an agreement to put a ceiling on salaries*
height • *when emigration was at its height*
most • *The most he'll make is a hundred pounds.*
upper limit • *the need to put an upper limit on spending*
utmost • *He did his utmost to make her agree.*

a
b
c
d
e
f
g
h
i
j
k
l
m
n
o
p
q
r
s
t
u
v
w
x
y
z

A
B
C
D
E
F
G
H
I
J
K
L
M
N
O
P
Q
R
S
T
U
V
W
X
Y
Z

ANTONYM:
• minimum

maybe ADVERB
it is possible that • *Maybe I should have done a bit more.*
conceivably • *The mission could conceivably be accomplished within a week.*
it could be • *It could be that's why he refused.*
perhaps • *Perhaps, in time, she'll understand.*
possibly • *Television is possibly to blame for this.*

MORE SYNONYMS:
• mayhap
• peradventure
• perchance

meagre ADJECTIVE
very small and inadequate • *his meagre pension*
inadequate • *inadequate portions*
measly (INFORMAL) • *The average British bathroom measures a measly 3.5 square metres.*
paltry • *a paltry fine of £150*
scant • *She berated the police for paying scant attention to the theft.*
sparse • *sparse vegetation*

MORE SYNONYMS:
• exiguous
• insubstantial
• scanty
• skimpy

meal NOUN
an occasion when people eat • *She sat next to him throughout the meal.*
banquet • *a state banquet at Buckingham Palace*
dinner • *a series of official dinners*
feast • *the wedding feast*
kai (AUSTRALIAN AND NEW ZEALAND; INFORMAL) • *a cheap kai in a local restaurant*

MORE SYNONYMS:
• repast
• spread

mean ① VERB
to convey a message • *The red signal means that you can shoot.*
denote • *Red eyes denote strain and fatigue.*
indicate • *Today's vote indicates a change in policy.*
signify • *Becoming a father signified that he was now an adult.*

mean ② VERB
to intend to do something • *I meant to phone you, but didn't have time.*
aim • *I aim to arrive early.*
intend • *She intended to move back to France.*
plan • *They plan to marry in the summer.*

mean ③ ADJECTIVE
unwilling to spend money • *Don't be mean with the tip.*
miserly • *He is miserly with both his time and his money.*
snoep (SOUTH AFRICAN; INFORMAL) • *Have you ever met anyone as snoep as him?*
tight (INFORMAL) • *He was so tight that he wouldn't even spend three roubles.*

MORE SYNONYMS:
• parsimonious
• penny-pinching
• stingy
• tight-fisted

ANTONYM:
• generous

meaning NOUN
the idea expressed by something • *the meaning of this dream*
drift • *Grace was beginning to get his drift.*
gist • *I could not get the gist of their conversation.*

message • *the message of the film*
significance • *The President's visit is loaded with symbolic significance.*

MORE SYNONYMS:
• connotation
• import

measure ① VERB
to check the size of something • *We measured how tall he was.*
gauge • *He gauged the wind at over 30 knots.*
survey • *geological experts who surveyed the cliffs*

MORE SYNONYMS:
• calibrate
• quantify

measure ② NOUN
an amount of something • *There has been a measure of agreement.*
amount • *a certain amount of disappointment*
degree • *a degree of success*
portion • *I have spent a considerable portion of my life here.*
proportion • *A large proportion of my time was spent abroad.*

measure ③ NOUN
an action in order to achieve something • *Tough measures are needed to maintain order.*
expedient • *I reduced my spending by the simple expedient of destroying my credit card.*
manoeuvre • *manoeuvres to block the electoral process*
means • *The move is a means to fight crime.*
procedure • *safety procedures*
step • *steps to discourage drink-driving*

medicine NOUN
something you take to make you better • *They prevent the food and medicine from reaching Iraq.*

drug • *Three new drugs recently became available.*
medication • *some medication for her ulcers*
muti (SOUTH AFRICAN; INFORMAL) • *muti for treating a fever*
remedy • *At the moment we are trying a herbal remedy.*

medium ① ADJECTIVE
average in size • *He was of medium height.*
average • *a ginger tomcat of average size*
medium-sized • *a medium-sized saucepan*
middling • *Small and middling flats have increased in price much more than luxury ones.*

medium ② NOUN
a means of communication • *the medium of television*
channel • *through diplomatic channels*
vehicle • *The play seemed an ideal vehicle for his music.*

MORE SYNONYMS:
• agency
• instrument

meek ADJECTIVE
quiet and timid • *a meek, mild-mannered fellow*
deferential • *the traditional requirement for Asian women to be deferential to men*
docile • *docile, obedient children*
mild • *a mild man*
submissive • *Most doctors want their patients to be submissive.*
timid • *a timid child*
unassuming • *He's very polite and unassuming.*

MORE SYNONYMS:
• acquiescent

a b c d e f g h i j k l m n o p q r s t u v w x y z

- compliant
- mild-mannered

ANTONYM:
- bold

meet ① VERB
to be in the same place as someone
• I met her quite by chance.
bump into (INFORMAL) • I bumped into a friend of yours today.
come across • where I came across a group of noisy children
come upon • We turned the corner and came upon a group of hikers.
encounter • the most gifted child he had ever encountered
run across • We ran across some old friends.
run into • You'll never guess who I ran into the other day.

meet ② VERB
to gather in a group • We meet for lunch once a week.
assemble • a convenient place for students to assemble between classes
congregate • Youngsters love to congregate here in the evening.
convene • Senior officials convened in October.
gather • We all gathered in the boardroom.
get together • the last time we all got together

meet ③ VERB
to fulfil a need • services intended to meet the needs of the elderly
answer • Would communism answer their needs?
fulfil • All the requirements were fulfilled.
satisfy • Candidates must satisfy the general conditions for admission.

meeting ① NOUN
an event at which people come together for a purpose • a business meeting
audience • an audience with the Pope
conference • a conference on education
congress • a medical congress
convention • the annual convention of the World Boxing Council
gathering • a social gathering
get-together (INFORMAL) • a get-together I had at my home
reunion • a family reunion

MORE SYNONYMS:
- conclave
- convocation

meeting ② NOUN
an occasion when you meet someone • a chance meeting
assignation (LITERARY) • She had an assignation with her boyfriend.
encounter • a remarkable encounter with a group of soldiers
rendezvous • Baxter arranged a six o'clock rendezvous.
tryst • a lovers' tryst

melodramatic ADJECTIVE
behaving in an exaggerated way
• Don't you think you're being rather melodramatic?
histrionic • She let out a histrionic groan.
sensational • sensational tabloid newspaper reports
theatrical • In a theatrical gesture Glass clamped his hand over his eyes.

melt ① VERB
to become liquid • The snow had melted.
dissolve • Heat gently until the sugar dissolves.
thaw • It's so cold the snow doesn't get a chance to thaw.

MORE SYNONYMS:
- deliquesce
- liquefy

melt ② VERB
to disappear • *Her inhibitions melted.*
disappear • *The immediate threat has disappeared.*
disperse • *The crowd dispersed peacefully.*
dissolve • *His new-found optimism dissolved.*
evaporate • *My anger evaporated.*
vanish • *All her fears suddenly vanished.*

memorable ADJECTIVE
likely to be remembered • *a memorable victory*
catchy • *a catchy tune*
historic • *a historic meeting*
notable • *with a few notable exceptions*
striking • *the most striking feature of those statistics*
unforgettable • *an unforgettable experience*

memory NOUN
the ability to remember • *Every detail is fresh in my memory.*
recall • *a man blessed with total recall*
remembrance (FORMAL) • *My remembrance of the incident is somewhat hazy.*

MORE SYNONYMS:
- recollection
- retention

mend VERB
to repair something broken • *I should have had the catch mended.*
darn • *a woman darning socks*
fix • *If something is broken, we get it fixed.*
patch • *They patched the barn roof.*
renovate • *The couple spent thousands renovating the house.*
repair • *to get her car repaired*

restore • *experts who specialize in restoring ancient parchments*

mention ① VERB
to talk about something briefly • *I may not have mentioned it to her.*
allude to • *She alluded to his absence in vague terms.*
bring up • *Why are you bringing it up now?*
broach • *I broached the subject of her early life.*
hint • *The President hinted that he might make some changes.*
intimate • *He did intimate that he is seeking legal action.*
refer to • *In his speech, he referred to a recent trip to Canada.*
touch on • *The film touches on these issues, but only superficially.*
touch upon • *I'd like to touch upon a more serious question now.*

mention ② NOUN
a brief comment about something • *There was no mention of elections.*
allusion • *She made an allusion to the events in Los Angeles.*
reference • *He made no reference to any agreement.*

merciful ① ADJECTIVE
showing kindness • *He is merciful and sympathetic to others.*
compassionate • *a deeply compassionate man*
humane • *the desire for a more humane society*
kind • *She is warm-hearted and kind to everyone.*

ANTONYM:
- merciless

merciful ② ADJECTIVE
showing forgiveness • *We can only hope the court is merciful.*

a
b
c
d
e
f
g
h
i
j
k
l
m
n
o
p
q
r
s
t
u
v
w
x
y
z

forgiving • *I don't think people are in a very forgiving mood.*
lenient • *He believes the government is already lenient with drug traffickers.*

ANTONYM:
• merciless

merciless ADJECTIVE
showing no kindness or forgiveness
• *the merciless efficiency of a modern police state*
callous • *his callous disregard for human life*
cruel • *Children can be so cruel.*
heartless • *I couldn't believe they were so heartless.*
implacable • *a powerful and implacable enemy*
ruthless • *his ruthless treatment of employees*

MORE SYNONYMS:
• hard-hearted
• pitiless
• unforgiving

ANTONYM:
• merciful

mercy ① NOUN
the quality of kindness • *He showed no mercy.*
compassion • *his compassion for a helpless woman*
kindness • *He was treated with kindness by numerous officials.*
pity • *She saw no pity in their faces.*

MORE SYNONYMS:
• benevolence
• charity

mercy ② NOUN
the quality of forgiveness • *He threw himself upon the mercy of the court.*
forgiveness • *He fell to his knees begging for forgiveness.*
leniency • *He said he would show no leniency towards them.*

MORE SYNONYMS:
• clemency
• forbearance

merit ① NOUN
worth or value • *Box-office success mattered more than artistic merit.*
excellence • *the top US award for excellence in journalism*
value • *The value of this work experience should not be underestimated.*
virtue • *There is little virtue in such an approach.*
worth • *people who had already proved their worth to their companies*

merit ② NOUN
a good quality that something has
• *Whatever its merits, their work would never be used.*
advantage • *The great advantage of home-grown oranges is their flavour.*
asset • *Her leadership qualities were her greatest asset.*
strength • *The book's strength lay in its depiction of modern-day Tokyo.*
strong point • *Science was never my strong point at school.*
virtue • *Its other great virtue is its hard-wearing quality.*

merit ③ VERB
to deserve something • *Such ideas merit careful consideration.*
be entitled to • *She is entitled to feel proud.*
be worthy of • *The bank might think you're worthy of a loan.*
deserve • *He deserves a rest.*
earn • *Companies must earn a reputation for honesty.*
warrant • *no evidence to warrant a murder investigation*

mess ① NOUN
a state of untidiness • *I'll clear up the mess later.*

chaos • *Their concerts often ended in chaos.*

disarray • *He found the room in disarray.*

disorder • *Inside all was disorder.*

mess ② NOUN

a situation that is full of problems • *the reasons why the economy is in such a mess*

fix (INFORMAL) • *The government has really got itself into a fix.*

jam (INFORMAL) • *They were in a real jam.*

muddle • *Our finances are in a muddle.*

turmoil • *Her marriage was in turmoil.*

mess ③ or **mess up** VERB

to spoil something • *He had messed up his career.*

botch up • *I hate having builders botch up repairs on my house.*

bungle • *Two prisoners bungled an escape bid.*

make a hash of (INFORMAL) • *The government made a total hash of things.*

muck up (SLANG) • *He always seemed to muck everything up.*

message ① NOUN

a piece of information for someone • *He left a message on her answerphone.*

bulletin • *a news bulletin*

communication • *The ambassador brought a communication from the President.*

despatch or **dispatch** • *this dispatch from our West Africa correspondent*

memo • *office memos*

memorandum • *a memorandum from the Ministry of Defence*

note • *I'll have to leave a note for Karen.*

word • *There is no word from the authorities on the reported attack.*

MORE SYNONYMS:
• communiqué
• missive

message ② VERB

to send information to • *He messaged dozens of friends.*

email or **e-mail** • *Gwyn and I emailed each other every week.*

IM • *chatting and IMing online*

instant message • *We instant messaged each other before meeting.*

text • *He texted a journalist with his comments.*

messenger NOUN

someone who carries a message • *There will be a messenger at the airport to collect the photographs.*

courier • *a motorcycle courier*

envoy • *an envoy to the King*

runner • *a bookie's runner*

MORE SYNONYMS:
• emissary
• go-between
• herald

method NOUN

a way of doing something • *the traditional method of making wine*

approach • *different approaches to gathering information*

mode • *the capitalist mode of production*

procedure • *He did not follow the correct procedure.*

technique • *the techniques of modern agriculture*

way • *a way of making new friends*

middle ① NOUN

the part furthest from the edges • *in the middle of the room*

centre • *the centre of the table*

halfway point • *Postle was third fastest at the halfway point.*

midst • *a house in the midst of huge trees*

MORE SYNONYMS:
• midpoint
• midsection

a
b
c
d
e
f
g
h
i
j
k
l
m
n
o
p
q
r
s
t
u
v
w
x
y
z

middle ② ADJECTIVE
furthest from the edges • *the middle house*
central • *central London*
halfway • *a point halfway between the two posts*

mild ① ADJECTIVE
not strong or powerful • *a mild shampoo*
insipid • *It tasted bland and insipid.*
weak • *weak beer*

ANTONYM:
• strong

mild ② ADJECTIVE
gentle and good-tempered • *a mild man*
gentle • *her gentle nature*
meek • *a meek, mild-mannered fellow*
placid • *a placid child who rarely cried*

MORE SYNONYMS:
• easy-going
• equable
• pacific
• peaceable

mild ③ ADJECTIVE
warmer than usual • *The area is famous for its mild winter climate.*
balmy • *balmy summer evenings*
temperate • *a temperate climate*

mind ① NOUN
your ability to think • *You have a very suspicious mind.*
brain • *Once you stop using your brain you soon go stale.*
head • *I can't get that song out of my head.*
imagination • *Africa was alive in my imagination.*
intellect • *good health and a lively intellect*
psyche • *disturbing elements of the human psyche*

RELATED WORD:
• ADJECTIVE mental

mind ② VERB
to be annoyed by something • *I don't mind what you do.*
be bothered • *I'm not bothered if he has another child.*
care • *young men who did not care whether they lived or died*
object • *I don't object to his smoking.*

mind ③ VERB
to look after something • *My mother is minding the shop.*
keep an eye on • *She asked me to keep an eye on the children.*
look after • *I looked after the dogs while she was away.*
take care of • *There was no one else to take care of the children.*
watch • *She bought the tickets while I watched the cases.*

minimum ADJECTIVE
being the least possible • *the minimum height for a policeman*
least possible • *I try to cause the least amount of trouble possible.*
minimal • *The aim is to incur minimal expense.*

ANTONYM:
• maximum

minor ADJECTIVE
less important • *a minor injury*
lesser • *They pleaded guilty to lesser charges.*
petty • *petty crime*
secondary • *matters of secondary importance*
slight • *We have a slight problem.*
trifling • *Outside California these difficulties may seem trifling.*
trivial • *trivial details*

ANTONYM:
• major

minute ① NOUN

a short period of time • *I'll be with you in just a minute.*

flash • *It was all over in a flash.*

instant • *For an instant, Catherine was tempted to flee.*

moment • *Stop for one moment and think about what you're doing!*

second • *Just a second. I'm coming.*

trice • *I'll be back in a trice.*

minute ② ADJECTIVE

extremely small • *Only a minute amount is needed.*

microscopic • *microscopic fibres*

negligible • *They are convinced the strike will have a negligible impact.*

slender • *We won the vote by a slender majority.*

small • *small particles of dust*

tiny • *a tiny fraction of US production*

MORE SYNONYMS:
• diminutive
• minuscule

ANTONYM:
• vast

miracle NOUN

a surprising and fortunate event • *the Italian economic miracle*

marvel • *a marvel of high technology*

wonder • *the wonders of science*

miserable ① ADJECTIVE

very unhappy • *a job which made me miserable*

dejected • *Everyone has days when they feel dejected.*

depressed • *He seemed somewhat depressed.*

down • *Try to support each other when one of you is feeling down.*

downcast • *After his defeat Mr Rabin looked downcast.*

low • *"I didn't ask for this job," he tells friends when he is low.*

melancholy • *It was in these hours that he felt most melancholy.*

mournful • *He looked mournful, even near to tears.*

sad • *It left me feeling sad and empty.*

unhappy • *She is desperately unhappy.*

wretched • *I feel really confused and wretched.*

MORE SYNONYMS:
• disconsolate
• sorrowful

ANTONYM:
• cheerful

miserable ② ADJECTIVE

causing unhappiness • *a miserable little flat*

gloomy • *Officials say the outlook for next year is gloomy.*

pathetic • *a pathetic sight*

sorry • *The fires have left the industry in a sorry state.*

wretched • *He died in wretched poverty.*

misery NOUN

great unhappiness • *All that money brought nothing but misery.*

depression • *He's been suffering from depression.*

despair • *feelings of despair*

grief • *her grief at her husband's suicide*

melancholy • *with an air of melancholy*

sadness • *with a mixture of sadness and joy*

sorrow • *a time of great sorrow*

unhappiness • *There was a lot of unhappiness in my adolescence.*

woe • *a tale of woe*

ANTONYM:
• joy

misfortune NOUN

an unfortunate event • *I had the misfortune to fall off my bike.*

adversity • *times of adversity*

a b c d e f g h i j k l m n o p q r s t u v w x y z

bad luck • *He has had his share of bad luck.*

misrepresent VERB

to give a false account of something • *Keynes deliberately misrepresented the views of his opponents.*

distort • *The minister said his remarks had been distorted by the press.*

falsify • *falsifying personal details on his CV*

twist • *You're twisting my words.*

miss ① VERB

to fail to notice • *It's on the second floor. You can't miss it.*

fail to notice • *He failed to notice that the lights had turned red.*

mistake • *There's no mistaking her sincerity.*

overlook • *a fact that we all tend to overlook*

miss ② VERB

to feel the loss of • *The boys miss their father.*

long for • *Steve longed for the good old days.*

pine for • *Make sure your pet won't pine for you while you're away.*

yearn for • *He yearned for his freedom.*

mistake ① NOUN

something that is wrong • *spelling mistakes*

blunder • *It had been a monumental blunder to give him the assignment.*

error • *a mathematical error*

gaffe • *a social gaffe*

oversight • *By an unfortunate oversight, full instructions do not come with the product.*

slip • *There must be no slips.*

MORE SYNONYMS:
• inaccuracy
• miscalculation

mistake ② VERB

to think one thing is another thing • *I mistook him for the owner of the house.*

confuse with • *I can't see how anyone could confuse you with your brother!*

misinterpret as • *She misinterpreted his remarks as a threat.*

mix up with • *People often mix me up with other actors.*

take for • *She had taken him for a journalist.*

mistreat VERB

to treat someone badly • *She had been mistreated by men in the past.*

abuse • *parents who abuse their children*

ill-treat • *They thought Mr Smith had been ill-treating his wife.*

mix VERB

to combine things • *Mix the ingredients together slowly.*

amalgamate • *a need to amalgamate the two companies*

blend • *Blend the butter with the sugar.*

combine • *Combine the flour with 3 tablespoons of water.*

merge • *how to merge the graphic with text*

mingle • *the mingled smell of flowers and cigar smoke*

MORE SYNONYMS:
• intermingle
• interweave

mixture NOUN

a combination of things • *a sticky mixture of flour and water*

alloy • *an alloy of copper and tin*

amalgamation • *an amalgamation of two organizations*

blend • *a blend of wine and sparkling water*

combination • *a fantastic combination of colours*

compound • *a compound of water, sugar, vitamins and enzymes*
fusion • *fusions of jazz and pop*
medley • *We communicated in a medley of foreign words and gestures.*

MORE SYNONYMS:
• amalgam
• composite
• conglomeration
• mix

mix-up VERB
to confuse two things • *People often mix us up.*
confuse • *Great care is taken to avoid confusing the two projects.*
muddle • *Critics have begun to muddle the two names.*

mix-up NOUN
a mistake in something planned • *a mix-up with the bookings*
mistake • *There must be some mistake.*
misunderstanding • *Ensure that there is no misunderstanding about the instructions.*
muddle • *There's been a muddle about whose responsibility it is.*

moan ① VERB
to make a low sound • *Laura moaned in her sleep.*
groan • *He began to groan with pain.*
grunt • *The driver grunted, convinced that Michael was crazy.*

moan ② VERB
to complain about something • *Carol is always moaning about her husband.*
complain • *People always complain that the big banks are unfriendly.*
groan • *His parents were beginning to groan about the price of college tuition.*
grumble • *A tourist grumbled that the waiter spoke too much Spanish.*
whine • *They come to me to whine about their troubles.*

whinge (INFORMAL) • *Stop whingeing and get on with it.*

MORE SYNONYMS:
• bleat
• carp

moan ③ NOUN
a low sound • *She let out a faint moan.*
groan • *a groan of disappointment*
grunt • *grunts of disapproval*

mock ① VERB
to make fun of someone • *Don't mock me.*
deride (FORMAL) • *Other countries are derided for selling arms to the enemy.*
laugh at • *I thought they were laughing at me because I was ugly.*
make fun of • *Don't make fun of me.*
poke fun at • *She poked fun at people's shortcomings.*
ridicule • *Mr Goss ridiculed that suggestion.*
scoff at • *Some people may scoff at the idea that animals communicate.*

mock ② ADJECTIVE
not genuine • *mock surprise*
artificial • *artificial limbs*
bogus • *their bogus insurance claim*
counterfeit • *counterfeit money*
dummy • *dummy weapons*
fake • *a fake fur*
false • *false teeth*
feigned • *with feigned indifference*
imitation • *imitation leather*
phoney or **phony** (INFORMAL) • *a phoney excuse*
pretended • *with pretended zeal*
sham • *sham marriages*

MORE SYNONYMS:
• ersatz
• pseudo

mockery NOUN
the act of mocking someone • *Was there a glint of mockery in his eyes?*

derision • *shouts of derision*
jeering • *there was a chorus of jeering, whistles and laughter*
ridicule • *Davis was subjected to public ridicule.*

model ① NOUN
a copy of something • *an architect's model of a wooden house*
dummy • *a tailor's dummy*
replica • *a replica of the Statue of Liberty*
representation • *a representation of a human figure*

MORE SYNONYMS:
• facsimile
• mock-up

model ② NOUN
a perfect example of something
• *The essay is a model of clarity.*
epitome • *the epitome of good taste*
example • *He is an example to the younger lads.*
ideal • *the Japanese ideal of beauty*
paragon • *a paragon of virtue*

MORE SYNONYMS:
• archetype
• exemplar

model ③ VERB
to make something into a shape
• *clay modelled into the shape of a bear*
carve • *One of the prisoners had carved a wooden chess set.*
fashion • *Stone Age settlers fashioned necklaces from sheep's teeth.*
form • *figures formed from modelling clay*
mould • *We moulded a chair out of mud.*
sculpt • *An artist sculpted a full-size replica of her head.*
shape • *Shape each half into a loaf.*

moderate ① ADJECTIVE
neither too much nor too little
• *moderate exercise*

average • *I was only average academically.*
fair • *Reimar had a fair command of English.*
medium • *a medium size*
middling • *The Beatles enjoyed only middling success until 1963.*
reasonable • *reasonable force*

moderate ② VERB
to become or make less extreme
• *They are hoping he can be persuaded to moderate his views.*
abate • *The storm had abated.*
curb • *You must curb your extravagant tastes.*
ease • *Tensions had eased.*
relax • *Rules have been relaxed recently.*
soften • *to soften the blow of steep price rises*
temper • *He had to learn to temper his enthusiasm.*
tone down • *He toned down his statements after the meeting.*

modern ① ADJECTIVE
relating to the present time • *modern society*
contemporary • *contemporary music*
current • *the current situation*
present • *the government's present economic difficulties*
present-day • *Even by present-day standards these were large aircraft.*
recent • *in recent years*

modern ② ADJECTIVE
new and involving the latest ideas
• *modern technology*
latest • *the latest fashions*
new • *new methods of treating cancer*
up-to-date • *Germany's most up-to-date electric power station*
up-to-the-minute • *up-to-the-minute information*

ANTONYM:
• old-fashioned

modest ① ADJECTIVE
small in size or amount • *a modest improvement*
limited • *They may only have a limited amount of time.*
middling • *The Beatles enjoyed only middling success until 1963.*
moderate • *moderate exercise*
small • *a relatively small problem*

modest ② ADJECTIVE
not boastful • *Lord Carrington is modest about his achievements.*
humble • *He gave a great performance, but he was very humble.*
unassuming • *She has a gentle, unassuming manner.*

MORE SYNONYMS:
• self-effacing
• unpretentious

ANTONYM:
• conceited

moment ① NOUN
a short period of time • *He paused for a moment.*
instant • *The pain disappeared in an instant.*
minute • *See you in a minute.*
second • *Seconds later, firemen reached the door.*
split second • *Her gaze met Michael's for a split second.*

MORE SYNONYMS:
• flash
• trice

moment ② NOUN
a point in time • *At that moment, the doorbell rang.*
instant • *At that instant the museum was plunged into darkness.*
point • *At this point Diana arrived.*
time • *It seemed like a good time to tell her.*

money NOUN
coins or banknotes • *I needed to earn some money.*
capital • *Companies are having difficulty in raising capital.*
cash • *We were desperately short of cash.*
dosh (BRITISH, AUSTRALIAN AND NEW ZEALAND) • *They'll have the dosh to pay for a new sign.*
dough (INFORMAL) • *He worked hard for his dough.*
funds • *The concert will raise funds for research into AIDS.*

RELATED WORD:
• ADJECTIVE pecuniary

mood NOUN
a state of mind • *She was in a really cheerful mood.*
frame of mind • *Lewis was not in the right frame of mind to continue.*
humour • *Could that have been the source of his good humour?*
spirits • *A bit of exercise will help lift his spirits.*
state of mind • *I want you to get into a whole new state of mind.*
temper • *I was in a bad temper last night.*

moody ① ADJECTIVE
depressed or unhappy • *Tony, despite his charm, could sulk and be moody.*
irritable • *He had missed his dinner, and grew irritable.*
morose • *She was morose and reticent.*
sulky • *a sulky adolescent*
sullen • *a sullen and resentful workforce*

MORE SYNONYMS:
• huffy
• ill-tempered
• testy
• tetchy

a
b
c
d
e
f
g
h
i
j
k
l
m
n
o
p
q
r
s
t
u
v
w
x
y
z

moody ② ADJECTIVE
liable to change your mood • *David's mother was unstable and moody.*
temperamental • *He is very temperamental.*
volatile • *He has a volatile temper.*
MORE SYNONYMS:
• capricious
• mercurial

more ADJECTIVE
greater than something else • *I've got more chips than you.*
added • *For added protection choose lipsticks with a sun screen.*
additional • *The US is sending additional troops to the region.*
extra • *Extra staff have been taken on.*
further • *There are likely to be further delays.*
ANTONYM:
• less

motivate VERB
to cause a particular behaviour • *What motivates athletes to take drugs?*
drive • *Jealousy drives people to murder.*
inspire • *What inspired you to change your name?*
lead • *His abhorrence of racism led him to write the book.*
move • *It was punk that first moved him to join a band.*
prompt • *Japan's recession has prompted consumers to cut back on buying cars.*
provoke • *The destruction of the mosque has provoked much anger.*

mountain NOUN
◆ TYPES OF MOUNTAIN
◆ alp
◆ ben (SCOTTISH)
◆ elevation
◆ height
◆ mount
◆ peak
◆ precipice
◆ range
◆ ridge

move ① VERB
to change position • *The train began to move.*
▶ see Word Study **move**, page 650

move ② VERB
to change residence • *She had often considered moving to London.*
migrate • *Peasants have migrated to the cities.*
move house • *They move house fairly frequently.*
relocate • *if the company was to relocate*

move ③ VERB
to cause a deep emotion • *Her story moved us to tears.*
affect • *Her loss still clearly affects him.*
touch • *Her enthusiasm touched me.*

movement ① NOUN
a change of position • *They monitor the movement of the fish going up river.*
flow • *the frantic flow of cars and buses along the street*
motion • *the wind from the car's motion*

movement ② NOUN
a group of people with similar aims • *the peace movement*
campaign • *the campaign against public smoking*
faction • *the leaders of the country's warring factions*
group • *members of an environmental group*
organization • *the International Labour Organization*

moving ADJECTIVE
causing deep emotion • *It was a moving moment.*

affecting • *one of the most affecting scenes in the film*
emotional • *an emotional reunion*
poignant • *a poignant love story*
stirring • *a stirring speech*
touching • *the touching tale of a wife who stood by the husband she loved*

muddle ① NOUN
a state of disorder • *Our finances are in a muddle.*
chaos • *Their concerts often ended in chaos.*
confusion • *There was confusion when a man fired shots.*
disarray • *He found the room in disarray.*
disorder • *Inside all was disorder.*
disorganization • *a state of complete disorganization*
jumble • *a meaningless jumble of words*
mess • *the reasons why the economy is in such a mess*
tangle • *a tangle of wires*

muddle ② VERB
to mix things up • *One or two critics have begun to muddle the two names.*
confuse • *Great care is taken to avoid confusing the two projects.*
jumble • *a number of animals whose remains were jumbled together*
mix up • *People often mix us up.*

multiply VERB
to increase in number • *The trip wore on and the hazards multiplied.*
increase • *The population continues to increase.*
proliferate • *Computerized databases are proliferating fast.*
spread • *Cholera is not spreading as quickly as it did in the past.*

mumble VERB
to speak quietly • *He mumbled a few words.*

murmur • *He murmured something to the professor.*
mutter • *He sat there muttering to himself.*

murder ① NOUN
the act of killing someone • *after being found guilty of murder*
assassination • *the assassination of John F. Kennedy*
homicide • *the scene of the homicide*
killing • *a brutal killing*
manslaughter • *She was found guilty of manslaughter.*
slaughter • *the imperial army's slaughter of Chinese civilians*
slaying (LITERARY) • *a trail of motiveless slayings*

murder ② VERB
to kill someone • *a thriller about two men who murder a third*
assassinate • *Robert Kennedy was assassinated in 1968.*
kill • *a man who killed his wife*
slaughter • *Thirty four people were slaughtered while queueing up to cast their votes.*
slay (LITERARY) • *David slew Goliath with a stone.*
take the life of • *He admitted to taking the lives of at least 35 more women.*

mysterious ① ADJECTIVE
strange and not well understood • *He died in mysterious circumstances.*
arcane (FORMAL) • *the arcane world of high finance*
baffling • *a baffling array of wires*
cryptic • *My father's notes are more cryptic here.*
enigmatic • *one of Orson Welles's most enigmatic films*
mystifying • *I find your attitude rather mystifying.*

a b c d e f g h i j k l m n o p q r s t u v w x y z

MORE SYNONYMS:
• abstruse
• obscure
• recondite

mysterious ② ADJECTIVE

secretive about something • *Stop being so mysterious.*
furtive • *with a furtive glance over her shoulder*
secretive • *the secretive world of spying*

mystery NOUN

something that is not understood
• *the mystery surrounding his death*
conundrum • *this theological conundrum*
enigma • *Iran remains an enigma for the outside world.*
puzzle • *"Women are a puzzle," he said.*
riddle • *the answer to the riddle of why it was never finished*

Nn

naked ① ADJECTIVE
not wearing any clothes • *a naked man diving into the sea*
bare • *her bare feet*
nude • *nude bathing*
stark-naked • *She didn't seem to notice I was stark-naked.*
unclothed • *an unclothed male body*
undressed • *She couldn't remember getting undressed.*

ANTONYM:
• clothed

naked ② ADJECTIVE
openly displayed or shown • *naked aggression*
blatant • *evidence of blatant discrimination*
evident • *the party's evident dislike of the president*
manifest • *his manifest enthusiasm*
open • *open opposition to the government*
unmistakable • *with unmistakable amusement in his eyes*

MORE SYNONYMS:
• overt
• patent
• stark

ANTONYM:
• secret

name ① NOUN
a word that identifies a person or thing • *My name is Joe.*
designation • *a level four alert, a designation reserved for very serious incidents*

epithet • *the common epithet for the Buddha*
nickname • *He's heard your nickname is Codfish.*
term • *I don't know the medical term for it.*
title • *Your actual title would be business manager.*

MORE SYNONYMS:
• appellation
• denomination
• sobriquet

RELATED WORD:
• ADJECTIVE nominal

name ② NOUN
the opinion people have about someone • *to protect Janet's good name*
character • *a series of personal attacks on my character*
reputation • *I know Chris has a bad reputation.*

name ③ VERB
to give a name to someone or something • *a little girl named Betsy*
baptize • *She could be baptized Margaret.*
call • *in a town called Fishingport*
christen • *He wanted to christen his son Arthur Albert.*
dub • *a girl cruelly dubbed "the Worm"*
style • *a character who styled himself the Memory Man*
term • *He had been termed a temporary employee.*

narrow ADJECTIVE
having a small distance from side to side • *a narrow stream*

fine • *the fine hairs on her arms*
slender • *long slender legs*
slim • *a slim volume of Auden's poems*
thin • *a thin layer of clay*

ANTONYM:
• wide

narrow-minded ADJECTIVE
unwilling to consider new ideas or
other people's opinions • *their own
narrow-minded view of the world*
biased • *a biased view*
bigoted • *bigoted opinions*
insular • *those insular British travellers*
opinionated • *the most opinionated
rubbish I have read*
prejudiced • *a whole host of prejudiced
and xenophobic ideas*

MORE SYNONYMS:
• parochial
• reactionary

ANTONYM:
• tolerant

nasty ADJECTIVE
very unpleasant • *a nasty taste*
disagreeable • *a disagreeable experience*
disgusting • *the most disgusting
behaviour*
foul • *They produce a foul smell of rotten
eggs.*
horrible • *I've got a horrible feeling about
this one.*
repellent • *the most repellent human
being I have ever met*
unpleasant • *some unpleasant surprises*
vile • *All the food is vile.*

ANTONYM:
• pleasant

natural ① ADJECTIVE
normal and to be expected • *the
natural reaction to a failed marriage*
common • *It is a common response.*
everyday • *the everyday drudgery of work*
normal • *Biting is normal for puppies
when they are teething.*

ordinary • *The cottage looks quite
ordinary from the road.*
typical • *typical symptoms of stress*
usual • *It was not usual for the women to
accompany them.*

ANTONYM:
• unnatural

natural ② ADJECTIVE
not trying to pretend • *He was so
natural with the children.*
candid • *rather candid about her marriage*
frank • *an unusually frank interview*
genuine • *He always seems so genuine.*
real • *She came across as a real person.*
unaffected • *She sang with unaffected
simplicity.*

MORE SYNONYMS:
• artless
• ingenuous

ANTONYM:
• false

natural ③ ADJECTIVE
existing from birth and not learned • *I
never had much natural rhythm.*
inborn • *an inborn sense of optimism*
inherent • *the inherent goodness of
people*
innate • *the innate conservatism of his
predecessor*
instinctive • *an instinctive distrust of
authority*
intuitive • *an intuitive understanding of
the market*
native • *He relies on his native wit to get
him through.*

MORE SYNONYMS:
• immanent
• indigenous

nature NOUN
someone's character • *It's not in my
nature to sit still.*
character • *the funny side of his character*
make-up • *Compromise was never part
of his make-up.*

personality • *his dominating personality*

naughty ① ADJECTIVE
tending to behave badly • *a naughty little boy*
bad • *the bad behaviour of their teenage children*
disobedient • *Lucy was similarly disobedient.*
impish • *an impish sense of humour*
mischievous • *a mischievous child*
wayward • *He tried to control his wayward son.*

ANTONYM:
• well-behaved

naughty ② ADJECTIVE
rude or indecent • *a programme all about naughty words*
bawdy • *a series of bawdy jokes*
lewd • *his arrest for lewd behaviour*
obscene • *making obscene gestures to the crowd*
vulgar • *The lyrics were vulgar.*

MORE SYNONYMS:
• ribald
• risqué
• smutty

near ① PREPOSITION
not far from • *He drew his chair nearer the fire.*
adjacent to • *a garden and maze adjacent to the castle*
alongside • *the huts set up alongside the river*
close to • *We parked close to the pavement.*
next to • *I realised someone was standing next to me.*
not far from • *a car park not far from the entrance*

near ② ADJECTIVE
not far away in distance • *A beautiful woman is near.*
adjacent • *an adjacent room*

adjoining • *A phone rang in an adjoining office.*
close • *a close neighbour*
nearby • *the nearby village*

ANTONYM:
• far

near ③ ADJECTIVE
not far away in time • *The time of judgment is near.*
approaching • *the approaching deadline*
forthcoming • *the forthcoming football season*
imminent • *He is in imminent danger.*
looming • *The students are panicking due to the looming exams.*
near at hand • *His death is near at hand.*
nigh • *The end of the world is nigh.*
upcoming • *the upcoming elections*

nearly ADVERB
not completely but almost • *The beach was nearly empty.*
almost • *Over the past decade their wages have almost doubled.*
as good as • *The World Championship is as good as over.*
just about • *We are just about finished with this section.*
practically • *The house was practically a wreck.*
virtually • *Their country is virtually bankrupt.*

neat ① ADJECTIVE
having everything arranged in a tidy way • *The house was clean and neat.*
orderly • *an orderly office*
smart • *a smart navy blue suit*
spruce • *Mundo was looking spruce in a suit.*
tidy • *He always kept his bedroom tidy.*
trim • *a street of trim little villas*

ANTONYM:
• untidy

neat ② ADJECTIVE
not mixed with anything else • *a small glass of neat vodka*

a
b
c
d
e
f
g
h
i
j
k
l
m
n
o
p
q
r
s
t
u
v
w
x
y
z

pure · *a carton of pure orange juice*
straight · *calling for a straight whisky*
MORE SYNONYMS:
• undiluted
• unmixed

necessary ① ADJECTIVE
needed so that something can
happen · *Make the necessary
arrangements.*
essential · *It is essential that you visit
a dentist.*
imperative · *It is imperative we end
up with a win.*
indispensable · *Jordan is an
indispensable part of the peace process.*
required · *That book is required
reading.*
vital · *Bone marrow is vital for
producing blood cells.*
MORE SYNONYMS:
• de rigueur
• requisite
ANTONYM:
• unnecessary

necessary ② ADJECTIVE (FORMAL)
certain to happen or exist · *a
necessary consequence of war*
certain · *one certain outcome of the
conference*
inevitable · *She now accepts that a
divorce is inevitable.*
inexorable · *The growth in travel has
been inexorable.*
unavoidable · *The union knows that
job losses are unavoidable.*

need VERB
to believe you must have or do
something · *You need some fresh air.*
demand · *The children demand her
attention.*
require · *If you require further
information, please telephone.*
want · *I want a drink.*

neglect ① VERB
to fail to look after someone or

something · *unhappy and neglected
children*
ignore · *They see the government
ignoring poor people.*
overlook · *Pensioners feel they are being
overlooked.*
turn your back on · *Do not turn your
back on the unemployed.*

neglect ② VERB (FORMAL)
to fail to do something · *He had
neglected to give her his address.*
fail · *I was shattered and I failed to tell her
about the good bits.*
forget · *She forgot to lock her door.*
omit · *He omitted to mention his
connection with the company.*

neglect ③ NOUN
lack of care · *Most of her plants died from
neglect.*
disregard · *a callous disregard for his
victims*
indifference · *Indifference to patients is
rare in America.*
unconcern · *the government's
unconcern for the environment*

nervous ADJECTIVE
worried about something · *She had
been nervous before the match.*
anxious · *I was very anxious about her
safety.*
apprehensive · *Their families are
apprehensive about the trip.*
edgy · *I was edgy and tired.*
jittery (INFORMAL) · *She still feels jittery
when she visits her sister.*
jumpy · *The Italians are getting jumpy
after drawing against the Swiss.*
tense · *too tense to sleep*
toey (AUSTRALIAN AND NEW ZEALAND;
SLANG) · *Dad's getting a bit toey.*
uptight (INFORMAL) · *an uptight British
couple*
worried · *You had me worried for a
moment.*
ANTONYM:
• calm

neutral ADJECTIVE

not supporting either side • *We stayed neutral during the war.*

disinterested • *a disinterested observer*

dispassionate • *a full and dispassionate account*

impartial • *How can he give impartial advice?*

nonaligned • *the Arab and nonaligned countries*

MORE SYNONYMS:
• nonpartisan
• unbiased
• unprejudiced

ANTONYM:
• biased

never ADVERB

at no time at all • *I never said I was leaving.*

at no time • *At no time did he see the helicopter.*

not ever • *The problem won't ever go away.*

new ADJECTIVE

recently created or discovered • *a new hotel*

advanced • *trial results of the company's most advanced drugs*

current • *all the current gossip on the stars*

fresh • *fresh footprints in the snow*

ground-breaking • *a ground-breaking discovery*

latest • *We review all the latest films.*

modern • *modern technology*

recent • *Lawson's most recent novel*

ultra-modern • *an ultra-modern shopping mall*

up-to-date • *the most up-to-date computers*

up-to-the-minute • *up-to-the-minute information*

ANTONYM:
• old

news NOUN

information about things that have happened • *news about the civil war*

bulletin • *the main evening bulletin*

disclosure • *disclosures about his private life*

dispatch • *the latest dispatches from the war zone*

information • *up-to-date information on weather*

intelligence • *military intelligence from behind Iraqi lines*

latest (INFORMAL) • *the latest on the bomb explosion*

tidings (FORMAL) • *the bearer of bad tidings*

word • *There is no word about casualties.*

next ① ADJECTIVE

coming immediately after something else • *Their next child was a girl.*

ensuing • *the ensuing years of violence*

following • *The following day I went to work as usual.*

subsequent • *As subsequent events showed, he was wrong.*

succeeding • *succeeding generations of students*

next ② ADVERB

coming immediately after something else • *Steve arrived next.*

afterwards • *I felt dizzy afterwards and had to sit down.*

subsequently • *She was subsequently married to his cousin.*

next ③ ADJECTIVE

in a position nearest to something • *in the next room*

adjacent • *I pulled into the adjacent driveway.*

adjoining • *in adjoining streets*

closest • *Britain's closest neighbours*

nearest • *the nearest Italian restaurant*

neighbouring • *Liberians fleeing to neighbouring countries*

a
b
c
d
e
f
g
h
i
j
k
l
m
n
o
p
q
r
s
t
u
v
w
x
y
z

nice ADJECTIVE
attractive or enjoyable • *Did you have a nice time, dear?*
▶ see Word Study **nice**, page 652

no INTERJECTION
not at all • *"Any problems?" - "No, everything's fine."*
absolutely not • *"Did they consult you?" - "Absolutely not."*
certainly not • *"Perhaps it would be better if I withdrew." - "Certainly not!"*
definitely not • *"Are you going to the party?" - "Definitely not."*
not at all • *"You're not upset, are you?" - "Not at all."*
of course not • *"I'd like to talk to the lads, if you don't mind." - "Of course not, Chief."*

ANTONYM:
• yes

noble ① ADJECTIVE
deserving admiration because of honesty, bravery and unselfishness • *a good and noble thing to do*
generous • *It reflects his generous nature.*
honourable • *His colleagues were honourable people.*
magnanimous • *Miss Balding is magnanimous in victory.*
upright • *a very upright, trustworthy man*
virtuous • *the virtuous Mrs Friendall*
worthy • *less worthy members of our profession*

ANTONYM:
• ignoble

noble ② NOUN
someone from the highest social rank • *The Scottish nobles were united.*
aristocrat • *All his sisters had married German aristocrats.*
lord • *They assumed that Amy was a snob because her father was a lord.*
nobleman • *a Spanish nobleman*
peer • *He was made a life peer in 1981.*

ANTONYM:
• peasant

noise NOUN
a loud or unpleasant sound • *He is making an awful noise.*
commotion • *There was a commotion in the corridor.*
din • *He'd never heard a din like it.*
hubbub • *the hubbub of Paris in the 1880s*
pandemonium • *There was pandemonium in the classroom.*
racket • *There was a terrible racket going on.*
row • *Whatever is that row?*
uproar • *The courtroom was in an uproar.*

MORE SYNONYMS:
• clamour
• rumpus
• tumult

ANTONYM:
• silence

noisy ADJECTIVE
making a lot of noise • *a noisy audience of schoolchildren*
deafening • *a deafening roar*
loud • *The disco music was a little too loud.*
piercing • *her piercing laugh*
strident • *the strident vocals of Joy Malcolm*
tumultuous • *He took the field to tumultuous applause.*
vociferous • *vociferous support from the Scottish fans*

MORE SYNONYMS:
• clamorous
• riotous
• uproarious

ANTONYM:
• quiet

nominate VERB
to suggest someone for a position • *The party refused to nominate him as its candidate.*
name • *He'll be naming a new captain.*

A B C D E F G H I J K L M N O P Q R S T U V W X Y Z

propose • *Cliff was proposed as chairman.*

recommend • *He recommended him as his successor at Boston.*

select • *no prospect of being selected to stand for Parliament*

submit • *Mr Heath submitted a list of 200 names.*

suggest • *Some commentators have suggested Clark for the job.*

nonsense NOUN
foolish words or behaviour • *I say the allegations are complete nonsense.*

bull (SLANG) • *They're teaching our kids a load of bull.*

drivel • *mindless drivel aimed at Middle America*

garbage (INFORMAL) • *One source claimed the rumours were complete garbage.*

inanity • *the burbling inanities of the tabloids*

rot • *She is talking complete rot.*

rubbish • *complete and utter rubbish*

waffle (BRITISH; INFORMAL) • *He writes smug, sanctimonious waffle.*

normal ADJECTIVE
usual and ordinary • *my normal routine*

average • *What's your average day like?*

conventional • *conventional tastes*

habitual • *their country of habitual residence*

ordinary • *It was just an ordinary weekend.*

regular • *It looks like a regular cigarette.*

routine • *a routine medical check*

standard • *standard practice*

typical • *A typical day begins at 8.30.*

usual • *She did not collect him at the usual time.*

ANTONYM:
• unusual

nosy ADJECTIVE
trying to find out about other people's business • *nosy neighbours watching us through the curtains*

curious • *surrounded by a group of curious villagers*

eavesdropping • *We don't want to be overheard by eavesdropping servants.*

inquisitive • *Bears are naturally inquisitive creatures.*

prying • *I hid it away, safe from prying eyes.*

note ① NOUN
a short letter • *I wrote him a note asking him to come round.*

communication (FORMAL) • *a communication from the President*

letter • *I have received a letter from a friend.*

memo • *a leaked memo to managers*

memorandum • *A memorandum has been sent to the members of the board.*

message • *He sent his mate round with a message for me.*

reminder • *We keep getting reminders from the garage to pay our bill.*

MORE SYNONYMS:
• epistle
• missive (OLD-FASHIONED)

note ② NOUN
a written record that helps you remember something • *I made a note of his address.*

account • *Keep an account of all your outgoings.*

jotting • *Carry a notebook with you for your jottings.*

record • *Keep a record of all payments.*

register • *She kept a register of each child's progress.*

note ③ NOUN
an atmosphere, feeling, or quality • *I detected a note of bitterness in his voice.*

hint • *Was there was a hint of irony in that remark?*

tone • *He laughed again, this time with a cold, sharp tone.*

touch • *There is an unmistakable touch of pathos in his last film.*

a
b
c
d
e
f
g
h
i
j
k
l
m
n
o
p
q
r
s
t
u
v
w
x
y
z

A
B
C
D
E
F
G
H
I
J
K
L
M
N
O
P
Q
R
S
T
U
V
W
X
Y
Z

trace • *He wrote on the subject without a trace of sensationalism.*

note ④ VERB
to become aware of or mention a fact • *I noted that the rain had stopped.*
mention • *I mentioned in passing that I liked her dress.*
notice • *Contact the police if you notice anything suspicious.*
observe (FORMAL) • *Hooke observed a reddish spot on the surface of the planet.*
perceive • *He perceived a certain tension between them.*
register • *The sound was so familiar that she didn't register it.*
remark • *Everyone has remarked what a lovely lady she is.*
see • *A lot of people saw what was happening but did nothing.*

notice ① VERB
to become aware of something • *Then I noticed Billy wasn't laughing.*
detect • *He detects signs of growing support for his plan.*
discern • *I did not discern any change in attitudes.*
note • *I noted that the rain had stopped.*
observe • *I've observed how hard he had to work.*
perceive • *gradually perceiving the possibilities*
see • *I saw that the lobby was swarming with police.*
spot • *Allen spotted me on the other side of the dance floor.*

notice ② NOUN
a written announcement • *a handwritten notice in the window*
advertisement • *one advertisement in a local paper*
bill • *students posting bills near the campus for a demo*
poster • *a poster advertising a charity concert*

sign • *a hand-written cardboard sign hung round his neck*

notice ③ NOUN
warning that something is going to happen • *She was transferred without notice.*
advance warning • *advance warning of the attack*
intimation • *He has given no intimation of an intention to resign.*
notification • *Official notification is expected to arrive today.*
warning • *I was sacked without warning.*

noticeable ADJECTIVE
obvious and easy to see • *a noticeable improvement*
conspicuous • *a conspicuous lack of sympathy*
evident • *He ate with evident enjoyment.*
obvious • *There are obvious dangers.*
perceptible • *Germany is showing a perceptible improvement.*
unmistakable • *a growing but unmistakable impatience*

MORE SYNONYMS:
• manifest
• salient

notify VERB
to officially inform someone of something • *The skipper notified the coastguard of the tragedy.*
advise (FORMAL) • *I think it best that I advise you of my decision first.*
inform • *They would inform him of any progress they made.*
tell • *He told me I was on a final warning.*
warn • *They warned him of the dangers.*

notorious ADJECTIVE
well-known for something bad • *The district was notorious for violent crime.*
disreputable • *a low and disreputable character*
infamous • *an industry infamous for late payment of debts*

scandalous • *her scandalous affair with the president*

now ADVERB
at the present time or moment • *I need to talk to him now.*
at once • *I really must go at once.*
currently • *The vaccines are currently being tested.*
immediately • *Please come immediately.*
nowadays • *I don't see much of Tony nowadays.*
right now • *Stop that noise right now!*
straightaway • *I think you should see a doctor straightaway.*
without delay • *We'll come round without delay.*

nuisance NOUN
someone or something that is annoying • *Sorry to be a nuisance.*
annoyance • *Snoring can be an annoyance.*
bother • *Most men hate the bother of shaving.*
hassle (INFORMAL) • *Writing out a cheque is a hassle.*
inconvenience • *the inconvenience of a rail strike*
irritation • *He describes the tourists as "an irritation".*
pain (INFORMAL) • *She found dressing up for the occasion a real pain.*
pest • *I didn't want to be a cry baby or a pest.*

MORE SYNONYMS:
• plague
• vexation

numb ① ADJECTIVE
unable to feel anything • *Your right arm goes numb.*
dead • *Hillier suffered a dead leg playing for the reserves.*
frozen • *a frozen shoulder*
insensitive • *The brain itself is insensitive to pain.*

paralysed • *He has been left with a paralysed arm.*

MORE SYNONYMS:
• benumbed
• insensible

numb ② VERB
to make you unable to feel anything • *The cold numbed my fingers.*
dull • *morphine to dull the pain*
freeze • *an epidural to freeze the hip area*
paralyse • *people paralysed by illness or injury*
stun • *the gun used to stun the animals*

MORE SYNONYMS:
• benumb
• deaden
• immobilize

number ① NOUN
a word or symbol used for counting • *Pick a number between one and ten.*
digit • *a six-digit password*
figure • *a figure between a hundred and a thousand*
numeral • *Roman numerals*

MORE SYNONYMS:
• character
• integer

number ② NOUN
a quantity of things or people • *Adrian has introduced me to a large number of people.*
collection • *a huge collection of books about Keats*
crowd • *a huge crowd of supporters*
horde • *a horde of drunken villagers*
multitude • *Bands can play to multitudes of fans.*

numerous ADJECTIVE
existing or happening in large numbers • *on numerous occasions*
lots of • *I've got lots of photos of the kids.*
many • *I have met Imran many times.*
several • *He is fluent in several languages.*

a b c d e f g h i j k l m **n** o p q r s t u v w x y z

Oo

oaf NOUN
a clumsy or aggressive person • *You drunken oaf!*
brute • *Custer was an idiot and a brute.*
lout • *a drunken lout*

oath NOUN
a formal promise • *He took an oath of loyalty to the government.*
pledge • *The meeting ended with a pledge to step up cooperation.*
promise • *If you make a promise, you should keep it.*
vow • *I made a silent vow to be more careful.*

obedient ADJECTIVE
tending to do what you are told • *He was always very obedient to his parents.*
law-abiding • *law-abiding citizens*
submissive • *Most doctors want their patients to be submissive.*
subservient • *her willingness to be subservient to her children*

MORE SYNONYMS:
• biddable
• compliant

ANTONYM:
• disobedient

obey VERB
to do what you are told • *Most people obey the law.*
abide by • *They have got to abide by the rules.*
adhere to • *All members adhere to a strict code of practice.*

comply with • *The army will comply with the ceasefire.*
follow • *Take care to follow the instructions carefully.*
observe • *forcing motorists to observe speed restrictions*

ANTONYM:
• disobey

object ① NOUN
anything solid and non-living • *everyday objects such as wooden spoons*
article • *household articles*
thing • *What's that thing in the middle of the fountain?*

object ② NOUN
an aim or purpose • *The object of the exercise is to raise money for the charity.*
aim • *The aim of the festival is to increase awareness of Hindu culture.*
goal • *The goal is to raise as much money as possible.*
idea • *The idea is to give children the freedom to explore.*
intention • *It is my intention to remain in my position.*
objective • *His objective was to win.*
purpose • *What is the purpose of your visit?*

object ③ VERB
to express disapproval • *A lot of people will object to the book.*
oppose • *Many parents oppose bilingual education in schools.*

protest • *He picked up the cat before Rosa could protest.*

MORE SYNONYMS:
• demur
• expostulate

ANTONYM:
• approve

objection NOUN
disapproval of something • *despite objections by the White House*
opposition • *Opposition to this plan has come from the media.*
protest • *protests against the government*

ANTONYM:
• support

obscene ADJECTIVE
indecent and likely to upset people • *obscene pictures*
bawdy • *a bawdy song*
blue • *a blue movie*
dirty • *a dirty book*
filthy • *a filthy joke*
indecent • *an indecent suggestion*
lewd • *lewd comments*
pornographic • *a pornographic magazine*

MORE SYNONYMS:
• ribald
• salacious
• smutty

obscure ① ADJECTIVE
known by only a few people • *an obscure Mongolian dialect*
little-known • *a little-known Austrian composer*
unknown • *an unknown writer*

ANTONYM:
• famous

obscure ② ADJECTIVE
difficult to understand • *The news was shrouded in obscure language.*

arcane • *the arcane world of contemporary classical music*
cryptic • *cryptic comments*
opaque • *the opaque language of the inspector's reports*

MORE SYNONYMS:
• abstruse
• esoteric
• recondite

ANTONYM:
• simple

obscure ③ VERB
to make something difficult to see • *His view was obscured by trees.*
cloak • *a land permanently cloaked in mist*
cloud • *Perhaps anger had clouded his vision.*
conceal • *The hat concealed her hair.*
hide • *The compound was hidden by trees and shrubs.*
mask • *A thick grey cloud masked the sun.*
screen • *Most of the road was screened by a block of flats.*
shroud • *Mist shrouded the outline of Buckingham Palace.*

ANTONYM:
• expose

observant ADJECTIVE
good at noticing things • *Painting makes you really observant of things.*
attentive • *the attentive audience*
perceptive • *a perceptive remark*
vigilant • *He warned the public to be vigilant.*
watchful • *Keep a watchful eye on babies and toddlers.*

MORE SYNONYMS:
• eagle-eyed
• sharp-eyed

observe ① VERB
to watch something carefully • *He has*

a
b
c
d
e
f
g
h
i
j
k
l
m
n
o
p
q
r
s
t
u
v
w
x
y
z

spent years observing their behaviour.
monitor • I have been monitoring his progress carefully.
scrutinize • She scrutinized his features to see if he was telling the truth.
study • Debbie studied her friend's face for a moment.
survey • He surveys American politics from an interesting standpoint.
view • You can view the lesson from the gallery.
watch • A man was watching him from across the square.

observe ② VERB
to notice something • I observed a number of strange phenomena.
discover • They discovered that they were being watched.
note • People noted how much care she took over her work.
notice • Contact the police if you notice anything unusual.
see • I saw a man coming towards me.
spot • Moments later, smoke was spotted coming out of the kitchen.
witness • Anyone who witnessed the attack should call the police.

observe ③ VERB
to make a comment about something • "You've had your hair cut," he observed.
comment • Stuart commented that this was true.
mention • I mentioned that I didn't like contemporary music.
remark • "Some people have more money than sense," he remarked.
say • She said that I looked tired.
state • He stated that this was, indeed, the case.

obsession NOUN
a compulsion to think about something • her obsession with Christopher

complex • I have never had a complex about my height.
fixation • the country's fixation on the war
mania • a mania for horror films
preoccupation • today's preoccupation with royal misdeeds
thing (INFORMAL) • He's got this thing about ties.

obstacle NOUN
something which makes it difficult to go forward • a large obstacle to improving housing conditions
barrier • Taxes are the most obvious barrier to free trade.
difficulty • the difficulties ahead
hindrance • The higher rates have been a hindrance to economic recovery.
hurdle • the first hurdle for many women returning to work
impediment • There was no legal impediment to the marriage.
obstruction • an obstruction in the road

MORE SYNONYMS:
• bar
• stumbling block

obstinate ADJECTIVE
unwilling to change your mind • He is obstinate and will not give up.
dogged • his dogged insistence on their rights
headstrong • He's young and very headstrong.
inflexible • His opponents viewed him as dogmatic and inflexible.
intractable • He protested but Wright was intractable.
stubborn • a stubborn character who is used to getting his own way
wilful • a wilful child

MORE SYNONYMS:
• intransigent

- recalcitrant
- refractory

ANTONYM:
- flexible

obstruct VERB
to block a road or path • *Lorries obstructed the road.*
bar • *He stood there, barring her way.*
block • *Some students blocked the highway.*
choke • *The roads are choked with cars.*
clog • *The traffic clogged the Thames bridges.*

obtain VERB
to get something • *He tried to obtain a false passport*
acquire • *I recently acquired a beautiful old lamp.*
get • *trying to get enough food to live*
get hold of • *It's hard to get hold of guns.*
get your hands on (INFORMAL) • *reading everything she could get her hands on*
procure (FORMAL) • *It became hard to procure fuel.*
secure (FORMAL) • *continuing their efforts to secure a ceasefire*

obvious ADJECTIVE
easy to see or understand • *an obvious injustice*
apparent • *It was apparent that he had lost interest.*
blatant • *a blatant foul*
clear • *a clear breach of the rules*
evident • *His love of nature is evident in his paintings.*
overt • *parents who showed us no overt affection*
palpable • *The tension between them is palpable.*
plain • *It was plain to him that I was having a nervous breakdown.*

self-evident • *The implications for this country are self-evident.*

MORE SYNONYMS:
- conspicuous
- manifest
- patent

occasion ① NOUN
an important event • *The launch of a ship was a big occasion.*
affair • *The visit was to be a purely private affair.*
event • *A new book by Grass is always an event.*

occasion ② NOUN
an opportunity to do something • *an important occasion for setting out government policy*
chance • *the chance to practise medicine in British hospitals*
opportunity • *I had an opportunity to go to New York.*
time • *This was no time to make a speech.*

occasion ③ VERB (FORMAL)
to cause something • *damage occasioned by fire*
bring about • *the only way to bring about peace*
give rise to • *The judge's decision gave rise to practical problems.*
induce • *an economic crisis induced by high oil prices*
produce • *The drug is known to produce side-effects in women.*
prompt • *The demonstration prompted fears of more violence.*
provoke • *The incident has provoked outrage in Okinawa.*

occasional ADJECTIVE
happening sometimes • *an occasional outing*
intermittent • *after three hours of intermittent rain*

a
b
c
d
e
f
g
h
i
j
k
l
m
n
o
p
q
r
s
t
u
v
w
x
y
z

odd • *at odd moments*
periodic • *periodic bouts of illness*
sporadic • *a year of sporadic fighting*

ANTONYM:
• frequent

occur ① VERB

to happen or exist • *The disease occurs throughout Africa.*

appear • *a test to reveal infection before symptoms appear*

arise • *A problem may arise later in pregnancy.*

be present • *This vitamin is present in breast milk.*

exist • *A conflict of interest may exist in such situations.*

happen • *The accident happened close to Martha's Vineyard.*

take place • *Elections will take place on the second of November.*

occur ② VERB

to come into your mind • *It didn't occur to me to check.*

cross your mind • *The possibility of failure did cross my mind.*

dawn on • *It dawned on me that I shouldn't give up without a fight.*

strike • *A thought struck her.*

odd ADJECTIVE

strange or unusual • *an odd coincidence*

bizarre • *his bizarre behaviour*

curious • *a curious mixture of the ancient and modern*

funny • *There's something funny about him.*

peculiar • *Rachel thought it tasted peculiar.*

queer (OLD-FASHIONED) • *There's something a bit queer going on.*

singular (FORMAL) • *Where he got that singular notion I just can't think.*

strange • *Then a strange thing happened.*

weird • *That first day was weird.*

ANTONYM:
• ordinary

offend VERB

to upset or embarrass someone • *He says he had no intention of offending the community.*

affront • *He pretended to be affronted, but inwardly he was pleased.*

insult • *Buchanan says he was insulted by the judge's remarks.*

outrage • *Many people have been outraged by what was said.*

ANTONYM:
• please

offensive ADJECTIVE

rude and upsetting • *offensive behaviour*

abusive • *abusive language*

insulting • *an insulting remark*

objectionable • *I find your tone highly objectionable.*

offer ① VERB

to ask if someone wants something • *Rhys offered him an apple.*

hold out • *I held out my ticket for him to check.*

tender • *She has tendered her resignation.*

MORE SYNONYMS:
• extend
• proffer
• submit

offer ② NOUN

something that someone offers you • *He had refused several excellent job offers.*

proposition • *I made her a proposition.*

tender • *a tender for a public contract*

official ① ADJECTIVE

approved by someone in authority • *the official figures*

authorized • *the authorized biography*
certified • *a certified accountant*
formal • *No formal announcement has been made.*
licensed • *a licensed doctor*

ANTONYM:
• unofficial

official ② NOUN
someone in authority • *a senior UN official*
executive • *a senior bank executive*
officer • *a local authority education officer*
representative • *trade union representatives*

MORE SYNONYMS:
• bureaucrat
• functionary

often ADVERB
happening many times • *They often spent Christmas at Prescott Hill.*
frequently • *He was frequently depressed.*
repeatedly • *Both men have repeatedly denied the allegations.*

okay or **OK** ADJECTIVE (INFORMAL)
acceptable or satisfactory • *Is it okay if I come by myself?*
acceptable • *It is becoming more acceptable for women to drink.*
all right • *if it's all right with you*

old ① ADJECTIVE
having lived for a long time • *an old lady*
▶ see Word Study **old**, page 654

ANTONYM:
• young

old ② ADJECTIVE
in the past • *my old art teacher*
▶ see Word Study **old**, page 654

ANTONYM:
• new

old-fashioned ADJECTIVE
no longer fashionable • *old-fashioned shoes*
antiquated • *an antiquated system*
archaic • *archaic practices such as these*
dated • *Some of the language sounds quite dated.*
obsolete • *So much equipment becomes obsolete almost as soon as it's made.*
outdated • *outdated attitudes*
outmoded • *toiling in outmoded factories*
out of date • *a make of car that is now out of date*
passé • *Punk is passé.*

MORE SYNONYMS:
• behind the times
• obsolescent
• old-time

ANTONYM:
• fashionable

omen NOUN
a sign of what will happen • *Her appearance at this moment is an omen of disaster.*
sign • *people who look to the skies for signs*
warning • *a warning of trouble to come*

MORE SYNONYMS:
• augury
• portent

ominous ADJECTIVE
suggesting that something bad will happen • *an ominous silence*
sinister • *a sinister message*
threatening • *a threatening sky*

MORE SYNONYMS:
• inauspicious
• portentous
• unpropitious

omit VERB
to not include something • *Omit the salt in this recipe.*

a
b
c
d
e
f
g
h
i
j
k
l
m
n
o
p
q
r
s
t
u
v
w
x
y
z

A
B
C
D
E
F
G
H
I
J
K
L
M
N
O
P
Q
R
S
T
U
V
W
X
Y
Z

exclude • *Women felt excluded from the workplace.*
leave out • *The Spaniard has been left out of the team.*
miss out • *What about Sally? You've missed her out!*
skip • *It is all too easy to skip meals.*

only ① ADVERB
involving one person or thing • *Only Keith knows whether he will continue.*
just • *It's not just a financial matter.*
merely • *Watson was far from being merely a furniture expert.*
purely • *a racing machine, designed purely for speed*
simply • *Most of the damage was simply because of fallen trees.*
solely • *decisions based solely upon what we see in magazines*

only ② ADJECTIVE
having no other examples • *their only hit single*
one • *My one aim is to look after the horses well.*
sole • *Our sole intention is to reunite her with her baby.*

open ① VERB
to cause something not to be closed • *She opened the door.*
uncover • *When the seedlings sprout, uncover the tray.*
undo • *I managed secretly to undo a corner of the parcel.*
unlock • *She unlocked the case.*

MORE SYNONYMS:
• unfasten
• unseal

ANTONYM:
• shut

open ② ADJECTIVE
not closed • *an open box of chocolates*
ajar • *He left the door ajar.*

uncovered • *The uncovered bucket in the corner stank.*
undone • *pictures of him with his shirt undone*
unlocked • *an unlocked room*

MORE SYNONYMS:
• unfastened
• unsealed

ANTONYM:
• shut

open ③ ADJECTIVE
not trying to deceive someone • *He had always been open with her.*
candid • *I haven't been completely candid with him.*
frank • *My client has been less than frank with me.*
honest • *He had been honest with her and she had tricked him!*

opening ① ADJECTIVE
coming first • *the opening day of the season*
first • *the first night of the play*
inaugural • *his inaugural address*
initial • *the aim of this initial meeting*
introductory • *an introductory offer*

opening ② NOUN
the first part of something • *the opening of the film*
beginning • *the beginning of the book*
commencement (FORMAL) • *at the commencement of the course*
start • *four years after the start of the Great War*

ANTONYM:
• conclusion

opening ③ NOUN
a hole or gap • *a narrow opening in the fence*
chink • *a chink in the wall*
cleft • *a narrow cleft in the rocks*
crack • *Kathryn had seen him through a*

crack in the curtains.
gap • *the wind tearing through gaps in the window frames*
hole • *a hole in the wall*
slot • *a slot in which to insert a coin*
space • *a half-inch space between the curtains*
vent • *Steam escaped from the vent at the front of the machine.*

MORE SYNONYMS:
• aperture
• fissure
• orifice

opinion NOUN
a belief or view • *I wasn't asking for your opinion.*
assessment • *What is your assessment of the situation?*
belief • *his religious beliefs*
estimation • *He has gone down considerably in my estimation.*
judgment • *In your judgment, what has changed?*
point of view • *Thanks for your point of view, John.*
view • *Make your views known to your local MP.*
viewpoint • *to include as many viewpoints as possible*

oppose VERB
to disagree with something
• *protesters opposing planned nuclear tests*
fight against • *a lifetime fighting against racism*
resist • *They resisted our attempts to modernize.*
speak out against • *He spoke out strongly against some of the radical ideas.*

MORE SYNONYMS:
• take a stand against
• take issue with

ANTONYM:
• support

opposite ① ADJECTIVE
completely different to something • *I take the opposite view to you.*
conflicting • *three powers with conflicting interests*
contrary • *He has a contrary opinion to mine.*
contrasting • *two men with completely contrasting backgrounds*
opposed • *This was a straight conflict of directly opposed aims.*
reverse • *The wrong attitude will have exactly the reverse effect.*

MORE SYNONYMS:
• antithetical
• diametrically opposed

opposite ② NOUN
a completely different person or thing • *He was the complete opposite of Raymond.*
antithesis (FORMAL) • *The antithesis of the Middle Eastern buyer is the Japanese.*
contrary • *I'm not a feminist, quite the contrary.*
converse • *Don't you think that the converse might also be possible?*
reverse • *This didn't upset him at all, in fact quite the reverse.*

MORE SYNONYMS:
• inverse
• obverse

opposition NOUN
disagreement about something
• *Much of the opposition to this plan has come from the media.*
disapproval • *His action had been greeted with almost universal disapproval.*
hostility • *There is hostility to this method among traditionalists.*
resistance • *Initially I met resistance from my own family.*

a
b
c
d
e
f
g
h
i
j
k
l
m
n
o
p
q
r
s
t
u
v
w
x
y
z

ANTONYM:
• support

oppressed ADJECTIVE
treated cruelly or unfairly • *a member of an oppressed minority*
abused • *those who work with abused children*
downtrodden • *the downtrodden, bored housewife*
MORE SYNONYMS:
• enslaved
• tyrannized

oppression NOUN
cruel or unfair treatment • *the oppression of black people throughout history*
persecution • *the persecution of minorities*
tyranny • *The 1930s was a decade of tyranny in Europe.*
MORE SYNONYMS:
• subjection
• subjugation

optimistic ADJECTIVE
hopeful about the future • *an optimistic mood*
buoyant • *She was in a buoyant mood.*
confident • *I am confident that everything will come out right in time.*
hopeful • *I am hopeful this misunderstanding will be rectified.*
positive • *a positive frame of mind*
sanguine • *They have begun to take a more sanguine view.*
ANTONYM:
• pessimistic

oral ADJECTIVE
spoken rather than written • *oral history*
spoken • *the spoken word*
verbal • *a verbal agreement*

orange NOUN or ADJECTIVE

◆ **SHADES OF ORANGE**
◆ amber
◆ apricot
◆ carrot
◆ ochre
◆ peach
◆ tangerine

ordeal NOUN
a difficult and unpleasant experience • *the ordeal of being arrested*
hardship • *One of the worst hardships is having so little time.*
nightmare • *Taking my son Peter to a restaurant was a nightmare.*
torture • *Waiting for the result was torture.*
trial • *the trials of adolescence*
tribulation (FORMAL) • *the trials and tribulations of everyday life*

order ① NOUN
a command by someone in authority • *I don't take orders from him any more.*
command • *The tanker failed to respond to a command to stop.*
decree • *He issued a decree ordering all armed groups to disband.*
dictate • *to ensure that the dictates of the Party are followed*
directive • *a new EU directive*
instruction • *MPs defied a party instruction to vote against the Bill.*

order ② NOUN
a well-organized situation • *the wish to impose order upon confusion*
harmony • *the ordered harmony of the universe*
regularity • *the chessboard regularity of their fields*
symmetry • *the beauty and symmetry of a snowflake*

ANTONYM:
• disorder

order ③ VERB
to tell someone to do something
• He ordered his men to stop firing.
command • He commanded his troops
to attack.
decree • the rule that decreed no
alcohol on the premises
direct • a court order directing the
group to leave the land
instruct • The family has instructed
solicitors to sue Thomson.
ordain • Nehru ordained that
socialism should rule.

ANTONYM:
• forbid

orderly ADJECTIVE
well-organized or well-arranged
• Their vehicles were parked in orderly
rows.
neat • She put her wet clothes in a neat
pile in the corner.
regular • regular rows of wooden huts
tidy • a tidy desk

ANTONYM:
• disorderly

ordinary ADJECTIVE
not special or different • an ordinary day
conventional • a respectable married
woman with conventional opinions
normal • He lives a normal life.
regular • the regular barman
routine • a routine procedure
standard • It was standard practice.
usual • all the usual inner-city problems

MORE SYNONYMS:
• run-of-the-mill
• unexceptional
• unremarkable

ANTONYM:
• special

organization ① NOUN
a group or business • charitable
organizations
association • research associations
body • the Chairman of the policemen's
representative body
company • the Ford Motor Company
confederation • the Confederation of
Indian Industry
group • an environmental group
institution • financial institutions
outfit (INFORMAL) • We are a
professional outfit.

organization ② NOUN
the planning and arranging of
something • He was involved in
the organization of conferences and
seminars.
organizing • His duties involved the
organizing of transport.
planning • The trip needs careful
planning.
structuring • improvements in the
structuring of courses

organize VERB
to plan and arrange something
• Organizing a wedding takes time.
arrange • The bank can arrange a loan
for students.
establish • How do you establish a
workable system?
jack up (NEW ZEALAND; INFORMAL) • to
jack up a demonstration
plan • A team meeting was planned for
last night.
set up • This tribunal was set up by the
government.

origin ① NOUN
the beginning or cause of something
• the origins of the custom
derivation • The derivation of its name
is obscure.
root • His sense of guilt had its roots in
his childhood.

source • *the source of the problem*

MORE SYNONYMS:
• genesis
• provenance

origin ② NOUN
someone's family background • *She was of Swedish origin.*
ancestry • *Noel can trace her ancestry to the 11th century.*
descent • *All the contributors were of African descent.*
extraction • *a Malaysian citizen of Australian extraction*
lineage • *a respectable family of ancient lineage*
stock • *people of Mediterranean stock*

original ① ADJECTIVE
being the first example of something
• *the original owner of the cottage*
first • *Her first reaction was disgust.*
initial • *His initial response was to disbelieve her.*

original ② ADJECTIVE
imaginative and clever • *a stunningly original idea*
fresh • *These designers are full of fresh ideas.*
new • *These proposals aren't new.*
novel • *a novel way of losing weight*

MORE SYNONYMS:
• innovative
• innovatory

ANTONYM:
• unoriginal

ornament NOUN
an object that you display • *a shelf containing ornaments*
adornment • *a building without any adornments*
bauble • *a Christmas tree decorated with coloured baubles*
decoration • *The only wall decorations are candles.*

knick-knack • *Her flat is spilling over with knick-knacks.*
trinket • *She sold trinkets to tourists.*

ostentatious ADJECTIVE
intended to impress people with appearances • *an ostentatious lifestyle*
extravagant • *They make extravagant shows of generosity.*
flamboyant • *flamboyant clothes*
flashy • *a flashy sports car*
grandiose • *the grandiose building which housed the mayor's offices*
pretentious • *This pub was smaller and less pretentious.*
showy • *large, showy flowers*

outbreak NOUN
a sudden occurrence of something
• *the outbreak of war*
eruption • *this sudden eruption of violence*
explosion • *the global explosion of interest in rugby*

outdo VERB
to do something better than another person • *She would love to outdo her sister Manuela.*
go one better than • *You always have to go one better than anyone else.*
outshine • *Jesse has begun to outshine me in sports.*
surpass • *determined to surpass the achievements of his older brothers*
top • *How are you going to top that?*

MORE SYNONYMS:
• best
• eclipse

outline ① VERB
to describe something in a general way • *The mayor outlined his plan to clean up the town's image.*
sketch • *Tudjman sketched his vision of a future Bosnia.*

summarize • *The article can be summarized in three sentences.*

MORE SYNONYMS:
• adumbrate
• delineate

outline ② NOUN
a general description of something
• *an outline of the survey's findings*
rundown (INFORMAL) • *Here's a rundown of the options.*
summary • *a summary of the report*
synopsis • *a brief synopsis of the book*

MORE SYNONYMS:
• résumé
• thumbnail sketch

outline ③ NOUN
the shape of something • *the hazy outline of the goalposts*
contours • *the contours of her body*
figure • *Alistair saw the dim figure of Rose in the chair.*
form • *She'd never been so glad to see his bulky form.*
shape • *dark shapes of herons silhouetted against the moon*
silhouette • *the dark silhouette of the castle ruins*

outlook ① NOUN
your general attitude towards life
• *I adopted a positive outlook on life.*
attitude • *Being unemployed produces negative attitudes to work.*
perspective • *It gave him a new perspective on life.*
view • *an optimistic view of the future*

outlook ② NOUN
the future prospects of something
• *The economic outlook is one of rising unemployment.*
future • *a conference on the country's political future*
prospects • *a detailed review of the company's prospects*

out of date ADJECTIVE
no longer useful • *The information is already out of date.*
antiquated • *an antiquated system*
archaic • *archaic practices such as these*
obsolete • *So much equipment becomes obsolete almost as soon as it's made.*
old-fashioned • *old-fashioned shoes*
outdated • *outdated attitudes*
outmoded • *toiling in outmoded factories*

ANTONYM:
• modern

outside ① NOUN
the outer part of something • *The moth was on the outside of the glass.*
exterior • *the exterior of the building*
facade • *the refurbishing of the cathedral's facade*
face • *the face of the watch*
surface • *the surface of the road*

ANTONYM:
• inside

outside ② ADJECTIVE
not inside • *an outside toilet*
exterior • *the oven's exterior surfaces*
external • *the external walls*
outdoor • *outdoor activities*
outer • *the outer suburbs of the city*
outward • *with no outward sign of injury*
surface • *Its total surface area was seven thousand square feet.*

ANTONYM:
• inside

outskirts PLURAL NOUN
the edges of an area • *the outskirts of New York*
edge • *We were on a hill, right on the edge of town.*
perimeter • *the perimeter of the airport*
periphery • *countries on the periphery of Europe*

a
b
c
d
e
f
g
h
i
j
k
l
m
n
o
p
q
r
s
t
u
v
w
x
y
z

A
B
C
D
E
F
G
H
I
J
K
L
M
N
O
P
Q
R
S
T
U
V
W
X
Y
Z

MORE SYNONYMS:
• environs
• purlieus

outspan VERB (SOUTH AFRICAN)
to relax • *Let's take a break and just outspan for a while.*
laze • *Fred lazed in an easy chair.*
relax • *I ought to relax and stop worrying.*
rest • *He rested for a while before starting work again.*
take it easy • *Try to take it easy for a week or two.*

outstanding ① ADJECTIVE
extremely good • *an outstanding tennis player*
brilliant • *a brilliant performance*
excellent • *the recording quality is excellent*
exceptional • *children with exceptional ability*
first-class • *first-class service*
first-rate • *The show was first-rate.*
great • *great cultural achievements*
superb • *a superb 18-hole golf course*

outstanding ② ADJECTIVE
still owed • *The total debt outstanding is $70 billion.*
due • *They sent me £100 and advised me that no further payment was due.*
overdue • *pay overdue salaries*
owing • *There is still some money owing for the rent.*
payable • *The amount payable is £175.*
unpaid • *a pile of unpaid bills*

over ① PREPOSITION
more than a particular amount • *It cost over a million dollars.*
above • *speeds above 50 mph*
exceeding • *a budget exceeding $700 million a year*
in excess of • *a fortune in excess of 150 million pounds*

more than • *The airport had been closed for more than a year.*
RELATED WORDS:
• PREFIXES hyper-, super-, supra-, sur-

over ② ADJECTIVE
completely finished • *I am glad it's all over.*
at an end • *The matter is now at an end.*
complete • *The work of restoring the farmhouse is complete.*
done • *When her deal is done, the client emerges with her purchase.*
finished • *once the season's finished*
gone • *Any chance of winning was now gone.*
past • *The time for loyalty is past.*
up • *when the six weeks were up*

overcome VERB
to manage to deal with something • *Molly had overcome her fear of flying.*
conquer • *He has never conquered his addiction to smoking.*
get the better of • *She didn't allow her emotions to get the better of her.*
master • *His genius alone has mastered every crisis.*
surmount • *I realized I had to surmount the language barrier.*
triumph over • *a symbol of good triumphing over evil*
vanquish (LITERARY) • *the man who helped vanquish Napoleon*

overlook VERB
to ignore or fail to notice something • *We tend to overlook warning signals about our health.*
disregard • *The police must not be allowed to disregard human rights.*
forget • *She never forgets his birthday.*
ignore • *For years her talents were ignored by the film industry.*
miss • *His searching eye never missed a detail.*

neglect • *She never neglects her duties.*
turn a blind eye to • *Are teachers turning a blind eye to these issues?*

overrule VERB
to reject a decision officially • *The Court of Appeal overruled this decision.*
overturn • *when the Russian parliament overturned his decision*
reverse • *They will not reverse the decision to increase prices.*

MORE SYNONYMS:
• countermand
• override

oversee VERB
to make sure a job is done properly • *Get a supervisor to oversee the work.*
be in charge of • *She is in charge of day-to-day operations.*
coordinate • *Government officials have been sent to coordinate the relief effort.*
direct • *his coolness in directing the rescue of the hostages*
manage • *Within two years, he was managing the project.*
preside • *Mr Brown will be presiding over the day's events.*
supervise • *He supervises the vineyards.*

overthrow VERB
to remove someone from power by force • *The government was overthrown in a military coup.*
bring down • *They brought down the government by withdrawing their support.*
depose • *He fled to Hawaii after being deposed as president.*
oust • *His opponents tried to oust him with a vote of no confidence.*
topple • *the revolution which toppled the regime*

overturn ① VERB
to knock something over • *Alex jumped up so violently that he overturned his glass.*
capsize • *I didn't count on his capsizing the raft.*
knock down • *Isabel rose so abruptly that she knocked down her chair.*
knock over • *Emma knocked over the box of cornflakes.*
tip over • *He tipped the table over in front of him.*
topple • *Winds and rain toppled trees and electricity lines.*
upset • *Don't upset the piles of sheets under the box.*

MORE SYNONYMS:
• upend
• upturn

overturn ② VERB
to reject a decision officially • *when the Russian parliament overturned his decision*
overrule • *The Court of Appeal overruled this decision.*
reverse • *They will not reverse the decision to increase prices.*

MORE SYNONYMS:
• countermand
• override

overweight ADJECTIVE
too fat, and therefore unhealthy • *Being overweight increases your risk of heart problems.*
fat • *I could eat what I liked without getting fat.*
hefty • *She was quite a hefty woman.*
obese • *Obese people tend to have higher blood pressure than lean people.*
stout • *a stout man with grey hair*

MORE SYNONYMS:
• corpulent
• rotund

own ① ADJECTIVE
belonging to a particular person or

thing • *She stayed in her own house.*
personal • *That's my personal opinion.*
private • *76 bedrooms, all with private bathrooms*

own ② VERB
to have something that belongs to you • *His father owns a local pub.*
have • *They have a house in France.*
keep • *His father kept a village shop.*
possess • *I would give her everything I possess.*

own ③ : **on your own** ADVERB
without other people • *I work best on my own.*

alone • *She lives alone.*
by oneself • *I didn't know if I could raise a child by myself.*
independently • *several people working independently*
unaided • *She brought us up completely unaided.*

owner NOUN
the person to whom something belongs • *the owner of the store*
possessor • *the proud possessor of a truly incredible voice*
proprietor • *the proprietor of a local restaurant*

A
B
C
D
E
F
G
H
I
J
K
L
M
N
O
P
Q
R
S
T
U
V
W
X
Y
Z

Pp

pacify VERB
to calm down someone who is angry
• *She shrieked again, refusing to be pacified.*
appease • *The offer has not appeased separatists.*
calm • *A business lunch helped calm her nerves.*
mollify • *The investigation was undertaken to mollify pressure groups.*
placate • *He went aboard to placate the angry passengers.*
soothe • *She took him in her arms and soothed him.*

MORE SYNONYMS:
• assuage
• propitiate

pain ① NOUN
an unpleasant feeling of physical hurt • *I felt a sharp pain in my lower back.*
ache • *Poor posture can cause neck aches.*
discomfort • *Steve had some discomfort but no real pain.*
irritation • *These oils may cause irritation to sensitive skin.*
soreness • *The soreness lasted for about six weeks.*
trouble • *back trouble*
twinge • *He felt a slight twinge in his hamstring.*

pain ② NOUN
a feeling of deep unhappiness • *the pain of rejection*
agony • *the agony of divorce*

anguish • *Mark looked at him in anguish.*
distress • *Jealousy causes distress and painful emotions.*
grief • *The grief soon gave way to anger.*
misery • *All that money brought nothing but sadness and misery.*

painful ① ADJECTIVE
causing emotional pain • *painful memories*
distressing • *one of the most distressing episodes in his life*
grievous • *Their loss would be a grievous blow to our industry.*
saddening • *a saddening experience*
unpleasant • *an unpleasant truth*

painful ② ADJECTIVE
causing physical pain • *a painful knock on the knee*
aching • *his aching joints*
excruciating • *an excruciating headache*
sore • *a sore throat*
tender • *My leg is very tender and sore.*

pale ADJECTIVE
rather white or without much colour
• *Migrating birds filled the pale sky.*
ashen • *He fell back, shocked, his face ashen.*
colourless • *a colourless liquid*
faded • *a girl in faded jeans*
sallow • *His face was sallow and shiny with sweat.*
wan • *He looked wan and tired.*

A
B
C
D
E
F
G
H
I
J
K
L
M
N
O
P
Q
R
S
T
U
V
W
X
Y
Z

white • *He turned white and began to stammer.*

panic ① NOUN
a very strong feeling of fear or anxiety • *The earthquake caused panic among the population.*
alarm • *She sat up in alarm.*
dismay • *She discovered to her dismay that she was pregnant.*
fear • *my fear of the dark*
fright • *To hide my fright I asked a question.*
hysteria • *mass hysteria*
terror • *She shook with terror.*

panic ② VERB
to become afraid or anxious • *Guests panicked when the bomb exploded.*
become hysterical • *Miss Brady became hysterical when he produced the gun.*
go to pieces • *England went to pieces when they conceded a goal.*
lose your nerve • *They lost their nerve and pulled out of the deal.*

parade NOUN
a line of people moving as a display • *A military parade marched through the streets.*
cavalcade • *a cavalcade of limousines and police motorcycles*
march • *Organizers expect 300,000 protesters to join the march.*
pageant • *a traditional Christmas pageant*
procession • *religious processions*
tattoo • *the world-famous Edinburgh military tattoo*

paragraph NOUN
◆ **PARTS OF A PARAGRAPH**
◆ clause
◆ phrase
◆ sentence
◆ word

paralyse VERB
to make someone lose feeling and movement • *Her sister had been paralysed in a road accident.*
cripple • *He heaved his crippled leg into an easier position.*
disable • *He was disabled by polio.*

parent NOUN
your father or your mother • *I told my parents I was moving out.*
father • *Her father was furious.*
mother • *the mother of two girls*
old (AUSTRALIAN AND NEW ZEALAND; INFORMAL) • *a visit to the olds*
patriarch • *a domineering patriarch*

parody NOUN
an amusing imitation of someone else's style • *a parody of an American sitcom*
imitation • *I can do a pretty good imitation of him.*
satire • *a sharp satire on the American political process*
spoof (INFORMAL) • *a spoof on Hollywood life*
takeoff (INFORMAL) • *She did a brilliant takeoff of the Queen.*
MORE SYNONYMS:
• lampoon
• skit

part ① NOUN
a piece or section of something • *I like that part of Edinburgh.*
bit • *a bit of paper*
fraction • *a fraction of a second*
fragment • *fragments of glass*
piece • *a piece of cheese*
portion • *Damage was confined to a small portion of the castle.*
section • *a large orchestra, with a vast percussion section*

part ② NOUN
a person's involvement in something

• He tried to conceal his part in the accident.

capacity • He has served the club in many capacities.

duty • My duty is to look after the animals.

function • Their main function is to raise capital for industry.

involvement • You have no proof of my involvement in anything.

role • the drug's role in preventing infection

part ③: take part in VERB

to do something with other people • Thousands took part in the demonstrations.

be instrumental in • He was instrumental in tracking down the killers.

be involved in • My grandparents were involved in the Methodist church.

have a hand in • He had a hand in three of the goals.

join in • I hope that everyone will be able to join in the fun.

participate in • They expected him to participate in the ceremony.

play a part in • He continued to play a part in drug operations from prison.

participate VERB

to take part in an activity • Over half the population participate in sport.

be involved in • HMS Cardiff was also involved in the exercise.

engage in • They have refused to engage in all-party talks.

enter into • We entered into discussions with them weeks ago.

join in • Their rivals refused to join in any price war.

take part • The oldest car taking part was built in 1907.

particular ① ADJECTIVE

relating to only one thing or person • That particular place is dangerous.

distinct • The book is divided into two distinct parts.

exact • Do you think I could get the exact thing I want?

express • I bought the camera for the express purpose of taking railway photographs.

peculiar • This is not a problem peculiar to London.

precise • the precise location of the ship

specific • There are several specific problems to be dealt with.

particular ② ADJECTIVE

especially great or intense • Pay particular attention to the forehead.

exceptional • children with exceptional ability

marked • a marked increase in crime in the area

notable • Two other notable events took place last week.

singular • It was a goal of singular brilliance.

special • a special occasion

uncommon • Both are blessed with an uncommon ability to fix things.

MORE SYNONYMS:
• especial
• noteworthy

particular ③ ADJECTIVE

not easily satisfied • Ted was very particular about the colours he used.

choosy (INFORMAL) • Skiers should be choosy about the insurance policy they buy.

exacting • exacting standards of craftsmanship

fastidious • He was fastidious about his appearance.

fussy • She is very fussy about her food.

meticulous • meticulous attention to detail

partly ADVERB

to some extent but not completely

a
b
c
d
e
f
g
h
i
j
k
l
m
n
o
p
q
r
s
t
u
v
w
x
y
z

• *This is partly my fault.*
in part (FORMAL) • *The levels of blood glucose depend in part on what you eat.*
in some measure (FORMAL) • *Power is in some measure an act of will.*
partially • *Jo is partially sighted.*
to some degree • *These statements are, to some degree, correct.*
to some extent • *Her concern is, to some extent, understandable.*

partner ① NOUN
either member of a couple in a relationship • *My partner moved in with me last year.*
husband • *Are husbands and wives included in the invitation?*
mate • *She has found her ideal mate.*
spouse • *Anything left to your spouse is free from inheritance tax.*
wife • *His wife is a lawyer.*

partner ② NOUN
the person someone is doing something with • *my tennis partner*
companion • *her travelling companion*
team-mate • *his team-mate at Ferrari*

part of speech NOUN

♦ **PARTS OF SPEECH**
♦ adjective
♦ adverb
♦ conjunction
♦ interjection
♦ noun
♦ plural noun
♦ preposition
♦ pronoun
♦ reflexive verb
♦ verb

party ① NOUN
a social event where people enjoy themselves • *Most teenagers like to go to parties.*
celebration • *a New Year's Eve celebration*

function • *a charity function at the hotel*
gathering • *a gathering of friends and relatives*
get-together (INFORMAL) • *a family get-together*
hooley or **hoolie** (NEW ZEALAND, SCOTTISH AND IRISH) • *a hooley down on the beach*
reception • *a wedding reception*

party ② NOUN
an organization for people with the same political beliefs • *his resignation as party leader*
alliance • *The two parties have agreed to form an electoral alliance.*
clique • *the clique attached to Prime Minister*
coalition • *a coalition of right-wing and religious factions*
faction • *the party's small pro-European faction*
grouping • *two main political groupings pressing for independence*

party ③ NOUN
a group who are doing something together • *a research party of scientists*
band • *a small but dedicated band of supporters*
crew • *a ship's crew*
gang • *a gang of criminals*
squad • *the West Indies squad to tour Australia*
team • *Each consultant has a team of doctors under him.*
unit • *the health services research unit*

pass ① VERB
to exceed or go past something • *He gave a triumphant wave as he passed the winning post.*
exceed • *The demand for places at some schools exceeds the supply.*
go beyond • *Did your relationship go*

beyond a close friendship?

outdo • *The Colombian fans outdid the home supporters in fervour.*

outstrip • *Demand continues to outstrip supply.*

overtake • *Britain's lottery will this year overtake Japan's as the world's biggest.*

surpass • *He was determined to surpass the achievements of his brothers.*

pass ② VERB

to be successful in a test • *Wendy has just passed her driving test.*

get through • *I got through my banking exams last year.*

graduate • *He graduated in engineering.*

qualify • *I qualified as a doctor.*

succeed • *the skills and qualities needed to succeed*

ANTONYM:
• fail

pass ③ NOUN

a document that allows you to go somewhere • *Don't let any cars onto the land unless they've got a pass.*

identification • *Passport control asked me if I had any further identification.*

passport • *You should take your passport with you when changing money.*

ticket • *I'm not going to renew my season ticket.*

passage ① NOUN

a space that connects two places • *He cleared a passage for himself through the crammed streets.*

channel • *a drainage channel*

course • *the river's twisting course*

path • *A group of reporters blocked the path.*

road • *the road between Jerusalem and Bethlehem*

route • *the most direct route to the town centre*

way • *This is the way in.*

passage ② NOUN

a narrow space that connects one place with another • *up some stairs and along a narrow passage towards a door*

aisle • *the frozen food aisle*

corridor • *They sat crowded together in the hospital corridor.*

hall • *The lights were on in the hall and in the bedroom.*

lobby • *the cramped pitch-dark lobby*

passage ③ NOUN

a section of a book or piece of music • *a passage from the Bible*

excerpt • *an excerpt from her speech*

extract • *an extract from his new book*

quotation • *a favourite quotation from St Augustine*

section • *a section from the first movement of Beethoven's 'Eroica' symphony*

passion ① NOUN

a strong feeling of physical attraction • *the passion had gone from their relationship*

desire • *sexual desire*

infatuation • *Daisy's infatuation with the doctor*

love • *our love for each other*

lust • *He is obsessed by his lust for her.*

passion ② NOUN

any strong emotion • *He spoke with great passion.*

emotion • *Her voice trembled with emotion.*

excitement • *I was in a state of great excitement.*

fire • *His speeches were full of fire.*

intensity • *His intensity alarmed me.*
warmth • *He greeted us both with warmth and affection.*
zeal • *his zeal for teaching*

passionate ADJECTIVE
expressing very strong feelings about something • *I'm a passionate believer in public art.*
ardent • *ardent supporters of capital punishment*
emotional • *an emotional farewell*
heartfelt • *My heartfelt sympathy goes out to all the relatives.*
impassioned • *He made an impassioned appeal for peace.*
intense • *intense hatred*
strong • *Many viewers have strong opinions about violence on TV.*

passive ADJECTIVE
submissive or not playing an active part • *His passive attitude made things easier for me.*
docile • *docile, obedient children*
receptive • *The voters had seemed receptive to his ideas.*
resigned • *She was already resigned to losing her home.*
submissive • *Most doctors want their patients to be submissive.*

MORE SYNONYMS:
• acquiescent
• compliant
• inactive
• quiescent

past ① : **the past** NOUN
the period of time before the present • *We would like to put the past behind us.*
antiquity • *famous monuments of classical antiquity*
days gone by • *This brings back memories of days gone by.*
former times • *In former times he*

would have been clapped in irons.
long ago • *The old men told stories of long ago.*

past ② ADJECTIVE
happening or existing before the present • *details of his past activities*
ancient • *ancient history*
bygone • *a bygone era*
former • *Remember him as he was in his former years.*
olden • *We were talking about the olden days on his farm.*
previous • *She has a teenage daughter from a previous marriage.*

MORE SYNONYMS:
• erstwhile
• quondam

ANTONYM:
• future

past ③ PREPOSITION
situated on the other side of somewhere • *It's just past the church there.*
beyond • *Beyond the garden was a small orchard.*
by • *He walked by her house every day.*
over • *He lived in the house over the road.*

pastime NOUN
a hobby or something done for pleasure • *His favourite pastime is snooker.*
activity • *activities range from canoeing to birdwatching*
diversion • *Finger painting is very messy but an excellent diversion.*
hobby • *My hobbies are squash and swimming.*
recreation • *Saturday afternoon is for recreation and outings.*

path ① NOUN
a strip of ground for people to walk on • *We followed the paths along the clifftops.*

footpath • *It is accessible only by footpath.*
pathway • *a pathway leading towards the nearby river*
towpath • *He took a cycle trip along a canal towpath.*
track • *We set off over a rough mountain track.*
trail • *He was following a broad trail through the trees.*
way • *the Pennine Way*

path ② NOUN
the space ahead of someone as they move along • *A group of reporters stood in his path.*
course • *obstacles blocking our course*
direction • *St Andrews was 10 miles in the opposite direction.*
passage • *Two men elbowed a passage through the shoppers.*
route • *All escape routes were blocked by armed police.*
way • *Get out of my way!*

pathetic ① ADJECTIVE
causing someone to feel pity • *She now looked small, shrunken, and pathetic.*
heartbreaking • *a heartbreaking succession of miscarriages*
sad • *He seemed a rather sad figure.*

MORE SYNONYMS:
• pitiable
• plaintive

pathetic ② ADJECTIVE
very poor or unsuccessful • *pathetic excuses*
feeble • *This is a particularly feeble argument.*
lamentable • *a lamentable display by the league leaders*
pitiful • *They are paid pitiful wages.*
poor • *The flat was in a poor state of repair.*

sorry • *Their oil industry is in a sorry state.*

patience NOUN
the ability to stay calm in a difficult situation • *It was exacting work and required all his patience.*
calmness • *calmness under pressure*
composure • *He regained his composure and went on to win the match.*
cool (SLANG) • *The big Irishman was on the verge of losing his cool.*
restraint • *They behaved with more restraint than I'd expected.*
tolerance • *a low tolerance of errors*

MORE SYNONYMS:
• equanimity
• forbearance
• imperturbability

patient ① ADJECTIVE
staying calm in a difficult situation • *Please be patient - your cheque will arrive.*
calm • *She is usually a calm and diplomatic woman.*
composed • *a composed and charming manner*
long-suffering • *long-suffering train commuters*
philosophical • *He is philosophical about the defeat.*
serene • *She looks dreamily into the distance, serene, calm and happy.*

ANTONYM:
• impatient

patient ② NOUN
a person receiving medical treatment • *patients who wish to change their doctor*
case • *He is a suitable case for treatment.*
invalid • *elderly invalids*

a b c d e f g h i j k l m n o p q r s t u v w x y z

A
B
C
D
E
F
G
H
I
J
K
L
M
N
O
P
Q
R
S
T
U
V
W
X
Y
Z

sick person • *a ward full of very sick people*
sufferer • *asthma sufferers*

pattern ① NOUN
a decorative design of repeated shapes • *red and purple thread stitched into a pattern of flames*
design • *tableware decorated with a blackberry design*
motif • *a rose motif*

pattern ② NOUN
a diagram or shape used as a guide for making something • *sewing patterns*
design • *They drew up the design for the house in a week.*
diagram • *Follow the diagram on page 20.*
plan • *a plan of the garden*
stencil • *flower stencils*
template • *Make a paper template of the seat of the chair.*

pause ① VERB
to stop doing something for a short time • *On leaving, she paused for a moment at the door.*
break • *They broke for lunch.*
delay • *Various problems delayed the launch.*
halt • *Striking workers halted production at the plant.*
rest • *He rested briefly before pressing on.*
take a break • *He needs to take a break from work.*
wait • *I waited to see how she responded.*

pause ② NOUN
a short period when activity stops • *There was a pause while the barmaid set down two plates.*
break • *Do you want to have a little break?*

halt • *Agricultural production was brought to a halt.*
interruption • *The sudden interruption stopped her in mid-flow.*
interval • *I had a drink during the interval.*
rest • *I think he's due for a rest now.*
stoppage • *Miners have voted for a one-day stoppage next month.*

MORE SYNONYMS:
• caesura
• entr'acte

pay ① VERB
to give money to someone to settle a debt • *You can pay by credit card.*
compensate • *Farmers could be compensated for their loss of subsidies.*
honour • *The bank refused to honour the cheque.*
settle • *I settled the bill for our drinks.*

MORE SYNONYMS:
• recompense
• reimburse
• remunerate

pay ② VERB
to give someone a benefit • *It pays to be honest.*
be advantageous • *It is easy to imagine cases where cheating is advantageous.*
be worthwhile • *He believed the operation had been worthwhile.*

pay ③ NOUN
money paid to someone for work done • *their complaints about pay and conditions*
earnings • *his earnings as an accountant*
fee • *solicitors' fees*
income • *a modest income*
payment • *a redundancy payment*
salary • *The lawyer was paid a good salary.*
wages • *His wages have gone up.*

MORE SYNONYMS:
- emolument
- recompense
- reimbursement
- remuneration
- stipend

payment NOUN
an amount of money that is paid to someone • *mortgage payments*
advance • *She was paid a £100,000 advance for her next two novels.*
deposit • *A $50 deposit is required when ordering.*
instalment • *The first instalment is payable on application.*
premium • *higher insurance premiums*
remittance • *Please make your remittance payable in sterling.*

peace ① NOUN
a state of undisturbed calm and quiet • *They left me in peace to recover from the funeral.*
calm • *the rural calm of Grand Rapids, Michigan*
quiet • *He wants some peace and quiet before his match.*
silence • *They stood in silence.*
stillness • *An explosion shattered the stillness of the night air.*
tranquillity • *The hotel is a haven of tranquillity.*

MORE SYNONYMS:
- quietude
- repose

peace ② NOUN
freedom from war • *The people do not believe that the leaders want peace.*
armistice • *the armistice between North Korea and the United Nations*
cessation of hostilities • *a resolution calling for an immediate cessation of hostilities*

truce • *an uneasy truce between the two sides*

ANTONYM:
- war

peaceful ADJECTIVE
quiet and calm • *a peaceful house in the heart of the countryside*
calm • *a calm spot amid the bustle of the city*
placid • *the placid waters of Lake Erie*
quiet • *The street was unnaturally quiet.*
serene • *a beautiful, serene park*
still • *In the room it was very still.*
tranquil • *the tranquil paradise of his native Antigua*

peak ① NOUN
the point at which something is at its greatest or best • *the peak of the morning rush hour*
climax • *The tournament is building up to a dramatic climax.*
culmination • *The marriage was the culmination of an eight-month romance.*
high point • *The high point of this trip was a day at the races.*
zenith • *His career is now at its zenith.*

MORE SYNONYMS:
- acme
- apogee
- ne plus ultra

peak ② NOUN
the pointed top of a mountain • *snow-covered peaks*
brow • *He overtook a car as he approached the brow of a hill.*
crest • *Burns was clear over the crest of the hill.*
pinnacle • *He plunged 25 metres from a rocky pinnacle.*
summit • *the first man to reach the summit of Mount Everest*
top • *the top of Mount Sinai*

a b c d e f g h i j k l m n o **p** q r s t u v w x y z

A
B
C
D
E
F
G
H
I
J
K
L
M
N
O
P
Q
R
S
T
U
V
W
X
Y
Z

MORE SYNONYMS:
• aiguille
• apex

peak ③ VERB
to reach the highest point or greatest level • *His career peaked during the 1970s.*
be at its height • *when trade union power was at its height*
climax • *a tour that climaxed with a three-night stint at Wembley Arena*
come to a head • *The siege came to a head with the death of a marshal.*
culminate • *The celebration of the centenary will culminate with a dinner.*
reach its highest point • *The stock market reached its highest point since the 1987 crash.*

peculiar ① ADJECTIVE
strange and perhaps unpleasant • *a very peculiar sense of humour*
bizarre • *bizarre behaviour*
curious • *a curious mixture of the ancient and modern*
funny • *Children get some funny ideas sometimes.*
odd • *Something odd began to happen.*
queer • *There's something queer going on.*
strange • *There was something strange about the flickering blue light.*
weird • *It must be weird to be so rich.*

peculiar ② ADJECTIVE
associated with one particular person or thing • *He has his own peculiar way of doing things.*
distinctive • *She has a very distinctive laugh.*
distinguishing • *Does he have any distinguishing features?*
individual • *all part of her very individual personality*
personal • *cultivating their own personal style*

special • *Everyone has their own special problems or fears.*
unique • *a feature unique to humans*

ANOTHER SYNONYM:
• idiosyncratic

peek ① VERB
to have a quick look at something • *She peeked at him through a crack in the wall.*
glance • *He glanced at his watch.*
peep • *Children came to peep at him round the doorway.*
snatch a glimpse • *Spectators lined the route to snatch a glimpse of the Queen.*
sneak a look • *We sneaked a look at his diary.*

peek ② NOUN
a quick look at something • *He took his first peek at the new course yesterday.*
glance • *Trevor and I exchanged a glance.*
glimpse • *Some people had waited all day to catch a glimpse of her.*
look • *She took a last look in the mirror.*
peep • *He took a peep at his watch.*

pent-up ADJECTIVE
held back for a long time without release • *She had a lot of pent-up anger to release.*
inhibited • *inhibited sexuality*
repressed • *repressed hostility*
suppressed • *Deep sleep allowed suppressed anxieties to surface.*

people ① PLURAL NOUN
men, women, and children • *Millions of people have lost their homes.*
human beings • *The disease can be transmitted to human beings.*
humanity • *crimes against humanity*
humans • *millions of years before humans appeared on earth*
mankind • *the evolution of mankind*

people ② PLURAL NOUN
all the men, women, and children of
a particular place • *It's a triumph for
the American people.*
citizens • *the citizens of New York City*
inhabitants • *the inhabitants of Hong
Kong*
population • *Africa's rapidly rising
population*
public • *the British public*

perceptive ADJECTIVE
good at noticing or realizing things
• *a perceptive account of the poet's life*
acute • *His relaxed exterior hides an
extremely acute mind.*
astute • *He made a series of astute
business decisions.*
aware • *They are politically very
aware.*
penetrating • *He never stopped
asking penetrating questions.*
sharp • *He has a sharp eye and an
excellent memory.*

MORE SYNONYMS:
• insightful
• percipient
• perspicacious

perfect ① ADJECTIVE
of the highest standard and without
fault • *His English was perfect.*
expert • *There is a great deal to learn
from his expert approach.*
faultless • *faultless technique*
flawless • *her flawless complexion*
masterly • *a masterly performance*
polished • *polished promotional skills*
skilled • *a skilled repair job*

ANTONYM:
• imperfect

perfect ② ADJECTIVE
complete or absolute • *They have a
perfect right to say so.*
absolute • *absolute nonsense*

complete • *The resignation came as a
complete surprise.*
consummate • *He acted the part with
consummate skill.*
sheer • *an act of sheer desperation*
unmitigated • *Last year's crop was an
unmitigated disaster.*
utter • *utter nonsense*

perfect ③ VERB
to make something as good as it can
be • *The technique was perfected during
the 1960s.*
hone • *a chance to hone their skills*
improve • *You must improve your
French.*
polish • *He spent time polishing the
script.*
refine • *Surgical techniques are
constantly being refined.*

perform ① VERB
to carry out a task or action
• *people who have performed acts of
bravery*
carry out • *Police believe the attacks
were carried out by nationalists.*
complete • *He completed the test in
record time.*
do • *He crashed trying to do a tricky
manoeuvre.*
execute • *The landing was skilfully
executed.*
fulfil • *Fulfil the tasks you have been
allocated.*

perform ② VERB
to act, dance, or play music in public
• *students performing Shakespeare's
Macbeth*
act • *acting in Tarantino's films*
do • *I've always wanted to do a one-man
show on Broadway.*
play • *His ambition is to play the part
of Dracula.*
present • *The company is presenting a
new production of "Hamlet".*

put on • *The band are hoping to put on a UK show.*
stage • *The group staged their first play in the late 1970s.*

perhaps ADVERB
maybe • *Perhaps you're right.*
conceivably • *The mission could conceivably be accomplished in a week.*
it could be • *It could be he's upset at what you said.*
maybe • *Maybe she is in love.*
possibly • *Do you think that he could possibly be right?*

period NOUN
a particular length of time • *a period of a few months*
interval • *a long interval when no-one spoke*
spell • *a long spell of dry weather*
stretch • *an 18-month stretch in the army*
term • *a 5-year prison term*
time • *At 15 he left home for a short time.*
while • *I haven't seen him for a long while.*

permanent ADJECTIVE
lasting for ever or present all the time • *a permanent solution to the problem*
abiding • *one of his abiding interests*
constant • *Inflation is a constant threat.*
enduring • *an enduring friendship*
eternal • *the quest for eternal youth*
lasting • *We are well on our way to a lasting peace.*
perpetual • *a perpetual source of worry*

MORE SYNONYMS:
• immutable
• imperishable
• steadfast

ANTONYM:
• temporary

permission NOUN
authorization to do something • *He asked permission to leave the room.*
approval • *The plan will require official approval.*
assent • *He requires the assent of parliament.*
authorization • *his request for authorization to use military force*
consent • *Can she be examined without my consent?*
go-ahead • *The government gave the go-ahead for five major road schemes.*
licence • *He has given me licence to do the job as I see fit.*

ANTONYM:
• ban

permit ① VERB
to allow something or make it possible • *The guards permitted me to bring my camera.*
allow • *Smoking will not be allowed.*
authorize • *They are expected to authorize the use of military force.*
enable • *The test should enable doctors to detect the disease early.*
give the green light to • *He has been given the green light to resume training.*
grant • *Permission was granted a few weeks ago.*
sanction • *The chairman will not sanction a big-money signing.*

ANTONYM:
• ban

permit ② NOUN
an official document allowing someone to do something • *a work permit*
authorization • *We didn't have authorization to go.*
licence • *a driving licence*
pass • *a rail pass*
passport • *My passport expires next year.*

permission • *Permission for the march has not been granted.*
warrant • *Police issued a warrant for his arrest.*

persecute VERB
to treat someone with continual cruelty and unfairness • *The Communists began by brutally persecuting the Church.*
hound • *He has been hounded by the press.*
ill-treat • *They thought Mr Smith had been ill-treating his wife.*
oppress • *Minorities here have been oppressed for generations.*
pick on • *She was repeatedly picked on by the manager.*
torment • *They were tormented by other pupils.*
torture • *He would not torture her further by trying to argue with her.*

person NOUN
a man, woman, or child • *The amount of sleep we need varies from person to person.*
human • *the common ancestor of humans and the great apes*
human being • *This protein occurs naturally in human beings.*
individual • *the rights and responsibilities of the individual*
living soul • *The nearest living soul was 20 miles away.*
soul • *a tiny village of only 100 souls*

personal ADJECTIVE
belonging to a particular person or thing • *personal belongings*
individual • *Divide the vegetables among four individual dishes.*
own • *My wife decided I should have my own shop.*
particular • *his own particular style of preaching*
peculiar • *her own peculiar talents*

private • *my private life*
special • *Every person will have his or her own special problems.*

personality ① NOUN
a person's character and nature • *She has such a kind, friendly personality.*
character • *a negative side to his character*
identity • *our own sense of cultural identity*
individuality • *People should be free to express their individuality.*
make-up • *There was some fundamental flaw in his make-up.*
nature • *She trusted people. That was her nature.*
psyche • *disturbing elements of the human psyche*

personality ② NOUN
a famous person in entertainment or sport • *television personalities*
big name • *the big names in French cinema*
celebrity • *Hollywood celebrities*
famous name • *a famous name from Inter Milan's past*
household name • *The TV series that made him a household name.*
star • *film stars*

persuade VERB
to make someone do something by reason or charm • *He persuaded the company to sign her up.*
bring round (INFORMAL) • *We will do what we can to bring them round to our point of view.*
coax • *She coaxed Bobby into talking about himself.*
induce • *I would do anything to induce them to stay.*
sway • *Don't ever be swayed by fashion.*
talk into • *He talked me into marrying him.*

win over • *By the end of the day he had won over the crowd.*

MORE SYNONYMS:
• impel
• inveigle

perverted ADJECTIVE
practising abnormal and unacceptable behaviour • *She has been a victim of perverted phone calls and letters.*

depraved • *the work of depraved and evil criminals*

deviant • *Not all drug abusers produce deviant offspring.*

immoral • *those who think that birth control is immoral*

unhealthy • *His interest developed into an unhealthy obsession.*

MORE SYNONYMS:
• debauched
• vitiated

pessimistic ADJECTIVE
believing that bad things will happen • *a pessimistic view of life*

despondent • *despondent about their children's future*

gloomy • *a gloomy view of the future*

glum • *They are not entirely glum about the car industry's prospects.*

hopeless • *Even able pupils feel hopeless about job prospects.*

ANTONYM:
• optimistic

pest ① NOUN
an insect or animal that damages crops or livestock • *10% of the crop was lost to a pest called corn rootworm.*

bane • *The bane of farmers across the country is the badger.*

blight • *potato blight*

scourge • *This parasitic mite is the scourge of honey bees.*

pest ② NOUN
an annoying person • *I didn't want to be a cry baby or a pest.*

bane • *Student journalists were the bane of my life.*

bore • *I don't enjoy his company. He's a bore and a fool.*

nuisance • *He could be a bit of a nuisance when he was drunk.*

pain (INFORMAL) • *She's been a real pain recently.*

pain in the neck (INFORMAL) • *I've always been a pain in the neck to publishers.*

pester VERB
to bother someone continually • *He gets fed up with people pestering him for money.*

annoy • *She kept on annoying me.*

badger • *She badgered her doctor time and again.*

bother • *We are playing a trick on a man who keeps bothering me.*

bug (INFORMAL) • *Stop bugging me.*

drive someone up the wall (SLANG) • *I sang in the bath and drove my sister up the wall.*

get on someone's nerves (INFORMAL) • *I was beginning to get on her nerves.*

MORE SYNONYMS:
• bedevil
• chivvy

petty ① ADJECTIVE
small and unimportant • *endless rules and petty regulations*

insignificant • *In 1949, Bonn was a small, insignificant city.*

measly (INFORMAL) • *The average bathroom measures a measly 3.5 square metres.*

trifling • *The sums involved are trifling.*

trivial • *trivial details*

unimportant · *It was an unimportant job, and paid very little.*

petty ② ADJECTIVE
selfish and small-minded · *I think that attitude is a bit petty.*
cheap · *politicians making cheap political points*
mean · *I'd feel mean saying no.*
small-minded · *their small-minded preoccupation with making money*

phone ① NOUN
a device that allows you to speak to someone in another place · *Will you please answer the phone.*
blower (BRITISH; INFORMAL) · *Get on the blower and speak to the boss.*
mobile · *Can I borrow your mobile?*
mobile phone · *I lost my mobile phone at the weekend.*
moby (INFORMAL) · *She put her keys and moby in her pocket and went out the door.*
telephone · *an old-fashioned black telephone*

phone ② VERB
to contact a person by phone · *Phone me when you get home.*
call · *You should call work to let them know you're ill.*
contact · *I've been trying to contact you all day.*
ring · *Joe rang the police station.*
Skype ® · *They Skype their son in Australia every week.*
telephone · *Mary telephoned when you were out.*

phoney ADJECTIVE (INFORMAL)
false and intended to deceive · *a phoney accent*
bogus · *a bogus insurance claim*
counterfeit · *counterfeit currency*
fake · *fake certificates*
false · *a false name and address*

forged · *forged documents*
sham · *a sham marriage*

MORE SYNONYMS:
• feigned
• spurious

ANTONYM:
• genuine

pick ① VERB
to choose something · *He picked ten people to interview for six sales jobs.*
choose · *There are several options to choose from.*
decide upon · *He decided upon a career in publishing.*
hand-pick · *He was hand-picked for his job by the Admiral.*
opt for · *I think we should opt for a more cautious approach.*
select · *the party's policy of selecting candidates*
settle on · *I finally settled on an Audi TT roadster.*

pick ② VERB
to remove a flower or fruit with your fingers · *He helps his mother pick fruit.*
gather · *We spent the afternoon gathering berries.*
harvest · *Many farmers are refusing to harvest the cane.*
pluck · *I plucked a lemon from the tree.*

pick ③ NOUN
the best · *the pick of the country's young athletes*
elite · *the elite of women's tennis*
flower · *the flower of Polish manhood*
pride · *the hovercraft, once the pride of British maritime engineering*

pick on VERB
to criticize someone unfairly or treat them unkindly · *Bullies pick on younger children.*
bait · *He delighted in baiting his mother.*

tease • *He teased me mercilessly about going to Hollywood.*
torment • *They were tormented by other pupils.*

picture ① NOUN

a drawing, painting, or photograph • *It's got a picture of me on the cover.*
drawing • *She did a drawing of me.*
illustration • *Tolkien's illustrations for The Hobbit*
painting • *his collection of Impressionist paintings*
photograph • *He wants to take some photographs of the house.*
portrait • *Velazquez's portrait of Pope Innocent X*
sketch • *pencil sketches*

RELATED WORD:
• ADJECTIVE **pictorial**

picture ② VERB

to imagine something clearly • *He pictured her with long black hair.*
conceive of • *I can't conceive of doing work that doesn't interest me.*
imagine • *It's difficult to imagine anything coming between them.*
see • *A good idea, but can you see Taylor trying it?*
visualize • *He could not visualize her as old.*

MORE SYNONYMS:
• envision
• see in the mind's eye

piece ① NOUN

a portion or part of something • *a piece of cheese*
bit • *a bit of paper*
chunk • *He was accused of stealing a tin of pineapple chunks.*
fragment • *There were fragments of cork in the wine.*
part • *The engine has got only three moving parts.*

portion • *Damage was confined to a small portion of the castle.*
slice • *a slice of bread*

piece ② NOUN

something that has been written, created, or composed • *his piece on fox hunting*
article • *a newspaper article*
composition • *Schubert's piano compositions*
creation • *the fashion designer's latest creations*
study • *Leonardo's studies of horsemen*
work • *In my opinion, this is Rembrandt's greatest work.*

piece together VERB

to assemble things or parts to make something complete • *Doctors painstakingly pieced together the broken bones.*
assemble • *He is assembling evidence concerning a murder.*
join • *Join all the sections together.*
mend • *I should have had it mended, but never got round to it.*
patch together • *A hasty deal was patched together.*
repair • *the cost of repairing earthquake damage*
restore • *The trust is playing a leading part in restoring old cinemas.*

pierce VERB

to make a hole in something with a sharp instrument • *Pierce the potato with a fork.*
bore • *tunnels bored into the foundations of the building*
drill • *I drilled five holes at equal distance.*
lance • *It's a painful experience having the boil lanced.*
penetrate • *The Earth's atmosphere was penetrated by a meteor.*

puncture • *The bullet punctured the skull.*

pig NOUN
a farm animal kept for meat • *the number of pigs at the trough*
hog • *He's as fat as a hog.*
piggy (INFORMAL) • *These two piggies are going to market!*
porker • *a 30kg Vietnamese potbellied porker*
swine • *herds of oxen, sheep, and swine*

RELATED WORDS:
• ADJECTIVE porcine
• MALE boar
• FEMALE sow
• YOUNG piglet
• COLLECTIVE NOUN litter
• HABITATION sty

pile ① NOUN
a quantity of things lying one on top of another • *a pile of books*
heap • *a compost heap*
hoard • *a hoard of jewels*
mound • *The bulldozers piled up huge mounds of dirt.*
mountain • *They have mountains of coffee to sell.*
stack • *a stack of magazines on the table*

pile ② NOUN
the raised fibres of a soft surface • *the carpet's thick pile*
down • *The whole plant is covered with fine down.*
fur • *This creature's fur is short and dense.*
nap • *The cotton is lightly brushed to heighten the nap.*

pile ③ VERB
to put things one on top of another • *A few newspapers were piled on the table.*
heap • *She heaped more carrots onto his plate.*
hoard • *They've begun to hoard gold and silver.*

stack • *They are stacked neatly in piles of three.*

pink NOUN or ADJECTIVE

◆ **SHADES OF PINK**
◆ coral
◆ flesh
◆ fuchsia
◆ oyster pink
◆ rose
◆ salmon
◆ shell pink
◆ shocking pink

pit NOUN
a large hole in something • *He lost his footing and began to slide into the pit.*
chasm • *The coach plunged down the chasm.*
hole • *The builders had cut holes into the soft stone.*
pothole • *She was seriously injured when she fell 90 feet down a pothole.*

pity ① VERB
to feel sorry for someone • *I don't know whether to hate or pity him.*
feel for • *She cried on the phone and I really felt for her.*
feel sorry for • *This is my biggest win but I don't feel sorry for the bookies.*
sympathize with • *I sympathize with you for your loss.*

pity ② NOUN
sympathy for other people's suffering • *She saw no pity in their faces.*
charity • *They showed a lack of charity and understanding to her.*
compassion • *his compassion for a helpless woman*
kindness • *He was treated with kindness by numerous officials.*
mercy • *Neither side showed any mercy.*
sympathy • *We expressed our sympathy for her loss.*
understanding • *We would like*

a
b
c
d
e
f
g
h
i
j
k
l
m
n
o
p
q
r
s
t
u
v
w
x
y
z

A
B
C
D
E
F
G
H
I
J
K
L
M
N
O
P
Q
R
S
T
U
V
W
X
Y
Z

to thank them for their patience and understanding.

MORE SYNONYMS:
• clemency
• forbearance

pity ③ NOUN
a regrettable fact • *It's a pity they can't all have the same opportunities.*
crime (INFORMAL) • *It would be a crime to travel to Australia and not stop in Sydney.*
crying shame • *It would be a crying shame to split up a winning partnership.*
shame • *It's a shame it had to close.*

place ① NOUN
any point or area • *The pain is always in the same place.*
area • *a picnic area*
location • *The first thing he looked at was his office's location.*
point • *The pain originated from a point in his right thigh.*
position • *the ship's position*
site • *a bat sanctuary with special nesting sites*
spot • *the island's top tourist spots*

place ②: take place VERB
to happen • *The meeting took place on Thursday.*
come about • *That came about when we went to Glastonbury last year.*
go on • *This has been going on for around a year.*
happen • *We cannot say for sure what will happen.*
occur • *The crash occurred when the crew shut down the wrong engine.*

place ③ VERB
to put something somewhere • *Chairs were placed in rows for the parents.*
deposit • *Imagine if you were suddenly deposited on a desert island.*

locate • *the best city in which to locate a business*
plant • *So far no one has admitted to planting the bomb.*
position • *plants which are carefully positioned in the alcove*
put • *She put the photograph on her desk.*
situate • *The hotel is situated next to the railway station.*

plain ① ADJECTIVE
very simple in style with no decoration • *It was a plain, grey stone house.*
austere • *The church was austere and simple.*
bare • *bare wooden floors*
spartan • *her spartan home in a tiny village*
stark • *a stark white, characterless fireplace*

ANTONYM:
• fancy

plain ② ADJECTIVE
obvious and easy to recognize or understand • *It was plain to him that I was having a nervous breakdown.*
clear • *The book is clear and readable.*
comprehensible • *a comprehensible manual*
distinct • *a distinct smell of burning coal*
evident • *His footprints were clearly evident in the heavy dust.*
obvious • *an obvious injustice*
unmistakable • *His voice was unmistakable.*

plain ③ NOUN

◆ **TYPES OF PLAIN**
◆ flat
◆ flatland
◆ grassland
◆ llano

- ◆ lowland
- ◆ mesa
- ◆ plateau
- ◆ prairie
- ◆ savannah
- ◆ steppe
- ◆ tableland

plan ① NOUN
a way thought out to do something
• *a plan to amalgamate the two parties*
method • *He did it by his usual method.*
proposal • *The proposals need careful study.*
scheme • *The scheme was an abject failure.*
strategy • *What should our marketing strategy achieve?*
system • *the advantages of the new system over the old one*

plan ② NOUN
a detailed diagram of something
• *a detailed plan of the prison*
blueprint • *a blueprint for a new bathroom*
diagram • *a circuit diagram*
layout • *He tried to recall the layout of the farmhouse.*
scale drawing • *scale drawings of locomotives*

plan ③ VERB
to decide in detail what is to be done
• *when we plan road construction*
arrange • *We arranged a social event once a year.*
design • *He approached me to design the restaurant.*
devise • *We devised a plan.*
draft • *The legislation was drafted by the committee.*
formulate • *He formulated his plan for escape.*

play ① VERB
to take part in games or use toys
• *Polly was playing with her teddy bear.*

amuse oneself • *He amused himself by rollerskating round the building.*
entertain oneself • *I used to entertain myself by building model planes.*
frolic • *Tourists sunbathe and frolic in the ocean.*
have fun • *having fun with your friends*

play ② VERB
to take part in a sport or game • *Alain was playing cards with his friends.*
compete • *Eight entrants competed for the prize.*
participate • *Sixteen teams participated in the tournament.*
take on • *Scotland take on South Africa at Murrayfield.*
take part • *The teams taking part are cricket's bitterest enemies.*
vie with • *Arsenal are vying with Leeds for second spot in the league.*

play ③ NOUN
a piece of drama performed on stage, radio, or television • *Chekhov's best play*
comedy • *a romantic comedy*
drama • *He also wrote radio dramas and film scripts.*
pantomime • *He regularly performs in Christmas pantomimes.*
show • *a one-woman show*
tragedy • *Shakespeare's tragedies*

plead VERB
to beg someone for something • *She pleaded with her daughter to come home.*
appeal • *The United Nations appealed for aid from the international community.*
ask • *I've asked you time and again not to do that.*
beg • *We are not going to beg for help any more.*
beseech (LITERARY) • *She beseeched him to show mercy.*
implore • *Opposition leaders implored the president to break the deadlock.*

a
b
c
d
e
f
g
h
i
j
k
l
m
n
o
p
q
r
s
t
u
v
w
x
y
z

A
B
C
D
E
F
G
H
I
J
K
L
M
N
O
P
Q
R
S
T
U
V
W
X
Y
Z

pleasant ① ADJECTIVE
enjoyable or attractive • *I've got a pleasant little flat.*
agreeable • *workers in more agreeable and better paid occupations*
delightful • *It was the most delightful garden I'd ever seen.*
enjoyable • *an enjoyable meal*
lekker (SOUTH AFRICAN; SLANG) • *a lekker little town*
lovely • *He had a lovely voice.*
nice • *It's nice to be here together again.*
pleasurable • *He found sailing more pleasurable than skiing.*
ANTONYM:
• unpleasant

pleasant ② ADJECTIVE
friendly or charming • *an extremely pleasant and obliging man*
affable • *He is an affable and approachable man.*
amiable • *She had been surprised at how amiable and polite he had seemed.*
charming • *He can be charming to his friends.*
friendly • *She has a friendly relationship with her customers.*
likable or **likeable** • *He's an immensely likable man.*
nice • *He's a nice fellow, very quiet and courteous.*
ANTONYM:
• unpleasant

please VERB
to give pleasure to • *I was tidying my bedroom to please mum.*
amuse • *The thought seemed to amuse him.*
charm • *He charmed all of us.*
delight • *music that has delighted audiences all over the world*
entertain • *Children's TV not only entertains but also teaches.*

pleased ADJECTIVE
happy or satisfied • *I'm pleased with the way things have been going.*
contented • *She had a contented smile on her face.*
delighted • *I know he will be delighted to see you.*
glad • *I'm glad he changed my mind in the end.*
happy • *She's a confident and happy child.*
satisfied • *satisfied customers*

pleasure NOUN
a feeling of happiness and satisfaction • *Everybody takes pleasure in eating.*
amusement • *Her impersonations provided great amusement.*
enjoyment • *her enjoyment of the countryside*
happiness • *My happiness helped to erase the bad memories.*
joy • *tears of joy*
satisfaction • *job satisfaction*

plentiful ADJECTIVE
existing in large amounts • *a plentiful supply*
abundant • *Birds are abundant in the tall vegetation.*
ample • *The design created ample space for a large kitchen.*
bountiful • *a bountiful harvest of fruits and vegetables*
copious • *He attended the lectures and took copious notes.*
infinite • *an infinite variety of landscapes*
MORE SYNONYMS:
• lavish
• profuse
ANTONYM:
• scarce

plenty NOUN
a lot of something • *There's plenty to go round.*

enough • *Have you had enough?*
great deal • *I've spent a great deal of time on this project.*
heaps (INFORMAL) • *You have heaps of time.*
lots (INFORMAL) • *He has made lots of amendments to the script.*
plethora • *a plethora of new products*

plot ① NOUN
a secret plan made by a group of people • *the plot to assassinate Martin Luther King*
conspiracy • *a conspiracy to steal nuclear missiles*
intrigue • *political intrigues*
plan • *a secret government plan to build a nuclear waste dump*
scheme • *an elaborate scheme to dupe the police*

MORE SYNONYMS:
• cabal
• machination
• stratagem

plot ② NOUN
the story of a novel or play • *The film has a ludicrously complicated plot.*
narrative • *a fast-moving narrative*
scenario • *The movie's scenario is nonsensical.*
story • *I doubt the appeal of cinematic sex without a story.*
story line • *It sounds like a typical story line from a soap opera.*

plot ③ VERB
to plan something secretly with others • *Prosecutors allege the defendants plotted to overthrow the government.*
conspire • *The countries had secretly conspired to acquire nuclear weapons.*
hatch • *He hatched a plot to murder his wife.*

plan • *I suspect they are secretly planning to raise taxes.*
scheme • *He claimed that they were scheming against him.*

MORE SYNONYMS:
• cabal
• collude
• machinate

plug ① NOUN
a small, round object for blocking a hole • *She put the plug in the sink and filled it with water.*
bung • *Remove the bung from the barrel.*
cork • *the sound of popping champagne corks*
stopper • *a bottle sealed with a cork stopper*

plug ② VERB
to block a hole with something • *working to plug a major oil leak*
block • *When the shrimp farm is built it will block the stream.*
fill • *Fill small holes with wood filler.*
seal • *She filled the containers and sealed them with a cork.*

plump ADJECTIVE
rather fat • *a plump, fresh-faced young woman*
beefy (INFORMAL) • *beefy bodyguards*
burly • *burly shipyard workers*
chubby • *I was quite chubby as a child.*
fat • *I could eat what I liked without getting fat.*
stout • *He was a tall, stout man of sixty.*
tubby • *He's a bit on the tubby side.*

point ① NOUN
the purpose or meaning something has • *Cutting costs is not the point of the exercise.*
aim • *The aim of this book is to inform you.*
goal • *The goal is to raise a lot of money.*
intention • *It was never my intention to injure anyone.*

object • *It was his object in life to find the island.*

purpose • *He did not know the purpose of Vincent's visit.*

point ② NOUN
a quality or feature • *Tact was never her strong point.*

attribute • *Cruelty is a regrettable attribute of human behaviour.*

characteristic • *their physical characteristics*

feature • *They're one of my best features.*

quality • *mature people with leadership qualities*

side • *the dark side of his character*

trait • *Creativity is a human trait.*

point ③ NOUN
the thin sharp end of something • *the point of a needle*

nib • *the nib of my pen*

prong • *the prongs of a fork*

tip • *the tip of my scissors*

poison NOUN
a substance that can kill people or animals • *Mercury is a known poison.*

toxin • *the liver's ability to break down toxins*

venom • *the cobra's deadly venom*

RELATED WORD:
• ADJECTIVE toxic

poisonous ADJECTIVE
containing something that causes death or illness • *a large cloud of poisonous gas*

noxious • *Many household products give off noxious fumes.*

toxic • *The cost of cleaning up toxic waste.*

venomous • *The adder is Britain's only venomous snake.*

poke ① VERB
to jab or prod someone or something • *She poked a fork into the turkey skin.*

dig • *His companions were digging him in the ribs.*

elbow • *As I tried to get past him he elbowed me in the face.*

jab • *Somebody jabbed an umbrella into his leg.*

nudge • *She nudged me awake after I dozed off.*

prod • *He prodded Murray with the shotgun.*

stab • *He stabbed at Frank with his forefinger.*

poke ② NOUN
a jab or prod • *She gave Richard a playful poke.*

dig • *She silenced him with a sharp dig in the small of the back.*

jab • *a quick jab of the brakes*

nudge • *She slipped her arm under his and gave him a nudge.*

prod • *He gave the donkey a mighty prod in the backside.*

polish ① VERB
to make smooth and shiny by rubbing • *He polished his shoes every morning.*

buff • *He was already buffing the car's hubs.*

shine • *Let him dust and shine the furniture.*

wax • *a Sunday morning spent washing and waxing the car*

polish ② VERB
to improve a skill or technique • *Polish up your writing skills.*

brush up • *She spent the summer brushing up on her driving.*

improve • *I want to improve my golf game.*

perfect • *We perfected a hand-signal system.*

refine • *Surgical techniques are constantly being refined.*

polish ③ NOUN

elegance or refinement • *The opera lacks the polish of his later work.*

class (INFORMAL) • *For sheer class, Mark Waugh is the best batsman of the World Cup.*

elegance • *The furniture combined practicality with elegance.*

finesse • *It's good but it lacks the finesse of vintage champagne.*

grace • *Ballet classes are important for learning poise and grace.*

refinement • *a girl who possessed both dignity and refinement*

style • *Paris, you have to admit, has style.*

MORE SYNONYMS:
• politesse
• suavity
• urbanity

polite ① ADJECTIVE

having good manners • *It's not polite to point at people.*

civil • *I have to force myself to be civil to him.*

courteous • *Her reply was courteous but firm.*

respectful • *Their children are always respectful to their elders.*

well-behaved • *well-behaved little girls*

well-mannered • *a very pleasant and well-mannered student*

ANTONYM:
• rude

polite ② ADJECTIVE

cultivated or refined • *Certain words are not acceptable in polite society.*

cultured • *He is immensely cultured and well-read.*

genteel • *two ladies with genteel manners and voices*

refined • *His speech and manner are very refined.*

sophisticated • *Recently her tastes have become more sophisticated.*

urbane • *She describes him as charming and urbane.*

politeness NOUN

the quality of being civil to someone • *She listened to him but only out of politeness.*

civility • *Handle customers with tact and civility.*

courtesy • *He did not even have the courtesy to reply to my fax.*

decency • *He should have had the decency to inform me.*

etiquette • *the rules of diplomatic etiquette*

pollute VERB

to contaminate with something harmful • *Heavy industry pollutes our rivers with noxious chemicals.*

contaminate • *Have any fish been contaminated in the Arctic Ocean?*

infect • *a virus which is spread mainly by infected blood*

poison • *Drilling operations have poisoned the Nile delta.*

taint • *blood tainted with the hepatitis viruses*

MORE SYNONYMS:
• adulterate
• befoul
• smirch

pompous ADJECTIVE

behaving in a way that is too serious and self-important • *a pompous man with a high opinion of his own capabilities*

arrogant • *an air of arrogant indifference*

grandiose • *grandiose plans which never got off the ground*

ostentatious • *an ostentatious wedding reception*

a b c d e f g h i j k l m n o **p** q r s t u v w x y z

A
B
C
D
E
F
G
H
I
J
K
L
M
N
O
P
Q
R
S
T
U
V
W
X
Y
Z

pretentious • *His response was full of pretentious nonsense.*
puffed up • *He is puffed up with own importance.*

MORE SYNONYMS:
• pontifical
• portentous
• vainglorious

ponder VERB
to think about something deeply • *I'm continually pondering how to improve the team.*
brood • *I guess everyone broods over things once in a while.*
consider • *You have to consider the feelings of those around you.*
contemplate • *He lay in bed contemplating his future.*
mull over • *I'll leave you alone here so you can mull it over.*
reflect • *I reflected on the child's future.*
think • *I have often thought about this problem.*

poor ① ADJECTIVE
having little money • *They see the government ignoring poor people.*
broke (INFORMAL) • *He was broke when I married him.*
destitute • *destitute people living on the streets*
hard up (INFORMAL) • *Her parents were very hard up.*
impoverished • *one of the most impoverished suburbs of Rio de Janeiro*
penniless • *a penniless refugee*
poverty-stricken • *a teacher of poverty-stricken kids*

ANTONYM:
• rich

poor ② ADJECTIVE
of a low quality or standard • *He was a poor actor.*

feeble • *a feeble attempt to save Figo's shot*
inferior • *The cassettes were of inferior quality.*
mediocre • *His school record was mediocre.*
second-rate • *Passengers are fed up using a second-rate service.*
shoddy • *shoddy goods*
unsatisfactory • *questions to which he received unsatisfactory answers*

popular ① ADJECTIVE
liked or approved of by a lot of people • *These delicious pastries will be very popular.*
fashionable • *fashionable wine bars*
favourite • *Britain's favourite soap opera*
in demand • *He was much in demand as a lecturer.*
in favour • *He is now back in favour with the manager.*
sought-after • *one of the most sought-after new names in Hollywood*
well-liked • *She was very sociable and well-liked by the other students.*

ANTONYM:
• unpopular

popular ② ADJECTIVE
involving or intended for ordinary people • *the popular press*
common • *Much of the countryside has fallen out of common ownership and into private hands.*
conventional • *a respectable married woman with conventional opinions*
general • *general awareness about bullying*
universal • *universal health care*

portion NOUN
a part or amount of something • *I have spent a considerable portion of my life here.*

bit · *I missed the first bit of the meeting.*
chunk · *Cut the melon into chunks.*
helping · *She gave them extra helpings of ice-cream.*
part · *A large part of his earnings went on repaying the loan.*
piece · *Do you want another piece?*
segment · *the middle segment of his journey*
serving · *Each serving contains 240 calories.*

pose ① VERB

to ask a question · *When I finally posed the question, "Why?" he merely shrugged.*
ask · *I wasn't the only one asking questions.*
put · *Some workers may be afraid to put questions publicly.*
submit · *Passengers are invited to submit questions.*

MORE SYNONYMS:
• posit
• propound

pose ② VERB

to pretend to be someone else · *The team posed as drug dealers to trap the ringleaders.*
impersonate · *He was once jailed for impersonating a policeman.*
masquerade as · *He masqueraded as a doctor and fooled everyone.*
pass oneself off as · *He frequently passed himself off as a lawyer.*
pretend to be · *We spent the afternoon pretending to be foreign tourists.*

posh ① ADJECTIVE (INFORMAL)

smart, fashionable and expensive · *a posh hotel*
classy (INFORMAL) · *expensive cars with classy brand names*
elegant · *an elegant society ball*
exclusive · *a member of Britain's most exclusive club*

fashionable · *fashionable restaurants*
smart · *smart London dinner parties*
stylish · *stylish décor*
up-market · *an up-market agency aimed at professional people*

posh ② ADJECTIVE

upper-class · *He sounded very posh on the phone.*
aristocratic · *a wealthy, aristocratic family*
genteel · *two ladies with genteel manners and voices*
upper-class · *upper-class speech*

MORE SYNONYMS:
• blue-blooded
• patrician (FORMAL)

ANTONYM:
• common

position ① NOUN

the place where someone or something is · *The ship's name and position were reported to the coastguard.*
location · *She knew the exact location of their headquarters.*
place · *The pain is always in the same place.*
point · *The pain originated from a point in his right thigh.*
whereabouts · *Finding his whereabouts proved surprisingly easy.*

position ② VERB

to put something somewhere · *Position trailing plants near the edges.*
arrange · *Arrange the books in neat piles.*
lay out · *Grace laid out the knives and forks at the table.*
locate · *the best city in which to locate a business*
place · *Chairs were placed in rows for the parents.*
put · *She put the photograph on her desk.*

a
b
c
d
e
f
g
h
i
j
k
l
m
n
o
p
q
r
s
t
u
v
w
x
y
z

positive ① ADJECTIVE
completely sure about something
• I was positive he'd known about that money.
certain • It wasn't a balloon – I'm certain about that.
confident • Mr Ryan is confident of success.
convinced • He was convinced that I was part of the problem.
sure • It is impossible to be sure about the value of the land.

positive ② ADJECTIVE
providing definite proof of the truth or identity of something • positive evidence
clear • a clear case of mistaken identity
clear-cut • The issue is not so clear-cut.
conclusive • Research on the matter is far from conclusive.
concrete • He had no concrete evidence.
firm • There is no firm evidence to prove this.

MORE SYNONYMS:
• incontrovertible
• indisputable
• unequivocal

positive ③ ADJECTIVE
tending to emphasize what is good
• I anticipate a positive response.
constructive • We welcome constructive criticism.
helpful • Camilla's helpful comments

ANTONYM:
• negative

possess ① VERB
to have something as a quality • He possesses both stamina and great technique.
be blessed with • She was blessed with a photographic memory.
be born with • Mozart was born with perfect pitch.
enjoy • I have always enjoyed good health.
have • They have talent in abundance.

possess ② VERB
to own something • He was said to possess a huge fortune.
acquire • I have acquired a new car.
control • He now controls the entire company.
hold • He does not hold a firearm certificate.
occupy • US forces now occupy part of the country.
seize • Troops have seized the airport and railway terminals.
take over • They plan to take over another airline.

possession NOUN
ownership of something • How did this picture come into your possession?
control • The restructuring involves his giving up control of the firm.
custody • She will have custody of their two children.
ownership • the growth of home ownership
tenure • his 28-year tenure of the house

possessions PLURAL NOUN
the things owned by someone
• People had lost all their possessions.
assets • The group had assets worth over 10 million dollars.
belongings • He was identified only by his personal belongings.
effects • His daughters were collecting his effects.
estate • She left her entire estate to a charity.
property • the rightful owner of the property
things • She told him to take all his things and not to return.

possibility NOUN
something that might be true or
might happen • *the possibility of a ban*
chance • *There's no chance of that
happening.*
hope • *We had absolutely no hope of
raising the money.*
likelihood • *the likelihood of infection*
odds • *What are the odds of that
happening?*
prospect • *There is little prospect of
peace.*
risk • *It reduces the risk of heart disease.*

possible ① ADJECTIVE
likely to happen or able to be done
• *I am grateful to the staff for making
this work possible.*
attainable • *I always thought
promotion was attainable.*
feasible • *Whether such cooperation
is feasible is a matter of doubt.*
practicable • *It was not reasonably
practicable for Mr Tyler to attend.*
viable • *commercially viable products*
workable • *This isn't a workable
solution in most cases.*

ANTONYM:
• impossible

possible ② ADJECTIVE
likely or capable of being true
or correct • *It's possible there's an
explanation for all this.*
conceivable • *It is just conceivable
that a survivor might be found.*
imaginable • *a place of no imagin
able strategic value*
likely • *Experts say a "yes" vote is still
the likely outcome.*
potential • *the channel's potential
audience*

postpone VERB
to put off to a later time • *The visit
has been postponed until tomorrow.*

adjourn • *The proceedings have been
adjourned until next week.*
defer • *Customers often defer payments
for as long as possible.*
delay • *I wanted to delay my departure
until June.*
put back • *The news conference has
been put back a couple of hours.*
put off • *The Association has put off the
event until October.*
shelve • *Sadly, the project has now been
shelved.*

potential ① ADJECTIVE
possible but not yet actual • *potential
sources of finance*
likely • *A draw is the likely outcome.*
possible • *Her family is discussing a
possible move to America.*
probable • *A bomb was the accident's
most probable cause.*

potential ② NOUN
ability to achieve future success
• *Denmark recognized the potential of
wind energy early.*
ability • *You have the ability to become a
good pianist.*
aptitude • *more aptitude for academic
work than the others*
capability • *We experience differences
in mental capability depending on the
time of day.*
capacity • *people's creative capacities*
power • *the power of speech*
wherewithal • *She didn't have the
financial wherewithal to do it.*

pour VERB
to flow quickly and in large quantities
• *Blood was pouring from his broken
nose.*
course • *The tears coursed down her
cheeks.*
flow • *compressor stations that keep the
gas flowing*
gush • *Piping-hot water gushed out.*

a
b
c
d
e
f
g
h
i
j
k
l
m
n
o
p
q
r
s
t
u
v
w
x
y
z

run • *Water was running down the walls.*
spout • *The water spouted 40 feet into the air.*
stream • *She came in, rain streaming from her clothes and hair.*

poverty NOUN
the state of being very poor • *Garvey died in loneliness and poverty.*
destitution • *refugees living in destitution*
hardship • *Many people are suffering economic hardship.*
insolvency • *Several companies are on the brink of insolvency.*
want • *We are fighting for freedom from want.*

MORE SYNONYMS:
• beggary
• indigence
• penury
• privation

power ① NOUN
control over people and activities • *a position of great power and influence*
ascendancy • *The extremists in the party are gaining ascendancy.*
control • *He has been forced to give up control over the company.*
dominion • *They truly believe they have dominion over us.*
sovereignty • *the resumption of Chinese sovereignty over Hong Kong in 1997*
supremacy • *The party has re-established its supremacy.*

power ② NOUN
authority to do something • *The police have the power of arrest.*
authority • *The judge had no authority to order a second trial.*
authorization • *I don't have the authorization to make such a decision.*
licence • *He has given me licence to do the job as I see fit.*

privilege • *the ancient powers and privileges of parliament*
right • *the right to vote*

power ③ NOUN
physical strength • *Power and bulk are vital to success in rugby.*
brawn • *He's got plenty of brains as well as brawn.*
might • *The might of the army could prove a decisive factor.*
strength • *He threw it forward with all his strength.*
vigour • *His body lacks the vigour of a normal two-year-old.*

powerful ① ADJECTIVE
able to control people and events • *Russia and India, two large, powerful countries*
commanding • *We're in a more commanding position than we've been in for ages.*
dominant • *He was a dominant figure in the Italian film industry.*
influential • *He had been influential in shaping economic policy.*

powerful ② ADJECTIVE
physically strong • *It's such a big powerful dog.*
mighty • *a mighty river*
strapping • *He was a bricklayer - a big, strapping fellow.*
strong • *I'm not strong enough to carry him.*
sturdy • *The camera was mounted on a sturdy tripod.*
vigorous • *He was a vigorous, handsome young man.*

ANTONYM:
• weak

powerful ③ ADJECTIVE
having a strong effect • *a powerful argument*

compelling • *a compelling reason to leave*
convincing • *convincing evidence*
effective • *Antibiotics are effective against this organism.*
forceful • *forceful action to stop the suffering*
persuasive • *Mr. Knight made a persuasive case for removing the tax.*
telling • *He spoke reasonably, carefully, and with telling effect.*

powerless ADJECTIVE
unable to control or influence events • *I was powerless to save her.*
helpless • *Many people felt helpless against the violence.*
impotent • *The West is impotent to influence the Balkan war.*
incapable • *He is incapable as a manager.*

practical ① ADJECTIVE
involving experience rather than theory • *practical suggestions for healthy eating*
applied • *plans to put more money into applied research*
pragmatic • *a pragmatic approach to the problems of Latin America*

practical ② ADJECTIVE
likely to be effective • *The clothes are lightweight and practical for holidays.*
functional • *The design is functional but stylish.*
sensible • *sensible footwear*
ANTONYM:
• impractical

practical ③ ADJECTIVE
able to deal effectively with problems • *the practical common sense essential in management*
accomplished • *an accomplished cook*
experienced • *a team packed with experienced professionals*

proficient • *A great number of them are proficient in foreign languages.*
seasoned • *The author is a seasoned academic.*
skilled • *amateur but highly skilled observers of wildlife*
veteran • *a veteran broadcaster*

practice ① NOUN
something that people do regularly • *a public inquiry into bank practices*
custom • *I have tried to adapt to local customs.*
habit • *a survey on eating habits*
method • *her usual method of getting through the traffic*
routine • *We had to change our daily routine and lifestyle.*
way • *a return to the old ways of doing things*

practice ② NOUN
regular training or exercise • *I need more practice.*
drill • *The teacher ran them through the drill again.*
exercise • *Lack of exercise can lead to feelings of exhaustion.*
preparation • *Behind any successful event lie months of preparation.*
rehearsal • *rehearsals for a concert tour*
training • *her busy training schedule*

practise ① VERB
to do something repeatedly so as to gain skill • *Lauren practises the piano every day.*
polish • *They just need to polish their technique.*
rehearse • *She was in her room rehearsing her lines.*
train • *He was training for the new season.*

practise ② VERB
to take part in the activities of a religion, craft, or custom

a
b
c
d
e
f
g
h
i
j
k
l
m
n
o
p
q
r
s
t
u
v
w
x
y
z

• *Acupuncture has been practised in China for thousands of years.*
do • *I used to do karate.*
follow • *Do you follow any particular religion?*
observe • *American forces are observing Christmas quietly.*

praise ① VERB
to express strong approval of someone • *Many others praised Sanford for taking a strong stand.*
admire • *All those who knew him will admire him for his work.*
applaud • *He should be applauded for his courage.*
approve • *Not everyone approves of the festival.*
congratulate • *I must congratulate the organizers on a well run event.*
pay tribute to • *He paid tribute to his captain.*

MORE SYNONYMS:
• acclaim
• eulogize
• extol
• laud

ANTONYM:
• criticize

praise ② NOUN
something said or written to show approval • *She is full of praise for the range of services available.*
accolade • *the ultimate international accolade, the Nobel Peace Prize*
approval • *an obsessive drive to gain her mother's approval*
commendation • *They received a commendation from the Royal Society of Arts.*
congratulation • *I offered her my congratulations.*
tribute • *We marched past in tribute to our fallen comrades.*

MORE SYNONYMS:
• encomium
• eulogy
• panegyric

ANTONYM:
• criticism

precaution NOUN
an action intended to prevent something from happening • *It's still worth taking precautions against accidents.*
insurance • *Farmers grew a mixture of crops as an insurance against crop failure.*
preventative measure • *a preventative measure against heart disease*
protection • *protection against damage to buildings*
provision • *People need to make decent provision for their old age.*
safeguard • *legislation that offers safeguards against discrimination*

precious ADJECTIVE
of great value and importance • *precious jewels*
expensive • *an expensive new coat*
invaluable • *I was to gain invaluable experience over that year.*
priceless • *his priceless collection of Chinese art*
prized • *These shells were very highly prized by the Indians.*
valuable • *valuable books*

ANTONYM:
• worthless

precise ADJECTIVE
exact and accurate • *We may never know the precise details.*
accurate • *an accurate description of his attackers*
actual • *The actual number of victims is higher than statistics suggest.*

correct · *This information was correct at the time of going to press.*
exact · *The exact number of protest calls has not been revealed.*
particular · *a very particular account of events*
specific · *I asked him to be more specific.*
very · *Those were his very words.*

ANTONYM:
• vague

predicament NOUN
a difficult situation · *The decision will leave her in a peculiar predicament.*
fix (INFORMAL) · *The government has really got itself into a fix.*
hot water (INFORMAL) · *His antics keep landing him in hot water with officials.*
jam (INFORMAL) · *We are in a real jam now.*
scrape (INFORMAL) · *He's had his fair share of scrapes with the law.*
tight spot · *This was one tight spot he couldn't get out of.*

predict VERB
to say that something will happen in the future · *The opinion polls are predicting a very close contest.*
forecast · *He forecasts that house prices will rise by 5% this year.*
foresee · *He did not foresee any problems.*
foretell · *prophets who have foretold the end of the world*
prophesy · *She prophesied a bad ending for the expedition.*

MORE SYNONYMS:
• forebode
• portend
• presage
• prognosticate
• soothsay

prediction NOUN
something that is forecast in advance · *He was unwilling to make a prediction for the coming year.*
forecast · *a forecast of heavy weather to come*
prophecy · *the interpreters of Biblical prophecy*

prefer VERB
to like one thing more than another thing · *Does he prefer a particular sort of music?*
be partial to · *I'm quite partial to mussels.*
favour · *Both sides favour a diplomatic solution.*
go for · *They went for a more up-market approach.*
incline towards · *The majority incline towards a forgiving attitude.*
like better · *I like the flat shoes better.*

prefix NOUN
◆ **PREFIXES**
◆ ante-
◆ anti-
◆ auto-
◆ bi-
◆ centi-
◆ co-
◆ contra-
◆ de-
◆ demi-
◆ dis-
◆ ex-
◆ extra-
◆ hyper-
◆ in-
◆ inter-
◆ intra-
◆ mega-
◆ micro-
◆ mid-
◆ milli-
◆ mini-

a b c d e f g h i j k l m n o **p** q r s t u v w x y z

- mono-
- multi-
- neo-
- non-
- over-
- poly-
- post-
- pre-
- pro-
- pseudo-
- re-
- self-
- semi-
- step-
- sub-
- super-
- tele-
- trans-
- tri-
- ultra-
- un-
- under-
- vice-

prejudice ① NOUN
an unreasonable or unfair dislike or preference • *prejudice against workers over 45*
bias • *Bias against women permeates every level of the judicial system.*
partiality • *She is criticized for her one-siddedness and partiality.*
preconception • *preconceptions about the sort of people who did computing*

prejudice ② NOUN
intolerance towards certain people or groups • *racial prejudice*
bigotry • *religious bigotry*
chauvinism • *the growth of Russian chauvinism*
discrimination • *sex discrimination*
racism • *the fight to rid sport of racism*
sexism • *sexism in the workplace*

premonition NOUN
a feeling that something unpleasant is going to happen • *He had a premonition that he would die.*
foreboding • *His triumph was overshadowed by an uneasy sense of foreboding.*
funny feeling (INFORMAL) • *I have a funny feeling something unpleasant is about to happen.*
omen • *Her appearance at this moment is an omen of disaster.*
sign • *a sign of impending doom*

MORE SYNONYMS:
- portent
- presage
- presentiment

preoccupied ADJECTIVE
totally involved with something or deep in thought • *I am preoccupied with my tennis career.*
absorbed • *They were completely absorbed in each other.*
engrossed • *Tom didn't notice because he was too engrossed in his work.*
immersed • *He's becoming really immersed in his studies.*
oblivious • *When he was in his car he was totally oblivious to everybody else.*
wrapped up • *She's wrapped up in her new career.*

present ① ADJECTIVE
being at a place or event • *He had been present at the birth of his son.*
at hand • *Having the right equipment at hand will be very useful.*
here • *He was here a minute ago.*
in attendance • *Police and several fire engines are in attendance.*
there • *The group of old buildings is still there today.*
to hand • *I haven't got the instructions to hand.*

ANTONYM:
- absent

present ② NOUN
something given to someone • *a birthday present*
bonsela (SOUTH AFRICAN) • *your kind bonsela to the hospital*
donation • *Employees make regular donations to charity.*
gift • *a Christmas gift*
offering • *Hindus kill turtles ritually as an offering to their gods.*

present ③ VERB
to give something to someone • *The Mayor presented the prizes.*
award • *For his dedication he was awarded a medal of merit.*
bestow • *The Queen bestowed on him a knighthood.*
donate • *He frequently donates large sums to charity.*
give • *She gave me a pen for my birthday.*
grant • *France has agreed to grant him political asylum.*
hand out • *One of my jobs was to hand out the prizes.*

press ① VERB
to apply force or weight to something • *Press the blue button.*
compress • *Poor posture compresses the body's organs.*
crush • *Peel and crush the garlic.*
mash • *Mash the bananas with a fork.*
push • *She pushed the door open.*
squeeze • *He squeezed her arm reassuringly.*

press ② VERB
to try hard to persuade someone to do something • *Trade Unions are pressing him to stand firm.*
beg • *I begged him to come back with me.*
implore • *"Tell me what to do!" she implored him.*
petition • *All the attempts to petition the government had failed.*

plead • *I pleaded to be allowed to go.*
pressurize • *He thought she was trying to pressurize him.*
urge • *He had urged her to come to Ireland.*

MORE SYNONYMS:
• entreat
• exhort
• importune

pretend VERB
to claim or give the appearance of something untrue • *Sometimes the boy pretended to be asleep.*
counterfeit • *the coins he is alleged to have counterfeited*
fake • *He faked his own death last year.*
falsify • *He was charged with falsifying business records.*
feign • *The striker was accused of feigning injury.*
pass oneself off as • *She tried to pass herself off as an actress.*

pretentious ADJECTIVE
making unjustified claims to importance • *Many critics thought her work and ideas pretentious and empty.*
affected • *She passed along with an affected air and a disdainful look.*
conceited • *I thought him conceited and arrogant.*
ostentatious • *an ostentatious wedding reception*
pompous • *He's pompous and has a high opinion of his own capabilities.*
snobbish • *a snobbish dislike for their intellectual inferiors*

MORE SYNONYMS:
• bombastic
• grandiloquent
• magniloquent
• vainglorious

pretty ① ADJECTIVE

attractive in a delicate way • She's a very charming and very pretty girl.
attractive • She has a round attractive face.
beautiful • a beautiful child
cute • a cute little baby
lovely • his lovely wife

pretty ② ADVERB (INFORMAL)

quite or rather • He spoke pretty good English.
fairly • Both ships are fairly new.
kind of (INFORMAL) • I was kind of embarrassed about it.
quite • It was quite hard.
rather • She's rather vain.

prevent VERB

to stop something from happening • the most practical way of preventing crime
avert • A fresh tragedy was narrowly averted yesterday.
foil • The plot was foiled by policemen.
hinder • Research is hindered by lack of cash.
impede • Fallen rocks are impeding the progress of the rescue workers.
stop • a new diplomatic initiative to try to stop the war
thwart • Her ambition to become an artist was thwarted by failing eyesight.

previous ADJECTIVE

happening or existing before something else • the previous year
earlier • His earlier works include impressive still lifes.
former • a former president of Mexico
one-time • the country's one-time military rulers
past • a return to the turbulence of past centuries
preceding • This is examined in detail in the preceding chapter.

prior • I can't make it. I have a prior engagement.

price ① NOUN

the amount of money paid for something • a sharp increase in the price of petrol
amount • I was asked to pay the full amount.
charge • an annual management charge of 1.25%
cost • the cost of a loaf of bread
fee • the annual membership fee
figure • A figure of £2000 was mentioned.
value • The company's market value rose to 5.5 billion dollars.

price ② VERB

to fix the price or value of something • I just can't imagine why it has been priced at this level.
cost • We hope it won't cost too much.
estimate • His personal riches were estimated at $368 million.
put a price on • The company has refused to put a price on its bid.
value • I had my jewellery valued for insurance purposes.

pride ① NOUN

a feeling of satisfaction about your achievements • We take pride in offering you the highest standards.
delight • Haig took obvious delight in proving his critics wrong.
pleasure • Our first win gave me great pleasure.
satisfaction • His success was a great source of satisfaction to him.

pride ② NOUN

an excessively high opinion of yourself • His pride may still be his downfall.
arrogance • He has a swaggering arrogance.

conceit · *He knew, without conceit, that he was considered a genius.*
egotism · *typical showbiz egotism*
smugness · *a trace of smugness in his voice*
snobbery · *intellectual snobbery*
vanity · *her vanity about her long hair*

MORE SYNONYMS:
• haughtiness
• hauteur
• hubris
• superciliousness

ANTONYM:
• humility

priest NOUN

◆ **TYPES OF PRIEST**
◆ guru (HINDUISM and SIKHISM)
◆ high priest or high priestess
◆ imam (ISLAM)
◆ lama (BUDDHISM)
◆ minister (CHRISTIANITY)
◆ priest
◆ rabbi (JUDAISM)
◆ shaman or medicine man
◆ vicar (CHRISTIANITY)

prim ADJECTIVE
behaving very correctly and easily shocked by anything rude · *We tend to assume the Victorians were very prim and proper.*
proper · *He was very pompous and proper.*
prudish · *I'm not prudish but I think those photos are obscene.*
puritanical · *He has a puritanical attitude towards sex.*
strait-laced · *He is very strait-laced and narrow-minded.*

prime ① ADJECTIVE
main or most important · *a prime cause of brain damage*
chief · *The job went to one of his chief rivals.*

leading · *a leading industrial nation*
main · *the city's main tourist area*
principal · *our principal source of foreign exchange earnings*

prime ② ADJECTIVE
of the best quality · *prime beef*
best · *He'll have the best care.*
choice · *our choicest chocolates*
first-rate · *He's a first-rate officer.*
select · *With that historic win he now joins a select band of golfers.*
superior · *superior coffee beans*

primitive ADJECTIVE
very simple or basic · *a very small primitive cottage*
crude · *crude stone carvings*
rough · *a rough wooden table*
rude · *He constructed a rude cabin for himself.*
rudimentary · *The bomb was rudimentary but lethal.*
simple · *a simple shelter*

principal ADJECTIVE
main or most important · *Their principal concern is that of winning the election.*
chief · *his chief reason for withdrawing*
first · *The first duty of this government is to tackle poverty.*
foremost · *one of the world's foremost scholars of classical poetry*
main · *What are the main differences between them?*
major · *the major factor in her decision*
primary · *the primary cause of his problems*
prime · *Police will see me as the prime suspect!*

principle ① NOUN
a set of moral rules guiding personal conduct · *a woman of principle*
conscience · *the law on freedom of conscience and religious organizations*

integrity • *He has always been a man of integrity.*
morals • *public morals*
scruples • *a man with no moral scruples*
sense of duty • *He did it out of a sense of duty to his men.*

principle ② NOUN

a general rule or scientific law • *the basic principles of Marxism*
axiom • *the long-held axiom that education leads to higher income*
canon • *the canons of political economy*
doctrine • *Christian doctrine*
fundamental • *the fundamentals of astronomy*
law • *the laws of motion*

MORE SYNONYMS:
• dictum
• precept
• verity

printing NOUN

◆ **PRINTING WORDS**
◆ bold print
◆ character
◆ fount *or* font
◆ italics
◆ lower case
◆ roman
◆ type size
◆ typeface
◆ upper case

prison NOUN

a building where criminals are kept in captivity • *a high-security prison*
dungeon • *The castle's dungeons haven't been used for years.*
jail • *Three prisoners escaped from the jail.*
nick (BRITISH, AUSTRALIAN AND NEW ZEALAND; SLANG) • *I was banged up in the nick for six months.*

penal institution • *Thirty years in a penal institution is indeed a harsh penalty.*

prisoner NOUN

someone kept in prison or captivity • *top-security prisoners*
captive • *the difficulties of spending four months as a captive*
convict • *convicts serving life sentences*
hostage • *negotiations to release the hostages*

private ① ADJECTIVE

for few people rather than people in general • *a private bathroom*
exclusive • *Many of our cheeses are exclusive to our shops in Britain.*
individual • *Divide the vegetables among four individual dishes.*
personal • *It's for my own personal use.*
special • *her own special problems*

private ② ADJECTIVE

taking place among a small number of people • *He was buried in a private ceremony.*
clandestine • *He had a clandestine meeting with his lover.*
confidential • *confidential information about her private life*
secret • *a secret love affair*

ANTONYM:
• public

prize ① NOUN

a reward given to the winner of something • *He won first prize at the Leeds Piano Competition.*
accolade • *the ultimate international accolade, the Nobel Peace Prize*
award • *the Booker Prize, Britain's top award for fiction*
honour • *He was showered with honours - among them an Oscar.*
trophy • *They haven't won a trophy since 1991.*

prize ② ADJECTIVE
of the highest quality or standard
• *a prize bull*
award-winning • *an award-winning restaurant*
first-rate • *a first-rate thriller writer*
outstanding • *an outstanding horse*
top • *Holland's top striker*

prize ③ VERB
to value highly • *These ornaments are prized by collectors.*
cherish • *We cherish our independence.*
esteem • *one of Europe's most esteemed awards*
treasure • *She treasures her memories of those joyous days.*
value • *I value the work he gives me.*

probability NOUN
the likelihood of something happening • *the probability of a serious earthquake*
chances • *The chances of success for the product are good.*
likelihood • *the likelihood of infection*
odds • *The odds are that you are going to fail.*
prospect • *the prospect for peace in Rwanda*

probable ADJECTIVE
likely to be true or to happen • *a misunderstanding about the probable cost*
apparent • *There is no apparent reason for the crime.*
feasible • *Whether this is feasible is a matter of doubt.*
likely • *Further delays are likely.*
on the cards • *A promotion is definitely on the cards for you.*
plausible • *a plausible explanation*
MORE SYNONYMS:
• credible

• ostensible
• verisimilar
ANTONYM:
• improbable

probably ADVERB
in all likelihood • *The wedding's probably going to be in late August.*
doubtless • *He will doubtless try to change my mind.*
in all probability • *Victory will, in all probability, earn France the title.*
likely • *The entire surplus will most likely be handed over.*
presumably • *The spear is presumably the murder weapon.*

problem ① NOUN
an unsatisfactory situation causing difficulties • *the economic problems of the inner city*
difficulty • *This company is facing great difficulties.*
predicament • *the once great club's current predicament*
quandary • *We're in a quandary over our holiday plans.*
trouble • *I had trouble parking this morning.*

problem ② NOUN
a puzzle that needs to be solved • *a mathematical problem*
conundrum • *an apparently insoluble conundrum*
puzzle • *The data has presented astronomers with a puzzle.*
riddle • *the riddle of the birth of the universe*

procedure NOUN
the correct or usual way of doing something • *He did not follow the correct procedure in applying for a visa.*
method • *new teaching methods*
policy • *It is our policy to prosecute shoplifters.*

a
b
c
d
e
f
g
h
i
j
k
l
m
n
o
p
q
r
s
t
u
v
w
x
y
z

practice • *a public inquiry into bank practices*
process • *the production process*
strategy • *a strategy for controlling malaria*
system • *an efficient filing system*

proceed ① VERB
to start doing or continue to do something • *I had no idea how to proceed.*
begin • *He stood up and began to move about the room.*
carry on • *"Can I start with a couple of questions?" - "Carry on."*
continue • *I need some advice before I can continue with this task.*
get under way • *The court case got under way last autumn.*
go on • *Go on with your work.*
start • *I started to follow him up the stairs.*
ANTONYM:
• cease

proceed ② VERB (FORMAL)
to move in a particular direction • *She proceeded along the hallway.*
advance • *I advanced slowly, one step at a time.*
continue • *He continued rapidly up the path.*
go on • *They went on through the forest.*
make your way • *He made his way to the marketplace.*
progress • *He progressed slowly along the coast in an easterly direction.*
travel • *You can travel to Helsinki tomorrow.*

process ① NOUN
a method of doing or producing something • *The building process was spread over three years.*
course of action • *It is important that we take the right course of action.*

means • *The move is a means to fight crime.*
method • *new teaching methods*
procedure • *the correct procedure for applying for a visa*
system • *an efficient filing system*

process ② VERB
to deal with or treat something • *Your application is being processed.*
deal with • *the way that banks deal with complaints*
dispose of • *They disposed of the problem quickly.*
handle • *She didn't know how to handle the situation.*
take care of • *They left it to me to try and take care of everything.*

produce ① VERB
to make something • *a white wine produced mainly from black grapes*
construct • *an inner frame constructed from timber*
create • *It was created from odds and ends.*
invent • *He invented the first electric clock.*
make • *One of my jobs was to make the tea.*
manufacture • *They manufacture plastics.*

produce ② VERB
to bring out something so it can be seen or discussed • *To hire a car you must produce a driving licence.*
advance • *Many new theories have been advanced recently.*
bring forward • *We will bring forward new proposals for legislation.*
bring to light • *new evidence brought to light by the police*
put forward • *He has put forward new peace proposals.*

product NOUN
something that is made to be sold

• Many household products give off noxious fumes.

commodity • basic commodities such as bread and milk

goods • imported goods

merchandise • The club sells a wide range of merchandise.

produce • locally grown produce

productive ① ADJECTIVE

producing a large number of things • Training makes workers highly productive.

fertile • a product of his fertile imagination

fruitful • a landscape that was fruitful and lush

prolific • She is a prolific writer of novels and short stories.

MORE SYNONYMS:
• fecund
• generative

ANTONYM:
• unproductive

productive ② ADJECTIVE

bringing favourable results • I'm hopeful the talks will be productive.

constructive • constructive criticism

useful • We made some progress during a useful exchange.

valuable • The experience was very valuable.

worthwhile • It had been a worthwhile discussion.

ANTONYM:
• unproductive

profession NOUN

a job that requires advanced education or training • Harper was a teacher by profession.

business • May I ask you what business you're in?

career • a career in journalism

occupation • her new occupation as an author

proficient ADJECTIVE

able to do something well • They tend to be proficient in foreign languages.

able • an able young rider

accomplished • an accomplished fundraiser

adept • an adept guitar player

capable • a very capable speaker

competent • a competent civil servant

efficient • a team of efficient workers

skilful • He is skilful at managing people.

skilled • a network of amateur but highly skilled observers of wildlife

ANTONYM:
• incompetent

profit ① NOUN

money gained in business or trade • The bank made pre-tax profits of $3.5 million.

earnings • his earnings as an accountant

proceeds • The proceeds from the concert will go to charity.

revenue • tax revenues

surplus • Japan's trade surplus

takings • the pub's weekly takings

ANTONYM:
• loss

profit ② VERB

to gain or benefit from something • They profited shamefully at the expense of my family.

capitalize on • The rebels are trying to capitalize on the public's discontent.

exploit • They are trying to exploit the troubles to their advantage.

make the most of • Happiness is the ability to make the most of what you have.

take advantage of • She took advantage of him even after their divorce.

a
b
c
d
e
f
g
h
i
j
k
l
m
n
o
p
q
r
s
t
u
v
w
x
y
z

program NOUN

a set of instructions that a computer follows to perform a task • *a program to convert dollars to pounds*

app • *This app allows you to search by date or location.*

application • *a great application for editing photographs*

killer app • *The game is this month's killer app.*

software • *a fairly simple software package*

programme ① NOUN

a planned series of events • *a programme of official engagements*

agenda • *This is sure to be an item on the agenda again next week.*

schedule • *We both have such hectic schedules.*

timetable • *We've finally managed to agree on a timetable for formal talks.*

programme ② NOUN

a broadcast on radio or television • *local news programmes*

broadcast • *a broadcast by the President*

show • *my favourite TV show*

progress ① NOUN

improvement or development • *progress in the fight against cancer*

advance • *dramatic advances in road safety*

breakthrough • *a breakthrough in their research*

headway • *The police are making little headway in the investigation.*

improvement • *considerable room for improvement in facilities for patients*

progress ② VERB

to become more advanced or skilful • *His reading is progressing well.*

advance • *Japan has advanced from a rural society to an industrial power.*

blossom • *In just a few years it has blossomed into an international event.*

develop • *workshops designed to develop acting skills*

improve • *Their French has improved enormously.*

prohibit VERB

to forbid something or make it illegal • *a law which prohibited trading on Sundays*

ban • *The country will ban smoking in all offices this year.*

forbid • *The country's constitution forbids the military use of nuclear energy.*

outlaw • *In 1975 gambling was outlawed.*

prevent • *Residents may be prevented from leaving the islands.*

ANTONYM:
• allow

prominent ① ADJECTIVE

important • *the children of very prominent or successful parents*

eminent • *an eminent scientist*

famous • *England's most famous modern artist*

important • *an important figure in the media*

notable • *the notable linguist, Henriette Walter*

noted • *a noted Hebrew scholar*

renowned • *Sir William Crookes, the renowned chemist*

well-known • *He liked to surround himself with well-known people.*

prominent ② ADJECTIVE

very noticeable, or sticking out a long way • *a prominent feature of the landscape*

conspicuous • *a conspicuous landmark*

eye-catching • *I outlined it in black to make it more eye-catching.*

jutting • *a jutting chin*

noticeable · *Squeezing spots only makes them more noticeable.*
obvious · *His cultural roots are most obvious in his poetry.*
pronounced · *The exhibition has a pronounced Scottish theme.*
striking · *a striking aspect of these statistics*

MORE SYNONYMS:
• blatant
• salient

promiscuous ADJECTIVE
having many casual sexual relationships · *a promiscuous teenager*
loose · *If you wear a short skirt in here you're considered a loose woman.*
wanton · *A woman with many sexual partners is still considered wanton.*

MORE SYNONYMS:
• libertine
• licentious
• of easy virtue

promise ① VERB
to say that you will definitely do or not do something · *I promise not to be back too late.*
assure · *She assured me that she would deal with the problem.*
give your word · *He had given us his word he would join the club.*
guarantee · *Most countries guarantee the right to free education.*
pledge · *They have pledged to support the opposition.*
vow · *I vowed that someday I would return to live in Europe.*

promise ② VERB
to show signs of · *This promised to be a very long night.*
hint at · *One finding hints at support for this theory.*
indicate · *His early work indicates talent.*

show signs of · *Already she shows signs of beauty.*

MORE SYNONYMS:
• augur
• bespeak
• betoken
• bid fair

promise ③ NOUN
an undertaking to do or not do something · *If you make a promise, you should keep it.*
assurance · *He gave written assurance that he would start work at once.*
guarantee · *They can give no guarantee that they will fulfil their obligations.*
pledge · *a pledge to step up cooperation between the two countries*
undertaking · *an undertaking that he would be a responsible parent*
vow · *I kept my marriage vows.*

promote ① VERB
to encourage the progress or success of something · *All attempts to promote a ceasefire have failed.*
back · *She backed the new initiative enthusiastically.*
support · *He thanked everyone who had supported the strike.*

promote ② VERB
to encourage the sale of a product by advertising · *She's in Europe promoting her new film.*
advertise · *She is contracted to advertise their beauty products.*
plug (INFORMAL) · *He was on the show to plug his latest film.*
publicize · *I was publicizing the book in London.*

promote ③ VERB
to raise someone to a higher rank or position · *He has been promoted twice in two years.*

elevate • *He was elevated to the post of Prime Minister.*
upgrade • *He was upgraded to supervisor.*

prompt ① VERB
to make someone decide to do something • *Falling rates of pay have prompted consumers to stop buying new cars.*
cause • *What caused you to change your mind?*
induce • *Many teachers were induced to take early retirement.*
inspire • *These herbs will inspire you to try out all sorts of dishes.*
motivate • *How do you motivate people to work hard?*
spur • *Is it the money that spurs these firefighters to risk their lives?*

prompt ② VERB
to encourage someone to say something • *"What was that you were saying about a guided tour?" he prompted her.*
coax • *"Tell us what happened next," he coaxed me.*
remind • *"You stopped in the middle of your story," I reminded mother.*

prompt ③ ADVERB
exactly at the time mentioned • *The invitation specifies eight o'clock prompt.*
exactly • *He arrived at exactly five o'clock.*
on the dot • *At nine o'clock on the dot, they have breakfast.*
precisely • *The meeting began at precisely 4.00 pm.*
sharp • *She planned to get up at 8.00 sharp.*

prompt ④ ADJECTIVE
done without any delay • *a serious condition which needs prompt treatment*

immediate • *These incidents had an immediate effect.*
instant • *He took an instant dislike to this woman.*
instantaneous • *This would result in his instantaneous dismissal.*
quick • *hoping for a quick end to the dispute*
rapid • *their rapid response to the situation*
swift • *make a swift decision*

prone ① ADJECTIVE
having a tendency to be affected by or do something • *She is prone to depression.*
disposed • *I might have been disposed to like him in other circumstances.*
given • *I am not very given to emotional displays.*
inclined • *Nobody felt inclined to argue with Smith.*
liable • *equipment that is liable to break*
susceptible • *She's very susceptible to colds and flu.*

prone ② ADJECTIVE
lying flat and face downwards • *We were lying prone on the grass.*
face down • *He was lying face down on his bed.*
prostrate • *The injured jockey lay prostrate on the ground.*

proof NOUN
evidence that confirms that something is true or exists • *You have to have proof of residence in the state of Texas.*
confirmation • *further confirmation that house prices are no longer falling*
evidence • *To date there is no evidence to support this theory.*
testimony • *His testimony was an important element of the prosecution case.*
verification • *verification of her story*

MORE SYNONYMS:
- authentication
- certification
- corroboration
- substantiation

proper ① ADJECTIVE
correct or most suitable • *the proper course of action*
appropriate • *a smart outfit appropriate to the job*
apt • *an apt title for the book*
correct • *the correct way to do things*
fitting • *His address was a fitting end to a bitter campaign.*
right • *He's the right man for the job.*
suitable • *She had no other dress suitable for the occasion.*

ANTONYM:
- improper

proper ② ADJECTIVE
accepted or conventional • *She wanted a proper wedding.*
accepted • *the accepted way of doing things*
conventional • *conventional surgical methods*
orthodox • *orthodox police methods*

property ① NOUN
the things that belong to someone • *her personal property*
assets • *The company has assets of 3.5 billion francs.*
belongings • *I collected my belongings and left.*
effects • *After the funeral he sorted his father's personal effects.*
estate • *His estate was valued at $150,000.*
possessions • *People had lost their homes and all their possessions.*

property ② NOUN
a characteristic or quality • *Mint has powerful healing properties.*

attribute • *a normal attribute of human behaviour*
characteristic • *their physical characteristics*
feature • *a feature of the local culture*
hallmark • *The killing had the hallmarks of a professional assassination.*
quality • *mature people with leadership qualities*
trait • *Creativity is a human trait.*

proportion NOUN
part of an amount or group • *a tiny proportion of the population*
percentage • *It has a high percentage of protein.*
quota • *Britain's fishing quota has been cut.*
segment • *a fast-growing segment of the market*
share • *I pay a share of the phone and gas bills.*

prospect NOUN
expectation or something anticipated • *There was no prospect of going home.*
expectation • *The hotel was being renovated in expectation of a tourist boom.*
hope • *There is little hope of improvement now.*
outlook • *Officials say the outlook for next year is gloomy.*
promise • *New Year brought the promise of better things to come.*

protect VERB
to prevent someone or something from being harmed • *Cash dispensers are protected by thick steel and glass.*
defend • *I had to defend myself against the attack.*
guard • *Soldiers guarded homes near the airport.*

safeguard • *action to safeguard the ozone layer*
shelter • *a wooden house, sheltered by a low pointed roof*
shield • *He shielded his head from the sun with a newspaper.*

protection NOUN

something that protects • *a diet believed to offer protection against some cancers*
barrier • *a flood barrier*
buffer • *Keep savings as a buffer against unexpected cash needs.*
cover • *air cover for ground operations*
safeguard • *a safeguard against weeds*
shelter • *an air-raid shelter*

protest ① VERB

to disagree with someone or object to something • *She protested that she was a patriot, not a traitor.*
complain • *People always complain that the big banks are unhelpful.*
disagree • *I disagree with the drug laws in general.*
disapprove • *Her mother disapproved of her working in a pub.*
object • *We objected strongly but were outvoted.*
oppose • *Many parents oppose bilingual education in schools.*

MORE SYNONYMS:
• demur
• expostulate
• remonstrate

protest ② NOUN

a strong objection • *The council has ignored their protests by backing the scheme.*
complaint • *the way that banks deal with complaints*
objection • *I questioned the logic of his objections.*

outcry • *The incident caused an international outcry.*

proud ADJECTIVE

feeling pleasure or satisfaction • *I was proud of our players today.*
gratified • *He was gratified by the audience's response.*
honoured • *I am honoured to work with her.*
pleased • *I was pleased to call him my friend.*

prove VERB

to provide evidence that something is definitely true • *History will prove him to have been right all along.*
ascertain • *They had ascertained that he was not a spy.*
confirm • *X-rays confirmed that he had not broken any bones.*
demonstrate • *You have to demonstrate that you are reliable.*
establish • *The autopsy established the cause of death.*
verify • *I can verify that it takes about thirty seconds.*

MORE SYNONYMS:
• authenticate
• corroborate
• evince
• substantiate

ANTONYM:
• disprove

provide VERB

to make something available to someone • *I'll be glad to provide a copy of this.*
contribute • *NATO agreed to contribute troops and equipment.*
equip • *proposals to equip all officers with body armour*
furnish • *They'll be able to furnish you with the rest of the details.*
outfit • *They outfitted him with artificial legs.*

supply • *the blood vessels supplying oxygen to the brain*

provoke ① VERB
to try to make someone angry • *I didn't want to do anything to provoke him.*
anger • *It's important not to anger her.*
annoy • *You're just trying to annoy me.*
enrage • *He enraged the government by going back on the agreement.*
goad • *My little brother was always goading me.*
insult • *I didn't mean to insult you.*
irritate • *If you go on irritating that dog, it'll bite you.*
tease • *I'm sorry, I shouldn't tease you like that.*

provoke ② VERB
to cause an unpleasant reaction • *His comments have provoked a shocked reaction.*
cause • *These policies are likely to cause problems.*
evoke • *The programme has evoked a storm of protest.*
produce • *The decision produced a furious reaction among fans.*
prompt • *The allegations prompted an indignant response from the accused.*
rouse • *This roused a feeling of rebellion in him.*
set off • *The arrival of the supply van set off a minor riot among waiting villagers.*
spark off • *a political crisis sparked off by religious violence*

pry VERB
to try to find out about someone else's private business • *We do not want people prying into our business.*
interfere • *I wish everyone would stop interfering and just leave me alone.*
intrude • *The press were intruding into my personal life.*

poke your nose in (INFORMAL) • *Who asked you to poke your nose in?*
poke your nose into (INFORMAL) • *strangers who poke their noses into our affairs*
snoop (INFORMAL) • *He was snooping around Kim's hotel room.*

pub NOUN
a place where alcoholic drinks are served • *He goes to the pub most nights.*
bar (BRITISH) • *He works in a bar.*
boozer (BRITISH, AUSTRALIAN AND NEW ZEALAND; INFORMAL) • *the local boozer*
inn • *a village inn*
lounge • *the hotel lounge*
public house • *a robbery at a public house in New Milton*
saloon • *a Wild West saloon*
tavern • *an old country tavern*

public ① NOUN
people in general • *the public's confidence in the government*
masses • *a quest to bring the internet to the masses*
nation • *The President spoke to the nation.*
people • *the will of the people*
populace • *a large proportion of the populace*
society • *a menace to society*

public ② ADJECTIVE
relating to people in general • *public support for the idea*
civic • *a sense of civic pride*
general • *The project should raise general awareness about bullying.*
popular • *Popular anger has been expressed in demonstrations.*
universal • *the universal outrage at the deaths*

public ③ ADJECTIVE
provided for everyone to use or open to anyone • *public transport*

communal • *a communal dining room*
community • *a village community centre*
open to the public • *Part of the castle is now open to the public.*
universal • *universal health care*

ANTONYM:
• private

publicity NOUN
information or advertisements about an item or event • *government publicity campaigns*
advertising • *tobacco advertising in women's magazines*
plug (INFORMAL) • *The whole interview was an unashamed plug for her new book.*
promotion • *They've spent a lot of money on advertising and promotion.*

publicize VERB
to advertise something or make it widely known • *The author appeared on TV to publicize her book.*
advertise • *The product has been much advertised in specialist magazines.*
plug (INFORMAL) • *another celebrity plugging their latest book*
promote • *a tour to promote his second solo album*

publish VERB
to make a piece of writing available for reading • *We publish a range of titles.*
bring out • *The newspapers all brought out special editions.*
print • *a letter printed in the Times yesterday*
put out • *a statement put out by the Iraqi news agency*

puke VERB (INFORMAL)
to vomit • *They got drunk and puked.*
be sick • *She got up and was sick in the handbasin.*
chunder (AUSTRALIAN AND NEW

ZEALAND; SLANG) • *the time you chundered in the taxi*
spew (INFORMAL) • *He's really drunk. I hope he doesn't start spewing.*
throw up (INFORMAL) • *She threw up after reading reports of the trial.*
vomit • *Anything containing cow's milk made him vomit.*

pull ① VERB
to draw an object towards you • *a wooden plough pulled by oxen*
drag • *He dragged his chair towards the table.*
draw • *He drew his chair nearer the fire.*
haul • *A crane was used to haul the car out of the stream.*
tow • *They threatened to tow away my van.*
tug • *She kicked him, tugging his thick hair.*
yank • *She yanked open the drawer.*

ANTONYM:
• push

pull ② NOUN
the attraction or influence of something • *The pull of Mexico was too strong.*
attraction • *The attraction of Hollywood began to pall.*
lure • *The lure of rural life is as strong as ever.*
magnetism • *the sheer magnetism of his presence*

punctual ADJECTIVE
arriving or leaving at the correct time • *The most punctual airline last year was Swissair.*
in good time • *It is now 5am and we are in good time.*
on time • *I'm generally early or on time for an appointment.*
prompt • *We expect you to be prompt for all your classes.*

punctuation NOUN

- ◆ **PUNCTUATION MARKS**
- ◆ apostrophe
- ◆ asterisk
- ◆ bracket
- ◆ bullet point
- ◆ colon
- ◆ comma
- ◆ dash
- ◆ exclamation mark
- ◆ full stop
- ◆ hyphen
- ◆ question mark
- ◆ semicolon
- ◆ slash
- ◆ speech marks *or* quotation marks

punish VERB

to make someone suffer a penalty for some misbehaviour • *I got punished for insolence.*

discipline • *He was disciplined by his company but not dismissed.*

penalize • *Bad teaching is not penalized in a formal way.*

rap someone's knuckles • *The company got its knuckles rapped for this advertisement.*

sentence • *He has admitted the charge and will be sentenced later.*

throw the book at • *The football authorities seem certain to throw the book at him.*

punishment NOUN

a penalty for a crime or offence • *The punishment must always fit the crime.*

penalty • *One of those arrested could face the death penalty.*

retribution • *He didn't want any further involvement for fear of retribution.*

MORE SYNONYMS:

- chastening
- chastisement
- just deserts

puny ADJECTIVE

very small and weak • *He's always been a puny lad.*

feeble • *He was old and feeble.*

frail • *She lay in bed looking frail.*

sickly • *He has been a sickly child.*

skinny • *a skinny little boy*

weak • *His arms and legs were weak.*

pupil NOUN

a student taught at a school • *She is a model pupil.*

scholar (SOUTH AFRICAN) • *a bunch of rowdy scholars*

schoolboy • *a group of ten-year-old schoolboys*

schoolchild • *The bus was packed with schoolchildren.*

schoolgirl • *an appealing role model for schoolgirls*

student • *The students are sorted into three ability groups.*

pure ① ADJECTIVE

clean and free from harmful substances • *The water is pure enough to drink.*

clean • *Tiled kitchen floors are easy to keep clean.*

germ-free • *chlorine gas used to keep water germ-free*

pasteurized • *The milk is pasteurized to kill bacteria.*

spotless • *She kept the kitchen spotless.*

sterilized • *sterilized surgical equipment*

MORE SYNONYMS:

- unadulterated
- unblemished
- uncontaminated
- unpolluted
- untainted

a b c d e f g h i j k l m n o **p** q r s t u v w x y z

ANTONYM:
• impure

pure ② ADJECTIVE
complete and total • *a matter of pure luck*
absolute • *You're talking absolute nonsense.*
complete • *complete and utter rubbish*
outright • *an outright rejection of the deal*
sheer • *acts of sheer desperation*
unmitigated • *Last year's crop was an unmitigated disaster.*
utter • *This, of course, is utter nonsense.*

purple NOUN OR ADJECTIVE

♦ **SHADES OF PURPLE**
♦ amethyst
♦ aubergine
♦ gentian
♦ heather
♦ heliotrope
♦ indigo
♦ lavender
♦ lilac
♦ magenta
♦ mauve
♦ mulberry
♦ plum
♦ puce
♦ royal purple
♦ violet

purpose ① NOUN
the reason for something • *What is the purpose of this meeting?*
aim • *the aim of the policy*
function • *Their main function is to raise capital for industry.*
intention • *The intention of the scheme is to encourage faster sales.*
object • *the object of the exercise*
point • *I don't see the point of it.*
reason • *What is the real reason for the delay?*

purpose ②: **on purpose** ADVERB
deliberately • *Did you do that on purpose?*
by design • *The pair met often - at first by chance but later by design.*
deliberately • *It looks as if the fire was started deliberately.*
intentionally • *I've never hurt anyone intentionally.*
knowingly • *He said that he'd never knowingly taken illegal drugs.*
purposely • *They are purposely withholding information.*

push ① VERB
to apply force to something in order to move it • *She pushed the door open.*
press • *He pressed his back against the door.*
ram • *He rammed the key into the lock.*
shove • *He shoved her aside.*
thrust • *They thrust him into the back of the jeep.*

ANTONYM:
• pull

push ② VERB
to persuade someone into doing something • *His mother pushed him into auditioning for a part.*
encourage • *She encouraged me to stick to the diet.*
persuade • *They persuaded him to moderate his views.*
press • *Trade unions are pressing him to stand firm.*
urge • *He had urged her to come to Ireland.*

pushy ADJECTIVE (INFORMAL)
unpleasantly forceful and determined • *a confident and pushy young woman*
aggressive • *a very aggressive business executive*
ambitious • *You have to be ambitious*

to make it in this business.

assertive • *Women have become more assertive over the last ten years.*

bossy • *She remembers being a rather bossy little girl.*

forceful • *Sarah is notorious for her forceful and quarrelsome nature.*

obtrusive • *"You are rude and obtrusive, Mr Smith," said Tommy.*

put ① VERB

to place something somewhere • *She put the photograph on the desk.*

deposit • *On his way out he deposited a glass in front of me.*

lay • *Lay a sheet of newspaper on the floor.*

place • *He placed it in the inside pocket of his jacket.*

position • *Plants were carefully positioned in the alcove.*

rest • *He rested his arms on the back of the chair.*

put ② VERB

to express something • *I think you put that very well.*

phrase • *I would have phrased it quite differently.*

word • *You misinterpreted his letter, or else he worded it poorly.*

put down ① VERB

to criticize someone and make them appear foolish • *Racist jokes come from wanting to put down other people.*

belittle • *She's always belittling her husband in public.*

criticize • *She rarely criticized any of her children.*

find fault with • *I wish you wouldn't find fault with me in front of the kids.*

humiliate • *His teacher continually humiliates him.*

put down ② VERB

to kill an animal that is ill or

dangerous • *Magistrates ordered the dog to be put down immediately.*

destroy • *The horse had to be destroyed.*

kill • *Animals should be killed humanely.*

put out of its misery • *The bird was so badly injured I decided to put it out of its misery.*

put to sleep • *Take the dog to the vet's and have her put to sleep.*

put off VERB

to delay something • *Ministers have put off making a decision until next month.*

defer • *Customers often defer payment for as long as possible.*

delay • *She wants to delay the wedding.*

postpone • *The visit has been postponed indefinitely.*

put back • *The news conference has been put back a couple of hours.*

put on ice • *The decision has been put on ice until October.*

reschedule • *Since I'll be away, I'd like to reschedule the meeting.*

put up with VERB

to tolerate something disagreeable • *They won't put up with a return to the bad old days.*

abide • *I can't abide arrogant people.*

bear • *He can't bear to talk about it.*

stand • *She cannot stand her boss.*

stand for • *We won't stand for it any more.*

stomach • *He could not stomach violence.*

tolerate • *She can no longer tolerate the position she is in.*

MORE SYNONYMS:
• brook
• countenance

puzzle ① VERB

to perplex and confuse • *There was something about her that puzzled me.*

A
B
C
D
E
F
G
H
I
J
K
L
M
N
O
P
Q
R
S
T
U
V
W
X
Y
Z

baffle • *An apple tree producing square fruit is baffling experts.*

bewilder • *His silence bewildered her.*

confuse • *German politics surprised and confused him.*

mystify • *The audience were mystified by the plot.*

stump • *I was stumped by an unexpected question.*

MORE SYNONYMS:
• confound
• flummox

• nonplus
• perplex

puzzle ② NOUN

a game or question that requires a lot of thought to solve • *a crossword puzzle*

brain-teaser (INFORMAL) • *It took me ages to solve that brain-teaser.*

poser • *Here is a little poser for you.*

problem • *a mathematical problem*

riddle • *See if you can answer this riddle.*

Qq

qualification ① NOUN
a skill or achievement • *His qualifications are impressive.*
ability • *a man of considerable abilities*
accomplishment • *Carl was proud of his son's accomplishments.*
achievement • *the highest academic achievement*
capability • *Her capabilities were not fully appreciated.*
quality • *Colley's leadership qualities*
skill • *a skill you can use*

MORE SYNONYMS:
• attribute
• endowment

qualification ② NOUN
something added to make a statement less strong • *The argument is not true without qualification.*
condition • *You can make any conditions you like.*
exception • *a major exception to this general argument*
modification • *to consider modifications to his proposal*
reservation • *men whose work I admire without reservation*

qualify VERB
to pass the tests necessary for an activity • *I qualified as a doctor 30 years ago.*
become licensed • *You can only become licensed by doing an accredited course.*
gain qualifications • *the opportunity to gain medical qualifications*
get certified • *They wanted to get certified as divers.*
graduate • *She graduated as a physiotherapist in 1960.*

quality ① NOUN
the measure of how good something is • *The quality of food is very poor.*
calibre • *a man of your calibre*
distinction • *a chef of great distinction*
grade • *high grade meat and poultry*
merit • *a work of real merit*
value • *He set a high value upon their friendship.*
worth • *a person's true worth*

quality ② NOUN
a characteristic of something • *These qualities are essential for success.*
aspect • *every aspect of our lives*
characteristic • *their physical characteristics*
feature • *the most striking feature of his work*
mark • *the mark of a great composer*
property • *the magnetic properties of iron*
trait • *the young Ms Rankine's personality traits*

MORE SYNONYMS:
• attribute
• peculiarity

quantity ① NOUN
an amount you can measure or count • *a large quantity of alcohol*

amount • *a small amount of mayonnaise*
number • *There are a limited number of seats available.*
part • *the greater part of his wealth*
sum • *a large sum of money*
MORE SYNONYMS:
• portion
• quota

quantity ② NOUN
the amount of something that there is • *emphasis on quality rather than quantity*
extent • *the extent of the damage*
measure • *The government has had a fair measure of success.*
size • *He gauged the size of the audience.*
volume • *the sheer volume of traffic and accidents*
MORE SYNONYMS:
• bulk
• expanse
• magnitude

quarrel ① NOUN
an angry argument • *I had a terrible quarrel with my brother.*
argument • *an argument about money*
disagreement • *My instructor and I had a brief disagreement.*
dispute • *Brand eavesdropped on the petty dispute.*
feud • *a two-year feud between neighbours*
fight • *It was a silly fight about where we parked the car.*
row • *Maxine and I had a terrible row.*
squabble • *minor squabbles about phone bills*
MORE SYNONYMS:
• altercation
• fracas
• fray

quarrel ② VERB
to have an angry argument • *My brother quarrelled with my father.*
argue • *They were still arguing later.*
bicker • *They bickered endlessly over procedure.*
clash • *She had clashed with Doyle in the past.*
fall out (INFORMAL) • *Mum and I used to fall out a lot.*
fight • *The couple often fought with their son.*
row • *He had rowed with his girlfriend.*
squabble • *The children were squabbling over the remote control.*

queasy ADJECTIVE
feeling slightly sick • *He already felt queasy.*
ill • *I was feeling ill.*
nauseous • *The medication may make you feel nauseous.*
queer • *Twenty minutes later, he began to feel queer.*
sick • *The very thought of food made him feel sick.*
unwell • *He felt unwell this afternoon.*

query ① NOUN
a question • *If you have any queries, please contact us.*
inquiry • *I'll be happy to answer all your inquiries, if I can.*
question • *The President refused to answer further questions on the subject.*
ANTONYM:
• response

query ② VERB
to question something because it seems wrong • *No one queried my decision.*
challenge • *The move was challenged by two countries.*
dispute • *He disputed the allegations.*
object to • *A lot of people objected to the plan.*

question • *It never occurred to me to question the doctor's decisions.*

question ① NOUN

a problem that needs to be discussed • *Can we get back to the question of the car?*

issue • *What is your view on this issue?*

motion • *The conference is now debating the motion.*

point • *There is another point to consider.*

subject • *He raised the subject of money.*

topic • *the topic of where to go on holiday*

question ② VERB

to ask someone questions • *A man is being questioned by police.*

examine • *Lawyers examined the witnesses.*

interrogate • *I interrogated everyone even slightly involved.*

probe • *tabloid journalists probing us for details*

quiz • *She quizzed me quite closely for a while.*

MORE SYNONYMS:
- cross-examine
- interview
- investigate

ANTONYM:
- answer

question ③ VERB

to express doubts about something • *He never stopped questioning his own beliefs.*

challenge • *Rose convincingly challenged the story.*

dispute • *Nobody disputed that Davey was clever.*

distrust • *I distrusted my ability to keep quiet.*

doubt • *Nobody doubted his sincerity.*

query • *No one queried my decision.*

suspect • *Do we suspect the motives of our friends?*

quick ① ADJECTIVE

moving with great speed • *You'll have to be quick to catch the flight.*

brisk • *a brisk walk*

fast • *a very fast driver*

hasty • *He spoke in a hasty, nervous way.*

rapid • *a rapid rise through the company*

speedy • *a speedy recovery*

swift • *She is as swift as an arrow.*

MORE SYNONYMS:
- express
- fleet
- headlong

ANTONYM:
- slow

quick ② ADJECTIVE

lasting only a short time • *a quick chat*

brief • *a brief meeting*

cursory • *a cursory glance inside the van*

hasty • *a hasty meal of bread and soup*

hurried • *He ate a hurried breakfast.*

perfunctory • *With a perfunctory smile, she walked past Jessica.*

ANTONYM:
- long

quick ③ ADJECTIVE

happening without any delay • *a quick response*

hasty • *This is no hasty decision.*

prompt • *Prompt action is needed.*

sudden • *this week's sudden cold snap*

quickly ADVERB

with great speed • *Stop me if I'm speaking too quickly.*

fast • *How fast were you driving?*

hastily • *sheltering in hastily erected tents*

hurriedly • *students hurriedly taking notes*

rapidly • *moving rapidly across the field*

a
b
c
d
e
f
g
h
i
j
k
l
m
n
o
p
q
r
s
t
u
v
w
x
y
z

speedily • She speedily recovered herself.
swiftly • They had to act swiftly to save him.

ANTONYM:
• slowly

quiet ① ADJECTIVE
making very little noise • The children were quiet and contented.
hushed • Tales were exchanged in hushed tones.
inaudible • a tiny, almost inaudible squeak
low • I spoke in a low voice to Sullivan.
silent • He could speak no English and was silent.
soft • There was some soft music playing.

MORE SYNONYMS:
• noiseless
• soundless

ANTONYM:
• noisy

quiet ② ADJECTIVE
peaceful and calm • a quiet evening at home
calm • The city seems relatively calm today.
mild • The night was mild.
peaceful • a peaceful old house
restful • a restful scene
serene • the beautiful, serene park
tranquil • a tranquil lake

MORE SYNONYMS:
• motionless
• placid
• untroubled

quiet ③ NOUN
silence or lack of noise • The teacher called for quiet.
calmness • the calmness of this area
peace • I enjoy peace and quiet.
serenity • the peace and serenity of a tropical sunset

silence • There was a silence around the table.
stillness • the stillness of the summer night
tranquillity • the tranquillity of village life

ANTONYM:
• noise

quit VERB
to leave a place or stop doing something • Leigh quit his job as a salesman.
discontinue • Do not discontinue the treatment without seeing your doctor.
give up • She gave up smoking last year.
leave • He left school with no qualifications.
resign • Scott resigned from the firm.
retire • Littlejohn was forced to retire from the race.
stop • I stopped working last year to have a baby.

MORE SYNONYMS:
• abandon
• cease

quite ① ADVERB
fairly but not very • He is quite old.
fairly • Both ships are fairly new.
moderately • a moderately attractive man
rather • I made some rather bad mistakes.
reasonably • I can dance reasonably well.
somewhat • He's somewhat deaf.

quite ② ADVERB
completely and totally • Jane lay quite still.
absolutely • I absolutely refuse to get married.
completely • something completely different
entirely • an entirely new approach

fully • He has still not fully recovered.
perfectly • They are perfectly safe to eat.
totally • The fire totally destroyed the house.

MORE SYNONYMS:
• precisely
• wholly

quote VERB
to repeat the exact words someone
has said • She quoted a great line from Shakespeare.
cite • She cites a favourite poem by George Herbert.
extract • This material has been extracted from the handbook.
recite • They recited poetry to one another.
repeat • Could you repeat the whole interview word for word?

a
b
c
d
e
f
g
h
i
j
k
l
m
n
o
p
q
r
s
t
u
v
w
x
y
z

Rr

race ① NOUN

a group of human beings with similar physical characteristics
• *Discrimination on the grounds of race is illegal.*

ethnic group • *Ethnic group and nationality are often different.*
nation • *a mature and cultured nation*
people • *an address to the American people*

race ② VERB

to move very quickly • *When school was over, Kate raced home.*

dash • *He dashed upstairs.*
fly • *I must fly or I'll miss my train.*
hurry • *They hurried down the street.*
run • *The gunmen escaped by running into the woods.*
speed • *speeding along as fast as I could*
tear • *The door flew open and she tore into the room.*

racket ① NOUN

a lot of noise • *The racket went on past midnight.*

clamour • *She could hear a clamour in the road.*
commotion • *He heard a commotion outside.*
din • *make themselves heard over the din of the crowd*
hubbub • *His voice was drowned out by the hubbub of the fans.*
noise • *There was too much noise in the room.*

row • *"Whatever is that row?" she demanded.*
rumpus • *There was such a rumpus, she had to shout to make herself heard.*

MORE SYNONYMS:
• cacophony
• tumult

racket ② NOUN

an illegal way of making money • *a drugs racket*

enterprise • *a money-laundering enterprise*
fraud • *tax frauds*
scheme • *a quick money-making scheme*

rage ① NOUN

a feeling of very strong anger
• *trembling with rage*

anger • *She felt deep anger at what he had said.*
frenzy • *Their behaviour drove her into a frenzy.*
fury • *Her face was distorted with fury and pain.*
wrath • *He incurred the wrath of the referee.*

rage ② VERB

to be angry or speak angrily about something • *He was raging at their lack of response.*

be furious • *He is furious at the way his wife has been treated.*
fume • *I was still fuming over her remark.*

lose your temper • *They had never seen me lose my temper before.*
rave • *She cried and raved for weeks.*
storm • *"It's a disaster!" he stormed.*

rage ③ VERB
to continue with great force • *The fire raged out of control.*
be at its height • *when the storm was at its height*
rampage • *a mob rampaging through the town*
storm • *armies storming across the continent*
surge • *The flood surged through the village.*

raid ① VERB
to attack something by force
• *Soldiers raided the capital.*
assault • *Their stronghold was assaulted by pirates.*
attack • *We are being attacked!*
break into • *No-one saw them break into the warehouse.*
invade • *The invading army took all their food supplies.*
plunder • *plundering the homes of the inhabitants*
MORE SYNONYMS:
• pillage
• rifle
• sack

raid ② NOUN
an attack on something • *a bank raid*
attack • *a surprise attack on the house*
break-in • *The break-in occurred last night.*
foray • *Guerrillas made forays into the territory.*
MORE SYNONYMS:
• incursion
• sortie

rain ① NOUN
water falling from the clouds • *A*

spot of rain fell on her hand.
deluge • *homes damaged in the deluge*
downpour • *A two-day downpour swelled water levels.*
drizzle • *The drizzle had stopped and the sun was shining.*
rainfall • *four years of below average rainfall*
showers • *bright spells followed by scattered showers*

rain ② VERB
to fall from the sky in drops • *It rained the whole weekend.*
drizzle • *It was starting to drizzle when I left.*
pour • *We drove all the way in pouring rain.*
teem • *It teemed the entire day.*

raise ① VERB
to make something higher • *a drive to raise standards of literacy*
elevate • *Emotional stress can elevate blood pressure.*
heave • *He heaved his crippled leg into an easier position.*
hoist • *He climbed on the roof to hoist the flag.*
lift • *She lifted the last of her drink to her lips.*
ANTONYM:
• lower

raise ② VERB
to look after children until they are grown up • *the house where she was raised*
bring up • *She brought up four children single-handed.*
nurture • *the best way to nurture a child to adulthood*
rear • *He reared his sister's family as well as his own.*

raise ③ VERB
to mention or suggest something

a
b
c
d
e
f
g
h
i
j
k
l
m
n
o
p
q
r
s
t
u
v
w
x
y
z

• He had raised no objections at the time.

advance • Some important ideas were advanced at the conference.

bring up • I hesitate to bring up this matter with you, but I have no choice.

broach • Eventually I broached the subject of her early life.

introduce • always willing to introduce a new topic

moot • The project was first mooted last year.

suggest • one possibility that might be suggested

ramble ① NOUN

a long walk in the countryside • They went for a ramble through the woods.

excursion • They organized an excursion into the hills.

hike • a long hike along the valley floor

stroll • The next day we took a stroll along the river bank.

walk • We often go for walks in the country.

ramble ② VERB

to go for a long walk • freedom to ramble across the moors

amble • ambling along a country lane

stray • You mustn't stray across the border.

stroll • whistling as he strolled along the road

walk • We finished the evening by walking along the beach.

wander • He loved to wander in the woods.

MORE SYNONYMS:
• perambulate
• rove

ramble ③ VERB

to talk in a confused way • He started rambling and repeating himself.

babble • She babbled on and on about the visitors.

chatter • I was so nervous that I chattered away like an idiot.

rampage ① VERB

to rush about angrily or violently • children rampaging round the garden

go berserk • The crowd went berserk at the sight of him.

rage • His shop was stormed by a raging mob.

run amok • He was arrested after running amok with a gun.

run riot • The prisoners ran riot after the announcement.

rampage ②: on the rampage ADJECTIVE

rushing about in a wild and violent way • a bull on the rampage

amok • The gunman ran amok and killed several people.

berserk • The fans went berserk and mobbed the stage.

wild • They just went wild after he left.

random ① ADJECTIVE

not based on a definite plan • random violence against innocent victims

aimless • after several hours of aimless searching

arbitrary • Arbitrary arrests and detention without trial were common.

haphazard • He had never seen such a haphazard approach to writing.

indiscriminate • the indiscriminate use of fertilisers

spot • picked up in a spot check

MORE SYNONYMS:
• desultory
• fortuitous
• unpremeditated

random ②: at random ADVERB

without any definite plan • chosen at random

aimlessly • wandering around aimlessly for hours

arbitrarily • *The questions were chosen quite arbitrarily.*
haphazardly • *The books were stacked haphazardly on the shelves.*
indiscriminately • *This disease strikes indiscriminately.*
randomly • *a randomly selected sample*

MORE SYNONYMS:
• adventitiously
• unsystematically
• willy-nilly

range ① NOUN
the maximum limits of something • *Tactical nuclear weapons have shorter ranges.*
bounds • *the bounds of good taste*
extent • *the full extent of my knowledge*
field • *The subject covers a very wide field.*
limits • *outside the city limits*
province • *This doesn't fall within our province.*
scope • *He promised to widen the scope of their activities.*

range ② NOUN
a number of different things of the same kind • *a wide range of colours*
assortment • *There was a good assortment to choose from.*
class • *Cars in this class are expensive.*
gamut • *I experienced the whole gamut of emotions.*
selection • *a wide selection of delicious meals*
series • *a completely new model series*
variety • *The shop stocks a variety of local craft products.*

range ③ VERB
to vary between two extremes • *goods ranging between the everyday and the exotic*
extend • *The reclaimed land extends from here to the river.*

go • *Their sizes go from very small to enormous.*
run • *Accommodation runs from log cabins to high-standard hotels.*
stretch • *with interests that stretched from chemicals to sugar*
vary • *The cycle of sunspots varies between 8 to 15 years.*

rank ① NOUN
someone's level in a group • *He rose to the rank of captain.*
class • *relationships between social classes*
echelon • *the upper echelons of society*
grade • *Staff turnover is high among the junior grades.*
level • *various levels of the judiciary system*
standing • *a woman of wealth and social standing*
station • *a humble station in life*
status • *promoted to the status of foreman*

rank ② NOUN
a row of people or things • *ranks of police in riot gear*
column • *a column of figures*
file • *They walked in single file to the top.*
line • *He waited in a line of slow-moving vehicles.*
row • *She lived in the middle of a row of pretty cottages.*

rank ③ ADJECTIVE
complete and absolute • *It was rank stupidity to go there alone.*
absolute • *not intended for absolute beginners*
complete • *her complete ignorance*
downright • *That was just downright rudeness.*
sheer • *his sheer stupidity*
unmitigated • *an unmitigated villain*
utter • *his utter disregard for other people*

a
b
c
d
e
f
g
h
i
j
k
l
m
n
o
p
q
r
s
t
u
v
w
x
y
z

A
B
C
D
E
F
G
H
I
J
K
L
M
N
O
P
Q
R
S
T
U
V
W
X
Y
Z

MORE SYNONYMS:
• arrant
• egregious

rare ADJECTIVE
not common or frequent • *a rare species of bird*
exceptional • *in exceptional circumstances*
few • *Genuine friends are few.*
scarce • *Jobs are becoming increasingly scarce.*
sparse • *Information about the tests is sparse.*
sporadic • *occurring at only sporadic intervals*
uncommon • *The disease is uncommon in younger women.*
unusual • *an unusual variety but a very attractive one*

ANTONYM:
• common

rash ① ADJECTIVE
acting in a hasty and foolish way
• *It would be rash to act on such flimsy evidence.*
foolhardy • *Some described his behaviour as foolhardy.*
hasty • *This is no hasty decision.*
impetuous • *As usual, he reacted in a heated and impetuous way.*
impulsive • *He is too impulsive to take this responsibility.*
reckless • *his reckless driving*

MORE SYNONYMS:
• heedless
• injudicious
• unthinking

rash ② NOUN
an irritated area on your skin • *I noticed a rash on my leg.*
eruption • *an unpleasant skin eruption*
outbreak • *an outbreak of blisters around his mouth*

rash ③ NOUN
a large number of events happening together • *a rash of strikes*
epidemic • *A victim of the recent epidemic of shootings.*
flood • *a flood of complaints about the programme*
plague • *Last year there was a plague of burglaries.*
spate • *a spate of attacks on horses*
wave • *the current wave of violent attacks*

rate ① NOUN
the speed or frequency of something
• *appearing at the rate of one a week*
frequency • *She phoned with increasing frequency.*
pace • *at an accelerated pace*
speed • *moving at the speed of light*
tempo • *They wanted to speed up the tempo of change.*
velocity • *changes in wind velocity*

rate ② NOUN
the cost or charge for something
• *phone calls at cheap rates*
charge • *An annual charge will be made for this service.*
cost • *a low-cost mortgage*
fee • *The work will be invoiced at the usual fee.*
price • *falling share prices*
tariff • *How much you pay depends on your tariff.*

rate ③ VERB
to give an opinion of someone's qualities • *He was rated as one of the best.*
appraise • *She gave me an appraising glance.*
class • *classed as one of the top ten athletes*
consider • *I considered myself to be quite good at maths.*

count • *That would be counted as wrong.*
rank • *The hotel was ranked as one of the world's best.*
regard • *a highly regarded member of staff*

MORE SYNONYMS:
- adjudge
- esteem
- evaluate

rather ADVERB
to a certain extent • *We got along rather well.*
fairly • *Both ships are fairly new.*
pretty (INFORMAL) • *I'm pretty tired now.*
quite • *The cottage looks quite ordinary from the road.*
relatively • *I think I'm relatively easy to get on with.*
slightly • *slightly startled by his sudden appearance*
somewhat • *He said, somewhat unconvincingly, that he would pay.*

rational ADJECTIVE
using reason rather than emotion • *to arrive at a rational conclusion*
enlightened • *enlightened companies who take a pragmatic view*
logical • *There must be a logical explanation for it.*
reasonable • *a perfectly reasonable decision*
sensible • *The sensible thing is to leave them alone.*

rave ① VERB
to talk in an uncontrolled way • *He started raving about being treated badly.*
babble • *She babbled on and on about her plans.*
rage • *He was raging at their lack of response.*
rant • *She started ranting about her boss's attitude.*

rave ② VERB (INFORMAL)
to be enthusiastic about something • *She raved about the facilities there.*
be wild about (INFORMAL) • *He was just wild about the play.*
enthuse • *She enthused about the local architecture.*
gush • *"It was brilliant!" he gushed.*

reach ① VERB
to arrive somewhere • *He did not stop until he reached the door.*
arrive at • *to arrive at an erroneous conclusion*
attain • *She worked hard to attain a state of calm.*
get as far as • *If we get as far as the coast we will be quite satisfied.*
get to • *You must get to the end before noon.*
make • *They didn't think they would make the summit.*

reach ② VERB
to extend as far as something • *Her cloak reached to the ground.*
extend to • *The boundaries extend to the edge of the lake.*
go as far as • *Try to make the ball go as far as the trees.*
touch • *I could touch both walls with my arms extended.*

reach ③ VERB
to arrive at a certain stage or level • *Unemployment has reached record levels.*
arrive at • *They planted a flag when they arrived at the trees.*
attain • *He was close to attaining his personal best.*
climb to • *Attendance climbed to a record level this year.*
fall to • *Profits are expected to fall to their lowest level.*
rise to • *She rose rapidly to the top of her profession.*

a
b
c
d
e
f
g
h
i
j
k
l
m
n
o
p
q
r
s
t
u
v
w
x
y
z

reaction ① NOUN
a person's response to something
• *Reaction to the visit was mixed.*
acknowledgment • *She made no acknowledgment of my question.*
answer • *In answer to speculation in the press, she declared her interest.*
feedback • *Continue to ask for feedback on your work.*
response • *in response to a request from the members*

reaction ② NOUN
a response to something unpopular
• *a reaction against religious leaders*
backlash • *the male backlash against feminism*
counterbalance • *an organization set up as a counterbalance to the official group*

read ① VERB
to look at something written • *I love to read in bed.*
glance at • *He just glanced briefly at the article.*
look at • *She was looking at the evening paper.*
pore over • *poring over a dictionary*
scan • *There's only time to scan through it quickly.*
study • *I'll study the text more closely later.*

read ② VERB
to understand what someone means
• *as if he could read her thoughts*
comprehend • *Her expression was difficult to comprehend.*
decipher • *She was still no closer to deciphering the code.*
interpret • *You have to interpret their gestures, too.*

ready ① ADJECTIVE
prepared for action or use • *The plums are ready to eat now.*

organized • *Everything is organized for the party tomorrow.*
prepared • *He was prepared for a tough fight.*
primed • *The other side is primed for battle.*
ripe • *Are those strawberries ripe yet?*
set • *We'll be set to go in five minutes.*

ready ② ADJECTIVE
willing to do something • *She was always ready to give interviews.*
agreeable • *We can go ahead if you are agreeable.*
eager • *Children are eager to learn.*
happy • *always happy to help*
keen • *He wasn't keen to get involved.*
willing • *questions which they were not willing to answer*

MORE SYNONYMS:
• minded
• predisposed

ready ③ ADJECTIVE
easily produced or obtained • *ready cash*
accessible • *The system should be accessible to everyone.*
available • *Food is available round the clock.*
convenient • *a convenient excuse*
handy • *Keep a pencil and paper handy.*

real ① ADJECTIVE
actually existing and not imagined
• *You're dealing with real life now.*
actual • *She was the actual basis for the leading character.*
authentic • *containing authentic details of what happened*
concrete • *I don't have any concrete evidence.*
factual • *a factual account*
genuine • *His worries about the future were genuine ones.*
legitimate • *These are legitimate concerns.*

tangible • *I cannot see any tangible benefits in these changes.*
true • *the true story of his life*

ANTONYM:
• imaginary

real ② ADJECTIVE

genuine and not imitation • *Is that a real gun?*
authentic • *an authentic French recipe*
bona fide • *We are happy to donate to bona fide charities.*
dinkum (AUSTRALIAN AND NEW ZEALAND; INFORMAL) • *a place which serves dinkum Aussie tucker*
genuine • *It's a genuine Rembrandt, all right.*
honest • *It was an honest attempt to set things right.*
sincere • *His remorse was completely sincere, not just an act.*
rightful • *the rightful heir to the throne*
true • *He is a true believer in human rights.*
unaffected • *her genuine and unaffected sympathy for the victims*

ANTONYM:
• fake

realistic ① ADJECTIVE

accepting the true situation • *It's only realistic to admit that things will go wrong.*
down-to-earth • *We welcomed her down-to-earth approach.*
level-headed • *a sensible, level-headed approach*
matter-of-fact • *He sounded matter-of-fact and unemotional.*
practical • *a highly practical attitude to life*
sensible • *I'm trying to persuade you to be more sensible.*
sober • *a more sober assessment of the situation*

realistic ② ADJECTIVE

true to real life • *His novels are more realistic than his short stories.*
authentic • *They have to look authentic.*
faithful • *faithful copies of old household items*
lifelike • *almost as lifelike as a photograph*
true • *It gave a true picture of how things were.*

MORE SYNONYMS:
• naturalistic
• representational
• vérité

reality NOUN

something that is true and not imagined • *Fiction and reality were increasingly blurred.*
authenticity • *The film's authenticity impressed the critics.*
fact • *No-one knew how much of what he said was fact.*
realism • *His stories had an edge of realism.*
truth • *I must tell you the truth about this situation.*

realize VERB

to become aware of something • *People don't realize how serious it is.*
appreciate • *He appreciates the difficulties we face.*
comprehend • *They do not comprehend the nature of the problem.*
grasp • *She still couldn't grasp what had really happened.*
recognize • *Of course I recognize that evil exists.*
understand • *I didn't understand what he meant until later.*

really ① ADVERB

very or certainly • *I've had a really good time.*

a
b
c
d
e
f
g
h
i
j
k
l
m
n
o
p
q
r
s
t
u
v
w
x
y
z

absolutely • *feeling absolutely exhausted*
certainly • *I am certainly getting tired of hearing about it.*
extremely • *My mobile phone is extremely useful.*
remarkably • *They have been remarkably successful.*
terribly • *I'm terribly sorry to bother you.*
truly • *a truly splendid man*
very • *learning very quickly*

really ② ADVERB
in fact • *He didn't really love her.*
actually • *I pretended I was interested, but I was actually half asleep.*
in fact • *It sounds simple, but in fact it's very difficult.*
in reality • *He came across as streetwise, but in reality he was not.*
truly • *I truly never minded caring for Rusty.*

reason ① NOUN
the cause of something that happens • *for a multitude of reasons*
cause • *The true cause of the accident may never be known.*
grounds • *some grounds for optimism*
incentive • *There is no incentive to adopt these measures.*
motive • *Police have ruled out robbery as a motive.*
purpose • *the purpose of their visit*

reason ② NOUN
the ability to think • *a conflict between emotion and reason*
intellect • *good health and a lively intellect*
judgment • *His judgment was impaired.*
rationality • *We live in an era of rationality.*
reasoning • *a lack of sound reasoning and logic*

sense • *He should have had more sense.*

reason ③ VERB
to try to persuade someone of something • *It's better to reason with them than to use force.*
bring round (INFORMAL) • *We'll try to bring you round to our point of view.*
persuade • *I had to persuade him of the advantages.*
win over • *They still hoped to win him over to their way of thinking.*

reasonable ① ADJECTIVE
fair and sensible • *a reasonable sort of chap*
fair • *You can be sure she will be fair with you.*
moderate • *an easygoing man of very moderate views*
rational • *Please try to be rational about this.*
sane • *No sane person wishes to see a war.*
sensible • *She was a sensible girl and did not panic.*
sober • *We are now more sober and realistic.*
steady • *a politician who was steady almost to the point of being boring*
wise • *You're a wise old man: tell me what to do.*

MORE SYNONYMS:
• judicious
• plausible

reasonable ② ADJECTIVE
based on good reasoning • *It seems reasonable to expect rapid urban growth.*
justifiable. • *Our violence was justifiable on the grounds of political necessity.*
legitimate • *That's a perfectly legitimate fear.*
logical • *There was a logical explanation.*

sensible • *a sensible solution*
sound • *sound advice*
understandable • *His unhappiness was understandable.*

reasonable ③ ADJECTIVE
not too expensive • *His fees were quite reasonable.*
cheap • *She said she'd share a flat if I could find somewhere cheap enough.*
competitive • *homes offered for sale at competitive prices*
fair • *It's a fair price for a car like that.*
inexpensive • *an inexpensive divorce settlement*
low • *The low prices and friendly service made for a pleasant evening.*
modest • *a modest charge*

reassure VERB
to make someone feel less worried • *She reassured me that everything was fine.*
bolster • *measures intended to bolster morale*
cheer up • *I wrote it just to cheer myself up.*
comfort • *He tried to comfort her as far as he could.*
encourage • *Investors were encouraged by the news.*
MORE SYNONYMS:
• buoy up
• hearten
• inspirit

rebel VERB
to fight against authority and accepted values • *I rebelled against everything when I was young.*
defy • *It was the first time she had defied her mother.*
mutiny • *Sailors mutinied against their officers.*
resist • *activists convicted of resisting apartheid*

revolt • *The islanders revolted against the prince.*

rebellion NOUN
an organized opposition to authority • *the ruthless suppression of the rebellion*
insurrection • *They were plotting to stage an armed insurrection.*
mutiny • *convicted of mutiny and high treason*
revolt • *The revolt ended in failure.*
revolution • *after the French Revolution*
uprising • *Isolated attacks turned into a full-scale uprising.*

receive ① VERB
to accept something from someone • *Did they receive my letter?*
accept • *They accepted the parcel gratefully.*
be given • *We were all given presents.*
get • *She got some lovely things.*
pick up • *He picked up an award for his performance.*
take • *Will you take this parcel for your neighbour?*

receive ② VERB
to experience something • *We received a very warm welcome.*
encounter • *He encountered some unexpected opposition.*
suffer • *He suffered some bangs and bumps.*
sustain • *She had sustained a cut on her arm.*
undergo • *You may have to undergo a bit of teasing.*

receive ③ VERB
to welcome visitors • *You must be there to receive your guests.*
entertain • *She loved to entertain friends at home.*
greet • *They greeted the visitors at the door.*

a
b
c
d
e
f
g
h
i
j
k
l
m
n
o
p
q
r
s
t
u
v
w
x
y
z

A
B
C
D
E
F
G
H
I
J
K
L
M
N
O
P
Q
R
S
T
U
V
W
X
Y
Z

meet • *I'll come down to meet you.*
take in • *The country took in many refugees.*
welcome • *Several people came by to welcome me.*

recent ADJECTIVE
happening a short time ago • *his most recent acquisition*
current • *a sound knowledge of current affairs*
fresh • *fresh footprints in the snow*
new • *the subject of a new film*
present-day • *Even by present-day standards these were large aircraft.*
up-to-date • *the most up-to-date computers*
MORE SYNONYMS:
• contemporary
• latter-day

recession NOUN
a decline in economic conditions • *companies which survived after the recession*
decline • *signs of economic decline*
depression • *the Great Depression of the 1930s*
downturn • *due to a sharp downturn in the industry*
slump • *Many jobs were lost during the slump.*

reckon ① VERB (INFORMAL)
to think or believe something is the case • *I reckon he's still fond of her.*
assume • *If mistakes occurred, they were assumed to be my fault.*
believe (FORMAL) • *"You've never heard of him?" "I don't believe so."*
consider • *Barbara considers that people who sell these birds are acting illegally.*
judge • *I would judge that my earnings are considerably below those of my sister.*
suppose • *I suppose I'd better do some homework.*

think • *I think there should be a ban on tobacco advertising.*
MORE SYNONYMS:
• deem (FORMAL)
• hold to be
• surmise (FORMAL)

reckon ② VERB
to calculate an amount • *The figure is now reckoned to be 15%.*
calculate • *We calculate that the average size farm in the county is 65 acres.*
count • *The years before their arrival in prison are not counted as part of their sentence.*
estimate • *Analysts estimate its current popularity at around ten per cent.*
figure out • *I roughly figured out the total.*
work out • *It is proving hard to work out the value of their assets.*

recognize ① VERB
to know who or what someone or something is • *I recognized him at once.*
identify • *She tried to identify the perfume.*
know • *You'd know him if you saw him again.*
place • *He couldn't place my voice immediately.*
spot • *I spotted the house quite easily.*

recognize ② VERB
to accept or acknowledge something • *He was recognized as an outstanding pilot.*
acknowledge • *Her great bravery was acknowledged.*
appreciate • *In time you'll appreciate his good points.*
honour • *achievements honoured with the Nobel Prize*
salute • *We salute your great courage.*

reconstruct ① verb

to rebuild something that has been damaged • *The city centre has been completely reconstructed.*
rebuild • *The task of rebuilding would be very expensive.*
recreate • *They try to recreate the atmosphere of former times.*
regenerate • *the ability to regenerate damaged tissues*
renovate • *The hotel was being renovated.*
restore • *experts who specialize in restoring old furniture*

MORE SYNONYMS:
• reassemble
• remodel

reconstruct ② verb

to build up from small details • *The police reconstructed the scene of the crime.*
build up • *They built up an image of him from several different descriptions.*
deduce • *The date can be deduced from other documents.*
piece together • *It was easy to piece together the shattered fragments.*

record ① noun

a stored account of something
• *medical records*
account • *The company keeps detailed accounts.*
archives • *Earlier issues are stored in the archives.*
file • *the right to inspect company files*
journal • *He kept a journal while he was travelling.*
minute • *Did you read the minutes of the last meeting?*
register • *a register of births, deaths and marriages*

record ② noun

what someone has done in the

past • *You will be rejected if you have a criminal record.*
background • *His background was in engineering.*
career • *His career spoke for itself.*
curriculum vitae • *I must update my curriculum vitae.*
track record (INFORMAL) • *Her track record as a teacher was impeccable.*

record ③ verb

to note and store information • *Her diary records her daily life in detail.*
blog • *If I'm getting paid by a client, I don't blog about it.*
document • *All these facts have been well documented.*
enter • *All the names are entered in this book.*
log • *They log everyone who comes in or out.*
note • *I must note your birthday.*
register • *We registered his birth straight away.*
write down • *If I don't write it down, I'll forget it.*

recover ① verb

to get better again • *He has still not fully recovered.*
convalesce • *those convalescing from illness or surgery*
get better • *He never really got better again.*
get well • *Get well soon!*
improve • *The condition of your hair will soon improve.*
recuperate • *recuperating from a serious injury*
revive • *Business soon revived once he came back.*

recover ② verb

to get something back again • *They took legal action to recover the money.*
get back • *We got everything back after the burglary.*

A
B
C
D
E
F
G
H
I
J
K
L
M
N
O
P
Q
R
S
T
U
V
W
X
Y
Z

recapture • *trying to recapture the atmosphere of our holiday*
recoup • *trying to recoup their losses*
regain • *It took him a while to regain his composure.*
retrieve • *I retrieved my bag from the back seat.*

recovery ① NOUN

the act of getting better again • *He made a remarkable recovery after his illness.*
healing • *Adams claims that humour is an integral part of healing.*
improvement • *Germany is showing a perceptible improvement.*
recuperation • *great powers of recuperation*
revival • *little chance of a revival of interest*

MORE SYNONYMS:
• convalescence
• rally

recovery ② NOUN

the act of getting something back • *a reward for the recovery of the painting*
recapture • *An offensive was launched for the recapture of the airbase.*
reclamation • *the reclamation of dry land from the marshes*
restoration • *She owed the restoration of her sight to this remarkable technique.*
retrieval • *electronic storage and retrieval systems*

recruit ① VERB

to persuade people to join a group • *He helped to recruit volunteers.*
draft • *drafted into the armed forces*
enlist • *I had to enlist the help of six people to move it.*
enrol • *She enrolled me on her evening course.*
muster • *trying to muster support for the movement*

recruit ② NOUN

someone who has recently joined a group • *the latest batch of recruits*
beginner • *The course is suitable for beginners.*
convert • *a recent convert to their religion*
novice • *I'm a novice at these things.*
trainee • *My first job was as a graduate trainee with a bank.*

MORE SYNONYMS:
• neophyte
• proselyte
• tyro

red NOUN OR ADJECTIVE

◆ **SHADES OF RED**
◆ burgundy
◆ cardinal
◆ carmine
◆ cerise
◆ cherry
◆ claret
◆ crimson
◆ cyclamen
◆ flame
◆ fuchsia
◆ magenta
◆ maroon
◆ poppy
◆ raspberry
◆ ruby
◆ scarlet
◆ strawberry
◆ titian
◆ vermilion

RELATED WORDS:
• ADJECTIVES rubicund, ruddy

reduce ① VERB

to make something smaller in size or amount • *Gradually reduce the dosage.*
curtail • *His powers will be severely curtailed.*
cut • *The first priority is to cut costs.*

cut down • *Try to cut down your coffee consumption.*
decrease • *The government plans to decrease interest rates.*
diminish • *to diminish the prestige of the monarchy*
lessen • *a diet that would lessen the risk of disease*
lower • *a commitment to lower taxes*
shorten • *taking steps to shorten queues*

ANTONYM:
• increase

reduce ② VERB
to bring to a weaker or inferior state • *The village was reduced to rubble.*
degrade • *I wouldn't degrade myself by going out with him.*
demote • *The Soviet team have been demoted to second place.*
downgrade • *The female role has been downgraded in the drive for equality.*
drive • *an old woman driven to shoplifting to survive*
force • *The men were so hungry they were forced to eat grass.*

refer ① VERB
to mention something • *In his speech, he referred to a recent trip to Canada.*
allude • *She alluded to his absence in vague terms.*
bring up • *Why are you bringing that up now?*
cite • *She cites a favourite poem by George Herbert.*
mention • *She did not mention her mother's illness.*

refer ② VERB
to look at to find something out • *I had to refer to the manual.*
consult • *He had to consult a dictionary.*
look up • *I looked up your file to get your address.*

refined ① ADJECTIVE
polite and well-mannered • *His speech and manner are very refined.*
civilized • *the demands of civilized behaviour*
genteel • *two ladies with genteel manners and voices*
gentlemanly • *Sopwith behaved in his usual gentlemanly manner.*
ladylike • *They are models of ladylike decorum.*
polite • *polite and correct behaviour*

ANTONYM:
• common

refined ② ADJECTIVE
processed to remove impurities • *refined sugar*
distilled • *distilled water*
filtered • *two pints of spring or filtered water*
processed • *a diet high in processed foods*
pure • *crisp pure air*
purified • *freshly purified drinking water*

reform ① NOUN
a major change or improvement • *radical economic reforms*
amendment • *an amendment to remove the ban on divorce*
correction • *a correction of social injustice*
improvement • *She is pressing for improvements to education.*
rehabilitation • *the rehabilitation of young offenders*

MORE SYNONYMS:
• amelioration
• betterment
• rectification

reform ② VERB
to make major changes or improvements to something • *his plans to reform the economy*

a
b
c
d
e
f
g
h
i
j
k
l
m
n
o
p
q
r
s
t
u
v
w
x
y
z

A
B
C
D
E
F
G
H
I
J
K
L
M
N
O
P
Q
R
S
T
U
V
W
X
Y
Z

amend • *They want to amend the current system.*

better • *industrial action to better their working conditions*

correct • *keen to correct injustices*

rectify • *measures suggested to rectify the financial situation*

rehabilitate • *a loan for Bulgaria to rehabilitate its railway system*

MORE SYNONYMS:
• ameliorate
• emend
• revolutionize

refresh VERB
to make you feel more energetic • *A glass of fruit juice will refresh you.*

brace • *a bracing walk*

enliven • *Music can enliven the spirit.*

rejuvenate • *He was told that the Italian climate would rejuvenate him.*

revive • *The cold water revived me a bit.*

stimulate • *a toner to stimulate the skin*

MORE SYNONYMS:
• freshen
• invigorate
• revitalize
• revivify

refuge NOUN
a place where you go for safety • *a mountain refuge*

asylum • *political asylum*

harbour • *Patches of gorse were a great harbour for foxes.*

haven • *The island is a haven for international criminals.*

sanctuary • *a sanctuary from the outside world*

shelter • *an underground shelter*

refuse ① VERB
to say you will not do something • *He refused to speculate about the contents of the letter.*

abstain • *people who abstain from eating meat*

decline • *He declined to comment on the story.*

withhold • *Financial aid for Britain has been withheld.*

refuse ② VERB
to say you will not allow or accept something • *He offered me a drink, which I refused.*

decline • *He declined their invitation.*

reject • *The court rejected their petition.*

spurn • *You spurned his last offer.*

turn down • *He has turned down the job.*

ANTONYM:
• accept

refuse ③ NOUN
rubbish or waste • *a weekly collection of refuse*

garbage • *rotting piles of garbage*

junk (INFORMAL) • *What are you going to do with all that junk?*

litter • *If you see litter in the corridor, pick it up.*

rubbish • *They had piled most of their rubbish into yellow skips.*

trash • *I forgot to take out the trash.*

waste • *a law that regulates the disposal of waste*

regard ① VERB
to have particular views about someone or something • *I regard creativity as a gift.*

consider • *I consider activities such as jogging a waste of time.*

judge • *This may or may not be judged as reasonable.*

look on • *A lot of people looked on him as a healer.*

see • *I don't see it as my duty to take sides.*

think of • *We all thought of him as a father.*
view • *They view the United States as a land of opportunity.*

regard ② VERB (LITERARY)
to look at someone in a particular way • *She regarded him curiously for a moment.*
contemplate • *He contemplated her in silence.*
eye • *We eyed each other thoughtfully.*
gaze • *gazing at herself in the mirror*
look • *She looked at him earnestly.*
scrutinize • *She scrutinized his features to see if he was to be trusted.*
watch • *Chris watched him sipping his brandy.*

region NOUN
a large area of land • *a remote mountainous region of Afghanistan*
area • *The area is renowned for its cuisine.*
district • *I drove around the business district.*
land • *a land permanently cloaked in mist*
locality • *All other factories in the locality went on strike.*
quarter • *We wandered through the Chinese quarter.*
sector • *the northeast sector of Bosnia*
territory • *the disputed territory of Kashmir*
tract • *They cleared large tracts of forest.*
zone • *a different time zone*

regret ① VERB
to be sorry something has happened • *I gave in to him, and I have regretted it ever since.*
be sorry • *I'm sorry you feel that way about it.*
grieve • *grieving over the death of his wife*

lament • *We lament the loss of a fine novelist.*
mourn • *to mourn the loss of a loved one*
repent • *He repents his past sins.*

MORE SYNONYMS:
• bemoan
• bewail
• rue

regret ② NOUN
the feeling of being sorry about something • *He expressed regret that he had caused any offence.*
grief • *his guilt and grief over the failed relationship*
pang of conscience • *He need not feel any pangs of conscience over his decision.*
penitence • *an abject display of penitence*
remorse • *He expressed remorse over his own foolishness.*
repentance • *an apparent lack of genuine repentance*
sorrow • *I feel real sorrow that my dad did this.*

MORE SYNONYMS:
• compunction
• contrition
• ruefulness
• self-reproach

regular ① ADJECTIVE
even or equally spaced • *soft music with a regular beat*
consistent • *a consistent heart-rate*
constant • *a constant temperature*
even • *an even level of sound*
periodic • *Periodic checks are carried out.*
rhythmic • *the rhythmic beating of the drum*
steady • *a steady pace*
uniform • *The Earth rotates on its axis at a uniform rate.*

ANTONYM:
• irregular

a
b
c
d
e
f
g
h
i
j
k
l
m
n
o
p
q
r
s
t
u
v
w
x
y
z

regular ② ADJECTIVE

usual or normal • *I was filling in for the regular bartender.*

customary • *her customary place at the table*

everyday • *part of everyday life*

habitual • *habitual practices*

normal • *a normal day*

ordinary • *It was just an ordinary weekend.*

routine • *a routine knee operation*

typical • *My typical day begins at 8.30.*

usual • *In a usual week I watch about 15 hours of television.*

reject VERB

to refuse to accept or agree to something • *We reject any suggestion that the law needs amending.*

decline • *They declined his proposal.*

deny • *He denied our offer of assistance.*

rebuff • *She rebuffed his advances.*

refuse • *He offered me a drink, which I refused.*

renounce • *She renounced her parents' religion.*

say no to • *Just say no to drugs.*

spurn • *He spurned the advice of management consultants.*

turn down • *She turned down his offer of marriage.*

unfollow • *I found him boring so I unfollowed him.*

unfriend • *We fell out and she unfriended me.*

MORE SYNONYMS:
• disallow
• repudiate

ANTONYM:
• accept

rejoice VERB

to be very happy about something • *Today we can rejoice in our success.*

be overjoyed • *I was overjoyed to see him.*

celebrate • *We should celebrate our victory.*

delight • *He delighted in her success.*

glory • *glorying in the achievement of his troops*

MORE SYNONYMS:
• exult
• revel

relation ① NOUN

a connection between two things • *This theory bears no relation to reality.*

bearing • *Diet has an important bearing on your general health.*

bond • *the bond between a mother and child*

connection • *a possible connection between BSE and human disease*

correlation • *the correlation between unemployment and crime*

link • *a link between obesity and heart problems*

relationship • *the relationship between success and effort*

relation ② NOUN

a member of your family • *I was staying with relations in Atlanta.*

kin • *She has gone to live with her husband's kin.*

kinsman • *the prince who murdered his father and kinsmen*

kinswoman • *She was a kinswoman of the Duke of Portland.*

relative • *Get a relative to look after the children.*

relationship ① NOUN

the way people act towards each other • *He has a friendly relationship with his customers.*

affinity • *the natural affinity between the female members of the community*

association • *the association between the two countries*

bond • *The experience created a bond between us.*

connection • *He felt a personal connection with her.*
rapport • *He has a terrific rapport with kids.*

relationship ② NOUN
a close friendship, especially a sexual one • *I found myself in a relationship I couldn't handle.*
affair • *an affair with a married man*
liaison • *Nobody knew of their brief liaison.*

relationship ③ NOUN
the connection between two things • *the relationship between humans and their environment*
connection • *the connection between age and ill-health*
correlation • *the correlation between unemployment and crime*
link • *the link between smoking and lung cancer*
parallel • *the parallel between painting and music*

relax VERB
to be calm and become less worried • *I never have any time to relax.*
laze • *I'm just going to laze around and do nothing.*
rest • *Try to rest as much as you can.*
take it easy • *the chance to just take it easy for a week or two*
unwind • *It helps them to unwind after a busy day at work.*

relaxed ① ADJECTIVE
calm and not worried or tense • *As soon as I made the decision, I felt more relaxed.*
at ease • *It is essential to feel at ease with your therapist.*
calm • *Diane felt calm and unafraid as she entered the courtroom.*
comfortable • *He liked me and I felt comfortable with him.*

cool • *He was marvellously cool, smiling as if nothing had happened.*
easy • *By then I was feeling a little easier about the situation.*
serene • *that serene smile of his*
unflustered • *He has a calm, unflustered temperament.*

ANTONYM:
• tense

relaxed ② ADJECTIVE
calm and peaceful • *The atmosphere at lunch was relaxed.*
calm • *The city appears relatively calm today.*
casual • *We have a very casual relationship.*
comfortable • *a comfortable silence*
informal • *an informal occasion*
peaceful • *Sundays are usually quiet and peaceful in our house.*

ANTONYM:
• tense

release ① VERB
to set someone or something free • *negotiations to release the hostages*
deliver • *I thank God for delivering me from that pain.*
discharge • *He may be discharged from hospital today.*
extricate • *They managed to extricate the survivors from the wreckage.*
free • *Israel is set to free more Lebanese prisoners.*
let go • *They held him for three hours and then let him go.*
liberate • *liberated under the terms of the amnesty*
set free • *birds set free into the wild*

MORE SYNONYMS:
• emancipate
• manumit
• unfetter

release ② VERB
to make something available • *The*

a b c d e f g h i j k l m n o p q r s t u v w x y z

new album is released next week.
issue • He has issued a press statement.
launch • The company has just launched a new range of products.
publish • His latest book will be published in May.
put out • putting out a series of novels by Nobel prize winners

release ③ NOUN
the setting free of someone or something • his release from prison
discharge • a discharge from the army
emancipation • the emancipation of slaves in the 19th century
freedom • Hinckley campaigned for his freedom.
liberation • their liberation from a Nazi concentration camp
liberty • her television appearances pleading for his liberty

MORE SYNONYMS:
• deliverance
• manumission

relentless ADJECTIVE
never stopping or becoming less intense • The pressure was relentless.
incessant • incessant rain
nonstop • nonstop background music
persistent • in the face of persistent criticism
sustained • a sustained attack
unrelenting • unrelenting protests
unremitting • the unremitting demands of duty

relevant ADJECTIVE
connected with what is being discussed • We have passed on all relevant information.
applicable • These fees are not applicable to mortgages in Scotland.
apposite • He could not think of anything apposite to say.
appropriate • The name seemed very appropriate.

apt • an apt comment
pertinent • She had asked some pertinent questions.

MORE SYNONYMS:
• appurtenant
• germane
• material

ANTONYM:
• irrelevant

reliable ADJECTIVE
able to be trusted • You have to demonstrate that you are reliable.
dependable • dependable information
faithful • a faithful friend
safe • It's all right, you're in safe hands.
sound • sound advice
staunch • a staunch supporter
sure • a sure sign of rain
true • a true account
trustworthy • a trustworthy and level-headed leader

ANTONYM:
• unreliable

religion NOUN
◆ **RELIGIONS**
◆ animism
◆ Baha'ism
◆ Buddhism
◆ Christianity
◆ Confucianism
◆ Hinduism
◆ Islam
◆ Jainism
◆ Judaism
◆ Rastafarianism
◆ shamanism
◆ Shinto
◆ Sikhism
◆ Taoism
◆ Zen
◆ Zoroastrianism or Zoroastrism

religious ① ADJECTIVE
connected with religion • religious worship

devotional • *an altar covered with devotional pictures*
divine • *a request for divine guidance*
doctrinal • *their doctrinal differences*
holy • *To Tibetans, this is a holy place.*
sacred • *Bach's sacred music*
scriptural • *scriptural and theological references*
spiritual • *We've got no spiritual values.*
theological • *theological studies*

religious ② ADJECTIVE
having a strong belief in a god or gods • *They are both very religious.*
devout • *She is a devout Catholic.*
God-fearing • *They brought up their children to be God-fearing Christians.*
godly • *a learned and godly preacher*
pious • *He was brought up by pious female relatives.*
righteous • *struggling to be righteous and chaste*

reluctant ADJECTIVE
unwilling to do something • *He was reluctant to ask for help.*
averse • *I'm not averse to going along with the idea.*
disinclined • *He was disinclined to talk about himself.*
hesitant • *His advisers are hesitant to let the United States enter the conflict.*
loath • *The finance minister is loath to cut income tax.*
slow • *The world community has been slow to respond to the crisis.*
unwilling • *For months I had been unwilling to go through with it.*

ANTONYM:
• eager

remain ① VERB
to stay somewhere • *You'll have to remain in hospital for the time being.*
be left • *He was left in the car.*

linger • *I lingered for a few days until he arrived.*
stay behind • *I was told to stay behind after the class.*
wait • *Wait here until I come back.*

remain ② VERB
to stay the same • *The men remained silent.*
continue • *This state of affairs cannot continue.*
endure • *Somehow their friendship endures.*
go on • *The debate goes on.*
last • *Nothing lasts forever.*
stay • *They could stay afloat without swimming.*
survive • *companies which survived after the recession*

remainder NOUN
the part that is left of something • *He gulped down the remainder of his coffee.*
balance • *pay the balance on delivery*
last • *He finished off the last of the wine.*
others • *She took one and put the others back.*
remnants • *The remnants of the force were fleeing.*
remains • *tidying up the remains of their picnic*
rest • *I'm going to throw a party, then invest the rest of the money.*

remains PLURAL NOUN
the parts of something left over • *the remains of an ancient mosque*
debris • *screws, bolts and other debris from a scrapyard*
dregs • *Colum drained the dregs from his cup.*
leftovers • *Refrigerate any leftovers.*
relics • *a museum of war relics*
remnants • *Beneath the present church were remnants of Roman flooring.*
residue • *Discard the milky residue left behind.*

a
b
c
d
e
f
g
h
i
j
k
l
m
n
o
p
q
r
s
t
u
v
w
x
y
z

scraps • *the scraps from the dinner table*
vestiges • *an attempt to destroy the last vestiges of evidence*

MORE SYNONYMS:
• detritus
• leavings

remark ① VERB
to mention or comment on something • *She had remarked on the boy's improvement.*
comment • *So far, he has not commented on these reports.*
mention • *I mentioned that I didn't like jazz.*
observe • *"You're very pale," he observed.*
say • *"Well done," he said.*
state • *We stated that he had resigned.*

remark ② NOUN
something you say • *a vulgar remark*
comment • *his abrasive wit and caustic comments*
observation • *a few general observations*
statement • *That statement puzzled me.*
utterance • *admirers who hung on her every utterance*
word • *No-one had an unkind word to say about him.*

remember VERB
to bring to mind something from the past • *I do not remember the exact words.*
call to mind • *He invited the congregation to call to mind their sins.*
recall • *He tried to recall the layout of the farmhouse.*
recognize • *I don't recognize that name.*
retain • *information which can be retained in the memory*

MORE SYNONYMS:
• recollect
• reminisce

ANTONYM:
• forget

remind VERB
to make someone remember something • *He reminds me of myself at that age.*
bring back to • *Talking about the accident brought it all back to me.*
jog someone's memory • *See if this picture helps jog your memory.*
make someone remember • *Your article made me remember my own traumas.*
put in mind • *His eagerness to please put her in mind of a puppy.*
refresh someone's memory • *I read through the list to refresh my memory.*

remote ① ADJECTIVE
far off in distance • *a remote farm in the hills*
distant • *in that distant land*
far-off • *start a new life in a far-off country*
inaccessible • *people living in inaccessible parts of the country*
isolated • *Many of the refugee villages are in isolated areas.*
lonely • *It felt like the loneliest place in the world.*
outlying • *Tourists can visit outlying areas by jeep.*

remote ② ADJECTIVE
far away in time • *It dates from the remote past.*
distant • *a glimpse into the more distant future*
far-off • *She has entirely forgotten those far-off days*

remote ③ ADJECTIVE
not wanting to be friendly • *She looked beautiful, but at the same time so remote.*

aloof • *He seemed aloof, standing watching the others.*
cold • *What a cold, unfeeling woman she was.*
detached • *He tries to remain emotionally detached from the prisoners.*
distant • *He is courteous but distant.*
reserved • *She's quite a reserved person.*
withdrawn • *Her husband had become withdrawn and moody.*

remote ④ ADJECTIVE
not very great • *The chances of his surviving are pretty remote.*
poor • *The odds of it happening again are very poor.*
slender • *There is a slender possibility that the plan might work.*
slight • *Is there even a slight hope that she might change her mind?*
slim • *There's still a slim chance that he may become Prime Minister.*
small • *There was still a small possibility that he might phone.*

remove VERB
to take something off or away • *I removed the splinter from her finger.*
delete • *He deleted files from the computer system.*
detach • *Detach and keep the bottom part of the form.*
eject • *He was ejected from the restaurant.*
eliminate • *Eliminate dairy products from your diet.*
erase • *She had erased the message.*
extract • *She is having a tooth extracted today.*
get rid of • *to get rid of raw sewage by pumping it out to sea*
take away • *She took away the tray.*
take off • *I won't take my coat off, I'm not staying.*
take out • *Take that dog out of here.*
withdraw • *She withdrew her hand from Roger's.*

MORE SYNONYMS:
• efface
• excise
• expunge

renew VERB
to begin something again • *Syria renewed diplomatic relations with Egypt.*
begin again • *The audience began the slow handclap again.*
recommence • *He recommenced work on his novel.*
re-establish • *He had re-established his close friendship with Anthony.*
reopen • *It is feared that this issue could re-open the controversy.*
resume • *Rebels have refused to resume peace talks.*

renounce VERB (FORMAL)
to reject something or give it up • *She renounced terrorism.*
disown • *The comments were later disowned by an official spokesman.*
give up • *He did not want to give up his right to the title.*
reject • *children who reject their parents' political and religious beliefs*
relinquish • *He does not intend to relinquish power.*

ANOTHER SYNONYM:
• eschew (FORMAL)

renovate VERB
to repair an old building or machine • *They spent thousands renovating the house.*
do up • *his father's obsession with doing up old cars*
modernize • *plans to modernize the refinery*
recondition • *The company specializes in reconditioning photocopiers.*
refurbish • *This hotel has been completely refurbished.*

repair • *He has repaired the roof to make the house more windproof.*
restore • *The old town square has been beautifully restored.*
revamp • *plans to revamp the airport*

repair ① NOUN
something you do to mend something that is damaged • *The landlord carried out the repairs himself.*
darn • *a sock with a big darn in it*
mend • *Spray the area with paint to make the mend invisible.*
patch • *jackets with patches on the elbows*
restoration • *the restoration of a war-damaged building*

repair ② VERB
to mend something that is damaged • *The money will be used to repair faulty equipment.*
fix • *If something is broken, get it fixed.*
mend • *They mended it without charge.*
patch • *They patched the barn roof.*
patch up • *Patch up those holes.*
renovate • *They spent thousands renovating the house.*
restore • *experts who specialize in restoring ancient parchments*

repay VERB
to give back money which is owed • *It will take me years to repay the loan.*
pay back • *I'll pay you back that money tomorrow.*
refund • *Any extra that you have paid will be refunded to you.*
settle up • *If we owe you anything we can settle up when you come.*

MORE SYNONYMS:
• make restitution
• recompense
• reimburse
• remunerate
• square

repeat VERB
to say or write something again • *Since you didn't listen, I'll repeat that.*
echo • *"Are you frightened?" "Frightened?" she echoed. "Of what?"*
reiterate • *The lawyer could only reiterate what he had said before.*
say again • *"I'm sorry," she said again.*

MORE SYNONYMS:
• iterate
• recapitulate
• restate

repel ① VERB
to horrify and disgust • *The thought of spiders repels me.*
disgust • *He disgusted everyone with his boorish behaviour.*
offend • *viewers who are easily offended*
revolt • *The smell revolted him.*
sicken • *What he saw there sickened him.*

ANTONYM:
• attract

repel ② VERB
to fight and drive back enemy forces • *troops along the border ready to repel an enemy attack*
drive off • *They drove the guerillas off with infantry and air strikes.*
repulse • *Cavalry and artillery were sent to repulse the enemy forces.*
resist • *The tribe resisted the Spanish invaders.*

replace VERB
to take the place of something else • *the man who replaced him as England skipper*
succeed • *He was succeeded by his son.*
supersede • *Horses were superseded by cars.*
supplant • *Anger supplanted all other feelings.*
take over from • *the man taking over from Mr Berry as chairman*

take the place of • *Debit cards are taking the place of cash and cheques.*

replacement NOUN
a person or thing that takes the place of another • *He has nominated Adams as his replacement.*
proxy • *They must nominate a proxy to vote on their behalf.*
stand-in • *He was a stand-in for my regular doctor.*
substitute • *an artificial substitute for silk*
successor • *He recommended him as his successor.*
surrogate • *They had expected me to be a surrogate for my sister.*

reply ① VERB
to give someone an answer • *He did not even have the courtesy to reply to my fax.*
answer • *He avoided answering the question.*
counter • *"It's not that simple," he countered in a firm voice.*
respond • *"Mind your manners, lady!" I responded.*
retort • *"Nobody asked you," he retorted.*
return • *"I can manage," she returned coldly.*

MORE SYNONYMS:
• reciprocate
• rejoin
• riposte

reply ② NOUN
an answer given to someone • *There was a trace of irony in his reply.*
answer • *She could not give him a truthful answer.*
response • *His response was brusque.*
retort • *His sharp retort clearly made an impact.*

MORE SYNONYMS:
• rejoinder
• riposte

report ① VERB
to tell about or give an official account of something • *He reported the theft to the police.*
cover • *The US news media will cover the trial closely.*
describe • *His condition was described as "improving".*
inform of • *Inform the police of any suspicious activity.*
notify • *The skipper notified the coastguard of the tragedy.*
state • *The police stated that he had been arrested.*

report ② NOUN
an account of an event or situation • *reports of serious human rights violations*
account • *a dishonest account of events*
description • *a detailed description of the match*
statement • *a deliberately misleading statement*

represent ① VERB
to stand for something else • *This rune represents wealth and plenty.*
mean • *This tarot card means the death of your present situation.*
stand for • *The olive branch stands for peace.*
symbolize • *a scene which symbolizes the movie's message*

MORE SYNONYMS:
• betoken
• equate with

represent ② VERB
to describe something in a particular way • *The popular press tends to represent him as a hero.*

a b c d e f g h i j k l m n o p q r s t u v w x y z

depict • *Children's books usually depict farm animals as lovable.*
describe • *She was always described as an intellectual.*
picture • *In the American press she was pictured as a heroine.*
portray • *She was portrayed as a heartless, terrible woman.*
show • *He was shown as an intelligent and courageous man.*

representative ① NOUN
a person who acts on behalf of another or others • *Employees from each department elect a representative.*
agent • *You are buying direct, rather than through an agent.*
delegate • *a union delegate*
deputy • *I can't make it so I'll send my deputy.*
proxy • *They must nominate a proxy to vote on their behalf.*
spokesman • *the party's education spokesman*
spokeswoman • *a spokeswoman for her generation*

representative ② ADJECTIVE
typical of the group to which it belongs • *fairly representative groups of adults*
characteristic • *a characteristic feature*
illustrative • *an illustrative example*
typical • *a typical Italian menu*

MORE SYNONYMS:
• archetypal
• emblematic
• indicative

reputation NOUN
the opinion that people have of a person or thing • *The college has a good reputation.*
character • *a man of good character*
name • *I have disgraced the family's name.*

renown • *a singer of great renown*
repute • *a writer and scholar of some repute*
standing • *This has done nothing to improve his standing.*
stature • *his stature as the world's greatest cellist*

request ① VERB
to ask for something politely or formally • *She requested that the door be left open.*
ask • *The government is being asked to consider the plan.*
beg • *May I beg a favour of you?*
seek • *You should seek a medical opinion.*

MORE SYNONYMS:
• entreat
• solicit

request ② NOUN
the action of asking for something politely or formally • *France had agreed to his request for political asylum.*
appeal • *an appeal for witnesses to come forward*
application • *Their application was vetoed.*
call • *calls to decrease income tax*
plea • *his plea for help in solving the killing*

MORE SYNONYMS:
• entreaty
• petition

require ① VERB
to need something • *A baby requires warmth and security.*
demand • *The task of reconstruction would demand patience and hard work.*
depend on • *I depend on this money to survive.*
be in need of • *The house was in need of modernization.*
need • *He desperately needed money.*

want (INFORMAL) • *The windows wanted cleaning.*

require ② VERB
to say that someone must do something • *The rules require employers to provide safety training.*
compel • *legislation that would compel cyclists to wear a helmet*
demand • *This letter demands an immediate reply.*
direct • *a court order directing the group to leave the area*
instruct • *They have instructed their solicitor to sue for compensation.*
oblige • *This decree obliges unions to delay strikes.*
order • *The court ordered him to pay the sum in full.*

requirement NOUN
something that you must have or do • *The products met all legal requirements.*
demand • *the demands and challenges of his new job*
essential • *the basic essentials for bachelor life*
necessity • *food and other daily necessities*
need • *special nutritional needs*
specification • *These companies will have to meet new European specifications.*
MORE SYNONYMS:
• prerequisite (FORMAL)
• stipulation (FORMAL)

research ① NOUN
the act of studying and finding out about something • *funds for research into AIDS*
analysis • *They collected blood samples for laboratory analysis.*
examination • *a framework for the examination of these topics*
exploration • *an exploration of classical myths*

investigation • *Further investigation was hindered by the loss of all documentation.*
study • *The study demonstrated a link between obesity and heart problems.*

research ② VERB
to study and find out about something • *I'm researching for an article on New England.*
analyse • *We haven't had time to analyse those samples yet.*
examine • *The spacecraft will examine how solar wind affects Earth's magnetic field.*
explore • *I would probably be wise to explore the matter further.*
google • *Google 'Greek islands' and see what you can find.*
investigate • *Gas officials are investigating the cause of the explosion.*
study • *She's been studying chimpanzees for thirty years.*

resemblance NOUN
a similarity between two things • *I can see a resemblance between you.*
analogy • *the analogy between racism and homophobia*
correspondence • *There's little correspondence between our lifestyles.*
likeness • *These myths have a startling likeness to one another.*
parallel • *There were parallels between the two murders.*
similarity • *similarities between mother and son*
MORE SYNONYMS:
• comparability
• parity
• semblance
• similitude

resemble VERB
to be similar to something else • *Venison resembles beef in flavour.*

A
B
C
D
E
F
G
H
I
J
K
L
M
N
O
P
Q
R
S
T
U
V
W
X
Y
Z

bear a resemblance to • *She bears a resemblance to Marilyn Monroe.*

be like • *The ground is like concrete.*

be similar to • *The gun was similar to an air pistol.*

look like • *He looks like his father.*

parallel • *His fate paralleled that of his predecessor.*

take after • *You take after your grandmother.*

resent VERB

to feel bitter and angry about something • *I resent the slur on my integrity.*

be angry about • *I was angry at the way he spoke to me.*

be offended by • *She was offended by his comments.*

dislike • *I dislike his patronizing attitude.*

object to • *I object to being treated like an idiot.*

take offence at • *She took offence at the implied criticism.*

resentful ADJECTIVE

bitter about something that has happened • *a sullen and resentful workforce*

aggrieved • *He is still aggrieved at the size of the fine.*

angry • *I was angry that I wasn't consulted.*

bitter • *a forsaken and bitter man*

embittered • *He had grown into an embittered, hardened adult.*

huffy • *He's so huffy if he doesn't get his own way.*

indignant • *They were indignant that they had not been consulted.*

offended • *He was offended at being left out.*

MORE SYNONYMS:
• in high dudgeon

• peeved
• piqued

resentment NOUN

a feeling of anger and bitterness • *There is growing resentment against newcomers.*

anger • *Perhaps anger had clouded his vision.*

animosity • *The animosity between the two men grew.*

bitterness • *I feel bitterness towards the person who knocked me down.*

grudge • *It was an accident and I bear no grudges.*

huff • *She went off in a huff.*

indignation • *He could hardly contain his indignation.*

rancour • *There was no trace of envy or rancour in her face.*

MORE SYNONYMS:
• pique
• umbrage

reserve ① VERB

to keep for a particular person or purpose • *Hotel rooms have been reserved for us.*

hoard • *They've begun to hoard food and petrol.*

hold • *The information is held in a database.*

keep • *Grate the lemon zest and keep it for later.*

put by • *She had enough put by for her fare.*

save • *Save me a seat.*

set aside • *funds set aside for education*

stockpile • *People are stockpiling food for the coming winter.*

store • *potatoes stored for sale out of season*

reserve ② NOUN

a supply kept for future use • *a drain on the cash reserves*

cache • *a cache of weapons and explosives*
fund • *a pension fund*
hoard • *a hoard of food and petrol*
stock • *stocks of paper and ink*
stockpile • *stockpiles of chemical weapons*
store • *a secret store of sweets*
supply • *food supplies*

resign ① VERB
to leave a job • *Scott resigned from the firm.*
abdicate • *The King abdicated to marry an American divorcee.*
hand in your notice • *I handed in my notice on Friday.*
leave • *I am leaving to become a teacher.*
quit • *He quit his job as an office boy.*
step down (INFORMAL) • *He headed the government until he stepped down in 1990.*

resign ②: **resign oneself** VERB
to accept an unpleasant situation • *She had resigned herself to losing her home.*
accept • *You've got to accept the fact that he's left you.*
bow • *He bowed to the inevitable and allowed her to go.*
reconcile oneself • *She had reconciled herself to never seeing him again.*

resist VERB
to refuse to accept something and try to prevent it • *They resisted our attempts to modernize.*
defy • *arrested for defying the ban on street trading*
fight • *He vigorously fought the proposal.*
oppose • *Many parents oppose bilingual education in schools.*
refuse • *The patient has the right to refuse treatment.*

struggle against • *nations struggling against Communist takeovers*

ANTONYM:
• accept

resolve ① VERB
to decide firmly to do something • *She resolved to report the matter.*
decide • *She decided to quit smoking.*
determine • *He determined to rescue his two countrymen.*
intend • *I intended to teach him a lesson he wouldn't forget.*
make up your mind • *Once he made up his mind to do it, there was no stopping him.*

resolve ② VERB
to find a solution to a problem • *We must find a way to resolve these problems.*
clear up • *The confusion was soon cleared up.*
find a solution to • *the ability to find an effective solution to the crisis*
overcome • *Find a way to overcome your difficulties.*
solve • *These reforms did not solve the problem of unemployment.*
sort out • *The two countries have sorted out their trade dispute.*
work out • *It seems like a nightmare, but I'm sure we can work it out.*

resolve ③ NOUN
absolute determination • *He doesn't weaken in his resolve.*
determination • *the expression of fierce determination on her face*
resolution • *"I'm going on a diet," she said with sudden resolution.*
tenacity • *Hard work and sheer tenacity are crucial to career success.*

MORE SYNONYMS:
• doggedness

• single-mindedness
• willpower

respect ① VERB

to have a good opinion of someone
• I want him to respect me as a career woman.

admire • I admire him for his honesty.
have a good opinion of • Nobody seems to have a good opinion of him.
have a high opinion of • He had a very high opinion of Neil.
honour • the Scout's promise to honour God and the Queen
look up to • He looks up to his dad.
think highly of • His boss thinks very highly of him.
venerate • My father venerated General Eisenhower.

MORE SYNONYMS:
• esteem
• revere
• reverence
• set store by

ANTONYM:
• disrespect

respect ② NOUN

a good opinion of someone • We have no respect for him at all.

admiration • I have always had the greatest admiration for him.
esteem • We have to win the trust and esteem of our clients.
regard • I hold him in high regard.
reverence • We did it out of reverence for the dead.

ANTONYM:
• disrespect

respectable ① ADJECTIVE

considered to be acceptable and correct • respectable families

decent • They married after a decent interval.
good • He comes from a good family.

honourable • His colleagues were honourable people.
proper • It was not proper for women to go on the stage.
reputable • a reputable firm
upright • an upright and trustworthy man
worthy • worthy citizens

respectable ② ADJECTIVE

adequate or reasonable • a respectable rate of economic growth

appreciable • making appreciable progress
considerable • a considerable amount
decent • a decent standard of living
fair • She had a fair command of English.
reasonable • He couldn't make a reasonable living from his writing.

responsibility ① NOUN

the duty to deal with or take care of something • The garden is your responsibility.

duty • My duty is to look after the animals.
obligation • You have an obligation to help him.
onus • The onus was on him to make sure he didn't fail.

responsibility ② NOUN

the blame for something which has happened • We must all accept responsibility for our mistakes.

blame • I'm not going to take the blame for this.
fault • This is all your fault.
guilt • He was not completely free of guilt.
liability • He admitted liability for the crash.

MORE SYNONYMS:
• accountability
• culpability

responsible ① ADJECTIVE
being the person in charge of
something • *The Cabinet is
collectively responsible for policy.*
in charge • *I wish someone else was
in charge of this inquiry.*
in control • *Who is in control of the
operation?*

responsible ② ADJECTIVE
being to blame for something • *I hold
you responsible for this mess.*
at fault • *I was not at fault as my
vehicle was stationary.*
guilty • *I still maintain that I am not
guilty.*
to blame • *Television is possibly to
blame for this.*

responsible ③ ADJECTIVE
sensible and dependable • *He had
to show that he would be a responsible
parent.*
dependable • *a dependable,
trustworthy teacher*
level-headed • *a sensible, level-
headed approach*
reliable • *You have to demonstrate
that you are reliable.*
sensible • *She's a sensible girl, if a bit
headstrong.*
sound • *sound advice*
trustworthy • *He is a trustworthy
leader.*
ANTONYM:
• irresponsible

rest ① NOUN
the remaining parts of something
• *Take what you want and leave the rest.*
balance • *You pay half now and the
balance on delivery.*
others • *She took one and put the
others back.*
remainder • *He gulped down the
remainder of his coffee.*

surplus • *Coat with seasoned flour,
shaking off the surplus.*

rest ② NOUN
a period when you relax and do
nothing • *I'll start again after a rest.*
break • *He needs to take a break from
work.*
holiday • *I could really do with a holiday.*
leisure • *We get no leisure, no time off,
no overtime pay.*
relaxation • *Make time for a bit of
relaxation.*
respite • *a respite from the rush of
everyday life*

rest ③ VERB
to relax and do nothing for a while
• *He rested briefly before going on.*
have a break • *Paul felt he had to have
a break.*
idle • *He sat idling in his room.*
laze • *lazing on the beach*
put your feet up • *Nobody's home, so I
can put my feet up for a while.*
relax • *Guests can relax in the cosy bar.*
sit down • *I'll have to sit down for a
minute.*
take it easy • *the chance to just take it
easy for a couple of weeks*

restless ADJECTIVE
unable to sit still or relax • *She had been
restless and irritable all day.*
edgy • *She was nervous and edgy, still
chain-smoking.*
fidgety • *bored, fidgety youngsters*
fretful • *The whole family was fretful
and argumentative.*
jumpy • *If she can't smoke she gets
jumpy and irritable.*
on edge • *She's been on edge for weeks.*
unsettled • *The staff were unsettled
and demoralized.*

restore ① VERB
to cause something to return to its

a
b
c
d
e
f
g
h
i
j
k
l
m
n
o
p
q
r
s
t
u
v
w
x
y
z

previous state • *He was anxious to restore his reputation.*
re-establish • *an attempt to re-establish diplomatic relations*
reinstate • *the failure to reinstate the ceasefire*
reintroduce • *the plan to reintroduce wolves to the Highlands*
return • *their attempts to return the country to an agrarian economy*

restore ② VERB
to clean and repair something
• *experts who specialize in restoring ancient parchments*
fix up • *It took us months to fix this house up.*
mend • *They finally got round to mending the roof.*
rebuild • *plans to rebuild the opera house*
reconstruct • *reconstructing paintings by old masters*
refurbish • *The city is refurbishing the cathedral's facade.*
renovate • *The hotel was being renovated in expectation of a tourist boom.*
repair • *The money will be used to repair faulty equipment.*

MORE SYNONYMS:
• recondition
• retouch

restrain VERB
to hold someone or something back
• *He had to be restrained by his friends.*
contain • *He could hardly contain his rage.*
control • *She tried to control her excitement.*
curb • *You must curb your extravagant tastes.*
hamper • *I was hampered by a lack of information.*
hinder • *Research is hindered by lack of cash.*

hold back • *He could no longer hold back his laughter.*
inhibit • *factors which inhibit growth*

MORE SYNONYMS:
• constrain
• rein
• straiten

restrict VERB
to limit the movement or actions of someone or something • *laws to restrict foreign imports*
confine • *Keep your dog confined to the house.*
contain • *The curfew had contained the violence.*
hamper • *I was hampered by a lack of information.*
handicap • *handicapped by the terms of the contract*
impede • *Their work was being impeded by shortages of supplies.*
inhibit • *factors which inhibit growth*
limit • *He limited payments on the country's foreign debt.*
restrain • *the need to restrain wage rises*

MORE SYNONYMS:
• circumscribe
• demarcate
• straiten

restriction NOUN
a rule or situation that limits what you can do • *a speed restriction*
constraint • *financial constraints*
control • *a call for stricter gun control*
curb • *support for a curb on migration from neighbouring countries*
limitation • *A slipped disc causes severe limitation of movement.*
regulation • *regulations outlawing child labour*
restraint • *new restraints on trade unions*
stipulation • *The only dress stipulation was "no jeans".*

result ① NOUN

the situation that is caused by something • *the result of lengthy deliberation*

consequence • *This could have disastrous consequences for industry.*

effect • *the intended effect of the revised guidelines*

outcome • *The ultimate outcome will be different.*

product • *the product of five years' work*

upshot • *The upshot is that our employees are all unhappy.*

result ② VERB

to be caused by something • *The crash resulted from a defect in the aircraft.*

arise • *the publicity that arises from incidents of this kind*

derive • *Poor health often derives from poverty.*

develop • *a determination which has developed from his new-found confidence*

ensue • *If the system collapses, chaos will ensue.*

follow • *the consequences which followed his release from prison*

happen • *What will happen if the test proves positive?*

stem • *Her hatred of cars stems from her mother's death in a crash.*

result in VERB

to cause something to happen • *50% of road accidents result in head injuries.*

bring about • *The Suez crisis brought about petrol rationing.*

cause • *The play caused a stir here.*

lead to • *brain damage which leads to paralysis*

retaliate VERB

to do something to someone in return for what they did • *The militia said it would retaliate against any attacks.*

get back at • *a desire to get back at our enemies*

get even with (INFORMAL) • *He wanted to get even with his former employers.*

get your own back (INFORMAL) • *the opportunity to get your own back on your husband*

hit back • *In this article he hits back at his critics.*

pay someone back • *I'll pay him back for what he's done.*

take revenge • *taking revenge for his father's murder*

retreat ① VERB

to move away from someone or something • *damage inflicted by the rebels as they retreated from the town*

back away • *He put up his hands in protest and began to back away.*

back off • *I stood up for myself and they backed off.*

draw back • *They drew back in fear.*

pull back • *Their forces have pulled back in all areas.*

withdraw • *Troops withdrew from the country last month.*

ANTONYM:
• advance

retreat ② NOUN

the action of moving away from someone or something • *the long retreat from Moscow*

departure • *the departure of all foreign forces from the country*

evacuation • *the evacuation of British troops from Dunkirk*

flight • *my panicked flight from London*

withdrawal • *French withdrawal from Algeria*

ANTONYM:
• advance

retreat ③ NOUN

a quiet place you can go to • *He spent*

a
b
c
d
e
f
g
h
i
j
k
l
m
n
o
p
q
r
s
t
u
v
w
x
y
z

the day hidden away in his country retreat.
haven • *The hotel is a haven of tranquillity.*
refuge • *a refuge from the harsh realities of the world*
sanctuary • *a sanctuary located on an island*

return ① VERB
to go back to a place • *The plane failed to return at the scheduled time.*
come back • *He said he'd come back later.*
go back • *I love going back home.*
reappear • *He reappeared two nights later.*
turn back • *We've come too far now to turn back.*

return ② VERB
to give something back • *They guarantee to return your original investment.*
give back • *He is refusing to give the dog back.*
pay back • *You have to pay back the loan, plus an arrangement fee.*
refund • *The company will refund the full cost.*
repay • *I can afford to repay the loan.*
MORE SYNONYMS:
• recompense
• reimburse

reveal ① VERB
to tell people about something • *They were not ready to reveal any of the details.*
announce • *She was planning to announce her engagement.*
disclose • *He will not disclose the name of his patient.*
divulge • *I do not want to divulge where the village is.*
get off your chest (INFORMAL) • *I feel it's done me good to get it off my chest.*

let on • *She never let on that anything was wrong.*

reveal ② VERB
to uncover something that is hidden • *The carpet was removed to reveal the original pine floor.*
bring to light • *The truth is unlikely to be brought to light.*
lay bare • *His real motives were laid bare.*
uncover • *Auditors said they had uncovered evidence of fraud.*
unearth • *Quarry workers have unearthed the skeleton of a mammoth.*
unveil • *The statue will be unveiled next week.*

revenge ① NOUN
vengeance for wrongs or injury received • *acts of revenge*
reprisal • *Witnesses are unwilling to testify through fear of reprisals.*
retaliation • *The attack was in retaliation for his murder.*
retribution • *They did not want their names used for fear of retribution.*
vengeance • *He swore vengeance on everyone involved in the murder.*

revenge ② VERB
to take vengeance on someone • *to revenge himself on the press*
avenge • *He was trying to avenge the death of his friend.*
get even • *I'm going to get even with you for this.*
get your own back (INFORMAL) • *I simply want to get my own back on him.*
hit back • *He hit back at those who criticized him.*
pay someone back • *Some day I'll pay you back for this.*
retaliate • *I was sorely tempted to retaliate.*

reverse ① VERB
to change into something different

or contrary • *They won't reverse the decision to increase prices.*

change • *They should change the law to make this practice illegal.*

invalidate • *A contract signed now might be invalidated at a future date.*

overrule • *In 1998 the Court of Appeal overruled the decision.*

overturn • *When the parliament overturned his decision, he backed down.*

retract • *He was asked to retract his comments but refused.*

MORE SYNONYMS:
• countermand
• negate
• rescind
• revoke

reverse ② NOUN
the opposite of what has just been said or done • *The reverse seldom applies.*

contrary • *I'm not a feminist, quite the contrary.*

converse • *In fact, the converse is true.*

opposite • *When I told him to do something he always did the opposite.*

review ① NOUN
a critical assessment of a book or performance • *We've never had a good review in the music press.*

commentary • *He'll be writing a weekly commentary on American culture.*

criticism • *literary criticism*

notice • *Richards's solo work received good notices.*

review ② NOUN
a general survey or report • *a review of safety procedures*

analysis • *an analysis of American trade policy*

examination • *an examination of the top 250 companies*

report • *the committee's annual report*

study • *a recent study of treatments for back pain*

survey • *a survey of 250 businessmen*

revise VERB
to alter or correct something • *The second edition was completely revised.*

amend • *They voted unanimously to amend the constitution.*

correct • *time spent correcting his students' work*

edit • *We have the right to edit this book once it's finished.*

refresh • *The page refreshes every three minutes.*

revamp • *It is time to revamp the system.*

update • *He was back in the office, updating the work schedule.*

revive VERB
to make or become lively or active again • *an attempt to revive the Russian economy*

rally • *Markets began to rally worldwide.*

resuscitate • *a bid to resuscitate the weekly magazine*

MORE SYNONYMS:
• invigorate
• reanimate
• rekindle
• revitalize

reward NOUN
something given in return for a service • *As a reward for good behaviour, treat your child to a new toy.*

bonus • *We don't get a Christmas bonus any more.*

bounty • *They paid bounties to people to give up their weapons.*

payment • *Players now expect payment for interviews.*

prize • *He won first prize.*

a
b
c
d
e
f
g
h
i
j
k
l
m
n
o
p
q
r
s
t
u
v
w
x
y
z

A
B
C
D
E
F
G
H
I
J
K
L
M
N
O
P
Q
R
S
T
U
V
W
X
Y
Z

rhythm NOUN

a regular movement or beat • *His body twists and sways to the rhythm.*

beat • *the thumping beat of rock music*

pulse • *the repetitive pulse of the drum beat*

tempo • *Elgar supplied his works with precise indications of tempo.*

time • *A reel is in four-four time.*

rich ① ADJECTIVE

having a lot of money and possessions • *You're going to be a very rich man.*

affluent • *an affluent neighbourhood*

loaded (SLANG) • *Of course he can afford it. He's loaded.*

opulent • *his opulent lifestyle*

prosperous • *the youngest son of a relatively prosperous family*

wealthy • *a wealthy international businessman*

well off • *My grandparents were quite well off.*

ANTONYM:
• poor

rich ② ADJECTIVE

abundant in something • *Bananas are rich in vitamin A.*

abundant • *the Earth's most abundant natural resources*

fertile • *a fertile imagination*

plentiful • *a plentiful supply of vegetables*

MORE SYNONYMS:
• copious
• fecund
• plenteous

rid: get rid of VERB

to remove or destroy something • *a senior manager who wanted to get rid of him*

dispose of • *He disposed of the murder weapon.*

dump • *We dumped our bags at the hotel.*

eject • *Officials used guard dogs to eject the protestors.*

jettison • *The crew jettisoned excess fuel.*

remove • *Most of her fears had been removed.*

weed out • *We must weed these people out as soon as possible.*

ridiculous ADJECTIVE

very foolish • *It is ridiculous to suggest we are having a romance.*

absurd • *absurd claims to have met big stars*

laughable • *He claims the allegations are "laughable".*

ludicrous • *It's a completely ludicrous idea.*

preposterous • *their preposterous claim that they had unearthed a plot*

right ① ADJECTIVE

in accordance with the facts • *That clock never tells the right time.*

accurate • *an accurate record of events*

correct • *The correct answers can be found at the bottom of the page.*

exact • *That clock never tells the exact time.*

factual • *His version of events is not strictly factual.*

genuine • *a genuine eyewitness account*

precise • *Officials did not give precise figures.*

strict • *He has never been a playboy in the strict sense of the word.*

true • *The true cost often differs from that.*

valid • *Your point is a valid one.*

MORE SYNONYMS:
• unerring
• veracious

ANTONYM:
• wrong

right ② ADJECTIVE
most suitable • *The time is right for our escape.*
acceptable • *This was beyond the bounds of acceptable behaviour.*
appropriate • *an appropriate outfit for the occasion*
desirable • *This goal is neither achievable nor desirable.*
done • *It just isn't done to behave like that in public.*
fit • *a subject which is not fit for discussion*
fitting • *a fitting end to an exciting match*
okay or **OK** (INFORMAL) • *Is it okay if I bring a friend with me?*
proper • *It was not thought proper for a woman to appear on the stage.*
seemly • *the rules of civility and seemly conduct*
suitable • *the most suitable man for the job*

right ③ NOUN
what is just and fair • *At least he knew right from wrong.*
fairness • *a decision based not on fairness but on expediency*
equity • *Income should be distributed with some sense of equity.*
honour • *His whole life was dominated by his sense of honour.*
integrity • *They always strove to maintain a high level of integrity.*
justice • *He has no sense of justice or fair play.*
legality • *They are expected to observe the principles of legality.*
morality • *standards of morality and justice in society*
virtue • *Virtue is not confined to the Christian world.*

MORE SYNONYMS:
• lawfulness

• rectitude
• righteousness
• uprightness

right-wing ADJECTIVE
believing in capitalist policies • *some right-wing politicians*
conservative • *the conservative manifesto*
reactionary • *reactionary army people*
Tory (BRITISH) • *a senior Tory peer*

rigid ① ADJECTIVE
unchangeable and often considered severe • *Hospital routines for nurses are very rigid.*
fixed • *fixed laws*
inflexible • *Workers said the system was too inflexible.*
set • *They have very set ideas about how to achieve this.*
strict • *a strict diet*
stringent • *stringent rules*

rigid ② ADJECTIVE
not easy to bend • *rigid plastic containers*
firm • *a firm platform*
hard • *Something cold and hard pressed into his back.*
solid • *The concrete will stay as solid as a rock.*
stiff • *Her fingers were stiff with cold.*
ANTONYM:
• flexible

ring ① VERB
to make a loud clear sound • *He heard the school bell ring.*
chime • *The clock chimed three o'clock.*
clang • *A little later the church bell clanged.*
peal • *Church bells pealed at the stroke of midnight.*
resonate • *a strap hung with bells and resonating gongs*
toll • *The pilgrims tolled the bell.*

a
b
c
d
e
f
g
h
i
j
k
l
m
n
o
p
q
r
s
t
u
v
w
x
y
z

A
B
C
D
E
F
G
H
I
J
K
L
M
N
O
P
Q
R
S
T
U
V
W
X
Y
Z

ring ② NOUN
an object or group of things in the shape of a circle • *a ring of blue smoke*
band • *a black arm-band*
circle • *Cut out four circles of pastry.*
hoop • *a steel hoop*
loop • *a loop of garden hose*
round • *small fresh rounds of goats' cheese*

ring ③ NOUN
a group of people involved in an illegal activity • *a drug-trafficking ring*
band • *a small band of plotters*
cell • *a cell of neo-Nazis*
clique • *A small clique of people is trying to take over the party.*
syndicate • *a major crime syndicate*

riot ① NOUN
a disturbance made by an unruly mob • *a prison riot*
anarchy • *a decade of civil war and anarchy*
disorder • *mass public disorder*
disturbance • *Three fans were injured in a violent disturbance outside a pub.*
mob violence • *last week's mob violence in Bucharest*
strife • *communal strife in Los Angeles*

riot ② VERB
to take part in a riot • *They rioted in protest against the Government.*
go on the rampage • *Rock fans went on the rampage after a concert.*
rampage • *A curfew was imposed as gangs rampaged through the streets.*
run riot • *hooligans running riot in the streets*
take to the streets • *Workers and students took to the streets in protest.*

rise ① VERB
to move upwards • *Wilson watched the smoke rise from his cigar.*

ascend • *He held her hand as they ascended the steps.*
climb • *We climbed up the steps on to the bridge.*
go up • *He went up the ladder quickly.*
move up • *They moved up to second place after their win.*

rise ② VERB
to increase • *House prices are expected to rise this year.*
go up • *Life expectancy has gone up from 50 to 58.*
grow • *The Chinese economy continues to grow.*
increase • *the decision to increase prices*
intensify • *The conflict is bound to intensify.*
mount • *For several hours the tension mounted.*
ANTONYM:
• fall

rise ③ NOUN
an increase in something • *a rise in prices*
improvement • *a major improvement in standards*
increase • *a substantial increase in workload*
upsurge • *an upsurge of interest in books*
ANTONYM:
• fall

risk ① NOUN
a chance that something unpleasant might happen • *That's a risk I'm happy to take.*
danger • *the dangers of smoking*
gamble • *Booking a holiday can be a gamble.*
peril • *the perils of starring in a TV commercial*
pitfall • *the pitfalls of working abroad*

risk ② VERB
to do something knowing that
something unpleasant might
happen • *If he doesn't play, he risks
losing his place in the team.*
chance • *No assassin would chance a
shot from amongst that crowd.*
dare • *Few people dared go anywhere
on foot.*
gamble • *gambling his life savings on
the stock market*
jeopardize • *The talks may still be
jeopardized by disputes.*
put in jeopardy • *A series of setbacks
have put the whole project in jeopardy.*

rival ① NOUN
the person someone is competing
with • *He is well ahead of his nearest
rival.*
adversary • *political adversaries*
antagonist • *Greece's key rival and
chief antagonist, Turkey*
challenger • *his only challenger for the
presidency*
opponent • *He's a tough opponent but
I'm too good for him.*

rival ② VERB
to be the equal or near equal of • *As a
holiday destination, South Africa rivals
Kenya for weather.*
be a match for • *On our day we are a
match for anyone.*
equal • *The victory equalled Portugal's
best in history.*
match • *I think we matched them in
every department.*

river NOUN

◆ **TYPES OF RIVER**
◆ beck
◆ brook
◆ burn (SCOTTISH)
◆ creek
◆ estuary

◆ rivulet
◆ stream
◆ tributary
◆ watercourse
◆ waterway

road NOUN
a route used by travellers and vehicles
• *There was very little traffic on the roads.*
motorway • *Britain's first motorway,
the M1*
route • *the most direct route to the town
centre*
street • *He walked briskly down the
street.*
track • *a rough mountain track*

rob VERB
to take something from a person
illegally • *He was beaten senseless and
robbed of all his money.*
burgle • *He admitted that he was trying
to burgle the surgery.*
con (INFORMAL) • *The businessman had
conned him of $10,000.*
defraud • *charges of conspiracy to
defraud the government*
loot • *thugs who have looted shops*
steal from • *trying to steal from a
woman in the street*
swindle • *two executives who swindled
their employer*

romantic ADJECTIVE
connected with sexual love • *a
romantic relationship*
amorous • *The object of his amorous
intentions is Wendy.*
loving • *a loving husband*
passionate • *a passionate love affair*
tender • *They embraced and kissed. It
was a tender moment.*

room ① NOUN
a separate section in a building • *You
can stay in my spare room.*
chamber • *the council chamber*

a
b
c
d
e
f
g
h
i
j
k
l
m
n
o
p
q
r
s
t
u
v
w
x
y
z

A
B
C
D
E
F
G
H
I
J
K
L
M
N
O
P
Q
R
S
T
U
V
W
X
Y
Z

office • *I'm in the office at the end of the corridor.*

room ② NOUN
unoccupied space • *There wasn't enough room for his gear.*
capacity • *a seating capacity of 17,000*
elbow room • *There wasn't too much elbow room in the cockpit.*
space • *the high cost of office space*

rot ① VERB
to become rotten • *The grain started rotting in the silos.*
decay • *The bodies buried in the fine ash slowly decayed.*
decompose • *The debris slowly decomposes into compost.*
fester • *The wound is festering and gangrene has set in.*
spoil • *Fats spoil by becoming rancid.*
RELATED WORD:
• ADJECTIVE putrid

rot ② NOUN
the condition that affects things when they rot • *The timber frame was not protected against rot.*
decay • *tooth decay*
deterioration • *gum deterioration*
mould • *He scraped the mould off the cheese.*
MORE SYNONYMS:
• putrefaction
• putrescence

rotten ① ADJECTIVE
decayed and no longer of use • *The front bay window is rotten.*
bad • *That milk in the fridge is bad.*
decayed • *teeth so decayed they need to be pulled*
decomposed • *The body was too badly decomposed to be identified at once.*
mouldy • *mouldy bread*
sour • *sour milk*

rotten ② ADJECTIVE (INFORMAL)
of very poor quality • *It's a rotten idea.*
inferior • *overpriced and inferior products*
lousy (SLANG) • *The menu is limited and the food is lousy.*
poor • *The wine was very poor.*
unsatisfactory • *if you have obtained unsatisfactory goods or services*

rough ① ADJECTIVE
uneven and not smooth • *My bicycle bumped along the rough ground.*
bumpy • *bumpy cobbled streets*
craggy • *craggy mountains*
rocky • *a bleak and rocky shore*
rugged • *a remote and rugged plateau*
uneven • *The ball bobbled awkwardly on the uneven surface.*
ANTONYM:
• smooth

rough ② ADJECTIVE
difficult or unpleasant • *Teachers have been given a rough time.*
difficult • *It's been a difficult month for us.*
hard • *I've had a hard life.*
tough • *She had a pretty tough childhood.*
unpleasant • *The last few weeks here have been very unpleasant.*

rough ③ ADJECTIVE
only approximately correct • *At a rough guess it is five times more profitable.*
approximate • *The times are approximate only.*
estimated • *There are an estimated 90,000 gangsters in the country.*
sketchy • *a sketchy account of the incident*
vague • *She could only give a vague description of the intruder.*

MORE SYNONYMS:
• imprecise
• inexact

round ① ADJECTIVE
shaped like a ball or a circle • *She has a round attractive face.*
circular • *a circular hole twelve feet wide*
cylindrical • *a cylindrical container*
rounded • *a low rounded hill*
spherical • *gold spherical earrings*

round ② NOUN
one of a series of events • *After round three, two Americans shared the lead.*
lap • *the last lap of the race*
period • *the second period of extra time*
session • *The World Champion was ahead after the first two sessions.*
stage • *the second stage of the Tour de France*

route NOUN
a way from one place to another • *the direct route to the town centre*
channel • *a safe channel avoiding the reefs*
course • *The ship was on a course that followed the coastline.*
itinerary • *The next place on our itinerary was Silistra.*
path • *We followed the path along the clifftops.*
road • *The coastal road is longer, but more scenic.*
way • *I'm afraid I can't remember the way.*

routine ① ADJECTIVE
ordinary, and done regularly • *a series of routine medical tests*
everyday • *an everyday occurrence*
normal • *The hospital claimed they were following their normal procedure.*
ordinary • *It was just an ordinary weekend for us.*

regular • *one of the regular checks we carry out*
standard • *It was standard practice for untrained clerks to do this work.*
typical • *This was a fairly typical morning scene in our house.*
usual • *The usual methods were not effective.*

routine ② NOUN
the usual way or order someone does things • *The players had to change their daily routine.*
order • *Babies respond well to order in their daily lives.*
pattern • *All three attacks followed the same pattern.*
practice • *a public inquiry into bank practices*
procedure • *The White House said there would be no change in procedure.*
programme • *It is best to follow some sort of structured programme.*
schedule • *He has been forced to adjust his schedule.*
system • *an efficient filing system*

row ① NOUN
several things arranged in a line • *He was greeted by a row of glum faces.*
bank • *a bank of video screens*
column • *a column of figures*
line • *a sparse line of spectators*
queue • *a queue of shoppers*
rank • *a rank of taxis*

row ② NOUN
a serious disagreement • *This could provoke a major diplomatic row with France.*
altercation • *He had an altercation with the umpire.*
argument • *an argument about money*
quarrel • *I had a terrible quarrel with my brother.*
squabble • *There have been minor squabbles about phone bills.*

rowdy ADJECTIVE

rough and noisy • *He complained to the police about rowdy neighbours.*

boisterous • *Most of the children were noisy and boisterous.*

noisy • *My neighbours are a noisy bunch.*

unruly • *a mother accompanied by her ghastly unruly child*

wild • *They loved fast cars and wild parties.*

MORE SYNONYMS:
• obstreperous
• uproarious

royal ADJECTIVE

concerning a king or a queen or their family • *the royal yacht*

imperial • *the Imperial palace in Tokyo*

regal • *Never has she looked more regal.*

sovereign • *the Queen's sovereign authority*

rubbish ① NOUN

unwanted things or waste material • *tons of rubbish waiting to be dumped*

garbage • *I found all kinds of garbage left behind by the tide.*

litter • *fines for dropping litter*

refuse • *The Council made a weekly collection of refuse.*

trash • *The yards are overgrown and covered with trash.*

waste • *the safe disposal of toxic waste*

rubbish ② NOUN

foolish words or speech • *Don't talk rubbish!*

drivel • *mindless drivel*

garbage • *I personally think this is complete garbage.*

hot air (INFORMAL) • *His justification was just hot air.*

nonsense • *all that poetic nonsense about love*

rot • *What a load of pompous rot!*

rude ① ADJECTIVE

not polite • *He is rude to her friends.*

disrespectful • *They shouldn't treat their mother in this disrespectful way.*

impertinent • *I don't like being asked impertinent questions.*

impudent • *his rude and impudent behaviour*

insolent • *a defiant, almost insolent look*

MORE SYNONYMS:
• churlish
• discourteous
• peremptory

ANTONYM:
• polite

rude ② ADJECTIVE

unexpected and unpleasant • *a rude awakening*

abrupt • *The recession brought an abrupt end to his happiness.*

unpleasant • *an unpleasant surprise*

violent • *violent mood swings*

ruin ① VERB

to destroy or spoil something • *The crops have been ruined.*

break • *He's broken all his toys.*

damage • *This could damage our chances of winning.*

destroy • *a recipe for destroying the economy*

devastate • *A fire had devastated large parts of the castle.*

impair • *The flavour is impaired by overcooking.*

mar • *The celebrations were marred by violence.*

mess up • *He's messed up his whole career.*

spoil • *Don't let a stupid mistake spoil your life.*

undo • *He intends to undo everything I have fought for.*

wreck • *He wrecked the garden.*

ruin ② NOUN

the state of being destroyed or spoiled • *The vineyards were falling into ruin.*

decay • *The house fell into a state of decay.*

destruction • *the destruction caused by the rioters*

devastation • *A bomb brought chaos and devastation to the city centre yesterday.*

disrepair • *Many of the buildings had fallen into disrepair.*

downfall • *His lack of experience led to his downfall.*

fall • *the fall of the Roman empire*

ruin ③ NOUN

the remaining parts of a severely damaged thing • *the burnt-out ruins of houses*

remains • *the remains of an ancient mosque*

shell • *the shells of burned buildings*

wreck • *We thought of buying the house as a wreck and doing it up.*

rule ① NOUN

a statement of what is allowed • *This was against the rules.*

decree • *a decree lifting sanctions against China*

guideline • *Are there strict guidelines for animal experimentation?*

law • *inflexible moral laws*

order • *He was sacked for disobeying orders.*

regulation • *new safety regulations*

MORE SYNONYMS:
• dictum
• ordinance
• precept

rule ② : **as a rule** ADVERB

usually or generally • *As a rule, I eat my meals in front of the TV.*

generally • *It is generally true that the darker the fruit the higher its iron content.*

mainly • *Mainly I work alone.*

normally • *Normally, the transport system carries 50,000 passengers a day.*

on the whole • *Their wines are, on the whole, of a very high standard.*

usually • *She is usually a calm and diplomatic woman.*

rule ③ VERB

to govern people • *For four centuries, he says, foreigners have ruled Angola.*

administer • *calls for the UN to administer the country until the election*

be in power • *They were in power for eighteen years.*

govern • *The citizens are thankful they are not governed by a dictator.*

lead • *He led the country between 1949 and 1984.*

reign • *Henry II reigned from 1154 to 1189.*

ruler NOUN

a person who rules or commands • *He was a weak-willed and indecisive ruler.*

commander • *He is commander of the US Fifth Fleet.*

governor • *He was governor of the province in the late 1970s.*

head of state • *the heads of state of all the countries in the European Union*

leader • *the leader of the German Social Democratic Party*

monarch • *the coronation of the new monarch*

sovereign • *the first British sovereign to set foot on Spanish soil*

rumour NOUN

a story which may or may not be true • *persistent rumours of quarrels within the movement*

gossip • *We spent the first hour exchanging gossip.*

hearsay • *Much of what was reported to them was hearsay.*

a
b
c
d
e
f
g
h
i
j
k
l
m
n
o
p
q
r
s
t
u
v
w
x
y
z

A
B
C
D
E
F
G
H
I
J
K
L
M
N
O
P
Q
R
S
T
U
V
W
X
Y
Z

whisper • *I've heard a whisper that the Bishop intends to leave.*
word • *What's the latest word from Washington?*

run ① VERB
to move on foot at a rapid pace • *I excused myself and ran back to the telephone.*
bolt • *The pig rose, squealing, and bolted.*
gallop • *The horses galloped away.*
jog • *He could scarcely jog around the block that first day.*
sprint • *She sprinted to the car.*

run ② VERB
to manage • *He ran a small hotel.*
administer • *the authorities who administer the island*
be in charge of • *He is in charge of public safety.*
control • *He now controls a large retail development empire.*
direct • *Christopher will direct day-to-day operations.*
look after • *I look after his finances for him.*
manage • *Within two years he was managing the store.*

rush ① VERB
to move fast or do something quickly • *Someone rushed out of the building.*
dash • *She dashed in from the garden.*
fly • *I must fly or I'll miss my train.*
gush • *Piping-hot water gushed out.*
hasten • *One of them hastened towards me.*

hurry • *She had to hurry home to look after her son.*
race • *He raced across town to her house.*
run • *I excused myself and ran to the door.*
scurry • *Reporters scurried to get to the phones.*
shoot • *The car shot out of a junction and smashed into them.*

rush ② VERB
to force into immediate action without sufficient preparation • *Ministers won't be rushed into a response.*
hurry • *I don't want to hurry you.*
hustle • *You won't hustle me into making a commitment.*
press • *attempting to press me into making a statement*
pressurize • *Do not be pressurized into making your decision immediately.*
push • *Don't be pushed into signing anything.*

rush ③ NOUN
a state of hurrying • *the rush not to be late for school*
bustle • *the bustle of modern life*
dash • *a 160-mile dash to the hospital*
hurry • *Eric left the house in a hurry.*
race • *a race to get the work finished before the deadline*
scramble • *the scramble to get a seat on the early morning flight*
stampede • *There was a stampede for the exit.*

Ss

sack ① VERB (INFORMAL)
to dismiss from a job • *sacked for punching his boss*
discharge • *discharged from the army*
dismiss • *the power to dismiss employees*
fire (INFORMAL) • *He was fired for poor timekeeping.*

sack ② : **the sack** NOUN (INFORMAL)
dismissal from a job • *He got the sack after three months.*
discharge • *He plans to appeal his discharge.*
dismissal • *the case for his dismissal*
termination of employment • *wrongful termination of employment*

sacrifice ① VERB
to give something up • *She sacrificed her family life for her career.*
forego • *If we forego our summer holiday we can afford a car.*
forfeit • *The company is forfeiting safety for the sake of profit.*
give up • *I gave up my job to be with you.*
surrender • *We have surrendered our political authority for economic gain.*

sacrifice ② NOUN
the action of giving something up • *He was willing to make any sacrifice for peace.*
renunciation • *religious principles of renunciation and dedication*
self-denial • *an unprecedented act of self-denial*

sad ① ADJECTIVE
feeling unhappy about something • *The loss of our friendship makes me sad.*
blue • *I don't know why I'm feeling so blue today.*
dejected • *Everyone has days when they feel dejected.*
depressed • *She's depressed about this whole situation.*
dismal • *What are you all looking so dismal about?*
down • *The old man sounded really down.*
downcast • *a downcast expression*
glum • *a row of glum faces*
gloomy • *Don't look so gloomy, Mr Todd. I'll do my best for you.*
grief-stricken • *comforting the grief-stricken relatives*
low • *He used to listen when I was feeling low.*
melancholy • *melancholy thoughts*
mournful • *the mournful expression on his face*
unhappy • *I hate to see you so unhappy.*
wistful • *I found myself feeling wistful at the memory of him.*

MORE SYNONYMS:
• disconsolate
• doleful
• heavy-hearted
• low-spirited
• lugubrious
• woebegone

ANTONYM:
• happy

sad ② ADJECTIVE
making you feel unhappy • *a sad song*
depressing • *a depressing film*
dismal • *a dark, dismal day*
gloomy • *a gloomy tale of a poor orphan*
harrowing • *a harrowing documentary about drug addicts*
heart-rending • *heart-rending pictures of the victims*
melancholy • *the melancholy music used throughout the film*
mournful • *a mournful ballad*
moving • *a deeply moving account of her life*
pathetic • *the pathetic sight of oil-covered sea birds*
poignant • *a poignant love story*
tragic • *his tragic death*
upsetting • *I'm afraid I have some upsetting news for you.*

sadness NOUN
the feeling of being unhappy • *I said goodbye with a mixture of sadness and joy.*
dejection • *a feeling of dejection and despair*
depression • *plunged into the deepest depression*
despondency • *Deep despondency set in again.*
melancholy • *Dean had shaken off his melancholy.*
unhappiness • *His unhappiness shows in his face.*

MORE SYNONYMS:
• cheerlessness
• dolefulness
• dolour

ANTONYM:
• happiness

safe ① ADJECTIVE
not causing harm or danger • *This is not a safe place for a woman on her own.*
harmless • *harmless substances*
innocuous • *Both mushrooms look innocuous but are in fact deadly.*
wholesome • *fresh, wholesome ingredients*

ANTONYM:
• dangerous

safe ② ADJECTIVE
not in any danger • *I felt warm and safe with him.*
all right • *I'll be all right on my own.*
in safe hands • *It's all right, you're in safe hands.*
okay or **OK** (INFORMAL) • *Could you check that the baby's okay?*
out of danger • *We were not out of danger yet.*
out of harm's way • *I'm keeping him well out of harm's way.*
protected • *Keep the plants dry and protected from frost.*
safe and sound • *I'm hoping he will come home safe and sound.*
secure • *I would like to feel financially secure.*

safeguard ① VERB
to protect something • *international action to safeguard the ozone layer*
defend • *his courage in defending religious and civil rights*
guard • *He closely guarded her identity.*
look after • *People tend to look after their own property.*
preserve • *We need to preserve the forest.*
protect • *What can we do to protect ourselves against heart disease?*
save • *This machine could help save babies from cot death.*
shield • *They moved to shield their children from adverse publicity.*

safeguard ② NOUN
something that protects people or things • *adequate safeguards for civil liberties*
barrier • *a barrier against the outside world*
cover • *Airlines are required to provide cover against such incidents.*
defence • *The immune system is our main defence against disease.*
protection • *Innocence is no protection from the evils in our society.*

safety NOUN
the state of being safe from harm or danger • *I was very anxious about her safety.*
immunity • *natural immunity to the disease*
protection • *protection from harmful rays*
security • *a false sense of security*
ANTONYM:
• danger

salty ADJECTIVE
tasting of or containing salt • *a good rasher of salty bacon*
brak (SOUTH AFRICAN) • *the brak shallow water near the dam wall*
briny • *the flow of the briny water*
salted • *8 ounces of slightly salted butter*

same ADJECTIVE
exactly like one another • *The two words sound the same but have different spellings.*
alike • *No two families are alike.*
equal • *Mix equal quantities of soy sauce and rice vinegar.*
equivalent • *One unit is roughly equivalent to a glass of wine.*
identical • *Nearly all the houses were identical.*
indistinguishable • *symptoms indistinguishable from those of AIDS*

ANTONYM:
• different

sanction ① VERB
to officially approve of or allow something • *He is ready to sanction the use of force.*
allow • *I cannot be seen to allow violence on school premises.*
approve • *The parliament has approved a programme of economic reforms.*
authorize • *We are willing to authorize a police raid.*
back • *persuading the government to back the plan*
endorse • *policies endorsed by the voting public*
permit • *Will he let the court's decision stand and permit the execution?*
support • *The party is under pressure to support the ban.*
ANTONYM:
• veto

sanction ② NOUN
official approval of something • *The king could not enact the law without the sanction of parliament.*
approval • *The chairman has given his approval.*
authorization • *You will need the authorization of a parent or guardian.*
backing • *He said the president had the backing of his government.*
blessing • *With the blessing of the White House, the group is meeting to identify more budget cuts.*
permission • *Finally she gave permission for him to marry.*
support • *The prime minister gave his support to the reforms.*
MORE SYNONYMS:
• assent
• mandate
• ratification (FORMAL)

sanctions NOUN
penalties for countries which
break the law • *The United States is
considering imposing sanctions against
the regime.*
ban • *After four years, he lifted the ban.*
boycott • *the lifting of the economic
boycott against the country*
embargo • *They called on the
government to lift its embargo on trade
with the country.*
penalties • *legally binding penalties
against treaty violators*

sane ① ADJECTIVE
having a normal healthy mind • *This
was not the act of a sane person.*
lucid • *She was lucid right up until her
death.*
normal • *the question of what
constitutes normal behaviour*
rational • *He seemed perfectly rational
to me.*

MORE SYNONYMS:
• compos mentis
• in your right mind
• of sound mind

ANTONYM:
• mad

sane ② ADJECTIVE
showing good sense • *a sane and
practical policy*
judicious • *the judicious use of military
force*
level-headed • *a sensible, level-headed
approach*
rational • *a rational analysis*
reasonable • *a reasonable course of
action*
sensible • *the sensible thing to do*
sound • *sound advice*

sarcastic ADJECTIVE
saying the opposite of what you
mean to make fun of someone • *A*

*sarcastic remark was on the tip of her
tongue.*
caustic • *his abrasive wit and caustic
comments*
ironic • *an ironic remark*
sardonic • *a sardonic sense of humour*
satirical • *a satirical TV show*

MORE SYNONYMS:
• derisive
• mordacious
• mordant

satisfactory ADJECTIVE
acceptable or adequate • *a
satisfactory explanation*
acceptable • *The air pollution exceeds
acceptable levels.*
adequate • *One in four people are
without adequate homes.*
all right • *The meal was all right, but
nothing special.*
good enough • *He's not good enough
for you.*
passable • *She speaks passable French.*
sufficient • *One teaspoon of sugar
should be sufficient.*

ANTONYM:
• unsatisfactory

satisfied ADJECTIVE
happy because you have got what
you want • *We are not satisfied with
these results.*
content • *I'm perfectly content where
I am.*
contented • *She led a quiet, contented
life.*
happy • *I'm not happy with the
situation.*
pleased • *He seemed pleased with the
arrangement.*

ANTONYM:
• disappointed

satisfy ① VERB
to give someone as much of

A B C D E F G H I J K L M N O P Q R S T U V W X Y Z

something as they want • *a solution which I hope will satisfy everyone*
gratify • *He was gratified by the audience's response.*
indulge • *I don't believe in indulging children.*
please • *Our prime objective is to please our customers.*
MORE SYNONYMS:
• assuage
• pander to
• sate
• satiate
• slake

satisfy ② VERB
to convince someone of something • *He had to satisfy the doctors that he was fit to play.*
convince • *trying to convince the public that its product is safe*
persuade • *I had to persuade him of the advantages.*
put someone's mind at rest • *He has done his best to put my mind at rest.*
reassure • *I tried to reassure them, but they knew I was lying.*

satisfy ③ VERB
to fulfil a requirement • *Candidates must satisfy the conditions for admission.*
fulfil • *All the minimum requirements were fulfilled.*
meet • *The current arrangements are inadequate to meet their needs.*

savage ① ADJECTIVE
cruel and violent • *a savage attack*
barbarous • *the barbarous customs of earlier times*
barbaric • *a particularly barbaric act of violence*
brutal • *a very brutal murder*
cruel • *the cruel practice of bullfighting*
ferocious • *the most ferocious violence*

ever seen on the streets of London
inhuman • *the inhuman slaughter of these beautiful creatures*
vicious • *a vicious blow to the head*
violent • *violent crimes*

savage ② NOUN
a violent and uncivilized person • *They really are a bunch of savages.*
barbarian • *Our maths teacher was a complete barbarian.*
beast • *You beast! Let me go!*
brute • *He was a brute and he deserved his fate.*
lout • *a drunken lout*
monster • *These men were total monsters.*

savage ③ VERB
to attack and bite someone • *He was savaged to death by the animal.*
attack • *A lion attacked him when he was a child.*
bite • *Every year thousands of children are bitten by dogs.*
maul • *The dog went berserk and mauled one of the girls.*

save ① VERB
to rescue someone or something • *He saved my life.*
come to someone's rescue • *His uncle came to his rescue.*
deliver • *I thanked God for delivering me from the pain.*
redeem • *to redeem souls from purgatory*
rescue • *rescued from the flames*
salvage • *salvaging equipment from the wreckage*

save ② VERB
to keep someone or something safe • *a new machine which could save babies from cot death*
keep safe • *to keep my home safe from germs*

preserve • *preserving old buildings*
protect • *What can we do to protect ourselves from heart disease?*
safeguard • *measures to safeguard the ozone layer*

save ③ VERB

to keep something for later use
• *They are saving for a house.*
hoard • *They've begun to hoard food and petrol.*
keep • *Grate the lemon zest and keep it for later.*
put by • *He's putting his money by in a deposit account.*
reserve • *Drain the fruit and reserve the juice.*
set aside • *£130 million would be set aside for repairs to schools.*

MORE SYNONYMS:
• economize
• husband
• retrench

ANTONYM:
• waste

say ① VERB

to speak words • *She said they were very impressed.*
▶ see Word Study **say**, page 655

say ② NOUN

a chance to express your opinion
• *voters who want a say in the matter*
voice • *Parents are given a voice in decision-making.*
vote • *Every employee felt he had a vote in the company's future.*

saying NOUN

a well-known sentence or phrase
• *the saying, "charity begins at home"*
adage • *the old adage, "the show must go on"*
axiom • *the long-held axiom that education leads to higher income*
maxim • *I believe in the maxim, "If it*

ain't broke, don't fix it".
proverb • *an old Chinese proverb*

MORE SYNONYMS:
• aphorism
• apophthegm
• dictum
• saw

scarce ADJECTIVE

rare or uncommon • *Jobs are becoming increasingly scarce.*
few • *Our options are few.*
rare • *Puffins are now rare in this country.*
uncommon • *an extreme but by no means uncommon case*
unusual • *To be appreciated as a parent is quite unusual.*

ANTONYM:
• common

scare ① VERB

to frighten someone • *You're scaring me.*
alarm • *We could not see what had alarmed him.*
frighten • *He knew that Soli was trying to frighten him.*
give someone a fright • *The snake moved and gave everyone a fright.*
intimidate • *Jones had set out to intimidate and dominate Paul.*
startle • *Sorry, I didn't mean to startle you.*
terrify • *Flying terrifies him.*
terrorize • *pensioners terrorized by anonymous phone calls*
unnerve • *We were unnerved by the total silence.*

scare ② NOUN

a short period of feeling very frightened • *We got a bit of a scare.*
fright • *the last time I had a real fright*
shock • *It gave me quite a shock to see his face on the screen.*
start • *The sudden noise gave me quite a start.*

scare ③ NOUN
a situation where people worry about something • *Despite the health scare there are no plans to withdraw the drug.*
alert • *a security alert*
hysteria • *Everyone was getting carried away by the hysteria.*
panic • *the panic over GM foods*

scary ADJECTIVE (INFORMAL)
frightening • *Prison is going to be a scary thing for him.*
alarming • *an alarming report on the rise of street crime*
chilling • *a chilling account of the accident*
creepy (INFORMAL) • *places that are really creepy at night*
eerie • *the eerie dark path*
frightening • *a very frightening experience*
hair-raising • *a hair-raising encounter with a wild boar*
spooky • *The whole place has a slightly spooky atmosphere.*
terrifying • *I find it terrifying to be surrounded by a crowd of people.*
unnerving • *It is very unnerving to find out that someone you know is carrying the virus.*

scatter VERB
to throw or drop things all over an area • *She scattered the petals over the grave.*
shower • *The bomb exploded, showering shrapnel over a wide area.*
sow • *Sow the seeds in a warm place.*
sprinkle • *Sprinkle a tablespoon of sugar over the fruit.*
throw about • *They started throwing food about.*
MORE SYNONYMS:
• broadcast
• disseminate
• strew
ANTONYM:
• gather

scene ① NOUN
a picture or view of something • *a village scene*
landscape • *Arizona's desert landscape*
panorama • *a panorama of fertile valleys*
view • *a view of the lake*
MORE SYNONYMS:
• outlook
• vista

scene ② NOUN
the place where something happens • *the scene of the crime*
location • *filmed in an exotic location*
place • *Can you show me the place where the attack happened?*
setting • *Rome is the perfect setting for romance.*
site • *the site of the battle*
spot • *the ideal spot for a picnic*

scene ③ NOUN
an area of activity • *the music scene*
arena • *the political arena*
business • *the potential to revolutionize the publishing business*
environment • *the Japanese business environment*
world • *the fashion world*

scenery NOUN
the things you see in the countryside • *drive slowly down the lane enjoying the scenery*
landscape • *Arizona's desert landscape*
panorama • *admiring the distant mountain panorama*
surroundings • *a holiday home in beautiful surroundings*
terrain • *The terrain changed from arable land to desert.*

view • *The view from our window was spectacular.*

MORE SYNONYMS:
• outlook
• vista

scold VERB
to tell someone off • *She scolded her daughter for being cheeky.*
chide • *Cross chided himself for worrying.*
lecture • *My mother always used to lecture me about not eating properly.*
rebuke • *I turned to him and sharply rebuked him.*
reprimand • *reprimanded for talking in the corridor*
tell off (INFORMAL) • *The teacher really told her off.*
tick off (INFORMAL) • *ticked off for being late*

MORE SYNONYMS:
• berate
• castigate
• reprove
• upbraid

scorn ① NOUN
great contempt felt for something • *The proposal was greeted with scorn.*
contempt • *I treated this remark with the contempt it deserved.*
derision • *shouts of derision*
disdain • *Janet looked at him with disdain.*
mockery • *his mockery of all things English*

scorn ② VERB
to treat with great contempt • *Eleanor scorns the work of others.*
despise • *She secretly despises him.*
disdain • *He disdained politicians.*
look down on • *I wasn't successful so they looked down on me.*
slight • *He felt slighted by this treatment.*

MORE SYNONYMS:
• be above
• contemn
• hold in contempt

scornful ADJECTIVE
showing contempt for something • *He is deeply scornful of his rivals.*
contemptuous • *She gave a contemptuous little laugh.*
disdainful • *He is disdainful of politicians.*
scathing • *He made some scathing comments about the design.*
sneering • *a sneering tone*
supercilious • *His manner is supercilious and arrogant.*
withering • *Her mother gave her a withering look.*

scrape ① VERB
to rub a rough or sharp object against something • *We had to scrape the frost from the windscreen.*
graze • *He had grazed his knees a little.*
scour • *Scour the pans.*
scratch • *The branches scratched my face and hands.*
scuff • *scuffed shoes*
skin • *I found that I had skinned my knuckles.*

scrape ② VERB
to make a harsh noise by rubbing • *his shoes scraping across the ground*
grate • *His chair grated as he got to his feet.*
grind • *Blocks of ice ground against each other.*
rasp • *The blade rasped over his skin.*
scratch • *He scratched his knife over the worktop.*

scream ① VERB
to shout or cry in a high-pitched voice • *If he says that again, I shall scream.*
cry • *a crying baby*

howl • *He howled like a wounded animal.*
screech • *"Get me some water!" I screeched.*
shout • *I shouted at mother to get the police.*
shriek • *She shrieked and leapt from the bed.*
squeal • *Jennifer squealed with delight.*
yell • *I pushed him away, yelling abuse.*

scream ② NOUN
a loud, high-pitched cry • *Hilda let out a scream.*
cry • *a cry of horror*
howl • *a howl of rage*
screech • *The figure gave a screech.*
shriek • *a shriek of joy*
squeal • *the squeal of piglets*
yell • *Something brushed Bob's face and he let out a yell.*

scrounge VERB (INFORMAL)
to get something by asking rather than working for it • *He's always scrounging lifts.*
beg • *They managed to beg a lift from a passing fisherman.*
bludge (AUSTRALIAN AND NEW ZEALAND; INFORMAL) • *They've come here to bludge food and money.*
cadge • *Can I cadge a cigarette?*
sponge (INFORMAL) • *I got tired of him sponging off me and threw him out.*

scruffy ADJECTIVE
dirty and untidy • *four scruffy youths*
ragged • *a ragged band of men*
seedy • *his seedy clothes*
shabby • *a shabby, tall man with dark eyes*
tatty • *a tatty old cardigan*
unkempt • *His hair was unkempt and filthy.*
MORE SYNONYMS:
• disreputable
• slovenly
• ungroomed
ANTONYM:
• smart

scrutinize VERB
to examine something very carefully • *She scrutinized his features.*
examine • *He examined her passport.*
inspect • *Cut the fruit in half and inspect the pips.*
pore over • *We spent hours poring over the files.*
scan • *She kept scanning the crowd for Paul.*
search • *Her eyes searched his face.*
study • *Debbie studied the document for a moment.*

scungy ADJECTIVE (AUSTRALIAN AND NEW ZEALAND; SLANG)
dirty • *living in some scungy flat on the outskirts of town*
dirty • *He was wearing a dirty old mac.*
filthy • *This flat is so filthy I can't possibly stay here.*
foul • *foul polluted water*
seedy • *a seedy hotel*
sleazy • *sleazy bars*
sordid • *sordid little rooms*
squalid • *a squalid bedsit*

search ① VERB
to look for something • *The security forces are searching for the missing men.*
comb • *Police combed the woods for the murder weapon.*
forage • *foraging for food*
fossick (AUSTRALIAN AND NEW ZEALAND) • *to help Gaston fossick for food around the hut*
google • *I went straight home from the party and googled him.*
hunt • *hunting for a job*
look • *He's looking for a way out of this situation.*

scour • *They had scoured the intervening miles of moorland.*

seek • *the man he had been seeking for weeks*

sift • *sifting through the wreckage for clues*

search ② NOUN

the action of looking for something • *Police will resume the search today.*

hunt • *the hunt for my lost boy*

quest • *his quest to find true love*

secret ADJECTIVE

known about by only a few people • *a secret location*

closet (INFORMAL) • *a closet Fascist*

confidential • *a confidential report*

covert • *She gave him a covert glance.*

furtive • *furtive meetings*

hidden • *a hidden camera*

undercover • *undercover FBI agents*

underground • *the underground communist movement* MORE

SYNONYMS:
• cloak-and-dagger
• conspiratorial
• undisclosed

RELATED WORD:
• ADJECTIVE cryptic

secretive ADJECTIVE

hiding your feelings and intentions • *Jake was very secretive about his family affairs.*

cagey (INFORMAL) • *He is cagey about what he was paid for the business.*

reserved • *He was unemotional and reserved.*

reticent • *She is very reticent about her achievements.*

MORE SYNONYMS:
• tight-lipped
• uncommunicative
• unforthcoming

section NOUN

one of the parts into which

something is divided • *this section of the motorway*

division • *the company's sales division*

instalment • *Payment can be made in instalments.*

part • *the upper part of the body*

piece • *The equipment was taken down the shaft in pieces.*

portion • *I had learnt a portion of the Koran.*

segment • *the third segment of the journey*

secure ① VERB (FORMAL)

to manage to get something • *His achievements helped him to secure the job.*

acquire • *General Motors recently acquired a 50% stake in the company.*

gain • *Hard work may not be enough to gain a place at university.*

get • *I got a job at the sawmill.*

obtain • *He tried to obtain a false passport.*

procure (FORMAL) • *trying to procure the release of the hostages*

secure ② VERB

to make something safe • *We need to secure the building against attack.*

fortify • *British soldiers are working to fortify the airbase.*

make impregnable • *Their intention was to make the old fort impregnable.*

make safe • *Crime Prevention Officers will suggest ways to make your home safe.*

strengthen • *In the 14th century they strengthened this wall against raiders.*

secure ③ VERB

to fasten or attach something firmly • *The frames are secured by rails to the wall.*

attach • *The gadget can be attached to any vertical surface.*

bind • *Bind the ends of the cord together with thread.*

fasten • *Her long hair was fastened by an elastic band.*

fix • *He fixed a bayonet to the end of his rifle.*

lock • *Are you sure you locked the front door?*

moor • *She moored her barge on the river bank.*

tie up • *They dismounted and tied up their horses.*

ANTONYM:
• release

secure ④ ADJECTIVE

tightly locked or well protected • *Make sure your home is as secure as possible.*

fortified • *The door is fortified against flooding.*

impregnable • *The old castle was completely impregnable against raids.*

protected • *the right of women to be protected from sexual harassment*

safe • *We want to go to a football match knowing we are safe from hooliganism.*

shielded • *The company is shielded from takeover attempts.*

secure ⑤ ADJECTIVE

firmly fixed in place • *Shelves are only as secure as their fixings.*

fastened • *Make sure the safety belt is fastened.*

firm • *If you have to climb up, use a firm platform.*

fixed • *Check the holder is fixed in its place on the wall.*

locked • *Leave doors and windows locked.*

solid • *I yanked on the bracket to see if it was solid.*

stable • *The structure must be stable.*

tight • *He kept a tight hold of her arm.*

secure ⑥ ADJECTIVE

feeling safe and happy • *She felt secure when she was with him.*

confident • *In time he became more confident.*

protected • *It's good to have a place in which you feel protected and loved.*

reassured • *I feel much more reassured when I've been for a health check.*

relaxed • *There are very few people he feels relaxed with.*

safe • *He kissed me and I felt warm and safe.*

ANTONYM:
• insecure

see ① VERB

to look at or notice something • *Did you see what happened?*

behold • *She looked into his eyes and beheld madness.*

discern • *We could just discern the outline of the island.*

glimpse • *She glimpsed the man's face briefly.*

look • *She turned to look at him.*

notice • *She noticed a bird sitting on the roof.*

observe • *He observed a reddish spot on the planet's surface.*

perceive • *Infants start to perceive objects at a very early age.*

sight • *A fleet of French ships was sighted.*

spot • *I think he spotted me but didn't want to be seen.*

MORE SYNONYMS:
• catch sight of
• descry
• espy

see ② VERB

to realize or understand something • *I see what you mean.*

appreciate • *He appreciates the difficulties.*

a
b
c
d
e
f
g
h
i
j
k
l
m
n
o
p
q
r
s
t
u
v
w
x
y
z

A
B
C
D
E
F
G
H
I
J
K
L
M
N
O
P
Q
R
S
T
U
V
W
X
Y
Z

comprehend • *They do not comprehend the nature of the problem.*

follow • *Do you follow what I'm saying?*

get • *You don't seem to get the point.*

grasp • *They have not grasped the seriousness of the crisis.*

realize • *They realized too late that they were wrong.*

understand • *I'm not sure I understand.*

see ③ VERB
to find something out • *I'll see what's happening outside.*

ascertain • *Ascertain what services your bank provides.*

determine • *The investigation will determine what really happened.*

discover • *Try to discover what you are good at.*

find out • *Watch the next episode to find out what happens.*

seek ① VERB
to try to find something • *The police were still seeking information.*

be after • *At last I found what I was after.*

hunt • *Police are hunting for clues.*

look for • *I'm looking for a lost child.*

search for • *searching for answers*

seek ② VERB
to try to do something • *De Gaulle sought to reunite the country.*

aim • *We aim to raise funds for charity.*

aspire to • *He aspired to work in music journalism.*

attempt • *He was forever attempting to arrange deals.*

endeavour • *They are endeavouring to protect trade union rights.*

strive • *The school strives to treat pupils as individuals.*

try • *We are trying to bring about a better world.*

seem VERB
to appear to be • *He seemed such a quiet man.*

appear • *She appeared intoxicated.*

give the impression • *He gave the impression of being the perfect husband.*

look • *The cottage looks quite ordinary from the road.*

look like • *You look like a nice guy.*

seize ① VERB
to grab something firmly • *He seized the phone.*

grab • *I grabbed him by the neck.*

grasp • *He grasped both my hands.*

snatch • *Mick snatched the cards from Archie's hand.*

seize ② VERB
to take control of something • *Rebels have seized the airport.*

annex • *the plan to invade and annex Kuwait*

appropriate • *The land was appropriated by Communists.*

confiscate • *The police confiscated weapons and ammunition.*

hijack • *Almost 250 trucks were hijacked.*

impound • *The ship was impounded under the terms of the trade embargo.*

MORE SYNONYMS:
• commandeer
• take possession of

select ① VERB
to choose something • *They selected only the brightest pupils.*

choose • *Houston was chosen as the site for the conference.*

decide on • *I'm still trying to decide on an outfit for the wedding.*

opt for • *You may wish to opt for one method straight away.*

pick • *He had picked ten people to interview for the jobs.*

settle on • *I finally settled on the estate car because it was so roomy.*
single out • *His boss has singled him out for a special mission.*
take • *"I'll take the grilled tuna," she told the waiter.*

select ② ADJECTIVE
of good quality • *a select band of top-ranking sportsmen*
choice • *We use only the choicest ingredients.*
exclusive • *Britain's most exclusive club*
first-class • *a first-class hotel*
first-rate • *The first-rate cast includes many famous names.*
hand-picked • *a hand-picked series of timeless classics*
prime • *one of the City's prime sites, with a view of several historic buildings*
special • *a special group of government officials*
superior • *a superior range of products*

selfish ADJECTIVE
caring only about yourself • *his greedy and selfish behaviour*
egoistic or **egoistical** • *egoistic motives*
egotistic or **egotistical** • *an intensely egotistic streak*
greedy • *greedy bosses awarding themselves big rises*
self-centred • *He was self-centred, but he wasn't cruel.*
MORE SYNONYMS:
• self-interested
• self-seeking
• ungenerous

sell ① VERB
to let someone have something in return for money • *I just sold my car.*
deal in • *They deal in antiques.*
hawk • *vendors hawking trinkets*
peddle • *arrested for peddling drugs*

trade in • *They trade in spices and all kinds of grain.*
ANTONYM:
• buy

sell ② VERB
to have available for people to buy • *a little shop that sells teapots*
deal in • *a business dealing in honey*
stock • *The shop stocks a variety of local craft products.*
trade in • *a company that trades in sporting memorabilia*
ANTONYM:
• buy

send ① VERB
to arrange for something to be delivered • *He sent a basket of fruit and a card.*
dispatch • *He dispatched a telegram of congratulation.*
forward • *A letter was forwarded from the clinic.*
remit • *Many immigrants regularly remit money to their families.*

send ② VERB
to transmit a signal or message • *The pilot was trying to send a distress signal.*
broadcast • *to broadcast a message to a whole group of people at once*
transmit • *the most efficient way to transmit data*

senior ADJECTIVE
the highest and most important in an organization • *senior jobs*
best • *These officers have traditionally taken the best jobs.*
better • *Well-qualified women are now attaining better positions.*
high-ranking • *a high-ranking officer in the medical corps*
superior • *negotiations between crew members and their superior officers*

a
b
c
d
e
f
g
h
i
j
k
l
m
n
o
p
q
r
s
t
u
v
w
x
y
z

ANTONYM:
• junior

sense ① NOUN
a feeling you have about something • *an overwhelming sense of guilt*
consciousness • *a consciousness of tension*
feeling • *It gave me a feeling of satisfaction.*
impression • *The music creates an impression of menace.*

sense ② NOUN
the ability to think and behave sensibly • *He had the good sense to call me at once.*
brains (INFORMAL) • *At least I had the brains to keep quiet.*
common sense • *completely lacking in common sense*
intelligence • *He didn't have the intelligence to understand what was happening.*
judgment • *I respect his judgment.*
reason • *a conflict between emotion and reason*
wisdom • *the wisdom that comes of old age*

MORE SYNONYMS:
• nous
• sagacity
• wit or wits

sense ③ VERB
to become aware of something • *She sensed he wasn't telling her the whole story.*
be aware of • *He was aware of her anger.*
feel • *Suddenly, I felt a presence behind me.*
get the impression • *I get the impression he's lying.*
have a hunch • *Lowe had a hunch he was on to something.*

realize • *We realized something was wrong.*

sensible ADJECTIVE
showing good sense and judgment • *a sensible, level-headed approach*
down-to-earth • *the most down-to-earth person I've ever met*
judicious • *the judicious use of military force*
practical • *practical suggestions*
prudent • *It is prudent to start any exercise programme gradually.*
rational • *a rational decision*
sound • *sound advice*
wise • *a wise move*

ANTONYM:
• foolish

sensitive ADJECTIVE
easily upset about something • *He was sensitive about his height.*
easily offended • *I am not a feminist, nor am I easily offended.*
easily upset • *He remained deeply neurotic and easily upset.*
thin-skinned • *I'm too thin-skinned - I want everyone to like me.*
touchy • *She is very touchy about her weight.*

sentimental ADJECTIVE
expressing exaggerated sadness or tenderness • *sentimental love stories*
maudlin • *Jimmy turned maudlin after three drinks.*
mushy (INFORMAL) • *I go completely mushy when I see a baby.*
nostalgic • *nostalgic for the good old days*
sloppy (INFORMAL) • *I hate sloppy romantic films.*
slushy (INFORMAL) • *slushy ballads*

MORE SYNONYMS:
• dewy-eyed

- mawkish
- overemotional

separate ① ADJECTIVE
not connected to something else
• *The question muddles up two separate issues.*
detached • *a detached house*
disconnected • *sequences of disconnected events*
discrete • *two discrete sets of nerves*
divorced • *speculative theories divorced from reality*
isolated • *He lives as if isolated from the rest of the world.*
unconnected • *The two murders are unconnected.*

ANTONYM:
• connected

separate ② VERB
to end a connection between people or things • *Police moved in to separate the two groups.*
detach • *Three of the carriages on the train became detached.*
disconnect • *Make sure supply plugs are disconnected from the mains.*
divide • *This was a ruse to divide them.*

MORE SYNONYMS:
• bifurcate
• sunder
• uncouple

ANTONYM:
• connect

separate ③ VERB
to end a relationship or marriage
• *Her parents separated when she was very young.*
break up • *She hadn't used his name since they broke up.*
divorce • *We divorced ten years ago.*
part • *He is parting from his Swedish-born wife Eva.*
split up • *I split up with my boyfriend last year.*

sequence ① NOUN
a number of events coming one after another • *an unbroken sequence of victories*
chain • *the chain of events leading to the assassination*
course • *a course of injections*
cycle • *the cycle of birth, growth, decay, and death*
progression • *The story of American freedom is anything but a linear progression.*
series • *a series of explosions*
string • *a string of burglaries*
succession • *He took a succession of jobs that stood him in good stead.*

sequence ② NOUN
a particular order in which things are arranged • *the colour sequence: yellow, orange, purple, blue*
arrangement • *a simple arrangement of coloured tiles*
order • *Music shops should arrange their recordings in alphabetical order.*
pattern • *a systematic pattern of behaviour*
progression • *the natural progression of the seasons*
structure • *The bricks had been arranged in a regular structure.*

series NOUN
a number of things coming one after the other • *a series of loud explosions*
chain • *a bizarre chain of events*
run • *The England skipper is haunted by a run of low scores.*
sequence • *a sequence of novels*
string • *a string of burglaries*
succession • *He had a succession of jobs.*

serious ① ADJECTIVE
very bad and worrying • *They survived their serious injuries.*
acute • *an acute attack of appendicitis*

a
b
c
d
e
f
g
h
i
j
k
l
m
n
o
p
q
r
s
t
u
v
w
x
y
z

alarming • *the alarming increase in drug abuse*
bad • *a bad bout of flu*
critical • *He remains in a critical condition in hospital.*
dangerous • *His wound proved more dangerous than it seemed at first.*
extreme • *the most extreme case doctors have ever seen*
grave • *We are all in grave danger.*
grievous • *grievous wounds*
grim • *Our situation is grim indeed.*
intense • *Intense fighting has broken out in the capital.*
precarious • *He is in a very precarious position.*
severe • *a severe shortage of drinking water*
worrying • *It is a worrying situation.*

serious ② ADJECTIVE
important and deserving careful thought • *I regard this as a serious matter.*
crucial • *Negotiations were at a crucial stage.*
deep • *This novel raises deep questions about the nature of faith.*
difficult • *The government faces even more difficult problems.*
far-reaching • *His actions will have far-reaching consequences.*
grave • *a grave situation*
important • *We've got more important things to worry about now.*
momentous • *the momentous decision to go to war*
pressing • *a pressing problem*
profound • *a man who thinks about the more profound issues of life*
significant • *the most significant question of all*
urgent • *He is not equipped to deal with an urgent situation like this.*
weighty • *a weighty problem*

ANTONYM:
• funny

serious ③ ADJECTIVE
sincere about something • *I was not quite sure whether he was serious.*
earnest • *It is my earnest hope that we can work things out.*
genuine • *a genuine offer*
heartfelt • *a full and heartfelt apology*
honest • *He looked at me in honest surprise.*
in earnest • *I can never tell if he is in earnest or not.*
resolute • *He was resolute about his ideals.*
resolved • *They are quite resolved about their decision.*
sincere • *He's sincere in his views.*

serious ④ ADJECTIVE
quiet and not laughing much • *He's quite a serious person.*
earnest • *She looked up at me with an earnest expression.*
grave • *He was looking unusually grave.*
humourless • *a dour, humourless Scotsman*
pensive • *We're both in a pensive mood today.*
sober • *sad, sober faces*
solemn • *His solemn little face broke into a smile.*
staid • *bored with her marriage to a staid country doctor*
stern • *a stern headmaster feared by all the pupils*

set ① NOUN
a group of things that belong together • *a set of tools*
batch • *the latest batch of recruits*
kit • *I forgot my gym kit.*
outfit • *She was wearing a brand new outfit.*
series • *a series of books covering the history of aviation*

MORE SYNONYMS:
- assemblage
- compendium
- ensemble

set ② VERB
to put or place something
somewhere • *He set his case down on
the floor.*
deposit • *Imagine if you were suddenly
deposited on a desert island.*
lay • *Lay a sheet of newspaper on the
floor.*
locate • *The restaurant is located near
the cathedral.*
place • *She placed a mug of coffee in
front of him.*
position • *Plants were carefully
positioned in the alcove.*
put • *He put the photograph on the desk.*
rest • *He rested one of his crutches
against the rail.*
stick • *Just stick your bag down
anywhere.*

set ③ ADJECTIVE
fixed and not varying • *a set charge*
arranged • *We arrived at the arranged
time.*
established • *the established order*
firm • *a firm booking*
fixed • *a fixed rate of interest*
predetermined • *His destiny was
predetermined from the moment of his
birth.*
scheduled • *The plane failed to return
at the scheduled time.*

set on ADJECTIVE
determined to do something • *She
was set on going to the States.*
bent on • *He's bent on suicide.*
determined • *His enemies are
determined to ruin him.*
intent on • *an actress who was intent
on making a comeback*

settle ① VERB
to put an end to an argument or
problem • *The dispute has been settled.*
clear up • *Eventually the confusion was
cleared up.*
decide • *None of the cases had been
decided.*
dispose of • *the way in which you
disposed of that problem*
put an end to • *I just want to put an
end to this situation.*
reconcile • *urging the two parties to
reconcile their differences*
resolve • *They hoped the crisis could be
resolved peacefully.*
straighten out • *doing their best to
straighten out this confusion*

settle ② VERB
to decide or arrange something • *Let's
settle where we're going tonight.*
agree • *We haven't agreed a date yet.*
arrange • *Have you arranged our next
appointment?*
decide on • *They decided on an evening
to meet.*
determine • *The final wording had not
yet been determined.*
fix • *He's going to fix a time when I can
see him.*

settle ③ VERB
to make your home in a place
• *refugees settling in Britain*
make your home • *those who had
made their homes in China*
move to • *His family moved to New
Zealand when he was 12.*
people • *The plateau was peopled by
nomadic tribes.*
populate • *The island was populated by
Native Americans.*
MORE SYNONYMS:
- colonize
- put down roots
- take up residence

set up VERB
to make arrangements for
something • *setting up a system of
communication*
arrange • *We have arranged a series of
interviews.*
establish • *We have established links
with industry and commerce.*
install • *I'm having cable installed next
week.*
institute • *to institute better levels of
quality control*
organize • *a two-day meeting
organized by the UN*

several ADJECTIVE
indicating a small number • *several
boxes filled with albums*
assorted • *overnight stops in assorted
hotels*
some • *some cheers from the gallery*
sundry • *He has won sundry music
awards.*
various • *a dozen trees of various sorts*

severe ① ADJECTIVE
extremely bad or unpleasant
• *severe cash flow problems*
acute • *an acute economic crisis*
critical • *if the situation becomes
critical*
deep • *We will be in deep trouble if this
goes on.*
dire • *This would have dire consequences
for domestic peace.*
extreme • *people living in extreme
poverty*
grave • *He said the situation was very
grave.*
intense • *A number of people collapsed
in the intense heat.*
serious • *The government faces very
serious difficulties.*
terrible • *terrible injuries*

ANTONYM:
• mild

severe ② ADJECTIVE
stern and harsh • *This was a dreadful
crime and a severe sentence is necessary.*
disapproving • *Janet gave him a
disapproving look.*
grim • *Her expression was grim and
unpleasant.*
hard • *His father was a hard man.*
harsh • *the cold, harsh cruelty of her
husband*
stern • *He said stern measures would
be taken.*
strict • *My parents were very strict.*

sexy ADJECTIVE
sexually attractive or exciting • *a sexy
voice*
erotic • *an erotic film*
seductive • *I love dressing up to look
seductive.*
sensual • *a wide, sensual mouth*
sensuous • *his sensuous young
mistress*
voluptuous • *a voluptuous figure*

shabby ① ADJECTIVE
ragged and worn in appearance • *a
shabby overcoat*
dilapidated • *a dilapidated old
building*
ragged • *dressed in a ragged coat*
scruffy • *a scruffy basement flat in
London*
seedy • *his seedy clothes*
tatty • *a tatty old cardigan*
threadbare • *a square of threadbare
carpet*
worn • *a worn corduroy jacket*

MORE SYNONYMS:
• down at heel
• run-down
• the worse for wear

shabby ② ADJECTIVE
behaving meanly and unfairly
• *shabby treatment*

contemptible • *contemptible behaviour*
despicable • *a despicable thing to do*
dirty • *That was a dirty trick.*
mean • *It was mean of you to hurt her like that.*
rotten (INFORMAL) • *That's a rotten thing to say!*

MORE SYNONYMS:
• dishonourable
• ignoble
• scurvy

shake ① VERB
to move something from side to side or up and down • *You have to shake the bottle before use.*
agitate • *Gently agitate the water.*
brandish • *He appeared brandishing a knife.*
flourish • *He flourished his glass to make the point.*
wave • *The crowd were waving flags and cheering.*

shake ② VERB
to move from side to side or up and down • *The whole building shook with the force of the blast.*
jolt • *The train jolted again.*
quake • *The whole mountain quaked.*
quiver • *Her bottom lip began to quiver.*
shiver • *shivering with fear*
shudder • *Elaine shuddered with cold.*
tremble • *The leaves trembled in the breeze.*
vibrate • *The engine began to vibrate alarmingly.*

MORE SYNONYMS:
• joggle
• oscillate

shake ③ VERB
to shock and upset someone • *The news shook me quite a bit.*
distress • *Her death had profoundly distressed me.*

disturb • *dreams so vivid that they disturb me for days*
rattle (INFORMAL) • *He was obviously rattled by events.*
shock • *Pictures of emaciated prisoners shocked the world.*
unnerve • *unnerved by the sight*
upset • *I was too upset to speak.*

MORE SYNONYMS:
• discompose
• traumatize

shaky ADJECTIVE
weak and unsteady • *threatening an already shaky economy*
rickety • *Mona climbed the rickety wooden stairway.*
tottering • *the baby's first tottering steps*
trembling • *She held out one frail, trembling hand.*
unstable • *an unstable lamp on top of an old tea-chest*
unsteady • *His voice was unsteady.*
wobbly • *I'm sorry, this table's a bit wobbly.*

shame ① NOUN
a feeling of guilt or embarrassment • *She felt a deep sense of shame.*
embarrassment • *He turned red with embarrassment.*
humiliation • *the humiliation of discussing her husband's affair*
ignominy • *the ignominy of being made redundant*

MORE SYNONYMS:
• abashment
• loss of face
• mortification

shame ② NOUN
something that makes people lose respect for you • *I don't want to bring shame on the family.*

a
b
c
d
e
f
g
h
i
j
k
l
m
n
o
p
q
r
s
t
u
v
w
x
y
z

A
B
C
D
E
F
G
H
I
J
K
L
M
N
O
P
Q
R
S
T
U
V
W
X
Y
Z

discredit • *It was to his discredit that he did nothing.*
disgrace • *He had to resign in disgrace.*
dishonour • *his sense of dishonour at his brother's conduct*
scandal • *They often abandoned their children because of fear of scandal.*

shame ③ VERB
to make someone feel ashamed • *Her son's affair had shamed her.*
disgrace • *I have disgraced my country.*
embarrass • *It embarrassed him that he had no idea of what was going on.*
humiliate • *His teacher continually humiliates him in maths lessons.*

MORE SYNONYMS:
• abash
• mortify

shameless ADJECTIVE
behaving badly without showing any shame • *shameless dishonesty*
barefaced • *a barefaced lie*
brazen • *a brazen theft*
flagrant • *a flagrant violation of the law*
unabashed • *an unabashed egotist*
unashamed • *blatant, unashamed hypocrisy*
wanton • *a wanton woman*

shape ① NOUN
the outline of something • *a round shape*
contours • *the contours of the mountains*
figure • *a trim figure*
form • *the form of the human body*
lines • *The belt spoilt the lines of her long dress.*
outline • *the dim outline of a small boat*

shape ② VERB
to make something in a particular form • *Shape the dough into a loaf.*
fashion • *buttons fashioned from bone*
form • *The polymer is formed into a thin sheet.*

make • *gold made into wedding rings*
model • *She began modelling animals from clay.*
mould • *Mould the cheese into small ovals.*

share ① VERB
to divide something between two or more people • *We shared a bottle of champagne.*
divide • *The prize money was divided between the two winners.*
split • *We split the bill between us.*

share ② NOUN
a portion of something • *a share of the profits*
allotment • *a daily allotment of three ounces of bread*
portion • *his portion of the inheritance*
quota • *a quota of four tickets per person*
ration • *their daily ration of water*

sharp ① ADJECTIVE
having a fine cutting edge or point • *a sharp knife*
jagged • *jagged rocks*
keen • *a keen edge*
pointed • *pointed teeth*
razor-sharp • *the razor-sharp blade*

ANTONYM:
• blunt

sharp ② ADJECTIVE
quick to notice or understand things • *a sharp intellect*
alert • *She is alert and sprightly despite her 85 years.*
astute • *He made a series of astute business decisions.*
bright • *an exceptionally bright child*
observant • *an observant eye*
perceptive • *a perceptive gaze*
quick • *His quick mind soon grasped the situation.*

quick-witted · *He is very alert and quick-witted.*

sharp ③ ADJECTIVE
sudden and significant · *a sharp rise in prices*
abrupt · *Her idyllic world came to an abrupt end when her parents died.*
marked · *a marked increase in crimes against property*
sudden · *a sudden change in course*

sheer ① ADJECTIVE
complete and total · *acts of sheer desperation*
absolute · *I think it's absolute nonsense.*
complete · *He shook his head in complete bewilderment.*
pure · *To have an uninterrupted night's sleep was pure bliss.*
total · *This is total madness!*
unqualified · *It has been an unqualified disaster.*
utter · *a look of utter confusion*
MORE SYNONYMS:
• unadulterated
• unmitigated (FORMAL)

sheer ② ADJECTIVE
vertical · *There was a sheer drop just outside my window.*
perpendicular · *the perpendicular wall of sandstone*
steep · *a narrow valley with steep sides*
vertical · *The climber inched up a vertical wall of rock.*

sheer ③ ADJECTIVE
very light and delicate · *sheer black tights*
delicate · *delicate fabric*
fine · *a fine, pale grey material*
lightweight · *lightweight materials with Lycra*
thin · *the thin silk of her blouse*

ANTONYM:
• thick

shelter ① NOUN
a place providing protection · *a bus shelter*
hostel · *She spent two years living in a hostel.*
refuge · *a mountain refuge*
sanctuary · *His church became a sanctuary for people fleeing the civil war.*

shelter ② NOUN
protection from bad weather or danger · *the hut where they were given food and shelter*
asylum · *refugees who sought political asylum*
cover · *They ran for cover from the storm.*
harbour · *Patches of gorse were a great harbour for foxes.*
haven · *The island is a haven for international criminals.*
protection · *Riot shields acted as protection against the attack.*
refuge · *They took refuge in an old barn.*
safety · *the safety of one's own home*
sanctuary · *Some of them sought sanctuary in the church.*

shelter ③ VERB
to stay somewhere in order to be safe · *a man sheltering in a doorway*
hide · *They hid behind a tree.*
huddle · *She huddled inside the porch.*
take cover · *Shoppers took cover behind cars as the shots rang out.*

shelter ④ VERB
to hide or protect someone · *A neighbour sheltered the boy for seven days.*
harbour · *He was accused of harbouring terrorist suspects.*
hide · *They hid me until the coast was clear.*

a
b
c
d
e
f
g
h
i
j
k
l
m
n
o
p
q
r
s
t
u
v
w
x
y
z

protect • *A purple headscarf protected her against the wind.*

shield • *He shielded his head from the sun with a sack.*

shine VERB

to give out a bright light • *The sun is shining.*

beam • *The spotlight beamed down on the stage.*

gleam • *The moonlight gleamed on the water.*

glow • *The lantern glowed softly in the darkness.*

radiate • *the amount of light radiated by an ordinary light bulb*

shimmer • *The lake shimmered in the sunlight.*

sparkle • *Diamonds sparkled on her wrists.*

shining ADJECTIVE

giving out or reflecting light • *shining stainless steel tables*

bright • *a bright star*

brilliant • *brilliant sunshine*

gleaming • *gleaming headlights*

luminous • *the luminous dial on the clock*

radiant • *He saw a figure surrounded by a radiant light.*

shimmering • *a shimmering gold fabric*

sparkling • *elegant cutlery and sparkling crystal*

MORE SYNONYMS:
• effulgent
• incandescent

shock ① NOUN

a sudden upsetting experience • *The extent of the damage came as a shock.*

blow • *It was a terrible blow when he was made redundant.*

bombshell • *His departure was a bombshell for the team.*

distress • *She wanted to save her mother all the distress she could.*

trauma • *the trauma of losing a parent*

shock ② VERB

to make you feel upset • *I was shocked by his appearance.*

numb • *numbed by suffering and terror*

paralyse • *He stood paralysed with horror.*

shake • *The news of her death has shaken us all.*

stagger • *The judge said he was staggered by the defendant's callousness.*

stun • *Audiences were stunned by the film's violent ending.*

traumatize • *My wife was traumatized by the experience.*

shock ③ VERB

to offend because of being rude or immoral • *She is very easily shocked.*

appal • *I was appalled by her rudeness.*

disgust • *He disgusted everyone with his boorish behaviour.*

offend • *Many people are offended by strong swearwords.*

outrage • *They were outraged by his racist comments.*

MORE SYNONYMS:
• nauseate
• scandalize

shop NOUN

a place where things are sold • *I had to race round the shops.*

boutique • *He owns a jewellery boutique.*

market • *He sold fruit on a stall at the market.*

store • *Within two years he was managing the store.*

supermarket • *Most of us do our food shopping in the supermarket.*

MORE SYNONYMS:
• emporium

- hypermarket
- mart

shore NOUN

♦ **TYPES OF SHORE**
- bank
- beach
- coast
- foreshore
- front
- lakeside
- sands
- seaboard
- seashore
- shingle
- strand
- waterside

short ① ADJECTIVE
not lasting very long • *a short break*
brief • *a brief meeting*
fleeting • *a fleeting glimpse*
momentary • *a momentary lapse of reason*
short-lived • *a short-lived craze*

ANTONYM:
- long

short ② ADJECTIVE
small in height • *a short, elderly man*
▶ see Word Study **short**, page 659

ANTONYM:
- tall

short ③ ADJECTIVE
not using many words • *a short speech*
brief • *a brief description*
concise • *a concise summary*
succinct • *a succinct account*
terse • *a terse comment*

MORE SYNONYMS:
- abridged
- laconic
- pithy

shortage NOUN
a lack of something • *a shortage of funds*

dearth • *the dearth of good fiction by English authors*
deficiency • *tests for vitamin deficiency*
lack • *I was hampered by a lack of information.*
scarcity • *a scarcity of water*
shortfall • *a shortfall in income*
want • *a want of manners and charm*

MORE SYNONYMS:
- insufficiency
- paucity

ANTONYM:
- abundance

shorten VERB
to make something shorter • *Smoking can shorten your life.*
abbreviate • *He abbreviated his name to Alec.*
cut • *The film was cut to two hours.*
trim • *I need to get my hair trimmed.*

MORE SYNONYMS:
- abridge
- downsize
- truncate

ANTONYM:
- lengthen

shout ① NOUN
a loud call or cry • *I heard a distant shout.*
bellow • *a bellow of rage*
cry • *She gave a cry of horror.*
roar • *a roar of approval*
scream • *screams of terror*
yell • *He let out a yell of delight.*

shout ② VERB
to call or cry loudly • *He shouted something to his brother.*
bawl • *Laura and Peter were bawling at each other.*
bellow • *He bellowed orders down the phone.*
call • *He could hear them calling his name.*

a
b
c
d
e
f
g
h
i
j
k
l
m
n
o
p
q
r
s
t
u
v
w
x
y
z

A
B
C
D
E
F
G
H
I
J
K
L
M
N
O
P
Q
R
S
T
U
V
W
X
Y
Z

cry • *"You're under arrest!" he cried.*
roar • *"I'll kill you for that!" he roared.*
scream • *screaming at them to get out of my house*
yell • *She pushed him away, yelling abuse.*

show ① NOUN
to prove something • *Tests show that smoking can cause cancer.*
demonstrate • *The study demonstrated a link between obesity and heart problems.*
prove • *History will prove him to be right.*

show ② VERB
to do something in order to teach someone else • *I'll show you how to set the video timer.*
demonstrate • *She demonstrated how to make ice cream.*
instruct • *He instructed us on how to give first aid.*
teach • *She taught me how to ride.*

show ③ VERB
to display a quality or characteristic • *Her sketches showed artistic promise.*
demonstrate • *He has demonstrated his ability.*
display • *He displayed remarkable courage.*
indicate • *Her choice of words indicated her real feelings.*
manifest • *Fear can manifest itself in many ways.*
reveal • *His reaction revealed a lack of self-confidence.*

MORE SYNONYMS:
• evince
• testify to

show ④ NOUN
a public exhibition • *a fashion show*
display • *a gymnastics display*
exhibition • *an art exhibition*

presentation • *Julie's successful presentation to the board*

show ⑤ NOUN
a display of a feeling or quality • *a show of affection*
air • *an air of indifference*
display • *a display of remorse*
pose • *a pose of injured innocence*
pretence • *They have given up all pretence of neutrality.*
semblance • *trying to maintain a semblance of order*

shrewd ADJECTIVE
showing intelligence and good judgment • *a shrewd businessman*
astute • *an astute judge of character*
canny • *He was far too canny to give himself away.*
crafty • *He is a clever man and a crafty politician.*
perceptive • *a perceptive analysis of the situation*
sharp • *He is very sharp, and a quick thinker.*
smart • *a very smart move*

MORE SYNONYMS:
• perspicacious
• sagacious

shrill ADJECTIVE
high-pitched and piercing • *the shrill whistle of the engine*
penetrating • *a penetrating voice*
piercing • *a piercing squawk*
sharp • *the sharp cry of a vixen*

shrink VERB
to become smaller • *All my jumpers have shrunk in the wash.*
contract • *The ribcage expands and contracts as you breathe.*
diminish • *The threat of nuclear war has diminished.*
dwindle • *The factory's workforce has dwindled from 4000 to 200.*

get smaller • *Electronic systems are getting smaller.*
narrow • *The gap between the two parties has narrowed.*

ANTONYM:
• grow

shut ① VERB
to close something • *Someone had forgotten to shut the door.*
close • *If you are cold, close the window.*
fasten • *He fastened the diamond clasp of the necklace.*
slam • *He slammed the gate shut behind him.*

ANTONYM:
• open

shut ② ADJECTIVE
closed or fastened • *A smell of burning came from behind the shut door.*
closed • *All the exits were closed.*
fastened • *The pockets are fastened with buttons.*
sealed • *a sealed envelope*

ANTONYM:
• open

shy ADJECTIVE
nervous in the company of other people • *a shy, quiet-spoken girl*
bashful • *Offstage, he is bashful and awkward.*
retiring • *He was the quiet, retiring type.*
self-conscious • *I felt a bit self-conscious in my swimming costume.*
timid • *a timid little boy*

MORE SYNONYMS:
• diffident
• self-effacing

ANTONYM:
• bold

sick ① ADJECTIVE
unwell or ill • *a ward full of very sick people*

ailing • *She tenderly nursed her ailing mother.*
poorly (INFORMAL) • *I called Julie and she's still poorly.*
under par (INFORMAL) • *The flu has left me feeling under par.*
under the weather • *Are you still a bit under the weather?*
unwell • *She had been unwell for some time.*

ANTONYM:
• well

sick ② ADJECTIVE
feeling as if you are going to vomit • *The very thought of food made him sick.*
ill • *The smell of curry always makes me ill.*
nauseous • *These drugs may make you feel nauseous.*
queasy • *The motion of the ship was already making him queasy.*

sick ③ : **sick of** ADJECTIVE (INFORMAL)
tired of something • *I'm sick of your complaints.*
bored • *I'm getting bored with the whole business.*
fed up • *He is fed up with this country.*
tired • *I am tired of this music.*
weary • *She was weary of being alone.*

side ① NOUN
the edge of something • *Her head hung over the side of the bed.*
edge • *She fell over the edge of the balcony.*
verge • *He parked on the verge of the road.*

RELATED WORD:
• ADJECTIVE lateral

side ② NOUN
one of two groups involved in a dispute or contest • *Both sides began to prepare for battle.*

a
b
c
d
e
f
g
h
i
j
k
l
m
n
o
p
q
r
s
t
u
v
w
x
y
z

A
B
C
D
E
F
G
H
I
J
K
L
M
N
O
P
Q
R
S
T
U
V
W
X
Y
Z

camp • *Most of his supporters had now defected to the opposite camp.*
faction • *leaders of the warring factions*
party • *the candidates for the three main parties*
team • *Both teams played well.*

side with VERB
to support someone in an argument • *Louise always sided with her sister.*
agree with • *She's bound to agree with her husband.*
stand up for • *I was the one who always stood up for my mother.*
support • *a fellow prisoner who supported her*
take the part of • *Why do you always take his part?*

sight ① NOUN
the ability to see • *My sight is so bad now that I can't read any more.*
eyesight • *He suffered from weak eyesight.*
visibility • *Visibility was very poor.*
vision • *It can cause blindness or serious loss of vision.*

RELATED WORDS:
• ADJECTIVES optical, visual

sight ② NOUN
something you see • *It was a ghastly sight.*
display • *These flowers make a colourful display in spring.*
scene • *a bizarre scene*
spectacle • *an impressive spectacle*

sight ③ VERB
to see something or someone • *He had been sighted in Cairo.*
see • *I saw a deer in the woods today.*
spot • *I drove round till I spotted her.*

sign ① NOUN
a mark or symbol • *The negative number is preceded by a minus sign.*

character • *the characters used in the hallmarking system*
emblem • *a small yellow hammer-and-sickle emblem*
logo • *the company's logo*
mark • *Put a tick mark against the statements you agree with.*
symbol • *the chemical symbol for mercury*

sign ② NOUN
a notice put up to give a warning or information • *a sign saying that the highway was closed*
board • *He studied the destination board on the front of the bus.*
notice • *a notice saying "no entry"*
placard • *The protesters sang songs and waved placards.*

sign ③ NOUN
evidence of something • *the first signs of recovery*
clue • *the only real clue that something was wrong*
evidence • *there has been no evidence of criminal activity*
hint • *He showed only the slightest hint of emotion.*
indication • *All the indications suggest that he is the murderer.*
symptom • *typical symptoms of stress*
token • *a token of goodwill*
trace • *No traces of violence were found on the body.*

signal ① NOUN
something which is intended to give a message • *a distress signal*
beacon • *an emergency beacon*
cue • *He gave me my cue to speak.*
gesture • *She made a menacing gesture with her fist.*
sign • *They gave him the thumbs-up sign.*

signal ② VERB
to make a sign as a message to

someone • *He was frantically signalling to her to shut up.*

beckon • *I beckoned her over.*

gesticulate • *He was gesticulating at a hole in the ground.*

gesture • *I gestured towards the house, and he went in.*

motion • *He motioned to her to go behind the screen.*

nod • *They nodded goodnight to the security man.*

sign • *She signed to me to come near.*

wave • *He waved the servants out of the tent.*

significant ADJECTIVE

large or important • *This drug seems to have a significant effect on the disease.*

considerable (FORMAL) • *Doing it properly makes considerable demands on our time.*

important • *The strike represents an important challenge to the government.*

impressive • *an impressive achievement*

marked • *a marked increase in crimes against property*

notable • *With a few notable exceptions, doctors are a pretty sensible lot.*

pronounced • *The exhibition has a pronounced Scottish theme.*

striking • *The most striking feature of these statistics is the rate of growth.*

ANTONYM:
• insignificant

silence ① NOUN

an absence of sound • *There was a momentary silence.*

calm • *He liked the calm of the evening.*

hush • *A hush fell over the crowd.*

lull • *a lull in the conversation*

peace • *I love the peace of the countryside.*

quiet • *The quiet of the flat was very soothing.*

stillness • *An explosion shattered the stillness of the night air.*

ANTONYM:
• noise

silence ② NOUN

an inability or refusal to talk • *breaking his silence for the first time about the affair*

dumbness • *a woman traumatized into dumbness*

muteness • *He retreated into stubborn muteness.*

reticence • *Fran didn't seem to notice my reticence.*

speechlessness • *He was shy to the point of speechlessness.*

MORE SYNONYMS:
• taciturnity
• uncommunicativeness
• voicelessness

silence ③ VERB

to make someone or something quiet • *The shock silenced her completely.*

deaden • *We hung up curtains to try and deaden the noise.*

gag • *I gagged him with a towel.*

muffle • *You can muffle the sound with absorbent material.*

quiet • *A look from her husband quieted her at once.*

quieten • *She tried to quieten her breathing.*

stifle • *He put his hand to his mouth to stifle a giggle.*

still • *He raised a hand to still Alex's protest.*

suppress • *She barely suppressed a gasp.*

silent ① ADJECTIVE

not saying anything • *The class fell silent as the teacher entered.*

dumb • *We were all struck dumb for a moment.*

mute • *a mute look of appeal*
speechless • *speechless with rage*
taciturn • *a taciturn man with a solemn expression*
wordless • *They exchanged a wordless look of understanding.*

MORE SYNONYMS:
• tongue-tied
• uncommunicative

silent ② ADJECTIVE
making no noise • *The room was silent except for the ticking of the clock.*
hushed • *the vast, hushed space of the cathedral*
quiet • *a quiet engine*
soundless • *My bare feet were soundless on the carpet.*
still • *The room was suddenly still.*

ANTONYM:
• noisy

silly ADJECTIVE
foolish or ridiculous • *I know it's silly to get so upset.*
absurd • *He found fashion absurd.*
daft • *That's a daft question.*
foolish • *It is foolish to risk injury.*
idiotic • *What an idiotic thing to say!*
inane • *He stood there with an inane grin on his face.*
ridiculous • *a ridiculous suggestion*
stupid • *a stupid mistake*

MORE SYNONYMS:
• asinine
• fatuous
• puerile
• witless

similar ADJECTIVE
like something else • *an accident similar to Hakkinen's*
alike • *You two are very alike.*
analogous • *a ritual analogous to those of primitive tribal cultures*
comparable • *paying the same wages*

for work of comparable value
like • *They're as like as two peas in a pod.*
uniform • *droplets of uniform size*

ANTONYM:
• different

similarity NOUN
the quality of being like something else • *the similarity of our backgrounds*
analogy • *the analogy between racism and homophobia*
likeness • *These myths have a startling likeness to one another.*
resemblance • *I could see the resemblance to his grandfather.*
sameness • *He grew bored by the sameness of the speeches.*

MORE SYNONYMS:
• comparability
• congruence
• similitude

ANTONYM:
• difference

simple ① ADJECTIVE
easy to understand or do • *a simple task*
easy • *This ice cream maker is cheap and easy to use.*
elementary • *elementary computer skills*
straightforward • *It was a straightforward question.*
uncomplicated • *an uncomplicated story*
understandable • *He writes in a clear, understandable style.*

ANTONYM:
• complicated

simple ② ADJECTIVE
plain in style • *a simple but stylish outfit*
classic • *classic designs which will fit in anywhere*
clean • *the clean lines of Shaker furniture*

plain • *Her dress was plain but hung well on her.*

severe • *hair scraped back in a severe style*

ANTONYM:
• elaborate

simplify VERB

to make something easier to do or understand • *measures intended to simplify the procedure*

make simpler • *restructuring the tax system to make it simpler*

streamline • *an effort to cut costs and streamline operations*

sin ① NOUN

wicked and immoral behaviour • *preaching against sin*

crime • *a life of crime*

evil • *You can't stop all the evil in the world.*

offence • *an offence which can carry the death penalty*

wickedness • *a sign of human wickedness*

wrong • *I intend to right that wrong.*

MORE SYNONYMS:
• iniquity
• misdeed
• transgression
• trespass

sin ② VERB

to do something wicked and immoral • *I admit that I have sinned.*

do wrong • *They have done wrong and they know it.*

sincere ADJECTIVE

saying things that you really mean • *my sincere apologies*

genuine • *a display of genuine emotion*

heartfelt • *heartfelt sympathy*

real • *the real affection between them*

wholehearted • *a wholehearted and genuine response*

ANTONYM:
• insincere

single ① ADJECTIVE

only one and no more • *A single shot was fired.*

lone • *A lone policeman guarded the doors.*

one • *I just had one drink.*

only • *My only regret is that I never knew him.*

sole • *the sole survivor of the accident*

solitary • *There is not one solitary scrap of evidence.*

single ② ADJECTIVE

not married • *I'm surprised you're still single.*

unattached • *I only know two or three unattached men.*

unmarried • *an unmarried mother*

single ③ ADJECTIVE

for one person only • *a single room*

individual • *an individual portion*

separate • *separate beds*

singular ADJECTIVE (FORMAL)

unusual and remarkable • *a smile of singular sweetness*

exceptional • *children with exceptional ability*

extraordinary • *The task requires extraordinary patience and endurance.*

rare • *a leader of rare strength and instinct*

remarkable • *a remarkable achievement*

uncommon • *She read Cecilia's letter with uncommon interest.*

unique • *a woman of unique talent and determination*

unusual • *He had an unusual aptitude for mathematics.*

sinister ADJECTIVE

seeming harmful or evil • *There was something cold and sinister about him.*

a
b
c
d
e
f
g
h
i
j
k
l
m
n
o
p
q
r
s
t
u
v
w
x
y
z

A
B
C
D
E
F
G
H
I
J
K
L
M
N
O
P
Q
R
S
T
U
V
W
X
Y
Z

evil • *an evil smile*
forbidding • *a huge, forbidding building*
menacing • *His dark eyebrows gave him a menacing look.*
ominous • *A dark and ominous figure stood in the doorway.*
threatening • *his threatening appearance*

MORE SYNONYMS:
• baleful
• bodeful
• disquieting

situation NOUN
what is happening • *a serious situation*
case • *a clear case of mistaken identity*
circumstances • *I wish we could have met in happier circumstances.*
plight • *the plight of Third World countries*
scenario • *a nightmare scenario*
state of affairs • *This state of affairs cannot continue.*

size ① NOUN
how big or small something is • *the size of the audience*
dimensions • *He considered the dimensions of the problem*
extent • *the extent of the damage*
proportions • *In the tropics, plants grow to huge proportions.*

size ② NOUN
the fact of something being very large • *the sheer size of Australia*
bulk • *Despite his bulk, he moved gracefully.*
immensity • *The immensity of the universe is impossible to grasp.*

MORE SYNONYMS:
• magnitude
• vastness

skilful ADJECTIVE
able to do something very well • *the country's most skilful politician*

able • *a very able businessman*
accomplished • *an accomplished pianist*
adept • *an adept diplomat*
competent • *a competent and careful driver*
expert • *He is expert at handling complex negotiations.*
masterly • *a masterly performance*
proficient • *proficient with computers*
skilled • *a skilled wine maker*

MORE SYNONYMS:
• adroit
• dexterous

ANTONYM:
• incompetent

skill NOUN
the ability to do something well • *This task requires great skill.*
ability • *a man of considerable abilities*
competence • *his high professional competence*
dexterity • *Reid's dexterity on the guitar*
expertise • *the expertise to deal with these problems*
facility • *a facility for languages*
knack • *the knack of getting on with people*
proficiency • *basic proficiency in English*

skilled ADJECTIVE
having the knowledge to do something well • *skilled workers, such as plumbers*
able • *an able craftsman*
accomplished • *an accomplished pianist*
competent • *a competent and careful driver*
experienced • *lawyers who are experienced in these matters*
expert • *It takes an expert eye to see the symptoms.*

masterly · *the artist's masterly use of colour*
professional · *professional people like doctors and engineers*
proficient · *He is proficient in several foreign languages.*
skilful · *the artist's skilful use of light and shade*
trained · *Our workforce is highly trained.*

ANTONYM:
• incompetent

skinny ADJECTIVE
extremely thin · *a skinny little boy*
bony · *a long bony finger*
emaciated · *television pictures of emaciated prisoners*
lean · *a tall, lean figure*
scrawny · *the vulture's scrawny neck*
thin · *He is small and very thin with white skin.*
underfed · *Kate still looks pale and underfed.*
undernourished · *undernourished children*

ANTONYM:
• plump

slander ① NOUN
something untrue and malicious said about someone · *He is now suing the company for slander.*
libel · *defendants seeking damages for libel*
scandal · *She loves spreading scandal.*
slur · *a vicious slur on his character*
smear · *He called the allegation "an evil smear".*

MORE SYNONYMS:
• aspersion
• calumny
• defamation
• obloquy

slander ② VERB
to say untrue and malicious things

about someone · *He has been charged with slandering the Prime Minister.*
libel · *The newspaper which libelled him had to pay compensation.*
malign · *He claims he is being unfairly maligned.*
smear · *an attempt to smear their manager*

MORE SYNONYMS:
• calumniate
• defame
• traduce
• vilify

slang NOUN

◆ **SOME SLANG WORDS**
◆ bang tidy
◆ beast
◆ chillax
◆ dyno
◆ fit
◆ hot
◆ ledge
◆ legit
◆ lolz
◆ mank
◆ minging
◆ sound
◆ soz
◆ swag
◆ yaldi

sleep ① NOUN
the natural state of rest in which you are unconscious · *They were exhausted from lack of sleep.*
doze · *I had a doze after lunch.*
hibernation · *Many animals go into hibernation during the winter.*
kip (BRITISH; SLANG) · *Mason went home for a couple of hours' kip.*
nap · *I might take a nap for a while.*
slumber · *He had fallen into exhausted slumber.*
snooze (INFORMAL) · *a little snooze after dinner*

A
B
C
D
E
F
G
H
I
J
K
L
M
N
O
P
Q
R
S
T
U
V
W
X
Y
Z

MORE SYNONYMS:
• dormancy
• repose
• siesta

sleep ② VERB
to rest in a natural state of unconsciousness • *The baby slept during the car journey.*
doze • *He dozed in an armchair.*
hibernate • *Dormice hibernate from October to May.*
kip (BRITISH; SLANG) • *He kipped on my sofa last night.*
slumber • *The girls were slumbering peacefully.*
snooze (INFORMAL) • *Mark snoozed in front of the television.*
take a nap • *Try to take a nap every afternoon.*

sleepy ① ADJECTIVE
tired and ready to go to sleep • *Do you feel sleepy during the day?*
drowsy • *This medicine may make you feel drowsy.*
lethargic • *He felt too lethargic to get dressed.*
sluggish • *I was still feeling sluggish after my nap.*

MORE SYNONYMS:
• somnolent
• torpid

sleepy ② ADJECTIVE
not having much activity or excitement • *a sleepy little village*
dull • *a dull town*
quiet • *a quiet rural backwater*

slender ① ADJECTIVE
attractively thin • *a tall, slender woman*
lean • *Like most athletes, she was lean and muscular.*
slight • *She is small and slight.*
slim • *Jean is pretty, with a slim build.*

MORE SYNONYMS:
• svelte
• sylphlike
• willowy

slender ② ADJECTIVE
small in amount or degree • *He won, but only by a slender majority.*
faint • *They now have only a faint chance of survival.*
remote • *a remote possibility*
slight • *There is a slight improvement in his condition.*
slim • *a slim hope*
small • *a small chance of success*

MORE SYNONYMS:
• inconsiderable
• tenuous

slight ADJECTIVE
small in amount or degree • *a slight dent*
insignificant • *an insignificant amount*
minor • *a minor inconvenience*
negligible • *The strike will have a negligible impact.*
small • *It only makes a small difference.*
trivial • *trivial details*

MORE SYNONYMS:
• inconsiderable
• paltry
• scanty

ANTONYM:
• large

slip ① VERB
to go somewhere quickly and quietly • *Amy slipped downstairs and out of the house.*
creep • *I crept up to my room.*
sneak • *Sometimes he would sneak out to see me.*
steal • *They can steal away at night to join us.*

slip ② NOUN
a small mistake • *There must be no slips.*

blunder • *an embarrassing blunder*
error • *a tactical error*
mistake • *Many people are anxious about making mistakes in grammar.*

MORE SYNONYMS:
• faux pas
• imprudence
• indiscretion

slogan NOUN
a short easily-remembered phrase • *a poster with the slogan, "Your country needs you"*
jingle • *a catchy advertising jingle*
motto • *"Who Dares Wins" is the motto of the Special Air Service.*

slope ① NOUN
a flat surface with one end higher than the other • *The street is on a slope.*
gradient • *a steep gradient*
incline • *The car was unable to negotiate the incline.*
ramp • *There is a ramp allowing access for wheelchairs.*

MORE SYNONYMS:
• declination
• declivity
• inclination

slope ② VERB
to be at an angle • *The bank sloped sharply down to the river.*
fall • *The road fell steeply.*
rise • *The climb is arduous, rising steeply through thick bush.*
slant • *His handwriting slanted to the left.*

slow ① ADJECTIVE
moving or happening with little speed • *slow, regular breathing*
gradual • *Losing weight is a gradual process.*
leisurely • *He walked at a leisurely pace.*
lingering • *a lingering death*

ponderous • *His steps were heavy and ponderous.*
sluggish • *a sluggish stream*
unhurried • *She rose with unhurried grace.*

ANTONYM:
• fast

slow ② ADJECTIVE
not very clever • *He got hit in the head and he's been a bit slow ever since.*
dense • *He's not a bad man, just a bit dense.*
dim • *He is rather dim.*
dumb (INFORMAL) • *too dumb to realise what was going on*
obtuse • *It should be obvious even to the most obtuse person.*
stupid • *He can't help being a bit stupid.*
thick • *I can't believe I've been so thick.*

slow (down) VERB
to go or cause to go more slowly • *The car slowed and then stopped.*
check • *attempts to check the spread of AIDS*
decelerate • *He decelerated when he saw the warning sign.*

slowly ADVERB
not quickly or hurriedly • *He turned and began to walk away slowly.*
by degrees • *By degrees, the tension passed out of him.*
gradually • *Their friendship gradually deepened.*
unhurriedly • *The islanders drift along unhurriedly from day to day.*

ANTONYM:
• quickly

sly ADJECTIVE
cunning and deceptive • *She is devious, sly and manipulative.*
crafty • *a crafty villain*
cunning • *Some of these kids can be very cunning.*

A
B
C
D
E
F
G
H
I
J
K
L
M
N
O
P
Q
R
S
T
U
V
W
X
Y
Z

devious • *an extremely dangerous, evil and devious man*
scheming • *You're a scheming little rat, aren't you?*
underhand • *underhand tactics*
wily • *a wily politician*

small ① ADJECTIVE
not large in size, number, or amount • *a small child*
▶ see Word Study **small**, page 660

ANTONYM:
• large

small ② ADJECTIVE
not important or significant • *small changes*
inconsequential • *a seemingly inconsequential event*
insignificant • *an insignificant village in the hills*
little • *Fancy making such a fuss over such a little thing!*
minor • *a minor detail*
negligible • *The impact of the strike will be negligible.*
petty • *Rows would start over the most petty things.*
slight • *It will only make a slight difference.*
trifling • *These are trifling objections.*
trivial • *Let's not get bogged down in trivial details.*
unimportant • *a comparatively unimportant event*

smart ① ADJECTIVE
clean and neat in appearance • *a smart navy blue outfit*
chic • *chic Parisian women*
elegant • *Patricia looked beautiful and elegant, as always.*
neat • *a neat grey flannel suit*
spruce • *Chris was looking spruce in his uniform.*
stylish • *stylish white shoes*

MORE SYNONYMS:
• modish
• natty
• snappy

ANTONYM:
• scruffy

smart ② ADJECTIVE
clever and intelligent • *a smart idea*
astute • *a series of astute business decisions*
bright • *She is not very bright.*
canny • *He was far too canny to give himself away.*
clever • *Nobody disputed that Davey was clever.*
ingenious • *an ingenious plan*
intelligent • *Dolphins are an intelligent species.*
shrewd • *a shrewd businessman*

ANTONYM:
• dumb

smell ① NOUN
the quality of something which you sense through your nose • *a smell of damp wood*
aroma • *the aroma of fresh bread*
fragrance • *the fragrance of his cologne*
odour • *a disagreeable odour*
perfume • *enjoying the perfume of the lemon trees*
pong (BRITISH AND AUSTRALIAN; INFORMAL) • *What's that horrible pong?*
reek • *the reek of whisky*
scent • *flowers chosen for their scent*
stench • *a foul stench*
stink • *the stink of stale beer on his breath*

MORE SYNONYMS:
• bouquet
• fetor
• malodour

smell ② VERB
to have an unpleasant smell • *Do my feet smell?*

pong (BRITISH AND AUSTRALIAN; INFORMAL) • *She said he ponged a bit.*
reek • *The whole house reeks of cigar smoke.*
stink • *His breath stinks of garlic.*

smell ③ VERB
to become aware of the smell of something • *I could smell liquor on his breath.*
scent • *The dog had scented something in the bushes.*
sniff • *He opened his window and sniffed the air.*

smelly ADJECTIVE
having a strong unpleasant smell
• *smelly socks*
foul • *His breath was foul.*
reeking • *poisoning the air with their reeking cigars*
stinking • *piles of stinking rubbish*

MORE SYNONYMS:
• fetid
• malodorous
• noisome

ANTONYM:
• fragrant

smile ① VERB
to move the corners of your mouth upwards because you are pleased
• *When he saw me, he smiled and waved.*
beam • *She beamed at him in delight.*
grin • *He grinned broadly.*
smirk • *The two men looked at me, nudged each other and smirked.*

smile ② NOUN
the expression you have when you smile • *She gave me a big smile.*
beam • *a strange beam of satisfaction on his face*
grin • *She looked at me with a sheepish grin.*
smirk • *a smirk of triumph*

smooth ADJECTIVE
not rough or bumpy • *a smooth wooden surface*
glassy • *glassy green pebbles*
glossy • *glossy dark fur*
polished • *He slipped on the polished floor.*
silky • *The sauce should be silky in texture.*
sleek • *her sleek, waist-length hair*

ANTONYM:
• rough

smug ADJECTIVE
pleased with yourself • *They looked at each other in smug satisfaction.*
complacent • *an aggravating, complacent little smile*
conceited • *They had grown too conceited and pleased with themselves.*
self-satisfied • *a self-satisfied little snob*
superior • *He stood there looking superior.*

snag NOUN
a small problem or disadvantage • *The snag was that he had no transport.*
catch • *It sounds too good to be true - what's the catch?*
difficulty • *The only difficulty may be the price.*
disadvantage • *The disadvantage is that this plant needs frequent watering.*
drawback • *The flat's only drawback was its size.*
problem • *The only problem about living here is the tourists.*

MORE SYNONYMS:
• downside
• stumbling block

sneak ① VERB
to go somewhere quietly • *Sometimes he would sneak out to see me.*
lurk • *I saw someone lurking outside.*

sidle • *He sidled into the bar, trying to look inconspicuous.*

slip • *Amy slipped downstairs and out of the house.*

steal • *They can steal out and join us later.*

MORE SYNONYMS:
• skulk
• slink

sneak ② VERB
to put or take something somewhere secretly • *I sneaked the books out of the library.*

slip • *He slipped me a note.*

smuggle • *We smuggled a camera into the concert.*

spirit • *treasures spirited away to foreign museums*

sneaky ADJECTIVE
doing things secretly or being done secretly • *He only won by using sneaky tactics.*

crafty • *the crafty methods used by salesmen to get people to sign up*

deceitful • *They claimed the government had been deceitful.*

devious • *He was devious, saying one thing to me and another to her.*

dishonest • *It would be dishonest to mislead people in that way.*

mean • *That was a mean trick.*

slippery • *She's a slippery customer, and should be watched.*

sly • *He's a sly old beggar.*

untrustworthy • *His opponents say he's untrustworthy.*

snooper NOUN
a person who interferes in other people's business • *a tabloid snooper*

meddler • *a meddler in the affairs of state*

stickybeak (AUSTRALIAN AND NEW ZEALAND; INFORMAL) • *She's just an old stickybeak.*

MORE SYNONYMS:
• busybody
• nosy parker

soak VERB
to make something very wet • *The water had soaked his jacket.*

bathe • *Bathe the infected area in a salt solution.*

permeate • *The water had permeated the stone.*

steep • *green beans steeped in olive oil*

wet • *Wet the hair and work the shampoo through it.*

MORE SYNONYMS:
• drench
• saturate

sociable ADJECTIVE
enjoying the company of other people • *She's usually outgoing and sociable.*

friendly • *The people here are very friendly.*

gregarious • *I'm not a gregarious person.*

outgoing • *He was shy and she was very outgoing.*

MORE SYNONYMS:
• companionable
• convivial

society ① NOUN
the people in a particular country or region • *a major problem in society*

civilization • *an ancient civilization*

culture • *people from different cultures*

society ② NOUN
an organization for people with the same interest or aim • *the school debating society*

association • *the Football Association*

circle • *a local painting circle*

club • *He was at the youth club.*

fellowship • *the Visual Arts Fellowship*

group • *an environmental group*

guild • *the Screen Writers' Guild*
institute • *the Women's Institute*
league • *the World Muslim League*
organization • *student organizations*
union • *the International Astronomical Union*

soft ① ADJECTIVE
not hard, stiff or firm • *a soft bed*
flexible • *a flexible material*
pliable • *a pliable dough*
squashy • *a squashy tomato*
supple • *supple leather*
yielding • *yielding cushions*

MORE SYNONYMS:
• bendable
• ductile
• gelatinous
• malleable
• tensile

ANTONYM:
• hard

soft ② ADJECTIVE
quiet and not harsh • *a soft tapping at my door*
gentle • *a gentle voice*
low • *She spoke to us in a low whisper.*
mellow • *mellow background music*
muted • *Their loud conversation became muted.*
quiet • *He always spoke in a quiet tone to which everyone listened.*
subdued • *His voice was more subdued than usual.*

MORE SYNONYMS:
• dulcet
• mellifluous

software NOUN
computer programs used on a particular system • *software for mobile phones*
app • *an app telling you where your seat is*
application • *Download the application here.*

killer app • *The company is working on the next killer app.*

soil ① NOUN
the surface of the earth • *The soil is reasonably moist after the rain.*
clay • *a thin layer of clay*
dirt • *The bulldozers piled up huge mounds of dirt.*
earth • *a huge pile of earth*
ground • *a hole in the ground*

soil ② VERB
to make something dirty • *He looked at her as though her words might soil him.*
dirty • *He was afraid the dog's hairs might dirty the seats.*
foul • *The cage was fouled with droppings.*
pollute • *chemicals which pollute rivers*
smear • *The pillow was smeared with makeup.*
spatter • *Her dress was spattered with mud.*
stain • *Some foods can stain the teeth.*

MORE SYNONYMS:
• befoul
• begrime
• besmirch
• defile
• smirch
• sully

ANTONYM:
• clean

solemn ADJECTIVE
not cheerful or humorous • *a taciturn man with a solemn expression*
earnest • *Ella was a pious, earnest woman.*
grave • *He was looking unusually grave.*
serious • *She looked at me with big, serious eyes.*
sober • *sad, sober faces*

a b c d e f g h i j k l m n o p q r **s** t u v w x y z

A
B
C
D
E
F
G
H
I
J
K
L
M
N
O
P
Q
R
S
T
U
V
W
X
Y
Z

staid • *He is boring, old fashioned and staid.*

solid ① ADJECTIVE
hard and firm • *a block of solid wax*
firm • *a firm mattress*
hard • *The snow was hard and slippery.*

solid ② ADJECTIVE
not likely to fall down • *a solid structure*
stable • *stable foundations*
strong • *a strong fence*
sturdy • *The camera was mounted on a sturdy tripod.*
substantial • *The posts are made of concrete and are fairly substantial.*

solitude NOUN
the state of being alone • *He went to the cottage for a few days of solitude.*
isolation • *the isolation he endured while in captivity*
loneliness • *I have a fear of loneliness.*
privacy • *the privacy of my own room*
seclusion • *She lived in seclusion with her husband.*

solve VERB
to find the answer to a problem or question • *attempts to solve the mystery*
clear up • *During dinner the confusion was cleared up.*
crack • *He finally managed to crack the code.*
decipher • *trying to decipher the symbols on the stone tablets*
get to the bottom of • *The police wanted to get to the bottom of the case.*
resolve • *Scientists hope this will finally resolve the mystery.*
work out • *I've worked out where I'm going wrong.*

sometimes ADVERB
now and then • *Her voice was so low she was sometimes mistaken for a man.*

at times • *She can be a little common at times.*
every now and then • *He checks up on me every now and then.*
every so often • *Every so often he does something silly.*
from time to time • *I go back to see my mum from time to time.*
now and again • *I enjoy a day out now and again.*
now and then • *These people like a laugh now and then.*
occasionally • *I know that I do put people down occasionally.*
once in a while • *It does you good to get out once in a while.*

soon ADVERB
in a very short time • *You'll be hearing from us very soon.*
any minute now • *Any minute now she's going to start crying.*
before long • *Interest rates will come down before long.*
in a minute • *I'll be with you in a minute.*
in the near future • *The controversy is unlikely to be resolved in the near future.*
presently • *I'll deal with you presently.*
shortly • *The trial will begin shortly.*
ANTONYM:
• later

sophisticated ① ADJECTIVE
having refined tastes • *a charming, sophisticated companion*
cosmopolitan • *The family are rich and extremely cosmopolitan.*
cultivated • *an elegant and cultivated woman*
cultured • *He is immensely cultured and well-read.*
refined • *a woman of refined tastes*
urbane • *a polished, urbane manner*

sophisticated ② ADJECTIVE
advanced and complicated • *a*

sophisticated piece of equipment
advanced • *the most advanced optical telescope in the world*
complex • *complex machines*
complicated • *a complicated voting system*
elaborate • *an elaborate design*
intricate • *intricate controls*
refined • *a more refined engine*

ANTONYM:
• simple

sore ADJECTIVE
causing pain and discomfort • *a sore throat*
inflamed • *Her eyes were red and inflamed.*
painful • *a painful knock on the knee*
raw • *Her hands were rubbed raw by the rope.*
sensitive • *the pain of sensitive teeth*
smarting • *My eyes were smarting from the smoke.*
tender • *My stomach feels very tender.*

sorrow ① NOUN
deep sadness or regret • *a time of great sorrow*
grief • *Their grief soon gave way to anger.*
heartache • *suffering the heartache of a divorce*
melancholy • *She has an air of melancholy.*
misery • *All his money brought him nothing but misery.*
mourning • *a day of mourning*
pain • *My heart is full of pain.*
regret • *She accepted his resignation with regret.*
sadness • *It is with a mixture of sadness and joy that I say farewell.*
unhappiness • *I had a lot of unhappiness in my adolescence.*
woe (FORMAL) • *a tale of woe*

ANTONYM:
• joy

sorrow ② NOUN
things that cause deep sadness and regret • *the joys and sorrows of family life*
heartache • *all the heartaches of parenthood*
hardship • *One of the worst hardships is having so little time with my family.*
misfortune • *She seems to enjoy the misfortunes of others.*
trouble • *She told me all her troubles.*
woe (WRITTEN) • *He did not tell his friends about his woes.*
worry • *a life with no worries*

MORE SYNONYMS:
• affliction
• tribulation (FORMAL)

ANTONYM:
• joy

sorry ① ADJECTIVE
feeling sadness or regret • *I'm terribly sorry to bother you.*
apologetic • *"I'm afraid I can't help," she said with an apologetic smile.*
penitent • *He sat silent and penitent in a corner.*
regretful • *Now I'm totally regretful that I did it.*
remorseful • *He was genuinely remorseful.*
repentant • *repentant sinners*

MORE SYNONYMS:
• conscience-stricken
• contrite
• guilt-ridden
• shamefaced

sorry ② ADJECTIVE
feeling sympathy for someone • *I was sorry to hear about your husband's death.*
moved • *I'm moved by what you say.*
sympathetic • *She gave me a sympathetic glance.*

a
b
c
d
e
f
g
h
i
j
k
l
m
n
o
p
q
r
s
t
u
v
w
x
y
z

A
B
C
D
E
F
G
H
I
J
K
L
M
N
O
P
Q
R
S
T
U
V
W
X
Y
Z

sorry ③ ADJECTIVE
in a bad condition • *He was in a pretty sorry state when we found him.*
deplorable • *living in deplorable conditions*
miserable • *a miserable existence*
pathetic • *the pathetic sight of oil-covered sea birds*
pitiful • *a pitiful creature*
poor • *the poor condition of the pitch*
sad • *a sad state of affairs*
wretched • *the wretched victims of war*

MORE SYNONYMS:
• piteous
• pitiable

sort ① NOUN
one of the different kinds of something • *a dozen trees of various sorts*
brand • *his favourite brand of whisky*
category • *The topics were divided into six categories.*
class • *a better class of restaurant*
group • *Weathermen classify clouds into several different groups.*
kind • *different kinds of roses*
make • *a certain make of car*
species • *400 species of fungi have been recorded.*
style • *Several styles of hat were available.*
type • *What type of dog should we get?*
variety • *many varieties of birds*

MORE SYNONYMS:
• ilk
• stamp

sort ② VERB
to arrange things into different kinds • *He sorted the material into three folders.*
arrange • *Arrange the books in neat piles.*
categorize • *ways to categorize information*

classify • *Rocks can be classified according to their mode of origin.*
divide • *The subjects were divided into four groups.*
grade • *musical pieces graded according to difficulty*
group • *The fact sheet is grouped into seven sections.*
separate • *His work can be separated into three main categories.*

sound ① NOUN
something that can be heard • *the sound of gunfire*
din • *make themselves heard over the din of the crowd*
hubbub • *the hubbub of excited conversation*
noise • *the noise of bombs and guns*
racket • *the racket of drills and electric saws*
tone • *the clear tone of the bell*
ANTONYM:
• silence

RELATED WORDS:
• ADJECTIVES acoustic, sonic

sound ② VERB
to produce or cause to produce a noise • *A young man sounded the bell.*
blow • *A guard was blowing his whistle.*
chime • *He heard the doorbell chime.*
clang • *The church bell clanged.*
peal • *Church bells pealed at the stroke of midnight.*
ring • *She heard the school bell ringing.*
set off • *Any escape sets off the alarm.*
toll • *The pilgrims tolled the bell.*

sound ③ ADJECTIVE
healthy, or in good condition • *His body was still sound.*
all right • *Does the roof seem all right?*
fine • *She told me her heart was perfectly fine.*
fit • *Exercise is the first step to a fit body.*

healthy • *His once healthy mind was deteriorating.*

in good condition • *The timbers were all in good condition.*

intact • *The boat did not appear damaged and its equipment seemed intact.*

robust • *He is in robust health for a man of his age.*

sound ④ ADJECTIVE
reliable and sensible • *a sound financial proposition*

down-to-earth • *Their ideas seem very down-to-earth.*

good • *Give me one good reason why I should tell you.*

reasonable • *a perfectly reasonable decision*

reliable • *It's difficult to give a reliable estimate.*

sensible • *sensible advice*

solid • *good solid information*

valid • *Both sides made some valid points.*

sour ① ADJECTIVE
having a sharp taste • *The stewed apple was sour even with sugar added.*

acid • *The wine had an acid taste.*

bitter • *a bitter drink*

pungent • *a pungent sauce*

sharp • *a clean, sharp flavour*

tart • *the tart qualities of citrus fruit*

MORE SYNONYMS:
• acerbic
• acetic

ANTONYM:
• sweet

sour ② ADJECTIVE
unpleasant in taste because no longer fresh • *This cream's gone sour.*

curdled • *curdled milk*

off • *This meat's gone off.*

rancid • *rancid butter*

sour ③ ADJECTIVE
bad-tempered and unfriendly • *a sour expression*

disagreeable • *a shallow, disagreeable man*

embittered • *an embittered old lady*

jaundiced • *a jaundiced attitude*

tart • *a tart reply*

MORE SYNONYMS:
• churlish
• peevish
• waspish

source NOUN
the place where something comes from • *the source of his confidence*

beginning • *the beginning of all the trouble*

cause • *the cause of the problem*

derivation • *The derivation of the name is obscure.*

origin • *the origin of life*

originator • *the originator of the theory*

MORE SYNONYMS:
• fount
• fountainhead
• wellspring

souvenir NOUN
something you keep as a reminder • *a souvenir of our holiday*

keepsake • *a cherished keepsake*

memento • *a memento of the occasion*

relic • *the threadbare teddy bear, a relic of childhood*

reminder • *a permanent reminder of this historic event*

space ① NOUN
an area which is empty or available • *a car with plenty of interior space*

accommodation • *We have accommodation for six people.*

capacity • *the capacity of the airliner*

room • *no room to manoeuvre*

A
B
C
D
E
F
G
H
I
J
K
L
M
N
O
P
Q
R
S
T
U
V
W
X
Y
Z

RELATED WORD:
• ADJECTIVE spatial

space ② NOUN
the gap between two things • *the space between the two tables*
blank • *I've left a blank here for your signature.*
distance • *the distance between the island and the mainland*
gap • *The wind was tearing through gaps in the window frames.*
interval • *the intervals between the trees*

space ③ NOUN
a period of time • *two incidents in the space of a week*
interval • *a long interval of silence*
period • *for a limited period only*
span • *The batteries have a life span of six hours.*
time • *At 15 he left home for a short time.*
while • *Sit down for a while.*

spacious ADJECTIVE
having or providing a lot of space • *a spacious lounge*
ample • *the city's ample car parks*
broad • *a broad expanse of green lawn*
expansive • *an expansive play area*
extensive • *The palace stands in extensive grounds.*
huge • *a huge apartment overlooking the park*
large • *a large detached house*
vast • *a vast chamber*

MORE SYNONYMS:
• capacious
• commodious
• roomy
• sizable or
• sizeable

spare ① ADJECTIVE
in addition to what is needed • *Luckily I had a spare pair of glasses.*

extra • *Allow yourself some extra time in case of emergencies.*
free • *I'll do it as soon as I get some free time.*
superfluous • *I got rid of all my superfluous belongings.*
surplus • *They sell their surplus produce.*

MORE SYNONYMS:
• leftover
• supernumerary

spare ② VERB
to make something available • *Can you spare some money for a cup of tea?*
afford • *It's all I can afford to give you.*
give • *It's good of you to give me some of your time.*
let someone have • *I can let you have some milk and sugar.*

spare ③ VERB
to save someone from an unpleasant experience • *I wanted to spare her that suffering.*
let off (INFORMAL) • *I'll let you off this time.*
pardon • *Relatives had begged authorities to pardon him.*
relieve from • *a machine which relieves you of the drudgery of housework*
save from • *I was trying to save you from unnecessary worry.*

sparkle VERB
to shine with small bright points of light • *Diamonds sparkled on her wrists.*
gleam • *sunlight gleaming on the water*
glisten • *The wall glistened with frost.*
glitter • *A million stars glittered in the black sky.*
shimmer • *In the distance the lake shimmered.*
twinkle • *The old man's eyes twinkled.*

MORE SYNONYMS:
- coruscate
- scintillate

speak VERB

to use your voice to say words • *She turned to look at the person who was speaking.*

▶ see Word Study **say**, page 655

special ① ADJECTIVE

more important or better than others of its kind • *You are very special to me.*

exceptional • *children with exceptional ability*

important • *This is an important occasion.*

significant • *of significant importance*

unique • *a unique talent*

ANTONYM:
- ordinary

special ② ADJECTIVE

relating to one person or group in particular • *the special needs of the chronically sick*

characteristic • *a characteristic feature*

distinctive • *the distinctive smell of chlorine*

individual • *Each family needs individual attention.*

particular • *Fatigue is a particular problem for women.*

peculiar • *This is not a problem peculiar to London.*

specific • *the specific needs of the elderly*

ANTONYM:
- general

specify VERB

to state or describe something precisely • *Specify which size and colour you want.*

be specific about • *She was never very specific about her date of birth.*

indicate • *Please indicate your preference below.*

name • *The victims of the fire have been named.*

spell out • *He spelled out the reasons why he was leaving.*

state • *Please state your name.*

stipulate • *His duties were stipulated in the contract.*

spectator NOUN

a person who watches something • *Spectators lined the route.*

bystander • *an innocent bystander*

eyewitness • *Eyewitnesses say the police opened fire in the crowd.*

observer • *a disinterested observer*

onlooker • *A small crowd of onlookers was there to greet her.*

witness • *There were scores of witnesses.*

speech NOUN

a formal talk given to an audience • *He delivered his speech in French.*

address • *an address to the American people*

discourse • *a lengthy discourse on strategy*

lecture • *a series of lectures on art*

talk • *a talk on Celtic mythology*

MORE SYNONYMS:
- disquisition
- harangue
- homily
- oration

speed ① NOUN

the rate at which something moves or happens • *a top speed of 200 mph*

haste • *the old saying "more haste, less speed"*

hurry • *the hurry and excitement of the city*

momentum • *This campaign is gaining momentum.*

a
b
c
d
e
f
g
h
i
j
k
l
m
n
o
p
q
r
s
t
u
v
w
x
y
z

pace • He walked at a leisurely pace.
rapidity • My moods alternate with alarming rapidity.
swiftness • Time is passing with incredible swiftness.
velocity • the velocity of light

speed ② VERB
to move quickly • The pair sped off when the police arrived.
career • His car careered into a river.
flash • The bus flashed past me.
gallop • galloping along the corridor
race • He raced across town.
rush • He rushed off, closely followed by Kemp.
tear • Miranda tore off down the road.

spin VERB
to turn quickly around a central point • as the earth spins on its axis
pirouette • She pirouetted in front of the mirror.
revolve • The satellite revolves around the planet.
rotate • rotating propellers
turn • a turning wheel
whirl • The fallen leaves whirled around.

spirit ① NOUN
the part of you that is not physical • His spirit had left his body.
life force • the life force of all animate things
soul • praying for the soul of her dead husband

spirit ② NOUN
a ghost or supernatural being • a protection against evil spirits
apparition • an apparition of her dead son
ghost • the premise that ghosts exist
phantom • People claimed to have seen the phantom.
spectre • a spectre from the other world
sprite • a water sprite

spirit ③ NOUN
liveliness and energy • They played with spirit.
animation • They both spoke with animation.
energy • At 80 her energy is amazing.
enthusiasm • They seem to be lacking in enthusiasm.
fire • His performance was full of fire.
force • She expressed her feelings with some force.
vigour • We resumed the attack with renewed vigour.
zest • He threw himself into the project with typical zest.

MORE SYNONYMS:
• brio
• mettle

spite ① : **in spite of** PREPOSITION
even though something is the case • In spite of all the gossip, Virginia stayed behind.
despite • They manage to enjoy life despite adversity.
even though • They did it even though I warned them not to.
notwithstanding • Notwithstanding his age, Sikorski had an important job.
regardless of • He led from the front, regardless of the danger.
though • I enjoy painting, though I am not very good at it.

spite ② NOUN
a desire to hurt someone • He just did it out of spite.
ill will • He didn't bear anyone any ill will.
malevolence • a streak of malevolence
malice • There was no malice in her voice.
spitefulness • petty spitefulness
venom • His wit had a touch of venom about it.

MORE SYNONYMS:
- malignity
- rancour

spiteful ADJECTIVE
saying or doing nasty things to hurt people • *a stream of spiteful telephone calls*

bitchy (INFORMAL) • *It's not just women who are bitchy.*

catty (INFORMAL) • *She's always making catty remarks.*

cruel • *They gave him a cruel nickname.*

malevolent • *a malevolent stare*

malicious • *spreading malicious gossip*

nasty • *What nasty little snobs you all are.*

snide • *He made a snide comment about her weight.*

venomous • *a venomous attack*

vindictive • *How can you be so vindictive?*

splendid ① ADJECTIVE
very good indeed • *I've had a splendid time.*

cracking (BRITISH, AUSTRALIAN AND NEW ZEALAND; INFORMAL) • *It's a cracking script.*

excellent • *The recording quality is excellent.*

fantastic (INFORMAL) • *a fantastic combination of colours*

fine • *a fine little fellow*

glorious • *a glorious career*

great (INFORMAL) • *a great bunch of guys*

marvellous • *a marvellous thing to do*

wonderful • *a wonderful movie*

splendid ② ADJECTIVE
beautiful and impressive • *a splendid old mansion*

gorgeous • *a gorgeous Renaissance building*

grand • *a grand hotel*

imposing • *imposing wrought-iron gates*

impressive • *an impressive spectacle*

magnificent • *magnificent views across the valley*

superb • *The hotel has a superb isolated location.*

split ① VERB
to divide into two or more parts • *The ship split in two.*

diverge • *Their paths began to diverge.*

fork • *Ahead of us, the road forked.*

part • *For a moment the clouds parted.*

separate • *Fluff the rice with a fork to separate the grains.*

MORE SYNONYMS:
- bifurcate
- cleave
- disunite

split ② VERB
to have a crack or tear • *His trousers split.*

burst • *A water pipe has burst.*

come apart • *My jacket's coming apart at the seams.*

crack • *A gas main cracked.*

rip • *I felt the paper rip as we pulled in opposite directions.*

split ③ NOUN
a crack or tear in something • *There's a split in my mattress.*

crack • *The larvae burrow into cracks in the floor.*

fissure • *Water trickled out of fissures in the limestone.*

rip • *the rip in her new dress*

tear • *the ragged edges of a tear*

split ④ NOUN
a division between two things • *the split between rugby league and rugby union*

breach • *a serious breach in relations between the two countries*

breakup • *the breakup of the Soviet Union in 1991*

divergence • *a divergence between France and its allies*

division • *the conventional division between "art" and "life"*

rift • *There is a rift between us and the rest of the family.*

schism • *the schism which divided the Christian world*

spoil ① VERB

to damage or destroy something • *Don't let it spoil your holiday.*

damage • *This could damage our chances of winning.*

destroy • *His criticism has destroyed my confidence.*

harm • *This product harms the environment.*

impair • *The flavour is impaired by overcooking.*

mar • *The celebrations were marred by violence.*

mess up • *He's messed up his life.*

ruin • *My wife was ruining her health through worry.*

wreck • *the injuries which nearly wrecked his career*

spoil ② VERB

to give someone everything they want • *Grandparents often spoil their grandchildren.*

cosset • *We did not cosset our children.*

indulge • *a heavily indulged youngest daughter*

pamper • *pampered pets*

MORE SYNONYMS:
• coddle
• mollycoddle
• overindulge

spoilsport NOUN

a person who spoils other people's fun • *They made me feel like a spoilsport for saying no.*

misery (BRITISH; INFORMAL) • *the miseries in the government*

wowser (AUSTRALIAN; SLANG) • *a small group of wowsers*

spooky ADJECTIVE

eerie and frightening • *The whole place had a slightly spooky atmosphere.*

creepy (INFORMAL) • *a place that is really creepy at night*

eerie • *The wind made eerie noises in the trees.*

frightening • *Whenever I fall asleep, I see these frightening faces.*

ghostly • *The moon shed a ghostly light on the fields.*

haunted • *a haunted house*

supernatural • *The blade glowed with a supernatural light.*

scary • *a scary ruined castle*

uncanny • *The strange, uncanny feeling was creeping all over me.*

spot ① NOUN

a small round mark on something • *a navy blue dress with white spots*

blemish • *A small blemish spoiled the surface.*

blot • *an ink blot*

blotch • *His face was covered in red blotches.*

mark • *a little red mark on my neck*

smudge • *There was a dark smudge on his forehead.*

speck • *a speck of dirt*

spot ② NOUN

a location or place • *an out-of-the-way spot*

location • *The hotel is in a superb isolated location.*

place • *Jerusalem is Christianity's most venerated place.*

point • *the point where the river had burst its banks*

position • *She moved the body to a position where it would not be seen.*

scene • *He left a note at the scene of the crime.*

site • *plans to construct a temple on the site*

spot ③ VERB
to see or notice something • *Her drama teacher spotted her ability.*
catch sight of • *I caught sight of an ad in the paper.*
detect • *The test should enable doctors to detect the disease early.*
discern • *I did not discern any change.*
observe • *Can you observe any difference?*
see • *I can see a resemblance between you.*
sight • *A fleet of French ships was sighted.*

MORE SYNONYMS:
• descry
• espy

spread ① VERB
to open out or extend over an area • *He spread his coat over the bed.*
extend • *The new territory would e xtend over one-fifth of Canada's land mass.*
fan out • *She spun, and her dress's full skirt fanned out in a circle.*
open • *She opened her arms and gave me a big hug.*
sprawl • *The recreation area sprawls over 900 acres.*
unfold • *When the bird lifts off, its wings unfold to a six-foot span.*
unfurl • *We began to unfurl the sails.*
unroll • *I unrolled my sleeping bag.*

spread ② VERB
to put a thin layer on a surface • *Spread the bread with the cream cheese.*
apply • *Apply the preparation evenly over the wood's surface.*
coat • *Coat the fish with the paste.*
cover • *I covered the table with a cloth.*
overlay • *The floor was overlaid with rugs.*

plaster • *She plastered herself in sun lotion.*
smear • *Smear a little oil over the inside of the bowl.*
smother • *He likes to smother his bread with butter.*

spread ③ VERB
to reach or affect more people gradually • *The sense of fear is spreading in the neighbourhood.*
circulate • *Rumours were circulating that the project was to be abandoned.*
grow • *Opposition grew and the government agreed to negotiate.*
expand • *The industry is looking for opportunities to expand into other countries.*
increase • *The population continues to increase.*
proliferate • *the free internet services that are proliferating across the world*
travel • *News of his work travelled all the way to Asia.*

spread ④ NOUN
the extent or growth of something • *the gradual spread of information*
diffusion • *the development and diffusion of ideas*
expansion • *the rapid expansion of private health insurance*
extent • *the growing extent of the problem*
growth • *the growth of nationalism*
increase • *an increase of violence along the border*
progression • *This drug slows the progression of HIV.*
proliferation • *the proliferation of nuclear weapons*
upsurge • *the upsurge in interest in these books*

squabble ① VERB
to quarrel about something trivial • *Mum and Dad squabble all the time.*

argue • *They went on arguing all the way down the road.*

bicker • *The two women bickered constantly.*

fall out • *Mum and I used to fall out a lot.*

feud • *feuding neighbours*

fight • *Mostly, they fight about paying bills.*

quarrel • *At one point we quarrelled over something silly.*

row • *They rowed all the time.*

wrangle • *The two sides spend their time wrangling over procedural problems.*

squabble ② NOUN

a quarrel • *There have been minor squabbles about phone bills.*

altercation • *an altercation with the referee*

argument • *a heated argument*

barney (BRITISH, AUSTRALIAN AND NEW ZEALAND; INFORMAL) • *We had such a barney that we nearly split up.*

disagreement • *My instructor and I had a brief disagreement.*

dispute • *a dispute between the two countries over farm subsidies*

fight • *He had a big fight with his dad that night.*

quarrel • *I had a terrible quarrel with my brother.*

row • *A man had been stabbed to death in a family row.*

tiff • *She was walking home after a tiff with her boyfriend.*

staff NOUN

the people who work for an organization • *She made little effort to socialize with other staff.*

employees • *a temporary employee*

personnel • *An announcement was made to all personnel.*

team • *The team worked well under his direction.*

workers • *weekend and night-shift workers*

workforce • *a sullen and resentful workforce*

stage ① NOUN

a part of a process • *the closing stages of the race*

lap • *The first lap was clocked at under a minute.*

period • *We went through a period of unprecedented change.*

phase • *a passing phase*

point • *a critical point in the campaign*

step • *the next step in the process*

stage ② VERB

to organize something • *Workers have staged a number of one-day strikes.*

arrange • *We're arranging a surprise party for her.*

engineer • *He was the one who engineered the merger.*

mount • *a security operation mounted by the army*

orchestrate • *a carefully orchestrated campaign*

organize • *a two-day meeting organized by the UN*

stain ① NOUN

a mark on something • *grass stains*

blot • *an ink blot*

mark • *I can't get this mark to come off.*

spot • *brown spots on the skin caused by the sun*

stain ② VERB

to make a mark on something • *Some foods can stain the teeth.*

dirty • *Sheets can be reused until they are damaged or dirtied.*

mark • *the places where Steve's boots had marked the wood*

soil • *a soiled white apron*

spot • *her coat was spotted with blood*

MORE SYNONYMS:
• discolour
• smirch

stale ADJECTIVE
no longer fresh • *a lump of stale bread*
flat • *flat beer*
old • *mouldy old cheese*
sour • *sour milk*
stagnant • *stagnant water*

MORE SYNONYMS:
• fusty
• musty

ANTONYM:
• fresh

standard ① NOUN
a particular level of quality or
achievement • *There will be new
standards of hospital cleanliness.*
calibre • *the high calibre of these
researchers*
criterion • *The most important
criterion for entry is excellence in your
chosen field.*
guideline • *The accord lays down
guidelines for the conduct of
government agents.*
level • *The exercises are marked
according to their level of difficulty.*
norm • *the commonly accepted norms
of democracy*
quality • *Everyone can improve their
quality of life.*
requirement • *These products meet
all legal requirements.*

standard ② ADJECTIVE
usual, normal, and correct • *It was
standard practice for them to consult the
parents.*
accepted • *It is accepted wisdom that
the state of your body impacts on your
state of mind.*
correct • *the correct way to produce a
crop of tomato plants*

customary • *It is customary to offer a
drink or a snack to guests.*
normal • *Some shops were closed, but
that's quite normal for a Thursday.*
orthodox • *orthodox police methods*
regular • *This product looks and tastes
like regular lemonade.*
usual • *It is usual to tip waiters.*

standards PLURAL NOUN
moral principles of behaviour • *My
father has always had high moral
standards.*
ethics • *the difference between our
personal and social ethics*
ideals • *The party has drifted too far
from its socialist ideals.*
morals • *Western ideas and morals*
principles • *He refused to do anything
that went against his principles.*
rules • *They were expected to adhere to
the rules of the convent.*
scruples • *a man with no moral scruples*
values • *the values of liberty and
equality*

star NOUN
a famous person • *a film star*
celebrity • *A host of celebrities attended
the premiere.*
idol • *the city's greatest soccer idol*
luminary (LITERARY) • *The event
attracted such pop luminaries as
Madonna.*

stare VERB
to look at something for a long
time • *He stared at the floor, lost in
meditation.*
gaze • *gazing at herself in the mirror*
look • *He looked at her with open
hostility.*
ogle • *ogling the girls as they went past*
MORE SYNONYMS:
• gawp
• goggle

a
b
c
d
e
f
g
h
i
j
k
l
m
n
o
p
q
r
s
t
u
v
w
x
y
z

start ① VERB
to begin to take place • *School starts again next week.*
arise • *A conflict is likely to arise.*
begin • *A typical day begins at 8.30.*
come into being • *The festival came into being in 1986.*
come into existence • *a club that came into existence only 30 years ago*
commence • *The academic year commences at the beginning of October.*
get under way • *The game got under way.*
originate • *The disease originated in Africa.*

ANTONYM:
• finish

start ② VERB
to begin to do something • *Susie started to cry.*
begin • *He began to groan with pain.*
commence • *The hunter commenced to skin the animal.*
embark upon • *He's embarking on a new career as a writer.*
proceed • *He proceeded to get drunk.*
set about • *How do you set about getting a mortgage?*

ANTONYM:
• stop

start ③ VERB
to cause something to begin • *a good time to start a business*
begin • *The US is prepared to begin talks immediately.*
create • *Criticism will only create feelings of failure.*
establish • *The school was established in 1899.*
found • *Baden-Powell founded the Boy Scouts in 1908.*
get going • *I've worked hard to get this business going.*
inaugurate (FORMAL) • *the company*

which inaugurated the first scheduled international flight
initiate • *They wanted to initiate a discussion.*
instigate • *The violence was instigated by a few people.*
institute • *We have instituted a number of measures.*
introduce • *The government has introduced other money-saving schemes.*
launch • *The police have launched an investigation into the incident.*
open • *We opened the service with a hymn.*
pioneer • *the man who invented and pioneered DNA testing*
set in motion • *Several changes have already been set in motion.*
set up • *A committee was set up to arbitrate in the dispute.*
trigger • *Nuts can trigger an allergic reaction in some people.*

ANTONYM:
• stop

start ④ NOUN
the beginning of something • *His career had an auspicious start.*
beginning • *the beginning of all the trouble*
birth • *the birth of modern art*
commencement • *Applicants should be at least 16 before the commencement of the course.*
dawn • *the dawn of a new age*
foundation • *the foundation of the National Organization for Women*
inauguration • *the inauguration of new exam standards*
inception (FORMAL) • *Since its inception the company has produced 53 different aircraft designs.*
initiation • *There was a year between initiation and completion.*
onset • *the onset of puberty*

opening • *the opening of the trial*
outset • *There were lots of problems from the outset.*

ANTONYM:
• finish

state ① NOUN
the condition or circumstances of something • *the pathetic state of the rail network*
circumstances • *He's in desperate circumstances.*
condition • *He remains in a critical condition in hospital.*
plight • *the plight of Third World countries*
position • *We are in a privileged position.*
predicament • *the once great club's current predicament*
shape • *Her finances were in terrible shape.*
situation • *a precarious situation*

state ② NOUN
a country • *the state of Denmark*
country • *a country where alcohol is prohibited*
kingdom • *The kingdom's power declined.*
land • *in that distant land*
nation • *a leading nation in world politics*
republic • *In 1918, Austria became a republic.*

MORE SYNONYMS:
• body politic
• commonwealth
• federation

state ③ VERB
to say something, especially in a formal way • *Please state your occupation.*
affirm • *a speech in which he affirmed his policies*

articulate • *an attempt to articulate his feelings*
assert • *He asserted his innocence.*
declare • *He declared that he would fight on.*
express • *He expressed regret that he had caused any offence.*
say • *The police said he had no connection with the security forces.*
specify • *Please specify your preferences below.*

MORE SYNONYMS:
• aver
• expound
• propound

statement NOUN
a short written or spoken piece giving information • *He was depressed when he made that statement.*
account • *He gave a detailed account of what happened that night.*
announcement • *He made his announcement after talks with the President.*
bulletin • *A bulletin was released announcing the decision.*
declaration • *a public declaration of support*
explanation • *They have given no public explanation for his dismissal.*
proclamation • *The proclamation of independence was broadcast over the radio.*
report • *A press report said that at least six people had died.*
testimony • *His testimony was an important part of the prosecution case.*

status NOUN
a person's social position • *the status of children in society*
position • *a privileged position*
prestige • *to diminish the prestige of the monarchy*
rank • *He was stripped of his rank.*

a b c d e f g h i j k l m n o p q r **s** t u v w x y z

standing • *This has done nothing to improve his standing.*

stay VERB

to remain somewhere • *She stayed in bed till noon.*

hang around (INFORMAL) • *I can't hang around here all day.*

linger • *I lingered on for a few days until he arrived.*

loiter • *We loitered around looking in shop windows.*

remain • *You'll have to remain in hospital for the time being.*

tarry • *The shop's aim is to persuade you to tarry and spend.*

wait • *I'll wait here till you come back.*

steadfast ADJECTIVE

refusing to change or give up • *He remained steadfast in his belief.*

constant • *He has been her constant companion for the last four months.*

faithful • *this party's most faithful voters*

firm • *He held a firm belief in the afterlife.*

immovable • *On one issue, however, she was immovable.*

resolute • *a decisive and resolute international leader*

staunch • *a staunch supporter of these proposals*

steady • *He was firm and steady, unlike many men she knew.*

unshakeable • *his unshakeable belief in the project*

steady ① ADJECTIVE

continuing without interruptions • *a steady rise in profits*

consistent • *consistent support*

constant • *under constant pressure*

continuous • *Japanese-style programmes of continuous improvement*

even • *an even level of sound*

nonstop • *nonstop background music*

regular • *a regular beat*

uninterrupted • *28 years of uninterrupted growth*

steady ② ADJECTIVE

not shaky or wobbling • *O'Brien held out a steady hand.*

firm • *Make sure the tree is securely mounted on a firm base.*

secure • *Check joints are secure and the wood is sound.*

stable • *stable foundations*

steady ③ VERB

to prevent something from shaking or wobbling • *Two men were steadying a ladder.*

brace • *the old timbers which braced the roof*

secure • *The frames are secured by horizontal rails.*

stabilize • *gyros which stabilize the platform*

support • *Thick wooden posts support the ceiling.*

steal ① VERB

to take something without permission • *He was accused of stealing a tin of pineapple chunks.*

appropriate • *Several other companies have appropriated the idea.*

nick (BRITISH, AUSTRALIAN AND NEW ZEALAND; SLANG) • *I nicked that money from the till.*

pilfer • *Staff were pilfering behind the bar.*

pinch (INFORMAL) • *Someone's pinched my wallet.*

swipe (SLANG) • *Did you just swipe that book?*

take • *The burglars took anything they could carry.*

MORE SYNONYMS:
• embezzle
• filch
• misappropriate

- purloin
- thieve

steal ② VERB
to move somewhere quietly and
secretly • *They can steal out and join
us later.*
creep • *We crept away under cover of
darkness.*
slip • *I wanted to duck down and slip
past but they saw me.*
sneak • *Sometimes he would sneak out
to see me.*
tiptoe • *She slipped out of bed and
tiptoed to the window.*

steep ① ADJECTIVE
rising sharply and abruptly • *a steep
hill*
sheer • *a sheer drop*
vertical • *The slope was almost vertical.*
ANTONYM:
• gradual

steep ② ADJECTIVE
larger than is reasonable • *steep prices*
excessive • *excessive charges*
extortionate • *an extortionate rate of
interest*
high • *high loan rates*
unreasonable • *unreasonable interest
charges*
MORE SYNONYMS:
• exorbitant
• overpriced

steep ③ VERB
to soak something in a liquid
• *green beans steeped in olive oil*
immerse • *Immerse the gammon in
cold water to remove the salt.*
marinate • *Marinate the chicken for
at least four hours.*
soak • *Soak the beans overnight.*

sterile ① ADJECTIVE
free from germs • *Protect the cut with
a sterile dressing.*

antiseptic • *an antiseptic hospital
room*
germ-free • *Keep your working surfaces
germ-free.*
sterilized • *a sterilized laboratory*

sterile ② ADJECTIVE
unable to produce • *He found out he
was sterile.*
barren • *a barren mare*
unproductive • *70 million acres of
unproductive land*
MORE SYNONYMS:
• infecund
• unfruitful
ANTONYM:
• fertile

stick ① NOUN
a long, thin piece of wood • *crowds
armed with sticks and stones*
bat • *a baseball bat*
cane • *He wore a grey suit and leaned
heavily on his cane.*
mace • *a statue of a king holding a
golden mace*
pole • *He reached up with a hooked pole
to roll down the shutter.*
rod • *a witch-doctor's rod*
truncheon • *a policeman's truncheon*
twig • *the sound of a twig breaking
underfoot*
wand • *You can't wave a magic wand
and make everything okay.*

stick ② VERB
to thrust something somewhere
• *They stuck a needle in my back.*
dig • *She dug her spoon into the
moussaka.*
insert • *He inserted the key into the
lock.*
jab • *A needle was jabbed into my arm.*
poke • *He poked his finger into the hole.*
push • *She pushed her thumb into his
eye.*

a
b
c
d
e
f
g
h
i
j
k
l
m
n
o
p
q
r
s
t
u
v
w
x
y
z

A
B
C
D
E
F
G
H
I
J
K
L
M
N
O
P
Q
R
S
T
U
V
W
X
Y
Z

put • *Just put it through my letter-box when you're finished with it.*
ram • *He rammed the jacket under the seat.*
shove • *We shoved a copy of the newsletter beneath their door.*
stuff • *I stuffed my hands in my pockets.*
thrust • *A small aerial thrust up from the grass verge.*

stick ③ VERB
to attach • *Stick down any loose bits of flooring.*
attach • *We attach labels to things before we file them away.*
bond • *Strips of wood are bonded together.*
fix • *Fix the photo to the card using double-sided tape.*
fuse • *The scientists fused immune cells with cancer cells.*
glue • *Glue the fabric around the window.*
paste • *The children were busy pasting stars on to a chart.*

stick ④ VERB
to become attached • *The soil stuck to my boots.*
adhere • *Small particles adhere to the seed.*
bond • *Diamond does not bond well with other materials.*
cling • *His sodden trousers were clinging to his shins.*
fuse • *The flakes fuse together and produce ice crystals.*

stick ⑤ VERB
to jam or become jammed • *The dagger stuck tightly in the silver scabbard.*
catch • *His jacket buttons caught in the net.*
jam • *Every few moments the machinery became jammed.*
lodge • *The car has a bullet lodged in the passenger door.*

snag • *The fishermen said their nets kept snagging on underwater objects.*

sticky ADJECTIVE
covered with a substance that sticks to other things • *She thrust her hand into the sticky mess.*
adhesive • *adhesive tape*
tacky • *covered with a tacky resin*

MORE SYNONYMS:
• glutinous
• viscid
• viscous

stiff ① ADJECTIVE
firm and not easily bent • *stiff metal wires*
firm • *a firm mattress*
hard • *the hard wooden floor*
rigid • *a rigid plastic container*
solid • *a block of solid wax*
taut • *He lifted the wire until it was taut.*

ANTONYM:
• limp

stiff ② ADJECTIVE
not friendly or relaxed • *the rather stiff and formal surroundings of the Palace*
cold • *Sharon was very cold with me.*
forced • *a forced smile*
formal • *His voice was grave and formal.*
stilted • *Our conversation was stilted and polite.*
unnatural • *a strained and unnatural atmosphere*
wooden • *a wooden performance*

MORE SYNONYMS:
• constrained
• prim
• standoffish

stiff ③ ADJECTIVE
difficult or severe • *a stiff exam*
arduous • *an arduous undertaking*
difficult • *a difficult job*
exacting • *exacting standards*
formidable • *a formidable task*

hard • *a hard day's work*
rigorous • *rigorous military training*
tough • *a tough challenge*

still ADJECTIVE
not moving • *The air was still.*
calm • *the calm waters of the harbour*
inert • *He covered the inert body with a blanket.*
motionless • *He stood there, motionless.*
stationary • *The train was stationary for 90 minutes.*
tranquil • *a tranquil lake*

stink ① VERB
to smell very bad • *His breath stinks of garlic.*
pong (BRITISH AND AUSTRALIAN; INFORMAL) • *She said he ponged a bit.*
reek • *The whole house reeks of cigar smoke.*

stink ② NOUN
a very bad smell • *the stink of stale beer on his breath*
pong (BRITISH AND AUSTRALIAN; INFORMAL) • *What's that horrible pong?*
stench • *a foul stench*
MORE SYNONYMS:
• fetor
• malodour

stock ① NOUN
shares bought in an investment company • *the buying of stocks*
bonds • *the recent sharp decline in bond prices*
investments • *Earn a rate of return of 8% on your investments.*
shares • *He was keen to buy shares in the company.*

stock ② NOUN
the total amount of goods for sale in a shop • *The shop withdrew a quantity of stock from sale.*

goods • *Are all your goods on display?*
merchandise (FORMAL) • *25% off selected merchandise*

stock ③ NOUN
a supply of something • *Troops have seized a large stock of weapons.*
reserve • *65% of the world's oil reserves*
reservoir • *the body's short-term reservoir of energy*
stockpile • *treaties to cut stockpiles of chemical weapons*
store • *my secret store of chocolate biscuits*
supply • *What happens when food supplies run low?*

stock ④ NOUN
an animal or person's ancestors • *We are both from working-class stock.*
ancestry • *a family who can trace their ancestry back to the sixteenth century*
descent • *All the contributors were of African descent.*
extraction • *Her father was of Italian extraction.*
lineage • *a respectable family of ancient lineage*
parentage • *She's a Londoner of mixed parentage.*
origin • *people of Asian origin*

stock ⑤ VERB
to keep a supply of goods to sell • *The shop stocks a wide range of paint.*
deal in • *They deal in kitchen equipment.*
sell • *It sells everything from hair ribbons to oriental rugs.*
supply • *We supply office furniture and accessories.*
trade in • *He had been trading in antique furniture for 25 years.*

stock ⑥ ADJECTIVE
commonly used • *National security is the stock excuse for government secrecy.*

a b c d e f g h i j k l m n o p q r **s** t u v w x y z

hackneyed • *It may be an old hackneyed phrase, but it's true.*
overused • *an overused catch phrase*
routine • *We've tried all the routine methods of persuasion.*
standard • *the standard ending for a formal letter*
stereotyped • *stereotyped ideas about women*
typical • *the typical questions journalists ask celebrities*
usual • *He came out with all the usual excuses.*

stockpile ① VERB
to store large quantities of something • *People are stockpiling food for the winter.*
accumulate • *Some people get rich by accumulating wealth very gradually.*
amass • *It is best not to enquire how he amassed his fortune.*
collect • *Two young girls were collecting firewood.*
gather • *We gathered enough wood to last the night.*
hoard • *They've begun to hoard food and petrol.*
save • *Scraps of material were saved for quilts.*
stash (INFORMAL) • *He had stashed money in an offshore account.*
store up • *Investors were storing up cash in anticipation of disaster.*

stockpile ② NOUN
a large store of something • *stockpiles of fuel*
arsenal • *a formidable arsenal of guns and landmines*
cache • *a cache of weapons and explosives*
hoard • *a hoard of silver and jewels worth $4om*
reserve • *The country's reserves of food are running low.*

stash (INFORMAL) • *her mother's stash of sleeping pills*
stock • *Stocks of ammunition were being used up.*
store • *his secret store of sweets*

stocky ADJECTIVE
short but solid-looking • *a stocky, middle-aged man*
chunky • *the chunky South African tennis player*
solid • *a solid build*
sturdy • *a short, sturdy woman in her early sixties*
MORE SYNONYMS:
• stubby
• thickset

stomach NOUN
the front part of the body around the waist • *Breathe out and flatten your stomach.*
belly • *the enormous belly of the Italian foreign minister*
paunch • *Nicholson surveyed his spreading paunch.*
puku (NEW ZEALAND) • *a pain in my puku*
tummy (INFORMAL) • *I'd like a flatter tummy, but then who doesn't?*

stop ① VERB
to cease doing something • *I stopped working last year to have a baby.*
cease • *A small number of firms have ceased trading.*
cut out (INFORMAL) • *Will you cut out that racket?*
desist • *boycotting Norwegian products until they desist from whaling*
discontinue • *Do not discontinue the treatment without seeing your doctor.*
end • *public pressure to end the embargo*
quit • *He's trying to quit smoking.*
ANTONYM:
• start

stop ② VERB
to come to an end • *He prayed for the blizzard to stop.*
cease • *At one o'clock the rain ceased.*
come to an end • *An hour later, the meeting came to an end.*
conclude • *The evening concluded with dinner and speeches.*
end • *The talks ended in disagreement.*
finish • *The teaching day finishes at around 4 pm.*
halt • *Discussions have halted again.*

ANTONYM:
• start

stop ③ VERB
to prevent something • *measures to stop the trade in ivory*
arrest • *trying to arrest the bleeding*
check • *a policy to check fast population growth*
prevent • *the most practical way of preventing crime*

MORE SYNONYMS:
• forestall
• nip something in the bud

store ① NOUN
a supply kept for future use • *I have a store of food and water here.*
cache • *a cache of weapons and explosives*
fund • *an extraordinary fund of energy*
hoard • *a hoard of supplies*
reserve • *the world's oil reserves*
reservoir • *the body's short-term reservoir of energy*
stock • *stocks of paper and ink*
stockpile • *stockpiles of nuclear warheads*
supply • *food supplies*

store ② NOUN
a place where things are kept • *a grain store*
depot • *a government arms depot*

storeroom • *a storeroom filled with furniture*
warehouse • *a carpet warehouse*

MORE SYNONYMS:
• depository
• repository
• storehouse

store ③ VERB
to keep something for future use • *The information can be stored in a computer.*
hoard • *They've begun to hoard food and petrol.*
keep • *Grate the lemon zest and keep it for later.*
save • *His allotment of gas had to be saved for emergencies.*
stash (INFORMAL) • *He had stashed money away in a secret offshore account.*
stockpile • *People are stockpiling food for the coming winter.*

story NOUN
a tale told or written to entertain people • *a poignant love story*
account • *a true account*
anecdote • *her store of theatrical anecdotes*
legend • *an old Scottish legend*
narrative • *a fast-moving narrative*
tale • *a fairy tale*
yarn • *a children's yarn about giants*

straight ① ADJECTIVE
upright or level • *Keep your arms straight.*
erect • *The upper back and neck are held in an erect position.*
even • *to ensure an even hem*
horizontal • *a horizontal line*
level • *a completely level base*
perpendicular • *Position your body perpendicular with the slope.*
upright • *He sat in an upright position in his chair.*
vertical • *Keep the spine vertical.*

A
B
C
D
E
F
G
H
I
J
K
L
M
N
O
P
Q
R
S
T
U
V
W
X
Y
Z

ANTONYM:
• crooked

straight ② ADJECTIVE
honest, frank and direct • They
wouldn't give me a straight answer.
blunt • She is blunt about her personal
life.
candid • I haven't been completely
candid with you.
forthright • a forthright reply
frank • a frank discussion
honest • Please be honest with me.
outright • This was outright rejection.
plain • plain talking
point-blank • a point-blank refusal

straightforward ① ADJECTIVE
easy and involving no problems
• The question seemed straightforward
enough.
basic • The film's story is pretty basic.
easy • The shower is easy to install.
elementary • elementary computer
skills
lo-fi • books on how to start your own
lo-fi radio station
routine • a fairly routine procedure
simple • simple advice on filling in your
tax form
uncomplicated • good British
cooking with its uncomplicated, natural
flavours

ANTONYM:
• complicated

straightforward ② ADJECTIVE
honest, open, and frank • I liked his
straightforward, intelligent manner.
candid • I haven't been completely
candid with you.
direct • He avoided giving a direct
answer.
forthright • He was known for his
forthright manner.
frank • They had a frank discussion
about the issue.

honest • I was totally honest about
what I was doing.
open • He had always been open with
her.
plain • I believe in plain talking.
straight • He never gives a straight
answer to a straight question.

ANTONYM:
• devious

strain ① NOUN
worry and nervous tension • the
stresses and strains of a busy career
anxiety • Her voice was full of anxiety.
pressure • the pressure of work
stress • the stress of exams
tension • Laughing relieves tension and
stress.

strain ② VERB
to make something do more than
it is able to do • You'll strain your eyes
reading in this light.
overwork • Too much food will
overwork your digestive system.
tax • He is beginning to tax my patience.

MORE SYNONYMS:
• overexert
• overtax
• push to the limit

strange ① ADJECTIVE
unusual or unexpected • A strange
thing happened.
abnormal • an abnormal fear of spiders
bizarre • a bizarre scene
curious • a curious mixture of ancient
and modern
extraordinary • an extraordinary
occurrence
funny • a funny feeling
odd • There was something odd about
her.
peculiar • It tasted very peculiar.
queer • I think there's something a bit
queer going on.

uncommon • *A 15-year lifespan is not uncommon for a dog.*
weird • *He's a really weird guy.*

MORE SYNONYMS:
• out-of-the-way
• outré
• unaccountable

strange ② ADJECTIVE
new or unfamiliar • *alone in a strange country*
alien • *transplanted into an alien culture*
exotic • *filmed in an exotic location*
foreign • *This was a foreign country, so unlike his own.*
new • *I'm always open to new experiences.*
novel • *a novel idea*
unfamiliar • *visiting an unfamiliar city*

strength ① NOUN
physical energy and power • *an astonishing display of physical strength*
brawn • *He's got plenty of brains as well as brawn.*
might • *the full might of the army*
muscle • *demonstrating both muscle and skill*
stamina • *The race requires a lot of stamina.*

MORE SYNONYMS:
• brawniness
• lustiness
• sinew

ANTONYM:
• weakness

strength ② NOUN
the degree of intensity • *an indication of the strength of feeling among parents*
force • *the force of his argument*
intensity • *the intensity of their emotions*
potency • *the extraordinary potency of his personality*
power • *the overwhelming power of love*

vehemence • *I was surprised by the vehemence of his criticism.*
vigour • *We resumed the attack with renewed vigour.*

ANTONYM:
• weakness

strengthen ① VERB
to give something more power • *This move will strengthen his political standing.*
consolidate • *to consolidate an already dominant position*
encourage • *encouraged by the shouts of their supporters*
harden • *evidence which hardens suspicions about their involvement*
stiffen • *This only stiffened his resolve to quit.*
toughen • *new laws to toughen police powers*

MORE SYNONYMS:
• fortify
• hearten
• invigorate

ANTONYM:
• weaken

strengthen ② VERB
to support the structure of something • *The builders had to strengthen the joists with timber.*
bolster • *steel beams used to bolster the roof*
brace • *tottering pillars braced by scaffolding*
fortify • *citadels fortified by high stone walls*
reinforce • *They had to reinforce the walls with exterior beams.*
support • *the thick wooden posts that supported the ceiling*

ANTONYM:
• weaken

A
B
C
D
E
F
G
H
I
J
K
L
M
N
O
P
Q
R
S
T
U
V
W
X
Y
Z

stress ① NOUN

worry and nervous tension • *the stresses and strains of a busy career*

anxiety • *Her voice was full of anxiety.*

hassle (INFORMAL) • *I don't think it's worth the money or the hassle.*

pressure • *I felt the pressure of being the first woman in the job.*

strain • *She was tired and under great strain.*

tension • *Laughing relieves tension.*

worry • *It was a time of worry for us.*

stress ② VERB

to emphasize something • *The leaders have stressed their commitment to the talks.*

accentuate • *make-up which accentuates your best features*

emphasize • *He flourished his glass to emphasize the point.*

repeat • *We are not, I repeat not, in the negotiating process.*

underline • *The report underlined his concern about falling standards.*

MORE SYNONYMS:
• belabour
• dwell on
• point up
• underscore

stretch ① VERB

to extend over an area or time • *an artificial reef stretching the length of the coast*

continue • *The road continued into the distance.*

cover • *The oil slick covered a total area of seven miles.*

extend • *The caves extend for some 18 kilometres.*

go on • *The dispute looks set to go on into the new year.*

hang • *The branches hang right down to the ground.*

last • *His difficulties are likely to last well beyond childhood.*

reach • *a caravan park which reached from one end of the bay to the other*

spread • *The estuary spreads as far as the eye can see.*

stretch ② VERB

to reach out with part of your body • *She arched her back and stretched herself.*

extend • *Stand straight with your arms extended at your sides.*

reach • *He reached up for an overhanging branch.*

straighten • *Point your toes and straighten both legs slowly.*

ANTONYM:
• bend

stretch ③ NOUN

an area of land or water • *It's a very dangerous stretch of road.*

area • *extensive mountainous areas of Europe and South America*

expanse • *a huge expanse of grassland*

extent • *a vast extent of fertile country*

sweep • *The ground fell away in a broad sweep down the river.*

tract • *They cleared large tracts of forest for farming.*

stretch ④ NOUN

a period of time • *He would study for eight hour stretches.*

period • *a long period of time*

run • *The show will transfer to the West End, after a month's run in Birmingham.*

space • *They've come a long way in a short space of time.*

spell • *a long spell of dry weather*

stint • *He is coming home after a five-year stint abroad.*

term • *She worked the full term of her pregnancy.*

time • *doing very little exercise for several weeks at a time*

strict ① ADJECTIVE
very firm in demanding obedience
• *My parents were very strict.*
authoritarian • *He has an authoritarian approach to parenthood.*
firm • *the guiding hand of a firm father figure*
rigid • *a rigid hospital routine*
rigorous • *rigorous military training*
stern • *Her mother was stern and hard to please.*
stringent • *stringent rules*

strict ② ADJECTIVE
precise and accurate • *He has never been a playboy in the strict sense of the word.*
accurate • *an accurate record of events*
exact • *I do not remember the exact words.*
meticulous • *meticulous attention to detail*
particular • *very particular dietary requirements*
precise • *precise instructions*
true • *a true account*

strive VERB
to make a great effort to achieve something • *He strives hard to keep himself fit.*
attempt • *He attempted to smile, but found it difficult.*
do your best • *I'll do my best to find out.*
do your utmost • *She was certain he would do his utmost to help her.*
endeavour (FORMAL) • *They are endeavouring to protect trade union rights.*
make an effort • *He made no effort to hide his disappointment.*
seek • *We have never sought to impose our views.*
try • *He tried to block her advancement in the Party.*

strong ① ADJECTIVE
having powerful muscles • *a strong, robust man*
athletic • *He was tall and athletic.*
brawny • *a brawny young rugby player*
burly • *a big, burly man*
muscular • *Like most female athletes, she was lean and muscular.*
powerful • *a powerful bodybuilder*
strapping • *He was a bricklayer - a big, strapping fellow.*
well-built • *a fit, well-built runner*

ANTONYM:
• weak

strong ② ADJECTIVE
able to withstand rough treatment
• *a strong casing, which won't crack or chip*
durable • *made of durable plastic*
hard-wearing • *hard-wearing cotton overalls*
heavy-duty • *a heavy-duty canvas bag*
reinforced • *reinforced concrete supports*
sturdy • *a camera mounted on a sturdy tripod*
substantial • *a substantial boat with a powerful rigging*
tough • *a tough vehicle designed for all terrains*
well-built • *You need a well-built fence all round the garden.*

ANTONYM:
• fragile

strong ③ ADJECTIVE
great in degree or intensity • *Despite strong opposition, she was victorious.*
acute • *an acute feeling of embarrassment*
ardent • *an ardent admirer*
deep • *a deep resentment*
fervent • *a fervent hope for peace*
fierce • *He inspires fierce loyalty in his friends.*

a b c d e f g h i j k l m n o p q r **s** t u v w x y z

keen • *a keen interest in tennis*
intense • *an intense dislike of jazz*
passionate • *a passionate believer in justice*
profound • *a profound distrust of bankers*
vehement • *the government's most vehement critic*
violent • *His plans met with violent hostility.*
zealous • *her zealous religious beliefs*
ANTONYM:
• faint

structure ① NOUN
the way something is made or organized • *the structure of this molecule*
arrangement • *an intricate arrangement of treadles, rods and cranks*
construction • *The chairs were light in construction but very strong.*
design • *The shoes were of good design and good quality.*
make-up • *the chemical make-up of the oceans and atmosphere*
organization • *the organization of the economy*
MORE SYNONYMS:
• configuration
• conformation

structure ② NOUN
something that has been built • *The museum is an impressive structure.*
building • *an ugly modern building*
construction • *an impressive steel and glass construction*
edifice • *historic edifices in the area*

struggle ① VERB
to try hard to do something • *They had to struggle to make ends meet.*
strain • *straining to lift heavy weights*
strive • *He strives hard to keep himself fit.*

toil • *toiling to make up for lost time*
work • *I had to work hard for everything I've got.*

struggle ② NOUN
something that is hard to achieve • *Life became a struggle for survival.*
effort • *It was an effort to finish in time.*
labour • *weary from their labours*
toil • *another day of toil and strife*
work • *It's been hard work, but rewarding.*

stubborn ADJECTIVE
determined not to change or give in • *a stubborn character who is used to getting his own way*
dogged • *his dogged insistence on his rights*
inflexible • *His opponents viewed him as dogmatic and inflexible.*
obstinate • *a wicked and obstinate child*
tenacious • *a tenacious and persistent interviewer*
wilful • *a headstrong and wilful young lady*
MORE SYNONYMS:
• intractable
• obdurate
• recalcitrant
• refractory

stuck-up ADJECTIVE (INFORMAL)
proud and conceited • *She was famous, but she wasn't a bit stuck-up.*
arrogant • *He was so arrogant, he never even said hello to me.*
conceited • *He's a very conceited young man.*
disdainful • *She cast a disdainful glance at me.*
haughty • *She looks haughty, but when you get to know her, she's very friendly.*
proud • *He's too proud to use public transport.*

snobbish • *I'd expected her to be snobbish, but she was warm and welcoming.*

study ① VERB

to spend time learning about something • *He is studying History and Economics.*

learn • *I'm learning French.*

read up • *She spent a year reading up on farming techniques.*

swot (BRITISH, AUSTRALIAN AND NEW ZEALAND; INFORMAL) • *swotting for their finals*

study ② VERB

to look at something carefully • *He studied the map in silence.*

contemplate • *He contemplated his hands, frowning.*

examine • *He examined her passport and stamped it.*

pore over • *We spent hours poring over travel brochures.*

MORE SYNONYMS:
• peruse
• scrutinize

study ③ NOUN

the activity of learning about a subject • *the serious study of medieval architecture*

lessons • *He was lagging behind in his lessons.*

research • *funds for research into AIDS*

school work • *She buried herself in school work.*

swotting (BRITISH, AUSTRALIAN AND NEW ZEALAND; INFORMAL) • *She put her success down to last-minute swotting.*

stuff ① NOUN

a substance or group of things • *"That's my stuff," he said, pointing to a bag.*

apparatus • *all the apparatus you'll need for the job*

belongings • *I collected my belongings and left.*

equipment • *outdoor playing equipment*

gear • *fishing gear*

kit • *I forgot my gym kit.*

material • *organic material*

substance • *The substance that's causing problems comes from barley.*

tackle • *Martin kept his fishing tackle in his room.*

things • *Sara told him to take all his things and not to return.*

MORE SYNONYMS:
• paraphernalia
• trappings

stuff ② VERB

to push something somewhere quickly and roughly • *He stuffed the newspapers into a litter bin.*

cram • *I crammed her hat into a waste-basket.*

force • *I forced the key into the ignition.*

jam • *Pete jammed his hands into his pockets.*

push • *Someone had pushed a tissue into the keyhole.*

ram • *He rammed his clothes into a drawer.*

shove • *We shoved a newsletter beneath their door.*

squeeze • *I squeezed everything into my rucksack.*

thrust • *She thrust a stack of photos into my hands.*

stuff ③ VERB

to fill something with a substance or objects • *He stood there, stuffing his mouth with popcorn.*

cram • *I crammed my bag full of clothes and set off.*

fill • *I filled the box with polystyrene chips.*

a
b
c
d
e
f
g
h
i
j
k
l
m
n
o
p
q
r
s
t
u
v
w
x
y
z

load • *They loaded all their equipment into backpacks.*
pack • *a lorry packed with explosives*

stuffy ① ADJECTIVE
formal and old-fashioned • *his lack of stuffy formality*
dull • *They are nice people but rather dull.*
formal • *an austere and formal family*
old-fashioned • *She was condemned as an old-fashioned prude.*
staid • *He is boring, old-fashioned and staid.*
strait-laced • *She is very strait-laced and narrow-minded.*

MORE SYNONYMS:
• fusty
• old-fogeyish
• priggish
• stodgy

stuffy ② ADJECTIVE
not containing enough fresh air • *It was hot and stuffy in the classroom.*
close • *The atmosphere was close.*
heavy • *The air was heavy, moist and sultry.*
muggy • *It was muggy and overcast.*
oppressive • *The little room was windowless and oppressive.*
stale • *A layer of smoke hung in the stale air.*
stifling • *the stifling heat of the room*

MORE SYNONYMS:
• fetid
• frowsty
• sultry
• unventilated

stupid ADJECTIVE
lacking intelligence or good judgment • *How could I have been so stupid?*
absurd • *absurd ideas*
daft (INFORMAL) • *That's a daft question.*

dim • *He is rather dim.*
foolish • *It is foolish to risk injury.*
idiotic • *What an idiotic thing to say!*
inane • *She's always asking inane questions.*
obtuse • *It should be obvious even to the most obtuse person.*
thick • *I must have seemed incredibly thick.*

MORE SYNONYMS:
• asinine
• crass
• cretinous
• fatuous
• imbecilic
• moronic

ANTONYM:
• clever

stupidity NOUN
lack of intelligence or good judgment • *I was astonished by his stupidity.*
absurdity • *the absurdity of the suggestion*
folly • *the danger and folly of taking drugs*
foolishness • *He expressed remorse over his own foolishness.*
inanity • *The inanity of the conversation.*
silliness • *He sounded quite exasperated by my silliness.*

MORE SYNONYMS:
• asininity
• fatuity
• imbecility
• obtuseness

sturdy ADJECTIVE
strong and unlikely to be damaged • *The camera was mounted on a sturdy tripod.*
durable • *Fine china is surprisingly durable.*

hardy • *He looked like a farmer, round-faced and hardy.*
robust • *very robust, simply-designed machinery*
solid • *The car feels very solid.*
substantial • *Jack had put on weight - he seemed more substantial.*
stout • *a stout oak door*
strong • *a strong casing which won't crack or chip*
well-built • *Mitchell is well-built and of medium height.*

ANTONYM:
• fragile

style ① NOUN
the way in which something is done
• *a dictatorial management style*
approach • *his blunt approach*
manner • *a satire in the manner of Dickens*
method • *a new method of education*
mode • *a cheap and convenient mode of transport*
technique • *his driving technique*
way • *He had a strange way of talking.*

style ② NOUN
smartness and elegance • *She has not lost her grace and style.*
chic • *French designer chic*
elegance • *Princess Grace's understated elegance*
flair • *dressed with typical Italian flair*
sophistication • *to add a touch of sophistication to any wardrobe*
taste • *impeccable taste*

MORE SYNONYMS:
• élan
• panache
• savoir-faire

subdue VERB
to bring people under control by force
• *The government have not been able to subdue the rebels.*

crush • *ruthless measures to crush the revolt*
defeat • *an important role in defeating the rebellion*
overcome • *working to overcome the enemy forces*
overpower • *The police eventually overpowered him.*
quell • *tough new measures to quell the disturbances*
vanquish • *his vanquished foe*

subject ① NOUN
the thing or person being discussed
• *They exchanged views on a wide range of subjects.*
issue • *an issue that had worried him for some time*
matter • *I don't want to discuss the matter.*
object • *the object of much heated discussion*
point • *There is another point to consider.*
question • *the difficult question of unemployment*
theme • *The book's central theme is power.*
topic • *The weather is a constant topic of conversation.*

subject ② VERB
to make someone experience something • *He was subjected to constant interruptions.*
expose • *people exposed to high levels of radiation*
put through • *My husband put me through hell.*
submit • *The old woman was submitted to a terrifying ordeal.*

submit ① VERB
to accept or agree to something unwillingly • *I submitted to their requests.*
agree • *Management has agreed to the union's conditions.*

a b c d e f g h i j k l m n o p q r **s** t u v w x y z

bow • *Some shops are bowing to consumer pressure and stocking the product.*
capitulate • *He capitulated to their ultimatum.*
comply • *The commander said his army would comply with the ceasefire.*
give in • *Officials say they won't give in to the workers' demands.*
surrender • *We'll never surrender to these terrorists.*
yield • *She yielded to her mother's nagging and took the child to a specialist.*

ANTONYM:
• resist

submit ② VERB
to formally present a document or proposal • *They submitted their reports to the Chancellor.*
hand in • *I'm supposed to hand in my dissertation on Friday.*
present • *The group intends to present this petition to the parliament.*
propose • *He has proposed a bill to abolish the House of Commons.*
put forward • *He has put forward new peace proposals.*
send in • *Applicants are asked to send in a CV and covering letter.*
table • *They've tabled a motion criticizing the Government for its actions.*
tender • *She tendered her resignation.*

ANTONYM:
• withdraw

substance NOUN
a solid, powder, liquid or gas • *Poisonous substances should be labelled as such.*
element • *a chart of the chemical elements*
fabric • *Condensation will rot the fabric of the building.*
material • *an armchair of some resilient plastic material*

stuff • *the stuff from which the universe is made*

substitute ① VERB
to use one thing in place of another • *You can substitute honey for the sugar.*
exchange • *exchanging one set of problems for another*
interchange • *Meat can be interchanged with pulses as a source of protein.*
replace • *We dug up the concrete and replaced it with grass.*
swap • *Some hostages were swapped for convicted prisoners.*
switch • *They switched the tags on the cables.*

substitute ② NOUN
something used in place of another thing • *an artificial substitute for silk*
deputy • *I can't make it so I'll send my deputy.*
proxy • *They must nominate a proxy to vote on their behalf.*
replacement • *He has nominated Adams as his replacement.*
representative • *Employees from each department elect a representative.*
surrogate • *They had expected me to be a surrogate for my sister.*

MORE SYNONYMS:
• locum
• locum tenens
• makeshift
• stopgap

subtract VERB
to take one number away from another • *If you subtract 3 from 5 you get 2.*
deduct • *Marks will be deducted for spelling mistakes.*
take away • *Take away the number you first thought of.*
take from • *Take the 5% discount from the total amount due.*

ANTONYM:
• add

succeed ① VERB
to achieve the result you intend • *To succeed, you must learn to overcome obstacles.*
be successful • *We must help our clubs to be successful in Europe.*
do well • *Their team did well.*
flourish • *The business flourished.*
make it (INFORMAL) • *It is hard for an English actress to make it in Hollywood.*
prosper • *His team have always prospered in cup competitions.*
thrive • *The company has thrived by selling cheap, simple products.*
triumph • *a symbol of good triumphing over evil*
work • *The plan worked.*

ANTONYM:
• fail

succeed ② VERB
to be the next person to have someone's job • *David is almost certain to succeed him as chairman.*
replace • *the man who replaced him as England skipper*
take over from • *Last year he took over from Bauman as chief executive.*

success ① NOUN
the achievement of a goal, fame, or wealth • *Do you believe that work is the key to success?*
celebrity • *I never expected this kind of celebrity when I was writing my novel.*
eminence • *a pilot who achieved eminence in the aeronautical world*
fame • *her rise to fame as a dramatist*
prosperity • *the country's economic prosperity*
triumph • *last year's Republican triumph in the elections*
victory • *Union leaders are heading for victory in their battle over workplace rights.*
wealth • *His hard work brought him wealth and respect.*

MORE SYNONYMS:
• ascendancy (FORMAL)
• coup

ANTONYM:
• failure

success ② NOUN
a person or thing achieving popularity or greatness • *Everyone who knows her says she will be a huge success.*
celebrity • *At the age of 12, Dan is already a celebrity.*
hit • *The song became a massive hit.*
sensation • *the film that turned her into an overnight sensation*
star • *I always knew she would be a star.*
triumph • *a triumph of modern surgery*
winner • *Selling was my game and I intended to be a winner.*

ANTONYM:
• failure

successful ADJECTIVE
having achieved what you intended to do • *Mr Singh was a highly successful salesman.*
flourishing • *a flourishing business*
lucrative • *a lucrative career*
profitable • *a profitable exchange of ideas*
rewarding • *a rewarding investment*
thriving • *a thriving housebuilding industry*
top • *a top model*

sudden ADJECTIVE
happening quickly and unexpectedly • *a sudden cry*
abrupt • *Her idyllic world came to an abrupt end when her parents died.*
hasty • *his hasty departure*

quick • *I had to make a quick decision.*
swift • *a swift blow to the stomach*
unexpected • *His death was totally unexpected.*

ANTONYM:
• gradual

suffer VERB
to be affected by pain or something unpleasant • *I knew he was suffering some discomfort.*
bear • *He bore his trials with dignity and grace.*
endure • *The writer endured a harsh life.*
experience • *Widows seem to experience more distress than do widowers.*
go through • *I wouldn't like to go through that again.*
sustain • *He had sustained massive facial injuries.*
undergo • *He had to undergo a body search.*

sufficient ADJECTIVE
being enough for a purpose • *He had sufficient time to prepare his speech.*
adequate • *an adequate income*
ample • *an ample supply of petrol*
enough • *enough cash to live on*

ANTONYM:
• insufficient

suffix NOUN

◆ **SUFFIXES**
◆ -able
◆ -ence
◆ -er
◆ -est
◆ -ful
◆ -hood
◆ -ism
◆ -ize or -ise
◆ -less
◆ -like
◆ -logy or -ology

◆ -ly
◆ -ness
◆ -phobia
◆ -ship
◆ -ward or -wards

suggest ① VERB
to mention something as a possibility or recommendation • *Clive suggested going out for tea.*
advise • *I advise you to keep quiet.*
advocate • *Mr Jones advocates longer school days.*
propose • *And where do you propose building such a huge thing?*
recommend • *I have no qualms about recommending this approach.*

suggest ② VERB
to hint that something is the case • *Reports suggested the factory would close.*
hint • *The President hinted that he might make some changes.*
imply • *The tone of the report implied that his death was inevitable.*
indicate • *She has indicated that she may resign.*
insinuate • *an article which insinuated that he was lying*
intimate • *He did intimate that he is seeking legal action.*

suggestion ① NOUN
an idea mentioned as a possibility • *practical suggestions*
plan • *The government is being asked to consider the plan.*
proposal • *the proposal to do away with nuclear weapons*
proposition • *a business proposition*
recommendation • *a range of recommendations for change*

suggestion ② NOUN
a slight indication of something • *a suggestion of dishonesty*

hint • *He showed only the slightest hint of emotion.*
indication • *He gave no indication of remorse.*
insinuation • *The insinuation is that I have something to hide.*
intimation • *He did not give any intimation that he was going to resign.*
trace • *No traces of violence were found on the body.*

suit VERB
to be acceptable • *They will only move if it suits them.*
be acceptable to • *The name chosen had to be acceptable to everyone.*
do • *A holiday at home will do me just fine.*
please • *I'll leave when it pleases me and not before.*
satisfy • *Nothing you can do will satisfy him.*

suitable ADJECTIVE
right or acceptable for a particular purpose • *Conditions were not suitable for life to flourish.*
acceptable • *a mutually acceptable new contract*
appropriate • *an appropriate outfit for the occasion*
apt • *an apt name*
fit • *the suggestion that she is not a fit mother*
fitting • *a fitting background for her beauty*
proper • *It was not thought proper for a woman to be on stage.*
right • *He always said just the right thing.*
satisfactory • *a satisfactory arrangement*
MORE SYNONYMS:
• apposite
• befitting
• pertinent
• seemly
ANTONYM:
• unsuitable

sulky ADJECTIVE
showing annoyance by being silent and moody • *a sulky adolescent*
huffy • *What are you being so huffy about?*
moody • *Her husband had become withdrawn and moody.*
petulant • *He's just being childish and petulant.*
resentful • *a resentful workforce*
sullen • *He lapsed into a sullen silence.*

summary NOUN
a short account of something's main points • *a summary of the report*
outline • *an outline of the proposal*
review • *a film review*
rundown • *Here's a rundown of the options.*
summing-up • *The judge concluded his summing-up.*
synopsis • *a brief synopsis of the book*
MORE SYNONYMS:
• abridgment
• digest
• précis
• recapitulation
• résumé

sum up VERB
to describe briefly • *He summed up his weekend in one word: "Disastrous".*
recapitulate • *Let's just recapitulate the essential points.*
summarize • *The article can be summarized in three sentences.*

superb ADJECTIVE
very good indeed • *With superb skill, he managed to make a perfect landing.*
breathtaking • *The house has breathtaking views.*

excellent • *You've done an excellent job.*
exquisite • *His photography is exquisite.*
magnificent • *a magnificent country house*
marvellous • *She is a marvellous cook.*
outstanding • *an outstanding performance*
splendid • *a splendid Victorian mansion*
superior • *a superior blend of the finest coffee beans*
unrivalled • *He has an unrivalled knowledge of British politics.*
wonderful • *The sun setting over the mountains was a wonderful sight.*

ANOTHER SYNONYM:
• superlative

superior ① ADJECTIVE
better than other similar things
• *superior coffee beans*
better • *I'd like to move to a better area.*
choice • *the choicest cuts of meat*
de luxe • *a de luxe model*
exceptional • *children with exceptional ability*
first-rate • *a first-rate thriller*
surpassing • *her surpassing achievements*
unrivalled • *colour printing of unrivalled quality*

ANTONYM:
• inferior

superior ② ADJECTIVE
showing pride and self-importance
• *He stood there looking superior.*
condescending • *I'm fed up with your condescending attitude.*
disdainful • *She passed along with a disdainful look.*
haughty • *He spoke in a haughty tone.*
lofty • *lofty disdain*
patronizing • *his patronizing attitude to the homeless*
snobbish • *a snobbish dislike for their*

intellectual inferiors
stuck-up (INFORMAL) • *She was a famous actress, but she wasn't a bit stuck-up.*
supercilious • *His manner is supercilious and arrogant.*

superior ③ NOUN
a person in a higher position than you
• *his immediate superior*
boss (INFORMAL) • *Her boss was very supportive.*
manager • *His plans found favour with his manager.*
senior • *He was described by his seniors as a model officer.*
supervisor • *Each student has a supervisor.*

ANTONYM:
• inferior

supervise VERB
to oversee a person or activity • *He supervised more than 400 volunteers.*
be in charge of • *He is in charge of the whole project.*
direct • *Christopher will direct day-to-day operations.*
have charge of • *He has charge of a three-acre estate.*
keep an eye on • *I told you to keep an eye on the children.*
manage • *I manage a small team of workers.*
oversee • *an architect to oversee the work*
run • *Each teacher will run a different workshop.*

MORE SYNONYMS:
• preside over
• superintend

supplement ① VERB
to add to something to improve it • *I suggest supplementing your diet with vitamin A.*

add to • *A good bathroom adds to the value of any house.*

augment • *a way to augment the family income*

complement • *an in-work benefit that complements earnings*

reinforce • *measures which will reinforce their current strengths*

top up • *compulsory contributions to top up pension schemes*

supplement ② NOUN

something added to something else • *a supplement to their basic pension*

addition • *an addition to the existing system*

appendix • *The report includes a six-page appendix.*

complement • *The photographs are a perfect complement to the text.*

extra • *an optional extra*

supplies PLURAL NOUN

food or equipment for a particular purpose • *I had only two pints of water in my emergency supplies.*

equipment • *vital medical equipment*

provisions • *provisions for two weeks*

rations • *Aid officials said food rations had been distributed.*

stores • *an important part of a ship's stores*

supply ① VERB

to provide someone with something • *an agreement not to supply chemical weapons*

equip • *plans for equipping the island with water*

furnish • *They'll be able to furnish you with the details.*

give • *We'll give you all the information you need.*

provide • *They'll provide all the equipment.*

MORE SYNONYMS:
• endow
• purvey

supply ② NOUN

an amount of something available for use • *a plentiful supply of vegetables*

cache • *a cache of weapons and explosives*

fund • *an extraordinary fund of energy*

hoard • *a hoard of food and petrol*

reserve • *The Gulf has 65% of the world's oil reserves.*

stock • *stocks of paper and ink*

stockpile • *stockpiles of chemical weapons*

store • *I have a store of food and water here.*

support ① VERB

to agree with someone's ideas or aims • *We supported his political campaign.*

back • *a new witness to back his claim*

champion • *He passionately championed the cause.*

defend • *He defended all of Clarence's decisions, right or wrong.*

promote • *He continued to promote the idea of Scottish autonomy.*

second • *The Prime Minister seconded the call for discipline.*

side with • *accused of siding with terrorists*

uphold • *We uphold the capitalist free economy.*

ANTONYM:
• oppose

support ② VERB

to help someone in difficulties • *Try to support each other when one of you is feeling down.*

encourage • *When things aren't going well, he encourages me.*

help • *He'd do anything to help a friend.*

a
b
c
d
e
f
g
h
i
j
k
l
m
n
o
p
q
r
s
t
u
v
w
x
y
z

A
B
C
D
E
F
G
H
I
J
K
L
M
N
O
P
Q
R
S
T
U
V
W
X
Y
Z

support ③ VERB
to hold something up from underneath • *Thick wooden posts support the ceiling.*
bolster • *steel beams used to bolster the roof*
brace • *The roll-over bar braces the car's structure.*
hold up • *Her legs wouldn't hold her up.*
prop up • *Use sticks to prop the plants up.*
reinforce • *They had to reinforce the walls with exterior beams.*
MORE SYNONYMS:
• buttress
• shore up

support ④ NOUN
an object that holds something up • *the metal supports which hold up the canvas*
brace • *He will have to wear a neck brace for several days.*
foundation • *the foundation on which the bridge was built*
pillar • *the pillars supporting the roof*
post • *The device is fixed to a post.*
prop • *a structural part such as a beam or prop*
MORE SYNONYMS:
• abutment
• stanchion

supporter NOUN
a person who agrees with or helps someone • *He is a strong supporter of the plan.*
adherent • *Communism was gaining adherents in Latin America.*
advocate • *a strong advocate of free market policies*
ally • *a close political ally*
champion • *a champion of women's causes*
fan • *fans of this football club*
follower • *followers of the Dalai Lama*

sponsor • *the first sponsor of Buddhism in Japan*
MORE SYNONYMS:
• patron
• protagonist

suppose VERB
to think that something is probably the case • *Where do you suppose he has gone?*
assume • *I assume you have permission to be here?*
believe • *We believe them to be hidden somewhere in the area.*
expect • *I don't expect you've had much experience in the job yet.*
guess • *I guess you're right.*
imagine • *We tend to imagine that the Victorians were prim and proper.*
presume • *I presume you're here on business.*
think • *Do you think she was embarrassed?*
MORE SYNONYMS:
• conjecture
• surmise (FORMAL)

supposed ① ADJECTIVE
planned, expected, or required to do something • *You're not supposed to leave a child on its own.*
expected • *You were expected to arrive much earlier than this.*
meant • *Parties are meant to be fun.*
obliged • *He is legally obliged to declare his interests.*
required • *Will I be required to come to every meeting?*

supposed ② ADJECTIVE
generally believed or thought to be the case • *What is his son supposed to have said?*
alleged • *The accused is alleged to have killed a man.*
assumed • *As usual, the mistakes were*

assumed to be my fault.
believed • *He is believed to have died in 1117.*
meant • *They are meant to be one of the top teams in the world.*
presumed • *This area is presumed to be safe.*
reputed • *The monster is reputed to live in the deep waters of a Scottish loch.*
rumoured • *They are rumoured to be on the verge of splitting up.*

suppress ① VERB
to prevent people from doing something • *international attempts to suppress drug trafficking*
crush • *a plan to crush the uprising*
quash • *It may help to quash these rumours.*
quell • *The army moved in to quell the uprising.*
stamp out • *steps to stamp out bullying in schools*
stop • *measures to stop the trade in ivory*

suppress ② VERB
to stop yourself from expressing a feeling or reaction • *She barely suppressed a gasp.*
conceal • *Robert could not conceal his relief.*
contain • *He could hardly contain his rage.*
curb • *He curbed his temper.*
repress • *people who repress their emotions*
restrain • *unable to restrain her anger*
smother • *I smothered a chuckle.*
stifle • *Miller stifled a yawn and looked at his watch.*

supreme ADJECTIVE
of the highest degree or rank • *They conspired to seize supreme power.*
chief • *his chief rival*
foremost • *the world's foremost scientists*

greatest • *the city's greatest soccer idol*
highest • *the highest academic achievement*
leading • *the world's leading basketball players*
paramount • *a factor of paramount importance*
pre-eminent • *a pre-eminent political figure*
principal • *the principal reason*
top • *the president's top military advisers*
ultimate • *the ultimate international accolade, the Nobel Prize*

sure ① ADJECTIVE
having no doubts • *She was no longer sure how she felt about him.*
certain • *certain of getting a place on the team*
clear • *He is not clear on how he will go about it.*
convinced • *He is convinced it's your fault.*
definite • *a definite answer*
positive • *I'm positive it will happen.*
satisfied • *We must be satisfied that the treatment is safe.*

ANTONYM:
• unsure

sure ② ADJECTIVE
reliable or definite • *a sure sign that something is wrong*
definite • *a definite advantage*
dependable • *dependable information*
foolproof • *a foolproof system*
infallible • *an infallible eye for detail*
reliable • *a reliable source*
trustworthy • *trustworthy reports*
undeniable • *a sad but undeniable fact*

surprise ① NOUN
something unexpected • *The resignation came as a complete surprise.*

a
b
c
d
e
f
g
h
i
j
k
l
m
n
o
p
q
r
s
t
u
v
w
x
y
z

A
B
C
D
E
F
G
H
I
J
K
L
M
N
O
P
Q
R
S
T
U
V
W
X
Y
Z

bombshell • *His departure was a bombshell for the team.*

revelation • *Degas's work had been a revelation to her.*

shock • *I got a shock when I saw her.*

start • *You gave me quite a start.*

surprise ② NOUN

the feeling caused by something unexpected • *an exclamation of surprise*

amazement • *He stared in baffled amazement.*

astonishment • *"What?" Meg asked in astonishment.*

incredulity • *The announcement has been met with incredulity.*

wonder • *Cross shook his head in wonder.*

surprise ③ VERB

to give someone a feeling of surprise • *I was surprised by the vehemence of his criticism.*

amaze • *Most of the cast were amazed by the play's success.*

astonish • *I was astonished to discover his true age.*

astound • *He was astounded at the result.*

jolt • *Henderson was jolted by the news.*

stagger • *I was staggered by his reaction.*

stun • *Audiences were stunned by the film's tragic end.*

take aback • *Derek was taken aback when a man answered the phone.*

MORE SYNONYMS:
• flabbergast
• nonplus

surrender ① VERB

to agree that the other side has won • *We'll never surrender to the terrorists.*

capitulate • *They had no choice but to capitulate.*

give in • *She gave in to him on everything.*

submit • *I refuse to submit to their demands.*

succumb • *The Minister said his country would never succumb to pressure.*

yield • *The government had to yield to local opinion.*

surrender ② VERB

to give something up to someone else • *We have surrendered our political authority for economic gain.*

cede • *After the war, Spain ceded the island to America.*

give up • *She is loath to give up her hard-earned liberty.*

relinquish • *He does not intend to relinquish power.*

renounce • *He renounced his claim to the throne.*

yield • *He was obliged to yield territory to France.*

surrender ③ NOUN

a situation in which one side gives in to the other • *unconditional surrender*

capitulation • *the German capitulation at the end of the First World War*

submission • *The army intends to starve the city into submission.*

surround VERB

to be all around a person or thing • *He was surrounded by bodyguards.*

encircle • *A forty-foot-high concrete wall encircles the jail.*

enclose • *The land was enclosed by a fence.*

encompass • *the largest lake in Canada wholly encompassed by a town*

envelop • *The rich smell of the forest enveloped us.*

hem in • *a valley hemmed in by mountains*

surroundings PLURAL NOUN

the area and environment around a

person or place • *He felt a longing for familiar surroundings.*
background • *a fitting background for her beauty*
environment • *a safe environment for marine mammals*
location • *filmed in an exotic location*
neighbourhood • *living in an affluent neighbourhood*
setting • *Rome is the perfect setting for romance.*

MORE SYNONYMS:
• environs
• milieu

survive VERB
to live or exist in spite of difficulties • *companies which survived after the recession*
endure • *Somehow their friendship endures.*
last • *Nothing lasts forever.*
live • *having lived through the 1930s depression*
outlive • *They have outlived the horror of the war.*
pull through • *He should pull through okay.*

suspect ① VERB
to think something is likely • *I suspect they are secretly planning to raise taxes.*
believe • *Police believe the attacks were carried out by nationalists.*
feel • *I somehow feel he was involved.*
guess • *As you probably guessed, I don't like him much.*
suppose • *The problem is more complex than he supposes.*

suspect ② VERB
to have doubts about something • *He suspected her motives.*
distrust • *I don't have any particular reason to distrust them.*

doubt • *Do you doubt my word?*
mistrust • *He mistrusts all journalists.*

suspect ③ ADJECTIVE
not to be trusted • *a rather suspect holy man*
dodgy (BRITISH, AUSTRALIAN AND NEW ZEALAND; INFORMAL) • *a dodgy car dealer*
doubtful • *These details are of doubtful origin.*
dubious • *dubious practices*
fishy (INFORMAL) • *There's something very fishy about it.*
questionable • *the questionable motives of politicians*

suspicion ① NOUN
a feeling of mistrust • *I was always regarded with suspicion because of my background.*
distrust • *an instinctive distrust of authority*
doubt • *I have my doubts about his ability to govern.*
misgiving • *His first words filled us with misgiving.*
mistrust • *a deep mistrust of banks*
scepticism • *The report has been greeted with scepticism.*

MORE SYNONYMS:
• dubiety
• qualm

suspicion ② NOUN
a feeling that something is true • *I have a strong suspicion they are lying.*
hunch • *Lowe had a hunch he was on to something.*
idea • *I had an idea that he joined the army later.*
impression • *I get the impression he's hiding something.*

suspicious ① ADJECTIVE
feeling distrustful of someone or

something • *He was rightly suspicious of their motives.*
apprehensive • *She was apprehensive of strangers.*
distrustful • *Voters are deeply distrustful of all politicians.*
doubtful • *At first I was doubtful about their authenticity.*
sceptical • *Other archaeologists are sceptical about his findings.*
wary • *Many people are wary of lawyers.*

suspicious ② ADJECTIVE
causing feelings of distrust
• *suspicious circumstances*
dodgy (BRITISH, AUSTRALIAN AND NEW ZEALAND; INFORMAL) • *He was a bit of a dodgy character.*
doubtful • *selling something of doubtful quality*
dubious • *This claim seems to us rather dubious.*
fishy (INFORMAL) • *There's something fishy going on here.*
funny • *There's something funny about him.*
questionable • *the questionable motives of politicians*
shady (INFORMAL) • *shady deals*
suspect • *The whole affair has been highly suspect.*

swap VERB
to replace one thing for another
• *Some hostages were swapped for convicted prisoners.*
barter • *bartering wheat for cotton and timber*
exchange • *exchanging one set of problems for another*
interchange • *Meat can be interchanged with pulses as a source of protein.*
switch • *They switched the tags on the cables.*

trade • *They traded land for goods and money.*

sweet ① ADJECTIVE
containing a lot of sugar • *a mug of sweet tea*
cloying • *a cloying apricot chutney*
sugary • *a sugary meringue pie*
sweetened • *sweetened shortcrust pastry*

ANTONYM:
• sour

sweet ② ADJECTIVE
having a pleasant smell • *the sweet smell of roses*
aromatic • *a plant with aromatic leaves*
fragrant • *fragrant clover*
perfumed • *perfumed soaps*
sweet-smelling • *cottage gardens filled with sweet-smelling flowers and herbs*

sweet ③ ADJECTIVE
pleasant-sounding and tuneful • *the sweet sounds of children's singing*
harmonious • *harmonious sounds*
mellow • *mellow background music*
melodious • *The melodious tones of the organ echoed around the great cathedral.*
musical • *He had a soft, musical voice.*
tuneful • *The band were noted for their tuneful backing vocals.*

MORE SYNONYMS:
• dulcet
• euphonious

sweet ④ NOUN
a sweet-tasting thing such as a toffee
• *His sack was full of packets of sweets.*
candy (AMERICAN) • *We were sick after eating some syrupy candies she had made.*
confectionery • *The company specializes in selling confectionery from all over the world.*

lolly (AUSTRALIAN AND NEW ZEALAND)
• *Avoid feeding him too many lollies.*
sweetie • *She presented him with a jar of his favourite sweeties as a thank-you.*

swerve VERB
to change direction suddenly to avoid hitting something • *He swerved to avoid a truck.*
swing • *The car swung off the road.*
turn • *He turned sharply to the left.*
veer • *The vehicle veered out of control.*

swift ADJECTIVE
happening or moving very quickly
• *make a swift decision*
brisk • *walking at a brisk pace*
express • *a special express service*
fast • *The question is how fast the process will be.*
hurried • *a hurried breakfast*
prompt • *Prompt action is needed.*
quick • *The country has been developing at a very quick pace.*
rapid • *Will the Tunnel provide more rapid transport than ferries?*
speedy • *We wish Bill a speedy recovery.*

ANTONYM:
• slow

symbol NOUN
a design or idea used to represent something • *the chemical symbol for mercury*
emblem • *His badge bore a small yellow hammer-and-sickle emblem.*
emoticon • *He signed off with a happy-face emoticon.*
figure • *the figure of a five-pointed star*
logo • *the company's logo*

mark • *a mark of identification*
representation • *This rune is a representation of a spearhead.*
sign • *a multiplication sign*
token • *He gave her a ring as a token of his love.*

sympathy NOUN
kindness and understanding towards someone in trouble • *My heartfelt sympathy goes out to all the relatives.*
compassion • *I was impressed by the compassion he showed for a helpless old woman.*
empathy • *They displayed an admirable understanding of the crime and empathy with the victim.*
pity • *He showed no pity for his victims.*
understanding • *I'd like to thank you for your patience and understanding.*

system NOUN
an organized way of doing or arranging something • *the advantages of the new system over the old one*
arrangement • *an intricate arrangement of treadles, rods and cranks*
method • *the methods employed in the study*
procedure • *This is now the standard procedure.*
routine • *his daily routine*
structure • *the structure of local government*
technique • *a new technique for processing sound*

MORE SYNONYMS:
• methodology
• modus operandi

a
b
c
d
e
f
g
h
i
j
k
l
m
n
o
p
q
r
s
t
u
v
w
x
y
z

Tt

tact NOUN
the ability not to offend people • *He has handled the affair with great tact.*
delicacy • *Both countries are behaving with rare delicacy.*
diplomacy • *It took all Minnelli's diplomacy to get him to return.*
discretion • *I appreciate your discretion.*
sensitivity • *The police treated the victims with great sensitivity.*

tactful ADJECTIVE
showing tact • *Sorry, that wasn't a very tactful question.*
diplomatic • *She is very direct. I tend to be more diplomatic.*
discreet • *They were gossipy and not always discreet.*
sensitive • *his sensitive handling of the situation*

ANTONYM:
• tactless

take ① VERB
to require something • *He takes three hours to get ready.*
demand • *The task of rebuilding would demand much patience.*
require • *The race requires a lot of stamina.*

take ② VERB
to carry something • *I'll take these papers home and read them.*
bear (FORMAL) • *They bore the hardwood box into the kitchen.*

bring • *He poured a brandy for Dena and brought it to her.*
carry • *She carried the shopping from the car.*
convey (FORMAL) • *The minibus conveyed us to the city centre.*
ferry • *A plane arrives to ferry guests to the island.*
fetch • *Sylvia fetched a towel from the bathroom.*
transport • *They use tankers to transport the oil to Los Angeles.*

take ③ VERB
to lead someone somewhere • *She took me to a Mexican restaurant.*
bring • *Come to my party and bring a girl with you.*
conduct (FORMAL) • *He asked if he might conduct us to the ball.*
escort • *I escorted him to the door.*
guide • *a young Egyptologist who guided us through the tombs*
lead • *She confessed to the killing and led police to his remains.*
usher • *I ushered him into the office.*

take care of ① VERB
to look after someone or something
• *There was no-one to take care of the children.*
care for • *They hired a nurse to care for her.*
look after • *I love looking after the children.*
mind • *Jim will mind the shop while I'm away.*

nurse • *All the years he was sick, my mother had nursed him.*

protect • *He vowed to protect her all the days of her life.*

tend • *He tends the flower beds that he has planted.*

watch • *Are parents expected to watch their children 24 hours a day?*

ANTONYM:
• neglect

take care of ② VERB
to deal with a problem, task, or situation • *"Do you need clean sheets?" "No, Mrs May took care of that."*

attend to • *We have business to attend to first.*

cope with • *A new system has been designed to cope with the increased demand.*

deal with • *the way that building societies deal with complaints*

handle • *She handled the president's travel arrangements during the campaign.*

manage • *He expects me to manage all the household expenses on very little.*

see to • *While Frank saw to the luggage, Sara took the children home.*

take in ① VERB
to deceive someone • *He was a real charmer who totally took me in.*

con (INFORMAL) • *The British public has been conned by the government.*

deceive • *He has deceived us all.*

dupe • *Some offenders dupe the psychologists who assess them.*

fool • *Art dealers fool a lot of people.*

mislead • *It appears we were misled by a professional con artist.*

trick • *He'll be upset when he finds out how you tricked him.*

take in ② VERB
to understand something • *She seemed to take in all he said.*

absorb • *It will take time for us to absorb the news.*

appreciate • *She never really appreciated the bitterness of the conflict.*

assimilate • *My mind could only assimilate one of these ideas at a time.*

comprehend • *He failed to comprehend the significance of this remark.*

digest • *They need time to digest the information they have learned.*

get • *You just don't get what I'm saying, do you*

grasp • *The Government has not yet grasped the seriousness of the crisis.*

understand • *They are too young to understand what is going on.*

talent NOUN
a natural ability • *Both her children have a talent for music.*

ability • *Her drama teacher spotted her ability.*

aptitude • *Alan has no aptitude for music.*

capacity • *people's creative capacities*

flair • *a dentist with a flair for invention*

genius • *his genius for chess*

gift • *a gift for teaching*

knack • *He's got the knack of getting people to listen.*

talk ① VERB
to say things • *They were talking about American food.*
▶ see Word Study **say**, page 655

talk ② NOUN
a conversation • *We had a long talk about her father.*

chat • *I had a chat with him.*

chatter • *idle chatter*

conversation • *We had a long conversation.*

talk ③ NOUN
an informal speech • *a talk about AIDS*

address • *an address to the American people*

A
B
C
D
E
F
G
H
I
J
K
L
M
N
O
P
Q
R
S
T
U
V
W
X
Y
Z

discourse • *a lengthy discourse on strategy*
lecture • *a series of lectures*
sermon • *a church sermon*
speech • *He delivered his speech in French.*

MORE SYNONYMS:
• disquisition
• oration

talkative ADJECTIVE
talking a lot • *His eyes grew bright and he suddenly became very talkative.*
chatty • *She's quite a chatty person.*
communicative • *She has become a lot more communicative.*
long-winded • *I hope I'm not being too long-winded.*

tall ADJECTIVE
higher than average • *tall buildings*
high • *a high wall*
lanky • *He was six foot four, all lanky and leggy.*
lofty • *lofty ceilings*
soaring • *the soaring spires of churches like St Peter's*
towering • *towering cliffs of black granite*

ANTONYM:
• short

tangle ① NOUN
a mass of long things knotted together • *a tangle of wires*
jumble • *a jumble of twisted tubes*
knot • *Her hair was full of knots.*
mass • *a flailing mass of arms and legs*
mat • *the thick mat of sandy hair on his chest*
muddle • *The back of the tapestry was a muddle of threads.*
web • *a thick web of fibres*

tangle ② VERB
to twist together or catch someone or something • *Dolphins can get tangled in fishing nets and drown.*
catch • *a fly caught in a spider's web*
jumble • *The wires were all jumbled together and tied in a knot.*
knot • *The kite strings had got knotted together.*
twist • *Her hands began to twist the handles of the bag.*

task NOUN
a job that you have to do • *Walker had the task of breaking the bad news.*
assignment • *written assignments and practical tests*
chore • *household chores*
duty • *I carried out my duties conscientiously.*
job • *He was given the job of tending the fire.*
mission • *Salisbury sent him on a diplomatic mission to North America.*
undertaking • *Organizing the show has been a massive undertaking.*

taste ① NOUN
the flavour of something • *I like the taste of wine.*
flavour • *a crumbly texture with a strong flavour*
tang • *the tang of lemon*

taste ② NOUN
a small amount of food or drink • *He swirled the brandy around before taking another small taste.*
bite • *Chew each mouthful fully before the next bite.*
mouthful • *She gulped down a mouthful of coffee.*
sip • *a sip of wine*

taste ③ NOUN
a liking for something • *a taste for adventure*
appetite • *his appetite for success*
fondness • *I've always had a fondness for jewels.*

liking • *She had a liking for good clothes.*
penchant (FORMAL) • *He had a penchant for playing jokes on people.*

MORE SYNONYMS:
• partiality
• predilection

tasteless ① ADJECTIVE
having little flavour • *The fish was mushy and tasteless.*
bland • *It tasted bland, like warmed cardboard.*
insipid • *a rather insipid meal*

ANTONYM:
• tasty

tasteless ② ADJECTIVE
vulgar and unattractive • *a house crammed with tasteless ornaments*
flashy • *a flashy sports car*
garish • *garish bright red boots*
gaudy • *her gaudy floral hat*
tacky (INFORMAL) • *tacky holiday souvenirs*
tawdry • *a tawdry seaside town*
vulgar • *a very vulgar house*

ANTONYM:
• tasteful

tasty ADJECTIVE
having a pleasant flavour • *The food was very tasty.*
appetizing • *a choice of appetizing dishes*
delicious • *a wide selection of delicious desserts*
lekker (SOUTH AFRICAN; SLANG) • *a lekker meal*
luscious • *luscious fruit*
palatable • *some very palatable wines*

MORE SYNONYMS:
• flavourful
• flavoursome

ANTONYM:
• tasteless

tax ① NOUN
money paid to the government • *the tax on new cars*
duty • *customs duties*
excise • *These products are excused VAT and excise.*
levy (FORMAL) • *an annual motorway levy on all drivers*
tariff • *America wants to eliminate tariffs on items such as electronics.*

tax ② VERB
to make heavy demands on someone • *They must be told not to tax your patience.*
drain • *conflicts that drain your energy*
exhaust • *She has exhausted my sympathy.*
sap • *The illness sapped his strength.*
strain • *The volume of flights is straining the air traffic control system.*
stretch • *The drought there is stretching American resources to their limits.*

teach VERB
to instruct someone how to do something • *She taught Julie to read.*
coach • *He coached the basketball team.*
drill • *He drills the choir to a high standard.*
educate • *He was educated at Haslingden Grammar School.*
instruct • *He instructed family members in nursing techniques.*
school • *He had been schooled to take over the family business.*
train • *They train teachers in counselling skills.*
tutor • *She was tutored at home by her parents.*

teacher NOUN
someone who teaches something • *a geography teacher*
coach • *her drama coach*

a
b
c
d
e
f
g
h
i
j
k
l
m
n
o
p
q
r
s
t
u
v
w
x
y
z

don • *a Cambridge don*
guru • *a religious guru*
instructor • *a driving instructor*
lecturer • *a lecturer in law*
master • *a retired maths master*
mistress • *like a school mistress presiding over an exam*
professor • *a professor of economics*
tutor • *He surprised his tutors by failing the exam.*

MORE SYNONYMS:
• educator
• pedagogue

team ① NOUN
a group of people • *the football team*
band • *a band of rebels*
crew • *the ship's crew*
gang • *a gang of workmen*
group • *The students work in groups.*
side • *Italy were definitely the better side.*
squad • *the England under-21 squad*
troupe • *troupes of travelling actors*

team ② or **team up** VERB
to work together • *A friend suggested that we team up for a working holiday.*
collaborate • *The two men met and agreed to collaborate.*
cooperate • *They would cooperate in raising their child.*
join forces • *The groups joined forces to fight against the ban.*
link up • *the first time the two armies have linked up*
pair up • *Men and teenage girls pair up to dance.*
unite • *The two parties have been trying to unite.*
work together • *We have always wanted to work together.*

tear ① NOUN
a hole in something • *I peered through a tear in the curtains.*

hole • *the hole in my shoe*
ladder • *There was a ladder in her tights.*
rip • *the rip in her new dress*
rupture • *a rupture in the valve*
scratch • *I pointed to a number of scratches in the tile floor.*
split • *the split in his trousers*

tear ② VERB
to make a hole in something • *She nearly tore my overcoat.*
ladder • *after she laddered her tights*
rip • *I tried not to rip the paper.*
rupture • *a ruptured appendix*
scratch • *Knives will scratch the worktop.*
shred • *They may be shredding documents.*
split • *I'd split my trousers.*

MORE SYNONYMS:
• rend
• sunder

tear ③ VERB
to go somewhere in a hurry • *He tore through busy streets in a high-speed chase.*
charge • *He charged through the door.*
dart • *Ingrid darted across the deserted street.*
dash • *He dashed upstairs.*
fly • *She flew to their bedsides when they were ill.*
race • *He raced across town.*
shoot • *Another car shot out of a junction.*
speed • *A low shot sped past Lukic.*
zoom • *We zoomed through the gallery.*

MORE SYNONYMS:
• bolt
• career

tease VERB
to make fun of someone • *He used to tease me about wanting to act.*
make fun of • *The kids at school made fun of me and my Cockney accent.*

mock • *Don't mock me!*
needle (INFORMAL) • *He used to enjoy needling people.*
taunt • *Other youths taunted him about his clothes.*

tell ① VERB
to let someone know something
• *They told us the dreadful news.*
inform • *My daughter informed me that she was pregnant.*
notify • *We have notified the police.*

MORE SYNONYMS:
• acquaint
• apprise

tell ② VERB
to give someone an order • *A passer-by told the driver to move his car.*
command • *He commanded his troops to attack.*
direct (FORMAL) • *They have been directed to give special attention to the problem.*
instruct • *The family has instructed solicitors to sue the company.*
order • *He ordered his men to cease firing.*

MORE SYNONYMS:
• call upon
• enjoin

tell ③ VERB
to judge something correctly • *I could tell he was scared.*
discern • *It was hard to discern why this was happening.*
see • *I could see she was lonely.*

temporary ADJECTIVE
lasting a short time • *a temporary loss of memory*
ephemeral • *a reminder that earthly pleasures are ephemeral*
fleeting • *a fleeting glimpse*
interim • *an interim measure*
momentary • *a momentary lapse*

passing • *a passing phase*
provisional • *a provisional coalition government*
transient • *Modelling is a transient career.*
transitory • *the transitory nature of political success*

MORE SYNONYMS:
• impermanent
• short-lived

ANTONYM:
• permanent

tempt VERB
to persuade someone to do something • *Children not attending schools may be tempted into crime.*
entice • *She resisted attempts to entice her into politics.*
lure • *The company aims to lure smokers back to cigarettes.*
seduce • *We are seduced into buying all these items.*

tend ① VERB
to happen usually or often • *I tend to forget things.*
be apt • *She was apt to raise her voice.*
be inclined • *He was inclined to self-pity.*
be liable • *equipment that is liable to break*
be prone • *We know males are more prone to violence.*
have a tendency • *Shetland jumpers have a tendency to be annoyingly itchy.*

tend ② VERB
to look after someone or something
• *the way we tend our cattle*
care for • *They hired a nurse to care for her.*
look after • *I love looking after the children.*
nurse • *In hospital they nursed me back to health.*

a
b
c
d
e
f
g
h
i
j
k
l
m
n
o
p
q
r
s
t
u
v
w
x
y
z

take care of • *There was no one else to take care of the animals.*

tendency NOUN
behaviour that happens very often
• *a tendency to be critical*
inclination • *his artistic inclinations*
leaning • *their socialist leanings*
propensity • *his propensity for violence*

MORE SYNONYMS:
• predisposition
• proclivity
• proneness

tender ① ADJECTIVE
showing gentle and caring feelings
• *tender, loving care*
affectionate • *She gave him an affectionate smile.*
caring • *He is a lovely boy, and very caring.*
compassionate • *a deeply compassionate film*
gentle • *Michael's voice was gentle and consoling.*
kind • *She is warmhearted and kind to everyone and everything.*
loving • *He was a most loving husband and father.*
sensitive • *He was always so sensitive.*
warm • *She was a very warm person.*

ANTONYM:
• tough

tender ② ADJECTIVE
painful and sore • *My tummy felt very tender.*
aching • *The weary holidaymakers soothed their aching feet in the sea.*
bruised • *bruised legs*
inflamed • *Her eyes were inflamed.*
painful • *Her glands were swollen and painful.*
raw • *the drag of the rope against the raw flesh of my shoulders*

sensitive • *Ouch! I'm sorry, my lip is still a bit sensitive.*
sore • *My chest is still sore from the surgery.*

tender ③ VERB
to offer something such as an apology or resignation • *She tendered her resignation.*
hand in • *All the opposition members have handed in their resignation.*
offer • *May I offer my sincere condolences?*

tender ④ NOUN
a proposal to provide something at a price • *Builders will be asked to submit a tender for the work.*
bid • *Sydney's successful bid for the 2000 Olympic Games*
estimate • *The firm is preparing an estimate for the work.*
package • *We opted for the package submitted by the existing service provider.*
submission • *A written submission has to be prepared.*

tense ① ADJECTIVE
nervous and unable to relax • *Never had she seen him so tense.*
anxious • *She had become very anxious and alarmed.*
edgy • *She was nervous and edgy, still chain-smoking.*
jittery (INFORMAL) • *Investors have become jittery about the country's economy.*
jumpy • *I told myself not to be so jumpy.*
nervous • *It has made me very nervous about going out.*
uptight (INFORMAL) • *Penny never got uptight about exams.*

ANTONYM:
• calm

tense ② ADJECTIVE
causing anxiety • *the tense atmosphere at the talks*
anxious • *They had to wait ten anxious days.*
nerve-racking • *It was more nerve-racking than taking a World Cup penalty.*
stressful • *a stressful job*

tense ③ ADJECTIVE
having tight muscles • *She lay, eyes shut, body tense.*
rigid • *Andrew went rigid whenever he saw a dog.*
strained • *His shoulders were strained with effort.*
taut • *when muscles are taut or cold*
tight • *It is better to stretch the tight muscles first.*

ANTONYM:
• relaxed

term ① NOUN
a fixed period of time • *a 12 month term of service*
period • *for a limited period only*
session • *The parliamentary session ends on October 4th.*
spell • *a six-month spell of practical experience*
stretch • *He did an 18-month stretch in prison.*
time • *He served the time of his contract and then left the company.*

MORE SYNONYMS:
• duration
• incumbency

term ② NOUN
a name or word for a particular thing • *the medical term for a heart attack*
designation • *Level Four Alert is a designation reserved for very serious incidents.*
expression • *She used some remarkably coarse expressions.*

name • *The correct name for this condition is bovine spongiform encephalopathy.*
word • *The word ginseng comes from the Chinese "Shen-seng".*

terms PLURAL NOUN
conditions that have been agreed • *the terms of the merger agreement*
conditions • *They may be breaching the conditions of their contract.*
provisions • *the provisions of the Amsterdam treaty*
proviso • *He left me the house with the proviso that it had to stay in the family.*
stipulations • *He left, violating the stipulations of his parole.*

terrible ① ADJECTIVE
serious and unpleasant • *a terrible illness*
appalling • *an appalling headache*
awful • *an awful crime*
desperate • *a desperate situation*
dreadful • *a dreadful mistake*
frightful (OLD-FASHIONED) • *He got himself into a frightful muddle.*
horrendous • *horrendous injuries*
horrible • *a horrible mess*
horrid (OLD-FASHIONED) • *What a horrid smell!*
rotten • *What rotten luck!*

terrible ② ADJECTIVE
of very poor quality • *Paddy's terrible haircut*
abysmal • *The standard of play was abysmal.*
appalling • *Her singing is appalling.*
awful • *Jeans look awful on me.*
dire • *Most of the poems were dire.*
dreadful • *My financial situation is dreadful.*
horrible • *a horrible meal*
rotten • *I think it's a rotten idea.*

a b c d e f g h i j k l m n o p q r s t u v w x y z

ANTONYM:
• excellent

territory NOUN
the land that a person or country controls • *gangs fighting to defend their territories*
area • *They claim that the entire area belongs to Syria.*
country • *He is an ambassador to a foreign country.*
district • *Stick to your own district and stay out of ours.*
domain • *He surveyed his domain from the roof of the castle.*
dominion • *men who ruled their dominions with ruthless efficiency*
land • *New mines were discovered on what had been Apache land.*
province • *debates about the political future of their province*
state • *This state remains suspended from the Commonwealth.*

test ① VERB
to find out what something is like • *travelling to Holland to test a British-built boat*
assess • *The test was to assess aptitude rather than academic achievement.*
check • *It's worth checking each item for obvious flaws.*
try • *Howard wanted me to try the wine.*
try out • *London Transport hopes to try out the system in September.*

test ② NOUN
an attempt to test something • *the banning of nuclear tests*
assessment • *He was remanded for assessment by doctors.*
check • *regular checks on his blood pressure*
trial • *clinical trials*

texture NOUN
the way that something feels • *Her skin is pale, the texture of fine wax.*

consistency • *Mix the dough to the right consistency.*
feel • *Linen raincoats have a crisp, papery feel.*

theft NOUN
the crime of stealing • *the theft of classified documents*
robbery • *The man was serving a sentence for robbery.*
stealing • *She was jailed for six months for stealing.*
thieving • *an ex-con who says he's given up thieving*

MORE SYNONYMS:
• larceny
• pilfering

theory NOUN
an idea that explains something • *Darwin's theory of evolution*
conjecture • *That was a conjecture, not a fact.*
hypothesis • *Different hypotheses have been put forward.*
supposition • *As with many such suppositions, no one had ever tested it.*
surmise (FORMAL) • *His surmise proved correct.*

therefore ADVERB
as a result • *Muscles need lots of fuel and therefore burn lots of calories.*
as a result • *I slept in, and, as a result, I was late for work.*
consequently • *He's more experienced, and consequently earns a higher salary.*
for that reason • *I'd never met my in-laws before. For that reason, I was a little nervous.*
hence (FORMAL) • *These products are all natural, and hence, better for you.*
so • *I was worried about her, so I phoned to check how she was.*
thus • *His men were getting tired, and thus, careless.*

thesaurus NOUN

- **PARTS OF A DICTIONARY OR**
- **THESAURUS**
- antonym
- definition
- entry
- example
- headword
- homonym
- homophone
- inflection
- label
- part of speech
- pronunciation
- root word
- synonym
- word derivation

thick ① ADJECTIVE
measuring a large distance from side to side • *a thick stone wall*
fat • *a fat book*
wide • *a desk that was almost as wide as the room*

ANTONYM:
- thin

thick ② ADJECTIVE
containing little water • *thick soup*
clotted • *clotted cream*
concentrated • *a glass of concentrated orange juice*
condensed • *tins of condensed milk*

ANTONYM:
- watery

thick ③ ADJECTIVE
grouped closely together • *thick dark hair*
bristling • *a bristling moustache*
dense • *a large dense forest*
lush • *the lush green meadows*
luxuriant • *the luxuriant foliage of Young Island*

ANTONYM:
- sparse

thicken VERB
to become thicker • *The clouds thickened.*
clot • *The patient's blood refused to clot.*
condense • *Water vapour condenses to form clouds.*
congeal • *The blood had started to congeal.*
set • *as the jelly starts to set*

MORE SYNONYMS:
- coagulate
- jell

ANTONYM:
- thin

thief NOUN
someone who steals something • *a car thief*
burglar • *Burglars broke into their home.*
crook (INFORMAL) • *a petty crook*
mugger (INFORMAL) • *after being threatened by a mugger*
pickpocket • *a gang of pickpockets*
robber • *armed robbers*
shoplifter • *a persistent shoplifter*

MORE SYNONYMS:
- housebreaker
- pilferer

thin ① ADJECTIVE
measuring a small distance from side to side • *The material was too thin.*
fine • *the fine hairs on her arms*
narrow • *a narrow strip of land*
slim • *a slim volume of verse*

ANTONYM:
- thick

thin ② ADJECTIVE
not carrying a lot of fat • *a tall, thin man with grey hair*
▶ see Word Study **thin**, page 661

ANTONYM:
- fat

a b c d e f g h i j k l m n o p q r s t u v w x y z

thin ③ ADJECTIVE
containing a lot of water • *thin soup*
dilute or **diluted** • *a dilute solution of bleach*
runny • *a runny soft cheese*
watery • *watery beer*
weak • *a cup of weak tea*

ANTONYM:
• thick

thing NOUN
a physical object • *What's that thing doing here?*
article • *household articles*
object • *everyday objects such as wooden spoons*

things PLURAL NOUN
someone's clothes or belongings
• *Sara told him to take all his things with him.*
belongings • *He was identified only by his personal belongings.*
effects • *His daughters were collecting his effects.*
gear • *They helped us put our gear back into the van.*
possessions • *People had lost all their possessions.*
stuff • *Where have you put all your stuff?*

think ① VERB
to consider something • *Let's think what we can do next.*
consider • *The government is being asked to consider the plan.*
contemplate • *He cried as he contemplated his future.*
deliberate • *She deliberated over the decision for a good few years.*
meditate • *He meditated on the problem.*
mull over • *I'll leave you alone so you can mull it over.*
muse (LITERARY) • *Many of the papers muse on the fate of the President.*

ponder • *I'm continually pondering how to improve the team.*
reflect • *I reflected on the child's future.*

MORE SYNONYMS:
• cogitate
• ruminate

think ② VERB
to believe something • *I think she has a secret boyfriend.*
believe • *Experts believe that the drought will be extensive.*
consider • *He considers that this is the worst recession this century.*
deem (FORMAL) • *Many people have ideas that their society deems to be dangerous.*
hold • *The theory holds that minor events are the trigger for larger events.*
imagine • *I imagine he was just showing off.*
judge • *He judged that this was the moment to say what had to be said.*
reckon • *Toni reckoned that it must be about three o'clock.*

thorough ADJECTIVE
careful and complete • *a thorough examination*
complete • *a complete overhaul of the engine*
comprehensive • *a comprehensive guide to the region*
exhaustive • *exhaustive enquiries*
full • *Mr Primakov gave a full account of his meeting with the President.*
intensive • *four weeks of intensive study*
meticulous • *A happy wedding day requires meticulous planning.*
painstaking • *a painstaking search*
scrupulous • *Observe scrupulous hygiene when preparing and cooking food.*

MORE SYNONYMS:
• all-embracing
• in-depth

thought ① NOUN

an idea or opinion • *his thoughts on love*

idea • *his ideas about democracy*

notion • *We each have a notion of what kind of person we'd like to be.*

opinion • *most of those who expressed an opinion*

view • *Make your views known to your MP.*

thought ② NOUN

the activity of thinking • *After much thought I decided to end my marriage.*

consideration • *There should be careful consideration of the BBC's future role.*

contemplation • *He was lost in contemplation of the landscape.*

deliberation • *the result of lengthy deliberation*

meditation • *He stared at the floor, lost in meditation.*

reflection • *after days of reflection*

thinking • *This is definitely a time for decisive action and quick thinking.*

MORE SYNONYMS:
• cogitation
• introspection
• rumination

thoughtful ① ADJECTIVE

quiet and serious • *He was looking very thoughtful.*

contemplative • *a quiet, contemplative sort of chap*

pensive • *He looked unusually pensive before the start.*

reflective • *I walked on in a reflective mood.*

MORE SYNONYMS:
• introspective
• meditative
• ruminative

thoughtful ② ADJECTIVE

showing consideration for others • *a thoughtful and caring man*

attentive • *an attentive husband*

caring • *a caring son*

considerate • *the most considerate man I've ever known*

kind • *She is warmhearted and kind to everyone.*

MORE SYNONYMS:
• solicitous
• unselfish

ANTONYM:
• thoughtless

thoughtless ADJECTIVE

showing a lack of consideration • *It was thoughtless of her to mention it.*

insensitive • *My husband is very insensitive about my problem.*

tactless • *a tactless remark*

MORE SYNONYMS:
• inconsiderate
• undiplomatic

ANTONYM:
• thoughtful

threat ① NOUN

a statement that someone will harm you • *death threats*

menace • *demanding money with menaces*

threatening remark • *He was overheard making threatening remarks to the couple.*

threat ② NOUN

something that seems likely to harm you • *the threat of tropical storms*

hazard • *a health hazard*

menace • *a menace to the public*

risk • *a fire risk*

threaten ① VERB

to promise to do something bad • *He threatened her with a knife.*

a
b
c
d
e
f
g
h
i
j
k
l
m
n
o
p
q
r
s
t
u
v
w
x
y
z

A
B
C
D
E
F
G
H
I
J
K
L
M
N
O
P
Q
R
S
T
U
V
W
X
Y
Z

make threats to • *despite all the threats he'd made to harm her*
menace • *She's being menaced by her sister's latest boyfriend.*

threaten ② VERB
to be likely to cause harm • *The newcomers threaten the livelihood of the workers.*
endanger • *Toxic waste could endanger lives.*
jeopardize • *He has jeopardized the future of his government.*
put at risk • *If they have the virus, they are putting patients at risk.*
put in jeopardy • *A series of setbacks have put the whole project in jeopardy.*

thrifty ADJECTIVE
careful not to waste money or resources • *Britain became a nation of thrifty consumers and bargain hunters.*
careful • *He's very careful with his money.*
economical • *a very economical way to travel*
frugal • *a frugal lifestyle*
prudent • *the need for a much more prudent use of energy*

thrill ① NOUN
a feeling of excitement • *the thrill of waking up on Christmas morning*
high (INFORMAL) • *the high of a win over New Zealand*
kick (INFORMAL) • *I got a kick out of seeing my name in print.*

thrill ② VERB
to cause a feeling of excitement • *It thrilled me to see her looking so happy.*
excite • *I only take on work that excites me.*
give a kick (INFORMAL) • *It gave me a kick to actually meet her.*

thrive VERB
to be successful • *His company continues to thrive.*

do well • *Connie did well at school.*
flourish • *Racism and crime still flourish in the ghetto.*
prosper • *His team have always prospered in cup competitions.*

throw VERB
to make something move through the air • *throwing a tennis ball against a wall*
cast • *He cast the stone away.*
chuck (INFORMAL) • *He chucked the paper in the bin.*
fling • *Peter flung his shoes into the corner.*
hurl • *Groups of angry youths hurled stones at police.*
lob • *Thugs lobbed a grenade into the crowd.*
pitch • *Simon pitched the empty bottle into the lake.*
sling • *He took off his anorak and slung it into the back seat.*
toss • *She tossed her suitcase onto one of the beds.*

thug NOUN
a very violent person • *a gang of armed thugs*
bandit • *terrorist acts carried out by bandits*
hooligan • *severe measures against soccer hooligans*
tough • *The neighbourhood toughs beat them both up.*
tsotsi (SOUTH AFRICAN) • *Many are too terrified of local tsotsis to protest.*

tidy ① ADJECTIVE
arranged in an orderly way • *a tidy desk*
neat • *She put her clothes in a neat pile.*
orderly • *a beautiful, clean and orderly city*

MORE SYNONYMS:
• shipshape
• spick-and-span

ANTONYM:
• untidy

tidy ② VERB
to make something neat • *He tidied his garage.*
spruce up • *Many buildings have been spruced up.*
straighten • *straightening cushions and organizing magazines*

ANTONYM:
• mess up

tie ① VERB
to fasten something • *They tied the ends of the bag securely.*
bind • *Bind the ends of the cord together with thread.*
fasten • *instructions on how to fasten the strap to the box*
knot • *He knotted the laces securely together.*
lash • *The shelter is built by lashing poles together.*
rope • *I roped myself to the chimney.*
secure • *He secured the canvas straps as tight as they would go.*
tether • *tethering his horse to a tree*
truss • *She trussed him quickly with a stolen bandage.*

ANTONYM:
• untie

tie ② VERB
to have the same score • *Rafferty tied with Nobilo.*
be level • *At the end of 90 minutes the teams were level.*
draw • *Holland and Ireland drew 1–1.*

tie ③ NOUN
a connection with something • *I had very close ties with the family.*

affiliation • *They asked her what her political affiliations were.*
affinity • *He has a close affinity with the landscape.*
bond • *The experience created a special bond between us.*
connection • *The police say he had no connection with the security forces.*
relationship • *family relationships*

tight ① ADJECTIVE
fitting closely • *The shoes are too tight.*
constricted • *His throat began to feel swollen and constricted.*
cramped • *families living in cramped conditions*
snug • *a snug black T-shirt*

ANTONYM:
• loose

tight ② ADJECTIVE
firmly fastened • *a tight knot*
firm • *He managed to get a firm grip of it.*
secure • *Check joints are secure and the wood is sound.*

tight ③ ADJECTIVE
not slack or relaxed • *Pull the elastic tight.*
rigid • *I went rigid with shock.*
taut • *The clothes line is pulled taut and secured.*
tense • *A bath can relax tense muscles.*

ANTONYM:
• slack

tilt ① VERB
to raise one end of something • *Leonard tilted his chair back on two legs.*
incline • *Jack inclined his head.*
lean • *Lean the plants against a wall.*
slant • *The floor slanted down to the window.*
slope • *The bank sloped down sharply to the river.*
tip • *She had to tip her head back to see him.*

a
b
c
d
e
f
g
h
i
j
k
l
m
n
o
p
q
r
s
t
u
v
w
x
y
z

MORE SYNONYMS:
• cant
• list

tilt ② NOUN
a raised position • *the tilt of the earth's axis*
angle • *The boat is now leaning at a 30 degree angle.*
gradient • *a gradient of 1 in 3*
incline • *at the edge of a steep incline*
slant • *The house is on a slant.*
slope • *The street must have been on a slope.*

MORE SYNONYMS:
• camber
• list
• pitch

time ① NOUN
a particular period • *I enjoyed my time in Durham.*
interval • *a long interval of silence*
period • *a period of calm*
spell • *a brief spell teaching*
stretch • *an 18-month stretch in the army*
while • *They walked on in silence for a while.*

RELATED WORD:
• ADJECTIVE temporal

time ② VERB
to plan when something will happen • *We had timed our visit for March 7.*
schedule • *The space shuttle had been scheduled to blast off at 04:38.*
set • *A court hearing has been set for December 16.*

timid ADJECTIVE
lacking courage or confidence • *a timid child*
bashful • *Offstage, he is bashful and awkward.*
cowardly • *I was too cowardly to complain.*

diffident • *Helen was diffident and reserved.*
nervous • *a very nervous woman*
shy • *a shy, quiet-spoken girl*

MORE SYNONYMS:
• faint-hearted
• pusillanimous
• timorous

ANTONYM:
• bold

tiny ADJECTIVE
very small • *The living room is tiny.*
diminutive • *a diminutive figure standing at the entrance*
microscopic • *a microscopic amount of the substance*
miniature • *He looked like a miniature version of his brother.*
minute • *Only a minute amount is needed.*
negligible • *The pay that the soldiers received was negligible.*
wee (SCOTTISH) • *a wee boy*

MORE SYNONYMS:
• infinitesimal
• Lilliputian

ANTONYM:
• huge

tire VERB
to use a lot of energy • *If driving tires you, take the train.*
drain • *My emotional turmoil had drained me.*
exhaust • *Walking in deep snow had totally exhausted him.*
fatigue • *He is easily fatigued.*

MORE SYNONYMS:
• enervate
• wear out
• weary

tired ADJECTIVE
having little energy • *She was too tired to take a shower.*

A B C D E F G H I J K L M N O P Q R S **T** U V W X Y Z

drained • *as United stalked off, stunned and drained*

drowsy • *He felt pleasantly drowsy.*

exhausted • *She was too exhausted and distressed to talk.*

fatigued • *Winter weather can leave you feeling fatigued.*

sleepy • *I was beginning to feel sleepy.*

tuckered out (AUSTRALIAN AND NEW ZEALAND; INFORMAL) • *You must be tuckered out after that bus trip.*

weary • *a weary traveller*

worn out • *He's just worn out after the drive.*

together ① ADVERB

with other people • *We went on long bicycle rides together.*

collectively • *The Cabinet is collectively responsible for policy.*

en masse • *The people marched en masse.*

in unison • *Michael and the landlady nodded in unison.*

jointly • *an agency jointly run by New York and New Jersey*

shoulder to shoulder • *They could fight shoulder to shoulder against a common enemy.*

side by side • *areas where different nationalities live side by side*

together ② ADVERB

at the same time • *Three horses crossed the finish line together.*

as one • *The 40,000 crowd rose as one.*

at once • *You can't do two things at once.*

concurrently • *There were three races running concurrently.*

simultaneously • *The two guns fired almost simultaneously.*

with one accord • *With one accord they turned and walked back.*

tolerable ① ADJECTIVE

able to be tolerated • *The pain was tolerable.*

acceptable • *a mutually acceptable new contract*

bearable • *A cool breeze made the heat bearable.*

ANTONYM:
• unbearable

tolerable ② ADJECTIVE

fairly satisfactory • *a tolerable salary*

acceptable • *We've made an acceptable start.*

adequate • *The level of service was adequate.*

okay or **OK** (INFORMAL) • *For a fashionable restaurant like this the prices are okay.*

passable • *Ms Campbell speaks passable French.*

reasonable • *able to make a reasonable living from his writing*

so-so (INFORMAL) • *Their lunch was only so-so.*

tolerant ADJECTIVE

accepting of different views and behaviour • *more tolerant attitudes to unmarried couples having children*

broad-minded • *a very fair and broad-minded man*

liberal • *She is known to have liberal views on divorce.*

open-minded • *I am very open-minded about that question.*

understanding • *Fortunately for John, he had an understanding wife.*

MORE SYNONYMS:
• forbearing
• latitudinarian

ANTONYM:
• narrow-minded

tolerate ① VERB

to accept something you disagree with • *We will not tolerate such behaviour.*

accept • *Urban dwellers often accept noise as part of city life.*

A
B
C
D
E
F
G
H
I
J
K
L
M
N
O
P
Q
R
S
T
U
V
W
X
Y
Z

put up with • *You're late again and I won't put up with it.*

tolerate ② VERB
to accept something unpleasant • *She can no longer tolerate the position that she's in.*
bear • *He can't bear to talk about it.*
endure • *unable to endure the pain*
stand • *He can't stand me smoking.*

tomb NOUN
a burial chamber • *Carter discovered Tutankhamun's tomb.*
grave • *They used to visit her grave twice a year.*
mausoleum • *the elaborate mausoleums of the Paris cemetery*
sarcophagus • *an Egyptian sarcophagus*
sepulchre (LITERARY) • *the ornate lid of the sepulchre*
vault • *the family vault*

too ① ADVERB
also or as well • *You were there too.*
as well • *She published historical novels as well.*
besides • *You get to take lots of samples home as well.*
in addition • *There are, in addition, other objections to the plan.*
into the bargain • *The machine can play CDs into the bargain.*
likewise • *She sat down and he did likewise.*
moreover • *He didn't know, and moreover, he didn't care.*

too ② ADVERB
more than a desirable or acceptable amount • *You've had too many late nights.*
excessively • *He had an excessively protective mother.*
over- • *I didn't want to seem over-eager.*
overly • *Most people consider him to be overly ambitious.*

unduly • *She's unduly concerned with what people think of her.*
unreasonably • *These prices seem unreasonably high to me.*

tool NOUN
a hand-held instrument for doing a job • *The best tool for the purpose is a pair of shears.*
implement • *knives and other useful implements*
instrument • *instruments for cleaning and polishing teeth*
utensil • *cooking utensils*

top ① NOUN
the highest part of something • *I waited at the top of the stairs.*
apex • *at the very apex of the pyramid*
brow • *the brow of the hill*
crest • *the crest of the wave*
crown • *the crown of the head*
culmination • *the culmination of his career*
head • *A different name was placed at the head of the chart.*
height • *at the height of his success*
high point • *the high point of his movie career*
peak • *at the peak of the morning rush hour*
pinnacle • *the pinnacle of sporting achievement*
ridge • *He died after falling from a ridge on Mount Snowdon.*
summit • *the summit of the mountain*
zenith (LITERARY) • *His career is now at its zenith.*

MORE SYNONYMS:
• acme
• apex
• apogee

ANTONYM:
• bottom

top ② NOUN
the lid of a container • *a bottle top*

cap • *She unscrewed the cap of her water bottle.*
lid • *the lid of the jar*
stopper • *a scent bottle with a stopper in blue frosted glass*

top ③ ADJECTIVE
being the best of its kind • *He was the top student in physics.*
best • *the best pupil of his year*
chief • *one of the world's chief nuclear scientists*
elite • *the elite troops of the presidential bodyguard*
foremost • *the foremost urban painter of his age*
head • *He was head boy when he was at school.*
highest • *He achieved one of the highest positions in the land.*
lead • *She has landed the lead role in a major film.*
leading • *a leading member of the community*
pre-eminent • *a pre-eminent political figure*
premier • *the country's premier theatre company*
prime • *The store will be built in a prime location.*
principal • *the principal singer with the Royal Opera House*

top ④ VERB
to be greater than something • *The temperature topped 90 degrees.*
cap • *He capped his display with two fine goals.*
exceed • *Its research budget exceeds $700 million a year.*
go beyond • *This goes beyond anything I've ever attempted before.*
outstrip • *Demand is outstripping supply.*
surpass • *He has surpassed the record of nine wins in one season.*

top ⑤ VERB
to be better than someone or something • *You'll never manage to top that story.*
beat • *Nothing beats a nice, long bath at the end of a day.*
better • *As an account of adolescence, this novel cannot be bettered.*
eclipse • *Nothing is going to eclipse winning the Olympic title.*
improve on • *We need to improve on our performance against France.*
outdo • *Both sides are trying to outdo each other.*
surpass • *He was determined to surpass the achievements of his brothers.*

total ① NOUN
several things added together • *The companies have a total of 1776 employees.*
aggregate • *three successive defeats by an aggregate of 12 goals*
sum • *the sum of all the angles*
whole • *taken as a percentage of the whole*

total ② ADJECTIVE
complete in all its parts • *a total failure*
absolute • *absolute beginners*
complete • *a complete mess*
out-and-out • *an out-and-out lie*
outright • *an outright rejection of the deal*
unconditional • *unconditional surrender*
undivided • *You have my undivided attention.*
unmitigated • *an unmitigated failure*
unqualified • *an unqualified success*
utter • *utter nonsense*

MORE SYNONYMS:
• all-out
• thoroughgoing

a
b
c
d
e
f
g
h
i
j
k
l
m
n
o
p
q
r
s
t
u
v
w
x
y
z

A
B
C
D
E
F
G
H
I
J
K
L
M
N
O
P
Q
R
S
T
U
V
W
X
Y
Z

total ③ VERB
to reach the sum of • *Their debts totalled over 300,000 dollars.*
add up to • *Profits can add up to millions of dollars.*
amount to • *Spending on sports-related items amounted to £9.75 billion.*
come to • *That comes to over a thousand pounds.*

touch ① VERB
to put your hand on something • *Don't touch that dial.*
feel • *The doctor felt his head.*
finger • *He fingered the few coins in his pocket.*
handle • *Wear rubber gloves when handling cat litter.*

touch ② VERB
to come into contact with • *Annie lowered her legs until her feet touched the floor.*
brush • *Something brushed against her leg.*
graze • *A bullet had grazed his arm.*
meet • *when the wheels meet the ground*

RELATED WORD:
• ADJECTIVE tactile

touch ③ VERB
to emotionally affect someone • *I was touched by his kindness.*
affect • *Jazza was badly affected by his divorce.*
move • *These stories surprised and moved me.*
stir • *She stirred something very deep in me.*

touching ADJECTIVE
causing sadness or sympathy • *a touching tale*
affecting (LITERARY) • *an affecting memorial to Countess Rachel*

moving • *It was a moving moment for Marianne.*
poignant • *a poignant love story*

touchy ADJECTIVE
easily upset • *She is very touchy about her past.*
easily offended • *viewers who are easily offended*
sensitive • *Young people are very sensitive about their appearance.*
toey (AUSTRALIAN AND NEW ZEALAND; SLANG) • *Don't be so toey.*

MORE SYNONYMS:
• oversensitive
• thin-skinned

tough ① ADJECTIVE
able to put up with hardship • *She is tough and ambitious.*
hardened • *hardened criminals*
hardy • *a hardy race of pioneers*
resilient • *a good soldier, calm and resilient*
robust • *Perhaps men are more robust than women?*
rugged • *Rugged individualism forged America's frontier society.*
strong • *Eventually I felt strong enough to look at him.*

tough ② ADJECTIVE
difficult to break or damage • *beans with a rather tough outer skin*
durable • *Fine bone china is both strong and durable.*
hard-wearing • *hard-wearing cotton shirts*
leathery • *leathery skin*
resilient • *an armchair of some resilient plastic material*
robust • *very robust machinery*
rugged • *You need a rugged, four-wheel drive vehicle.*
solid • *The car feels very solid.*
strong • *a strong casing, which won't crack or chip*

sturdy • *The camera was mounted on a sturdy tripod.*
ANTONYM:
• fragile

tough ③ ADJECTIVE
full of hardship • *She had a pretty tough childhood.*
arduous • *an arduous journey*
difficult • *We're living in difficult times.*
exacting • *an exacting task*
hard • *a hard life*
ANTONYM:
• easy

trace ① VERB
to look for and find something • *Police are trying to trace the owner.*
locate • *We've simply been unable to locate him.*
track down • *She had spent years trying to track down her parents.*

trace ② NOUN
a sign of something • *No trace of his father had been found.*
evidence • *He'd seen no evidence of fraud.*
hint • *I saw no hint of irony on her face.*
indication • *He gave no indication of remorse.*
record • *There's no record of any marriage or children.*
sign • *Sally waited for any sign of illness.*
suggestion • *a faint suggestion of a tan*
whiff • *Not a whiff of scandal has ever tainted his private life.*

trace ③ NOUN
a small amount of something • *to write without a trace of sensationalism*
dash • *a story with a dash of mystery*
drop • *a drop of sherry*
remnant • *Beneath the present church were remnants of Roman flooring.*
suspicion • *large blooms of white with a suspicion of pale pink*

tinge • *Could there have been a slight tinge of envy in Eva's voice?*
touch • *a touch of flu*
vestige • *the last vestige of a UN force that once numbered 30,000*
MORE SYNONYMS:
• iota
• jot
• soupçon

trade ① NOUN
the buying and selling of goods • *foreign trade*
business • *a career in business*
commerce • *They have made their fortunes from industry and commerce.*
RELATED WORD:
• ADJECTIVE mercantile

trade ② NOUN
the kind of work someone does • *He learnt his trade as a diver in the North Sea.*
business • *the music business*
line • *Are you in the publishing line too?*
line of work • *In my line of work I often get home too late for dinner.*
occupation • *her new occupation as an author*
profession • *Harper was a teacher by profession.*

trade ③ VERB
to buy and sell goods • *They had years of experience of trading with the West.*
deal • *They deal in antiques.*
do business • *the different people who did business with me*
traffic • *those who traffic in illegal drugs*

trader NOUN
someone who trades in goods • *a timber trader*
broker • *a financial broker*
dealer • *dealers in commodities*
merchant • *a wine merchant*

a
b
c
d
e
f
g
h
i
j
k
l
m
n
o
p
q
r
s
t
u
v
w
x
y
z

A
B
C
D
E
F
G
H
I
J
K
L
M
N
O
P
Q
R
S
T
U
V
W
X
Y
Z

tradition NOUN
a long-standing custom • *the rich traditions of Afro-Cuban music*
convention • *It's just a social convention that men don't wear skirts.*
custom • *an ancient Japanese custom*

traditional ADJECTIVE
existing for a long time • *her traditional Indian dress*
conventional • *conventional family planning methods*
established • *the established church*
ANTONYM:
• unconventional

tragic ADJECTIVE
very sad • *a tragic accident*
distressing • *distressing news*
heartbreaking • *a heartbreaking succession of miscarriages*
heart-rending • *heart-rending pictures of refugees*

train VERB
to teach someone how to do something • *We train them in bricklaying and other building techniques.*
coach • *He coached the basketball team.*
drill • *He drills the choir to a high standard.*
educate • *I was educated at the local grammar school.*
instruct • *All their members are instructed in first aid.*
school • *He has been schooled to take over the family business.*
teach • *This is something they teach us to do in our first year.*
tutor • *She decided to tutor her children at home.*

transfer VERB
to move something from one place to another • *It's easy to transfer money between accounts.*

carry • *I carried the box to the table.*
download • *You can download free games from this website.*
move • *I think we should move the TV to the other side of the room.*
upload • *The boy uploaded a video of the puppies to the internet.*

transform VERB
to change something completely • *This technology has transformed our society.*
alter • *New curtains can completely alter the look of a room.*
change • *alchemists attempting to change base metals into gold*
convert • *They have converted the church into a restaurant.*
reform • *He was totally reformed by this experience.*
revolutionize • *a device which will revolutionize the way you cook*

transparent ADJECTIVE
able to be seen through • *a sheet of transparent plastic*
clear • *a clear glass panel*
crystalline (LITERARY) • *crystalline lakes*
sheer • *a sheer black shirt*
translucent • *translucent corrugated plastic*
MORE SYNONYMS:
• diaphanous
• see-through
ANTONYM:
• opaque

transport ① NOUN
the moving of goods and people • *The prices quoted include transport costs.*
removal • *the furniture removal business*
shipment • *transported to the docks for shipment overseas*
transportation • *the transportation of refugees*

transport ② VERB
to move people or goods
somewhere • *They use tankers to
transport the oil to Los Angeles.*
carry • *The ship could carry seventy
passengers.*
convey (FORMAL) • *a branch line to
convey fish direct to Billingsgate*
ship • *the food being shipped to Iraq*
transfer • *She was transferred to
another hospital.*

trap ① NOUN
a device for catching animals • *a
rabbit trap*
net • *a fishing net*
snare • *a snare for catching birds*

trap ② VERB
to catch animals • *The locals were
encouraged to trap and kill the birds.*
catch • *an animal caught in a trap*
corner • *like a cornered rat*
snare • *He'd snared a rabbit earlier
in the day.*

trap ③ VERB
to trick someone • *Were you trying to
trap her into making some admission?*
dupe • *a plot to dupe stamp collectors
into buying fake rarities*
trick • *His family tricked him into going
to Pakistan.*

MORE SYNONYMS:
• ensnare
• entrap

trash ① NOUN
waste material • *He picks up your
trash on Mondays.*
garbage • *rotting piles of garbage*
refuse • *a weekly collection of refuse*
rubbish • *They had piled most of their
rubbish into yellow skips.*
waste • *a law that regulates the
disposal of waste*

trash ② NOUN
something of poor quality • *Don't read
that awful trash.*
garbage (INFORMAL) • *He spends his
time watching garbage on TV.*
rubbish • *He described her book as
absolute rubbish.*

travel VERB
to make a journey somewhere • *You
had better travel to Helsinki tomorrow.*
go • *We went to Rome.*
journey (FORMAL) • *He intended to
journey up the Amazon.*
make your way • *He made his way
home at last.*
take a trip • *We intend to take a trip
there sometime.*

MORE SYNONYMS:
• proceed
• voyage

treacherous ① ADJECTIVE
likely to betray someone • *He
denounced the party's treacherous
leaders.*
disloyal • *disloyal Cabinet colleagues*
faithless • *an oppressive father and
faithless husband*
unfaithful • *his unfaithful wife*
untrustworthy • *Jordan has tried to
brand his opponents as untrustworthy.*

MORE SYNONYMS:
• perfidious
• traitorous

ANTONYM:
• loyal

treacherous ② ADJECTIVE
dangerous or unreliable • *treacherous
mountain roads*
dangerous • *a dangerous stretch of
road*
hazardous • *hazardous seas*
perilous (LITERARY) • *The roads grew
even steeper and more perilous.*

A
B
C
D
E
F
G
H
I
J
K
L
M
N
O
P
Q
R
S
T
U
V
W
X
Y
Z

treasure VERB
to consider something very precious • *He treasures his friendship with her.*
cherish • *The previous owners had cherished the house.*
hold dear • *forced to renounce everything he held most dear*
prize • *one of the gallery's most prized possessions*
value • *if you value your health*

MORE SYNONYMS:
• revere
• venerate

treat ① VERB
to behave towards someone • *Artie treated most women with indifference.*
act towards • *the way you act towards other people*
behave towards • *He always behaved towards me with great kindness.*
deal with • *in dealing with suicidal youngsters*

treat ② VERB
to give someone medical care • *the doctor who treated her*
care for • *They hired a nurse to care for her.*
nurse • *All the years he was sick my mother had nursed him.*

trendy ADJECTIVE (INFORMAL)
fashionable • *a trendy night club*
fashionable • *a very fashionable place to go on holiday*
in (SLANG) • *what's in and what's not*
in fashion • *Calf-length skirts are in fashion this season.*
in vogue • *African art is in vogue at the moment.*
latest • *the latest thing in camera technology*
stylish • *This city has got a lot more stylish in recent years.*

tribute NOUN
something that shows admiration • *Police paid tribute to her courage.*
accolade (FORMAL) • *To play for your country is the ultimate accolade.*
compliment • *We consider it a compliment to be called "conservative".*
honour • *Only two writers are granted the honour of a solo display.*
praise • *That is high praise indeed.*
testimony • *a testimony to her dedication*

trick ① NOUN
something that deceives someone • *We are playing a trick on a man who keeps bothering me.*
con (INFORMAL) • *Slimming snacks that offer miraculous weight loss are a con.*
deception • *the victim of a cruel deception*
hoax • *a bomb hoax*
ploy • *a cynical marketing ploy*
ruse • *This was a ruse to divide them.*

MORE SYNONYMS:
• stratagem
• subterfuge

trick ② VERB
to deceive someone • *They tricked me into giving them all my money.*
con (INFORMAL) • *We have been conned for 20 years.*
deceive • *He deceived me into thinking the money was his.*
dupe • *I was duped into letting them in.*
fool • *They tried to fool you into coming after us.*
take in (INFORMAL) • *I wasn't taken in for a minute.*

MORE SYNONYMS:
• hoax
• hoodwink

tricky ADJECTIVE
difficult to do or to deal with • *This could be a very tricky problem.*

complex • *the whole complex issue of crime and punishment*

complicated • *a complicated operation*

delicate • *This brings us to the delicate question of his future.*

difficult • *It was a difficult decision to make.*

hard • *That's a hard question to answer.*

problematic • *It's a very problematic piece to play.*

puzzling • *a puzzling case to solve*

sensitive • *The death penalty is a very sensitive issue.*

trip ① NOUN

a journey to a place • *a business trip*

excursion • *a coach excursion to Trondheim*

jaunt • *a jaunt in the car*

journey • *the journey to Bordeaux*

outing • *a school outing*

voyage • *Columbus's voyage to the West Indies*

trip ② VERB

to fall over • *I tripped on the stairs.*

fall over • *Plenty of top skiers fell over.*

lose your footing • *He lost his footing and slid into the water.*

stumble • *He stumbled and almost fell.*

triumph ① NOUN

a great success • *The championships proved to be a personal triumph for the coach.*

success • *The jewellery was a great success.*

victory • *a victory for common sense*

MORE SYNONYMS:
• coup
• feather in your cap
• tour de force

ANTONYM:
• failure

triumph ② VERB

to be successful • *a symbol of good triumphing over evil*

come out on top (INFORMAL) • *The only way to come out on top is to adopt a different approach.*

prevail • *I do hope he will prevail over the rebels.*

succeed • *if they can succeed in America*

win • *The top four teams all won.*

ANTONYM:
• fail

trivial ADJECTIVE

not important • *She doesn't concern herself with such trivial details.*

insignificant • *The dangers are insignificant compared with those of smoking.*

minor • *a minor inconvenience*

negligible • *The strike will have a negligible impact.*

paltry • *They had no interest in paltry domestic concerns.*

petty • *I wouldn't indulge in such petty schoolboy pranks.*

slight • *It's only a slight problem.*

trifling • *The sums involved were trifling.*

unimportant • *Too much time is spent discussing unimportant matters.*

MORE SYNONYMS:
• frivolous
• inconsequential

ANTONYM:
• important

trouble ① NOUN

a difficulty or problem • *financial troubles*

bother • *Vince is having a spot of bother with the law.*

difficulty • *economic difficulties*

hassle (INFORMAL) • *We had loads of hassles trying to find somewhere to rehearse.*

a
b
c
d
e
f
g
h
i
j
k
l
m
n
o
p
q
r
s
t
u
v
w
x
y
z

A
B
C
D
E
F
G
H
I
J
K
L
M
N
O
P
Q
R
S
T
U
V
W
X
Y
Z

problem • *The main problem is unemployment.*

trouble ② VERB
to make someone feel worried • *He was troubled by the lifestyle of his son.*
agitate • *The thought agitates her.*
bother • *Is something bothering you?*
disturb • *dreams so vivid that they disturb me for days*
worry • *I didn't want to worry you.*

trouble ③ VERB
to cause someone inconvenience • *Can I trouble you for some milk?*
bother • *I don't know why he bothers me with this kind of rubbish.*
disturb • *a room where you won't be disturbed*
impose upon • *I was afraid you'd feel we were imposing on you.*
inconvenience • *He promised to be quick so as not to inconvenience them further.*
put out • *I've always put myself out for others.*

true ① ADJECTIVE
not invented • *The film is based on a true story.*
accurate • *an accurate assessment of the situation*
correct • *a correct diagnosis*
factual • *any comparison that is not strictly factual*

ANTONYM:
• inaccurate

true ② ADJECTIVE
real or genuine • *She was a true friend.*
authentic • *authentic Italian food*
bona fide • *We are happy to donate to bona fide charities.*
genuine • *There was a risk of genuine refugees being returned to Vietnam.*
real • *No, it wasn't a dream. It was real.*

ANTONYM:
• false

trust VERB
to believe that someone will do something • *The president can't be trusted.*
count on • *I can always count on you to cheer me up.*
depend on • *You can depend on me.*
have confidence in • *We have the utmost confidence in your abilities.*
have faith in • *I have no faith in him any more.*
place your trust in • *I would never place my trust in one so young.*
rely upon • *I know I can rely on you to sort it out.*

trusty ADJECTIVE
considered to be reliable • *a trusty member of the crew*
dependable • *a dependable and steady worker*
faithful • *his faithful black Labrador*
firm • *Betty became a firm friend of the family.*
reliable • *the problem of finding reliable staff*
solid • *one of my most solid supporters*
staunch • *He proved himself a staunch ally.*
true • *a true friend*
trustworthy • *trying to find a trustworthy adviser*

truth NOUN
the facts about something • *Marcel is keen to get to the truth of what happened.*
fact • *How much was fact and how much fancy no one knew.*
reality • *Fiction and reality were increasingly blurred.*

RELATED WORDS:
• ADJECTIVES veritable, veracious

try ① VERB
to make an effort to do something
• I tried hard to persuade him to stay.
attempt • They are accused of
attempting to murder British soldiers.
endeavour (FORMAL) • I will
endeavour to arrange it.
make an attempt • He made three
attempts to break the record.
make an effort • He made no effort to
hide his disappointment.
seek • We have never sought to impose
our views.
strive • The school strives to treat pupils
as individuals.

try ② VERB
to test the quality of something
• Howard wanted me to try the wine.
check out • We went to the club to
check it out.
sample • We sampled a selection of
different bottled waters.
test • The drug was tested on rats.
try out • London Transport hopes to
try out the system in September.

try ③ NOUN
an attempt to do something • After
a few tries he pressed the right button.
attempt • a deliberate attempt to
destabilize the defence
effort • his efforts to improve
endeavour (FORMAL) • His first
endeavours in the field were wedding films.
go (INFORMAL) • She won on her first go.
shot (INFORMAL) • I have had a shot at
professional cricket.

tubby ADJECTIVE
rather fat • He's a bit on the tubby side.
chubby • She was very chubby as a
child.
fat • He was short and fat.
overweight • Being overweight is bad
for your health.
plump • a plump, good-natured little

woman
podgy • Eddie is a little podgy round the
middle.
portly • a portly gentleman
stout • His wife was a small, stout lady.

tug ① VERB
to give something a quick, hard pull
• A little boy tugged at her skirt excitedly.
drag • He grabbed my ankle and dragged
me back.
draw • She took his hand and drew him
along.
haul • I gripped his wrist and hauled
him up.
heave • They heaved the last bag into
the van.
jerk • He jerked his hand out of mine
angrily.
pluck • The beggar plucked at her sleeve
as she passed.
pull • She pulled down the hem of her
skirt over her knees.
wrench • The horse wrenched its head
free.
yank • He grabbed my arm and yanked
me out of the car.

tug ② NOUN
a quick, hard pull • He felt a tug at his
arm.
heave • With a mighty heave, she pulled
herself away from him.
jerk • He gave a sudden jerk of the reins.
pull • Give the cord three sharp pulls.
wrench • He lowered the flag with a
quick wrench.
yank • He gave the phone a savage yank.

tune NOUN
a series of musical notes • She was
humming a merry little tune.
melody • a beautiful melody
strains • She could hear the tinny strains
of a chamber orchestra.

a
b
c
d
e
f
g
h
i
j
k
l
m
n
o
p
q
r
s
t
u
v
w
x
y
z

MORE SYNONYMS:
• air
• theme

turn ① VERB

to change the direction or position of something • *She had turned the bedside chair to face the door.*

rotate • *Take each foot in both your hands and rotate it.*

spin • *He spun the wheel sharply and made a U-turn.*

swivel • *She swivelled her chair round.*

twirl • *Bonnie twirled her empty glass in her fingers.*

twist • *She twisted her head sideways.*

turn ② VERB

to become or make something different • *A hobby can be turned into a career.*

change • *She has now changed into a happy, self-confident woman.*

convert • *a table that converts into an ironing board*

mutate • *Overnight, the gossip begins to mutate into headlines.*

transform • *the speed at which your body transforms food into energy*

MORE SYNONYMS:
• metamorphose
• transfigure
• transmute

turn ③ NOUN

someone's right or duty to do something • *Tonight it's my turn to cook.*

chance • *All eligible people would get a chance to vote.*

go • *Whose go is it?*

opportunity • *Now is your opportunity to say what you've always wanted.*

twist ① VERB

to turn something round • *Her hands began to twist the handles of the bag.*

bend • *Bend the bar into a horseshoe.*

curl • *She sat with her legs curled under her.*

twine • *He had twined his chubby arms around Vincent's neck.*

weave • *He weaves his way through a crowd.*

wring • *after wringing the chicken's neck*

MORE SYNONYMS:
• entwine
• wreathe

twist ② VERB

to bend into a new shape • *The car was left a mess of twisted metal.*

distort • *A painter may exaggerate or distort shapes and forms.*

mangle • *the mangled wreckage*

screw up • *Amy screwed up her face.*

MORE SYNONYMS:
• contort
• warp

twist ③ VERB

to injure a part of your body • *I've twisted my ankle.*

sprain • *He fell and sprained his wrist.*

wrench • *He had wrenched his back badly from the force of the fall.*

MORE SYNONYMS:
• rick
• turn

two-faced ADJECTIVE

not honest in dealing with other people • *a two-faced, manipulative woman*

deceitful • *a deceitful, conniving liar*

dishonest • *He's been dishonest in his dealings with us both.*

disloyal • *I can't stand people who are disloyal.*

false • *He had been betrayed by his false friends.*

hypocritical • *a hypocritical and*

ambitious careerist
insincere • *They are still widely seen as insincere and untrustworthy.*
treacherous • *He has been consistently treacherous to both sides.*

type NOUN

a group of things that have features in common • *There are various types of dog suitable as pets.*
brand • *his favourite brand of whisky*
breed • *a rare breed of cattle*
class • *a better class of restaurant*
group • *Weather forecasters classify clouds into several different groups.*
kind • *I don't like that kind of film.*
make • *He'll only drive a certain make of car.*
sort • *a dozen trees of various sorts*
species • *a rare species of moth*
style • *Several styles of hat were available.*
variety • *Many varieties of birds live here.*

typical ADJECTIVE

having the usual characteristics of something • *a typical American child*
average • *The average adult man burns 1500 to 2000 calories per day.*
characteristic • *a characteristic feature of the landscape*
normal • *a normal day*
regular • *He describes himself as just a regular guy.*
representative • *fairly representative groups of adults*
standard • *It was standard practice in cases like this.*
stock • *He had a stock answer for all problems.*
usual • *a neighbourhood beset by all the usual inner-city problems*

MORE SYNONYMS:
• archetypal
• archetypical
• stereotypical

ANTONYM:
• uncharacteristic

a
b
c
d
e
f
g
h
i
j
k
l
m
n
o
p
q
r
s
t
u
v
w
x
y
z

Uu

ugly ADJECTIVE
having a very unattractive
appearance • *She makes me feel dowdy
and ugly.*
plain • *a shy, plain girl with a pale
complexion*
unattractive • *painted in an
unattractive shade of green*
unsightly • *The view was spoiled by
some unsightly houses.*

MORE SYNONYMS:
• unlovely
• unprepossessing

ANTONYM:
• beautiful

ultimate ① ADJECTIVE
being the final one of a series • *It
is not possible to predict the ultimate
outcome.*
eventual • *Reunification is the
eventual aim.*
final • *the fifth and final day*
last • *This is his last chance to do
something useful.*

ultimate ② ADJECTIVE
the most important or powerful
• *the ultimate goal of any player*
greatest • *Our greatest aim was to
take the gold medal.*
paramount • *His paramount ambition
was to be an actor.*
supreme • *the supreme test of his
abilities*
utmost • *This has to be our utmost
priority.*

ultimate ③ NOUN
the finest example of something
• *This hotel is the ultimate in luxury.*
epitome • *She was the epitome of the
successful businesswoman.*
extreme • *This was shyness taken to
the extreme.*
height • *the height of bad manners*
peak • *roses at the peak of perfection*

unaware ADJECTIVE
not knowing about something
• *Many people are unaware of how much
they eat.*
ignorant • *They are completely
ignorant of the relevant facts.*
oblivious • *John appeared oblivious to
his surroundings.*
unconscious • *totally unconscious of
my presence*
unsuspecting • *The cars were then
sold to unsuspecting buyers.*

ANTONYM:
• aware

unbearable ADJECTIVE
too unpleasant to be tolerated
• *Life was unbearable for the remaining
citizens.*
intolerable • *The heat and humidity
were intolerable.*
oppressive • *An oppressive sadness
weighed upon him.*
unacceptable • *She left her husband
because of his unacceptable behaviour.*

MORE SYNONYMS:
• insufferable
• unendurable

ANTONYM:
• tolerable

unbelievable ① ADJECTIVE
extremely great or surprising • *He showed unbelievable courage.*
colossal • *There has been a colossal waste of public money.*
incredible • *You're always an incredible help on these occasions.*
stupendous • *It cost a stupendous amount of money.*

unbelievable ② ADJECTIVE
so unlikely it cannot be believed • *He came up with some unbelievable story.*
implausible • *a film with an implausible ending*
improbable • *highly improbable claims*
inconceivable • *It was inconceivable that he'd hurt anyone.*
incredible • *It seems incredible that anyone would want to do that.*
preposterous • *The whole idea was preposterous.*
unconvincing • *In response he was given the usual unconvincing excuses.*

ANTONYM:
• believable

uncertain ① ADJECTIVE
not knowing what to do • *For a moment he looked uncertain as to how to respond.*
doubtful • *He was a bit doubtful about starting without her.*
dubious • *We were a bit dubious about it at first.*
unclear • *I'm unclear about where to go.*
undecided • *Even then she was still undecided about her future plans.*

MORE SYNONYMS:
• irresolute
• vacillating

ANTONYM:
• certain

uncertain ② ADJECTIVE
not definite • *facing an uncertain future*
ambiguous • *The wording of the contract was ambiguous.*
doubtful • *The outcome of the match is still doubtful.*
indefinite • *suspended for an indefinite period*
indeterminate • *a woman of indeterminate age*

MORE SYNONYMS:
• conjectural
• undetermined

ANTONYM:
• certain

unclear ADJECTIVE
confusing and not obvious • *It is unclear how much popular support they have.*
ambiguous • *in order to clarify the earlier ambiguous statement*
confused • *The situation remains confused, as no clear victor has emerged.*
vague • *The description was pretty vague.*

ANTONYM:
• clear

uncomfortable ① ADJECTIVE
feeling or causing discomfort • *an uncomfortable bed*
awkward • *Its shape made it awkward to carry.*
cramped • *living in very cramped conditions*
disagreeable • *designed to make flying a less disagreeable experience*
ill-fitting • *Walking was difficult*

a
b
c
d
e
f
g
h
i
j
k
l
m
n
o
p
q
r
s
t
u
v
w
x
y
z

A
B
C
D
E
F
G
H
I
J
K
L
M
N
O
P
Q
R
S
T
U
V
W
X
Y
Z

because of her ill-fitting shoes.
painful • *a painful back injury*

ANTONYM:
• comfortable

uncomfortable ② ADJECTIVE
not relaxed or confident • *Talking about money made her uncomfortable.*
awkward • *Offstage, he is bashful and awkward.*
embarrassed • *an embarrassed silence*
ill at ease • *I always feel ill at ease in their company.*
self-conscious • *She was always self-conscious about her height.*
uneasy • *He looked uneasy and refused to answer any more questions.*

ANTONYM:
• comfortable

uncommon ① ADJECTIVE
not happening or seen often • *This type of cancer is uncommon among young women.*
exceptional • *These are exceptional circumstances.*
extraordinary • *an act of extraordinary generosity*
few • *Genuine friends are few.*
infrequent • *one of the infrequent visitors to the island*
out of the ordinary • *My story is nothing out of the ordinary.*
scarce • *places where jobs are scarce*
sparse • *Traffic is sparse on this stretch of road.*
rare • *a rare occurrence*
unusual • *an unusual sight these days*

ANOTHER SYNONYM:
• unprecedented

ANTONYM:
• common

uncommon ② ADJECTIVE
unusually great • *She had read Cecilia's*

last letter with uncommon interest.
acute • *He has an acute dislike of children.*
exceptional • *a woman of exceptional beauty*
extraordinary • *a young player of extraordinary energy*
extreme • *regions suffering from extreme poverty*
great • *They share a great love of Bach's music.*
intense • *intense heat*
remarkable • *a musician of remarkable talent*

ANOTHER SYNONYM:
• unparalleled

unconscious ① ADJECTIVE
in a state similar to sleep • *By the time the ambulance arrived, he was unconscious.*
asleep • *They were fast asleep in their beds.*
senseless • *He was beaten senseless and robbed of all his money.*
stunned • *stunned by a blow to the head*

MORE SYNONYMS:
• comatose
• insensible

ANTONYM:
• conscious

unconscious ② ADJECTIVE
not aware of what is happening • *quite unconscious of their presence*
oblivious • *He seemed oblivious of his surroundings.*
unaware • *He was unaware of the chaos he was causing.*
unknowing • *unknowing accomplices in his crimes*
unsuspecting • *She was an unsuspecting victim of his deceit.*

a
b
c
d
e
f
g
h
i
j
k
l
m
n
o
p
q
r
s
t
u
v
w
x
y
z

ANTONYM:
• aware

uncover ① VERB
to find something out • *Auditors said they had uncovered evidence of fraud.*
bring to light • *The truth is unlikely to be brought to light.*
expose • *His lies were exposed in court.*
reveal • *He will reveal the truth behind the scandal.*
show up • *His true character has been shown up for what it is.*
unearth • *a campaign to unearth supposed conspiracies*

uncover ② VERB
to remove the lid or cover from something • *When the seedlings sprout, uncover the tray.*
expose • *The wreck was exposed by the action of the tide.*
lay bare • *Layers of paint and flaking plaster were laid bare.*
open • *I opened a new jar of coffee.*
reveal • *His shirt was open, revealing a tattooed chest.*
unearth • *Quarry workers have unearthed the skeleton of a mammoth.*
unveil • *The statue will be unveiled next week.*
unwrap • *unwrapping Christmas presents*

under PREPOSITION
at a lower level than something • *a labyrinth of tunnels under the ground*
below • *The sun had already sunk below the horizon.*
beneath • *the frozen grass crunching beneath his feet*
underneath • *people trapped underneath the wreckage*

ANTONYM:
• above

undergo VERB
to have something happen to you • *He had to undergo major surgery.*
be subjected to • *She was subjected to constant interruptions.*
endure • *The company endured heavy losses.*
experience • *They seem to experience more distress than the others.*
go through • *I wouldn't like to go through that again.*
suffer • *The peace process had suffered a serious setback.*

undermine VERB
to make something less secure or strong • *You're trying to undermine my confidence again.*
impair • *Their actions will impair France's national interests.*
sap • *I was afraid the illness had sapped my strength.*
subvert • *an attempt to subvert their culture from within*
weaken • *Her authority had been fatally weakened.*

ANTONYM:
• strengthen

understand ① VERB
to know what someone means • *Do you understand what I'm saying?*
catch on (INFORMAL) • *I didn't catch on immediately to what he meant.*
comprehend • *Whenever she failed to comprehend, she just laughed.*
follow • *I don't follow you at all.*
get • *Did you get that joke?*
grasp • *He instantly grasped that they were talking about him.*
see • *"I see," she said at last.*
take in • *too much to take in at once*

understand ② VERB

to know why or how something is happening • *too young to understand what was going on*

appreciate • *You must appreciate how important this is.*

comprehend • *I just cannot comprehend your viewpoint.*

fathom • *His attitude was hard to fathom.*

grasp • *We immediately grasped the seriousness of the crisis.*

realize • *People just don't realize how serious it could be.*

MORE SYNONYMS:
• conceive
• discern

understand ③ VERB

to hear of something • *I understand she hasn't been well.*

believe • *She's coming back tomorrow, I believe.*

gather • *We gather the report is critical of the judge.*

hear • *I hear you've been having some problems.*

learn • *On learning who he was, I wanted to meet him.*

understanding ① NOUN

a knowledge of something • *a basic understanding of computers*

appreciation • *some appreciation of the problems of consumers*

comprehension • *completely beyond our comprehension*

grasp • *a good grasp of foreign languages*

knowledge • *I have no knowledge of his business affairs.*

perception • *Her questions showed a shrewd perception.*

understanding ② NOUN

an informal agreement • *There was an understanding between us.*

accord • *trying to reach an accord*

agreement • *A new defence agreement was signed last month.*

pact • *an electoral pact between the parties*

understanding ③ ADJECTIVE

having a sympathetic nature • *Fortunately he had an understanding wife.*

compassionate • *a deeply compassionate man*

considerate • *They should be more considerate towards the prisoners.*

sensitive • *He was always sensitive and caring.*

sympathetic • *a sympathetic listener*

undertaking NOUN

a task which you have agreed to do • *Organizing the show has been a massive undertaking.*

affair • *It's going to be a tricky affair to arrange.*

business • *Livestock farming is an arduous and difficult business.*

endeavour • *an endeavour that was bound to end in failure*

enterprise • *a risky enterprise such as horse breeding*

job • *What made you decide to take this job on?*

operation • *the man in charge of the entire operation*

project • *I can't take responsibility for such a huge project.*

task • *a task I do not feel equipped to take on*

venture • *a venture that few were willing to invest in*

uneasy ADJECTIVE

worried that something may be wrong • *I was very uneasy about these developments.*

agitated • *She seemed agitated about something.*

anxious • *He admitted he was still anxious about the situation.*
nervous • *Consumers say they are nervous about their jobs.*
perturbed • *I am not too perturbed at this setback.*
worried • *If you're worried about it, just ask for more details.*

MORE SYNONYMS:
• apprehensive
• discomposed
• restive

ANTONYM:
• comfortable

unemployed ADJECTIVE
not having a job • *an unemployed mechanic*
idle • *He has been idle for almost a month.*
jobless • *One in four people are now jobless.*
redundant • *aid for the 30,000 redundant miners*

ANTONYM:
• employed

uneven ① ADJECTIVE
having an unlevel or rough surface • *I tripped and fell on an uneven pavement.*
bumpy • *bumpy cobbled streets*
not level • *It was hard to walk because the road was not level.*
not smooth • *The icing isn't smooth enough.*
rough • *She picked her way across the rough ground.*

ANTONYM:
• level

uneven ② ADJECTIVE
not the same or consistent • *six lines of uneven length*
fluctuating • *a fluctuating temperature*
inconsistent • *Their performance was inconsistent over the whole season.*
irregular • *at irregular intervals*
patchy • *Her career has been patchy.*
variable • *The potassium content of food is very variable.*

ANTONYM:
• even

unexpected ADJECTIVE
not considered likely to happen • *His death was completely unexpected.*
astonishing • *What an astonishing piece of good luck!*
chance • *a chance meeting*
surprising • *a most surprising turn of events*
unforeseen • *The show was cancelled due to unforeseen circumstances.*

MORE SYNONYMS:
• fortuitous
• unanticipated

unfair ADJECTIVE
without right or justice • *It was unfair that he should suffer so much.*
unjust • *an unjust decision*
wrong • *It would be wrong to allow the case to go any further.*
wrongful • *his claim for wrongful dismissal*

MORE SYNONYMS:
• inequitable
• iniquitous

ANTONYM:
• fair

unfaithful ADJECTIVE
not being faithful to your partner • *He was unfaithful to her for years.*
adulterous • *an adulterous relationship*
two-timing (INFORMAL) • *She called him a two-timing rat.*

ANTONYM:
• faithful

unfamiliar ADJECTIVE
not having been seen or heard of before • *She grew many plants which were unfamiliar to me.*
alien • *transplanted into an alien culture*
exotic • *filmed in an exotic location*
foreign • *This was a foreign country, so unlike his own.*
new • *This was a new experience for me.*
novel • *having to cope with many novel situations*
strange • *All these faces were strange to me.*
unknown • *I'd discovered a writer quite unknown to me.*

unfriendly ADJECTIVE
not showing any warmth or kindness • *He can expect an unfriendly welcome.*
aloof • *His manner was aloof.*
antagonistic • *They were always antagonistic to newcomers.*
cold • *She was a cold, unfeeling woman.*
disagreeable • *He may be clever but he's most disagreeable.*
hostile • *The prisoner eyed him in hostile silence.*
unkind • *They're always unkind to newcomers.*

MORE SYNONYMS:
• ill-disposed
• uncongenial

ANTONYM:
• friendly

ungrateful ADJECTIVE
not appreciating the things you have • *the most miserable and ungrateful people on earth*
unappreciative • *He was unappreciative of our efforts.*

unthankful • *mercenary players and unthankful supporters*

ANTONYM:
• grateful

unhappy ADJECTIVE
feeling sad or depressed • *He was a shy, sometimes unhappy man.*
depressed • *She's depressed about this whole situation.*
despondent • *After the interview John was despondent.*
down • *They felt really down after they spoke to him.*
miserable • *My job made me really miserable sometimes.*
sad • *I felt sad to leave our little house.*

MORE SYNONYMS:
• crestfallen
• disconsolate
• sorrowful

ANTONYM:
• happy

unhealthy ① ADJECTIVE
likely to cause illness • *an unhealthy lifestyle*
bad for you • *the argument that eating meat is bad for you*
harmful • *Try to avoid harmful habits like smoking.*
insanitary • *the insanitary conditions of slums*
noxious • *factories belching out noxious fumes*
unwholesome • *an epidemic originating from the unwholesome food they ate*

ANTONYM:
• healthy

unhealthy ② ADJECTIVE
not well • *an unhealthy looking man with a bad complexion*
ailing • *The President is said to be ailing.*

crook (Australian and New Zealand; informal) • *I'm sorry to hear you've been crook, mate.*

ill • *He didn't look at all ill when I last saw him.*

not well • *When I'm not well, she looks after me.*

poorly (British; informal) • *She's still poorly after that bout of pneumonia.*

sick • *He's very sick and he needs treatment.*

unwell • *an infection which could make you very unwell*

ANTONYM:
• healthy

unimportant ADJECTIVE
having little significance or importance • *The difference in their ages seemed unimportant at the time.*

insignificant • *In 1949, Bonn was a small, insignificant city.*

minor • *a minor inconvenience*

paltry • *They had little interest in paltry domestic concerns.*

slight • *We have a slight problem.*

trivial • *She waved aside the trivial details.*

ANTONYM:
• important

uninterested ADJECTIVE
not interested in something • *I'm completely uninterested in anything you have to say.*

apathetic • *apathetic about politics*

bored • *She looked bored with the whole performance.*

impassive • *He remained impassive while she ranted on.*

indifferent • *He is totally indifferent to our problems.*

nonchalant • *"Suit yourself," I said, trying to sound nonchalant.*

passive • *That passive attitude of his drives me mad.*

unconcerned • *She is unconcerned about anything except herself.*

ANTONYM:
• interested

union ① NOUN
an organization of people or groups with mutual interests • *a trades union*

association • *a member of several different associations*

coalition • *governed by a coalition of three parties*

confederation • *a confederation of mini-states*

federation • *a federation of six separate agencies*

league • *the League of Nations*

union ② NOUN
the joining together of two or more things • *The majority voted for union with Russia.*

amalgamation • *an amalgamation of two organizations*

blend • *a blend of traditional charm and modern amenities*

combination • *the combination of science and art*

fusion • *fusions of jazz and pop*

mixture • *a mixture of nuts, raisins, and capers*

MORE SYNONYMS:
• amalgam
• conjunction
• synthesis

unite VERB
to join together and act as a group • *We must unite to fight our common enemy.*

collaborate • *They all collaborated on the project.*

combine • *The companies have combined to form a multinational.*

join • *People of all kinds joined to make a dignified protest.*

a
b
c
d
e
f
g
h
i
j
k
l
m
n
o
p
q
r
s
t
u
v
w
x
y
z

join forces • *The two parties are joining forces.*

link up • *the first time the two armies have linked up*

merge • *The media group hopes to merge with its rival company.*

pull together • *The staff and management are pulling together to save the company.*

work together • *industry and government working together*

ANTONYM:
• divide

universal ADJECTIVE

relating to everyone or to the whole universe • *These programmes have a universal appeal.*

common • *The common view is that it is a good thing.*

general • *This project should raise general awareness about the problem.*

unlimited • *destruction on an unlimited scale*

widespread • *Food shortages are widespread.*

worldwide • *the fear of a worldwide epidemic*

MORE SYNONYMS:
• catholic
• omnipresent
• overarching

unkind ADJECTIVE

lacking in kindness and consideration • *It's very unkind to describe her in those terms.*

cruel • *Children can be so cruel.*

malicious • *spreading malicious gossip*

mean • *I'd feel mean saying no.*

nasty • *What nasty little snobs you are!*

spiteful • *How can you say such spiteful things about us?*

thoughtless • *a small minority of thoughtless and inconsiderate people*

ANTONYM:
• kind

unknown ADJECTIVE

not familiar or famous • *He was an unknown writer at that time.*

humble • *He started out as a humble fisherman.*

obscure • *an obscure Greek composer*

unfamiliar • *There were several unfamiliar names on the list.*

unsung • *among the unsung heroes of our time*

ANTONYM:
• famous

unlike PREPOSITION

different from • *She was unlike him in every way.*

different from • *I've always felt different from most people.*

dissimilar to • *a cultural background not dissimilar to our own*

distinct from • *Their cuisines are quite distinct from each other.*

divergent from (FORMAL) • *That viewpoint is not much divergent from that of his predecessor.*

far from • *His politics are not all that far from mine.*

ANTONYM:
• like

unlikely ADJECTIVE

probably not true or likely to happen • *a military coup seems unlikely*

implausible • *a film with an implausible ending*

incredible • *an incredible pack of lies*

unbelievable • *I know it sounds unbelievable, but I wasn't there that day.*

unconvincing • *He came up with a very unconvincing excuse.*

ANTONYM:
• likely

unlucky ADJECTIVE
having bad luck • *He was unlucky not to score during the first half.*
cursed • *the most cursed family in history*
hapless • *a hapless victim of chance*
luckless • *the luckless parents of a difficult child*
unfortunate • *Some unfortunate person nearby could be injured.*
wretched • *wretched people who had to sell or starve*

ANTONYM:
• lucky

unnecessary ADJECTIVE
completely needless • *He frowns upon unnecessary expense.*
needless • *causing needless panic*
pointless • *pointless meetings*
uncalled-for • *uncalled-for rudeness*

ANTONYM:
• necessary

unpleasant ① ADJECTIVE
causing feelings of discomfort or dislike • *It has a very unpleasant smell.*
bad • *I have some bad news.*
disagreeable • *a disagreeable experience*
distasteful • *I find her gossip distasteful.*
nasty • *This divorce could turn nasty.*
repulsive • *repulsive fat white slugs*
unpalatable • *Only then did I learn the unpalatable truth.*

ANTONYM:
• pleasant

unpleasant ② ADJECTIVE
rude or unfriendly • *a thoroughly unpleasant person*
disagreeable • *He may be clever, but he's a very disagreeable man.*
horrid • *I must have been a horrid little girl.*

objectionable • *His tone was highly objectionable.*
obnoxious • *Clarissa's obnoxious brother James*
rude • *He was frequently rude to waiters and servants.*
unfriendly • *spoken in a rather unfriendly voice*

ANTONYM:
• pleasant

unpopular ADJECTIVE
disliked by most people • *an unpopular idea*
detested • *The rebels toppled the detested dictator.*
disliked • *one of the most disliked choices on offer*
shunned • *the shunned former minister*
undesirable • *all sorts of undesirable effects on health*

ANTONYM:
• popular

unpredictable ADJECTIVE
unable to be foreseen • *Britain's notoriously unpredictable weather*
chance • *A chance meeting can change your life.*
doubtful • *The outcome remains doubtful.*
hit and miss (INFORMAL) • *Farming can be a very hit and miss affair.*
unforeseeable • *unforeseeable weather conditions*

ANTONYM:
• predictable

unsatisfactory ADJECTIVE
not good enough • *His work was judged unsatisfactory.*
disappointing • *The results were disappointing.*
inadequate • *The problem goes far beyond inadequate staffing.*

A
B
C
D
E
F
G
H
I
J
K
L
M
N
O
P
Q
R
S
T
U
V
W
X
Y
Z

mediocre • *a mediocre string of performances*

poor • *Her school record was poor at first.*

unacceptable • *The quality of his work was unacceptable.*

ANTONYM:
• satisfactory

unsteady ADJECTIVE

not held or fixed securely and likely to fall over • *a slightly unsteady item of furniture*

precarious • *The beds are precarious-looking hammocks strung from the walls.*

rickety • *She stood on a rickety old table.*

shaky • *He climbed up the shaky ladder to the scaffold.*

tottering • *a tottering pile of bricks*

unsafe • *That bridge looks decidedly unsafe to me.*

unstable • *funds used to demolish dangerously unstable buildings*

wobbly • *cat-scratched upholstery and wobbly chairs*

ANTONYM:
• steady

unsuitable ADJECTIVE

not appropriate for a purpose • *Her shoes were unsuitable for walking any distance.*

improper • *an improper diet*

inappropriate • *inappropriate use of the internet*

unacceptable • *using completely unacceptable language*

unfit • *unfit for human habitation*

MORE SYNONYMS:
• inapposite
• unseemly

ANTONYM:
• suitable

untidy ADJECTIVE

not neatly arranged • *The place quickly became untidy.*

bedraggled • *My hair was a bedraggled mess.*

chaotic • *the chaotic mess of papers on his desk*

cluttered • *There was no space on the cluttered worktop.*

jumbled • *We moved our supplies into a jumbled heap.*

messy • *She was a good, if messy, cook.*

unkempt • *the unkempt grass in front of the house*

MORE SYNONYMS:
• disordered
• shambolic

ANTONYM:
• tidy

untrue ADJECTIVE

not true • *The allegations were completely untrue.*

erroneous • *an erroneous description*

false • *He gave a false name and address.*

fictitious • *the source of the fictitious rumours*

inaccurate • *the passing on of inaccurate or misleading information*

incorrect • *an incorrect account of the sequence of events*

misleading • *It would be misleading to say we were friends.*

mistaken • *I had a mistaken idea of what had happened.*

ANTONYM:
• true

unusual ADJECTIVE

not occurring very often • *many rare and unusual plants*

curious • *a curious mixture of ancient and modern*

exceptional • *exceptional circumstances*

extraordinary • *What an extraordinary thing to happen!*
rare • *one of the rarest species in the world*
uncommon • *It's a very uncommon surname.*
unconventional • *produced by an unconventional technique*

MORE SYNONYMS:
• atypical
• unwonted

ANTONYM:
• common

unwell ADJECTIVE
ill or sick • *He felt unwell and had to go home early.*
ailing • *The President is said to be ailing.*
crook (AUSTRALIAN AND NEW ZEALAND; INFORMAL) • *I'm sorry to hear you've been crook, mate.*
ill • *Payne was seriously ill with pneumonia.*
poorly (BRITISH; INFORMAL) • *Julie is still poorly after her bout of flu.*
queasy • *I always feel queasy on boats.*
sick • *He's very sick and he needs treatment.*

MORE SYNONYMS:
• indisposed
• under the weather

ANTONYM:
• well

unwilling ADJECTIVE
not wanting to do something • *an unwilling participant in school politics*
averse • *I'm not averse to going along with the suggestion.*
grudging • *a grudging acceptance of the situation*
loath • *She is loath to give up her hard-earned liberty.*
reluctant • *They were reluctant to get involved at first.*

ANTONYM:
• willing

unwise ADJECTIVE
foolish or not sensible • *It would be unwise to expect too much of her.*
daft • *You'd be daft to get on the wrong side of him.*
foolish • *It was foolish to risk injury like that.*
idiotic • *What an idiotic thing to do!*
irresponsible • *irresponsible plans for tax cuts*
rash • *Don't panic or do anything rash.*
senseless • *It would be senseless to try and stop him now.*
silly • *You're not going to go and do something silly, are you?*
stupid • *I've had enough of your stupid suggestions.*

MORE SYNONYMS:
• imprudent
• injudicious

ANTONYM:
• wise

upkeep NOUN
the process and cost of maintaining something • *The money will be used for the upkeep of the grounds.*
keep • *He does not contribute towards his keep.*
maintenance • *the regular maintenance of government buildings*
overheads • *We must cut our overheads or we shall have to close.*
preservation • *the preservation of historical sites*
running • *The running of the house took up all her time.*

upset ① ADJECTIVE
feeling unhappy about something • *She was very upset when she heard the news.*

agitated • *in an excited and agitated state*
distressed • *The animals were distressed by the noise.*
frantic • *frantic with worry*
hurt • *I was very hurt when they refused.*
troubled • *He sounded deeply troubled.*
unhappy • *The divorce made him very unhappy.*

upset ② VERB
to make someone worried or unhappy • *The whole incident upset me terribly.*
agitate • *The thought agitates her.*
bother • *Don't let his manner bother you.*
distress • *The whole thing really distressed him.*
disturb • *These dreams disturb me for days afterwards.*
grieve • *deeply grieved by their suffering*
ruffle • *She doesn't get ruffled by anything.*

MORE SYNONYMS:
• discompose
• faze
• perturb

upset ③ VERB
to turn something over accidentally • *Don't upset that pile of papers.*
capsize • *He capsized the boat through his carelessness.*
knock over • *The kitten knocked over the vase.*
overturn • *She overturned her glass of wine as she stood up.*
spill • *The waiter spilled the drinks all over the table.*

urge ① NOUN
a strong wish to do something • *stifling the urge to scream*

compulsion • *a compulsion to write*
desire • *I had a strong desire to help and care for people.*
drive • *a demonic drive to succeed*
impulse • *Peter resisted an impulse to smile.*
longing • *his longing to return home*
wish • *She had a genuine wish to make amends.*

urge ② VERB
to try hard to persuade someone • *He urged the government to change the law.*
beg • *I begged him to leave me alone.*
beseech • *Her eyes beseeched him to show mercy.*
implore • *He left early, although they implored him to stay.*
plead • *kneeling on the floor pleading for mercy*
press • *The unions are pressing him to stand firm.*

MORE SYNONYMS:
• entreat
• exhort
• solicit

urgent ADJECTIVE
needing to be dealt with quickly • *an urgent need for food and water*
compelling • *There are compelling reasons to act swiftly.*
immediate • *The immediate problem is transportation.*
imperative • *It is imperative we end up with a win.*
pressing • *one of our most pressing problems*

use ① VERB
to perform a task with something • *Use a sharp knife to trim the edges.*
apply • *The company applies this technology to solve practical problems.*

employ • *the methods employed in the study*
operate • *Can you operate a fax machine?*
utilize • *The body utilizes many different minerals.*

MORE SYNONYMS:
• avail oneself of
• ply

use ② NOUN
the act of using something • *the use of force*
application • *Her theory was put into practical application.*
employment • *the employment of completely new methods*
operation • *the operation of the computer mouse*
usage • *Parts of the motor wore out because of constant usage.*

use ③ NOUN
the purpose for which something is utilized • *of no practical use whatsoever*
end • *The police force was manipulated for political ends.*
object • *the object of the exercise*
point • *I don't see the point of a thing like that.*
purpose • *It is wrong to use it for military purposes.*

useful ADJECTIVE
something which helps or makes things easier • *a great deal of useful information*
beneficial • *It may be beneficial to study the relevant guidelines.*
effective • *Antibiotics are effective against this organism.*
helpful • *a number of helpful booklets*
practical • *practical suggestions for healthy eating*
valuable • *Here are a few valuable tips to help you to succeed.*

worthwhile • *a worthwhile source of income*

ANTONYM:
• useless

useless ADJECTIVE
not suitable or useful • *We realized that our money was useless here.*
futile • *It would be futile to make any further attempts.*
impractical • *A tripod is impractical when following animals on the move.*
unproductive • *increasingly unproductive land*
unsuitable • *This tool is completely unsuitable for use with metal.*
worthless • *The old skills are worthless now.*

MORE SYNONYMS:
• disadvantageous
• ineffectual
• unavailing

ANTONYM:
• useful

usual ADJECTIVE
done or happening most often • *sitting at his usual table*
accustomed • *She acted with her accustomed shrewdness.*
common • *the commonest cause of death*
customary • *It's customary to offer guests a drink.*
habitual • *He soon recovered his habitual geniality.*
normal • *That's quite normal for a Friday.*
regular • *samples from one of their regular suppliers*
standard • *It was standard practice to put them outside.*

utter ADJECTIVE
complete or total • *scenes of utter chaos*

a
b
c
d
e
f
g
h
i
j
k
l
m
n
o
p
q
r
s
t
u
v
w
x
y
z

absolute • *This is absolute madness!*
complete • *a complete mess*
consummate • *a consummate professional*
out-and-out • *an out-and-out lie*
outright • *an outright rejection of the deal*
perfect • *a perfect stranger*

pure • *She did it out of pure malice.*
sheer • *an act of sheer stupidity*
thorough • *She is a thorough snob.*
total • *a total failure*

MORE SYNONYMS:
• unconditional
• unmitigated
• unqualified

Vv

vague ADJECTIVE
not clearly expressed or clearly visible • *vague promises about raising standards*
hazy • *Many details remain hazy.*
indefinite • *at some indefinite time in the future*
indistinct • *The lettering was worn and indistinct.*
loose • *a loose translation*
uncertain • *Students are facing an uncertain future.*
unclear • *The proposals were sketchy and unclear.*

MORE SYNONYMS:
• ill-defined
• indeterminate
• nebulous

ANTONYM:
• definite

vain ① ADJECTIVE
very proud of your looks or qualities • *I think he is shallow and vain.*
conceited • *They had grown too conceited and pleased with themselves.*
egotistical • *an egotistical show-off*
ostentatious • *He was generous with his money without being ostentatious.*
proud • *She was said to be proud and arrogant.*
stuck-up (INFORMAL) • *She was a famous actress, but she wasn't a bit stuck-up.*

MORE SYNONYMS:
• narcissistic

• overweening
• swaggering

vain ② ADJECTIVE
not successful in achieving what was intended • *He made a vain effort to cheer her up.*
abortive • *the abortive coup attempt*
fruitless • *It was a fruitless search.*
futile • *their futile attempts to avoid publicity*
unproductive • *an unproductive strategy*
useless • *a useless punishment which fails to stop crime*

ANTONYM:
• successful

vain ③: **in vain** ADJECTIVE
unsuccessful in achieving what was intended • *Her complaints were in vain.*
fruitless • *Four years of negotiation were fruitless.*
to no avail • *His protests were to no avail.*
unsuccessful • *Previous attempts have been unsuccessful.*
wasted • *Their efforts were wasted.*

valley NOUN

◆ **TYPES OF VALLEY**
◆ canyon
◆ chasm
◆ coomb
◆ cwm (WELSH)
◆ dale
◆ defile

- dell
- depression
- dingle
- glen
- gorge
- gulch
- gully
- hollow
- ravine
- strath (Scottish)
- vale

valuable ① ADJECTIVE
having great importance or usefulness • *The experience was very valuable.*
beneficial • *Using computers has a beneficial effect on learning.*
helpful • *a number of helpful booklets*
important • *Her sons are the most important thing in her life.*
prized • *one of the gallery's most prized possessions*
useful • *a mine of useful information*
worthwhile • *a worthwhile source of income*

MORE SYNONYMS:
- cherished
- esteemed
- treasured

ANTONYM:
- useless

valuable ② ADJECTIVE
worth a lot of money • *valuable old books*
costly • *a small and costly bottle of scent*
expensive • *exclusive, expensive possessions*
precious • *rings set with precious jewels*

ANTONYM:
- worthless

valuables PLURAL NOUN
the things you own that cost a lot
of money • *Leave your valuables in the hotel safe.*
heirlooms • *family heirlooms*
treasures • *The house was full of art treasures.*

value ① NOUN
the importance or usefulness of something • *Studies are needed to see if these therapies have any value.*
advantage • *the great advantage of this method*
benefit • *They see no benefit in educating these children.*
effectiveness • *the effectiveness of the new system*
importance • *They have always placed great importance on live performances.*
merit • *the artistic merit of their work*
use • *This is of no use to anyone.*
usefulness • *the usefulness of the internet in disseminating new ideas*
virtue • *the great virtue of modern technology*
worth • *This system has already proved its worth.*

value ② NOUN
the amount of money that something is worth • *The value of his house has risen by more than 100%.*
cost • *the cost of a loaf of bread*
market price • *buying shares at the current market price*
price • *a sharp increase in the price of petrol*
selling price • *the average selling price of a new home*
worth • *He sold the car for less than half its worth.*

value ③ VERB
to appreciate something and think it is important • *Do you value your friends enough?*
appreciate • *I would appreciate your advice.*

cherish • *Cherish every moment you have with your children.*
have a high opinion of • *Your boss seems to have a high opinion of you.*
prize • *These items are prized by collectors.*
rate highly • *He is an excellent keeper and I rate him highly.*
respect • *I respect his talent as a pianist.*
treasure • *memories I will treasure for the rest of my life*

value ④ VERB

to decide how much money something is worth • *I have had my jewellery valued for insurance purposes.*
appraise • *He was called in to appraise and sell the cottage.*
assess • *Experts are now assessing the cost of the restoration.*
cost • *an operation costed at around $649m*
estimate • *a personal fortune estimated at more than $400m*
evaluate • *The company needs to evaluate the cost of leasing the building.*
price • *The property was priced at less than £1m.*

vanish ① VERB

to disappear • *The moon vanished behind a cloud.*
become invisible • *The plane became invisible in the clouds.*
be lost to view • *They watched the ship until it was lost to view.*
disappear • *The aircraft disappeared off the radar.*
fade • *We watched the harbour fade into the mist.*
recede • *Gradually Luke receded into the distance.*
ANTONYM:
• appear

vanish ② VERB

to cease to exist • *Dinosaurs vanished from the earth millions of years ago.*
become extinct • *Without help, these animals will become extinct.*
cease • *At one o'clock the rain ceased.*
cease to exist • *Without trees, the world as we know it would cease to exist.*
die out • *Britain's bear population died out about 2,000 years ago.*
dissolve • *The crowds dissolved and we were alone.*
evaporate • *All my pleasure evaporated when I saw him.*
fade away • *Her black mood faded away.*
go away • *All she wanted was for the pain to go away.*
melt away • *All my cares melted away.*
pass • *Breathe deeply and the panic attack will pass.*

vanquish VERB

to defeat someone completely • *a happy ending in which the hero vanquishes the monsters*
beat • *the team that beat us in the finals*
conquer • *a great warrior who conquers the enemies of his people*
crush • *their bid to crush the rebels*
defeat • *His guerrillas defeated the colonial army in 1954.*
overcome • *They overcame the opposition to win the cup.*
rout • *the battle at which the Norman army routed the English*
trounce • *Australia trounced France by 60 points to 0.*

variation NOUN

a change from the normal or usual pattern • *a variation of the same route*
alteration • *some alterations in your diet*
change • *a change of attitude*
departure • *Her new novel is a departure from her previous work.*

a b c d e f g h i j k l m n o p q r s t u v w x y z

A
B
C
D
E
F
G
H
I
J
K
L
M
N
O
P
Q
R
S
T
U
V
W
X
Y
Z

deviation • *Deviation from the norm is not tolerated.*
difference • *a noticeable difference in his behaviour*
diversion • *a welcome diversion from the daily grind*

variety ① NOUN
a number of different kinds of things • *a wide variety of readers*
array • *an attractive array of bright colours*
assortment • *an assortment of pets*
collection • *a huge collection of books*
medley • *a medley of vegetables*
mixture • *a mixture of sweets*
range • *a range of sun-care products*

MORE SYNONYMS:
• cross section
• miscellany
• multiplicity

variety ② NOUN
a particular type of something • *a new variety of celery*
category • *There are three broad categories of soil.*
class • *several classes of butterflies*
kind • *different kinds of roses*
sort • *several articles of this sort*
strain • *a new strain of the virus*
type • *What type of guns were they?*

various ADJECTIVE
of several different types • *trees of various sorts*
assorted • *swimsuits in assorted colours*
different • *different brands of drinks*
disparate • *the disparate cultures of India*
diverse • *Society is more diverse than ever before.*
miscellaneous • *a hoard of miscellaneous junk*
sundry • *sundry journalists and lawyers*

MORE SYNONYMS:
• heterogeneous
• manifold

vary ① VERB
to change to something different • *weather patterns vary greatly*
alter • *During the course of a day the light alters constantly.*
alternate • *My moods alternate with alarming rapidity.*
change • *My feelings haven't changed.*
fluctuate • *Weight may fluctuate markedly.*

vary ② VERB
to introduce changes in something • *Vary your routes as much as possible.*
alternate • *Alternate the chunks of fish with chunks of vegetable.*
diversify • *They decided to diversify their products.*
modify • *The government refuses to modify its position.*

MORE SYNONYMS:
• permutate
• reorder

vast ADJECTIVE
extremely large • *farmers who own vast stretches of land*
colossal • *a colossal statue*
enormous • *The main bedroom is enormous.*
giant • *a giant meteorite heading for the earth*
gigantic • *a gigantic shopping mall*
great • *a great hall as long as a church*
huge • *a huge crowd*
immense • *an immense castle*
massive • *a massive theme park*

ANTONYM:
• tiny

verdict NOUN
a decision or opinion on something • *The doctor's verdict was that he was fine.*

conclusion • *I've come to the conclusion that she's lying.*
decision • *The editor's decision is final.*
finding • *The court announced its findings.*
judgment • *My judgment is that things are going to get worse.*
opinion • *You should seek a medical opinion.*

very ADVERB
to a great degree • *very bad dreams*
deeply • *I was deeply sorry to hear about your loss.*
extremely • *My mobile phone is extremely useful.*
greatly • *I was greatly relieved when he finally arrived.*
highly • *Mr Singh was a highly successful salesman.*
really • *I know her really well.*
terribly • *I'm terribly sorry to bother you.*
MORE SYNONYMS:
• exceedingly
• profoundly
• remarkably

veto ① VERB
to forbid something • *Treasury officials vetoed the plans.*
ban • *The authorities have banned the advertisement.*
forbid • *Most airlines forbid the use of mobile phones on their planes.*
prohibit • *The government intends to prohibit all trade with the country.*

veto ② NOUN
the act of forbidding or power to forbid something • *Dr. Baker has the power of veto.*
ban • *the arms ban on the Bosnian government*
prohibition • *a prohibition on nuclear testing*

victory NOUN
a success in a battle or competition • *his 15th consecutive victory in a doubles final*
laurels • *a former British champion took the laurels in this event*
success • *league and cup successes*
superiority • *United Nations air forces won air superiority.*
triumph • *last year's Republican triumph in the elections*
win • *eight wins in nine games*
ANTONYM:
• defeat

view ① NOUN
a personal opinion • *his political views*
attitude • *other people's attitudes towards you*
belief • *people's beliefs about crime*
conviction • *a firm conviction that things have improved*
feeling • *It is my feeling that Klein is right.*
opinion • *a favourable opinion of our neighbours*
point of view • *an unusual point of view on the subject*

view ② NOUN
the things you can see from a particular place • *There was a beautiful view from the window.*
aspect • *the Yorkshire hills which give the cottage a lovely aspect*
landscape • *Arizona's desert landscape*
panorama • *a panorama of fertile valleys*
perspective • *the aerial perspective of St Paul's Cathedral*
scene • *Wright surveyed the scene from his chosen seat.*
spectacle • *a sweeping spectacle of rugged peaks*

a b c d e f g h i j k l m n o p q r s t u **v** w x y z

A
B
C
D
E
F
G
H
I
J
K
L
M
N
O
P
Q
R
S
T
U
V
W
X
Y
Z

MORE SYNONYMS:
• prospect
• vista

view ③ VERB
to think of something in a particular way • *They viewed me with contempt.*
consider • *We consider them to be our friends.*
deem (FORMAL) • *His ideas were deemed unacceptable.*
judge • *His work was judged unsatisfactory.*
regard • *They regard the tax as unfair.*

viewpoint NOUN
an attitude towards something • *We all have our own personal viewpoints.*
attitude • *other people's attitudes towards you*
belief • *people's beliefs about crime*
conviction • *a very personal, political conviction*
feeling • *What are your feelings on this matter?*
opinion • *a favourable opinion of our neighbours*
point of view • *an unusual point of view on the subject*

violence ① NOUN
behaviour which is intended to hurt people • *Twenty people were killed in the violence.*
bloodshed • *The government must avoid further bloodshed.*
brutality • *the brutality of the war in Vietnam*
cruelty • *Human beings are capable of such cruelty to each other.*
force • *If you use any force, I shall inform the police.*
savagery • *acts of vicious savagery*
terrorism • *political terrorism in the 19th century*

violence ② NOUN
force and energy • *Amy spoke with sudden violence.*
fervour • *views he had put forward with fervour*
force • *She expressed her feelings with some force.*
harshness • *the harshness of her words*
intensity • *His voice hoarsened with intensity.*
severity • *the severity of her scoldings*
vehemence • *Tweed was taken aback by her vehemence.*

violent ① ADJECTIVE
intending to hurt or kill people • *violent criminals*
bloodthirsty • *a bloodthirsty monster*
brutal • *a brutal crime*
cruel • *He is cruel towards animals.*
murderous • *a murderous bank-robber*
savage • *savage warriors*
vicious • *He was a cruel and vicious man.*

ANTONYM:
• gentle

violent ② ADJECTIVE
happening unexpectedly and with great force • *violent storms*
powerful • *He was caught by a powerful blow.*
raging • *a raging flood*
rough • *A wooden ship sank in rough seas.*
strong • *strong winds and rain*
turbulent • *the turbulent events of the century*
wild • *the wild gales sweeping up from the channel*

MORE SYNONYMS:
• tempestuous
• tumultuous

violent ③ ADJECTIVE
said, felt, or done with great force • *the violent reaction to his plans*

acute • *pain which grew more and more acute*

furious • *a furious row*

intense • *a look of intense dislike*

powerful • *a powerful backlash against the government*

severe • *a severe emotional shock*

strong • *strong words*

MORE SYNONYMS:
• forcible
• passionate
• vehement

virtue ① NOUN

the quality of doing what is morally right • *He is a paragon of virtue.*

goodness • *He has faith in human goodness.*

integrity • *He was praised for his fairness and integrity.*

morality • *standards of morality and justice in society*

MORE SYNONYMS:
• probity
• rectitude
• righteousness

virtue ② NOUN

an advantage something has • *the virtue of neatness*

advantage • *the advantages of the new system*

asset • *The one asset the job provided was contacts.*

attribute • *a player with every attribute you could want*

merit • *the merits of various football teams*

plus (INFORMAL) • *The nutrients in milk have pluses and minuses.*

strength • *the strengths and weaknesses of our position*

virtue ③ : **by virtue of** PREPOSITION

because of • *The article stuck in my mind by virtue of one detail.*

as a result of • *People will feel better as a result of their efforts.*

because of • *She was promoted because of her experience.*

by dint of • *He succeeds by dint of hard work.*

on account of • *The city is popular with tourists on account of its many museums.*

thanks to • *Thanks to recent research, new treatments are available.*

visible ① ADJECTIVE

able to be seen • *The warning lights were clearly visible.*

clear • *the clearest pictures ever of Pluto*

conspicuous • *He felt more conspicuous than he'd have liked.*

distinguishable • *colours just distinguishable in the dark*

in sight • *There wasn't another vehicle in sight.*

observable • *the observable part of the Universe*

perceptible • *Daniel gave a barely perceptible nod.*

ANTONYM:
• invisible

visible ② ADJECTIVE

noticeable or evident • *There was little visible excitement.*

apparent • *There is no apparent reason for the crime.*

evident • *He ate with evident enjoyment.*

manifest • *his manifest enthusiasm*

noticeable • *subtle but noticeable changes*

obvious • *There are obvious dangers.*

plain • *It is plain a mistake has been made.*

MORE SYNONYMS:
• conspicuous
• discernible
• patent

a
b
c
d
e
f
g
h
i
j
k
l
m
n
o
p
q
r
s
t
u
v
w
x
y
z

A
B
C
D
E
F
G
H
I
J
K
L
M
N
O
P
Q
R
S
T
U
V
W
X
Y
Z

vision ① NOUN

a mental picture in which you imagine things • *my vision of the future*

conception • *my conception of a garden*

daydream • *He learned to escape into daydreams.*

dream • *his dream of becoming a pilot*

fantasy • *fantasies of romance and true love*

ideal • *your ideal of a holiday*

image • *an image in your mind of what you are looking for*

vision ② NOUN

the ability to imagine future developments • *a total lack of vision and imagination*

foresight • *They had the foresight to invest in technology.*

imagination • *He had the imagination to foresee dangers.*

insight • *the development of insight and understanding*

intuition • *Her intuition told her something was wrong.*

vision ③ NOUN

an experience in which you see things others cannot • *She was convinced her visions were real.*

apparition • *One of the women was the apparition he had seen.*

hallucination • *The drug can cause hallucinations.*

illusion • *Perhaps the footprint was an illusion.*

mirage • *The girl was a mirage, created by his troubled mind.*

phantom • *People claimed to have seen the phantom.*

spectre • *a spectre from the other world*

MORE SYNONYMS:

• chimera
• phantasm
• wraith

visit ① VERB

to go to see and spend time with someone • *He wanted to visit his brother in Sydney.*

call on • *Don't hesitate to call on me.*

go to see • *I'll go to see him in the hospital.*

look up • *She looked up friends she had not seen for a while.*

visit ② NOUN

a trip to see a person or place • *Helen had recently paid him a visit.*

call • *He decided to pay a call on Tommy.*

stay • *An experienced guide is provided during your stay.*

stop • *The last stop in Mr Cook's tour was Paris.*

vital ① ADJECTIVE

necessary or very important • *a blockade which cut off vital fuel supplies*

central • *He is central to the whole project.*

critical • *This decision will be critical to our future.*

crucial • *the man who played a crucial role in the negotiations*

essential • *It is essential that you see a doctor soon.*

important • *the most important piece of evidence in the case*

indispensable • *an indispensable piece of equipment*

necessary • *the skills necessary for survival*

pivotal • *He played a pivotal role in the match.*

vital ② ADJECTIVE

energetic and full of life • *Old age has diminished a once vital person.*

active • *an active youngster*

dynamic • *a dynamic and exciting place*

energetic • *She became a shadow of her happy, energetic self.*

lively • *a beautiful, lively young girl*
spirited • *the spirited heroine of this film*
sprightly • *a sprightly old man*
vivacious • *She is vivacious and charming.*

vomit VERB
to have food and drink come back up through the mouth • *Any product made from milk made him vomit.*
be sick • *She was sick in the handbasin.*
bring up • *Certain foods are difficult to bring up.*
chunder (AUSTRALIAN AND NEW ZEALAND; SLANG) • *the time you chundered in the taxi*
heave • *He gasped and heaved and vomited again.*
puke (INFORMAL) • *They got drunk and puked out of the window.*
regurgitate • *swallowing and regurgitating large quantities of water*

vote ① NOUN
a decision made by allowing people to state their preference • *Do you think we should have a vote on that?*
ballot • *The result of the ballot will be known soon.*
plebiscite (FORMAL) • *A plebiscite made Hitler the Chancellor.*
polls • *In 1945, Churchill was defeated at the polls.*
referendum • *Estonia planned to hold a referendum on independence.*

vote ② VERB
to indicate a choice or opinion • *It seems that many people would vote for the opposition.*
cast a vote • *90% of those who cast a vote*
go to the polls • *Voters are due to go to the polls on Sunday.*
opt • *The mass of Spaniards opted for democracy.*

return • *Members will be asked to return a vote for or against the motion.*

vote ③ VERB
to suggest that something should happen • *I vote that we all go to Holland.*
propose • *I propose that we all try to get some sleep.*
recommend • *I recommend that he be sent home early.*
suggest • *I suggest we go round the table and introduce ourselves.*

vulgar ① ADJECTIVE
socially unacceptable or offensive • *vulgar language*
coarse • *coarse humour*
crude • *crude pictures*
dirty • *dirty jokes*
indecent • *an indecent suggestion*
rude • *a rude gesture*
uncouth • *that oafish, uncouth person*

MORE SYNONYMS:
• improper
• ribald
• unrefined

ANTONYM:
• refined

vulgar ② ADJECTIVE
showing a lack of taste or quality • *I think it's a very vulgar house.*
common • *She could be a little common at times.*
flashy • *flashy clothes*
gaudy • *a gaudy purple-and-orange hat*
tasteless • *a house with tasteless decor*
tawdry • *a tawdry seaside town*

ANTONYM:
• sophisticated

a
b
c
d
e
f
g
h
i
j
k
l
m
n
o
p
q
r
s
t
u
v
w
x
y
z

vulnerable ADJECTIVE
weak and without protection
• *vulnerable old people*
exposed • *The west coast is very exposed to Atlantic winds.*
sensitive • *Most people are highly sensitive to criticism.*

susceptible • *an area that is susceptible to attack*
weak • *He spoke up for the weak and defenceless.*

MORE SYNONYMS:
• assailable
• defenceless
• unprotected

Ww

wait ① VERB
to spend time before something
happens • *Wait until we get there.*
linger • *I lingered on for a few days
until he arrived.*
pause • *The crowd paused for a
minute, wondering what to do next.*
remain • *You'll have to remain in
hospital for the time being.*
stand by • *Ships are standing by to
evacuate the people.*
stay • *Stay here while I go for help.*

wait ② NOUN
a period of time before something
happens • *They faced a three-hour wait
before they could leave.*
delay • *The accident caused some
delay.*
interval • *a long interval when
no-one spoke*
pause • *There was a pause before he
replied.*

wake VERB
to make or become conscious again
after sleep • *It was still dark when he
woke.*
awake • *We were awoken by the
doorbell.*
come to • *When she came to she
found it was raining.*
rouse • *We roused him at seven so he
would be on time.*
stir • *She shook him and he started to
stir.*
waken • *wakened by the thunder*

walk ① VERB
to go on foot • *I walked slowly along
the road.*
▶ see Word Study **walk**, page 662

walk ② NOUN
a journey made by walking • *We'll have
a quick walk while it's fine.*
hike • *a long hike in the country*
march • *a day's march north of their
objective*
ramble • *They went for a ramble
through the woods.*
stroll • *After dinner we took a stroll
around the city.*
trek • *He's on a trek across the Antarctic.*

MORE SYNONYMS:
• constitutional
• perambulation
• saunter

walk ③ NOUN
the way someone moves when
walking • *Despite his gangling walk he
was a good dancer.*
carriage • *her regal carriage*
gait • *an awkward gait*
pace • *moving at a brisk pace down the
road*
stride • *He lengthened his stride to
catch up with her.*

wander VERB
to move about in a casual way • *They
wandered aimlessly around the village.*
cruise • *A police car cruised by.*
drift • *The balloon drifted slowly over the
countryside.*

A
B
C
D
E
F
G
H
I
J
K
L
M
N
O
P
Q
R
S
T
U
V
W
X
Y
Z

ramble • *freedom to ramble across the moors*
range • *They range widely in search of food.*
roam • *Barefoot children roamed the streets.*
stroll • *We strolled down the street, looking at the shops.*

want ① VERB
to feel a desire for something • *I want a red car for a change.*
covet • *He coveted his boss's job.*
crave • *Sometimes she still craved chocolate.*
desire • *He could make them do whatever he desired.*
wish • *I don't wish to know that.*

want ② VERB
to need something • *My hair wants cutting.*
be deficient in • *Their diet was deficient in vitamins.*
demand • *The task of reconstruction demanded much sacrifice.*
lack • *training to give him the skills he lacked*
need • *My car needs servicing.*
require • *He knows exactly what is required of him.*

want ③ NOUN
a lack of something • *becoming weak from want of rest*
absence • *a complete absence of evidence*
deficiency • *They did blood tests for signs of vitamin deficiency.*
lack • *He got the job in spite of his lack of experience.*
scarcity • *an increasing scarcity of water*
shortage • *A shortage of funds is holding them back.*

MORE SYNONYMS:
• dearth
• insufficiency
• paucity

ANTONYM:
• abundance

war ① NOUN
a period of armed conflict between countries • *The war dragged on for five years.*
combat • *men who died in combat*
conflict • *The conflict is bound to intensify.*
fighting • *He was killed in the fighting which followed the treaty.*
hostilities • *in case hostilities break out*
strife • *The country was torn with strife.*
warfare • *chemical warfare*

ANTONYM:
• peace

RELATED WORDS:
• ADJECTIVES belligerent, martial

war ② VERB
to fight against something • *The two countries had been warring with each other for years.*
battle • *Thousands of people battled with the police.*
clash • *The two armies clashed at first light.*
combat • *measures to combat smuggling*
fight • *The tribe fought with its rivals.*

warm ① ADJECTIVE
having some heat but not hot • *a warm spring day*
balmy • *balmy summer evenings*
heated • *a heated swimming pool*
lukewarm • *Heat the milk until lukewarm.*
pleasant • *After a chilly morning, the afternoon was very pleasant.*
tepid • *a bath full of tepid water*

ANTONYM:
• cold

warm ② ADJECTIVE
friendly and affectionate • *a warm and likable personality*
affectionate • *with an affectionate glance at her children*
amiable • *He was very amiable company.*
cordial • *We were given a most cordial welcome.*
friendly • *All her colleagues were very friendly.*
genial • *a warm-hearted friend and genial host*
loving • *He is a loving husband and father.*

ANTONYM:
• unfriendly

warm ③ VERB
to heat something gently • *The sun came out and warmed his back.*
heat • *Heat the bread in the oven.*
heat up • *The fire soon heated up the room.*
melt • *He melted the butter in a small pan.*
thaw • *Always thaw pastry thoroughly.*
warm up • *You must begin gently to warm up the muscles.*

ANTONYM:
• cool

warn VERB
to give advance notice of something unpleasant • *I warned him about those loose tiles.*
alert • *The siren alerted them to the danger.*
caution • *Their reaction cautioned him against any further attempts.*
forewarn • *We were forewarned of what to expect.*
notify • *The weather forecast notified them of the coming storm.*

MORE SYNONYMS:
• admonish
• apprise

warning NOUN
something that tells people of possible danger • *advance warning of the attack*
alarm • *They heard the fire alarm and ran to safety.*
alert • *a security alert*
caution • *a note of caution*
notice • *three months' notice*
premonition • *He had a premonition of bad news.*

MORE SYNONYMS:
• augury
• caveat
• presage

wary ADJECTIVE
showing lack of trust in something • *She was wary of marriage.*
cautious • *His experience has made him cautious.*
distrustful • *Voters are deeply distrustful of all politicians.*
guarded • *The boy gave him a guarded look.*
suspicious • *He was rightly suspicious of their motives.*
vigilant • *He warned the public to be vigilant.*

MORE SYNONYMS:
• chary
• circumspect
• heedful

wash ① VERB
to clean something with water • *He got a job washing dishes.*
bathe • *She bathed her blistered feet.*
cleanse • *the correct way to cleanse the skin*
launder • *freshly laundered shirts*

a
b
c
d
e
f
g
h
i
j
k
l
m
n
o
p
q
r
s
t
u
v
w
x
y
z

A
B
C
D
E
F
G
H
I
J
K
L
M
N
O
P
Q
R
S
T
U
V
W
X
Y
Z

rinse • *Rinse several times in clear water.*
scrub • *I was scrubbing the bathroom floor.*
shampoo • *You must shampoo your hair first.*

wash ② VERB
to carry something by the force of water • *washed ashore by the waves*
carry off • *The debris was carried off on the tide.*
erode • *Exposed soil is quickly eroded by wind and rain.*
sweep away • *The floods swept away the houses by the river.*

waste ① VERB
to use too much of something unnecessarily • *I wouldn't waste my money on something like that.*
fritter away • *He just fritters his time away.*
squander • *He had squandered his chances of winning.*
throw away • *You're throwing away a good opportunity.*

ANTONYM:
• save

waste ② NOUN
using something excessively or unnecessarily • *What a complete waste of money!*
extravagance • *widespread tales of his extravagance*
misuse • *This project is a misuse of public funds.*
squandering • *a squandering of his valuable time*

MORE SYNONYMS:
• dissipation
• misapplication
• prodigality

waste ③ ADJECTIVE
not needed or wanted • *waste paper*
leftover • *leftover pieces of fabric*

superfluous • *She got rid of many superfluous belongings.*
unused • *spoiled or unused ballot papers*

wasteful ADJECTIVE
using something in a careless or extravagant way • *wasteful duplication of effort*
extravagant • *an extravagant lifestyle*
uneconomical • *the uneconomical duplication of jobs*

MORE SYNONYMS:
• improvident
• profligate
• spendthrift

ANTONYM:
• thrifty

watch ① NOUN
a period of time when a guard is kept on something • *Keep a close watch on the prisoners.*
observation • *In hospital she'll be under observation night and day.*
supervision • *A toddler requires close supervision.*
surveillance • *kept under constant surveillance*

MORE SYNONYMS:
• vigilance
• watchfulness

watch ② VERB
to look at something for some time • *I don't watch television very often.*
gaze at • *gazing at herself in the mirror*
look at • *They looked closely at the insects.*
observe • *Researchers observed the behaviour of small children.*
pay attention • *Pay attention or you won't know what to do.*
see • *We went to see the semi-finals.*
view • *The police have viewed the video recording of the incident.*

watch ③ VERB
to look after something • *You must watch the baby carefully.*
guard • *They were guarded the whole time they were there.*
look after • *I looked after her cat while she was away.*
mind • *Can you mind the store for a couple of hours?*
take care of • *Can you take care of the kids while I get my hair done?*

watch out VERB
to be careful or alert for something • *You have to watch out for snakes in the swamp.*
be alert • *The bank is alert to the danger.*
be watchful • *Be watchful for any warning signs.*
keep your eyes open • *They kept their eyes open for any troublemakers.*
look out • *What are the symptoms to look out for?*

waterfall NOUN

◆ TYPES OF WATERFALL
◆ cascade
◆ cataract
◆ chute
◆ fall
◆ linn (SCOTTISH)
◆ rapids
◆ torrent
◆ white water

wave ① VERB
to move or flap to and fro • *The doctor waved a piece of paper at him.*
brandish • *He appeared brandishing a knife.*
flap • *He flapped his hand at me to be quiet.*
flourish • *He flourished his glass to emphasize the point.*
flutter • *a fluttering white lace handkerchief*

shake • *Shake the rugs well to air them.*
MORE SYNONYMS:
• oscillate
• undulate

wave ② NOUN
a ridge of water on the surface of the sea • *the sound of the waves breaking on the shore*
breaker • *The foaming breakers crashed on to the beach.*
ripple • *gentle ripples on the surface of the lake*
swell • *We bobbed gently on the swell of the incoming tide.*

wave ③ NOUN
an increase in a type of activity • *the crime wave*
flood • *a flood of complaints about the programme*
movement • *a growing movement towards democracy*
rush • *He felt a sudden rush of panic at the thought.*
surge • *the recent surge in inflation*
trend • *This is a growing trend.*
upsurge • *There was an upsurge of business confidence after the war.*

way ① NOUN
a manner of doing something • *an excellent way of cooking meat*
approach • *different approaches to gathering information*
manner • *in a friendly manner*
means • *The move is a means to fight crime.*
method • *using the latest teaching methods*
procedure • *He failed to follow the correct procedure when applying for a visa.*
technique • *The tests were performed using a new technique.*

A
B
C
D
E
F
G
H
I
J
K
L
M
N
O
P
Q
R
S
T
U
V
W
X
Y
Z

way ② NOUN

the customs or behaviour of a person or group • *Their ways are certainly different.*

conduct • *People judged him by his social skills and conduct.*

custom • *an ancient Japanese custom*

manner • *His manner was rather abrupt.*

practice • *a public enquiry into bank practices*

style • *Behaving like that isn't his style.*

MORE SYNONYMS:
• idiosyncrasy
• wont

way ③ NOUN

a route taken to a particular place • *I can't remember the way.*

channel • *a safe channel avoiding the reefs*

course • *The ship was on a course that followed the coastline.*

lane • *the busiest shipping lanes in the world*

path • *The lava annihilates everything in its path.*

road • *the road into the village*

route • *the most direct route to the town centre*

weak ① ADJECTIVE

lacking in strength • *She had a weak heart.*

delicate • *She was physically delicate and mentally unstable.*

faint • *Feeling faint is one of the symptoms of angina.*

feeble • *old and feeble and unable to walk far*

frail • *in frail health*

puny • *He was puny as a child but grew up to be a top athlete.*

sickly • *a sickly baby with no resistance to illness*

wasted • *muscles which were wasted through lack of use*

MORE SYNONYMS:
• debilitated
• decrepit
• enervated
• infirm

ANTONYM:
• strong

weak ② ADJECTIVE

likely to break or fail • *a weak economy*

deficient • *The plane had a deficient landing system.*

faulty • *The money will be used to repair faulty equipment.*

inadequate • *inadequate safety measures*

weak ③ ADJECTIVE

easily influenced by other people • *He was a weak man who wouldn't stick his neck out.*

powerless • *a powerless ruler governed by his advisers*

spineless • *bureaucrats and spineless politicians*

MORE SYNONYMS:
• indecisive
• irresolute

ANTONYM:
• resolute

weaken VERB

to make or become less strong • *His authority was weakened by their actions.*

diminish • *to diminish the prestige of the monarchy*

fail • *His strength began to fail after a few hours.*

flag • *Her enthusiasm was in no way flagging.*

lessen • *The drugs lessen the risk of an epidemic.*

reduce • *Reduced consumer demand caused the company to collapse.*

sap • *I was afraid the illness had sapped my strength.*
undermine • *They were accused of trying to undermine the government.*
wane • *His interest in sport began to wane.*

MORE SYNONYMS:
• debilitate
• enervate
• mitigate

ANTONYM:
• strengthen

weakness ① NOUN
a lack of physical or moral strength • *His extreme weakness caused him to collapse.*
defect • *a serious character defect*
flaw • *His main flaw is his bad temper.*
fragility • *They are at risk because of the fragility of their bones.*
frailty • *the triumph of will over human frailty*
imperfection • *He concedes that there are imperfections in the system.*
vulnerability • *the extreme vulnerability of the young chicks*

MORE SYNONYMS:
• Achilles' heel
• debility
• infirmity

ANTONYM:
• strength

weakness ② NOUN
a great liking for something • *a weakness for chocolate*
fondness • *a fondness for good wine*
liking • *a liking for tripe and onions*
passion • *His other great passion was his motorbike.*
penchant • *a stylish woman with a penchant for dark glasses*

MORE SYNONYMS:
• partiality
• predilection

ANTONYM:
• dislike

wealth ① NOUN
a large amount of money • *Economic reform brought them wealth.*
affluence • *the trappings of affluence*
fortune • *He made a fortune in the property boom.*
means • *a person of means*
money • *All that money brought nothing but sadness and misery.*
prosperity • *Japan's economic prosperity*
riches • *His Olympic medal brought him fame and riches.*
substance • *run by local men of substance*

wealth ② NOUN
a lot of something • *a wealth of information*
abundance • *This area has an abundance of safe beaches.*
bounty • *autumn's bounty of fruits and berries*
plenty • *He grew up in a time of plenty.*
store • *She dipped into her store of theatrical anecdotes.*

MORE SYNONYMS:
• copiousness
• cornucopia
• plenitude
• profusion

ANTONYM:
• shortage

wealthy ADJECTIVE
having plenty of money • *She came from a very wealthy background.*
affluent • *living in an affluent neighbourhood*
comfortable • *from a stable, comfortable family*

a
b
c
d
e
f
g
h
i
j
k
l
m
n
o
p
q
r
s
t
u
v
w
x
y
z

opulent • *Most of the cash went on supporting his opulent lifestyle.*
prosperous • *The place looks more prosperous than ever.*
rich • *I'm going to be very rich one day.*
well-to-do • *a rather well-to-do family in the shipping business*

ANTONYM:
• poor

wear ① VERB
to be dressed in something • *He was wearing a brown uniform.*
be clothed in • *She was clothed in a flowered dress.*
be dressed in • *The women were dressed in their finest attire.*
don • *The police responded by donning riot gear.*
have on • *I had my new shoes on that night.*
put on • *He had to put on his glasses to read the paper.*
sport (INFORMAL) • *sporting a red tie*

wear ② VERB
to become worse in condition with use or age • *The old stone steps were worn in the middle.*
corrode • *The underground pipes were badly corroded.*
erode • *Exposed rock is quickly eroded by wind and rain.*
fray • *fraying edges on the stair carpet*
rub • *The inscription had been rubbed smooth by generations of hands.*
wash away • *The topsoil had been washed away by the incessant rain.*

MORE SYNONYMS:
• abrade
• deteriorate

wear ③ NOUN
the type of use which causes something to be damaged • *The tyres showed signs of wear.*

corrosion • *Zinc is used to protect other metals from corrosion.*
deterioration • *The building is already showing signs of deterioration.*
erosion • *erosion of the river valleys*
use • *The carpet must be able to cope with heavy use.*

MORE SYNONYMS:
• abrasion
• attrition

wear out VERB
to make someone tired • *The past few days have really worn me out.*
exhaust • *The long working day exhausted him.*
tire • *If driving tires you, take the train.*
weary • *wearied by the constant demands on his time*

weary ADJECTIVE
very tired • *She sank to the ground, too weary to walk another step.*
drained • *He's always completely drained after a performance.*
exhausted • *She was too exhausted and upset to talk.*
fatigued • *Winter weather can leave you feeling fatigued.*
tired • *He was too tired even to take a shower.*
tuckered out (AUSTRALIAN AND NEW ZEALAND; INFORMAL) • *You must be tuckered out after that bus trip.*
worn out • *He's just worn out after the long drive.*

weather NOUN

◆ **TYPES OF WEATHER**
◆ cloud
◆ drought
◆ fog
◆ freeze
◆ frost
◆ hail
◆ haze

- heatwave
- ice
- lightning
- rain
- sleet
- snow
- sunshine
- thaw
- thunder

◆ WORDS USED TO DESCRIBE THE
◆ WEATHER
- arctic
- baltic
- balmy
- blustery
- breezy
- clammy
- clear
- close
- cloudy
- cold
- drizzly
- dry
- dull
- fine
- foggy
- freezing
- hot
- humid
- icy
- mild
- misty
- muggy
- overcast
- rainy
- showery
- snowy
- stormy
- sultry
- sunny
- thundery
- wet
- windy

◆ WORDS FOR RAIN AND SNOW
- drizzle
- rain
- shower
- sleet
- slush
- snow

◆ WORDS FOR STORM
- blizzard
- hailstorm
- snowstorm
- squall
- storm
- superstorm
- tempest
- thunderstorm

◆ WORDS FOR WIND
- breeze
- cyclone
- gale
- gust
- hurricane
- squall
- tornado
- twister
- typhoon
- whirlwind
- wind

◆ WORDS FOR FOG
- fog
- haar
- haze
- mist
- pea-souper
- smog

weird ADJECTIVE
strange or odd • *I had such a weird dream last night.*
bizarre • *his bizarre behaviour*
curious • *What a curious thing to say!*
extraordinary • *an extraordinary occurrence*

a
b
c
d
e
f
g
h
i
j
k
l
m
n
o
p
q
r
s
t
u
v
w
x
y
z

funny • *There's something funny about him.*

odd • *an odd coincidence*

singular (FORMAL) • *I can't think where you got such a singular notion.*

strange • *Didn't you notice anything strange about her?*

peculiar • *It tasted very peculiar.*

queer • *I think there's something queer going on here.*

ANTONYM:
• ordinary

weirdo NOUN (INFORMAL)

a person who behaves in a strange way • *All the other kids thought I was a weirdo.*

crank (INFORMAL) • *He kept quiet in case people thought he was a crank.*

eccentric • *a local eccentric who wears shorts all year round*

freak (INFORMAL) • *Barry's always been looked on as a bit of a freak.*

loony (SLANG) • *I realize I must sound like a complete loony.*

nut (SLANG) • *There's some nut out there with a gun.*

nutter (BRITISH; SLANG) • *She was being stalked by a real nutter.*

well ① ADVERB

in a satisfactory way • *The interview went well.*

satisfactorily • *The system should work satisfactorily.*

smoothly • *So far, the operation is going smoothly.*

splendidly • *They have behaved splendidly.*

successfully • *The changeover is working successfully.*

well ② ADVERB

with skill and ability • *He draws well.*

ably • *He was ably assisted by the other members of staff.*

admirably • *dealing admirably with a difficult situation*

adequately • *He speaks French very adequately.*

competently • *They handled the situation very competently.*

effectively • *In the first half he operated effectively in defence.*

efficiently • *He works efficiently and accurately.*

expertly • *Shopkeepers expertly rolled spices up in bay leaves.*

professionally • *These tickets have been forged very professionally.*

skilfully • *He skilfully exploited his company's strengths.*

MORE SYNONYMS:
• adeptly
• proficiently

ANTONYM:
• badly

well ③ ADVERB

fully and with thoroughness • *They should be well washed and well dried.*

amply • *I was amply rewarded for my trouble.*

closely • *He studied the documents closely.*

completely • *Make sure you defrost it completely.*

fully • *The new system is now fully under way.*

highly • *one of the most highly regarded authors*

meticulously • *He had planned his trip meticulously.*

rigorously • *Their duties have not been performed as rigorously as they might have been.*

thoroughly • *Add the oil and mix thoroughly.*

well ④ ADVERB

in a kind way • *He treats his employees well.*

compassionately • *He always acted compassionately towards her.*
considerately • *I expect people to deal with me considerately and fairly.*
favourably • *companies who treat men more favourably than women*
humanely • *They treat their livestock humanely.*
kindly • *Children are capable of behaving kindly.*
with consideration • *He was treated with consideration and kindness.*

well ⑤ ADJECTIVE
having good health • *I'm not very well today.*
blooming • *She felt confident, blooming, and attractive.*
fit • *He keeps himself really fit.*
healthy • *Most people want to be healthy and happy.*
in good condition • *He's in good condition for his age.*
in good health • *He seemed to be in good health and spirits.*
robust • *He's never been a very robust child.*
sound • *a sound body*
strong • *Eat well and you'll soon be strong again.*

MORE SYNONYMS:
• able-bodied
• hale
• in fine fettle

ANTONYM:
• sick

wet ① ADJECTIVE
covered in liquid • *Don't get your feet wet.*
damp • *Her hair was still damp.*
drenched • *getting drenched by icy water*
moist • *The soil is reasonably moist after the September rain.*
saturated • *The filter has been saturated with oil.*

soaked • *soaked to the skin*
sodden • *We took off our sodden clothes.*
waterlogged • *The game was called off because the pitch was waterlogged.*

ANTONYM:
• dry

wet ② ADJECTIVE
in rainy weather conditions • *It was a miserable wet day.*
humid • *hot and humid weather conditions*
misty • *The air was cold and misty.*
rainy • *The rainy season starts in December.*
showery • *The day had been showery with sunny intervals.*

ANTONYM:
• dry

wet ③ VERB
to put liquid on to something • *Wet the edges and stick them together.*
dampen • *You must dampen the laundry before you iron it.*
irrigate • *irrigated by a system of interconnected canals*
moisten • *Take a sip of water to moisten your throat.*
soak • *The water had soaked his jacket and shirt.*
spray • *It can spray the whole field in half an hour.*
water • *We have to water the plants when the weather is dry.*

MORE SYNONYMS:
• drench
• humidify
• saturate

ANTONYM:
• dry

whim NOUN
a sudden fancy for something • *We decided to go more or less on a whim.*

A
B
C
D
E
F
G
H
I
J
K
L
M
N
O
P
Q
R
S
T
U
V
W
X
Y
Z

craze • *the latest fitness craze*
fad (INFORMAL) • *just a passing fad*
fancy • *I had a fancy for some strawberries.*
impulse • *He resisted the impulse to buy a new one.*
urge • *He had an urge to open a shop of his own.*

MORE SYNONYMS:
• caprice
• vagary
• whimsy

white NOUN OR ADJECTIVE

◆ **SHADES OF WHITE**
◆ cream
◆ ecru
◆ ivory
◆ magnolia
◆ off-white
◆ oyster white
◆ pearl
◆ snow-white

whole ① ADJECTIVE
indicating all of something • *We spent the whole summer abroad.*
complete • *The list filled a complete page.*
entire • *There are only ten in the entire country.*
full • *a full week's notice*
total • *The evening was a total fiasco.*
uncut • *the uncut version of the film*
undivided • *He has my undivided loyalty.*

whole ② NOUN
the full amount of something • *the whole of Asia*
aggregate • *the aggregate of the individual scores*
all • *All is not lost.*
everything • *Everything that happened is my fault.*
lot • *He lost the lot within five minutes.*

sum total • *The small room contained the sum total of their possessions.*
total • *The eventual total was far higher.*

wicked ① ADJECTIVE
very bad or evil • *That was a wicked thing to do.*
atrocious • *He had committed atrocious crimes against the refugees.*
bad • *Please forgive our bad behaviour.*
depraved • *the work of depraved criminals*
evil • *the country's most evil terrorists*
sinful • *"This is a sinful world," he said.*
vicious • *He was a cruel and vicious man.*

MORE SYNONYMS:
• egregious
• iniquitous
• nefarious

wicked ② ADJECTIVE
mischievous in an amusing or attractive way • *She always felt wicked when eating chocolate.*
impish • *an impish sense of humour*
mischievous • *like a mischievous child*
naughty • *little boys using naughty words*

wide ① ADJECTIVE
measuring a large distance from side to side • *It should be wide enough to give plenty of working space.*
ample • *a large woman with an ample bosom*
baggy • *He was wearing ridiculously baggy trousers.*
broad • *His shoulders were broad and his waist narrow.*
expansive • *The park has swings and an expansive play area.*
extensive • *The grounds were more extensive than the town itself.*
full • *She was wearing a dress with a full skirt.*

immense • *an immense body of water*
large • *This fish lives mainly in large rivers and lakes.*
roomy • *I like roomy jackets with big pockets.*
spacious • *The house has a spacious kitchen.*
sweeping • *the long sweeping curve of the bay*
vast • *The farmers there own vast stretches of land.*
voluminous • *a voluminous trench coat*

ANTONYM:
• narrow

wide ② ADJECTIVE
extensive in scope • *a wide range of colours*
ample • *There is ample scope here for the imagination.*
borad • *A broad range of issues was discussed.*
catholic • *He has very catholic tastes in music.*
comprehensive • *a comprehensive guide to the region*
encyclopedia • *He has an encyclopedic knowledge of the subject.*
exhaustive • *The author's treatment of the topic is exhaustive.*
extensive • *The question has received extensive press coverage.*
far-ranging • *the plan to introduce far-ranging reforms*
immense • *an immense range of holiday activities*
inclusive • *an inclusive survey*
large • *a large selection of goods at reasonable prices*
vast • *a vast range of products*
wide-ranging • *The aims of the redesign are wide-ranging but simple.*

ANTONYM:
• narrow

wide ③ ADVERB
as far as possible • *Open wide!*
completely • *He opened the map out completely so we could see.*
dilated • *I could tell from his dilated pupils that he was on drugs*
fully. • *Extend the aerial fully.*
fully open • *His mouth was fully open in astonishment.*
right out • *Spread it right out to the edges.*

widespread ADJECTIVE
existing over a large area • *Food shortages are widespread.*
broad • *The agreement won broad support among the people.*
common • *the common view that treatment is ineffective*
extensive • *The bomb caused extensive damage.*
pervasive • *the pervasive influence of the army in national life*
prevalent • *Smoking is becoming more prevalent among girls.*
rife • *Bribery and corruption were rife in the industry.*

wild ① ADJECTIVE
not cultivated or domesticated • *a meadow of wild flowers*
fierce • *Fierce hyenas scavenged for food after the kill.*
free • *stunning pictures of wild and free animals*
natural • *In the natural state this animal is not ferocious.*
uncultivated • *developed from an uncultivated type of grass*
undomesticated • *These cats lived wild and were completely undomesticated.*
untamed • *the untamed horses of the Camargue*
warrigal (AUSTRALIAN; LITERARY) • *a warrigal mare*

A
B
C
D
E
F
G
H
I
J
K
L
M
N
O
P
Q
R
S
T
U
V
W
X
Y
Z

wild ② ADJECTIVE
in stormy conditions • *They were not deterred by the wild weather.*
howling • *a howling gale*
raging • *The trip involved crossing a raging torrent.*
rough • *The two ships collided in rough seas.*
stormy • *a dark and stormy night*
violent • *That night they were hit by a violent storm.*

wild ③ ADJECTIVE
without control or restraint • *wild with excitement*
boisterous • *Most of the children were noisy and boisterous.*
rowdy • *The television coverage revealed their rowdy behaviour.*
turbulent • *five turbulent years of rows and reconciliations*
uncontrolled • *His uncontrolled behaviour disturbed the entire group.*
wayward • *wayward children with a history of emotional problems*
MORE SYNONYMS:
• disorderly
• riotous
• uproarious

will ① VERB
to leave something to someone when you die • *He had willed his fortune to his daughter.*
bequeath • *She bequeathed her collection to the local museum.*
leave • *Everything was left to the housekeeper.*
pass on • *He passed on much of his estate to his eldest son.*

will ② NOUN
the strong determination to achieve something • *the will to win*
determination • *Determination has always been a part of his make-up.*

purpose • *They are enthusiastic and have a sense of purpose.*
resolution • *He began to form a resolution to clear his name.*
resolve • *This will strengthen the public's resolve.*
willpower • *succeeding by sheer willpower*

will ③ NOUN
what someone wants • *the will of the people*
choice • *It's your choice.*
inclination • *She showed no inclination to go.*
mind • *You can go if you have a mind to do so.*
volition • *a product of our volition*
wish • *done against my wishes*
RELATED WORD:
• ADJECTIVE voluntary

willing ADJECTIVE
ready and eager to do something • *a willing helper*
agreeable • *We can go ahead if you are agreeable.*
eager • *Children are eager to learn.*
game (INFORMAL) • *He still had new ideas and was game to try them.*
happy • *That's a risk I'm happy to take.*
prepared • *I'm not prepared to take orders from her.*
ready • *ready to die for their beliefs*
MORE SYNONYMS:
• amenable
• compliant
• desirous
ANTONYM:
• unwilling

win ① VERB
to defeat your opponents • *The top four teams all won.*
be victorious • *Despite the strong opposition she was victorious.*

come first • *They unexpectedly came first this year.*
prevail • *the votes he must win in order to prevail*
succeed • *the skills and qualities needed to succeed*
triumph • *a symbol of good triumphing over evil*

ANTONYM:
• lose

win ② VERB
to succeed in obtaining something • *moves to win the support of the poor*
achieve • *We have achieved our objective.*
attain • *He's half-way to attaining his pilot's licence.*
gain • *After three weeks the hostages finally gained their freedom.*
get • *My entry got a commendation this year.*
secure • *Her achievements helped secure her the job.*

win ③ NOUN
a victory in a contest • *a run of seven games without a win*
success • *his success in the Monaco Grand Prix*
triumph • *their World Cup triumph*
victory • *the 3-1 victory over Switzerland*

ANTONYM:
• defeat

winner NOUN
a person who wins something • *The winners will be notified by post.*
champion • *a former Olympic champion*
conqueror • *This time they easily overcame their former conquerors.*
victor • *He emerged as the victor by the second day.*

ANTONYM:
• loser

wisdom NOUN
judgment used to make sensible decisions • *the wisdom that comes from experience*
discernment • *Her keen discernment made her an excellent collector.*
insight • *a man of considerable insight and diplomatic skills*
judgment • *He respected our judgment on this matter.*
knowledge • *the quest for scientific knowledge*
reason • *a conflict between emotion and reason*

MORE SYNONYMS:
• astuteness
• erudition
• sagacity

ANTONYM:
• foolishness

RELATED WORD:
• ADJECTIVE sagacious

wise ADJECTIVE
able to make use of experience and judgment • *a wise old man*
informed • *an informed guess at his wealth*
judicious • *the judicious use of military force*
perceptive • *the words of a perceptive political commentator*
rational • *You must look at both sides before you can reach a rational decision.*
sensible • *The sensible thing is to leave them alone.*
shrewd • *a shrewd deduction about what was going on*

ANTONYM:
• foolish

wish ① NOUN
a desire for something • *She was sincere in her wish to make amends.*
desire • *her desire for a child of her own*

A
B
C
D
E
F
G
H
I
J
K
L
M
N
O
P
Q
R
S
T
U
V
W
X
Y
Z

hankering • *She had always had a hankering to be an actress.*

hunger • *a hunger for success*

longing • *He felt a longing for familiar surroundings.*

urge • *He had an urge to open a shop of his own.*

want • *Supermarkets respond to the wants of their customers.*

wish ② VERB
to want something • *We wished to return.*

desire • *He was bored and desired to go home.*

hunger • *She hungered for adventure.*

long • *I'm longing for the holidays.*

thirst • *thirsting for knowledge*

want • *people who know exactly what they want in life*

yearn • *The younger ones yearned to be part of a normal family.*

withdraw ① VERB
to take something out • *He withdrew some money from the bank.*

draw out • *I'll have to draw out some of my savings.*

extract • *She extracted another dress from the wardrobe.*

remove • *I removed the splinter from her finger.*

take out • *There was a fee for taking out money from the account.*

withdraw ② VERB
to back out of an activity • *They withdrew from the conference.*

back out • *He backed out of the agreement.*

leave • *Davis left the game to go to hospital.*

pull out • *The general pulled out of the talks after two days.*

retire • *The jury retired three hours ago.*

retreat • *retreating from the harsh realities of life*

MORE SYNONYMS:
• disengage
• secede

wither ① VERB
to become weaker and fade away • *Will the company flourish or wither?*

decline • *The church's influence has declined.*

fade • *Prospects for peace have already started to fade.*

wither ② VERB
to shrivel up and die • *Crops withered under the sun.*

droop • *plants drooping in the heat*

shrivel • *They watched their crops shrivel and die in the drought.*

wilt • *The roses wilted the day after she bought them.*

witness ① NOUN
someone who has seen something happen • *The police appealed for witnesses to come forward.*

bystander • *Seven other innocent bystanders were injured.*

eyewitness • *Eyewitnesses say the soldiers opened fire on the crowd.*

observer • *A casual observer would not have noticed them.*

onlooker • *a small crowd of onlookers*

spectator • *carried out in full view of spectators*

witness ② VERB
to see something happening • *Anyone who witnessed the attack should call the police.*

be present at • *Many men are now present at the birth of their children.*

observe • *We observed them setting up the machine gun.*

see • *I saw him do it.*

watch • *She had watched them drinking heavily before the accident.*

witty ADJECTIVE

amusing in a clever way • *He's so witty I could listen to him for hours.*

amusing • *He provided an irreverent and amusing commentary to the film.*

brilliant • *a brilliant after-dinner speaker*

clever • *He raised some smiles with several clever lines.*

funny • *a film packed with incredibly funny dialogue*

humorous • *a satirical and humorous parody*

sparkling • *He's famous for his sparkling conversation.*

woman NOUN

an adult female human being • *women over 75 years old*

dame (SLANG) • *Who does that dame think she is?*

female • *The average young female is fairly affluent.*

girl • *a night out with the girls*

lady • *Your table is ready, ladies, so please come through.*

lass • *a lass from the country*

sheila (AUSTRALIAN AND NEW ZEALAND; INFORMAL) • *his role as a sheila in his own play*

vrou (SOUTH AFRICAN) • *Have you met his vrou yet?*

ANTONYM:

• man

wonder ① VERB

to think about something with curiosity • *I wondered what that noise was.*

ask oneself • *You have to ask yourself what this really means.*

ponder • *pondering how to improve the team*

puzzle • *Researchers continue to puzzle over the origins of the disease.*

speculate • *He refused to speculate about the contents of the letter.*

wonder ② VERB

to be surprised and amazed • *He wondered at her anger.*

be amazed • *Most of the cast were amazed by the play's success.*

be astonished • *I was astonished to discover his true age.*

boggle • *The mind boggles at what might be in store for us.*

marvel • *We marvelled at her endless energy.*

wonder ③ NOUN

something that amazes people • *one of the wonders of nature*

marvel • *a marvel of high technology*

miracle • *It's a miracle no one was killed.*

phenomenon • *a well-known geographical phenomenon*

spectacle • *a spectacle not to be missed*

wonderful ① ADJECTIVE

extremely good • *It's wonderful to see you.*

excellent • *The recording quality is excellent.*

great (INFORMAL) • *a great bunch of guys*

marvellous • *What a marvellous time we had!*

superb • *The hotel has a superb isolated location.*

tremendous • *I thought it was a tremendous book.*

wonderful ② ADJECTIVE

very impressive • *The sunset was a truly wonderful sight.*

amazing • *containing some amazing special effects*

astounding • *The results are quite astounding.*

incredible • *The intensity of colour was incredible.*

magnificent • *magnificent views across the valley*

remarkable • *It was a remarkable*

a
b
c
d
e
f
g
h
i
j
k
l
m
n
o
p
q
r
s
t
u
v
w
x
y
z

achievement to complete the course.

MORE SYNONYMS:
• phenomenal
• wondrous

word ① NOUN

PARTS OF A WORD
♦ capital letter
♦ consonant
♦ grapheme
♦ letter
♦ phoneme
♦ prefix
♦ suffix
♦ syllable
♦ vowel

RELATED WORDS:
• ADJECTIVES lexical, verbal

word ② NOUN

a remark • *I'd like to say a word of thanks to everyone who helped me.*
comment • *He left without any further comment.*
remark • *Apart from that one remark, he stayed quiet all evening.*
statement • *Verity issued a brief statement to the press.*
utterance • *a crowd of admirers who hung on his every utterance*

word ③ NOUN

a brief conversation • *James, could I have a quick word with you?*
chat • *We need to have a chat about the arrangements some time.*
conversation • *He recalled his brief conversation with the Queen.*
discussion • *We had a very short discussion about what to do.*
talk • *I bumped into him yesterday and we had a quick talk.*

word ④ NOUN

a message • *Since then we've had no word from them.*
announcement • *There has been*

no formal announcement from either government.
bulletin • *A spokesperson said no bulletin would be issued.*
communication • *The ambassador brought a communication from the President.*
information • *They will issue written information in due course.*
intelligence • *He wanted to pass this intelligence on to her.*
message • *Did he leave any message for me?*
news • *Is there any news from the embassy?*

word ⑤ NOUN

a promise or guarantee • *He gave me his word that he would be there.*
assurance • *Do I have your assurance that you'll take responsibility?*
oath • *She gave her solemn oath not to tell anyone.*
pledge • *He gave his personal pledge that he would help.*
promise • *I'll support you - you have my promise on that.*
word of honour • *I want your word of honour that you'll respect my anonymity.*

work ① VERB

to do the tasks required of you • *I had to work twelve hours a day.*
labour • *peasants labouring in the fields*
slave • *slaving over a hot stove*
slog away • *They are still slogging away at algebra.*
toil • *Workers toiled long hours in the mills.*

ANTONYM:
• laze

work ② NOUN

someone's job • *She's trying to find work.*
business • *We have business to attend to first.*

craft • *He learned his craft from an expert.*
employment • *unable to find employment*
job • *I got at a job at the sawmill.*
livelihood • *fishermen who depend on the seas for their livelihood*
occupation • *Please state your occupation.*
profession • *a dentist by profession*

MORE SYNONYMS:
• calling
• métier
• pursuit

work ③ NOUN
the tasks that have to be done
• *Sometimes he had to take work home.*
assignment • *written assignments and practical tests*
chore • *We share the household chores.*
duty • *My duty is to look after the animals.*
job • *It turned out to be a bigger job than expected.*
task • *catching up with administrative tasks*
yakka (AUSTRALIAN AND NEW ZEALAND; INFORMAL) • *a decade of hard yakka on the land*

worker NOUN
a person who works • *seeking a reliable research worker*
craftsman • *furniture made by a local craftsman*
employee • *Many of its employees are women.*
labourer • *a farm labourer*
workman • *Workmen are building a steel fence.*

MORE SYNONYMS:
• artisan
• hand
• proletarian

work out ① VERB
to find the solution to something • *It took us some time to work out what was happening.*
calculate • *First, calculate your monthly living expenses.*
figure out • *You don't need to be a detective to figure that one out.*
resolve • *They hoped the crisis could be quickly resolved.*
solve • *We'll solve the case ourselves and surprise everyone.*

work out ② VERB
to happen in a certain way • *Things didn't work out that way after all.*
develop • *Wait and see how the situation develops.*
go • *Did it all go well?*
happen • *Things don't happen the way you want them to.*
turn out • *Sometimes life doesn't turn out as we expect.*

worn-out ① ADJECTIVE
no longer usable because of extreme wear • *a worn-out pair of shoes*
broken-down • *Broken-down cars lined the road.*
tattered • *tattered clothes*
threadbare • *a square of threadbare carpet*
worn • *Worn tyres cost lives.*

worn-out ② ADJECTIVE
extremely tired • *You must be worn-out after the journey.*
exhausted • *too exhausted to do any more*
fatigued • *Winter weather can leave you feeling fatigued.*
prostrate • *He lay prostrate with exhaustion.*
tired • *I need to rest because I'm tired.*
weary • *a weary traveller*

a
b
c
d
e
f
g
h
i
j
k
l
m
n
o
p
q
r
s
t
u
v
w
x
y
z

worried ADJECTIVE

being anxious about something • *His parents were worried about his lack of progress.*

anxious • *I was very anxious about her safety.*

bothered • *I'm not bothered about it at all.*

concerned • *a phone call from a concerned neighbour*

nervous • *Consumers say they are nervous about their jobs.*

troubled • *He was troubled by the lifestyle of his son.*

uneasy • *an uneasy feeling that everything was going wrong*

MORE SYNONYMS:
• overwrought
• perturbed
• unquiet

ANTONYM:
• unconcerned

worry ① VERB

to feel anxious about something • *Don't worry, it's bound to arrive soon.*

be anxious • *They admitted they were still anxious about the situation.*

brood • *constantly brooding about her family*

feel uneasy • *I felt very uneasy at the lack of response.*

fret • *You mustn't fret about someone else's problems.*

worry ② VERB

to disturb someone with a problem • *I didn't want to worry the boys with this.*

bother • *I hate to bother you again so soon.*

hassle (INFORMAL) • *Then my boss started hassling me.*

pester • *I wish they'd stop pestering me for an answer.*

plague • *I'm not going to plague you with more questions.*

trouble • *Don't trouble me while I'm working.*

MORE SYNONYMS:
• harry
• importune
• perturb

worry ③ NOUN

a feeling of anxiety • *a major source of worry*

anxiety • *anxieties about money*

apprehension • *real anger and apprehension about the future*

concern • *growing concern for the environment*

fear • *His fears might be groundless.*

misgiving • *She had some misgivings about what she was about to do.*

unease • *a deep sense of unease about the coming interview*

worsen VERB

to become more difficult • *My relationship with my mother worsened.*

decline • *Hourly output declined in the third quarter.*

degenerate • *The whole tone of the campaign began to degenerate.*

deteriorate • *The weather conditions are deteriorating.*

go downhill (INFORMAL) • *Things have gone steadily downhill since he left.*

ANTONYM:
• improve

worship ① VERB

to praise and revere something • *People go to church to pray and worship their god.*

glorify • *The monks devoted their days to glorifying God.*

honour • *the Scout's promise to honour God*

praise • *She asked the church to praise God.*

pray to • *They prayed to their gods to bring them rain.*

venerate • *the most venerated religious figure in the country*

MORE SYNONYMS:
• deify
• exalt
• revere

ANTONYM:
• dishonour

worship ② VERB
to love and admire someone • *She had worshipped him from afar for years.*
adore • *an adoring husband*
idolize • *She idolized her father as she was growing up.*
love • *He genuinely loved and cherished her.*

ANTONYM:
• despise

worship ③ NOUN
a feeling of love and admiration for something • *the worship of the ancient Roman gods*
admiration • *Her eyes widened in admiration.*
adoration • *He had been used to female adoration all his life.*
adulation • *The book was received with adulation by the critics.*
devotion • *flattered by his devotion*
homage • *The emperor received the homage of every prince.*
praise • *singing hymns in praise of their god*

MORE SYNONYMS:
• deification
• exaltation

◆ **PLACES OF WORSHIP**
◆ altar
◆ basilica (CHRISTIANITY)
◆ cathedral (CHRISTIANITY)
◆ chapel (CHRISTIANITY)
◆ church (CHRISTIANITY)
◆ gurdwara (SIKHISM)
◆ meeting house (QUAKERISM)

◆ mosque (ISLAM)
◆ pagoda (HINDUISM and BUDDHISM)
◆ shrine
◆ synagogue (JUDAISM)
◆ tabernacle (JUDAISM and CHRISTIANITY)
◆ temple

worthless ADJECTIVE
having no real value or worth • *a worthless piece of junk*
meaningless • *their sense of a meaningless existence*
paltry • *a paltry amount*
poor • *a poor reward for his effort*
trifling • *We were paid a trifling sum.*
trivial • *She would go to the doctor for any trivial complaint.*
useless • *I felt useless and a failure.*
valueless • *commercially valueless trees*

MORE SYNONYMS:
• negligible
• nugatory

ANTONYM:
• valuable

write VERB
to record something in writing • *Write your name and address on a postcard and send it to us.*
inscribe • *Their names were inscribed on the front of the pillar.*
record • *Her letters record the domestic and social details of her life.*
take down • *notes taken down in shorthand*

writing NOUN

◆ **TYPES OF WRITING**
◆ autobiography
◆ ballad
◆ biography
◆ blog or weblog
◆ column
◆ dissertation
◆ editorial

A
B
C
D
E
F
G
H
I
J
K
L
M
N
O
P
Q
R
S
T
U
V
W
X
Y
Z

- epitaph
- essay
- fable
- feature
- fiction
- legend
- letter
- lyric
- memoir
- myth
- narrative
- non-fiction
- novel
- obituary
- parable
- play
- poem
- report
- review
- rhyme
- riddle
- script
- story
- thesis
- verse
- **STYLES USED IN WRITING**
- alliteration
- cliché
- idiom
- metaphor
- narrative
- parody
- pun
- satire
- simile
- **FEATURES OF WRITING**
- character
- dialogue
- imagery
- motif
- plot
- setting
- subplot
- theme

wrong ① ADJECTIVE

not correct or truthful • *That was the wrong answer.*

false • *We don't know if the information is true or false.*

faulty • *His diagnosis was faulty from the outset.*

incorrect • *a decision based on figures which were incorrect*

mistaken • *a mistaken view of the situation*

unsound • *The thinking is good-hearted, but muddled and unsound.*

untrue • *The remarks were completely untrue.*

MORE SYNONYMS:
- erroneous
- fallacious

ANTONYM:
- right

wrong ② ADJECTIVE

morally unacceptable • *It's wrong to hurt people.*

bad • *I may be a thief but I'm not a bad person.*

crooked • *crooked business deals*

evil • *the country's most evil terrorists*

illegal • *It is illegal to intercept radio messages.*

immoral • *Many would consider such practices immoral.*

unfair • *It was unfair that he should suffer so much.*

unjust • *unjust treatment*

MORE SYNONYMS:
- felonious
- iniquitous
- reprehensible
- unethical

ANTONYM:
- right

wrong ③ NOUN
an unjust action • *the wrongs of our society*
abuse • *controversy over human rights abuses*
crime • *crimes against humanity*

grievance • *He had a deep sense of grievance.*
injustice • *A great injustice had been done to him in the past.*
sin • *He admitted the many sins of his youth.*

Yy

yellow NOUN or ADJECTIVE

- ◆ **SHADES OF YELLOW**
- ◆ amber
- ◆ canary yellow
- ◆ champagne
- ◆ citrus yellow
- ◆ daffodil
- ◆ gold
- ◆ lemon
- ◆ mustard
- ◆ primrose
- ◆ saffron
- ◆ sand
- ◆ straw
- ◆ topaz

yes INTERJECTION

an expression used to agree with something or say it is true • *"Are you a friend of his?" "Yes."*
aye (SCOTTISH; INFORMAL) • *"Can I borrow this?" "Aye, but I want it back."*
okay • *"Will we leave now?" "Okay, if you like."*
sure • *"Can I come too?" "Sure."*
ya (SOUTH AFRICAN) • *"Are you a runaway?" "Ya," the child replied.*
yeah (INFORMAL) • *Yeah, I think we've met once.*

ANTONYM:
• no

yokel NOUN

a person who lives in the country • *a bunch of those yokels*

bushie or **bushy** (AUSTRALIAN AND NEW ZEALAND; INFORMAL) • *"I'm a bit of a bushie at heart," she said.*
countryman • *They are true old-fashioned countrymen.*
peasant • *In rural Mexico a peasant is rarely without his machete.*

young ① ADJECTIVE

not yet mature • *young people*
adolescent • *He spent his adolescent years playing guitar.*
immature • *an immature female whale*
infant • *his infant daughter*
junior • *a junior member of the family*
juvenile • *a juvenile delinquent*
little • *What were you like when you were little?*
youthful • *the youthful stars of the film*

ANTONYM:
• old

young ② PLURAL NOUN

the babies an animal has • *The hen may not be able to feed its young.*
babies • *animals making nests for their babies*
brood • *a hungry brood of fledglings*
family • *a family of weasels*
litter • *a litter of pups*
little ones • *a family of elephants with their little ones*
offspring • *female rats' offspring*

Zz

zero NOUN
nothing or the number 0 • *I will now count from zero to ten.*
nil • *They beat Argentina one-nil.*

nothing • *Some weeks I earn nothing.*
nought • *How many noughts are there in a million?*

Word Studies

BAD

BAD is such a commonly-used word that is has come to lose much of its effectiveness. Depending on the sense and context of what you are saying, there are many other much more expressive words that can be used instead.

1. If you are describing something that has a harmful effect, you could try:
   - extremely **damaging**
   - **destructive** effect
   - **detrimental** impact
   - **harmful** effects
   - **unhealthy** lifestyle
   - **unpleasant** side effects

2. If you are describing something upsetting, you could try:
   - **distressing** images
   - **disturbing** news
   - **grim** days
   - **painful** memories
   - a **traumatic** period
   - an **unsettling** atmosphere
   - an **upsetting** experience

3. If you are describing physical pain, you could try:
   - an **acute** attack
   - an **agonizing** death
   - **excruciating** pain
   - **intense** cramps
   - a **painful** knee
   - **serious** back problems
   - **severe** stomach pains
   - **terrible** migraine

4. If you are describing something of poor quality, you could try:
   - a **defective** engine
   - a **deficient** diet
   - **faulty** goods
   - an **imperfect** copy
   - an **inadequate** response
   - an **inferior** product
   - a **pathetic** excuse
   - **poor** housing
   - a **sorry** effort
   - an **unsatisfactory** reply

5. If you are describing someone or something that lacks skill, you could try:
   - an **incompetent** workman
   - an **inept** performance
   - a **poor** judge
   - a **useless** committee

6. If you are describing something or someone evil, you could try:
   - **corrupt** practices
   - **criminal** actions
   - **depraved** criminals
   - an **evil** man
   - an **immoral** act
   - **sinful** behaviour
   - a **villainous** character
   - a **wicked** stepmother
   - something **wrong**

BIG

Try not to use **BIG** to describe the size or importance of a person or thing. Use one of the many alternatives available.

1. If you are describing the size of something, you could try:
   - *a **colossal** statue*
   - *an **enormous** building*
   - *a **gigantic** creature*
   - *a **great** forest*
   - *a **huge** cake*
   - *an **immense** wall*
   - *a **large** map*
   - *a **massive** display*
   - *a **significant** difference*
   - *a **vast** cathedral*

2. If you are describing the importance of something or someone, you could try:
   - *an **eminent** politician*
   - *an **important** influence*
   - *an **influential** figure*
   - *a **leading** thinker*
   - *a **major** role*
   - *a **powerful** businessman*
   - *the **principal** guest*
   - *a **prominent** scientist*
   - *a **significant** investor*

3. If you are describing an important issue or problem, you could try:
   - *a **critical** moment*
   - *a **grave** crisis*
   - *a **momentous** decision*
   - *a **serious** disadvantage*
   - *an **urgent** need*
   - *a **weighty** problem*

Word Studies

There are lots of words you can use instead of **BREAK**, which give additional information about the way in which something breaks or is broken.

1. If something hard **cracks**, or you **crack** it, it becomes slightly damaged, with lines appearing on its surface:
    • *To get at the coconut flesh, **crack** the shell with a hammer.*

2. If something **fractures**, or you **fracture** it, it gets a slight crack in it:
    • *You've **fractured** a rib.*

3. If something **snaps**, or you **snap** it, it breaks suddenly, with a sharp cracking noise:
    • *She gripped the pipe in both hands, trying to **snap** it in half.*

4. If something **splits**, or you **split** it, it breaks into two or more parts:
    • *In the severe gale, the ship **split** in two.*

5. If something **splinters**, or you **splinter** it, it breaks into thin, sharp pieces:
    • *The ruler **splintered** into pieces.*

6. If something **fragments**, or is **fragmented**, it breaks or separates into small parts:
    • *The rock began to **fragment** and crumble.*

7. If something **crumbles**, or you **crumble** it, it breaks into many small pieces:
    • ***Crumble** the cheese into a bowl.*

8. If something **shatters**, it breaks into many small pieces:
    • *Safety glass won't **shatter** if it's hit.*

9. If something **disintegrates**, it breaks into many pieces and is destroyed:
    • *The car's windscreen **disintegrated** with the impact of the crash.*

10. If you **smash** something, or it **smashes**, it breaks into many small pieces, often because it has been hit or dropped:
    • *Two glasses fell off the table and **smashed** into pieces.*

11. If you **wreck** or **demolish** something, you completely destroy it:
    • *The bridge was **wrecked** by the storms.*
    • *The hurricane **demolished** houses across the area.*

CRY

If you want to give a little more detail about how a person cries, there are words you can use instead of CRY.

Word Studies

1. If you **weep**, you cry. This is quite a literary word:
   • *The woman began to **weep** uncontrollably.*

2. If you **whimper**, you make a low, unhappy sound as if you are about to cry:
   • *He huddled in a corner, **whimpering** with fear.*

3. If you **sob**, you cry in a noisy way, with short breaths:
   • *Her sister broke down and began to **sob** into her handkerchief.*

4. If you **blubber**, you cry noisily and in an unattractive way:
   • *To our surprise, he began to **blubber** like a child.*

5. If you **howl** or **wail**, you cry with a long, loud noise:
   • *The baby was **howling** in the next room.*
   • *The woman was **wailing** for her lost child.*

6. If you **bawl**, you cry very loudly:
   • *One of the toddlers was **bawling**.*

CUT

There are many useful alternatives for CUT, depending on what is being cut, what device is doing the cutting, and how deep the cutting is.

1. If you **nick** something, you make a small cut on its surface:
   • He **nicked** his chin while he was shaving.

2. If you **score** something, you cut a line or lines on its surface:
   • Lightly **score** the surface of the steaks with a cook's knife.

3. If you **slit** something, you make a long narrow cut in it:
   • He began to **slit** open each envelope.

4. If you **clip** something, you cut small pieces from it in order to shape it:
   • I saw an old man out **clipping** his hedge.

5. If you **trim** something, you cut off small amounts of it to make it look neater:
   • I have my hair **trimmed** every eight weeks.

6. If you **slice** something, you cut it into thin pieces:
   • I **sliced** the beef into thin strips.

7. If you **chop** something, you cut it into pieces with strong downward movements of a knife or axe:
   • You will need to **chop** the onions very finely.

EAT

Instead of using **EAT**, use one of the many other words that describe how a person eats.

1. If you **consume** something, you eat it. This is a formal word:
   • *Andrew would **consume** nearly a pound of cheese a day.*

2. When an animal **feeds**, or **feeds on** something, it eats:
   • *After a few days the caterpillars stopped **feeding**.*
   • *Slugs **feed on** decaying plant material.*

3. If you **swallow** something, you make it go from your mouth into your stomach:
   • *Snakes **swallow** their prey whole.*

4. If you **snack**, you eat things between meals:
   • *Instead of **snacking** on crisps and chocolate, eat fruit.*

5. If you **chew** something, you break it up with your teeth so that it is easier to swallow:
   • *I pulled out a filling while I was **chewing** a toffee.*

6. If you **nibble** food, you eat it by biting very small pieces of it, perhaps because you are not very hungry:
   • *She **nibbled** at a piece of dry toast.*

7. If you **munch** food, you eat it by chewing it slowly, thoroughly, and rather noisily:
   • *Luke **munched** his sandwiches appreciatively.*

8. If you **stuff yourself**, you eat a lot of food:
   • *They'd **stuffed themselves** with sweets before dinner.*

9. If you **gobble**, **guzzle**, **wolf (down)**, or **scoff** food, you eat it quickly and greedily. **Guzzle, wolf (down)**, and **scoff** are all informal words:
   • *Pete **gobbled** all the stew before anyone else arrived.*
   • *one of those people who **guzzle** chocolate whenever they are unhappy*
   • *I was back in the changing room **wolfing** sandwiches.*
   • *You greedy so-and-so! You've **scoffed** the lot!*

10. If you **devour** something, you eat it quickly and eagerly:
    • *She **devoured** half an apple pie.*

There are a number of alternatives to FAT, depending on how overweight the person is and how sensitive you are to the possibility of hurting the person's feelings.

1. Someone who is **overweight** weighs more than is considered attractive. However, you can be just a little overweight as well as very overweight:
   • *Since having my baby, I feel slightly **overweight**.*

2. If you say someone is **podgy**, you mean that they are slightly fat. This is an informal word:
   • *Eddie's getting a little **podgy** round the middle.*

3. If you describe someone as **fleshy**, you mean that they are slightly too fat:
   • *He was well-built, but too **fleshy** to be an imposing figure.*

4. A **chubby**, **tubby**, or **stout** person is rather fat:
   • *I was greeted by a small **chubby** man.*
   • *He had been a short **tubby** child who was taunted about his weight.*
   • *a tall **stout** man with grey hair*

5. A **portly** person is rather fat. This word is mostly used to describe men:
   • *a **portly** middle-aged man*

6. You can use the word **plump** to describe someone who is rather fat or rounded, usually when you think this is a good quality:

   • *Maria was a pretty little thing, small and **plump** with a mass of dark curls.*

7. If you describe a woman's figure as **rounded**, you mean that it is attractive because it is well-developed and not too thin:
   • *a beautiful woman with blue eyes and a **rounded** figure*

8. A **roly-poly** person is pleasantly fat and round. This is an informal word:
   • *a **roly-poly** little woman with laughing eyes*

9. If you describe a woman as **buxom**, you mean that she looks healthy and attractive and has a rounded body and big breasts:
   • *Melissa was a tall **buxom** blonde.*

10. If you describe someone as **obese**, you mean that they are extremely fat, perhaps to the point of being unhealthy:
    • ***Obese** people tend to have higher blood pressure than lean people.*

11. If you describe someone as **gross**, you mean that they are extremely fat and unattractive. This is a very insulting word to use:
    • *He tried to raise his **gross** body from the sofa.*

GOOD

Like **bad**, GOOD is used in so many ways to describe so many things that it has lost much of its effectiveness. Explore the wide range of alternative words available.

1. If you are describing the quality of something, you could try:
   • an **acceptable** standard
   • an **excellent** meal
   • a **fine** match
   • a **first-class** game
   • a **first-rate** dinner
   • a **great** concert
   • a **splendid** hotel
   • a **superb** performance

2. If you are describing an experience, you could try:
   • an **agreeable** evening
   • a **delightful** party
   • an **enjoyable** trip
   • a **lovely** holiday in Paris
   • a **pleasant** stay

3. If you are describing someone's behaviour, you could try:
   • **disciplined** behaviour
   • a **docile** child
   • three **obedient** sons
   • an **orderly** queue
   • **well-behaved** pupils

4. If you are describing someone who is skilled at something, you could try:
   • an **able** student
   • an **accomplished** pianist
   • He is **adept** at manipulating the press.
   • a **capable** employee

   • a **clever** negotiator
   • a **competent** worker
   • an **efficient** manager
   • an **expert** painter
   • an **first-rate** teacher
   • a **proficient** driver
   • a **skilled** carpenter
   • a **talented** musician

5. If you are describing an effect, you could try:
   • **advantageous** changes
   • **beneficial** effects
   • **favourable** conditions
   • **positive** results

6. If you are describing advice or an idea, you could try:
   • **constructive** input
   • a **helpful** suggestion
   • a **judicious** approach
   • a **prudent** strategy
   • **sound** advice
   • **practical** help
   • a **sensible** way
   • a **useful** tip
   • a **wise** plan

7. If you are describing a person or an action, you could try:
   • a **benevolent** parent
   • a **charitable** donation
   • a **considerate** son
   • a **generous** nature
   • a **humane** person

- *a **kind** woman*
- *a **kind-hearted** friend*
- *an **obliging** neighbour*
- *a **thoughtful** child*

8. If you are describing someone or something, you could try:

- *a **commendable** idea*
- *a thoroughly **decent** human being*
- *an **ethical** stance*
- *an **honourable** man*
- *an **upright** citizen*
- *a **virtuous** life*
- *a **worthy** cause*

HAPPY

There are many other words you can use in your writing in order to avoid using HAPPY.

Word Studies

1. If you would like to describe someone or something as displaying a cheerful nature or mood, you could try:
   • a **cheerful** disposition
   • a **cheery** face
   • You're very **chirpy** today.
   • a **jolly** fat man
   • a **merry** laugh
   • her unfailingly **sunny** nature

2. If you would like to describe something that causes joy, you could try:
   • the **agreeable** task
   • their **blissful** marriage
   • a truly **festive** occasion
   • a **gratifying** relationship
   • a **joyful** event
   • the **joyous** news
   • a **pleasurable** memory

3. If you would like to describe someone who is willing to do something, you could try:
   • She was **content** to sit and wait.
   • He is always **glad** to be of service.
   • I would be **pleased** to take you there myself.
   • She would be **prepared** to talk to them.
   • He's **ready** to help anyone.
   • I'm **willing** to wait.

4. If you would like to describe a feeling of joy at something, you could try:
   • They are **delighted** with their new home.
   • I was **ecstatic** to see George again.
   • She was **elated** that she had won.
   • He is understandably **euphoric** at the result.
   • We are all **glad** to be back.
   • She takes a **joyful** pride in her work.
   • They were **jubilant** over their victory.
   • The sisters are **overjoyed** to be reunited.
   • The players are **over the moon** with this result.
   • We're very **pleased** at the news.
   • I'm just **thrilled** about the job.

HIT

There is a wide range of words you can use instead of HIT, allowing you to find the one that describes exactly what is happening.

1. If you **strike** someone or something, you hit them deliberately. This is a formal word:
   • *She stepped forward and struck him across the mouth.*

2. If you **tap** something, you hit it with a quick light blow or series of blows:
   • *Tap the egg gently with a teaspoon to crack the shell.*

3. If you **pat** something or someone, you tap them lightly, usually with your hand held flat:
   • *'Don't worry about it,' he said patting me on the knee.*

4. If you **rap** something, or **rap on** it, you hit it with a series of quick blows:
   • *He rapped the glass with the knuckles of his right hand.*

5. If you **slap** or **smack** someone, you hit them with the palm of your hand:
   • *I slapped him hard across the face.*
   • *She smacked the child on the side of the head.*

6. If you **swat** something such as an insect, you hit it with a quick, swinging movement using your hand or a flat object:
   • *Every time a fly came near, I swatted it with a newspaper.*

7. If you **knock** someone or something, you hit it roughly, especially so that it falls or moves:
   • *She accidentally knocked the tin off the shelf.*

8. If you **knock** something such as a door or window, you hit it, usually several times, to attract someone's attention:
   • *She went to his apartment and knocked the door loudly.*

9. If you **beat** something, you hit it hard, usually several times or continuously for a period of time:
   • *a circle of men beating drums*

10. If you **hammer** something, you hit it hard several times to make a noise:
    • *We had to hammer the door and shout to attract their attention.*

11. If you **pound** something, you hit it with great force, usually loudly and repeatedly:
    • *He pounded the table with both fists.*

12. If you **batter** someone or something, you hit them very hard, using your fists or a heavy object:
    • *He battered the empty oil drum with a club.*

HIT

13. If you **bang** something, you hit it hard, making a loud noise:
    • *We banged on the door and shouted to be let out.*

14. If you **bang** a part of your body, you accidentally knock it against something and hurt it:
    • *She'd fainted and banged her head.*

15. If you **belt** someone, you hit them very hard. This is an informal word:
    • *She drew back her fist and belted him right in the stomach.*

16. If you **bash** someone or something, you hit them hard. This is an informal word:
    • *The chef was bashed over the head with a bottle.*

17. If you **whack** someone or something, you hit them hard. This is an informal word:
    • *Someone whacked me with a baseball bat.*

18. If you **wallop** someone or something, you hit them very hard, often causing a dull sound. This is an informal word:
    • *Once, she walloped me over the head with a frying pan.*

19. If you **thump** someone or something, you hit them hard, usually with your fist:
    • *I'm warning you, if you don't shut up, I'll thump you.*

20. If you **punch** someone or something, you hit them hard with your fist:
    • *After punching him on the chin, she ran off.*

LAUGH

Rather than using **LAUGH**, try one of the alternatives to express exactly how a person is laughing.

1. If you **chuckle**, you laugh quietly:
   • *I chuckled to myself at the look on his face.*

2. If you **chortle**, you laugh in a pleased or amused way:
   • *He sat there chortling at my predicament.*

3. If you **snigger**, you laugh in a quiet, sly way, perhaps at something rude or unkind:
   • *The boys sniggered when the teacher dropped his glasses on the floor.*

4. If you **giggle**, you laugh in a high-pitched way because you are nervous or embarrassed:
   • *They followed me around, giggling every time I spoke.*

5. If you **titter**, you give a short, nervous laugh, often at something rude or because you are embarrassed:
   • *The audience began to titter when the speaker couldn't find his notes.*

6. If you **cackle**, you laugh in a loud, harsh, and unpleasant way, often at something bad which happens to someone else:
   • *Her staff all cackled when they heard that she had been fired.*

7. If you **guffaw**, **howl**, or **roar**, you laugh very loudly because you think something is very funny:
   • *They guffawed at the comedian's jokes.*
   • *The crowd howled at his antics.*
   • *We roared when she told us the story.*

LOOK

All the words below mean **LOOK** but each one expresses a slightly different way of looking. Find the one that captures just what you mean.

1. If you **glance**, **peek**, or **peep** at something, you look at it quickly, and often secretly:
   • He **glanced** at his watch as she spoke.
   • She **peeked** at him through the curtains.
   • He **peeped** at me to see if I was watching him.

2. If you **scan** something written or printed, you look at it quickly:
   • She **scanned** the advertisement pages of the newspapers.

3. If you **eye** or **regard** someone or something, you look at them carefully:
   • The waiters **eyed** him with suspicion.
   • He **regarded** me curiously.

4. If you **gaze** or **stare** at someone or something, you look at them steadily for a long time, for example because you find them interesting or because you are thinking about something else. **Staring** is often thought to be rude, but **gazing** is not:
   • She sat **gazing** into the fire for a long time.
   • They **stared** silently into each other's eyes.

5. If you **observe** or **watch** someone or something, you look at them for a period of time to see what they are doing or what is happening:
   • A man was **observing** him from across the square.
   • I hate people **watching** me while I eat.

6. If you **survey** or **view** someone or something, you look at the whole of them carefully:
   • He stood up and **surveyed** the crowd.
   • The mourners filed past to **view** the body.

7. If you **examine**, **scrutinize**, or **study** something, you look at it very carefully, often to find out information from it:
   • He **examined** all the evidence.
   • He **scrutinized** her passport and stamped it.
   • We **studied** the menu for several minutes.

8. If you **glare**, **glower**, or **scowl** at someone, you stare at them angrily:
   • He **glared** resentfully at me.
   • She stood **glowering** at me with her arms crossed.
   • She **scowled** at the two men as they came into the room.

9. If you **peer** or **squint** at something, you try to see it more clearly by narrowing or screwing up your eyes as you look at it:
   • *He was **peering** at me through the keyhole.*
   • *She **squinted** at the blackboard, trying to read what was on it.*

10. If you **gape** at someone or something, you look at them in surprise, usually with your mouth open:
    • *She was **gaping** at the wreckage, lost for words.*

11. If you **goggle** at someone or something, you look at them with your eyes wide open, usually because you are surprised by them:
    • *He **goggled** at me in disbelief.*

12. If you **ogle** someone, you look at them in a way that makes it very obvious that you find them attractive:
    • *I hate the way he **ogles** every woman who goes by.*

Word Studies

MOVE

There are many ways to **MOVE**, and as many words to describe the way it is done. Use one of the alternatives below.

1. When a person **crawls**, they move forwards on their hands and knees:
   • *As he tried to **crawl** away, he was kicked in the head.*

2. When an insect **crawls** somewhere, it moves there quite slowly:
   • *I watched the moth **crawl** up the outside of the lampshade.*

3. If a person or animal **creeps** somewhere, they move quietly and slowly:
   • *I tried to **creep** upstairs without being heard.*

4. To **inch** somewhere means to move there very carefully and slowly:
   • *He began to **inch** along the ledge.*

5. If you **edge** somewhere, you move very slowly in that direction:
   • *He **edged** closer to the telephone.*

6. If a person or animal **slithers** somewhere, they move by sliding along the ground in an uneven way:
   • *Robert lost his footing and **slithered** down the bank.*

7. If you **wriggle** somewhere, for example through a small gap, you move there by twisting and turning your body:
   • *I **wriggled** through a gap in the fence.*

8. When people or small animals **scamper** or **scuttle** somewhere, they move there quickly with small, light steps:
   • *The children got off the bus and **scampered** into the playground.*
   • *The crabs **scuttled** along the muddy bank.*

9. When people or small animals **scurry** somewhere, they move there quickly and hurriedly, often because they are frightened:
   • *The attack began, sending residents **scurrying** for cover.*

10. If you **hurry**, **race**, or **rush** somewhere, you go there as quickly as you can:
    • *Claire **hurried** along the road.*
    • *He **raced** across town to the hospital.*
    • *A schoolgirl **rushed** into a burning building to save a baby.*

11. If you **hasten** somewhere, you hurry there. This is a literary word:
    • *He **hastened** along the corridor to Grace's room.*

12. If you **dash**, **dart**, or **shoot** somewhere, you run or go there quickly and suddenly:
    • She jumped up and **dashed** out of the room.
    • The girl turned and **darted** away through the trees.
    • They had almost reached the boat when a figure **shot** past them.

13. If you say that someone or something **flies** in a particular direction, you are emphasizing that they move there with a lot of speed and force:
    • I **flew** downstairs to answer the door.

14. If you **tear** somewhere, you move there very quickly, often in an uncontrolled or dangerous way:
    • Without looking to left or right, he **tore** off down the road.

15. When you **run**, you move quickly because you are in a hurry to get somewhere:
    • I excused myself and **ran** back to the house.

16. If you **jog**, you run slowly:
    • She **jogged** off in the direction he had indicated.

17. If you **sprint**, you run as fast as you can over a short distance:
    • The sergeant **sprinted** to the car.

18. If you **gallop**, you run somewhere very quickly:
    • They were **galloping** round the garden playing football.

19. If a person or animal **bolts**, they suddenly start to run very fast, often because something has frightened them:
    • I made some excuse and **bolted** towards the exit.

20. If a group of animals or people **stampede**, they run in a wild, uncontrolled way:
    • The crowd **stampeded** out of the hall.

NICE

Instead of using **NICE**, think carefully about what you are trying to describe. Is it a person, object, quality, or event? Then consider the many alternatives you can use.

1. If you are describing someone's appearance, you could try:
   • an **attractive** young lady
   • a **beautiful** baby boy
   • a very **cute** girl
   • her **dishy** brother
   • a **good-looking** guy
   • her **gorgeous** boyfriend
   • a **handsome** young man
   • a **lovely** woman
   • two **pretty** girls

2. If you are describing an object, place, or view, you could try:
   • a **beautiful** old church
   • a **charming** little fishing village
   • a **delightful** room
   • a **lovely** walled garden
   • a **pretty** cottage

3. If you are describing an item of clothing, you could try:
   • a **chic** black suit
   • an **elegant** evening dress
   • a **fetching** outfit
   • a **smart** wool jacket
   • She wears such **stylish** clothes.

4. If you are describing an event or occasion, you could try:
   • a very **agreeable** dinner party
   • a **delightful** wedding
   • an **enjoyable** evening
   • a **fantastic** party
   • a **lovely** holiday
   • a **pleasurable** experience

5. If you are describing someone's personality, you could try:
   • an **amiable** woman
   • a **considerate** neighbour
   • always **friendly** to strangers
   • unfailingly **good-natured**
   • **kind** to everyone
   • a **kindly** old man
   • an immensely **likeable** chap
   • a **thoughtful** girl

6. If you are describing food or drink, you could try:
   • an **appetizing** smell
   • some **delectable** raspberries
   • a **delicious** meal
   • a bowl of **luscious** peaches
   • a **mouthwatering** dessert
   • a **tasty** soup

NICE

7. If you are describing the weather, you could try:
   - *a **beautiful** morning*
   - *a **fine** afternoon*
   - *a **glorious** summer day*

8. If you are describing a room, flat, or house, you could try:
   - *a **comfortable** bungalow*
   - *a **cosy** sitting room*
   - *a **homely** atmosphere*
   - *a **welcoming** home*

Word Studies

OLD

Whether you are writing about an OLD person or an OLD thing, there are other words you can use to make your writing more interesting.

1. If you are describing someone who has lived for a long time, you could try:
   - an **aged** parent
   - her **ancient** grandparents
   - an **elderly** man
   - a **venerable** professor

2. If you are describing something in the past, you could try:
   - relics of **ancient** cultures
   - rituals of a **bygone** civilization
   - an **earlier** marriage
   - the **early** days of advertising
   - his **ex**-wife
   - a **former** colleague
   - in **olden** times
   - **one-time** president
   - **past** grievances
   - **previous** tenants
   - **prior** arrangements
   - those **remote** days of the Wild West

SAY

If you avoid SAY, you can be more creative by using one of the words which describe the way in which a person says something.

1. If someone **utters** sounds or words, they say them. This is a literary word:
   • *They left without **uttering** a single word.*

2. If you **comment** on something, you say something about it:
   • *He has refused to **comment** on these reports.*

3. If you **remark** that something is the case, you say that it is the case:
   • *'I don't see you complaining,' he **remarked**.*

4. If you **state** something, you say it in a formal or definite way:
   • *Could you please **state** your name for the record?*

5. If you **mention** something, you say something about it, usually briefly:
   • *He never **mentioned** that he was married.*

6. If you **note** something, you mention it in order to bring people's attention to it:
   • *'It's already getting dark,' he **noted**.*

7. If you **observe** that something is the case, you make a comment about it, especially when it is something you have noticed or thought about a lot:
   • *'He's a very loyal friend,' Daniel **observed**.*

8. If you **point out** a fact or mistake, you tell someone about it or draw their attention to it:
   • *'You've not done so badly out of the deal,' she **pointed out**.*

9. If you **announce** something, you tell people about it publicly or officially:
   • *'We're engaged!' she **announced**.*

10. If you **affirm** something, you state firmly that it is the case:
    • *'I'm staying right here,' he **affirmed**.*

11. If someone **asserts** a fact or belief, they state it firmly:
    • *'The facts are clear,' the Prime Minister **asserted**.*

12. If you **declare** that something is true, you say that it is true in a firm, deliberate way:
    • *'I'm absolutely thrilled with the result,' he **declared**.*

SAY

13. If you **add** something when you are speaking, you say something more:
    • *'Anyway, it serves you right,'* she **added** defiantly.

14. If you **interrupt**, you say something while someone else is speaking:
    • *'I don't think you quite understand,'* James **interrupted**.

15. If you **put in** a remark, you interrupt someone or add to what they have said with the remark:
    • *'Not that it's any of your business,'* Helen **put in**.

16. When people **chat**, they talk to each other in a friendly and informal way:
    • *We were just standing* **chatting** *in the corridor.*

17. If you **converse** with someone, you talk to them. This is a formal word:
    • *They were* **conversing** *in German.*

18. When people **natter**, they talk casually for a long time about unimportant things:
    • *Susan and her friend were still* **nattering** *when I left.*

19. If you **gossip** with someone, you talk informally, especially about other people or events:
    • *We sat and* **gossiped** *well into the evening.*

20. If you **explain** something, you give details about it so that it can be understood:
    • *'We weren't married at that point,'* she **explained**.

21. If you **ask** something, you say it in the form of a question because you want to know the answer:
    • *'How is Frank?'* he **asked**.

22. If you **inquire** about something, you ask for information about it. This is a formal word:
    • *'Is something wrong?'* he **inquired**.

23. To **query** or **question** means to ask a question:
    • *'Can I help you?'* the assistant **queried**.
    • *'What if something goes wrong?'* he **questioned** anxiously.

24. When you **answer** or **reply** to someone who has just spoken, you say something back to them:
    • *'When are you leaving?'* she asked. *'Tomorrow,'* he **answered**.
    • *'That's a nice outfit,'* he commented. *'Thanks,'* she **replied**.

25. When you **respond** to something that has been said, you react to it by saying something yourself:
   • *'Are you well enough to carry on?' 'Of course,' she **responded** scornfully.*

26. To **retort** means to reply angrily to someone. This is a formal word:
   • *'I don't agree,' James said. 'Who cares what you think?' she **retorted**.*

27. If someone **babbles**, they talk in a confused or excited way:
   • *'I'm so excited I don't know what I'm doing,' she **babbled**.*

28. If you **chatter**, you talk quickly and excitedly about things which are not important:
   • *Everyone was **chattering** away in different languages.*

29. If you **gabble**, you say things so quickly that it is difficult for people to understand you:
   • *Marcello sat on his knee and **gabbled** excitedly.*

30. If you **prattle**, you talk a great deal about something unimportant:
   • *She was **prattling** on about this guy she had met the night before.*

31. If someone **rambles**, they talk but do not make much sense because they keep going off the subject:
   • *The old man **rambled** about his feud with his neighbours.*

32. If someone **breathes** something, they say it very quietly. This is a literary word:
   • *'Oh, thank God you're here,' he **breathed**.*

33. When you **whisper**, you say something very quietly, using your breath rather than your throat:
   • *'Keep your voice down,' I **whispered**.*

34. If you **hiss** something, you say it forcefully in a whisper:
   • *'Stay here and don't make a sound,' he **hissed**.*

35. If you **mumble**, you speak very quietly and not at all clearly, so that your words are hard to make out:
   • *'I didn't know I was meant to do it,' she **mumbled**.*

36. If you **murmur** something, you speak very quietly, so that not many people can hear you:
   • *'How convenient,' I **murmured**.*

37. If you **mutter**, you speak very quietly, often because you are complaining about something:
   • *'Oh great,' he **muttered**, 'That's all I need.'*

38. If you **croak** something, you say it in a low, rough voice:
   • *'Water!' he **croaked**.*

SAY

39. If you **grunt** something, you say it in a low voice, often because you are annoyed or not interested:
    • 'Rubbish,' I **grunted**, 'You just didn't try hard enough.'

40. If you **rasp** something, you say it in a harsh, unpleasant voice:
    • 'Get into the car,' he **rasped**.

41. If you **wheeze** something, you say it with a whistling sound, for example because you cannot get your breath:
    • 'I'm really out of condition,' I **wheezed**.

42. If you **gasp** something, you say it in a short, breathless way, especially because you are surprised, shocked, or in pain:
    • 'What do you mean?' she **gasped**.

43. If you **pant** something, you say it while breathing loudly and quickly with your mouth open because you have been doing something energetic:
    • 'Let me get my breath back,' he **panted**, 'I'm not as young as I used to be.'

44. If you **groan** or **moan** something, you say it in a low voice, usually because you are unhappy or in pain:
    • 'My leg - I think it's broken,' Eric **groaned**.
    • 'I can't stand it any longer,' she **moaned**.

45. When someone **growls** something, they say it in a low, rough, and angry voice:
    • 'I ought to kill you for this,' Sharpe **growled**.

46. If you **snarl** something, you say it in a fierce, angry way:
    • 'Get out of here,' he **snarled**.

47. If you **snap** at someone, you speak to them in a sharp, unfriendly way:
    • 'Of course you can't have it,' he **snapped**.

SHORT

The are a number of words you can use instead of SHORT, although you should be aware that some are more likely to hurt a person's feelings than others.

1. A **little** or **small** person is not large in physical size:
   • *She was too **little** to reach the books on the top shelf.*
   • *She is **small** for her age.*

2. A **diminutive** person is very small:
   • *a **diminutive** figure standing at the entrance*

3. A **tiny** person is extremely small:
   • *Though she was **tiny**, she had a loud voice.*

4. If you describe a woman as **petite**, you are politely saying that she is small and not fat. This is a complimentary word:
   • *a **petite** blonde woman*

5. If you describe someone as **dumpy**, you mean they are short and fat. This is an uncomplimentary word:
   • *a **dumpy** woman in a baggy tracksuit*

6. If you describe someone as **squat**, you mean that they are short and thick, usually in an unattractive way:
   • *Eddie was a **squat** fellow in his mid-forties.*

Word Studies

SMALL

Before using SMALL in your writing, think about what you are describing, and then try one of the alternatives offered here.

1. If you are describing an object or the physical size of something, you could try:
   • *a **little** table*
   • *a **miniature** camera*
   • *a pair of **minuscule** shorts*
   • *a **minute** amount*
   • *a **tiny** room*

2. If you are describing an area, you could try:
   • *a **little** distance from the station*
   • *a **narrow** space*
   • *a **restricted** habitat*

3. If you are describing the size of a person, you could try:
   • *a **diminutive** figure*
   • *a **dumpy** man*
   • *too **little** to reach the shelf*
   • *a **petite** blonde*
   • *a **short** bald fellow*
   • *a **tiny** girl*

4. If you are describing a person's age, you could try:
   • *my **baby** brother*
   • *an **infant** prodigy*
   • *Her boys are only **little**.*
   • *a **young** child*

THIN

There are different ways of calling a person **THIN**. Some are complimentary, some are neutral, and some are definitely uncomplimentary. Remember this when you are choosing.

1. A **slender** person is attractively thin and graceful:
   • *a tall **slender** lady in a straw hat*

2. A **slim** person has an attractively thin and well-shaped body:
   • *a pretty **slim** girl with hazel eyes*

3. A **slight** person has a fairly thin and delicate-looking body:
   • *He is a **slight**, bespectacled, intellectual figure.*

4. A **light** person does not weigh very much:
   • *You need to be **light** to be a dancer.*

5. Someone who is **spare** is tall and not at all fat. This is a literary word:
   • *She was thin and **spare**, with a sharp, intelligent face.*

6. If you describe someone as **lean**, you mean that they are thin but look strong and healthy:
   • *Like most long-distance runners, she was **lean** and muscular.*

7. If you say someone is **lanky**, you mean that they are tall and thin and move rather awkwardly:
   • *He had grown into a **lanky** teenager.*

8. A **skinny** person is extremely thin, in a way that you find unattractive. This is an informal word:
   • *I don't think these **skinny** supermodels are very attractive.*

9. If you say a person is **scraggy** or **scrawny**, you mean that they look unattractive because they are so thin:
   • *a **scraggy** old man*
   • *a **scrawny** child of fifteen*

10. Someone who is **bony** has very little flesh covering their bones:
    • *a **bony** old woman dressed in black*

11. If someone is **underweight**, they are too thin and therefore not healthy:
    • *Nearly a third of the girls were severely **underweight**.*

12. A person or animal that is **emaciated** is very thin and weak from illness or lack of food:
    • *horrific television pictures of **emaciated** prisoners*

WALK

Instead of using **WALK**, use another word that describes exactly how the person walks.

1. If you **step** in a particular direction, you move your foot in that direction:
   • I **stepped** carefully over the piles of rubbish.

2. If you **tread** in a particular way, you walk in that way. This is rather a literary word:
   • She **trod** carefully across the grass.

3. If you **amble** or **stroll**, you walk in a slow, relaxed way:
   • We **ambled** along the beach hand in hand.
   • They **strolled** down the High Street, looking in shop windows.

4. If you **saunter**, you walk in a slow, casual way:
   • He was **sauntering** along as if he had all the time in the world.

5. If you **wander**, you walk around in a casual way, often without intending to go anywhere in particular:
   • Khachi was **wandering** aimlessly about in the garden.

6. If you **tiptoe**, you walk very quietly without putting your heels on the ground, so as not to be heard:
   • She slipped out of bed and **tiptoed** to the window.

7. If you **toddle**, you walk unsteadily, with short quick steps. This word is most often used of babies or small children:
   • My daughter **toddles** around after me wherever I go.

7. If you **pace**, you walk up and down a small area, usually because you are anxious or impatient:
   • As he waited, he **paced** nervously around the room.

8. If you **stride**, you walk with quick, long steps:
   • He turned abruptly and **strode** off down the corridor.

9. If you **march**, you walk quickly and in a determined way, perhaps because you are angry:
   • She **marched** into the office and demanded to see the manager.

10. If you **stamp**, you put your feet down very hard when you walk, usually because you are angry:
    • *'I'm leaving!' she shouted as she* **stamped** *out of the room.*

11. If you **flounce**, you walk quickly and with exaggerated movements, in a way that shows you are annoyed or upset about something:
    • *He* **flounced** *out of the room in a huff.*

12. If you **stalk**, you walk in a stiff, proud, or angry way:
    • *He* **stalked** *out of the meeting, slamming the door.*

13. If you **lurch**, you walk with sudden, jerky movements:
    • *He* **lurched** *around the room as if he was drunk.*

14. If you **stagger** or **totter**, you walk very unsteadily, often because you are ill or drunk:
    • *He* **staggered** *home from the pub every night.*
    • *I had to* **totter** *around on crutches for six weeks.*

15. If you **reel**, you walk about in an unsteady way as if you are going to fall:
    • *He lost his balance and* **reeled** *back.*

16. If you **stumble**, you trip while you are walking and almost fall:
    • *I* **stumbled** *into the phone box and dialled 999.*

17. If you **hike** or **ramble**, you walk some distance in the countryside for pleasure:
    • *They* **hiked** *along a remote trail.*
    • *a relaxing holiday spent* **rambling** *over the fells*

18. If you **trek**, you make a journey across difficult country by walking:
    • *This year we're going* **trekking** *in Nepal.*

19. You can also use **trek** to describe someone walking rather slowly and unwillingly, usually because they are tired:
    • *We* **trekked** *all round the shops looking for white shoes.*

20. If you **plod**, **tramp**, or **trudge**, you walk slowly, with heavy steps, often because you are tired:
    • *He* **plodded** *about after me, looking bored.*
    • *They spent all day* **tramping** *through the snow.*
    • *We had to* **trudge** *all the way back up the hill.*

423.